THE PENGUIN
DICTIONARY OF MUSIC

780.03

KT-178-880

Arthur Jacobs was born in Manchester in 1922 and educated at
Manchester Grammar School and Merton College, Oxford. After war
service he became music critic of the *Daily Express* at the age of twenty-
five and subsequently worked for many British and overseas newspapers
and magazines. He was a member of the editorial board of *Opera* and
for more than twenty years was a record reviewer for the *Sunday Times*.

Among his books are two acclaimed biographies, *Arthur Sullivan: A
Victorian Musician* (1984) and *Henry J. Wood: Maker of the Proms*
(1994). He is the author of *The Pan Book of Orchestral Music* and,
jointly with Stanley Sadie, *The Pan Book of Opera*, which has gone
through several British, American, Spanish and Portuguese editions.
He edited *Choral Music* (Penguin), which was translated into Spanish
and Japanese, and Penguin also publish *A Short History of Western
Music* (1972) and *The Penguin Dictionary of Musical Performers* (1990).
His translations of operas from French, German, Italian and Russian
have been performed by the English National Opera and other leading
companies.

For fifteen years he lectured in music history at the Royal Academy of
Music before becoming head of the department of music, and professor,
at Huddersfield Polytechnic (now University), from 1979 to 1984. He
was Visiting Scholar at Wolfson College, Oxford, and a visiting lecturer
at several universities in the United States, Canada and Australia.
Arthur Jacobs died in Oxford in December 1996.

THE PENGUIN
DICTIONARY OF MUSIC

ARTHUR JACOBS

SIXTH EDITION

This edition revised by Fiona Maddox

PENGUIN BOOKS

PENGUIN BOOKS

Published by the Penguin Group
Penguin Books Ltd, 27 Wrights Lane, London W8 5TZ, England
Penguin Putnam Inc., 375 Hudson Street, New York, New York 10014, USA
Penguin Books Australia Ltd, Ringwood, Victoria, Australia
Penguin Books Canada Ltd, 10 Alcorn Avenue, Toronto, Ontario, Canada M4V 3B2
Penguin Books (NZ) Ltd, Private Bag 102902, NSMC, Auckland, New Zealand

Penguin Books Ltd, Registered Offices: Harmondsworth, Middlesex, England

First published 1958
Reprinted with revisions 1960, 1961, 1963
Second edition 1967
Reprinted with revisions 1968, 1970
Third edition 1973
Fourth edition 1977
Reprinted with revisions 1978, 1982
Fifth edition 1991
Sixth edition 1996
Reprinted with revisions 1997, 1998
10 9 8 7 6 5 4

Filmset in 8½/10 pt Monotype Photina
Typeset by Datix International Limited, Bungay, Suffolk
Printed in England by Clays Ltd, St Ives plc

Introduction

More than thirty-five years after its first edition (1958), the *Penguin Dictionary of Music* is offered by its compiler in a thoroughly revised form. It has been updated not merely by the addition of new names and new musical terms, but by a scrutiny and amendment of all previously existing entries. Fully half of such existing entries have accordingly been altered in order to anticipate the inquiries of the student, the concert-goer, the opera-goer, the radio listener and the CD collector.

The obvious limitation is that of size in conformity with the general format of Penguin Reference Books – though it will be noted that each edition of the book (including this one) is longer than the previous. The second limitation confines the focus of the book to *classical music* as generally understood – that is, the western classical tradition central to the teaching of music colleges, cultivated by symphony orchestras and opera-houses and supported by magazines and radio stations including (in Britain) those significantly called *Classical Music* and *Classic FM*. Within this is embraced a whole range of tastes normally graded from 'heavy' (the music of the so-called avant-garde composers) to 'light' (including American musicals

of pre-rock vintage and nearly all brass band music).

Outside this range (e.g. in jazz, rock, the music of Asian and African cultures) the compiler has not strayed except to define some commonly encountered terms of those cultures (e.g. *jazz* itself, *gamelan*). As to performers and composers, not even the leading ones of these non-classical traditions are included unless (e.g. Duke Ellington, the Beatles) their names are commonly encountered in discussion of classical music.

Two sub-areas, however, are given a new degree of attention. While previous editions have embraced what might be called *classical operetta* such as *Die Fledermaus*, the doors have been further widened to welcome the titles of such newer works of the light musical theatre as *Fiddler on the Roof* and *Les Misérables*, with entries also for their composers. Likewise with the names of solo singers, instrumentalists and conductors both present and past: many more are now included, and also the names of many more orchestras and chamber ensembles. Such entries borrow freely from my *Dictionary of Musical Performers* (Penguin, 1990), but in all cases have been updated.

Both the hunter of specific fact and the browser-for-pleasure should benefit

Introduction

from an improved system of cross-referencing which involves the symbol ➤: see 'How to use this book' below, p. viii.

Another change from previous editions will be noted. As between *Le Nozze di Figaro* and *The Marriage of Figaro* (and hundreds of other analogous cases), my former practice was to make the English-language title the main one, the foreign-language title bearing simply a cross-reference to the other. But this usage no longer corresponds to the most frequent practice: even such a familiar title as *The Creation* has begun to yield on CD to *Die Schöpfung*, and many operas even when performed in English are now advertised under their original titles (*La Cenerentola* rather than *Cinderella*). In the present edition, conforming to this prevalent usage, the main entry will usually be found in the original language of the title (*Nozze* ...) while the English equivalent (*Marriage* ...) bears the cross-reference.

An exception is made, however, in retaining English forms for titles which begin with a biblical name: thus *Elijah* (Mendelssohn) has its principal entry in that form and not as the German *Elias*; similarly with Bach's *St John* and *St Matthew* Passions. Moreover, as in the general use of recording companies and the BBC, the general precedence given to original foreign titles is confined to those in French, German, Italian and Spanish. Works of other languages, notably Hungarian and Russian, are entered under their recognized English equivalents. Thus a principal entry will be found for (Tchaikovsky's) *The Queen of Spades*, with only a brief cross-referenced entry for *Pikovaya Dama*.

*

Due attention has been paid to differences between British and North American usage (for an example, see *bar*). For note-lengths, the more logical North American nomenclature of *half-note*, *quarter-note*, etc., has been followed: entries for the British equivalents (*minim*, *crochet*) carry a cross-reference. In the spelling of Russian names and others of original non-roman script, the example of *The New Grove Dictionary of Music and Musicians* (1980) has generally been followed – as in 'Rakhmaninov', 'Skryabin', 'Tchaikovsky'.

For a further explanation of forms of names and their alphabetical order, see the section which follows, 'How to use this book'.

In personal entries, State honours are sparingly indicated. It may be useful, especially for readers outside the United Kingdom, to clarify the relevant British terminology. Next in rank to a *peer*, marked by the title 'Lord' or 'Lady', is a *baronet* (male only), a title now almost obsolete. Next in rank is the *knight* (male) or *dame* (female), with the title 'Sir' or 'Dame'; then come the awards of CBE (Commander of the British Empire) and OBE (Order of the British Empire). All these are 'political' honours, government-controlled; royal patronage more directly governs the award of OM (Order of Merit) and CH (Companion of Honour), limited respectively to twenty-four and sixty-five at any one time, both recognizing special intellectual distinction.

All dictionary-compilers purloin from previous workers in the field, the debt in my case being greater and sweeter through personal contact with Stanley Sadie, Michael Kennedy, David

Cummings and the late Nicolas Slonimsky, tireless practitioners of the craft. Among important publications since the previous (1991) edition of the present work the following have been particularly helpful:

Anthony Baines, *The Oxford Companion to Musical Instruments*, 1992

Stanley Sadie (ed.), *The New Grove Dictionary of Opera*, 1992

Loris M. Marchetti & Cristina Santarelli, *Dizionario degli interpreti musicali* [UTET, Turin], 1993

Amanda Holden (ed.), *The Viking Opera Guide*, 1993

For the rapidly developing techniques of *electro-acoustic music* (a term which has now largely displaced *electronic music*), I have consulted standard texts as recent as that of Trevor Wishart (*Audible Design*, 1994) and am grateful for the personal advice of the composers Denis Smalley and Robert Sherlaw Johnson.

Note to the 1998 edition   This sixth edition has been further revised and corrected by Fiona Maddocks.

How to use this book

A single alphabetical list covers all entries. 'A' and 'The' and their equivalents in other languages are alphabetically ignored. Names beginning 'Mc' are alphabetized as if spelt 'Mac'; terms consisting of initials (e.g. BBC) are treated as if forming a word; entries beginning 'St' are listed as if spelt 'Saint'.

Most abbreviations are in common use or self-explanatory. Languages are abbreviated as Cz(ech), Dan(ish), Du(tch), Eng(lish), Fr(ench), Gael(ic), Ger(man), G(ree)k, Heb(rew), Hung-(arian), It(alian), Lat(in), Norw(e-gian), Pol(ish), Port(uguese), Rus-(sian), Swe(dish).

Dates may be qualified by *c.* (*circa*, i.e. approximately) – referring only to the figure immediately following. Thus '*c.* 1603–52' would indicate 'born about 1603, known definitely to have died in 1652'.

Whereas in previous editions SMALL CAPITAL LETTERS in the course of an entry indicated a cross-reference to another entry, in this edition the symbol ➤ is used, meaning: 'Look up this entry for further related information'.

Where a composer's name is mentioned in the course of any entry, that composer receives his or her own entry in the appropriate alphabetical place. In case of such mentions, therefore, it has not been necessary to add the cross-referencing symbol ➤.

Comments on the book and suggestions for its future revision will be welcome: they should be sent to me, care of Penguin Books, 27 Wrights Lane, London W8 5TZ.

ARTHUR JACOBS
Oxford, September 1995

A

A, note of the scale (commonly used for mutual tuning-up of orchestras and other ensembles using stringed instruments). So *A* ➤*flat*, *A* ➤*sharp*, semitonally adjacent notes; *A* ➤*major*, *A* ➤*minor*, keys or chords defined by having A as point of stability (➤tonic). So also *in A*, (1, of a composition or part of it) indication that the music belongs in that key (major unless indicated as minor); (2, of a wind instrument) indication of length of air-column which gives A as the fundamental of its harmonic series: the indication usually but not always implies a ➤transposing instrument. So *clarinet in A* or (colloquially) *A clarinet*.

A, abbr. for Associate (in musical diplomas – e.g. ARCM, Associate of the Royal College of Music).

A, term used in analysis to symbolize the first section of a piece. So ABA represents a piece containing one section followed by a different section followed by a repeat of the first.

a (lower-case letter), indication of the key of A minor as distinct from upper-case *A* for A major – a logical but not universal usage.

a, à (It., Fr.,), to, at, with, etc. So *a 2, a 3*, etc., indication either that a piece is written in so many parts, or that a single line of music is to be played by so many instruments in unison; so also *a* ➤ *cappella*, *a* ➤ *piacere*, *a* ➤ *tempo*, etc.

ab (Ger.), off, away. So *Dämpfer ab*, take mute(s) off.

ABA (and similar combinations of letters in musical analysis), see A (third entry).

Abbado, Claudio (b. 1933), Italian conductor: musical director, La Scala (opera), Milan, 1968–86; principal conductor, London Symphony Orchestra, 1979–87; in 1989 he succeeded Karajan as artistic director of the Berlin Philharmonic orchestra, until 2002.

Abduction from the Seraglio, The, opera by Mozart. ➤*Entführung aus dem Serail*.

'Abegg' Variations, Schumann's opus 1 for piano (1830), dedicated by him to a 'Countess Abegg' and consisting of variations on a theme made up of the notes A–B♭–E–G–G (German B = English B♭). Meta von Abegg was a friend of his, but the rank of Countess was imaginary.

Abel, Carl Friedrich (1723–87), German player of the bass viol (also of the harpsichord) and composer of chamber music, symphonies, etc. Trained in boyhood under J. S. Bach: settled in London (where he died) and gave concerts there with J. C. Bach.

Abrahamsen, Hans (b. 1952), Danish composer of *Nacht und Trompeten* (Ger., 'Night and Trumpets') for orchestra, *Märchenbilder* (Ger., 'Fairy-Tale Pictures') for chamber ensemble, 2 string quartets (no. 1 entitled *Preludes*).

Absil, Jean (1893–1974), Belgian composer of four symphonies, Divertimento for four saxophones and chamber orchestra, three piano concertos, ballets, etc.

absolute music, music without direct reference to anything outside itself, i.e. not having words and not being ➤illustrative music, depicting story, scene, etc.

absolute pitch, ➤pitch.

abstract music, same as ➤absolute music.

Abt, Franz (1819–85), German composer, especially of songs and part-songs in the German style of his period; also conductor in Germany and Switzerland.

Abu Hassan, one-act comic opera by Weber, produced in Munich, 1811. Libretto by F. C. Hiemer, after an *Arabian Nights* adventure of escaping debtors.

Academic Festival Overture, concert-overture by Brahms. ➤*Akademische Fest-Ouvertüre*.

Academy (1) a teaching institution, e.g. Royal Academy of Music; (2, actually the earlier meaning) a society for the promotion of science or art, hence a performing organization. The *Academy of St Martin-in-the-Fields* is a London chamber orchestra, named after a London church, founded (1959) and directed by Neville Marriner, originally with a speciality in string music of the Bach–Vivaldi period; the *Academy of Ancient Music*, founded in 1973 by Christopher Hogwood (and taking its title from an 18th-century organization) is a London group of expandable forces, using period instruments to perform mainly 18th-century music. Similarly in other languages: ➤Singakademie.

Accardo, Salvatore (b. 1941), Italian violinist particularly associated with Paganini; he was the first to record all six of Paganini's concertos. Also conductor.

accelerando (It.), quickening the pace.

acciaccatura (It., a crushing), an 'extra' note struck just before (or simultaneously with) the main note, but immediately released. Notated with the stem of the note crossed through ( ).

accidental, a sharp, flat, double-sharp, double-flat, or natural sign occurring temporarily in the course of a piece, and not forming part of the key-signature. It conventionally refers only to the bar where it occurs – not to any succeeding bars, unless repeated there.

accompanied recitative (or, It., *recitativo accompagnato*), ➤recitative.

accompany, to perform with another performer, but in a subordinate capacity; so *accompanist*, *accompaniment* – a piano being commonly understood as the instrument unless another is specified. (So *unaccompanied song*, *sonata for unaccompanied violin*, etc., indicating absence of piano or other keyboard instrument.) The term is avoided when the performers are thought of as equal partners, e.g. in a violin and piano sonata.

accordion, portable, box-shaped instrument having metal reeds which are made to vibrate by the access of air from bellows, actuated by the player's hands pushing and pulling. The notes are selected through the action of the player's fingers on studs or (*piano-accordion*) on studs for the left hand and a piano-like keyboard for the right. An instrument using only studs is sometimes called a *button-accordion*. On the standard piano-accordion some of the left-hand studs actuate individual bass-notes while others actuate pre-set chords; the *free-bass accordion* is one where all left-hand studs actuate individual notes. Much used in informal music-making, the instrument makes rare appearances in the concert-hall: as in works by ➤Harris (R.), ➤Lindberg, ➤Skempton.

achtel (Ger., eighth part), ➤eighth-note, quaver.

Acis and Galatea, dramatic cantata by Handel with text probably by John Gay, variously called a 'mask' (➤*masque*), 'serenata' and 'pastoral'; first performed privately near London, 1718. It had then no connection with Handel's earlier Italian cantata on the same story (of two pastoral lovers and a villainous giant); but when reviving the English work in 1732, Handel incorporated part of the Italian one.

acoustic, term sometimes used to distinguish a 'normal' (non-electric) instrument from its electric counterpart – e.g. *acoustic* ➤*guitar*, ➤electro-accoustic.

acoustic bass, a type of organ pedal stop which makes use of an acoustic phenomenon, the ➤resultant tone, to produce notes an octave lower than the pipes seemingly permit. When the note ordinarily representing 16-foot C is depressed, this stop brings into action that note together with the G above it; this then appears to sound the C an octave below, i.e. 32-foot C.

acoustics, (1) the science of sound, considered a branch of physics; (2) the sound-properties of a building, etc.

action, the operation of mechanical or other devices used in construction of musical instruments – e.g. *tracker action*, a direct mechanical link between an organ key and the sounding of the pipe, as alternative to *pneumatic* or *electric action*.

act tune, piece played between the scenes of an English 17th-century theatrical work; similar meanings are found in ➤*entr'acte*, ➤*intermezzo*.

adagietto (It., a little adagio), not quite so slow as ➤*adagio*; used as title of the fourth movement (out of five) of Mahler's Symphony no. 5, often played separately, being scored only for harp and strings.

adagio (It.), slow, a slow movement – slower than ➤ *andante*, faster than ➤ *largo*. *Adagio for Strings*, title of an orchestral work (in elegiac vein) by Barber, first performed in 1938 – originally the slow movement of a string quartet. ➤ Albinoni.

Adam, Adolphe [Charles] (1803–56), French composer of operas including *Si j'étais roi* ('If I were King'); ballets including ➤*Giselle*; choral and church music; etc. Also a critic.

Adam, Theo (b. 1926), German bass-baritone eminent in Wagner: for 45 years a member of the Dresden Opera; sang at Bayreuth Festival from 1952. Also stage director.

Adamis, Michael [George] (b. 1929), Greek composer and conductor who studied in USA. Works include *Apocalypse* (*The Sixth Seal*) for chorus, narrator, piano and tape; *Genesis* for three choruses, reciter, tape, painter and dance.

Adams, John [Coolidge] (b. 1947), American composer, also conductor and formerly clarinettist. Works include operas ➤*Nixon in China, The Death of Klinghoffer*, and *I was looking at the ceiling and then I saw the sky*; also *Grand Pianola Music* for two sopranos, two pianos and small orchestra; violin concerto, *Shaker Loops* for strings; piano quintet, etc.

Adaskin, Murray (b. 1906), Canadian composer and university teacher. Works include opera *Grant, Warden of the Plains*; *Qalala and Nilaula of the North* for woodwind, strings and percussion, based on Inuit tunes; Trio for flute, cello, piano.

added sixth, the major sixth added to the major or minor triad –

e.g. or , A being the

added note, the result being called an *added-sixth chord*. Used e.g. by Mahler and Delius and in jazz and later popular music.

Addinsell, Richard [Stewart] (1904–77), British composer of music particularly for films and plays – including *Warsaw Concerto* (fragment for piano and orchestra) in film *Dangerous Moonlight* (1941).

'Adélaïde' Concerto, a violin concerto falsely claimed to have been written by Mozart, aged 10, and dedicated to a French princess, Adélaïde.

Adès, Thomas [originally Thomas Joseph Edmund Ades, without accent] (b. 1971), British composer and pianist, pupil of Goehr and others at Cambridge. Works include *The Origin of the Harp* for violas, cellos, clarinets and percussion, *Five Eliot Landscapes* for soprano and piano, opera *Powder her Face, Asyla* for orchestra.

Adieux, Les (in full *Les Adieux, l'absence et le retour*), title given by Beethoven to his Piano Sonata in E♭, op. 81a (1809); the 'farewell, absence and return' are depicted successively in three movements.

Adler, Larry [originally Lawrence Cecil Adler] (b. 1914), American player of the harmonica (mouth-organ) – an instrument which he elevated to concert rank, works having been specially written for him by Milhaud, Vaughan Williams, M. Arnold, etc. Resident in England since 1949 and still performing at 80.

ad lib. (Lat., *ad libitum*), at discretion, to be performed as the performer wishes – especially meaning that strict time need not be observed, or that the inclusion of a particular voice or instrument in the ensemble is optional.

Adriana Lecouvreur, opera by Cilèa, produced in Milan, 1902. Libretto by A. Colautti, about an (historical) actress of the Comédie Française, 1730.

aeolian harp, primitive instrument with strings of different thicknesses, but all tuned to the same note, across which the wind is allowed to blow: various ➤harmonics are heard. Named from Aeolus, legendary keeper of the winds. A modern electronic simulation using vibrating metal strips has been made by Hugh ➤Davies.

Aeolian mode, the ➤mode which may be represented by the white keys of the piano from A to A.

aerophone, term used scientifically to classify an instrument in which a vibrating column of air produces the musical sound – including pipe-organ, accordion, etc., as well as conventional mouth-blown woodwind and brass instruments.

Aesop (*c.* 6th century BC), Greek fabulist. ➤Castiglioni.

affettuoso (It.), with feeling.

affrettando (It.), becoming faster or more agitated.

Africaine, L', opera by Meyerbeer, produced in Paris, 1865, with libretto mainly by Scribe. The (female) 'African', who loves the explorer Vasco da Gama, would appear to be the product of geographical aberration: her community is Hindu.

Afternoon of a Faun, The, orchestral work by Debussy. ➤*Après-midi d'un faune*.

Age of Anxiety, The, title (from W. H. Auden's poem) of Bernstein's Symphony no. 2, for piano and orchestra, first performed in 1949 and used for ballet (choreography by J. Robbins) in 1950.

Age of Enlightenment, Orchestra of the, self-governing London orchestra (with no permanent conductor) founded 1986, devoted principally to the 18th century and using period instruments. Absorbed London Classical Players, 1997.

agitato (It.), agitated, restless.

Agnus Dei (Lat., [O] Lamb of God), part of the ➤Mass.

Agon (Gk., contest), ballet with music by Stravinsky, choreography by Balanchine, produced in New York, 1957.

agrément (Fr.), an ➤ornament.

Agricola, Alexander (1446–1506), Flemish composer of church and secular music, possibly pupil of Ockeghem; died while employed in Spain.

Agrippina, opera by Handel, produced in Venice, 1710. Libretto by Vincenzo Grimani. Nero's mother successfully schemes to promote his accession to the Roman imperial throne.

Ahronovitch, Yuri Mikhailevich (b. 1932), Russian-born Israeli conductor; conductor of the Stockholm Philharmonic Orchestra, 1982–7.

Aichinger, Gregor (1564–1628), German composer who visited Rome and Venice, and became cathedral choir-master in Augsburg. Wrote Latin church music.

Aida, opera by Verdi, produced in Cairo, 1871. Libretto by A. Ghislanzoni, set in ancient Egypt and named after the Ethiopian princess who is its heroine. (The spelling 'Aïda', with diaeresis, is incorrect in Italian.)

air, a simple tune for voice or instrument. (The old English spelling ➤*ayre*, and the Italian equivalent ➤*aria*, have acquired more specialized meanings.) *Air on the G String* is a name given to an arrangement by Wilhelmj (1871) of the second movement of Bach's Suite no. 3 in D for orchestra; in this arrangement, for violin and piano, the piece is transposed from D to C and the violinist plays on the lowest (G) string.

Akademische Fest-Ouvertüre (Ger., 'Academic Festival Overture'),

5

concert-overture by Brahms, first performed in 1881, composed in acknowledgement of a doctorate from Breslau University, 1879. Made up of favourite German student songs.

Akhnaten, opera by Glass, produced in Stuttgart, 1984. Libretto by the composer and others, about the Pharaoh Akhnaten of *c*.1350 BC.

al (It.), to the. (For *al rovescio* and other phrases beginning thus, see under the word following.)

Alagna, Roberto (b. 1964) French-Sicilian tenor. Won Pavarotti competition, Philadelphia 1988. Debut, GTO 1988 as Alfredo in *La Traviata*, La Scala 1990, Royal Opera 1992. Married ➤Gheorgiu.

Alain, Jehan (1911–40), French organist and composer mainly of organ and choral music. See the following.

Alain, Marie-Claire (b. 1926), French organist, noted exponent of music by her brother (preceding), Bach and other composers.

Alban Berg Quartet Austrian string quartet founded in 1971; dedicatees of quartets by Schnittke and Rihm. Current members: Günter Pichler, Gerhard Schulz, Thomas Kakuska, Valentin Erben.

Albee, Edward (b. 1928), American dramatist. ➤Flanagan.

Albéniz, Isaac (1860–1909), Spanish composer of music in Spanish 'national' style. Child prodigy as composer and pianist; pupil of Liszt in Weimar; spent much of later life in London and Paris. Works include operas (two in English), songs and many piano pieces, e.g. the cycle ➤*Iberia*.

Albéniz, Mateo [Antonio Perez de] (*c*. 1755–1831), Spanish organist, composer and author of a musical treatise.

Albert, Eugène [Francis Charles] d' (1864–1932), Scottish-born composer-pianist, French-English by descent and German by adoption (therefore known also as Eugen d'Albert). Pupil of Liszt; teacher in Berlin; died in Riga. Composed *Tiefland* (Ger., 'Lowland') and 20 other operas, etc.

Albert Herring, comic opera by Britten, produced at Glyndebourne, 1947; libretto by E. Crozier, after a story by Maupassant about a male 'May Queen'.

Albert, Stephen [Joel] (1941–92), American composer, killed in a car crash shortly after completing a cello concerto for Yo-Yo Ma. Several of his works, including symphony entitled *RiverRun*, are based on Joyce's *Finnegans Wake*; other works include *Wind Canticle* for clarinet and orchestra.

Alberti bass, the spreading-out of a left-hand keyboard chord in a rhythmical pattern – e.g. [musical notation] from [musical notation]. Named after Domenico Alberti (1710–40), Italian composer, who used it extensively.

Albinoni, Tomaso (1671–1750), Italian violinist and composer of works of ➤*concerto grosso* type; also of more than 50 operas, etc. Bach studied, and adapted from, his music. An *Adagio* ascribed to him is principally the work of his biographer. Remo Giazotto (b. 1910).

alborada (Sp.), morning song (corresponding to Fr. ➤*aubade*); *Alborada del gracioso* (. . . of the Jester), piano piece by Ravel in the set ➤*Miroirs* (1905).

Albrecht, Gerd (b. 1935), German conductor whose first performances include that of Reimann's opera ➤*Lear*; made Covent Garden début 1986; principal conductor of Czech Philharmonic Orchestra since 1992.

Albrechtsberger, Johann Georg (1736–1809), Austrian composer and theorist under whom Beethoven studied counterpoint.

Alceste, opera by Gluck, produced (in Italian) in Vienna, 1767. Libretto by R. Calzabigi after Euripides' tragedy: Alcestis, wife of King Admetus, volunteers to die in his place. (The composer's French version, 1776, is substantially different.)

Alceste, ou Le Triomphe d'Alcide (Fr., 'Alcestis, or the Triumph of Hercules'), opera by Lully, produced in Paris, 1674. Libretto by P. Quinault after Euripides' tragedy: Alcestis, who has volunteered to die in place of her husband King Admetus, is rescued from Hades by Hercules.

Alcina, opera by Handel, produced in London, 1735. Libretto (after Ariosto's narrative poem of chivalry, *Orlando Furioso*) about an enchantress.

alcuna licenza, ➤*licenza*.

Aldrich, Henry (1648–1710), English composer of church music, the round 'Great Tom is Cast', etc.; also theologian and architect.

aleatoric, malformed word (presumably from Ger. *Aleatorik*, noun not adjective) ignorantly used in place of the standard English term ➤*aleatory*.

aleatory, dependent on chance or on the throw of the dice (Lat., *alea*). This is rather loosely applied to a tendency (since the 1950s) of some composers to leave elements in their compositions in an indeterminate state (➤ indeterminacy). But it might be more strictly confined to compositions in which random chance genuinely plays a part in performance (as pioneered by Cage), not to those in which a decision of the performer replaces a decision of the composer.

Aleko, opera by Rakhmaninov, produced in Moscow, 1893. Libretto by V. Nemirovich-Danchenko, after a story by Pushkin. The hero has gone to live with the gipsies but after stabbing his unfaithful lover is exiled by them.

Alexander Nevsky, cantata (drawn from film score) by Prokofiev, first performed in 1939, celebrating the victories of the 13th-century Russian prince.

Alexander, Roberta (b. 1949), American soprano who first appeared at the Metropolitan Opera 1983, Glyndebourne 1989; has recorded songs by Ives, Barber, Bernstein.

Alexander's Feast, cantata by Handel, first performed in 1736; words mainly from Dryden's poem, referring to Alexander the Great and celebrating the power of music.

Alexeev [more correctly Alexeyev], **Dmitry** (b. 1947), Russian pianist who won the Moscow (International Tchaikovsky) and Leeds competitions and has pursued concert and recording careers both in the former Soviet Union and in the West.

Alfano, Franco (1875–1954), Italian composer of operas including *Cyrano de Bergerac* (after Rostand); also symphonies, string quartets, etc. Completed Puccini's *Turandot* from sketches left by the composer.

Alfonso X, king of Portugal (1221–84), known as El Sabio ('the Wise'), patron of literature, music and the other arts; possibly himself a composer (➤*cantiga*).

Alfonso und Estrella, Schubert's only all-sung opera (D732), produced posthumously in Weimar, 1854. Libretto by F. von Schober, about two lovers, children of a deposed king and a usurping one.

Alfred, masque by T. A. Arne, produced at Cliveden, Bucks, 1740. Words by J. Thomson and D. Mallet, celebrating King Alfred. It contains 'Rule, Britannia!' (➤*Fantasia on British Sea Songs*).

Alfvén, Hugo (1872–1960), Swedish composer of five symphonies and three orchestral *Swedish Rhapsodies* (no. 1, *Midsummer Vigil*, is the one sometimes called simply *Swedish Rhapsody*); also of cantatas, a violin sonata, etc.

Aliabiev, ➤Alyabiev.

Alison, Richard (16th–17th century), English composer of songs, lute solos, etc.

Alkan (original surname Morhange), **Charles-Valentin** (1813–88), French pianist and composer of works for the normal piano and the ➤pedal-piano; his music has some 'advanced' chromatic harmonies.

Alkestis, alternative to Alcestis as British form of the Greek heroine's name. ➤*Alceste*.

alla (It.), to the, at the; in the manner of (like Fr. *à la*). ➤*alla breve*.

alla breve, a tempo-direction (chiefly 18th-century) indicating that, in a bar nominally of four beats, the pace is to be so fast that it is heard as having two beats only (on the original first and third beats).

allargando (It.), broadening, becoming slower.

allegretto (It., a little allegro), not quite so lively as ➤*allegro*.

Allegri, Gregorio (1582–1652), Italian composer, and singer in the Papal chapel. His *Miserere* was written down by Mozart, aged 14, after one hearing (and checked after a second hearing).

Allegri Quartet, London-based string quartet founded in 1953, re-formed 1968, now with 'resident' status at Oxford University. Repertory embraces many modern British composers including Lefanu, Osborne, Woolrich. Current members: Peter Carter, David Roth, Jonathan Barritt, Pál Banda.

allegro (It.), lively, i.e. rather fast (but not as fast as ➤*presto*).

alleluia, the Italian and Church Latin equivalent to 'Hallelujah'; ➤*Exsultate, jubilate*.

allemande, dance-movement often opening the baroque ➤suite, in moderate 4–4 time. It is divided into two sections and usually begins with a short note just before the bar-line. The term is French for 'German', but this is not the same as a ➤*German Dance*.

Allen, Thomas [Boaz] (b. 1944), British baritone, noted in opera; at Covent Garden from 1972, Metropolitan Opera from 1981.

Allende(-Sarón), [Pedro] **Humberto** (1985–1959), Chilean composer (also violinist, teacher and folk-music researcher). Works include 12 *Tonadas*, of popular Chilean character, for piano (some also orchestrated); *La voz de las calles* ('The voice of the streets') for orchestra; songs.

All Night Vigil, ➤Vigil.

almain, almand, almond, old English equivalents of ➤*allemande*.

Almaviva, ossia L'inutile precauzione, ➤*Barbiere di Siviglia*.

Alpensinfonie, Eine (Ger., 'An Alpine Symphony'), the last of R. Strauss's descriptive orchestral works, first performed in 1915.

alphorn, wind instrument having a straight wooden tube sometimes as much as 12 ft long. It sounds one ➤harmonic series only (like a bugle) with very powerful tone, and is used in Switzerland for attracting cattle (and tourists). The German name is *Alpenhorn*. Extremely rare in the concert-hall: ➤Alsina, ➤Schwertsik.

Alpine Symphony, An, ➤*Alpensinfonie*.

Alsina, Carlos Roqué (b. 1941), Argentinian composer, also pianist and conductor (in Germany 1964–6). Works include piano solos, chamber music (his *Rendezvous* uses an ➤alphorn) and *Schichten* (Ger., 'Layers') for orchestra.

Also sprach Zarathustra (Ger., 'Thus Spake Zarathustra'), symphonic poem by R. Strauss, first performed in 1896; after a literary text by Nietzsche, who used a variant name for the ancient Persian prophet Zoroaster.

alt, term signifying high in special vocal sense – *in alt*, in the octave written immediately above the treble clef, beginning with G; *in altissimo*, in the octave above that.

altissimo (It., very high), ➤*alt*.

alto (It., high), (1) an unusually high type of adult male voice, employing falsetto (➤counter-tenor); (2) the lower type of female voice – so designated in choirs, elsewhere usually ➤contralto (see also next entry); also, sometimes, the corresponding child's voice; (3) in a 'family' of instruments, having a range approximately that of an alto voice – e.g. *alto* ➤*flute*, alto ➤*saxophone*; (4, *alto clef*) type of ➤clef, written ; it is the normal clef for viola but is otherwise little used; (5, Fr.) = viola.

Alto Rhapsody, usual English title for Brahms's Rhapsody for contralto solo, male chorus and orchestra, first performed in 1870; it has a philosophical text by Goethe.

Alva, Luigi [originally Luis Ernesto Alva Talledo] (b. 1927), Peruvian tenor who studied in Milan and made an international operatic career with speciality in Mozart and Rossini (Covent Garden from 1960).

Alwyn, William (1905–85), British composer, in earlier career flautist. Works include four symphonies; opera *Miss Julie* (after Strindberg); two string quartets; also much film music.

Alyabiev, Alexander Alexandrovich (1787–1851), Russian composer of operas, etc.; his song 'The Nightingale' was formerly often interpolated into the Lesson Scene of Rossini's *Il barbiere di Siviglia*.

Amadeus Quartet, British string quartet (three of its members Austrian–Jewish refugees from the Nazis) which took Mozart's middle name; made its London début in 1948 and continued with unbroken membership. It disbanded on the death of its viola-player, Peter Schidlof, in 1987.

Amahl and the Night Visitors, opera for television by Menotti, produced in New York, 1951; later on stage. Libretto by composer, on the legend of the Magi.

Amati, family of violin-makers of Cremona, active from mid 16th to early 18th century.

Ambrosian chant, type of ➤plainsong associated with Bishop (St) Ambrose of Milan (340–97), differing from ➤Gregorian.

Ameling, Elly [originally Elisabeth Sara] (b. 1934), Dutch soprano well known in German and French song, Bach's church music, etc., with a few appearances in opera. Awarded Dutch knighthood, 1971.

American in Paris, An, descriptive piece for orchestra (including four taxi-horns) by Gershwin, first performed in 1928.

American organ, type of ➤reed-organ in which air is sucked in through bellows. (US term: cabinet-organ.)

'American' Quartet, nickname for Dvořák's String Quartet in F, op. 96 (1893), composed in USA and partly prompted by Negro melodies: hence also called 'Negro' Quartet and (in former usage) 'Nigger' Quartet.

Amfiparnaso, L' (It., 'The Amphiparnassus'), name given by Vecchi to a sequence of madrigals in the form of a dramatic comedy; published 1597, but not intended to be staged, therefore not a forerunner of opera. Title means 'The lower slopes of Parnassus' (mountain sacred to the Muses).

Amid Nature (Cz., *V přírodě*), overture by Dvořák, 1891; ➤Carnival.

Amor brujo, El (Sp., 'Love, the Sorcerer'), ballet with music by Falla (later revised), choreography by Pastora Imperio, first performed in 1915. (Title is often translated 'Love, the Magician': *brujo* indicates a 'male witch', and the ballet is about a young woman malevolently haunted by a dead lover.) It was written for a ballerina who can also sing. A suite for orchestra (properly with contralto) is drawn from it, one movement being the *Ritual Fire Dance*, also well known in the composer's piano arrangement.

amore, d'; amour, d' (It., Fr.), term applied to some old instruments, indicating an ingratiating tone (literally, 'of love'); as in the ➤*viola d'amore*.

amoroso (It., lovingly), tenderly.

Amsterdam Baroque Orchestra, ➤Koopman.

Amy, Gilbert (b. 1936), French composer, conductor and writer on music; director of Lyons Conservatory; pupil of Boulez. Works include *Trajectoires* for violin and orchestra, *Jeu* for 1–4 oboes, *Cycle* for six percussionists.

anacrusis (term borrowed from the analysis of verse), an initial upbeat, which may be one note or more – i.e. whatever is heard before the first strong accent (downbeat). A phrase beginning *on* the downbeat has no anacrusis.

Anchieta, Juan de (1462–1523), Spanish composer in service to Spanish royal family (also priest); wrote Latin church music and Spanish secular songs.

ancora (It.), still, yet more: *ancora più presto*, still more quickly. The word corresponds to Fr. ➤*encore*.

Anda, Geza (1921–76), Hungarian pianist, pupil of E. Dohnányi; noted in Bartók's music. Took Swiss nationality.

andante (It., going), at a walking pace, at moderate speed – not so fast as ➤*allegro* (or ➤*allegretto*) but not so slow as ➤*adagio*.

andantino (It., a diminutive of ➤*andante*), term apparently indicating either a little slower than *andante*, or (now more usually) not quite so slow as *andante*.

Anderson, Hans Christian (1805–75), Danish writer. ➤Hartmann (J. P. E.), ➤Henriques, ➤Høffding.

Anderson, Julian (b. 1967), British composer, pupil of John Lambert at the Royal College of Music, Tristan Murail in Paris and Alexander Goehr at Cambridge; professor of composition, RCM. Works include *Dyptych* for orchestra, *Kohorovod*, *The Crazed Moon*, *The Stations of the Sun*.

Anderson, June (b. 1950), American soprano, made her opera début with New York City Opera, 1978, and developed a speciality in coloratura roles.

Anderson, Marian (1902–93), American contralto; in 1955 became the first black singer to perform in the Metropolitan Opera, New York.

Andrea Chénier, opera by Giordano, produced in Milan, 1896. Libretto by L. Illica, about the historical French Revolutionary poet André Chénier.

André, Maurice (b. 1933), French trumpeter, noted soloist in baroque and modern music; Blacher and other composers have written works for him.

Andriessen, Hendrik [Franciscus] (1892–1981), Dutch composer of much Roman Catholic church music, also of opera, four symphonies, etc. Father of the two following composers.

Andriessen, Juriaan (b. 1925), Dutch composer, pupil of his father (preceding), also pianist and conductor. Works include Sinfonietta Concertante for four trumpets and orchestra; *Homage to Milhaud* for 11 instruments.

Andriessen, Louis (b. 1939), Dutch composer, pupil of his father (Hendrik, above), and of Berio. Collaborator with Peter ➤Schat; his own works include *The Nine Symphonies of Beethoven* for light orchestra and ice-cream bell; *Contra Tempus* (Lat., 'Against Time') for 23 musicians, *Sweet* for recorder.

Anerio, Felice (1560–1614), Italian composer, mainly of church music: Palestrina's successor as composer to the Papal Chapel. Brother of the following.

Anerio, Giovanni (c. 1577–1630), Italian composer (also priest), brother of the preceding. Worked as choirmaster in Italy; also visited Poland and died in Austria on a journey from Poland to Italy. Wrote masses , motets, madrigals, etc.

Anfossi, Pasquale (1727–97), Italian composer, especially of operas – including *La Finta Giardiniera* ('The Pretended Garden-Maid') to a libretto later used by Mozart: also church musician in Rome.

Angel of Fire, The, ➤*Fiery Angel*.

Anglican chant, type of harmonized melody used for psalm-singing in the Church of England. The melody is four-square in itself, but made metrically irregular by having to accommodate a varying number of syllables.

animato (It.), animated, lively.

Anisimova, Nina (b. 1909), Russian choreographer. ➤*Gayaneh*.

Anna Bolena (It., 'Anne Boleyn'), opera by Donizetti, produced in Milan, 1830. Libretto, by F. Romani, culminates in Anne's execution.

Années de pèlerinage (Fr., 'Years of Pilgrimage'), title of four sets of piano pieces by Liszt, alluding to his experiences of Italy and Switzerland – arranged in three 'years', plus a supplementary set, published 1855–83. The ➤*Dante Sonata* is included in it.

Annie Get Your Gun, musical comedy with text by Herbert and Dorothy Fields; music by Irving Berlin. Produced in New York, 1946. Its heroine is the historic markswoman Annie Oakley (1860–1926).

Anonymous IV, name by which scholars label a manuscript treatise on music, evidently by an English writer of about 1270–80. Name also adopted by an American female-voice quartet (founded 1986) devoted to medieval music.

Ansermet, Ernest (1883–1969), Swiss conductor – worked with Diaghilev, then (1918) founder-conductor of the Geneva orchestra (Orchestre de la Suisse Romande); gave many first performances of important modern works, especially of Stravinsky. Also writer on music.

answer, a musical phrase appearing to respond to another – particularly in a ➤fugue, where the first entry of the main theme is called the subject and the second (at the interval of a fifth upwards from the subject) is called the answer, and so on alternately. If the answer exactly reproduces the subject (apart from the displacement of a fifth), it is called a *real answer* and the fugue a 'real fugue'; if the internal intervals of the subject are (as usually) slightly modified in the answer, so as to keep the music within the key, then the answer is a *tonal answer* and the fugue a 'tonal fugue'.

Antar, orchestral work by Rimsky-Korsakov, originally (1867) designated as his Symphony no. 2, on second revision (1897) called a symphonic suite. Name is that of a 6th-century Arabian hero.

Antartica, ➤*Sinfonia Antartica*.

Antheil, George (1900–1959), American composer and pianist; also author of fiction and an autobiography. Wrote *Ballet Mécanique* (for aeroplane propellers, bells, motor-horns, etc.), 1927, opera *Volpone* (after Jonson) and many film scores.

anthem, short solemn vocal composition (hence *national anthem*, authorized for expression of patriotic sentiment): specifically, a short choral work, to a text not necessarily forming part of the liturgy, included in Church of England services – sometimes with organ accompaniment and either with or without solo parts (➤motet).

anticipation, the sounding of a note before the chord of which it forms part, so that at first it is heard as a discord with the preceding chord.

Antigone, title (after Sophocles' play) of operas by various composers, including one by Honegger, produced in Brussels, 1927 (libretto by Cocteau); another by Orff (with unorthodox, mainly percussive orchestra), directly setting Hölderlin's German version of Sophocles, produced in Salzburg, 1949.

antiphon (from Gk. for 'sounding across'), part of Roman Catholic and Greek Orthodox church services sung as responses between single and many voices or between two groups of singers; hence *antiphonal*, descriptive term for musical effects drawn from the use of groups of performers stationed apart.

antique cymbal, ➤*crotale*.

Antony and Cleopatra, opera by Barber, produced in New York, 1966, with libretto after Shakespeare by Franco Zeffirelli (libretto later revised by Menotti).

anvil, orchestra bar-and-striker instrument imitating real anvil; first used by Auber, 1825. Wagner's *Das Rheingold* demands 18.

Apollinaire, Guillaume (1880–1918), French poet. ➤*Mamelles de Tirésias*.

Apollo Musagetes (Gk., 'Apollo, Leader of the Muses'), ballet with music by Stravinsky, choreography by Adolph Bolm, produced in Washington, 1928. The French version of the title, *Apollon Musagète*, is sometimes used.

Apostel, Hans Erich (1901–72), German-born Austrian composer, pupil of Schoenberg and Berg. Works include two string quartets (no. 1, variations on a theme from ➤*Wozzeck* for Berg's birthday), a Requiem and piano solos.

Apostles, The, oratorio by Elgar (text from the Bible), first performed in 1903. The first part of Elgar's intended trilogy of oratorios; no. 2 is *The Kingdom*, no. 3 was never completed.

Appalachian Spring, ballet with music by Copland, choreography by Martha Graham, produced in 1944. The setting is a 'primitive' American rural community.

appoggiatura (It., a leaning), (1) musical ornament (chiefly 18th-century, now obsolete) consisting of unharmonized auxiliary note falling (or, less frequently, rising) to an adjacent note which is harmonized or implied to be so. Appoggiatura can be either *written* using an auxiliary note in smaller type

– e.g. played or

unwritten, i.e. to be inserted by performer according to conventions of the period – e.g. a recitative in Handel or Mozart ending was intended to be sung as ; (2, derived from above) term used in modern harmonic analysis for an accented non-harmonized note like the D in the first example (whether or not notated in the above obsolete way) adjacent to following harmonized note less accented than itself.

Apprenti sorcier, L' (Fr., 'The Sorcerer's Apprentice'), symphonic poem by Dukas, also called a 'scherzo'; first performed 1897. It humorously illustrates Goethe's story (based on Lucian, second century AD) of the apprentice who finds he can start a spell but not stop it.

Après-midi d'un faune, L' (Fr., 'The Afternoon of a Faun'), orchestral work by Debussy, composed as a musical illustration of Mallarmé's poem. Strictly called *Prélude à l'après-midi d'un faune*: Debussy originally intended two other pieces to follow it.

Arabella, opera by R. Strauss, produced in Dresden, 1933. Libretto by H. von Hofmannsthal: aristocratic debt and sexual mis-identity are resolved by true love.

arabesque (Fr., Eng.; also *Arabeske*, Ger.), title borrowed from visual art and sometimes given to short piece with decorative qualities – e.g. by Schumann and Debussy, for piano.

Aragall, Giacomo (originally Jaime Aragall y Garriga) (b. 1939), Spanish tenor who made an international reputation particularly in Italian opera, from the 1960s.

Aranjuez, Concierto de, guitar concerto by Rodrigo (named after a town near Madrid), first performed in 1940.

Arányi, Jelly [Eva] d' (1893–1966), Hungarian-born British violinist, great-niece of Joachim; works by Bartók, Ravel and Vaughan Williams were dedicated to her.

Araujo or **Arauxo, Francisco Correa de**, ➤Correa de Araujo.

Arbós, Enrique Fernandez (1863–1939), Spanish violinist, conductor and arranger; orchestrated part of ➤*Iberia* by Albéniz.

Arcadelt, Jacob (*c*. 1505–68), Flemish composer of Masses, motets, madrigals etc. (one of the earliest practitioners of the madrigal), working in Rome as Papal musician.

Arcadians, The, musical play with text by Mark Ambient and Alexander M. Thompson; lyrics by Arthur Wimperis; music by Howard Talbot and Lionel Monckton. Produced in London, 1909. People from Arcady, a land where lying is punished by immersion in the Well of Truth, venture to London.

'Archduke' Trio, nickname of Beethoven's Piano Trio in B♭ (1811), op. 97, dedicated to Archduke Rudolph of Austria.

Archer, Violet [Balestreri] (b. 1913), Canadian composer (also university teacher) who studied with Hindemith and Bartók. Works include piano concerto, violin concerto, many choral and solo vocal settings.

archlute, generic name for a long-necked ➤*lute* with extra bass strings: the ➤*theorbo* and (even longer-necked) ➤*chitarrone* are examples.

arco (It.), bow (of a stringed instrument); (instruction to) play with the bow (cancelling the instruction ➤*pizzicato*).

Arden muss sterben (Ger., 'Arden Must Die'), opera by Goehr, with libretto by Erich Fried, produced in Hamburg, 1967; the plot of violent intrigue is based on the (anonymous) Elizabethan play *Arden of Faversham*.

Arditi, Luigi (1822–1903), Italian composer of waltz-song *Il Bacio* ('The Kiss'), etc., and conductor; settled in England, 1858, and died there.

Arditti Quartet, British string quartet, founded 1974 and led by Irving Arditti; its high reputation rests on its devotion to the most complex modern works, e.g. by Ferneyhough and Xenakis. Current other members David Alberman, Levine Andrade, Rohan de Saram.

Arensky, Anton Stepanovich (1861–1906), Russian composer, pupil of Rimsky-Korsakov but not sharing his teacher's pronounced 'nationalism' in music; works include three operas, two symphonies, and piano pieces, chamber music including quartet for violin, viola, two cellos.

Argento, Dominick [Joseph] (b. 1927), American composer of 10 operas, including *Postcard from Morocco* and *The Aspern Papers* (after Henry James): *Letters from Composers* for tenor and guitar; incidental music for plays, etc. His teachers included Dallapiccola.

Argerich, Martha (b. 1941), Argentinian pianist, pupil of Gulda, Michelangeli and others; prizewinner in Geneva at 16, then internationally prominent partnering Rostropovich, Kremer and others; since 1978 not giving solo recitals.

aria (It.), air, song, especially one of some complexity in opera or oratorio; '*da capo*' *aria* (as used, e.g., by Handel), one in which the first section is finally repeated after a contrasting section.

Ariadne auf Naxos (Ger., 'Ariadne on [the island of] Naxos'), opera by Richard Strauss with libretto by H. von Hofmannsthal – original version, 1912, designed to be performed after Molière's play *Le Bourgeois Gentilhomme* (with Strauss's incidental music); longer, self-contained version, 1916. (To satisfy a patron, the serious drama of Ariadne's desertion by Theseus is mixed with a harlequinade.)

Ariadne on Naxos, opera by Richard Strauss. ➤*Ariadne auf Naxos*.

arietta (It.), a little or a light ➤aria.

ariette (Fr.), literally a 'little air', but historically (e.g. in Rameau) a term indicating an operatic song of considerable dimensions and great vocal display.

arioso (It.), aria-like, i.e. 'normally' sung (as distinct from ➤recitative) though not necessarily constructed according to the formal balance usually accorded to an ➤aria.

Ariosto, Ludovico (1474–1533), Italian poet. ➤*Alcina*.

Arkhipova, Irina [Konstantinovna] (b. 1925), Russian mezzo-soprano, prominent in opera in USSR and (since appearing in Milan, 1967) in the West. Still performing in 1994.

Arlésienne, L' (Fr., 'The Woman of Arles'), play by Alphonse Daudet, 1872, for which Bizet wrote incidental music including a ➤*farandole*; the second of the two suites drawn from this is an arrangement made by Guiraud after Bizet's death.

Armida (or, Fr., *Armide*), name of operas by several composers, based on Tasso's poem of the Crusades, *Jerusalem Delivered*; e.g. (1) by Lully, produced in Paris, 1686 (libretto by P. Quinault); (2) by Gluck, Paris, 1777 (libretto by P. Quinault); (3) by Haydn, Eszterháza, 1784 (Hob. XXVIII: 12; libretto, in Italian, by J. Durandi); (4) by Rossini, Naples, 1817 (libretto by G. Schmidt); (5) by

Dvořák, Prague, 1904 (libretto by J. Vrchlitzký). Armida is a pagan enchantress opposed by a Christian champion (➤*Rinaldo*).

armonica, Italian name for the ➤glass harmonica.

Armstrong, Karan (b. 1941), American soprano well known in opera, notably in title-role of Berg's *Lulu*. Sang in first performance of Berio's *Un re in ascolto*, 1984.

Armstrong, Richard (b. 1943), British conductor, music director of Welsh National Opera 1973–86, of Scottish Opera from 1993; concert appearances in Rome, Tokyo, at the Proms (first 1989), etc.

Arne, Michael (b. 1740 or 1741; d. 1786), British singer and, from childhood, a composer. Works include song 'The Lass with the Delicate Air', and much music for the stage. Illegitimate son of T. A. Arne.

Arne, Thomas Augustine (1710–78), British composer of *Artaxerxes* and other operas (one in Italian), other stage works, and songs; also of oratorio ➤*Judith*. Wrote masques ➤*Alfred* (in which 'Rule, Britannia!' occurs) and ➤*Comus*; the opera ➤*Love in a Village* is mostly his. Composed much music for the London pleasure gardens, Drury Lane Theatre, etc. D. Mus., Oxford, 1759. Was generally known as Dr Arne. Father of Michael Arne.

Arnell, Richard [Anthony Sayer] (b. 1917), British composer of seven symphonies, a *Symphonic Portrait: Lord Byron*, chamber music, etc. Lived for a time in USA.

Arnold, Malcolm [Henry] (b. 1921), British composer, pupil of Jacob; formerly orchestral trumpeter. Works include nine symphonies and a ➤*Toy Symphony*; various concertos (one for harmonica, one for piano duet and orchestra); a number of instrumental sonatas; many film scores. Knighted, 1993.

Arnold, Matthew (1822–88), British poet. ➤*Dover Beach*.

Arnold, Samuel (1740–1802), British composer of many operas and plays with music, church music, harpsichord pieces, etc. Was also organist and editor of first collected edition of Handel.

arpa (It.), harp.

arpeggio (It., from preceding), chord (on piano, etc.) which is performed 'spread out' – i.e. the notes sounded not simultaneously but in succession (nearly always starting at the bottom) as normally on the harp.

arpeggione, a six-stringed instrument invented in 1824, fretted and tuned like a guitar but bowed like a cello. The sonata that Schubert wrote for it (with piano) in that year (D821) is now commonly taken over by cellists and identified as the 'Arpeggione' Sonata.

arr., abbr. for *arranger, arranged*. ➤arrange.

arrange, to set out for one performing medium a composition written for another. Normally this indicates stricter fidelity to the composer's notes, and less artistic licence, than does ➤transcribe.

Arrau, Claudio (b. 1903–91), Chilean pianist who gave first recital at age five, and studied in Berlin under Krause (pupil of Liszt); appeared in USA, 1924, and then began world tours. Continued to perform into his 80s; returned in 1974 to Chile after a 17-year absence. His authority in the classics was considered unsurpassed.

Arriaga [y Balzola], **Juan Crisostomo Antonio** (1806–26), Spanish composer who studied in Paris and, before early death, wrote opera, symphony and three string quartets.

Arrigo, Girolamo (b. 1930), Italian composer resident in Paris. Has written many vocal works (texts in French, Italian, Spanish); *Infra-red* for 16 instruments; *Dalla nebbia verso la nebbia* ('From the mist to the mist') for 16 cellos and six double-basses; etc.

Arroyo, Martina (b. 1936), American soprano whose Aida at the Metropolitan Opera, New York, 1965, began her celebrity in heavier Italian operatic roles. She has also performed works by Stockhausen and other modern composers.

ars antiqua (Lat., old art), term for the style of Western European medieval music (based on ➤*plainsong* and ➤*organum*) practised, e.g., by Pérotin and preceding the ➤ars nova.

ars nova (Lat., new art), the musical style current in 14th-century France and Italy, free from the restrictions of ➤*ars antiqua*, introducing duple (instead of only triple) time and having much independence of part-writing; practised, e.g., by ➤Landini, ➤Machaut.

Artaxerxes, opera by Arne, produced in London, 1762; libretto by composer, translated from Metastasio, about the ancient Persian king Artaxerxes I (5th century BC).

arte (It.), art in various senses, as in ➤*commedia dell'arte*; so *L'arte del violino* ('The Art of the Violin'), title of a set of twelve concertos with other pieces by Locatelli, opus 3, published 1773.

articulation, the characteristics of a note or chord with respect to attack and decay, e.g. the quality of ➤*staccato*. Also more generally used: 'Even in rapid passages her articulation was outstanding.'

Art of Fugue, The, work by Bach. ➤*Kunst der Fuge*.

Arts Florissants, Les, ensemble directed by W. ➤Christie.

art-song, term sometimes used in contradiction to ➤folk-song or popular song to indicate a 'serious' composition intended for formal concert performance.

Arutiunian, Alexander Grigorievich (b. 1920), Armenian composer of a piano concerto, trumpet concerto, horn concerto, opera *Savat-Nova*, etc.; also writer on music.

Asafiev, Boris (1884–1949), Russian composer (*The Fountain of Bakhchisarai* and other ballets; also operas, five symphonies, etc.); and, under the name Igor Glebov, music critic and writer.

ASCAP, (name formed from the initials of) American Society of Composers, Authors and Publishers, a performing-rights agency, created in 1914.

Ashkenazy, Vladimir [Davidovich] (b. 1937), Russian pianist, naturalized Icelandic, 1972; joint winner, with John Ogdon, of the International Tchaikovsky Contest in Moscow, 1962. Emigrated to the West in 1963, won acclaim as pianist-conductor, later as conductor alone; music director of Royal Philharmonic Orchestra, 1987–95, and of Deutsche Sinfonie-Orchester (Berlin), since 1989.

Ashley, Robert [Reynolds] (b. 1930), American composer with special interest in film, multimedia, electronics, etc. Works include *The Wolfman Motorcity Revue* and other 'electronic music theatre' pieces; also *Quartet for any Number of Instruments*, etc.

Ashton, Sir Frederick (1904–88), British choreographer. ➤*Façade*.

assai (It.), very; *allegro assai*, very quick.

Aston, Hugh (*c.*1485–1522), English composer of a ➤hornpipe – the earliest known piece for virginals – and of Masses and other vocal works.

Atherton, David (b. 1944), British conductor, principal conductor of the Royal Liverpool Philharmonic Orchestra, 1980–83, of Hong Kong Philharmonic Orchestra since 1989; noted in modern music, including opera.

Atlantov, Vladimir (b. 1939), Russian tenor, formerly a member of the Kirov Opera (Leningrad/St Petersburg), one of the most prominent Russian opera singers of his generation, known in the Italian repertory (title-role in *Otello* at Covent Garden début, 1987) as well as the Russian classics.

atonal, not in any key: hence *atonality*, *atonalism*. (The term *pantonal*, indicating the synthesis of all keys rather than the absence of any, was preferred by Schoenberg but never won general acceptance.) ➤twelve-note music developed as a systematization of atonal music.

attacca(It.),attack(imperative),proceed to the next section without a break; so also *attacca subito* (immediately).

Atterberg, Kurt [Magnus] (1887–1974), Swedish composer, conductor and critic. Wrote nine symphonies, five operas, etc., sometimes making direct use of Swedish folk-music.

Attila, opera by Verdi, produced in Venice, 1846. Libretto by T. Solera, altered by F. M. Piave, on the fifth-century invasion of Italy by Attila and the Huns.

Attwood, Thomas (1765–1838), British organist (at St Paul's Cathedral, London, from 1796), and composer of church and other music, including notable songs. Pupil of Mozart in Vienna.

au, aux (Fr.), at the, to the, etc.

aubade (Fr.), morning song (complementary to ➤serenade and corresponding to Sp. ➤alborada).

Auber, Daniel François Esprit (1782–1871), French composer of more than 40 operas including *Masaniello*, ➤ *Manon Lescaut*, ➤*Fra Diavolo*; also of a violin concerto, etc. Director of the Paris Conservatory.

Auden, W. H. [Wystan Hugh] (1907–73), British-born US poet. ➤*Age of Anxiety*, ➤*Bassarids*, ➤*Elegy for Young Lovers*, ➤*Hymn to St Cecilia*, ➤*Paul Bunyan*, ➤*Rake's Progress*.

Audran, Edmond (1840–1901), French composer chiefly of operettas including *La Mascotte* ('The Mascot').

Auer, Leopold (1845–1930), Hungarian violinist who settled in St Petersburg and became a performer and teacher of worldwide renown; moved to USA, 1918.

Aufforderung zum Tanz (Ger., 'Invitation to the Dance'), piano piece by Weber, in the form of a waltz with slow introduction and slow epilogue, 1819. Orchestrated, e.g. by Berlioz and by Weingartner; used for the ballet Le ➤*Spectre de la rose* (choreography by M. Fokin), 1911.

Aufstieg und Fall der Stadt Mahagonny (Ger., 'Rise and Fall of the City of Mahagonny'), opera by Kurt Weill, produced in Leipzig, 1930. Libretto by Brecht, satirizing capitalist morality: 'Mahagonny' is the city of material pleasure. An earlier version was produced at Baden-Baden in 1927.

aug., abbr. for ➤*augmented* as applied to intervals.

Augér, Arleen [Joyce; she added the accent to the surname] (1939–93), American soprano internationally known in opera; made more than 160 recordings; sang at the Duke of York's wedding in 1986.

augment (1) to supplement the numbers of a performing group; so *augmented choir*, etc.; (2) to 'increase' certain intervals (➤augmented interval); (3) to subject a melody to ➤augmentation.

augmentation, the treatment of a melody in such a way as to lengthen (usually doubling) the time-values of its notes. The device is used, e.g., in some fugues.

augmented interval, a type of interval regarded as an 'increased' version of a certain other interval. So *augmented first* (e.g. C up to C♯); *augmented second* (C up to D♯); *augmented fourth* (C up to F♯); *augmented fifth* (C up to G♯); *augmented sixth* (C up to A♯

– distinguished as ➤French, ➤German and ➤Italian sixths); *augmented eighth* or *augmented octave* (C up to next C♯ but one). Note that the *augmented fifth* carries the harmonic implication of the major third too; e.g. the *augmented-fifth chord* on C is C-E-G♯, which chord is referred to in popular music, etc., as *C augmented* (abbr. *C aug.*).

Auletta, Pietro (1698–1771), Italian composer, whose opera Il ➤*maestro di musica* was formerly mis-attributed to Pergolesi.

aulos, ancient Greek oboe-like wind instrument always played in pairs, the player holding two reed-pipes in V-formation, one hand fingering each.

Aumer, Jean (1774–1883), French choreographer. ➤*Manon Lescaut*.

Auric, Georges (1899–1983), French composer, youngest member of Les ➤*Six*. Wrote much for ballet (e.g. *Phèdre*, after Racine's play) and for films; also a piano concerto, piano sonata, etc. Administrator of the two Paris opera-houses, 1962–8.

Austin, Frederic (1872–1952), British baritone and composer; arranged the music of The ➤*Beggar's Opera* for its exceptionally successful London revival, 1920. Made a similar arrangement of ➤*Polly*.

Austin, Larry [Don] (b. 1930), American composer (pupil of Milhaud) with special interest in electronics and multimedia, also in co-ordinated improvisation. Works include *Plastic Surgery* for piano, percussion, tape and film; *Clarini!* for 20 trumpets. Also writer on music and university teacher.

authentic, authenticity, terms broadly referring to correctness in performance achieved by observing the conventions that apply to the composer's period – e.g. 'They played it with authentic trills.' Specifically, from the 1970s, *authenticity* has referred to the use of the instruments (and the instrumental and vocal techniques) of a bygone period for performing music of the same era. In this sense no differentiation is made between genuine old instruments and modern replicas.

authentic modes, ➤mode.

autograph, term used by literary and musical scholars to denominate a manuscript (not just a signature) written in an author's or composer's own hand, with the implication that it carries authority over a mere copy. Hence, 'No autograph exists of Mozart's Clarinet Quintet.' The term 'holograph' is sometimes used to indicate a manuscript text completely, not partially, written in its originator's hand.

autoharp, type of zither invented in the 1870s, with pads depressed by spring-loaded bars, silencing certain strings and leaving the others to sound a ready-made chord; used by folk-singers to provide their own accompaniment.

auxiliary note, in harmony, a note which forms a discord with the chord with which it is heard, but is 'justified' because it lies adjacent (higher or lower) to a note of the chord which is heard immediately before and after – e.g. the D in the following example:

Ave Maria (Lat., Hail, Mary), Roman Catholic prayer of partly biblical source. It has been variously set to music. The setting usually described as 'Bach-Gounod' consists of the first prelude of Bach's ➤*Wohltemperirte* Clavier plus a melody which Gounod wrote over this (with the title 'Meditation'); to this melody the words of the 'Ave Maria' were fitted by someone else.

Avison, Charles (1709–70), British composer and organist who worked in Newcastle-on-Tyne, and probably studied with Geminiani in London. Works include concertos for string orchestra; also edited Marcello's psalm-settings with English texts. Collaborator with ➤Giardini.

Avni, Zvi [Jacob] (b. 1927), German-born Israeli composer, pupil of Copland, Foss and Ben-Haim. Works include *Summer Strings* for string quartet; *Collage* for voice, flute, percussion and electric guitar; *Meditations on a Drama* for orchestra.

Avodath hakodesh, choral work by E. Bloch. ➤*Sacred Service*.

Avshalomov, Aaron (1894–1965), Russian-born composer-conductor, active in Shanghai, 1928–46; died in New York. Wrote a piano concerto on Chinese themes and other works attempting an integration of Chinese and Western music. Father of ➤Jacob Avshalomov.

Avshalomov, Jacob [David] (b. 1919), American composer and conductor; born in China of a Russian father (preceding). Works include Sinfonietta; *Inscriptions at the City of Brass* for narrator, chorus and orchestra without strings.

ayre, old spelling of 'air', retained in modern English for a type of English song composed (e.g. by J. Dowland) about 1600: usually ➤strophic, its main melodic interest is focused in the top vocal line, with accompaniment for lute (or other voices).

B

B, note of the scale. So B ➤*flat*, B ➤*sharp*, semitonally adjacent notes; B ➤*major*, B ➤*minor*, keys or chords defined by having B as point of stability (➤tonic). So also *in B flat*, (1, of a composition or part of it) indication that the music belongs in that key (major unless indicated as minor); (2, of a wind instrument) indication of length of air-column that gives B flat as the fundamental of its harmonic series: the indication usually but not always implies a ➤transposing instrument. So *clarinet in B flat* or (colloquially) *B flat clarinet*. In German the note represented in English by B is represented by H, the Germans using B to mean what is in English B flat. Hence clarinets in German scores may be marked *in B*, etc.

B., abbr. for (1) Bachelor (in university degrees, e.g. B.Mus. or Mus.B., Bachelor of Music); (2) British (as in ➤BBC); (3) Bach, as in BWV (➤Bach, J. S.).

b (lower-case letter), indication of the key of B minor as distinct from upper-case B for B major – a logical but not universal usage.

Baal Shem, suite for violin and piano by E. Bloch, subtitled 'Three Pictures of Chassidic Life'; named after Baal Shem Tov (Master of the Good Name), 17th-century founder of the Jewish pietist sect of Chassidism.

Baaren, Kees van (1906–70), Dutch composer who studied in Germany. Works include Variations for orchestra, a piano concerto, wind quartet.

Baba Yaga, orchestral work by Lyadov, 1904, describing the flight of the legendary Russian witch so named (who is also alluded to in 'The Hut on Fowls' Legs', one of Musorgsky's ➤*Pictures at an Exhibition*).

Babbitt, Milton [Byron] (b. 1916), American composer (also influential theorist and teacher), pupil of Sessions. Works include piano concerto, *Beaten Paths* for marimba, *Philomel* for soprano, recorded soprano and synthesized accompaniment on tape.

Babi Yar, nickname for Shostakovich's Symphony no. 13 for bass voice, male chorus and orchestra, with words by Yevtushenko, first performed in 1962. 'Babi Yar' is actually the title of the first movement, referring to the place in Ukraine where thousands of Jews were killed by the Nazis in 1941.

baby grand, a grand piano of the smallest size.

Baccaloni, Salvatore (1900–1969), Italian bass whose long operatic career from 1922 was distinguished by his performances in Italian comic roles.

bacchanal, (in opera) a scene of intoxication and sexual licence, as in Act 1 of Wagner's *Tannhäuser*.

bacchetta (It., stick), drumstick.

Bacchus et Ariane (Fr., 'Bacchus and Ariadne'), ballet with music by Roussel, choreography by Serge Lifar, produced in Paris, 1931. Two orchestral suites are drawn from it.

Bacewicz, Grażyna (1909–69), Polish composer of symphonies, cello concerto, seven violin concertos, seven string quartets, etc.; she was also a violinist.

Bach, German family of musicians, some of whom are listed below; *Bach* without prefaced name or initials indicates Johann Sebastian Bach. (Used attributively, but not always correctly, with instruments: Bach ➤bow, Bach ➤trumpet.) The letters B-A-C-H happen to represent, in German nomenclature, the notes B♭-A-C-B♮; J. S. Bach himself conceived the idea of using these notes as a theme of the unfinished final fugue of *Die* ➤*Kunst der Fuge*, and the same combination has been used by many subsequent composers (e.g. Schumann, Liszt, Busoni), generally in tribute to Bach.

Bach, Anna Magdalena (1701–60), second wife of J. S. Bach, who compiled two books of music (by himself and others) for her musical instruction, 1722 and 1725.

Bach, Carl [in modern German references **Karl**] **Philipp Emanuel** (1714–88), German composer, fifth child of J. S. Bach, pupil of his father. Domestic musician to Frederick the Great of Prussia until assuming a church post at Hamburg in 1767. Noted keyboard-player, adapting his music progressively to suit trend from harpsichord to piano; wrote treatise on keyboard-playing. Works, showing departure from J. S. Bach's style towards that of Haydn and Mozart, include keyboard concertos and sonatas, symphonies, chamber music; also oratorio and church music. His work is indexed by 'Wq' numbers, referring to the thematic catalogue made by Alfred Wotquenne in 1905.

Bach, Johann Christian (1735–82), German composer, 18th child of J. S. Bach; studied under his father and under his brother C. P. E. Bach. Went in 1756 to Italy, in 1762 to London where he remained and was known as 'the English Bach'; influenced Mozart on his visit (aged eight) to London. Works include Italian operas, English songs, about 40 piano concertos and other orchestral works, church music in Latin and English.

Bach, Johann Christoph (1642–1703), German composer, cousin of J. S. Bach's father. Wrote organ music, cantatas, motets including *Ich lasse dich nicht* (literally 'I leave thee not', but in English usually known as *I wrestle and pray*), formerly ascribed in error to J. S. Bach.

Bach, Johann Sebastian (1685–1750), German composer, the best-known of a distinguished musical family. Of high repute in his time as organist, but only with posthumous (19th-century) revival winning recognition as one of the greatest of all composers. Born at Eisenach; studied under his brother Johann Christoph (not the preceding): held organist's or other posts at Weimar, 1703;

Arnstadt, later in 1703; Mühlhausen, 1707; Weimar, 1708; Köthen, 1717; then in 1723 in Leipzig as Cantor (director of music) at St Thomas's church, in which post he died shortly after becoming blind. Twice married, father of 20 children. Works, mostly written as official duty or with some other definite performance in view, include over 200 church cantatas (Lutheran), with instrumental accompaniment; ➤ St John Passion and ➤ St Matthew Passion, both using his harmonizations of Lutheran chorales; ➤ Christmas and ➤ Easter Oratorios; the so-called Mass in B minor (➤ Mass); ➤ Coffee Cantata and various other secular vocal works; preludes, fugues and other works for organ; ➤ Chromatic Fantasia and Fugue, ➤ Goldberg Variations, ➤ Italian Concerto, Das ➤ Wohltemperirte Clavier and other works for harpsichord and/or clavichord including ➤ English Suites, ➤ French Suites; concertos for one, two, three and (arranged from Vivaldi) four harpsichords, also for one and two violins; six ➤ Brandenburg Concertos; partita for unaccompanied violin (including famous ➤ Chaconne), six suites for unaccompanied cello. In Das ➤ Musikalisches Opfer and Die ➤ Kunst der Fuge, he demonstrated prodigious contrapuntal skill. Works which have acquired their own familiar names in English include ➤ Air on the G String, ➤ Jesu, joy of man's desiring, ➤ Sheep may safely graze. His music is indexed by BWV numbers (Bach Werke-Verzeichnis – i.e. Index to Bach's Works), according to the thematic catalogue made by Wolfgang Schmieder, 1950.

Bach, K. P. E. or K. Ph. E., the customary German way (modernizing Carl to Karl) of referring to the composer known as C. P. E. Bach in general non-German usage.

Bach, Wilhelm Friedemann (1710–84), German composer; eldest son and second child of J. S. Bach, who wrote some music specially for his instruction. Became church organist, died in poverty; wrote church cantatas, nine symphonies, organ and harpsichord music, etc.

Bachianas Brasileiras, title given by Villa-Lobos to a set of nine works (for various instrumental groups with or without voice) intended to combine the spirit of J. S. Bach's music and that of the traditional music of Villa-Lobos's native Brazil.

Bäck, Sven-Erik (b. 1919), Swedish composer, pupil of Petrassi in Rome. Works include Sinfonia sacra for choir and orchestra; opera Crane Feathers; Time Present for two violins with electronics.

Backhaus, Wilhelm (1884–1969), German pianist (latterly became Swiss citizen), renowned for playing Beethoven; taught in Manchester, 1905–9; performed up to a few days before his death.

Bacon, Francis (1909–92), British painter. ➤ Schurmann.

Bacquier, Gabriel [originally Gabriel-Augustin - Raymond - Théodore - Louis] (b. 1924), French baritone, internationally celebrated in opera (Covent Garden from 1962; Metropolitan Opera, New York, from 1964).

badinerie (Fr., a jest), title of certain 2/4 movements in the 18th century, e.g. in Bach's Suite in B minor (BMV 1067) for flute and strings.

Badings, Henk (1907–87), Dutch composer, born in Java; largely self-taught at first, then pupil of Pijper. Works include 14 symphonies, four violin concertos; Sonata for carillon, electronic music.

Badura-Skoda [originally Badura], **Paul** (b. 1927), Austrian pianist; toured widely and became well known as writer on music, an authority on Mozart and composer of cadenzas for his concertos.

Baer [or Bär], **Olaf** (b. 1957), German baritone, well known as recitalist; made British début (Wigmore Hall), 1983, US début 1987. Also sings in opera – at Covent Garden, Glyndebourne (1987 as the Count in *Capriccio*), etc.

Baermann [or Bärmann], **Heinrich** [Joseph] (1789–1847), German clarinettist for whom Weber wrote his clarinet concertos; held a court appointment at Munich and toured with Weber at the piano. Composer of an *Adagio* for clarinet and piano wrongly ascribed to Wagner.

bagatelle (Fr., trifle), short, light piece, often for piano – Beethoven wrote 26.

bagpipe(s), reed-pipe instrument for which wind is stored in a bag, either (e.g. Scottish Highland pipes) mouth-filled, or (e.g. Northumbrian pipes and Irish 'Uillean' or 'Union' pipes) filled by bellows under player's arm; the former type is louder. Similar types are found in other countries (➤*musette*); most have one or more drone pipes (giving unaltered bass-notes) as well as a pipe for the melody (chanter). The Scottish Highland pipe, though its scale does not correspond exactly to the normal one of the concert-hall, is used with orchestra in P. M. Davies's ➤*Orkney Wedding with Sunrise*.

baguette (Fr.), (1) drumstick; (2) a conductor's baton (the French do not use the word *bâton* in this sense).

Bailey, Norman [Stanley] (b. 1933), British baritone celebrated in Wagner roles sung in English and German; made Covent Garden début in 1969. CBE, 1977.

Baillot, Pierre [Marie François de Sales] (1771–1842). French violinist. composer of violin music and writer of an instructional textbook on his instrument.

Bainbridge, Simon (b. 1952), British composer. Works include a viola concerto, wind quintet, *Landscape and Woods* for soprano and instrumental ensemble.

Bainton, Edgar L[eslie] (1880–1956), British composer and educationist; went to Sydney, 1934, as director of the Conservatorium, and died there.

Baird, Tadeusz (1928–81), Polish composer of *Erotics* (six songs for soprano and orchestra), *Variations without a theme* and other orchestral works, a piano concerto, theatre and film music, etc.

Bairstow, Edward Cuthbert (1874–1946), British organist (at York Minster from 1913), composer chiefly of church music, conductor, and professor at Durham University; knighted, 1932.

Baker, Janet [Abbott] (b. 1933), British mezzo-soprano, formerly styling herself contralto; noted in concerts (Edinburgh Festival, 1960; first New York recital, 1966) and in operas, especially Handel's and Britten's. Retired in 1989. Created Dame, 1976; Companion of Honour, 1994.

Balakirev, Mily Alexeyevich (1837–

25

1910), Russian composer, leader of the 'nationalist' group of composers called the ➤*Mighty Handful*; also conductor and musical organizer. After nervous breakdown, retired from music, 1871–6, becoming railway official; 1883, director of music to the Russian court. Works include two symphonies; symphonic poem *Tamara*; much piano music, including ➤*Islamey* and a sonata; songs and folk-song arrangements.

balalaika, type of Russian plucked, fretted instrument usually with three strings and triangular body; made in various sizes, and used singly and in bands for folk-music, etc. The ➤*domra* is similar.

Balanchine, George (1904–83), Russian–American choreographer. ➤*Agon*, ➤*Apollo Musagetes*, ➤*Orpheus*, ➤Françaix.

Balfe, Michael William (1808–70), Irish composer, also baritone singer; came to London as a boy and later studied in Italy. Composed operas in French, Italian and English, including *The* ➤*Bohemian Girl* (internationally successful, combining a cosmopolitan operatic style with provision for the Victorian English taste for 'ballads'), *The Maid of Artois* (➤*Manon*), *The Rose of Castile*; also songs, cantatas, etc.

ballabile (It.), to be danced; in a dancing manner, analogously with ➤*cantabile*.

ballad (derived as 'ball', i.e. from dancing), (1) old song (often a ➤*folk-song*) telling a story, the music being repeated for each verse; hence – (2) a self-contained song of a narrative nature, e.g. Goethe's ➤*Erlkönig* as set by Schubert and Loewe; (3) song of narrative, explanatory type character-

istically found in French opera and also, e.g., in Wagner's *Der fliegende Holländer* ('Senta's Ballad'); so Stravinsky called his narrative cantata on Abraham and Isaac a 'sacred ballad'; (4) sentimental English song of 19th-century 'drawing-room' type (also found in English operas of the period); so *ballad concert*, mainly devoted to such songs. The terms ➤*ballade* and ➤*ballad opera* are related to these.

ballade (1) instrumental piece, suggesting narrative, e.g. four written for piano by Chopin, said to be inspired by (but certainly not being literal interpretations of) Polish poems by Mickiewicz. (The word is the French version of ➤*ballad*; its use in English may be justified by the convenience of differentiating the instrumental from the vocal term.) (2) a form of French medieval poetry and music; certain polyphonic works, e.g. by Machaut, are so described,

Ballad of Baby Doe, The, opera by Douglas Moore, produced in Central City, Colorado, 1956, with libretto by John Latouche; the 19th-century story revolves round the historical Elizabeth 'Baby' Doe, married to a Colorado goldmine-owner.

ballad opera, opera having spoken dialogue and using popular tunes of the day adapted to new words (➤ballad, 1), the prototype being *The* ➤*Beggar's Opera*, 1728. (The term is also used in various looser senses; Vaughan Williams's ➤*Hugh the Drover*, described as 'a romantic ballad opera', has no spoken dialogue, and is not made up of traditional tunes, but it is intended to evoke such tunes.)

ballata (It.), a form of 14th-century Italian poetry and music, found, e.g., in Landini's works. Not the same form as the French ➤*ballade* (2).

ballet (1) form of dancing of Italian origin, established at the French court in the 16th century and evolving into a recognized art-form with its own traditional technique and conventions; it normally uses orchestral music (specially composed or otherwise) and appropriately full resources of stage decoration. The term was long employed for almost any piece of stage dancing having an artistic purpose and substantial length but is now commonly withheld from works not based on the 'classical' technique of dancing – e.g. the so-called 'modern dance'. Hence *opéra-ballet* and *ballet-pantomime*, 18th-century French terms differentiating ballet scores with and without sung words. The term *opera-ballet* is also applied to certain modern ballets with singing, e.g. Prokofiev's ➤*Cinderella*, but the simple classification *ballet* does not exclude the use of voices – as in Ravel's score for ➤*Daphnis et Chloé*. (2) an alternative spelling of ➤*ballett*, and so pronounced.

ballett, type of concerted vocal composition prominent in England and Italy (*balletto*) about 1600 and similar to the madrigal, but having a dance-like lilt (as the name suggests) and a 'fa-la' refrain.

ballo (It.), a dance; *Il ballo delle ingrate* (It., 'The Dance of the Ungrateful Women'), stage work, with voices, by Monteverdi, 1608; *Overtura di ballo*, idiosyncratic title of a concert-overture by Sullivan, 1870, using a succession of dance rhythms.

Ballo in maschera, Un (It., 'A Masked Ball'), opera by Verdi, produced in Rome, 1859. Libretto by A. Somma, on a plot based on the assassination of Gustav III of Sweden, 1792. To comply with censorship the action was incongruously changed to Boston (Mass.), but some productions have reverted to the historical Swedish setting.

Baltsa, Agnes (b. 1944), Greek mezzo-soprano who established an operatic career in Germany, then internationally (Covent Garden from 1976).

Bamert, Matthias (b. 1942), Swiss conductor (also composer), resident in London since 1957; music director of Swiss Radio Orchestra (Basle) 1977–83, of London Mozart Players since 1993. With various orchestras, has conducted first performances of works by Takemitsu, Denisov and others. Director, Lucerne Festival, since 1992.

Banchieri, Adriano (1568–1634), Italian composer, also organist, musical theorist and priest. Works include Masses, instrumental works and 'madrigal comedies' (➤madrigal).

band, a numerous body of players, especially if mainly composed of wind instruments, e.g. ➤brass, ➤military, ➤dance bands, etc. The use of the term for a full or string orchestra is obsolete or colloquial, and the prestige of the term 'orchestra' was borrowed by dance bands from the 1930s onwards. The term *big band* now refers to the type of dance band of 20 or more musicians which became a theatrical attraction in the 1930s and has undergone a post-1960 revival.

bandoneon, German type of ➤concertina (invented by H. Band, 1845), which takes a leading role in Argentinian ➤tango bands; among concert composers, Kagel has written for it – and David Tudor plays it.

bandora, ➤pandora.

bandurría (Sp.), Spanish plucked instrument, usually with six pairs of strings, each pair tuned to a unison.

Banister, John (c. 1625–79), English violinist, composer, and organizer of the first concerts in London to be open to the public on payment of an admission fee, 1672.

banjo, fretted instrument usually of five strings, plucked with fingers or plectrum; taken over from Afro-Americans by black-faced minstrel shows, and also used in early jazz – otherwise not much played in public, except to provide local 'atmosphere', e.g. in the orchestration of Gershwin's ➤Porgy and Bess and Delius's ➤Koanga.

Bantock, Granville (1868–1946), British composer of Fifine at the Fair and other symphonic poems; also of Hebridean Symphony, song-cycles, unaccompanied choral works including a setting of Swinburne's Atlanta in Calydon (➤choral symphony), etc. Professor at Birmingham University, 1908; knighted, 1930.

bar (1) a metrical division of music, marked on paper as the distance between two vertical lines; so 'two beats in the bar', etc.; (2) such a vertical line itself. (In general the first of these uses is British, the second American – British bar equals US 'measure'; US bar equals British bar-line. But two vertical lines close together, indicating the end of a piece or section, are called even in English double bar, not double bar-line.) (3, a meaning unconnected with previous two), a medieval German pattern of song-construction, two similar sections being followed by one in contrast.

bar., abbr. of ➤baritone (voice).

Bär, ➤Baer.

Barbe-bleue (Fr., 'Bluebeard'), operetta by Offenbach, produced in Paris, 1866. Libretto by H. Meilhac and L. Halévy, a comic version of the legend of the ogre who murdered his successive wives.

Barber, Samuel (1910–81), American composer, also singer (e.g. in his own setting, for voice and string quartet, of Matthew Arnold's ➤Dover Beach). Works include operas Vanessa, A Hand of Bridge, Antony and Cleopatra; two symphonies; two Essays for Orchestra; Adagio for Strings (➤adagio); Capricorn Concerto (flute, oboe, trumpet and strings); piano sonata; ballet Medea (also known as Cave of the Heart); cantata Prayers of Kierkegaard.

Barber of Baghdad, The, opera by Cornelius. ➤Barbier von Bagdad.

Barber of Seville, The, operas by Paisiello and Rossini: ➤Barbiere di Siviglia.

Barberillo de Lavapiés, El (Sp., 'The Little Barber of Lavapiés'), operetta (➤zarzuela) by Francisco Barbieri, with libretto by Mariano de Larra. Produced in Madrid, 1874. The barber-factotum is unwittingly involved in political revolution in Madrid, 1770.

barber-shop, type of close-harmony singing (originally, in USA from 1938) by male-voice quartet, with sentimental popular repertory of c.1890–1930 and with concentration on certain harmonies; now extended to larger groups with or without female component.

Barbiere di Siviglia, Il, ovvero La precauzione inutile (It., 'The Barber of Seville, or the Useless Precaution'), opera by Paisiello, produced (in Italian) in St Petersburg, 1782, with libretto by G. Petrosellini; achieved international success until superseded in popularity by Rossini's opera (next entry) on the same plot.

Barbiere di Siviglia, Il (It., 'The Barber of Seville'), opera by Rossini, produced in Rome, 1816, with libretto by C. Sterbini; originally titled *Almaviva, ossia L'inutile precauzione* ('Almaviva, or the Useless Precaution') to distinguish it from Paisiello's opera (preceding entry; general allusions to *Il Barbiere di Siviglia* always refer to the Rossini version). The plot is that of Beaumarchais's French play, the cunning barber-factotum of the title being Figaro: the plot of Mozart's *Le* ➤*Nozze di Figaro* is a sequel. Formerly subjected in performance to interpolations of music by other composers, among them ➤Alyabiev.

Barbieri, Fedora (b. 1920), Italian contralto prominent in opera 1942–70, with more than 100 roles; first appeared at Covent Garden in visiting company from La Scala, Milan, 1950. Made many recordings, some with Callas.

Barbieri, Francisco [Asenjo] (1823–94), Spanish composer, also singer, instrumentalist and writer on music; composed Spanish comic operas of ➤zarzuela type, such as *El* ➤*Barberillo de Lavapiés*.

Barbier von Bagdad, Der (Ger., 'The Barber of Baghdad'), opera by Cornelius, produced in Weimar, 1858. Libretto by the composer, a comic tale of intrigue (after the *Arabian Nights' Entertainment*).

Barbirolli, John [originally Giovanni Battista] (1899–1970), British conductor of Italian and French parent-

age, previously cellist. Conductor of the New York Philharmonic-Symphony Orchestra, 1936–42, of the Hallé Orchestra (Manchester), 1943–70, and of the Houston (Texas) Symphony Orchestra, 1961–7. Knighted, 1949; Companion of Honour, 1969. Married Evelyn Rothwell (b. 1911), oboist.

barcarolle (Fr., from It. *barca*, boat), boating-song, especially of the kind associated with Venetian gondoliers; songs or instrumental piece suggestive of this, in swaying 6/8 time, e.g. Chopin's for piano, 1846, or the vocal duet in Offenbach's *Les* ➤*Contes d'Hoffmann*.

Barenboim, Daniel (b. 1942), Israeli pianist and conductor, born in Argentina; studied in Salzburg, Paris, Rome; boy prodigy as pianist (London, 1955; New York, 1957). Conductor, Orchestre de Paris, 1975–90; of Chicago Symphony Orchestra since 1991; cond. Deutsche Staatsoper, Berlin from 1992 and is highly reputed Wagner conductor, e.g. at Bayreuth since 1981. Married Jacqueline du Pré, 1967.

baritone (1) man's voice of a range intermediate between tenor and bass; (2, of 'families' of instruments) indication of a range below the 'tenor' type (➤saxhorn, ➤saxophone); (3) name used in brass bands as abbreviation for *baritone saxhorn*. The spelling ➤*baryton* carries a different meaning.

Bärmann, ➤Baermann.

Barnby, Joseph (1838–96), British conductor and composer (of part-song 'Sweet and Low', etc.). Principal of Guildhall School of Music, London; knighted, 1892.

Barnett (original surname Beer), **John** (1802–90), British composer (a relative of Meyerbeer), whose works include opera *The Mountain Sylph*, operettas, symphony.

barocco, Barock (It., Ger.), ➤*baroque*.

Baroni, Leonora (1611–70), Italian singer and lutenist; her singing won praise in Naples (when she was 16) and elsewhere in Italy. Attached to the French court, 1644–5.

baroque, term borrowed from architecture (where it has connotations of a twisting, elaborate, heavy, involved construction) and used to describe characteristics of musical style roughly corresponding to this, *c.* 1600–1750. Applied, e.g., to Monteverdi, Purcell and J. S. Bach, though the liberality of such application makes precise definition awkward – the use of ➤*continuo*, however, being a consistent ingredient. So *baroque* ➤*organ*, ➤*trumpet*, ➤*violin* etc., modern names for instruments of the period.

barrage (Fr.), the use of chords played ➤*barré* on the guitar.

Barraqué, Jean (1928–73), French composer, pupil of Messiaen. Works include a piano sonata; concerto for clarinet, vibraphone and six instrumental ensembles; *Chant après chant* ('Song after Song') for six percussionists, voice and piano.

Barraud, Henry (b. 1900), French composer of orchestral works, *Lavinia* and other operas, three symphonies, a piano concerto, etc.; also critic.

barré (Fr.), (chord on guitar, etc.) played with one finger laid like a rigid bar across all strings, raising the pitch of all these equally.

barrel-organ, automatic organ in which projections on a hand-rotated barrel bring into action the notes re-

quired – i.e. a genuine pipe-organ though limited to a number of pre-set tunes, like a musical box; formerly used in some English churches. The ➤hurdy-gurdy is different.

barrel-piano, alternative name for the ➤street piano.

Barrett, Richard (b. 1959), British composer resident in the Netherlands; gives improvisatory performances of live electronics. Works include *Vanity* for orchestra, *Earth* for trombone and percussion (one of several pieces called *Fictions*), and *I open and close* for amplified string quartet.

Barrie, [Sir] **James** (1860–1937), British novelist and dramatist. ➤O'Neill (N.).

Barry, Gerald [Anthony] (b. 1952), Irish composer of opera *The Intelligence Park*, *A Piano Concerto*, *Sweet Punishment* for brass quintet, etc. Also organist and painter.

Barshai, Rudolf (b. 1924), Russian viola-player and conductor who founded the Moscow Chamber Orchestra; conductor of the Bournemouth Symphony Orchestra, 1982–8; naturalized British, 1983.

Barstow, Josephine [Clare] (b. 1940), British soprano celebrated in opera, with first performances of works by Tippett, Penderecki and Henze. created Dame, 1995.

Bart [originally Begleiter], **Lionel** (b. 1930), British composer of musical shows including *Fings Ain't Wot They Used T'Be* (1959) and ➤*Oliver!*

Bartered Bride, The (Cz., *Prodaná nevěsta*), comic opera by Smetana, produced in Prague, 1866. Libretto by K. Sabina, about a village intrigue.

The Czech title actually means 'The Sold Fiancée'.

Bartók, Béla (1881–1945), Hungarian composer, settled in USA 1940, dying there a poor man. From youth, a virtuoso pianist. Cultivated and developed Hungarian national musical style; partly in association with Kodály, collected and edited Hungarian folk-songs, showing them to be different from the gipsy music borrowed by Liszt, Brahms, etc. Active in investigating other folk-music too. His own works – often atonal and cultivating extreme dissonance, especially in his middle life – include opera ➤*Duke Bluebeard's Castle*, mime-plays *The Wooden Prince* and *The* ➤*Miraculous Mandarin*; much piano music, such as *Allegro barbaro*, ➤*Mikrokosmos*, *Out of Doors* and works for children; orchestral *Dance Suite*; Concerto for Orchestra (➤Concerto); ➤*Music for Strings, Percussion and Celesta*; three piano concertos, two violin concertos; a viola concerto (posthumous, edited by T. Serly); six string quartets (➤pizzicato); trio ➤*Contrasts*; songs and folk-song arrangements; ➤cantata.

Bartók Quartet, name assumed in 1963 by a Hungarian string quartet, till then named after its leader Peter Komlós; other present members Géza Hargitai, Géza Nemeth, László Mezö. Has recorded not only all Bartók's quartets but all Beethoven's and Brahms's, etc.

Bartoli, Cecilia (b. 1966), Italian mezzo-soprano whose appearance at the Verona Arena in 1987 led swiftly to an international career, especially in such roles as Rosina in *Il barbiere di Siviglia*; starred in six opera recordings before she was 27.

Bartolozzi, Bruno (1911–80), Italian composer, also violinist and author of important book on new woodwind techniques. Works include Concerto for orchestra; *The Hollow Man* (after Eliot) for any woodwind instrument; *Images* for women's voices and 17 instruments.

baryton, stringed instrument resembling bass viol but having sympathetic strings like the viola d'amore. Haydn wrote extensively for it, because his patron, Prince Nicholas Esterházy, played it; disused thereafter until a modest post-1950 revival (➤Veress).

Bashmet, Yuri [Abramovich] (b. 1953), Russian viola-player for whom Schnittke, Tavener and others have written works specially; internationally prominent soloist, and founder of the ensemble 'Moscow Soloists'.

basic set, term used in ➤twelve-note technique for the note-row or series (comprising all 12 notes within the octave) in its original chosen order – i.e. not in an order arrived at by using the row backwards, or upside-down, or both (➤inversion, ➤retrograde).

bass (1) the lowest male voice; (2) the lowest note or part in a chord, a composition, etc.; (3) the lower regions of musical pitch generally – especially in antithesis to ➤treble; (4, of a 'family' of instruments) having low range, e.g. *bass* ➤*clarinet*, ➤*bass drum*, *bass* ➤*oboe*, *bass* ➤*saxophone*; also (predecessor of the cello), *bass* ➤*violin*; *bass flute*, usually a misnomer for 'alto flute' (➤flute); (5) colloquial abbreviation for double-bass, or (in military and brass bands) for the tuba (either size); (6, *bass clef*) clef written 𝄢 and indicating F below middle C as the top line but one of the staff (and so sometimes also called *F clef*); it is normally used for bass voice, for most lower-pitched instruments, for the left-hand part of piano music, etc. So also ➤*bass fiddle*.

Bassarids, The, opera by Henze, produced in Salzburg, 1966. Libretto by W. H. Auden and Chester Kallman, founded on Euripides' *The Bacchae*. Title means 'the [male or female] followers of Bacchus'.

bass drum (or 'long drum'), large, shallow drum of low but indefinite pitch; used in symphony orchestras, military bands (where it may be carried), dance bands (the drum-stick usually worked by pedal), etc.

basse (Fr.), bass; *bass chantante* = ➤*basso cantante*.

basset-clarinet, the modern name for a clarinet of standard size equipped with a downward extension, such as was used by Mozart's soloist Anton Stadler for the former's clarinet concerto and clarinet quintet.

basset-horn, instrument of same type as clarinet but lower in pitch (down to the F at the bottom of the bass staff). Used, e.g., by Mozart in his *Requiem*; also by R. Strauss (the opera *Elektra* and later works) but otherwise very rare since Mozart's day. It is a ➤transposing instrument in F.

bass fiddle, colloquial term for double-bass; or a substitute term (as used by ➤Grainger) for cello.

basso (It.), bass. So *basso cantante* ('singing'), a bass voice suitable for lyrical rather than dramatic parts in opera; *basso* ➤*continuo*; *basso ostinato*,

➤ground bass; *basso profondo* (incorrectly *profundo*), a bass voice of unusually low range.

bassoon, bass woodwind instrument found in the orchestra and military band, occasionally also as soloist and in chamber music; having a double reed, thus related to the oboe. Compass from the B♭ below the bass stave upwards for about three and a half octaves. The *double-bassoon*, rarely encountered before the 19th century, has a compass an octave lower; it is more often called contra-bassoon, on the analogy of It. *contrafagotto*, from *fagotto*, bassoon. (The obsolete *Russian bassoon* was not a bassoon at all but a kind of straightened-out ➤serpent.)

Bastien und Bastienne, German opera (K50) by Mozart (aged 12), produced in Vienna, 1768. Libretto by F. W. Weiskern and A. Schachtner (after a French original), about a pair of pastoral lovers separated and reunited.

Bate, Jennifer [Lucy] (b. 1944), British organist (also composer) who met Messiaen in 1975 and remained favoured by him as an interpreter of his music; has also given first performances of works by Dickinson and Mathias and recorded Vivaldi, Samuel Wesley, etc.

Bateson, Thomas (*c.* 1570–1630), English composer of madrigals, also organist (latterly in Dublin, where he died).

Bathori, Jane [originally Jeanne-Marie Berthier] (1877–1970), French soprano (sometimes her own accompanist) to whom Debussy, Ravel and Satie dedicated works; also writer on her art and, during World War I, theatre director.

baton (from the French *bâton*, though in French usage the conductor's stick is a *baguette*), stick used by conductor to indicate time and expression.

battaglia (It., 'battle'), general name for pieces suggesting armed conflict by a form of musical imitation, as in Isaac's instrumental *La Battaglia* (*c*.1485) and Janequin's chanson *La guerre* (Fr., 'war') of 1515. Such 'warlike' pieces as Beethoven's ➤*Wellingtons Sieg* and Tchaikovsky's ➤*Eighteen-Twelve* may be considered successors.

battery, an obsolete collective term for percussion instruments.

Battistini, Mattia (1856–1928), Italian baritone, among the most prominent operatic performers of his day; won acclaim in Britain and (every season from 1888 to 1914) in Russia.

Battle, Kathleen (b. 1948), American soprano, prominent in opera (Glyndebourne from 1979) and the concert repertory.

Battle of Victoria, Battle Symphony, work by Beethoven. ➤*Wellingtons Sieg*.

battuta (It.), (1) beat; (2) bar; *ritmo di tre battute*, literally 'rhythm of three bars', i.e. with the main accent falling at the beginning of every three bars.

Bauld, Alison (b. 1944), Australian composer, resident in Britain. Various theatrical works include *Exiles* for four actors, mezzo-soprano, tenor, chorus and instruments; has also written *Mad Moll* for soprano alone; *My Own Island* for clarinet and piano; *Van Diemen's Land* for unaccompanied chorus; etc.

Baumann, Hermann [Rudolf Conrad] (b. 1934), German horn-player who occasionally performs on the old valveless horn and has revived long-forgotten works.

Bax, Arnold [Edward Trevor] (1883–1953), British composer – not Irish, but influenced by Irish literature and lore. Also visited Russia, 1910. Knighted, 1937; Master of the King's (later Queen's) Music, 1941. Works include seven symphonies; *Tintagel* and other symphonic poems; *Overture to a Picaresque Comedy*; many piano solos.

bayan (Rus.), a Russian type of button-➤accordion.

Bayle, François (b. 1932), French composer, born in Madagascar; pupil of Stockhausen and others. Much of his music is electronic and includes *Motion-Emotion* and *The Acoustic Experience*, designed to last about 10 hours.

Bayreuth, a Bavarian town where a festival theatre was built to Wagner's designs. It opened in 1876 with *Der* ➤*Ring des Nibelungen* and has remained devoted to his music.

Bazelon, Irwin (b. 1922), American composer of *De-Tonations* for brass quintet and orchestra; *Triple Play* for two trombones and solo percussion; a piano concerto, etc.

Bazzini, Antonio (1818–97), Italian violinist and composer of *La ronde des Lutins* (Fr., 'The Dance of the Goblins') for violin and piano; also opera, six string quartets, etc.

BB♭ bass, ➤tuba.

BBC, British Broadcasting Corporation; the *BBC Symphony Orchestra*, its chief orchestra, is maintained in London – founded in 1930, first conducted by Boult; from 1983, Andrew Davis. Outside London it maintains, among others, the *BBC Philharmonic* (Manchester), till 1983 called the *BBC Northern Symphony Orchestra* (principal conductor, 1980–92, Edward Downes, then Yan Pascal Tortelier); *BBC Scottish Symphony Orchestra* (Glasgow; chief conductor since 1996, Osmo Vänskä); *BBC National Orchestra of Wales* (Cardiff, till 1993 called the *BBC Symphony Orchestra*; principal conductor since 1996 (succeeding Tadaaki Otaka), Mark Wigglesworth.

Beach, Mrs H. H. A., style of name used as a composer by Amy Marcy Beach (born Cheney; 1867–1944), whose works include *Gaelic Symphony*, a piano concerto, Mass, etc. – the first American woman to achieve a reputation as composer of such music.

Bear, The, nickname of Haydn's Symphony no. 82 in C, 1786 (Hob. I: 82), one of the ➤Paris Symphonies; its last movement supposedly suggests a captive bear dancing to a bagpipe.

Bear, The, one-act opera by Walton (libretto by Paul Dehn) based on a Chekhov play about a boorish character; produced in Aldeburgh, 1967.

beat (1) rhythmic pulse ('the waltz has three beats to the bar'), or the physical action corresponding to this ('watch the conductor's beat'); so ➤*down-beat*, ➤*up-beat*; (2, acoustics) appreciable regular increase and decrease of loudness caused by discrepancy in vibrations of adjacent notes sounded together (a phenomenon utilized, e.g., in piano-tuning); (3) (obsolete word for) ➤*appoggiatura*; (4) ornament found in old music,

probably meaning something similar to ➤*mordent*.

Beatles, The, British rock group, winning prodigious fame, 1962–70; the long-term (though not the first) membership was of Paul ➤McCartney, John Lennon, George Harrison, Ringo Starr. Lennon's and McCartney's songs in particular penetrated the world of 'classical' performers and composers, Brouwer and Takemitsu being among those who have arranged them instrumentally.

Béatrice et Bénédict (Fr., 'Beatrice and Benedict'), opera by Berlioz, produced in Baden-Baden, 1862. Libretto by composer, after Shakespeare's *Much Ado About Nothing*. (Shakespeare's spelling of his hero's name, Benedick, might well be retained in English-language performances.)

Beaumarchais, Pierre Augustin Caron de (1732–99), French dramatist. *Il* ➤*Barbiere di Siviglia*, *Le* ➤*Nozze di Figaro*,

Beaux Arts Trio, American piano trio founded 1955, in its most famous period (1968–87) having as members Isidore Cohen (violin), Bernard Greenhouse (cello), Menahem Pressler (piano).

Bebung, type of touch on the ➤clavichord.

bécarre (Fr.), ➤natural, the sign ♮.

Becken (Ger.), cymbals.

Beckett, Samuel (1906–89), Anglo-Irish dramatist and novelist. ➤Haubenstock-Ramati, ➤Kurtág, ➤Mihalovici, ➤Wilkinson.

Beckwith, John (b. 1927), Canadian composer, pupil of N. Boulanger in Paris; also writer and university teacher. Works include *Canada Dash, Canada Dot*, words-and-music collage for singers, speakers and orchestra; *Circle with Tangents* for harpsichord and 13 strings.

Bedford, David [Vickerman] (b. 1937), British composer, pupil of Berkeley and Nono. Works include *Star Clusters, Nebulae and Places in Devon* for chorus and brass; *Sun Paints Rainbows on Vast Waves* for wind band; *With 100 Kazoos* for instrumental ensemble and (in audience) kazoos. His brother is the conductor Steuart [John Rudolf] Bedford (b. 1939); they are grandsons of the following.

Bedford, Herbert (1867–1945), British composer (also author, painter); married the singer and composer Liza Lehmann. Works include unaccompanied songs and music for wind band.

Beecham, Thomas (1879–1961), British conductor; knighted in 1916 and later that year became baronet in succession to his father, Sir Joseph Beecham (manufacturing chemist and patron of music and ballet). First London orchestral season, 1905–6; important opera seasons, 1910, 1911 (first British performances of *Elektra* and *Salome*); founder-conductor in 1932 of London Philharmonic Orchestra, which parted company with him in 1940; founder-conductor of Royal Philharmonic Orchestra, 1946. Champion and biographer of Delius.

Beecroft, Norma [Marian] (b. 1934), Canadian composer (pupil of Copland and Maderna), also organizer of new music concerts, etc. Compositions include *Contrasts* for oboe, viola, harp, marimba, vibraphone, other percussion; choral work *The Living Flame of Love* (words from St John of the Cross);

ballet score *Hedda* (after Ibsen's *Hedda Gabler*).

Beerbohm, [Sir] **Max** (1872–1956), British writer. ➤Ghedini.

Beeson, Jack [Hamilton] (b. 1921), American composer of *Lizzie Borden, My Heart's in the Highlands* and other operas, symphony, etc.; had some informal tuition from Bartók. Also university teacher.

Bees' Wedding, The, piano piece by Mendelssohn. ➤*Lieder ohne Worte*.

Beethoven, Ludwig van (1770–1827), German composer whose greatness was acknowledged in his own time and ever since; born in Bonn, son and grandson of musicians. Published a piano piece at the age of 12; worked shortly afterwards as pianist, organist, viola-player. Went to Vienna, 1792 (to study with Haydn, but did not stay with him), and remained and died there. Many love-affairs, but never married. Brought up as a Roman Catholic but came to hold unorthodox deistical views. From 1801 suffered from increasing deafness, which became total by about 1824 – after composition of Symphony no. 9 (➤*Choral*) but before the last five quartets. Vastly extended the form and scope of the symphony (he wrote nine: no. 3, ➤*Eroica*, no. 6, ➤*Pastoral*): a conjectural reconstruction of a tenth symphony has been unconvincingly made. Likewise innovative was his treatment of the piano concerto (he wrote five, no. 5 being the so-called ➤*Emperor*), the string quartet (16, including the ➤*Razumovsky* set, plus ➤*Grosse Fuge*), the piano sonata (32, including ➤ *Moonlight*, ➤*Pathétique*, ➤ *Waldstein*). Other works include opera ➤*Fidelio*, ballet score *Die* ➤*Geschöpfe des*

Prometheus, Mass (➤*Missa solemnis*) in D and a smaller Mass in C; oratorio *Christus am Oelberge* ('Christ on the Mount of Olives'); a violin concerto and a triple concerto (piano, violin, cello); ➤*Choral Fantasia*; theatre music – ➤*Egmont*, ➤*Coriolan, Die* ➤*Weihe des Hauses* and concert overture ➤*Namensfeier*, descriptive 'Battle Symphony' (➤*Wellingtons Sieg*); 10 violin sonatas (op. 24, ➤*Spring*; op. 47, ➤*Kreutzer*); ➤*Archduke* and ➤*Geister* piano trios; songs; piano pieces including ➤*Diabelli* and *Prometheus* Variations, ➤*Equali* for trombones. The so-called ➤*Jena* Symphony is not by him. His works are indexed by Kinsky, some as ➤*WoO*.

Beethoven Quartet, Russian string quartet based in Moscow, active 1923–75; it gave the premières of nearly all Shostakovich's quartets. Final members: Dmitry Tsiganov, Sergey Shirinsky, Nikolay Zabaknikov, Fyodor Drusinin.

Beggar's Opera, The, work of ➤*ballad opera* type, with words by John Gay, set to tunes then current, produced in London, 1728. Musical arrangements by Pepusch. Later musical arrangements include those of F. Austin (1920, record London run of 1,463 performances) and Britten (Cambridge, 1948, libretto adapted by Tyrone Guthrie). ➤*Polly*, ➤*Dreigroschenoper*.

Beggar Student, The, operetta by Millöcker. ➤*Bettelstudent*.

Begleitung (Ger.), accompaniment.

Behrens, Hildegard (b. 1937), German soprano noted for her opera performances (title-role in *Salome* under Karajan at Salzburg, 1977; also recorded) and as song-recitalist.

Beinum, Eduard [Alexander] van (1901–59), Dutch conductor, associated with the London Philharmonic Orchestra and principal conductor of the (Royal) Concertgebouw Orchestra of Amsterdam from 1945 until his death.

bel canto (It., beautiful singing), term used – often vaguely – by teachers, 'authorities' on singing, etc., with reference to the finely cultivated voice, especially to the agile yet smooth voice-production demanded in the operas of Bellini, Donizetti, etc.

Belkin, Boris (b. 1948), Russian violinist who emigrated to Israel and made his 'western' début there with the Israel Philharmonic Orchestra under Mehta, 1974. Now an international soloist, he has recorded both Prokofiev's concertos.

bell (1) heavy resonating vessel in hollow cup-shape found in churches, etc., and rung either directly by hand-ropes (➤change-ringing) or by ➤carillon; (2) orchestral instrument usually in the form of a free-hanging tube (*tubular bell*) struck by hand with small hammer – a set of such bells sometimes spanning as much as an octave; (3) the open end of a wind instrument, at the opposite extremity to the mouthpiece (named for its shape). See also following entry.

Bell Anthem, nickname for Purcell's *Rejoice in the Lord Alway* (Z49, composed *c*. 1684–5), alluding to bell-like descending scales in the introduction (for strings).

Bell, Joshua (b. 1967), American violinist who performed with Philadelphia Orchestra at 14; gave first performance of Maw's concerto, dedicated to him (1993) and has recorded chamber music as well as concertos.

Belle Hélène, La (Fr., 'The Beautiful Helen'), operetta by Offenbach, produced in Paris, 1864. Libretto by Meilhac and L. Halévy, mocking the classical story of Helen of Troy.

Bellini, Vincenzo (1801–35), Italian composer of opera, pupil of Zingarelli. Visited London and Paris, 1833; wrote his last completed opera, *I* ➤*Puritani*, for performance in Paris, and died near there. The other operas he composed in his short life include *I Capuleti e i Montecchi* ('The Capulets and the Montagues' – but not based on Shakespeare's *Romeo and Juliet*), *La* ➤*Sonnambula* and ➤*Norma*.

Bell Rondo (It., *Rondo alla campanella*), the finale of Paganini's Violin concerto in B minor (*c*.1824), with bell-like effect. Liszt's *La campanella* for piano (1838, revised in 1851) is based on it.

Bells, The (Rus., *Kolokola*), cantata by Rakhmaninov, first performed in St Petersburg, 1915: text, translated from Poe, imagines the 'voices' of bells.

belly, the upper surface (i.e. that lying directly under the strings) of a stringed instrument.

Belshazzar's Feast (1) suite by Sibelius drawn from his incidental music to a play by H. Procope (1906); (2) work for baritone, chorus and orchestra by Walton (words arranged by Osbert Sitwell, based on the Bible), first performed in Leeds, 1931.

bémol (Fr.), ➤flat, the sign ♭.

ben, bene (It.), well, very.

bend, (especially in modern popular music) to shift a note temporarily sharp or flat for expressive reasons, e.g. in singing or guitar-playing.

Benda, Jiří Antonín (1722–95), Bohemian oboist, keyboard-player and composer, one of a family of many musicians. Worked in Germany (known there as Georg Benda) and died there. Notable for his cultivation of ➤melodrama (in its technical sense); also wrote symphonies, operas, church music, etc.

Benedetti Michelangeli, ➤Michelangeli.

Benedicite (Lat., Bless ye . . .), a name in Anglican Church use for the canticle taken from the 'Song of the Three Holy Children' found in the Apocrypha. This text is combined with a poem by J. Austin (1613–69) in Vaughan Williams's cantata *Benedicite* (first performed 1930). Text also used in an electronic work by Stockhausen (➤*Gesang*).

Benedict, Julius (1804–85), German-born composer (also conductor), pupil of Weber, who settled in England 1835, becoming naturalized; knighted, 1871. Works include two symphonies, two piano concertos, and operas in Italian and English including *The* ➤*Lily of Killarney*, formerly a favourite of the British public.

Benedictus (1) part of the Mass (starting '*Benedictus qui venit*', 'Blessed is he that cometh'); (2) canticle sung during Anglican morning service and based on Luke i. 68ff.

Ben-Haim, Paul (1897–1984), Israeli composer, German-born, who changed his surname from Frankenburger after emigrating to Palestine, 1933. Works include two symphonies, a piano concerto, chamber music, setting of biblical Hebrew texts.

Benjamin, Arthur (1893–1960), Australian composer and pianist resident in London and for a time in Vancouver. Wrote comic operas *The Devil Take Her* and *Prima Donna*, a piano concerto, film music, and many smaller pieces including *Jamaican Rumba* (➤rumba).

Benjamin, George [William John] (b. 1960; no relation to the preceding), British composer, also pianist and conductor; precociously gifted, he had an orchestral work performed at the Proms before he was 21 – *Ringed by the Flat Horizon*. Has also written *Sudden Time* for orchestra; *Flight* for unaccompanied flute; *Sortilèges* (Fr., 'Spells') for piano, etc.

Bennet, John (*c.* 1575–?), English composer of madrigals (contributor to *The* ➤*Triumphs of Oriana*) and church music, etc.

Bennett, Richard Rodney (b. 1936), British composer of operas *The Ledge*, *The* ➤*Mines of Sulphur*, *A Penny for a Song*, *Victory*; various concertos; chamber works – some called ➤*commedia*; more than 40 film scores. Studied with H. Ferguson and (in Paris) Boulez. Also jazz pianist (and occasional singer) who plays his own transcriptions of Cole Porter, etc. CBE, 1977. Knighted 1998.

Bennett, Robert Russell (1894–1981), American composer (symphonies, film music, etc.) and arranger of 'symphonic pictures' drawn from the scores of musicals by Gershwin, Kern, etc.

Bennett, William Sterndale (1816–75), British composer and pianist, pupil of Mendelssohn at Leipzig; friend of Schumann, who dedicated his *Symphonic Studies* (for piano) to him. Professor at Cambridge; knighted, 1871.

Works include cantata *The May Queen*, five piano concertos, overture *The Naiads*, piano pieces and songs.

Bentzon, Jørgen (1897–1951), Danish composer; wrote chamber music, including *Racconti* (one-movement works using 3–5 instruments suggesting narrative, hence this Italian title), and *A Dickens Symphony*. Cousin of the following.

Bentzon, Niels Viggo (b. 1919), Danish composer and pianist (also writer on music), cousin of preceding. Very prolific: works include 18 symphonies, 8 piano concertos, tuba concerto, five sets of 24 preludes and fugues for piano, variations on *The Volga Boatmen* for unaccompanied cello.

Benvenuto Cellini, opera by Berlioz, produced in Paris, 1838. Libretto by L. de Wailly and A. Barbier, after Cellini's autobiography (*c.*1560). Source of the concert-overture *Le* ➤*Carnaval romain*.

bequadro (It.), ➤natural, the sign ♮.

Berberian, Cathy (1925–83), American mezzo-soprano, mainly devoted to modern music, e.g. by Cage, Bussotti, Pousseur and especially Berio (to whom she was married, 1950–65) and of whose music she gave many first performances. Also composer of *Stripsody* (for unaccompanied voice, based on comic-strip sounds), 1966.

berceuse (Fr.), cradle-song, lullaby; instrumental piece suggestive of this.

Berenice, opera by Handel, produced in London, 1737. Libretto by A. Salvi; Berenice is the wife of an ancient Egyptian king. The well-known minuet occurs in the overture.

Berezovsky, Boris (b. 1969), Russian pianist, winner of the 1990 Tchaikovsky competition in Moscow; made first appearance in London (Wigmore Hall) 1988, in USA 1991. Has since toured widely and made recordings of Rakhmaninov, Chopin, etc.

Berezovsky (also spelt Berezowsky), **Nikolai** (1900–1953), Russian-born composer who settled in USA, 1922; also conductor, violinist, viola-player (soloist in first performance of his Viola Concerto, 1941). Other works include four symphonies, oratorio *Gilgamesh* (text from Babylonian poem of 1750 BC); children's opera *Babar the Elephant*.

Berg, Alban [Maria Johannes] (1885–1935), Austrian composer; born, worked and died in Vienna; pupil of Schoenberg, whose methods he developed. Used a free-atonal idiom combined with very closely worked structures (passacaglia, variations, etc.) in opera ➤*Wozzeck*, completed in 1922; shortly afterwards turned to strict ➤twelve-note technique, e.g. in his Chamber Concerto (piano, violin, wind), completed in 1925. Other works include 12-note opera, ➤*Lulu*; a string quartet and (also for string quartet) *Lyric Suite*; songs with orchestra and with piano; a violin concerto 'In memory of an angel' (i.e. Manon Gropius, 18-year-old daughter of Mahler's widow by her second marriage), written shortly before his own death and not performed till after it (1936).

Berg Quartet, ➤Alban Berg Quartet.

bergamasca (It.; also Fr., *bergamasque*, and Eng., *bergomask*), (1) tune and chord-sequence apparently from Bergamo, Italy, widely used in 16th and 17th centuries, e.g. as ground bass; (2) folk-dance from Bergamo; (3) now a term used by composers with only the vaguest picturesque significance – e.g. by Debussy in *Suite Bergamasque* for piano (composed at intervals between 1890 and 1905), which includes 'Clair de lune'.

Berganza, Teresa (b. 1935), Spanish mezzo-soprano noted in florid roles of Italian opera; at La Scala, Milan, from 1957, Glyndebourne from 1958, etc.

Berger, Arthur [Victor] (b. 1912), American composer, pupil of N. Boulanger (in Paris) and others; works include *Ideas of Order* for orchestra, and much chamber music. Also music critic and university professor.

Berger, Jean (b. 1909), German-born composer resident in France and then (from 1941) in USA – naturalized, 1943. Also writer. Works include *Brazilian Psalm* and other pieces for choir; *Caribbean Concerto* for harmonica and orchestra.

bergerette (Fr.), light French song cultivating a pastoral style that is highly idealized (like Dresden-china shepherdesses). From Fr., *berger*, shepherd.

Berglund, Paavo [Allan Engelbert] (b. 1929), Finnish conductor; principal conductor of Bournemouth Symphony Orchestra, 1972–9, and of Royal Danish Orchestra since 1993.

Bergman, Erik [Valdemar] (b. 1911), Finnish composer of opera *The Singing Tree*, piano concerto, violin concerto, *Poseidon* for orchestra, cantata *The Birds* (Swedish text) for vocal soloists, celesta and percussion; is also conductor and formerly music critic.

Bergonzi, Carlo (b. 1924), Italian tenor (originally sang as baritone); noted in Italian opera, especially Verdi – heard in London from 1953, New York (Metropolitan Opera) from 1956. Gave farewell recital at Covent Garden, 1991.

Bergsma, William (1921–94) American composer of two symphonies; *Blatant Hypotheses* for trombone and piano; opera *The Wife of Martin Guerre*, etc.

Berio, Luciano (b. 1925), Italian composer, internationally distinguished. He has employed spatial effects, e.g. in *Circles* (text by e.e. cummings) for voice, harp and two percussion instruments; has also written electronic music and works allowing free choice by performers (➤indeterminacy). Wrote much for the vocal virtuosity of Cathy Berberian, to whom he was married. His operas include *Un re in ascolto* (*A King Listening*). A series of pieces each called *Sequence* (It., *Sequenza*) is for different solo instruments – no. 5 for trombone, no. 6 for viola. His Sinfonia (orchestra, organ, piano, harpsichord, chorus, reciters) incorporates a section of Mahler's Symphony no. 2. Has taught widely, with Harvard professorship 1993–4.

Bériot, Charles [Auguste] **de** (1802–70), Belgian violinist and composer, chiefly for his instrument. Toured much; first visited London in 1826.

Berkeley, Lennox [Randall Francis] (1903–89), British composer, pupil of N. Boulanger in Paris. Wrote operas including *Nelson* and *A ➤Dinner Engagement*; four symphonies; *Four Poems of St Teresa* for contralto and orchestra. Knighted, 1974.

Berkeley, Michael [Fitzhardinge] (b. 1948), British composer, son of Lennox Berkeley. Works include concertos for oboe, horn, cello, organ; political oratorio *Or Shall We Die?*; opera *Baa-baa, Black Sheep* (after Kipling).

Berkoff, Steven (b. 1937), British playwright. ➤*Greek*.

Berlin, Irving (originally Israel Baline) (1888–1989), Russian-born composer, resident in USA from 1893. Composer of popular songs markedly successful from 'Alexander's Ragtime Band' (1911) and including the now perennial 'I'm Dreaming of a White Christmas' (from film *Holiday Inn*, 1942); also of musicals including ➤*Annie Get Your Gun* and ➤*Call Me Madam*.

Berlin Philharmonic Orchestra, orchestra founded in 1882; conductor 1955–89, Herbert von Karajan (succeeding Furtwängler); Abbado is his current successor (until 2002).

Berlin Radio Symphony Orchestra. ➤Deutsches Symphonie-Orchester.

Berlioz, [Louis] **Hector** (1803–69), French composer, also noted as conductor and music críic. Learnt guitar and had general musical training at Paris Conservatoire, but became proficient neither on piano nor on any orchestral instrument – yet masterly innovator in orchestration (on which he wrote a book). His works show extraordinary originality of form and harmony, and nearly all bear some literary or other extra-musical allusion: his love for the English Shakespearian actress Harriet Smithson is expressed in his ➤*Symphonie fantastique*, 1830; he married her in 1833 and separated from her in 1842.

other works include operas ➤*Benvenuto Cellini*, ➤*Béatrice et Bénédict*, *Les* ➤*Troyens*; choral works including *La* ➤*Damnation de Faust* (in which occurs his arrangement of the ➤*Rákóczi March*), *L'*➤*Enfance du Christ* and ➤*Grande Messe des Morts* (➤*Requiem*); symphony ➤*Roméo et Juliette*; ➤*Harold en Italie* for viola and orchestra; *Lélio* (intended sequel to the *Symphonie fantastique*) for reciter, singers and orchestra; ➤*Carnaval romain, Le* ➤*Corsaire*, ➤*King Lear* and other overtures; songs with orchestra and with piano. A Mass composed in 1824 was rediscovered in 1992.

Berman, Lazar [Naumovich] (b. 1930), Russian pianist, pupil of S. Richter, who played in London in 1958 but was politically prevented from developing his major international career until after 1970.

Bernac (real surname Bertin), **Pierre** (1899–1979), French baritone, particularly distinguished in recitals of French songs: Poulenc was often his accompanist.

Bernanos, Georges (1888–1948). French novelist. ➤*Dialogues des Carmélites*.

Bernart de Ventadorn (*c.* 1135–*c.*1195), French troubadour, of whom 18 poems survive complete with their musical settings – more than for any other troubadour of that period.

Berners, Lord [Gerald Hugh Tyrwhitt-Wilson] (1883–1950), British composer (also painter, author, diplomat). Works include ballets *The Wedding Bouquet* (words by Gertrude Stein, stage-settings of Berners's own design) and *The Triumph of Neptune; Valses bourgeoises* for piano duet; and songs.

Bernstein, Leonard (1918–90), American composer, also conductor, pianist and celebrated television presenter of music. Pupil of Piston and others; conductor of the New York Philharmonic Orchestra, 1958; 'laureate conductor', 1969. Works include 'Jeremiah' Symphony; Symphony no. 2 with piano; Symphony no. 3 (➤*Kaddish*); *Prelude, Fugue and Riffs* (➤riff) for orchestra; theatre piece ➤*Mass*; opera *Trouble in Tahiti*; operetta ➤*Candide* (after Voltaire); musicals ➤*On the Town* (based on his ballet *Fancy Free*) and ➤*West Side Story*; songs; chamber music; ➤*Chichester Psalms* (in Hebrew) for Chichester Cathedral (choir and orchestra).

Béroff, Michel (b. 1950), French pianist, noted in Messiaen's works and other modern music.

Berry, Walter (b. 1929), Austrian baritone, formerly often appearing with his wife (divorced 1970) Christa ➤Ludwig; prominent at Vienna State Opera from 1953, he recorded with such conductors as Karajan and Boulez.

Bertini, Gary (b. 1927), Israeli (Russian-born) conductor (also composer); conductor of Jerusalem Symphony Orchestra 1977–86, music director of Frankfurt Opera 1987–91, music director of New Israeli Opera from 1994.

Berwald, Franz Adolf (1796–1868), Swedish composer and violinist who studied in Germany; little appreciated in his lifetime, only no. 1 (*Sérieuse*) of his four symphonies receiving performance. Also wrote opera *Estrella di Soria*, a violin concerto, chamber music, etc. in an individual ➤Romantic style.

Bésard, Jean-Baptiste (b. 1567; d. after 1617), French lutenist and composer whose publications include music for lute by himself and others.

Besuch der alten Dame, Der (Ger., 'The Visit of the Old Lady'), opera by von Einem, produced in Vienna, 1971; libretto by Friedrich Dürrenmatt based on his own play of that title about a long-delayed revenge.

Bethlehem, 'choral drama' by Boughton, produced in Glastonbury, 1916. Libretto from the medieval Coventry play.

Betrothal in a Monastery, The, ➤*Duenna*.

Bettelstudent, Der (Ger., 'The Beggar Student'), operetta by Millöcker with libretto by F. Zell and Richard Genée, produced in Vienna, 1882. In Krakow, 1704, an impoverished rebel student is released from prison to carry out an amorous intrigue.

Betterton, Thomas (1635–1710), English actor and playwright. ➤*Dioclesian*.

Bibalo, Antonio (b. 1922), Italian composer (also pianist), resident in Norway; has written operas *The Smile at the Foot of the Ladder* (after Henry Miller) and *Ghosts* (after Ibsen), orchestral and piano works, etc.

Biber, Heinrich Johann Franz von (1644–1704), Austrian violinist, musical director at the Archbishop of Salzburg's court, and composer of violin sonatas and chamber music; also wrote opera and church music. An early exploiter of ➤*scordatura*.

big band, ➤band.

Biggs, E. [Edward George] **Power** (1906–77), British-born concert organist who settled in USA and had international career; also editor of organ music.

Billings, William (1746–1800), one of the earliest American-born composers, but a tanner by trade; wrote 'fuguing tunes' (with primitive ➤imitation), words and music of hymns, music to American patriotic songs, etc. Also concert promoter. ➤Cowell, ➤Schuman.

Billy Budd, opera by Britten, produced in London, 1951; libretto by E. M. Forster and E. Crozier, after Melville's novel of the British navy at the time of the mutiny of the Nore (1797). Also opera by Ghedini, 1949, after the same source.

Billy the Kid, ballet (about an outlaw) with choreography by Eugene Loring and music by Copland, 1938; a well-known orchestral suite is drawn from the score.

Bilson, Malcolm (b. 1935), American harpsichordist and pianist who studied in Vienna and Paris; noted in performance of Mozart's, Chopin's and other music on instruments of its period. Professor at Cornell University.

binary, in two sections; *binary form*, classification used of a simple movement (e.g. in an early 18th-century keyboard suite) which is in two sections, the first modulating to another key and the second returning to the original key. (Distinguished from ➤ternary form.) The above form developed historically into ➤sonata-form, an alternative name for which is, accordingly, *compound binary form*.

Binchois, Gilles [Egidius] (*c.* 1400–1460), Netherlands composer of chansons, motets, etc., who worked at the court of Burgundy.

Birds, The, orchestral work by Respighi. ➤*Uccelli*.

Bird-Seller, The, operetta by Zeller. ➤*Vogelhändler*.

Birmingham Symphony Orchestra, ➤City of Birmingham Symphony Orchestra.

Birtwistle, Harrison (b. 1934), British composer; professor, King's College, London, 1994; associated with (Royal) National Theatre 1976–88. Works include *The Triumph of Time*, *Earth Dances: Exody* for orchestra; *Panic* for saxophone and orchestra; *Grimethorpe Aria* for brass band; *Refrains and Choruses* for wind quintet; *Tragoedia* for 10 players: *Harrison's Clocks* for solo piano; operas ➤*Punch and Judy*, *The Mask of Orpheus*, ➤*Gawain* and *The* ➤*Second Mrs Kong* (and, arising from it, *Anubis* for tuba and orchestra). Knighted, 1987.

bis (Fr., twice), word actually used in French where the English use 'encore'; so *bisser*, to encore. When written, it is an instruction that a section of music is to be performed twice.

bisbigliando (It., whispering), repeating the notes softly and quickly, as a special effect in playing the harp.

biscroma (It.), ➤thirty-second note, demisemiquaver.

Bishop, Henry [Rowley] (1786–1855), British composer, chiefly of operas; also adapted Mozart's and other operas. Prominent as conductor; knighted in 1842, the first musician to receive knighthood at the hands of a British sovereign. His opera *Clari, or*

The Maid of Milan (1823) includes his song 'Home, Sweet Home', used in a recurrent way (➤reminiscence-motive).

Bishop-Kovacevich, Stephen, ➤Kovacevich.

bitonality, the use of two keys simultaneously; e.g. by Stravinsky (a famous early use in ➤*Petrushka*, 1911), Holst, Milhaud. (➤tonality.)

Bitter-Sweet, operette [*sic*] with text and music by Noël Coward. Produced in London, 1929. Aristocratic London and (in flashback) Viennese café society put constraints on true love.

biwa, a Japanese form of lute, normally with four silk strings.

Bizet, Georges (forenames originally Alexandre César Léopold) (1838–75), French composer, pupil of Halévy, whose daughter he married after Halévy's death. At 19 won prize for an operetta, *Doctor Miracle*; later composed operas including *Les* ➤*Pêcheurs de perles*, *La* ➤*Jolie Fille de Perth*, ➤*Ivan IV* (not performed till 1946) and finally ➤*Carmen* – at first only a moderate success (Bizet died three months after its first performance), then acknowledged among the greatest masterpieces of opera. His other works include incidental music to Daudet's play *L'*➤*Arlésienne*; symphony (written at age 17 but not performed until 1935); suite ➤*Jeux d'enfants* for piano duet.

Björling, Jussi [originally Johan] (1911–60), Swedish tenor, eminent in Italian opera at Metropolitan Opera House (New York) and elsewhere.

Bjørnson, Bjørnstjerne (1832–1910), Norwegian writer. ➤Grieg, ➤*Homage March*.

Blacher, Boris (1903–75), German

43

composer born of Russian parents in China; from 1953 director of the (West) Berlin High School of Music. Works include operas (one based on Shakespeare's *Romeo and Juliet*); oratorio *The Grand Inquisitor* (after Dostoyevsky's *Crime and Punishment*); two piano concertos; orchestral *Variations on a Theme of Paganini* (➤Paganini).

Black Angels, work by Crumb, 1970, for 'electric string quartet' (i.e. instruments with individual amplification), the performers also playing maracas, tam-tams and water-tuned glasses.

Blades, James (b. 1901), British percussionist, pioneer in new effects (working with Britten); author of historical textbook on percussion.

Blake, David [Leonard] (b. 1936), British composer (and York University teacher), pupil of Eisler in Berlin. Works include Variations for piano, Chamber Symphony, unaccompanied choral music, opera *Toussaint*.

Blake, Howard [David] (b. 1938), British composer of works appealing to young audiences, e.g. *The Snowman* for narrator, boy soprano and orchestra; also of a clarinet concerto, sinfonietta for 10 brass, etc. OBE, 1994.

Blake, Rockwell [originally Robert] (b. 1951), American tenor, in demand for particularly high tenor roles, e.g. in Rossini operas; Metropolitan Opera from 1981.

Blake, William (1757–1827), British poet and artist. ➤*Job*, ➤*Serenade* (Britten); ➤Smirnov, ➤Weber (B.).

Blaník, ➤*My Country*.

blasen (Ger.), to blow; *Bläser*, wind instruments, wind-players; *Blasinstru-*

ment(e), wind instrument(s); *Blasmusik*, music for wind.

Blavet, Michel (1700–1768), French flautist and composer of flute music, operas, etc.

Blech (Ger.), brass (section of an orchestra); *Blechmusik*, brass band, music for brass.

Blech, Harry (b. 1910), British conductor, formerly violinist; founder-conductor of London Mozart Players (chamber orchestra), 1949–84. OBE, 1962.

Blessed Damozel, The, cantata by Debussy. ➤*Damoiselle élue*.

Bliss, Arthur (1891–1975), British composer; BBC director of music, 1941–5; knighted, 1950; Master of the Queen's Music, 1953. Works include ballet ➤ *Checkmate*; opera *The Olympians* (libretto by J. B. Priestley); symphony *Morning Heroes* (with speaker and chorus); piano concerto, violin concerto; *Music for Strings*; *A Colour Symphony*; piano sonata; clarinet quintet and other chamber music; *Seven American Poems* and other songs, and one of the first important film scores, *The Shape of Things to Come* (1935).

Blitheman, John (1525–91), English organist (at the Chapel Royal, London), and composer of church music and keyboard pieces; teacher of J. Bull.

Blitzstein, Marc (1905–64), American composer (pupil of N. Boulanger and Schoenberg) and pianist. Composed music expressing militantly socialist ideas – e.g. operas *The Cradle Will Rock* and *Regina*, symphonic poem *Freedom Morning*. Killed in Martinique, apparently as the result of a political brawl.

Bloch, Augustyn [Hippolit] (b. 1929), Polish composer of *Thou Shalt Not Kill* for baritone, cello, choir and orchestra, also of *Dialogues* for violin and orchestra, *Wordsworth Songs* for baritone and chamber ensemble.

Bloch, Ernest (1888–1959), Swiss-born composer; naturalized American in 1924. Much of his work has specific Jewish associations – e.g. ➤*Schelomo* ('Solomon') for cello and orchestra; ➤*Sacred Service*; ➤*Baal Shem* for violin and piano; *Israel Symphony* (with voices). Other works include opera ➤*Macbeth*; rhapsody *America*; violin concerto (➤*Szigeti*), a piano quintet (1923, introducing quarter-tones); five string quartets.

block (percussion instrument), ➤temple block, ➤wood block.

Blockflöte (Ger.), ➤recorder.

Blockx, Jan (1851–1912), Belgian composer of music mainly with Flemish nationalist associations – operas and cantatas with Flemish words, overture *Rubens*, etc.

Blomdahl, Karl-Birger (1916–68), Swedish composer (also conductor), pupil of Rosenberg. Works include three symphonies (no. 3 called *Facets*); cantata *In the Hall of Mirrors*; chamber music; piano pieces; operas *Aniara* (set on a space-ship) and *Herr von Hancken*.

Blomstedt, Herbert [Thorson] (b. 1927), American-born Swedish conductor; music director, San Francisco Symphony Orchestra 1985–95; appointed music director of Gewandhaus Orchestra (Leipzig) from 1998.

Blondel [de Nesle], 12th-century French ➤*trouvère* (minstrel) of whom

some songs survive; according to legend he discovered (by singing and being answered) the place where Richard Cœur de Lion was held captive.

Blow, John (1649–1708), English composer, pupil of H. Cooke and others; teacher of Purcell; organist of Westminster Abbey, 1668–79 (Purcell succeeding him) and again, 1695–1708. Works include English and Latin anthems, services, odes on the death of Purcell and on other occasions (10 for New Year's Day); keyboard pieces and songs; masque ➤*Venus and Adonis*.

Bluebeard, operetta by Offenbach. ➤*Barbe-bleue*.

Bluebeard's Castle, opera by Bartók. ➤*Duke Bluebeard's Castle*.

Blue Danube, The (Ger., *An der schönen blauen Donau*, 'By the beautiful blue Danube'), waltz by Johann Strauss the younger, composed 1867; originally with chorus.

bluegrass, type of American 'country music' (in the pop sense) featuring fiddle, banjo, guitar: ➤Butler.

blue note, a note of the scale (especially the third and seventh) characteristically flattened in jazz and in light and serious music indebted to jazz idiom.

blues, type of slow, sad Afro-American song, becoming widely known about 1911; strictly *12-bar blues* in three lines of four bars each, the second line exactly or nearly repeating the first and the whole following a set chord-sequence. (Also used loosely, e.g. by Copland, as indication of mood only.)

Blumine (an invented German word

of the early 19th century, representing the goddess Flora), title of the original second movement of Mahler's Symphony no. 1 (1889); discarded by the composer, this movement has none the less been reinstated in some modern performances.

B.Mus., abbr. of Bachelor of Music.

Boccaccio, operetta by Suppé with libretto by F. Zell and Richard Genée based on a play by Bayard, Leuven, Lhérie and Beauplan; produced in Vienna, 1879. The 14th-century Florentine author of the *Decameron* is the hero of an amorous intrigue.

Boccherini, Luigi (1743–1805), Italian composer and cellist. By invitation, of the Spanish ambassador in Paris, visited Spain in 1768–9; and was there again from 1797 until dying there in poverty, lacking a patron. Works include 11 cello concertos; 30 symphonies; 125 string quintets (from one of which – op. 13, no. 5, in E – comes 'the' Boccherini minuet); 91 string quartets and much other chamber music; Spanish opera *Clementina*; church music.

Bock, Jerry [originally Jerrold Lewis Bock] (b. 1928), American composer of musical shows including *She Loves Me* (1963) and ➤*Fiddler on the Roof*, subsequently translated into many languages.

Bodanzky, Artur (1877–1939), Austrian conductor, an associate of Mahler; conducted London's first stage performance of *Parsifal* (1914) and was prominent at the Metropolitan Opera, New York.

bodhrán (Gaelic), Irish drum similar to a large tambourine without the

jingles; used in Irish traditional music and in Cage's *Roaratorio*.

Boehm, ➤Böhm (alternative spelling).

Boehm, Theobald (1794–1881), German flautist, composer for his instrument, and inventor. His key-mechanism (replacing finger-holes) spread from the flute to oboe, clarinet and bassoon and became standard.

Boehm system, woodwind key-mechanism; see preceding entry.

Boëllmann, Léon (1862–97), French organist (latterly at church of St Vincent de Paul, Paris) and composer, principally for organ; also wrote a symphony, Symphonic Variations for cello and orchestra, etc.

Bogusławski, Eduard (b. 1940), Polish composer. Works include *Apocalypse* for narrator, chorus and orchestra; *Polonia* for violin and orchestra; opera *The Dream Play* (after Strindberg).

Bohème, La (Fr., 'Bohemian Life', in artistic sense), name of Italian operas based on Murger's French novel *Scènes de la vie de Bohème* – (1) by Puccini, produced in Turin, 1896; libretto by G. Giacosa and L. Illica; (2) by Leoncavallo, produced in Venice, 1897; libretto by composer. The two were composed contemporaneously, but the latter missed Puccini's success.

Bohemian Girl, The, opera by Balfe, produced in London, 1843. Libretto by A. Bunn; the high-born heroine is abducted as a child by gipsies ('Bohemians') and finally restored.

Böhme, Kurt (1908–89), German bass, whose membership of Dresden Opera 1930–50 embraced various premières including R. Strauss's *Arabella*. Appeared at Bayreuth, Metropolitan

Opera (début 1954), etc. and sang Ochs in *Der Rosenkavalier* more than 500 times.

Böhm, Georg (1661–1733), German organist and composer of a 'St John' Passion, organ music, keyboard suites, etc.; from 1698 at Lüneburg, where J. S. Bach, as a boy chorister at another church, apparently came to know his music.

Böhm, Karl (1894–1981), Austrian conductor, director of Vienna State Opera, 1943–5 and 1954–6. Noted in Mozart and R. Strauss.

Böhm, Theobald, ➤Boehm.

Boïeldieu, François Adrien (1775–1834), French composer, pupil of Cherubini and others. Wrote a piano concerto, chamber music and especially operas – including *La Dame blanche* ('The White Lady'), after two novels of Scott, which contains Scottish tunes, and *Le* ➤*Calife de Bagdad*. Also conductor, e.g. at St Petersburg.

Boismortier, Joseph Bodin de (1689–1755), French composer of much instrumental music especially for recorder and for flute, also for ➤hurdy-gurdy; cantatas, etc.

Boito, Arrigo (1842–1918), Italian composer (operas ➤*Mefistofele*, *Nerone* etc.) and librettist, e.g. for Verdi's *Otello* and *Falstaff*.

Bolcom, William [Elden] (b. 1938), American composer, pupil of Milhaud (in California and in Paris); works include *Dynamite Tonite* (a 'pop opera' for actors and 11 instruments), four symphonies, nine string quartets, *Frescoes* for two pianists each doubling on harmonium and harpsichord.

bolero, Spanish dance in triple time,

usually with a triplet on the second half of the first beat of bar; accompaniment includes dancers' voices and castanets. Ravel's purely orchestral *Boléro*, 1928, is for ballet, not for dancing a real bolero. Chopin's *Bolero* is for piano, published in 1834. A quite different dance-type, in duple time but bearing the same name, originated in Cuba and spread elsewhere in Latin America.

Bolet, Jorge (1914–90), Cuban-American pianist, pupil of Godowsky, of commanding ability in large-scale Romantic works; his reputation did not peak until the mid-1970s.

Bolshoi Theatre, Moscow's principal opera and ballet theatre; the present building opened in 1856. (*Bolshoi* means 'large', 'great'.)

Bolton, Ivor (b. 1958), British conductor; music director of English Touring Opera 1990–93, then of Glyndebourne Touring Opera; also conductor of Scottish Chamber Orchestra since 1994.

bombard(e), name given to the larger instruments of the ➤shawm family. ('Pommer' is an alternative form.)

bombarde, a 16-➤foot reed stop on the organ.

bombardon (1) name formerly given in brass and military bands to the two types of bass ➤tuba used in those bands; (2) organ stop similar to ➤bombarde.

Bond, Capel (1730–90), British organist, leader of festival performances, and composer of anthems and a set of six concertos (1775), including one each for trumpet and bassoon.

Bond, Carrie Jacobs (1862–1946),

Bond, Edward

American composer of 'The End of a Perfect Day' (which sold over five million copies) and similar popular sentimental songs.

Bond, Edward (b. 1934), British playwright. ➤*We Come to the River*.

bones, percussion instrument used in black-faced minstrel shows, etc.; a pair of small bones (or wood or plastic substitutes) held between the fingers and clicked together.

bongo, single-headed small drum (tunable or non-tunable) struck with the fingers; familiar in Latin-American dance bands and occasionally used elsewhere. Usually in sets of two or three (plural *bongos*).

Bonney, Barbara (b. 1956), Canadian soprano, prominent in opera (Covent Garden 1984, Metropolitan 1989), and with recordings of Handel, Schoenberg and others.

Bononcini (or Buononcini), **Giovanni** (1670–1747), Italian composer and cellist, one of a family of musicians; worked in Rome, Vienna, Berlin and (1720–32) London, where he rivalled Handel for a time, leaving eventually when plagiarism was proved against him. Works include operas, Masses, funeral anthem for the Duke of Marlborough. Died in poverty in Vienna.

Bonynge, Richard [Alan] (b. 1930), Australian conductor who coached and advised the young Joan Sutherland, married her in 1954 and was conductor of almost all her performances; also revived unfamiliar ballet scores. CBE, 1977; Officer of the Order of Australia, 1983.

boobam, modern percussion instrument (the name an inversion of *bamboo*), a length of bamboo tubing cut to length in order to sound a defined pitch when struck by fingers or beater; used by composers in a set of differing pitches.

book, the story and dialogue of a musical show – as distinct from the lyrics, i.e. the words to the songs.

Borge, Victor [originally Borge Rosenbaum] (b. 1909), Danish-born American musical comedian (and pianist) who settled in New York, 1940, and became famous for his comic act. He was still performing and touring in his eighties.

Borg, Kim (b. 1919), Finnish bass of multilingual international career (début at Metropolitan, New York, 1959), also composer of a trombone concerto, two symphonies, etc.

Boris Godunov, opera by Musorgsky, produced in St Petersburg, 1874; libretto by composer, after Pushkin's drama of the historic tsar (d. 1605). The opera was afterwards edited and altered by Rimsky-Korsakov, in which form it first became known outside Russia, sometimes incorporating the additional 'St Basil scene' revised and altered by Ippolitov-Ivanov. A version has also been made by Shostakovich which (unlike Rimsky-Korsakov's) respects the composer's harmonies but provides new orchestration.

Börlin, Jean (1893–1930), Swedish choreographer. ➤*Création du monde*.

Borodin, Alexander [Porfyrevich] (1833–87), Russian composer – also professor of chemistry, so could spare little time for music. Illegitimate son of a prince; pupil of Balakirev; one of the 'nationalist' group of composers known as the ➤*Mighty Handful*. His opera ➤*Prince Igor*, unfinished; brought to a complete (but arbitrary) shape by Rimsky-Korsakov and Glazunov, includes the 'Polovtsian Dances'. He also wrote three symphonies (no. 3 unfinished, but two movements of it advanced enough to be completed by Glazunov); symphonic poem ➤*In the Steppes of Central Asia*; two string quartets; songs. ➤*Kismet*.

Borodin Quartet, Russian string quartet founded as Moscow Philharmonic Quartet in 1946, taking its present name in 1955; had close association with Shostakovich, though the ➤Beethoven Quartet gave most of his quartets their premières. Current members: Mikhail Kopelman, Andrei Abramenkov, Dmitri Shebalin, Valentin Berlinsky.

Borodina, Olga (b. 1960), Russian mezzo-soprano prominent in such roles as Olga in *Yevgeny Onegin*, Marfa in *Khovanshchina*; after beginning her career in Russia she sang with distinction in Rome, at Covent Garden (1992), etc.

Bortnyansky, Dmitri Stepanovich (1751–1825), Russian composer who studied in Italy, returned to Russia and became director of the court church choir, which he reformed. Composed chiefly church music, but also Italian operas.

Boscovich, Alexander Uriah (1907–64), Romanian-born Israeli composer who emigrated to Palestine, 1937. Works include a violin concerto, an oboe concerto, songs.

Boskovsky, Willy (1909–91), Austrian violinist and orchestra leader, famous for his appearances at Vienna's New Year Concerts (1954–80), which he directed in traditional fashion with the violin bow.

Bossi, [Marco] **Enrico** (1861–1925), Italian composer and organist; works include an organ concerto and many organ solos, also operas, oratorios, etc.

Boston Pops Orchestra, an offshoot of the Boston Symphony Orchestra; founded 1885, it has an annual season presenting the lighter repertory. Conductor 1988–95, John [Tower] Williams.

Boston Symphony Orchestra, an orchestra founded in Boston, Mass., 1881. Koussevitzky's conductorship (1924–49) made it especially famous. Conductor since 1973, Seiji Ozawa.

Bottesini, Giovanni (1821–89), Italian double-bass virtuoso who appeared as soloist in London and elsewhere; also composer and conductor.

bouche fermée (Fr.), with the mouth closed, i.e. (as instruction to singers) humming.

Boucourechliev, André (b. 1925), Bulgarian composer, naturalized French in 1956; also critic. Has written several chamber works, each called *Archipelago* (Fr., *Archipel*), which are performable in more than one version; also a piano sonata and *Musiques Nocturnes* for clarinet, harp and piano.

bouffe, (Fr.), comic; so ➤*opéra bouffe*.

Boughton, Rutland (1878–1960), British composer (also conductor and writer on music). In emulation of Wagner at Bayreuth, organized a festival operatic centre (not only for his own works) at Glastonbury, 1914–25; it opened with his *The➤ Immortal Hour* which later ran for 216 successive performances in London. None of his later stage works – including ➤*Bethlehem* – achieved such success.

Boulanger, Lili [originally Marie-Juliette] (1893–1918), French composer, pupil of her sister Nadia and others; first woman to win the 'Rome Prize', principal French award to young composers. Works include cantata *Faust et Hélène* (after Goethe), psalms with orchestra. Died at 24.

Boulanger, Nadia (1887–1979), French composer (orchestral works, songs, etc.), conductor, and teacher of distinguished musicians from many countries, especially USA (e.g. Copland, Piston). Sister of preceding.

Boulez, Pierre (b. 1925), French composer, pupil of Messiaen; also conductor; in both respects one of the leading musicians of his generation. Extended the methods of ➤twelve-note technique to the 'organizing' (in mathematical relationships) of rhythms, volume, etc., and has also employed spatial effects. Works include piano pieces (often of great complexity, with some choice of order left to performer); *Le ➤Marteau sans maître* for contralto and chamber orchestra; two works for soprano and instrumental ensemble called *Improvisation sur Mallarmé*. Noted conductor at Bayreuth Wagner Festival; principal conductor of BBC Symphony Orchestra, 1971–5, of New York Philharmonic Orchestra, 1971–7; director of musical-acoustical research centre in Paris (➤IRCAM). Conducted first complete performance of Berg's *Lulu*, Paris, 1979.

Boult, Adrian [Cedric] (1889–1983), British conductor who studied in Germany. Musical director of BBC, 1930–42; formed and conducted BBC Symphony Orchestra, 1931–50, then chief conductor of London Philharmonic Orchestra till 1957. Knighted, 1937.

bourdon, a 16-➤foot organ stop of stopped ➤*diapason* type.

Bourgeois, Louis (*c.* 1510–*c.* 1561), French musician who contributed harmonizations (including that of the 'Old Hundredth') to Calvin's Genevan Psalter, 1551.

Bourgeois Gentilhomme, Le (Fr., 'The Tradesman as Gentleman'), (1) play by Molière (1670) with incidental music by Lully; (2) incidental music by R. Strauss to a shortened version of Molière's play, intended to precede the original version of ➤*Ariadne auf Naxos*.

Bourguignon, Francis de (1890–1961), Belgian composer (also pianist, formerly accompanist to Melba) and critic; works, some using polytonality, include piano concertos, songs, chamber music.

Bournemouth Municipal Orchestra, ➤Bournemouth Symphony Orchestra.

Bournemouth Sinfonietta, a chamber orchestra founded 1968 under the same management as the Bournemouth Symphony Orchestra; principal conductor 1989–97, Tamás Vásáry from 1997/8 season, Alexander Polianichko.

Bournemouth Symphony Orchestra, the successor in 1954 to the former Bournemouth Municipal Orchestra, founded in 1893 under Sir Dan Godfrey's conductorship. Conductor from

1995, Yakov Kreizberg, succeeding Andrew Litton.

bourrée (Fr.), dance-movement (found, e.g., in the baroque ➤suite) in quick duple time beginning with an up-beat.

bouzouki (Gk.), a modern Greek type of mandolin.

bow, stick with horsehair stretched across it, used to set in vibration the strings of the violin and related instruments, also the viols; *Tourte bow*, name for the ordinary modern kind of bow (after François Tourte, inventor, 1747–1835), with stick curved inward to the hair. The earlier type (sometimes called baroque bow), with an outward-curving stick, has been revived for 'old' music (but the idea that it could play simultaneous four-string chords as written by Bach is false). The term *Bach bow* sometimes alludes to a discredited 20th-century invention associated with the violinist Emil Telmányi (1892–1988). So also *to bow*, i.e. to play with the bow or to mark an instrumental part indicating up-bow and down-bow.

Bowen, [Edwin] **York** (1884–1961), British pianist and composer (also played violin and horn); composer of three piano concertos, many piano solos, etc.

Bowles, Paul [Frederic] (b. 1910), American composer, pupil of N. Boulanger, Sessions and others; studied folk-music in Spain and Latin America. Works include orchestral *Danza Mexicana*, operas, chamber music, theatre and film scores. Also novelist.

Bowman, James [Thomas] (b. 1941), British counter-tenor, formerly boy chorister; London concert début,

1967, followed by operatic appearances in works of Handel, Britten, etc., winning him international distinction. CBE, 1997.

Boyce, William (1711–79), British composer and organist; D.Mus., Oxford. Boy chorister at St Paul's Cathedral, London, later a pupil of Greene and (1755) Master of the King's Band; organist of the Chapel Royal, 1758. Works include church and stage music, eight symphonies, songs including 'Heart of Oak'; editor of a notable collection of English cathedral music.

Boyd, Anne [Elizabeth] (b. 1946), Australian composer who trained in Britain; in 1990 became head of music department at Sydney University. Works include *Summer Nights* for voice and small orchestra (with a musical saw and other rare instruments); *The Voice of the Phoenix* for piano, guitar, harp, harpsichord and orchestra with synthesizer.

Boy Friend, The, musical comedy with text and music by Sandy Wilson. Produced in London, 1953. In a pastiche of the style of the 1920s, a messenger-boy turns out to be a rich aristocrat.

Bozay, Attila (b. 1939), Hungarian composer of *Outcries* for tenor and chamber ensemble; Variations for piano; *Symphonic Piece* for orchestra, etc.

Br., abbr. of Ger. *Bratsche(n)*, i.e. viola(s).

Brade, William (1560–1630), English viol-player and musical director who worked mainly in Germany and died in Hamburg. Composed dance-music for instrumental ensemble, etc.

Braga, Gaetano (1829–1907), Italian cellist, composer of popular vocal 'Serenade', also of operas, etc.

Braham (real surname Abraham), **John** (1774–1856), British tenor, the original male lead in Weber's ➤*Oberon*; sang also on the Continent; composer of · songs including the once very popular 'The Death of Nelson'.

Brahms, Johannes (1833–97), German composer, also pianist; reinvigorated the symphonic tradition and resisted the widely prevalent Lisztian ideal of ➤programme music; composed no opera. Born in Hamburg, where as a youngster he played in sailors' taverns. In 1853 attracted the interest of Joachim, Liszt and Schumann; settled in Vienna, 1863. Never married. Entirely devoted to composition from 1864, but did not write the first of his four symphonies till 1875. Composed two piano concertos, violin concerto, double concerto for violin and cello; ➤*Akademische Fest-Ouvertüre* and ➤*Tragische Ouvertüre*; ➤'St Anthony' *Variations* (formerly known as *Variations on a Theme of Haydn*) for orchestra or two pianos. His chamber music includes three piano quartets, piano quintet, two sonatas for clarinet and piano. Wrote also variations for piano on themes by Handel and by ➤Paganini; songs (including ➤*Vier ernste Gesänge*), part-songs (including ➤*Liebeslieder-Walzer*), and choral works including *Ein* ➤*deutsches Requiem*, *Nänie* (➤*nenia*) and ➤*Alto Rhapsody*.

Brain, Dennis (1921–57), British horn-player, son of an equally eminent horn-player, Aubrey Brain (1893–1955). Works by Britten (*Serenade for Tenor, Horn and Strings*), Hindemith, and others were written for him. Died in a car crash.

Brand, Max (1896–1980), Polish-born Austrian composer of opera *Maschinist Hopkins* (1929, later banned by the Nazis) and other works. Lived in USA, 1940–75.

Brandenburg Concertos, six works by J. S. Bach, 1721 (BWV 1046–51), for varying instrumental combinations, no two alike; dedicated to the Margrave of Brandenburg. Often classified as ➤*concerto grosso* type, they are not really typical, having a wide variety of styles and forms.

branle, bransle, French dance-movement in 2/2 time, something like the gavotte; it is called *brawl* in Shakespeare.

Brant, Henry [Dreyfus] (b. 1913), Canadian composer resident in USA. Works include *Antiphony I* for five separated orchestral groups and five conductors; *The Grand Universal Circus*, spatial theatre piece for eight singing and speaking voices, 32 choristers, 16 instruments; concerto for trumpet and nine instruments.

brass, collective term for musical instruments made of brass or other metals and blown directly though a cup-shaped or funnel-shaped mouthpiece. (This excludes, e.g., saxophone, because the air is actuated through a reed and not directly; it excludes flute, even if made of metal, because it has no such mouthpiece; ➤woodwind.) Basic brass requirements of the symphony orchestra are four horns, two or three trumpets, two tenor and one bass trombone, and one tuba; *heavy brass*, inexact and unhelpful term for trombones and tuba. See also ➤brass band.

brass band, combination of ➤brass instruments only (as distinct from military and other bands having woodwind too – ➤wind band) with or without percussion; in Britain made up of a fairly rigid combination of cornets, flugelhorn, tenor and baritone saxhorns, euphoniums, trombones, tubas and percussion.

Bratsche (Ger., pl. -en), viola.

bravo (It., brave, fine), interjection used to express approval – invariable in English-speaking countries, but *brava, bravi, brave* in Italian for a female performer, male performers, female performers, respectively.

bravura (It.), courage, swagger; *bravura passage*, one calling for a bold and striking display of an executant's technique.

brawl, ➤branle.

break (1) a change in tone-quality encountered in some voices and wind instruments in passing between different ➤registers; (2) a short solo passage, usually improvised, in a concerted jazz piece – i.e. a ➤cadenza; (3, verb) of the voice, to undergo that change in quality and compass which comes to a young male's voice in puberty (better spoken of as 'to change', as *break* suggests that something has been destroyed and lost).

Bream, Julian [Alexander] (b. 1933), British guitarist who made début at age 12 and won international eminence; also lutenist, as soloist and formerly as recital partner of Peter Pears. Britten, Takemitsu, Tippett and others wrote works for him. CBE, 1985.

Breasts of Tiresias, The, opera by Poulenc. ➤Mamelles de Tirésias.

Brecht, Bertolt (1898–1956), German dramatist and poet. ➤Dessau, ➤Eisler, ➤Aufstieg und Fall der Stadt Mahagonny, ➤Dreigroschenoper.

breit (Ger.), broadly, grandly – an indication of manner of performance, not (except incidentally) of speed.

Brendel, Alfred (b. 1931), Czech-born pianist, resident in Austria, then (since 1972) in Britain. Noted in Mozart and Beethoven; has also recorded Prokofiev, Schoenberg, etc.; is also occasional writer on music. Honorary KBE, 1989.

breve (Lat., short – the medieval significance of a note-value now very long), ➤double whole-note. This meaning has no connection with the tempo-direction ➤alla breve.

brevis (Lat.), short; *missa brevis*, ➤missa.

Brian, Havergal (1876–1972), British composer of 32 symphonies (some using voices; no. 1, ➤Gothic), operas, songs, etc.; also writer on music. Mainly self-taught. His music was little performed until his last years.

bridge (1) on a violin, viol, guitar, etc., the supporting piece of wood which holds the strings up from the belly of the instrument, and transmits their vibrations to the body of the instrument; (2) in a composition, a section (usually *bridge passage*) serving to link together two passages more important than itself.

Bridge, Frank (1879–1941), British composer (pupil of Stanford, teacher of Britten), chiefly of chamber music; other works include *The Sea* for orchestra and ➤Oration (cello concerto); songs, including 'Go not, happy day' (Tennyson).

Bridge, [John] Frederick (1844–1924), British organist (Westminster Abbey), choral conductor, composer of church music, author of textbooks; knighted, 1897.

Brigadoon, musical play with text by Alan Jay Lerner; music by Frederick Loewe. Produced in New York, 1947. Set in a Scottish village in which time has miraculously stood still.

Brigg Fair, 'English rhapsody' by Delius (being variations on a Lincolnshire folk-song) for orchestra; first performed in 1908. It is dedicated to Grainger, who acquainted Delius with the song.

brillant, brillante (Fr., It.), brilliant (as a direction for performance, particularly in solo music).

brindisi (It.), a toast, drinking-song (e.g. in *La* ➤*Traviata*).

Brindle, Reginald Smith, ➤Smith Brindle.

brio (It.), spirit, dash; *con brio*, spiritedly.

brisé (Fr., broken), term applied to notes of a chord played successively (➤*arpeggio*), especially in 17th–18th-century French keyboard music borrowing style from guitar or lute.

Britten, [Edward] Benjamin (1913–76), British composer, the first in the 20th century to achieve international success in opera; noted also as pianist (often in duo-recital with his permanent companion, Peter ➤Pears) and conductor; chief creator of Aldeburgh Festival (1948) and English Opera Group. The first composer to be raised to the peerage. Pupil of Frank Bridge from age 12; much influenced (especially in vocal setting) by Purcell. While in USA and Canada, 1939–42, he wrote operetta ➤*Paul Bunyan*, but his operatic fame began in 1945 with ➤*Peter Grimes*, followed by The ➤*Rape of Lucretia* and ➤*Albert Herring* (operas with small cast, chamber orchestra, no chorus), ➤*Billy Budd* (all-male), ➤*Gloriana* and (again small-scale) The ➤*Turn of the Screw*. Later theatrical works include *Let's Make an Opera!* for children; ➤*Noye's Fludde*, ➤*Curlew River*, *The Burning Fiery Furnace* and *The Prodigal Son* (all for church performance); *A* ➤*Midsummer Night's Dream*, *Owen Wingrave* (for television), ➤*Death in Venice*; ballet *The* ➤*Prince of the Pagodas*. He edited *The* ➤*Beggar's Opera* (with the tunes very freely treated). Other works include ➤*Simple Symphony*, ➤*Sinfonia da Requiem*, Cello Symphony (cello and orchestra), *The* ➤*Young Person's Guide to the Orchestra*, choral ➤*War Requiem* and ➤*Spring Symphony*, *Cantata Academica* (➤cantata); five ➤canticles; settings of Auden (➤*Hymn to St Cecilia*), Rimbaud (*Les* ➤*Illuminations*), Michelangelo, Donne, Pushkin, and others (➤*Serenade*, ➤*Nocturne*); folk-song arrangements. OM, 1965; life peer (Lord Britten), 1976.

Brixi, František Xaver (1732–71), Bohemian organist and composer of much church music, also of instrumental works.

Brodsky Quartet, a modern British string quartet named after Adolf Brodsky (1851–1929), Russian-born violinist who became principal of the Royal Manchester (now Royal Northern) College of Music. Current members: Michael Thomas, Ian Belton, Paul Cassidy, Jacqueline Thomas.

broken chord, a chord of which the notes are not all played simultaneously, but one after the other (or a few followed by another few). Similarly *broken octaves*, a passage of alternate notes an octave apart – especially in piano-writing.

broken consort, ➤consort.

Brontë, Charlotte (1816–55) and **Emily** (1818–48), British novelists. ➤Floyd, ➤Herrmann, ➤Joubert, ➤Landowski, ➤Muldowney.

Brouwer, Leo (b. 1939), Cuban composer (also guitarist and conductor) who trained in New York and has held official musical posts in Cuba. Has written many film scores; *Songs of the New Era* for actors, children's chorus, piano, harp and two percussion instruments; a guitar concerto.

Brown, Earle (b. 1926), American composer, a pioneer of time-notation (➤graphic) and ➤open forms. Works include *25 Pages* for 1–25 pianos; *Available Forms II* for 98 specified instruments divided between two conductors; *Tracer* for ensemble and 4-track tape.

browning, a type of English variation-form current about 1600, based on a tune 'The leaves be green, the nuts be brown'.

Browning, Elizabeth Barrett (1806–61), British poet. ➤Naylor.

Browning, Robert (1812–89), British poet. ➤Galuppi, ➤Vogler.

Brubeck, Dave [originally David Warren Brubeck] (b. 1920), American jazz composer and pianist, leader of a celebrated jazz quartet (1951–67), who studied under Milhaud and Schoenberg in California; has composed cantata *Truth is Fallen*, a *Festival Mass to Hope*, etc.

Bruch, Max (1838–1920), German composer; also conductor – of Liverpool Philharmonic Society, 1880–83. Works include three violin concertos (no. 1 is well known); ➤*Kol Nidrei* for cello and orchestra; also three symphonies, operas, choral works.

Bruckner, Anton (1824–96), Austrian composer; also organist – played at Royal Albert Hall, London, 1871. At first church choirboy; went to Vienna and studied with Sechter (with whom Schubert had intended to study) and from 1868 settled in Vienna, becoming professor at the Conservatory there. Heard *Tristan und Isolde*, 1865, and became Wagner's fervent disciple; wrote, however, no operas but nine symphonies (no. 3 nicknamed his 'Wagner' Symphony; no. 4, ➤Romantic), not including two unnumbered early works later rejected by him. Symphony no. 9 (only three out of four movements finished) is dedicated 'to God'. Symphonies nos. 7, 8, 9 use ➤Wagner tubas. Only from the mid 20th century came a wide appreciation of his symphonies; there are important differences between the shortened published versions of some symphonies and the 'authentic' texts published after his death. Other works include five Masses, a Te Deum, string quintet.

Brüggen, Frans (b. 1934), Dutch player of the recorder (also of flute); prominent as soloist and in ensembles reviving 17th- and 18th-century music.

Bruhns, Nikolaus (1665–97), German organist and composer of church music, etc.; pupil of Buxtehude.

Brüll, Ignaz (1846–1907), Austrian pianist and composer of 10 operas, two piano concertos, etc.

Brumel, Antoine (*c.* 1460–*c.* after 1520), Flemish composer of church music, etc.; choirmaster of Notre Dame in Paris, 1498–1500, afterwards going to Italy.

Bruneau, [Louis Charles Bonaventure] **Alfred** (1857–1934), French composer of operas (two with librettos by Zola, whose political and social ideas he shared), three choral symphonies, etc.; also writer on music.

Brunswick, Mark (1902–71), American composer who died in London. Works include choral symphony *Eros and Death*; Quartet for violin, viola, cello and double-bass; unfinished opera *The Master Builder* (after Ibsen).

Bruscantini, Sesto (b. 1919), Italian bass famous mainly for comic roles in opera, with a total of 130 parts in 108 works; prominent in the 1950s at La Scala, Glyndebourne etc., he was still singing on stage in the 1990s.

Bruson, Renato (b. 1936), Italian baritone much esteemed in operas by Donizetti (including rare revival of his *Torquato Tasso*, 1985) and by Verdi (many recordings; title-role of *Falstaff* at Covent Garden, 1982).

Brustwerk (Ger.), ➤choir-organ.

Bryars, [Richard] **Gavin** (b. 1943), British composer of *The Green Ray* for saxophone and orchestra, operas *Medea* and *Doctor Ox's Experiment* for ENO, vocal/instrumental ensemble works *Jesus' Blood Never Failed Me Yet* and *The Sinking of the Titanic*, etc.; also Leicester University professor and director of his own performing group.

Brymer, Jack (b. 1915), British clarinettist, principal in London orchestras to 1987, noted solo performer, also radio speaker and autobiographer. OBE, 1960.

Bryn-Julson, Phyllis [Mae] (b. 1945), American soprano who first trained as pianist; distinguished for first (and many other) performances of such American composers as Sessions, Carter, Crumb, and for 20th-century repertory in general; gave masterclasses at Moscow Conservatory, 1987.

Btb., Ger. abbr. of bass ➤tuba, i.e. the normal orchestral tuba.

Bucchi, Valentino (1916–76), Italian composer and conservatory director, pupil of Dallapiccola. Works include opera *Il contrabbasso* (*The Double-bass*, after Chekhov); *Concerto lirico* for violin and string orchestra; film scores.

Büchner, Georg (1813–37), German dramatist. ➤*Wozzeck*; ➤Lopatnikoff.

Buck, Dudley (1839–1909), American composer and organist who studied in Germany; wrote opera *Deseret*, choral works, chamber music, etc.

Budapest Quartet, string quartet founded in 1917, originally Hungarian; but during its celebrated period (from 1936 until it disbanded in 1967) its members were Russian-Jewish, led by Josef Roisman.

buffo, buffa (It.), comic; *basso buffo*, *tenore buffo*, comic bass, comic tenor (in opera). (So also *buffo* by itself is sometimes found, e.g. in the list of singers required for an Italian opera, and then indicates a comic bass.) So also *opera buffa* – literally 'comic opera' (➤opera).

bugle, brass instrument without

valves and so producing only one ➤harmonic series (normally in B flat), used by armies, etc., both as a band instrument and to signal movements, etc. *Key bugle, keyed bugle, Kent bugle* – ➤ophicleide.

Bühnenweihfestspiel, ➤*Parsifal*.

Bulgakov, Mikhail Afanasyevich (1891–1940), Russian novelist and playwright. ➤*Meister und Margarita*.

Bull, John (1562/3–1628), English composer and organist – at Chapel Royal, London; first professor of music at Gresham College, London, 1596. Left England, 1613; in 1617 became cathedral organist at Antwerp, where he died. Wrote notable pieces for keyboard (➤*Parthenia*), one of them the probable source of 'God Save the Queen'; also music for viols, and church music.

Bull, Ole (1810–80), Norwegian violinist, composer (two violin concertos, etc.), and enthusiast for Norwegian folk-music; gave Grieg early encouragement.

Buller, John [Stuart] (b. 1927), British composer, previously an architectural surveyor. Works include opera *Bacchae*, after Euripides (the orchestral *Bacchae Metres* is derived from it), *Proença* (Provence) for orchestra, *Poor Jenny* for flute and percussion, and a series of works based on Joyce's *Finnegans Wake*.

bull-roarer, primitive musical instrument found in Australian aboriginal and other cultures; a sound is produced by the whirling of an object at the end of a rope, the other end being held in the hand.

Bülow, Hans [Guido] **von** (1830–94), German pianist, music-editor and conductor – reckoned the first 'virtuoso' conductor; disciple of Liszt and Wagner, but enthusiast also for Brahms. Married Liszt's daughter Cosima, who afterwards left him for Wagner. Died in Cairo.

Bulwer-Lytton, Edward George Earle Lytton [Lord Lytton] (1803–73), British novelist and dramatist. ➤*Rienzi*.

Bumbry, Grace [Ann Melzia] (b. 1937), American mezzo-soprano, prominent in opera (first black singer to appear at Bayreuth Festival, 1961), latterly has taken some soprano roles.

bumper, (orchestral colloquialism for) an extra player, especially a fifth horn-player, engaged to relieve the leading player and reinforce ('bump up') *tutti* passages.

Bunyan, John (1628–88), English writer. ➤*Pilgrim's Progress*.

Buononcini, Giovanni, ➤Bononcini.

Burchuladze, Paata (b. 1951), Georgian bass who first graduated in engineering; began operatic career at Tbilisi (Georgia) and Moscow, with subsequent appearances at Covent Garden (1984), Salzburg Festival under Karajan, etc.

burden (1) the refrain of a song; (2) in 14th- and 15th-century English music, the lowest strand in a polyphonic complex.

Burgess, Sally (b. 1953), British (South African-born) mezzo-soprano with distinguished career at English National Opera (as Carmen, etc.) from the 1970s; has also sung at Covent Garden (1983), at Glyndebourne, and in *Show Boat* for Royal Shakespeare Co. with Opera North.

Burgmüller, [Johann] **Friedrich** [Franz] (1806–74), German composer who settled in Paris and wrote two supplementary numbers for the ballet *Giselle* (mainly by Adam) as well as his own ballet *La Péri*. Also composed many piano pieces.

Burgon, Geoffrey (b. 1941), British composer, formerly trumpeter. Works include a Requiem, trumpet concerto, oboe quartet, television theme music for *Brideshead Revisited* and orchestral *Brideshead Variations*.

Burian, Emil František (1904–59), Czech composer (also singer, author, playwright, producer); inventor of 'voice band', an ensemble of voices using vowels as concords, consonants as discords (demonstrated, 1928). Works include operas, ballets, chamber music.

Burkhard, Willy (1900–1955), Swiss composer (also pianist and conductor); pupil of Karg-Elert and somewhat influenced by Hindemith. Works include *Das Gesicht Jesajas* ('The Vision of Isaiah'), and other Protestant oratorios; three symphonies; Toccata for four wind instruments with percussion and strings; Mass; opera *Die Schwarze Spinne* ('The Black Spider').

Burleigh, Henry Thacker (1866–1914), American baritone, composer and arranger of Negro spirituals; pupil of Dvořák.

burlesque (Fr., Eng.), **burlesca** (It.), **Burleske** (Ger.), terms indicating a humorous, playful vein (It., *burla*, joke), applied variously in musical titles, usually without an implication of parody. R. Strauss's *Burleske* is for piano and orchestra (1886).

burletta (It.), term used in Britain around 1800 for a light Italian comic opera, or a work in that style.

Burnand, [Sir] **Francis Cowley** (1836–1917), British writer. ➤*Cox and Box*; ➤Savoy Operas.

Burney, Charles (1726–1814), British author of a famous history of music and other books; also organist and composer.

Burns, Robert (1759–96), British poet. ➤Sviridov.

Burrell, Diana (b. 1948), British composer, formerly orchestral viola-player; works include viola concerto, *Scene with Birds* for orchestra, *Arched Forms with Bells* for organ, and a Mass (*Missa Sancte Endeliente*).

Burt, Francis (b. 1926), British composer, pupil of Ferguson and (in Berlin) of Blacher; resident since 1957 mostly in Vienna. Works include *Iambics* for orchestra; two string quartets; opera *Volpone* (after Ben Jonson).

Busch, Adolf [Georg Wilhelm] (1891–1952), German-born violinist who, as anti-Nazi, took Swiss nationality; died in New York. Well known as soloist, leader of the Busch String Quartet and partner of Rudolf ➤Serkin (who became his son-in-law). Also composer. Brother of Fritz Busch.

Busch, Fritz (1890–1951), German-born conductor who, as anti-Nazi, settled in Denmark; noted also as the first opera conductor at Glyndebourne (1934–9, returning 1950–51). Died in London. Brother of Adolf Busch.

Bush, Alan [Dudley] (1900–1995), British composer (also pianist, conductor, writer on music and teacher); studied under John Ireland, and also in Berlin. Communist sympathies give clues to many of his works including operas ➤*Wat Tyler* and *Men of Blackmoor* (both produced in East Germany), a piano concerto (with male chorus declaiming leftist text in finale), string quartet entitled *Dialectic*, and *Lyric Interlude* for violin and piano.

Bush, Geoffrey (1920–98), British composer (also writer and university teacher), formerly Salisbury Cathedral choirboy. Works include *Lord Arthur Savile's Crime* (after Wilde) and other operas, two symphonies, songs (some with orchestra).

Busnois, the name by which Antoine de Busne (*c.* 1430–1492) was known: he was a Flemish (Netherlandish) composer in service to the dukes of Burgundy. Wrote Masses and other church music, also secular ➤*chansons*.

Busoni, Ferruccio [Benvenuto] (1866–1924), Italian pianist and composer; travelled widely; from 1894 lived mainly in Berlin (was himself of a German mother) and died there. Made wider appeal as a pianist, piano-teacher and arranger (e.g. editions for piano of J. S. Bach's organ works) than as composer. Works include operas *Arlecchino*, ➤*Doktor Faust*, and ➤*Turandot*; a piano concerto (using male choir); a violin concerto; many piano solos; *Fantasia Contrappuntistica* (It., Contrapuntal Fantasia) for two pianos, based on J. S. Bach's *Die* ➤*Kunst der Fuge*.

Büsser, Paul Henri (1872–1973), French composer, also conductor. Works include seven operas, church and organ music, and orchestrations of piano pieces by Debussy.

Bussotti, Sylvano (b. 1931), Italian composer of *La Passion selon Sade*

('The Passion according to [the Marquis of] Sade'), a 'staged concert for voice, instruments, narrator'; piano pieces; *Rara Requiem* (for voices and chamber orchestra), etc. Employs highly individualized ➤graphic notation.

Butler, Martin (b. 1960), British composer who trained partly in USA. Works include opera *Craig's Progress*, *Piano Piano* for two pianos and tape, *Still Breathing* for wind orchestra. Several works including *Bluegrass Variations* for unaccompanied violin are in folkish vein. (➤bluegrass).

Butt, Clara [Ellen] (1872–1936), British contralto for whom Elgar wrote his *Sea Pictures*; chiefly famous for ballad singing, and the first musician to be created Dame (1920).

Butterfly, Butterfly's Wing(s), unauthorized nicknames for Chopin's Study in G flat for piano, op. 25, no. 9.

Butterley, Nigel [Henry] (b. 1935), Australian composer who studied in London. Works include opera *Lawrence Hargrave Flying Alone*; *Meditations of Thomas Traherne* for children's recorder group and orchestra; *Explorations* for piano and orchestra; three string quartets.

Butterworth, George [Sainton Kaye] (1885–1916), British composer; collected English folk-songs and shows their influence in, e.g., *A Shropshire Lad* (after Housman) for orchestra. Killed in action as a soldier.

Buxtehude, Diderik (*c.* 1637–1707), Danish organist and composer; from 1668 organist at Lübeck, Germany, and therefore better known by the German form of his name as Dietrich Buxtehude. Wrote organ and harpsichord pieces, also church cantatas, etc. Much esteemed in his own day; visited by Bach and Handel as young men, influencing them both.

BWV, the accepted system of numbering Bach's works; ➤Bach.

Bychkov, Semyon (b. 1952), Russian-born conductor, naturalized American, 1983. Left USSR in 1975. Appointed conductor of the Orchestre de Paris from 1990. His brother is ➤Kreizberg.

Byrd, William (1543–1623), English composer; organist of Lincoln Cathedral, 1563, of the Chapel Royal (jointly with Tallis), 1572. Jointly with Tallis, held from Queen Elizabeth a monopoly of music printing. Roman Catholic; composed for both his own and the Anglican Church. Works,

mainly in serious vein and mainly church music, include Masses for three, four and five voices; more than 200 Latin motets (17 in ➤*Cantiones Sacrae*, 1575); five Anglican services (one incomplete); also madrigals, rounds and other secular vocal music, many pieces for keyboard (some contributed to ➤*Parthenia*), and ➤fancies, etc., for viols.

Byron, George Gordon [Lord] (1788–1824), British poet. ➤*Corsaire*, ➤*Harold en Italie*, ➤*Manfred*, ➤*Mazeppa*, ➤*Ode to Napoleon Buonaparte*, ➤Holbrooke, ➤Nathan, ➤Thomson (V.).

Byzantine music, the music of the liturgical chant of the Eastern Orthodox Churches, so named from the former city of Byzantium (later Constantinople, now Istanbul).

C

C, note of the scale. So C ➤*flat*, C ➤*sharp*, semitonally adjacent notes; C ➤*major*, C ➤*minor*, keys or chords defined by having C as point of stability (➤tonic). So also *in C* (1, of a composition or part of it) indication that the music belongs in that key (major unless indicated as minor); (2, of a wind instrument) indication of length of air-column which gives C as the fundamental of its harmonic series: the indication usually but not always implies a non-transposing instrument in cases where otherwise a ➤transposing instrument might seem to be indicated. So *trumpet in C* (to differentiate from trumpet in B flat). So also *middle C*, the C situated about the middle of the piano, and notated on the line below the treble staff; *cello C*, the C below the bass staff (tuning of the cello's lowest note); *C clef*, any one of the clefs which indicate the position of the middle C – e.g. the ➤alto and ➤tenor clefs, and the obsolete ➤soprano clef.

c (lower-case letter), indication of the key of C minor as distinct from capital C for C major – a logical but not universal usage.

cabaletta (It.), in 19th-century Italian opera (and, by analogy, in other operatic contexts), the final, quicker section of an aria or duet made up of several (usually two) sections. ➤*cavatina*.

Caballé, Montserrat (b. 1933), Spanish (Catalan) soprano, prominent in operas by Donizetti and other Italian composers, with a total of 88 roles. At La Scala, Milan, from 1960, Covent Garden from 1972.

Cabaret, musical with text by Joe Masteroff based on the play *I Am a Camera* by John van Druten and the stories of Christopher Isherwood; lyrics by Fred Ebb; music by John Kander. Produced in New York, 1966. A Berlin cabaret provides a metaphor for the advent of Nazism.

Cabezón, Antonio de (1510–66), Spanish organist, harpsichordist and composer of keyboard music, musician at the Spanish court; he was blind, apparently from birth. Wrote keyboard variations, etc.

cabinet organ, ➤American organ.

caccia (It., hunt), an Italian poetic and musical form of the 14th and early 15th centuries, usually for two voices and dealing with real-life scenes such as the hunt. So *corno di caccia* (➤horn) and, a disputed term, *oboe di caccia* (➤oboe).

Caccini, Giulio (c. 1545–1618), Italian composer (and lutenist) whose *Euridice*

61

(1600) is one of the earliest operas; as a pioneer of a newly expressive type of music, he called his collection of madrigals and canzonets (1601) *Le nuove musiche* ('the new music(s)'). His daughters, Francesca (*c.* 1587–1640) and Settimia (*c.* 1591–1638), were celebrated singers as well as composers, an opera by the former being performed in Florence in 1625.

cachucha, a lively Spanish dance (from Andalusia) in triple time, borrowed by Sullivan in *The Gondoliers*.

cadence, a progression of chords (usually two) giving an effect of closing a 'sentence' in music. Thus *perfect cadence*, progression of dominant chord to tonic chord; *plagal cadence*, subdominant to tonic; *imperfect cadence*, tonic (or other chord) to dominant: *interrupted cadence*, dominant to submediant (or to some other chord suggesting a substitution for the expected tonic chord); *Phrygian cadence*, progression (deriving from the Phrygian ➤mode) which, in the key of C major, leads to the chord of E major (and correspondingly with other keys). Note that (1) some of these definitions are open to differences between authorities; (2) the *feminine cadence* is not a specific kind of harmonic progression, as the above, but any cadence in which the final chord comes on a weaker beat than its predecessor (instead of, as normally, the other way round). See also the following.

cadenza (It., cadence; but pronounced as English and used in different sense), solo vocal or instrumental passage, either of an improvised nature or in some other way suggesting an interpolation in the flow of the music – particularly, today, in concertos for solo instrument and orchestra. In the performance of such works, however, genuine improvisation has for 150 years been very rare, cadenzas being written out in full instead by either the composer, the actual performer, or a third person.

Cadman, Charles Wakefield (1881–1946), American composer of *Pennsylvania Symphony* (orchestration includes banging on iron plate); opera *Shanewis*, based on an American–Indian story; songs (including 'At Dawning'); etc.

Cage aux Folles, La, musical with text by Harvey Fierstein based on the play by Jean Poiret; music and lyrics by Jerry Herman. Produced in New York, 1983. The title is that of a night-club in St Tropez; off-duty, the entertainers confront homosexuality and cross-dressing.

Cage, John (1912–92), American composer (also pianist and writer), pupil of Schoenberg; inventor of the musical 'happening'. Wrote for normal instruments and for his invention, the ➤prepared piano; noted for works which seem to involve the abdication of the composer, e.g. his *Imaginary Landscape No. 4* for 12 radio sets, first performed in 1951, requiring 24 performers (two to each set) and conductor – dynamics, and the ratio of sound to silence, are stipulated but the result obviously depends on chance (➤aleatory). His *4'33"* requires the piano to be *silent* for that period of time. Other works include *Roaratorio* (1979), after Joyce's *Finnegans Wake* (the instrumentation includes a ➤bodhran).

Cain, James M. (1892–1977), American novelist. ➤Paulus (Stephen).

caisse (Fr.), drum; *grosse caisse*, bass drum; *caisse claire*, side-drum; *caisse roulante* or *caisse sourde*, tenor drum.

cakewalk, US dance originating among ex-African slaves in Southern plantations, with musical elements foreshadowing ➤ragtime; became generally known from late 19th century. Adopted by Debussy in ➤*Children's Corner*.

calando (It.), getting weaker and slower.

Caldara, Antonio (*c.* 1670–1736), Italian composer who settled in Vienna, 1716, where he died; works include more than 80 operas, also oratorios, chamber music, church music.

Calderón, Pedro (1600–1681). Spanish dramatist. ➤Wimberger.

Calife de Bagdad, Le (Fr., 'The Caliph of Baghdad'), opera by Boïeldieu, produced in Paris in 1800. Libretto by C. H. d'A. de Saint-Just; the Caliph assumes a disguise to learn people's real feelings about him.

Calinda, La, orchestral piece by Delius (excerpt from his opera ➤*Koanga*), taking its name from a Negro dance imported by African slaves to the American continent.

Caliph of Baghdad, The, opera by Boïeldieu. ➤*Calife de Bagdad*.

Calisto, opera by Cavalli, produced in Venice, 1651: libretto by Faustini, about the nymph of Roman legend who is metamorphosed into a constellation. ('Callisto' is correct Latin spelling; 'Calisto' is the Italian form.)

Callas, Maria (form of name used by Maria Anna Kalogeropoulos) (1923–77), American-born soprano of Greek parentage, at first with career based mainly in Italy, then achieving highest international reputation, especially in bringing new dramatic power to works by Rossini, Verdi, etc. Rare operas, e.g. Cherubini's *Médée*, were revived for her. Gave concerts sporadically after last stage appearance in 1965.

Call Me Madam, musical comedy with text by Howard Lindsay and Russel Crouse; music and lyrics by Irving Berlin. Produced in New York, 1950. Satire concerning a female American ambassador to the fictitious European 'Lichtenburg': on stage an ➤ocarina is played.

Calvé, Emma (originally Rose-Noémie Calvet de Roquer), (1858–1942), French soprano, celebrated in the (normally mezzo-soprano) role of Carmen. Sang at Covent Garden from 1892.

Cambert, Robert (*c.* 1628–77), French composer who lived in London from 1673, and died there. His *Pomone* (1671) is one of the earliest French operas.

cambiata, ➤*nota cambiata*.

Camelot, musical with text by Alan Jay Lerner based on *The Once and Future King* by T. H. White; music by Frederick Loewe. Produced in New York, 1960. King Arthur forgives his wife and her lover for their elopement, though the newly civilized values of his court in Camelot are imperilled.

camera, da (It.), for the room – either (1) as distinct from *da chiesa*, for the church, or (2) as implying music for a small gathering, exactly as 'chamber music' does. So *sonata da camera* (➤sonata).

camerata (1, It.) a historical name for

a club or society, in musical history usually referring to that which centred on Count Giovanni Bardi in Florence shortly before 1600, the composers Caccini and Peri being members. In this group but also in others at Florence the new concepts of ►monody and of opera were shaped; (2) modern name sometimes used (in various countries) for a chamber orchestra.

Camidge, Matthew (1758–1844), British organist, composer of piano sonatas, editor of a collection of cathedral music.

Camilleri, Charles [Mario] (b. 1931), Maltese composer who has used Maltese, African and other musical sources. Works include opera *Melita*; three piano concertos; *Missa Mundi* (Lat., 'Mass of the World') for organ.

campana, campane (It.), bell, bells.

Campanella, La, ►Bell Rondo.

campanology, the study of bells.

Campion (or **Campian**), **Thomas** (1567–1620), English composer of more than 100 songs to lute accompaniment; also of masques, etc. Wrote poems set to music by himself and others, and was also lawyer and physician.

Campra, André (1660–1744), French composer of operas including *Tancrède* and *Idoménée* (same plot as Mozart's ►*Idomeneo*), opera-ballets, church music etc.; in charge of music at the church of Notre Dame, Paris.

canarie, canaries, canary, an old dance in triple time (a type of ►jig) having a prominent dotted rhythm.

can-can, Parisian dance, sometimes supposedly salacious, in quick 2/4 time; used by Offenbach in ►*Orphée aux enfers*.

cancion (Sp.), song; so *cancionero*, song-book.

cancrizans (made-up Lat.), crab-wise. The term is used (apparently through defective observation of crabs, which move sideways) to indicate a back-to-front order of notes (i.e. retrograde motion); *canon cancrizans*, a canon in which the imitating voice gives out the theme not as the first voice gave it but with the notes in reverse order.

Candide, operetta with text by Lillian Hellman based on the satire by Voltaire; lyrics by Richard Wilbur; music by Leonard Bernstein. Produced in New York, 1956. Voltaire himself introduces this story of the naïve Candide and his blindly optimistic tutor Dr Pangloss.

Cannabich, Johann Christian (1731–98), German composer of symphonies (adherent of the so-called ►Mannheim School) and of operas, ballets, chamber music, etc.; also violinist and conductor.

Cannon, Philip (b. 1929), British composer of partly French descent. Works include string quartet, songs, choral symphony *Son of Man* (after Isaiah).

canon, contrapuntal composition, or section of a composition, in which a melody announced by one voice (or instrument) is repeated by one or more other voices (or instruments), each entering before the previous voice has finished so that overlapping results. A *canon at the unison* is when the 'imitating' (i.e. following) voice enters at the same pitch as the first voice; a *canon at the fifth* is when the imitating voice enters a fifth higher than the original. A *canon four in one* indicates four voices entering successively on the same melody; a *canon four in two* (or *double canon*) has two different simultaneous canons for two voices each. So also *accompanied canon*, when there are simultaneous other voices or instruments performing but not taking part in the canon; *perpetual canon*, when each voice as it comes to the end begins again (➤round); *canon by* ➤augmentation, ➤diminution, ➤inversion, etc., one in which the theme is treated in the imitating voice in one of those ways; *riddle* (or *enigma* or *puzzle*) *canon*, one in which only the opening voice is written out, leaving the notation of the other entries to be deduced.

cantabile (It.), in a 'singing' fashion; flowingly and clearly.

cantata (It., a sung piece), an extended choral work with or without solo voices, and usually with orchestral accompaniment. This is the later meaning of the term, but in Italian baroque usage it implies solo voice(s) and ➤continuo, and Bach's cantatas have solo voice(s) with accompanying instruments, with or without chorus. The term is much more rarely used as an actual title than its counterpart, ➤sonata – but Stravinsky composed a *Cantata* (two solo singers, female chorus, five instrumentalists) to old English texts, 1952, and Bartók a *Cantata profana* (subtitle 'The Enchanted Stags', on a legend symbolizing a plea for political freedom) for two soloists, chorus and orchestra, 1930. Britten's *Cantata academica* (in Latin) was written for the 500th anniversary of Basle University, 1960.

cantatrice (It.), woman singer.

cante flamenco, cante hondo (or *jondo*), ➤*flamenco*, ➤*hondo*.

Cantelli, Guido (1920–56), Italian conductor. He appeared at the 1950 Edinburgh Festival and was chosen as music director of La Scala, Milan, shortly before being killed in an air crash; his gifts were considered outstanding.

Canteloube [de Malaret], **Marie-Joseph** (1879–1957), French pianist, composer and folk-song collector, chiefly known for his ➤*Chants d'Auvergne* (region of France).

canticle (1) a hymn with biblical words, other than from the Psalms, used in Christian liturgy (distinct from ➤anthem, which is not on a liturgically obligatory text); so, analogously, (2) a concert work with a religious or quasi-religious text – term used, e.g., as title of five works by Britten.

cantiga, type of Spanish or Portuguese medieval song; *Cantigas de Santa María*, a 13th-century collection of more than 400 such songs (some in praise of the Virgin Mary) collected under the auspices of ➤Alfonso X and surviving in manuscript.

cantilena (It.), a smooth song-like melodic line.

cantillation, unaccompanied chanting in free rhythm – term used particularly of Jewish liturgical chanting.

Cantiones Sacrae (Lat., Sacred Songs), title sometimes formerly applied to collections of Latin motets (e.g. one composed by Tallis and Byrd, 1575).

canto (It.), song; melody; *marcato il canto*, bring out the melody; *col canto*, let the tempo of the accompaniment be accommodated to that of the soloist's tune; *canto fermo*, ➤*cantus firmus*. Plural *canti*, as in Dallapiccola's *Canti di Liberazione* ('Songs of Liberation') for chorus and orchestra, first performed 1955.

cantor (Lat., singer) (1) director of music in a German Lutheran church (in modern German, *Kantor*) – e.g. Bach's position at St Thomas's, Leipzig; (2) the leader of the chanting in a synagogue.

cantoris (Lat., of the singer, i.e. of the precentor), that section of the choir in a cathedral, etc., which is stationed on the north (i.e. precentor's) side of the chancel; opposite of ➤*decani*.

cantus (Lat.), (1) song, melody; *cantus firmus* (pl. *cantus firmi*), fixed song, i.e. the 'given' melody borrowed from religious or secular sources which 14th–17th-century composers used as a basis of works by setting other melodies in counterpoint against it – similarly, a melody given to a student, even today, to set a counterpoint against; (2) in, e.g., the 16th century, the upper voice-line of a choir; (3) title sometimes given to a vocal work, e.g. Pärt's *Cantus in memoriam Benjamin Britten*.

canzona, canzone (It.), (1) any song; e.g. 'Canzone del salce', the 'Willow Song' from Verdi's *Otello*; (2) specifically, a type of medieval Italian poem, and hence a musical setting of this; (3) type of short instrumental piece, especially of the 16th to early 18th centuries, often less strongly polyphonic than the ➤*ricercar* – developed from the contemporary French ➤*chanson*.

canzonet (Anglicized from It. *can-*

zonetta), term used *c*. 1600 for a light song for one or more voices, and later (e.g. Haydn's English canzonets) for an English solo song not from an opera.

canzonetta (It. diminutive of ➤*canzona*), little song, light song.

caoine, ➤keen (lament).

Čapek, Karel (1890–1938), Czech novelist and dramatist. ➤*Makropoulos Affair*.

capella, incorrect spelling for ➤*cappella*.

Caplet, André (1878–1925), French composer of unaccompanied Mass, song-cycles, etc.; also conductor – at Boston, USA, 1910–14; friend of Debussy, some of whose work he arranged for orchestra.

capo (It., head) (1) ➤*da capo*; (2) a device used on the fingerboard of a guitar to shorten the strings equally in order to facilitate playing in various keys – i.e. a form of movable nut (➤nut, 1).

cappella (It.), chapel; in 17th-century usage, a near-synonym for ➤*ripieno*, i.e. full performing forces; *a cappella, alla cappella*, 'in the chapel style', i.e. unaccompanied (of choral music).

Cappuccilli, Piero (b. 1929), Italian baritone, distinguished in Verdi; sang at La Scala, Milan, from 1964.

Capriccio, opera by R. Strauss, produced in Munich, 1942. Styled 'a conversation piece in one act' (2 hours). Libretto by composer and Clemens Krauss, in which a poet and a musician are rival suitors to a young widowed countess; set in the 18th century.

capriccio (It.), **caprice** (Fr., Eng.), term

applied to various types of lively, light piece; and specifically to a 17th-century keyboard work in lively fugal style. See also following.

Capriccio espagnol (It. and Fr., 'Spanish Caprice'), orchestral work by Rimsky-Korsakov (first performed in 1887) on themes of Spanish national character.

Capriccio italien (It. and Fr., 'Italian Caprice'), orchestral work by Tchaikovsky, composed in 1879 in Italy, based on popular tunes heard there.

Capriol, suite for strings by Warlock, 1926, also arranged for full orchestra; in six movements based on old French dances from Thoinot Arbeau's *Orchésographie*, a book on dancing, 1589. ('Capriol' is an imaginary character in the book.)

Carafa [full surname Carafa di Colobrano], **Michele Enrico** (1787–1872). Italian opera-composer who settled in France. ➤*Masaniello*.

Cardew, Cornelius (1936–81), British composer, pupil of Howard Ferguson, later associated with Stockhausen; works include *Octet 1961* with diagrammatic notation and free choice for performers (➤indeterminacy). Also composed more conventional music for piano, string trio, etc., and some later works with 'popular' simplification in pursuance of Maoist political ideas.

Cardillac, opera by Hindemith, produced at Dresden, 1926. Libretto by F. Lion; it was later revised – the text extensively, the music rather less. Title is the name of the hero, a 17th-century French goldsmith.

Cardoso, Manuel (1556–1650), Portu-guese composer, monk, and chapel music director. Three books of Masses and motets by him were published, but some of his work in manuscript was destroyed in the fire following the Lisbon earthquake of 1755.

Carey, Henry (*c.* 1689–1743), English composer (also poet and playwright); wrote words and music of *Chrononhotonthlogos* (burlesque of pompous tragedy) and other stage pieces including *True Blue*; also composed cantatas and songs. Wrote words and a tune (not the best-known one) of 'Sally in our Alley'.

carillon (originally Fr.), (1) set of bells, e.g. in a tower, on which tunes are played either by heavy manual and pedal keyboards or mechanically; (2) bell-like organ stop; (3) title of work by Elgar (1914) for reciter with orchestra, based on a bell-like short theme.

Carissimi, Giacomo (1605–74), Italian composer and church musician who wrote early examples of oratorio (➤*Jephtha*); also cantatas, Masses, vocal duets, etc.

Carmelites, The, ➤*Dialogues des Carmélites*.

carmen (Lat.), song; the plural is *carmina*, as in ➤*Carmina Burana*.

Carmen, Bizet's most successful opera, produced in Paris, 1875. Libretto by H. Meilhac and L. Halévy. Title from the name of the heroine, a gipsy working in a cigarette factory. The opera's well-known *habanera* is taken from a song by Yradier. Adaptations of the score include works by ➤Constant and ➤Shchedrin.

Carmen Jones, musical play with text by Oscar Hammerstein II based on Bizet's ➤*Carmen* with an updated story. Produced in New York, 1943. The heroine works in a wartime parachute factory, meets a boxer called Hunky Miller (= Bizet's Escamillo), etc.

Carmina Burana (Lat., 'Songs of Beuren') (1) title given in the 19th century to a collection of medieval (mainly Latin) poems about love, liquor, etc., found at the monastery of Benediktbeuren, Bavaria; (2) cantata by Orff using a selection of these poems, intended for mimed action; first performed in Frankfurt, 1937. (*Carmina* is accented on the first syllable.)

Carnaval (Fr., 'Carnival'), piano work by Schumann, having a thematic connection with his ➤*Papillons*. The ballet so titled, with choreography by Fokin, 1910, used Schumann's music in an orchestration by Glazunov and other Russian composers.

Carnaval des animaux, Le (Fr., 'The Carnival of the Animals'), 'grand zoological fantasy' for two pianos and orchestra by Saint-Saëns, 1886 (withheld from public performances in his lifetime); 14 movements, of which no. 11 is 'Pianists' and no. 13 'The Swan'.

Carnaval romain, Le (Fr. 'The Roman Carnival'), concert overture (based on a scene from his opera *Benvenuto Cellini*) by Berlioz, 1844.

Carnevale di Venezia, Il (It., 'The Carnival of Venice'), the name given to a set of variations for violin and orchestra by Paganini, apparently on a popular song.

Carnival (with variant forms ➤*carnaval*, ➤*carnevale*), title of works alluding to traditional pre-Lenten festivities, or more generally to public merry-making, as in (1) concert-overture (Cz., *Karneval*) by Dvořák, 1891, the second of his cycle of three overtures, *Nature, Life and Love* (no. 1 ➤*Amid Nature*; no. 3 ➤*Othello*); (2) concert overture by Glazunov, 1894.

Carnival Jest from Vienna, piano work by Schumann. ➤*Faschingsschwank aus Wien*.

Carnival of the Animals, The, work for two pianos and orchestra by Saint-Saëns. ➤*Carnaval des animaux*.

carol, an English traditional song of joyful character (apparently, in its medieval origins, a danced song). The *Christmas carol* (most of the current examples dating from the 19th–20th centuries) is only one type.

Carousel, musical play with text by Oscar Hammerstein II based on *Liliom* by Ferenc Molnar; music by Richard Rodgers. Produced in New York, 1945. Title (= roundabout) refers both to a New England fairground (1873) and to the changes life brings.

Carpenter, John Alden (1876–1951), American composer of orchestral suite *Adventures in a Perambulator*, two symphonies (no. 2 incorporating Algerian tunes), ballet *Krazy Kat*, etc.; he combined music with a business career.

Carreras, José [Maria] (b. 1946), Spanish (Catalan) tenor prominent in Italian opera; at Covent Garden since 1974, at La Scala, Milan from 1975. His career was interrupted by leukaemia, 1987–8.

Carrillo, Julián (1875–1965), Mexican composer of three operas, Masses, symphonies, etc., of 'normal' musical structure; also deviser of harps and other instruments producing intervals such as quarter-, eighth- and 16th-tones, and composer of more than 50 works for them.

Carroll, Lewis [C. L. Dodgson] (1832–98), British writer. ➤Del Tredici, ➤Evangelista, ➤Horovitz, ➤Taylor (D.).

Carter, Elliott [Cook] (b. 1908), American composer, pupil in Paris of N. Boulanger. Winner of many US and other awards. In early career was music director of ballet company. Works include ballet score *The Minotaur*, Double Concerto (harpsichord, piano, two chamber orchestras), piano concerto, violin concerto, five string quartets; *A Mirror on Which to Dwell* for soprano and nine instrumentalists.

Carulli, Fernando (1770–1841), Italian guitarist, composer of nearly 400 pieces for his instrument; settled in Paris, taught and died there.

Caruso, Enrico (1873–1921), Italian tenor who made his first public appearance in 1894 in Naples (where he was born and died); appeared in Britain from 1902, USA from 1903. One of the first artists whose enormous success owed much to recording.

Cary, Tristram [Ogilvie] (b. 1925), British composer of electronic music on tape (e.g. *Birth is Life is Power is Death is God is*), also sonata for guitar, film and television scores, etc. Writer on electronic technology, holder of university post in Adelaide.

Casadesus, Robert [Marcel] (1899–1972), French pianist, noted as soloist and also forming two-piano team with his wife, Gaby; also composer of piano concertos, symphonies, etc.

Casals, Pablo (he also used the Catalan form of his first name: Pau) (1876–1973), Spanish (Catalan) cellist; also pianist, conductor and composer, e.g. of oratorio *El Pessebre* ('The Manger'), who made his first London appearance in 1898. Won unsurpassed reputation, particularly in J. S. Bach's unaccompanied cello works, and received high state honours from many countries. From 1940 lived outside Spain in protest against Franco's government (latterly in Puerto Rico), founding annual festival at Prades in the French Pyrenees.

Casella, Alfredo (1883–1947), Italian composer and pianist; pupil of Fauré in Paris. Works include operas, symphonies, *Pupazzetti* ('Puppets') for piano duet, many piano solos; chamber music including Concerto for string quartet. Also wrote oratorio *Il deserto tentato* ('The Desert Challenged') (idealizing Mussolini's conquest of Ethiopia) and other works with topical links.

Casken, John [Arthur] (b. 1949), British composer and professor at Manchester University since 1992. Works include string quartet, cello concerto, *Darting the Skiff* (title from Gerard Manley Hopkins) for orchestra, opera *Golem*.

cassa (It.), drum; *gran cassa*, bass drum; *cassa rullante*, tenor drum.

cassation (derivation uncertain), 18th-century type of composition (e.g. by Mozart) in several movements and in ➤*divertimento* style for an orchestra or small group of instruments.

Casse-noisette, ➤*Nutcracker*.

castanets, percussion instruments made of two hollowed-out wooden surfaces rhythmically clicked together by the fingers of Spanish dancers; in the orchestra the clicking pieces of wood are often mounted for convenience at the end of a small stick. (Derivation from Sp. *castaño*, chestnut, but this wood is not used in their manufacture.)

Castelnuovo-Tedesco, Mario (1895–1968), Italian composer, pupil of Pizzetti; settled in USA, 1939, when banned as a Jew from Italian cultural life. Works include operas, oratorio *The Book of Jonah*, three violin concertos, a guitar concerto, song-settings of Shakespeare, music for the synagogue.

Castiglioni, Niccolò (1932–96), Italian composer and pianist who has worked at US universities. Works include *Granulation* for two flutes, two clarinets; Symphony in C with choral text by Jonson, Dante, Shakespeare and Keats; *Le favole di Esopo* ('Aesop's Fables') for chorus and orchestra.

castrato (It., castrated), male singer castrated at puberty to allow development of a powerful voice in soprano or contralto range. Such singers were employed in Italian churches in the 17th and 18th centuries and became prominent in Italian operas – Handel's for instance being written for their participation.

Catalani, Alfredo (1854–93), Italian composer who studied in Paris and wrote *La* ➤*Wally* and other successful operas; also Mass, symphonic poem *Ero e Leandro* ('Hero and Leander'), etc.

catch, type of ➤round with tricky, amusing (sometimes bawdy) words, cultivated by Purcell and other English composers from 17th to 19th century.

Cat Duet, a piece for two female voices and piano, falsely ascribed to Rossini; it mocks the Italian operatic style with miaowing sounds.

Cats, musical based on *Old Possum's Book of Practical Cats* by T. S. Eliot; music by Andrew Lloyd Webber. Produced in London, 1981. On a set representing a gigantic rubbish dump, cats with such names as Bustopher Jones and Jennyanydots reveal their personalities.

Cat's Fugue, nickname of one of D. Scarlatti's so-called 'sonatas' for harpsichord (no. 30 in Kirkpatrick's catalogue; published in 1738). Its theme of oddly rising intervals is dubiously said to originate from the steps of a cat on the keyboard.

Catullus, Caius Valerius (*c.* 84–54 BC), Roman poet. ➤Orff.

Causton, Thomas (*c.* 1525–1569), English composer of church music, etc.

Cavalieri, Emilio de' (*c.* 1550–1602), Italian composer, mainly at the Medici court in Florence; as well as incidental music for court festivities, he composed *La* ➤*Rappresentazione di anima e di corpo* – type of 'morality play' set to music, now reckoned the first oratorio (but using costumes and action).

Cavalleria Rusticana (It., 'The Rustic Code of Honour'), opera by Mascagni, produced in Rome, 1890. Libretto by G. Menasci and G. Targioni-Tozzetti: a tale of revenge in a Sicilian village. It is performed without an interval, the well-known Intermezzo being traditionally played with the curtain up at a point in the middle when the stage is empty of characters.

Cavalli, Pietro Francesco (1602–76), Italian composer of more than 40 operas, including ➤*Ormindo*, ➤*Calisto*, *Eritrea* and *Erismena*, also of church music; worked in Venice as singer (at first under Monteverdi) and organist.

cavatina (It.) (1) operatic song in slow tempo, either complete in itself or (e.g. in Bellini and Verdi) followed by faster, more resolute section (➤*cabaletta*); hence (2) a rather slow, song-like instrumental movement – title, e.g., of a movement in Beethoven's String Quartet in B flat, op. 130 (1826); also of a once-famous piece (originally for violin and piano) by Raff.

Cavazzoni, Girolamo (1510 – after 1565), Italian composer of keyboard works, including some in the forms of ➤*ricercar* and ➤*canzona*. Son of the following.

Cavazzoni, Marco Antonio (*c.* 1490– after 1570), Italian composer, singer and organist, in service to Pope Leo X; works include a collection of keyboard pieces. Father of the preceding.

Cavendish, Michael (*c.*1565–1628), English composer of psalms, madrigals (one in *The* ➤*Triumphs of Oriana*), ayres, etc.

cebell, dance of the gavotte type, found in English music around 1700.

Ceccato, Aldo (b. 1934), Italian conductor, formerly pianist. Prominent in opera, and principal conductor of Bergen Symphony Orchestra since 1985.

Cecilia, Christian saint (now no longer recognized by Roman Catholic Church), supposedly executed in Sicily under the Romans in the second or third century AD. Later called the patron saint of music (commemorated annually on 22 November), though

her connection with music is purely legendary and dates only from the 16th century, apparently through the misreading of a Latin text. ➤*Hymn to St Cecilia*; ➤*Ode for St Cecilia's Day*.

cédez (Fr., yield), hold the tempo back (usually implying that a return to the previous tempo will shortly follow).

celesta (pronounced as English word; it is not Italian), instrument looking like small upright piano but having hammers striking metal bars giving bell-like sound; used, a few years after its invention in Paris, by Tchaikovsky in the 'Dance of the Sugar-Plum Fairy' (in *The* ➤*Nutcracker*) and afterwards by various composers, usually for 'picturesque' effects in the orchestra. Its compass is from middle C upwards for four octaves.

Celibidache, Sergiu (1912–96), Romanian conductor, trained in Germany; was attached to Berlin Philharmonic Orchestra, 1945–52. Chief conductor, Munich Philharmonic Orchestra from 1979.

Cellier, Alfred (1844–91), British composer, especially of operettas – including *Dorothy* (1886), with a record London run; also organist and conductor.

cello (It.; see end of entry), bowed four-stringed instrument, one of the family (of which the principal member is the violin) that superseded the viols in the 17th century; an early form is sometimes called *bass* ➤*violin*. The modern instrument has compass from C two octaves below middle C, upwards for more than three octaves. The five-stringed cello sometimes demanded, e.g. by Bach, is now obsolete. (The word *cello* is abbr. from *violoncello*, meaning a small violone, this being a large viol; hence it was formerly given the apostrophe, as 'cello. But it has been accepted, without the apostrophe, as a standard English word on its own, like 'piano', since no 'really English' alternative for it has been recognized, though ➤Grainger proposed one.

Celtic harp, ➤harp.

cembalo (It.), literally, a dulcimer but used as abbr. for *clavicembalo*, i.e. keyed dulcimer, i.e. ➤harpsichord. Also the standard German name for the instrument.

cencerro (Sp.), ➤cow-bell.

Cendrillon (Fr., 'Cinderella'), opera by Massenet based on Perrault's fairy-tale, produced in Paris, 1899 (libretto by H. Cain). Also opera by Isouard, 1810, and ballet score by Sors.

Cenerentola, La, ossia La bontà in trionfo (It., 'Cinderella, or Goodness Triumphant'), opera by Rossini, based on Perrault's fairy-tale produced in Rome, 1817 (libretto by J. Ferretti).

Cerha, Friedrich [Paul] (b. 1926), Austrian composer, also violinist, conductor and writer. (➤*Lulu*.) Works include *Spiegel* ('Mirrors') nos. 1–8 for orchestra.

Certon, Pierre (*c*.1510–72), French composer, choirmaster in Paris; works include Masses, psalm-settings, chansons.

Cervantes [Saavedra], **Miguel de** (1547–1616), Spanish writer. ➤*Don Quichotte*, ➤*Don Quixote*, ➤*Retablo de maese Pedro*; ➤Minkus.

Cesti, Marc'Antonio (1623–69), Italian composer and Franciscan monk holding church and court musical posts; pupil of Carissimi. Works include operas, solo cantatas, motets.

Cetra, La (It., 'The Lyre'), title of a set of 12 violin concertos by Vivaldi, published in 1727.

Ch-, Russian names beginning with this sound are listed (by convention rather than consistency) under **Tch** . . . e.g., Tchaikovsky.

ch., abbr. for choir (as a manual on the organ); *chm.*, abbr. for choirmaster (in some musical diplomas).

Chabrier, [Alexis] **Emmanuel** (1841–94), French composer, also pianist and conductor; originally civil servant. He visited Spain, 1882, and afterwards wrote orchestral rhapsody ➤*España*. Wrote also *Joyeuse Marche* for orchestra; piano and two-piano works; opera *Le Roi malgré lui* ('King Despite Himself'); etc. In late life suffered melancholic near-madness.

chaconne (Fr., from Sp. *chacona*), type of dance-piece in slow three-beat time, originating in the late 16th century. Using this form, composers often chose to repeat a given theme over and over again in the bass (i.e. a ground bass). In such examples as the Chaconne which forms the final movement of Bach's Partita no. 2 in D minor for violin alone (*c*.1720), the theme is harmonically implied even at those points when it is not actually present. The term is applied by modern historians also to vocal numbers (e.g. 'When I am laid in earth' in *Dido and Aeneas*) with a similar pattern of repetition. ➤*passacaglia*.

chacony, term formerly used in England, e.g. by Purcell, for ➤*chaconne*.

Chadwick, George Whitefield (1854–1931), American composer of three symphonies, five string quartets, etc.; pioneer of a distinctively American type of symphonic composition; pupil of Rheinberger in Germany.

Chailly, Luciano (b. 1920), Italian composer of *Una domanda di matrimonio* (*The Proposal*, after Chekhov) and other operas, chamber works, etc. Artistic director of La Scala opera house, Milan, 1968–71. Father of the following.

Chailly, Riccardo (b. 1953), Italian conductor, son of Luciano Chailly. Assistant conductor at La Scala, Milan, from age 19; after rapid international rise, became conductor of the (Royal) Concertgebouw Orchestra (Amsterdam) in 1988.

Chaliapin(e), ➤Shalyapin.

chalumeau (Fr.) (1) an obsolete instrument, forerunner of the clarinet; (2) the lowest register of the clarinet, with a distinctively 'dark' tone-colour.

chamber music, music intended for a room (in fact, called by Grainger 'room music', very sensibly), as distinct from a large hall, theatre, church, bandstand, ballroom, etc.; hence, particularly, music calling for 'intimate' presentation, having only a few performers, and treating all these as soloists on equal terms. Conventionally, works for one or two performers only are excluded. (The term is not a precisely defined one; see also following entries. There is every reason for including in it the appropriate kind of vocal music, e.g. madrigal-singing with one to two voices to each part.) Hindemith gave the actual title *Chamber Music* (Ger. *Kammermusik*) to each of a set of seven compositions for various instrumental combinations, 1922–30.

chamber opera, term sometimes used for an opera with few singers and a small orchestra (e.g. *The* ➤*Rape of Lucretia* and some others by Britten); an inaccurate term, because it falsely suggests (by analogy with ➤chamber music) that such work should be capable of being performed in an ordinary room, not a theatre.

chamber orchestra, an orchestra small in size, and therefore capable of playing in a room (or anyway a small hall), but not merely a string orchestra.

chamber sonata, ➤sonata.

Chamber Symphony, title of two works by Schoenberg which use only a few players and treat them as soloists (➤chamber music). No. 1 (1906) he scored also (1935) for normal orchestra; no. 2, begun 1906, was put aside, completed in USA and first performed in 1940. There are also works of this title by Schreker and others.

Chaminade, Cécile (1857–1944), French composer (pupil of Godard) and pianist, performing much in England; mainly known for her light piano pieces but also wrote opera, ballet, orchestral suites, etc.

Chamisso, Adalbert von (1781–1838), German poet. ➤*Frauenliebe und -leben*.

Champagne, Claude (1891–1965), Canadian composer of *Altitude* for chorus, Ondes Martenot and orchestra; Concerto for piano with chamber orchestra; French-Canadian folk-song arrangements, etc.

Chandos Anthems, 12 anthems (with orchestra) composed by Handel for his patron James Brydges (later Duke of Chandos), 1717–18.

Chang, Sarah (b. 1980), American violinist of Korean parentage, prodigiously gifted. Soloist with New York Philharmonic Orchestra at age 8, then with other US orchestras, making her London début in 1992.

change-ringing, the British practice of ringing church bells by teams, of which each member pulls the rope controlling one bell; thus with three bells the number of available *changes* (i.e. variations of the order of pulling) is six (= 3 × 2 × 1), with four bells it is 24 (= 4 × 3 × 2 × 1), etc.

changing-note, ➤*nota cambiata*.

chanson (Fr.), song, in particular a type of polyphonic song, sometimes with instruments, current in France from 14th to 16th century. The *chanson de geste*, however, was a type of heroic verse chronicle set to music, current in the 11th and 12th centuries. There are various non-specific uses in 19th- and 20th-century music, e.g. Elgar's *Chanson de matin*, *Chanson de nuit* for violin with piano or orchestra, published 1899, Ravel's *Chansons madécasses* (= of Madagascar), for voice and piano, 1926.

chant (1, Eng.) ➤Anglican chant, ➤plainsong, ➤*znammeny chant*; (2, Fr.) song, singing.

Chants d'Auvergne (Fr., 'Songs of Auvergne' [region of France]), a series of folksongs with dialect texts collected and arranged by Canteloube; a suite of nine for soprano and orchestra has become well known.

chanty, ➤shanty.

chapel-master, the director of music in a church – made-up English equivalent for *maître de chapelle*, *Kapellmeister*, *maestro di cappella* (Fr., Ger., It.). But the German sense is much wider: ➤Kapelle, ➤Kapellmeister.

Chapel Royal, the English court chapel (i.e. a corporate body, not a building) with records going back to 1135; many leading English musicians have been associated with it as choirboys, choir-men or organists.

Chapí [y Lorente], Ruperto (1851–1909), Spanish composer who for a time lived in Rome; wrote ➤*zarzuelas*, also a symphony and other orchestral works, piano pieces, etc.

characteristic piece, Charakterstück (Eng., Ger.), a musical representation of a mood, a place, etc.

charango (Sp.), the South American small guitar (with body traditionally made from an armadillo shell), a folk instrument strummed with the fingers across its five ➤courses of strings.

Charpentier, Gustave (1860–1956), French composer, pupil of Massenet; wrote notably successful opera ➤*Louise* and unsuccessful sequel *Julien*. Expressed his sympathy for the socially underprivileged both in these works and in founding a music school for working-class girls. Wrote also orchestral *Impressions d'Italie*, songs, etc.

Charpentier, Marc-Antoine (*c.* 1645–1704), French composer, pupil of Carissimi in Rome; held church posts in France and wrote Masses and other church music, as well as operas, ballets, incidental music to plays by Molière (with whom he collaborated) and Racine, etc.

chasse (Fr.), hunt; *La Chasse* (nickname of a Haydn symphony), ➤*Hunt*; *cor de chasse* (hunting-horn), ➤horn.

Chaucer, Geoffrey (1340–1400), English poet. ➤lay; ➤*Troilus and Cressida*; ➤de Koven; ➤Finney; ➤Stevenson; ➤Wood (T.).

Chausson, Ernest (1855–99), French composer, pupil of Massenet and then of Franck, stylistically bridging the gap between that generation and Debussy's. Works include ➤*Poème* for violin and orchestra; a piano quartet; Concerto for violin and piano with string quartet; *Poème de l'amour et de la mer* (Poem of Love and the Sea) for voice and orchestra; and many songs.

Chávez, Carlos (1899–1976), Mexican composer (also conductor, musical organizer and folk-song researcher) who studied in Europe and New York. Used Mexican native instruments, writing for an ensemble of them, e.g. in *Xochipilli-Macuilxochitl* (name of the Aztec god of music). Other works include seven symphonies; *HP* (i.e. Horse-power) and other ballets; piano pieces. Cultivated a Mexican national idiom.

Checkmate, ballet with choreography by Ninette de Valois, music by Bliss, produced in Paris, 1937. (A game of chess between Love and Death.)

chef d'attaque (Fr., leader of the attack), an orchestra's first violinist (Eng., leader; US, concertmaster).

chef d'orchestre (Fr.), conductor.

Chekhov, Anton (1806–1904), Russian writer. ➤*Bear*, ➤Bucchi, ➤Chailly (L.).

Cherevichki, ➤*Slippers*.

Cherkassky, Shura, professional name of Alexander (for which Shura is a diminutive) Cherkassky (1909–95), Russian-born pianist who studied in USA and took US nationality; cele-

brated as virtuoso from the 1930s to the 1990s.

Cherubini, [Maria] **Luigi** [Carlo Zenobio Salvatore] (1760–1842), Italian-born composer, permanently in Paris from 1788 and head of the Paris Conservatory from 1822; met Beethoven, who admired his music and whose *Fidelio* was a 'rescue opera' influenced by Cherubini's *Faniska*. Wrote various other operas in French and Italian including ➤*Médée*, *Lodoiska* and *The Water-Carrier* (French title, *Les Deux Journées*, i.e. 'The Two Days'); also symphony, chamber music, two Requiems and other church music.

chest (of viols), a set of various sizes – usually six instruments in all and so called because in the 16th century they were often stored together in a chest or cupboard – for which composers often wrote as an ensemble.

chest voice, that 'register' of the voice which gives the feeling to the singer of coming from the chest – i.e. the lower register, contrasted with ➤head voice.

Chicago Symphony Orchestra, American orchestra founded in 1891. Conductor since 1991, Barenboim, succeeding Solti.

Chichester Psalms, cantata by Bernstein on Hebrew psalm-texts, commissioned for Chichester Cathedral and first performed there in 1965.

chiesa, da (It.), for the church (as opposed, e.g., to *da camera*, for the room); so *sonata da chiesa* (➤sonata).

Chilcot, Thomas (*c.* 1700–1766), English organist and composer of harpsichord concertos, songs, etc.

Child, William (1606–97), English composer, particularly of church music, including about 25 services; court musician to Charles II.

Child and the Spells, The, opera by Ravel. ➤*Enfant et les sortilèges*.

Childhood of Christ, The, oratorio by Berlioz. ➤*Enfance du Christ*.

Child of our Time, A, oratorio by Tippett, first performed in 1944. Text (by the composer) forms a modern plea for the oppressed, with special reference to the Nazi persecutions, and the music incorporates Negro spirituals to parallel the traditional chorales in Bach's ➤Passions.

Children's Corner, suite of six piano pieces by Debussy, 1906–8, dedicated to his daughter. No. 1 is *Doctor* ➤*Gradus ad Parnassum*; titles of the other pieces, as of the whole suite, are in English (as Debussy conceived it), no. 2 being 'Jimbo's [i.e. Jumbo's] Lullaby' and no. 6 'The Golliwogg's [*sic*] Cakewalk'.

Children's Games, suite for piano duet by Bizet. ➤*Jeux d'enfants*.

Children's Overture, orchestral work by Quilter, based on English nursery-rhyme tunes, composed 1914.

Childs, Barney [Sanford] (b. 1926), American composer, also university teacher and writer on music. Writes for unusual combinations (*Mary's Idea* for tuba and harpsichord) and employs ➤indeterminacy – e.g. *Any Five* which leaves players to perform any five of eight written parts indicated as 'high strings', 'low wind', etc.

Chilingirian Quartet, British string quartet founded by Levon Chilingirian, 1971; other current members, Charles Sewart, Simon Rowland-Jones, Philip de Groote. Quartet-in-resi-

dence, Royal College of Music, since 1986. It has recorded works by Panufnik, Pärt, Hugh Wood, etc. as well as the standard repertory.

Chinese block, ➤wood block.

Chinese pavilion, ➤Jingling Johnny.

Chisholm, Erik (1904–65), British composer – also pianist, conductor and professor at the University of Cape Town. Works include two piano concertos, no. 2 subtitled 'The Indian' (indebted to Indian music); trilogy of short operas *Murder in Three Keys*.

chitarra (It.), guitar.

chitarrone (It., big guitar), largest ➤archlute with greatly extended neck, cultivated in 16th and 17th centuries; much used as a ➤*continuo* instrument in opera.

chiuso (It.), closed; (of horn notes) 'stopped' by the placing of the hand in the bell.

Chocolate Soldier, The, operetta by Oscar Straus. ➤*Tapfere Soldat*.

choir (1) a body of singers, especially in a place of worship ('chorus' or 'choral society' being more used in other contexts); (2) part of a church where singers are seated; (3) usual abbreviation for ➤choir-organ.

choir-organ (or simply *choir*), division of an organ (a manual and the equipment controlled by it) having predominantly soft stops. (Originally 'chair-organ', the pipes being placed behind the organist's chair or stool.)

choke cymbals, ➤cymbal.

Chopin, Frédéric François (French form of Polish 'Fryderyk Franciszek') (1810–49), Polish composer and pianist of partly French descent. Born at

Żelazowa Wola, near Warsaw; studied in Warsaw; settled in Paris, touring from there (e.g. to England and Scotland). Never revisited Poland (under Russian occupation) but was keen patriot and student of Polish literature. Never married; met 'George Sand' (real name Aurore Dudevant) in 1838, and lived with her till 1847; suffered from consumption, gave his last public concert in 1848, and died in Paris. Works – nearly all for piano, and equally remarkable for harmonic imagination and for use of piano technique – constitute a peak of ➤Romantic music. Composed three sonatas (no. 2, in B flat minor, including a funeral march), four scherzos, 25 preludes, 27 studies, 19 nocturnes, 19 waltzes, 10 polonaises, at least 55 mazurkas (these and some other works influended by Polish folkmusic), four ballades; also two piano concertos, sonata for cello and piano, songs, etc. Contributor to the ➤Hexameron. ➤barcarolle; ➤Sylphides.

Chopiniana, ballet score. ➤Sylphides.

Chopsticks, anonymous short quickwaltz tune for piano, playable with two outstretched forefingers, or with the little fingers if the hand is held vertically like a chopper. Variations have been written on it by, e.g., Borodin, Rimsky-Korsakov and Liszt. The French and German names for it mean 'cutlets' – thus the reference is to chopping (not to chopsticks in the Chinese sense).

choragus, musical office-holder at Oxford University, subordinate to professor – office revived in 1926, after lapsing.

choral (1, Eng.) relating to a choir or chorus; ➤*Choral Fantasia*; ➤choral

symphony); (2, Ger.) original form of the English (mock-foreign) word *Chorale* (in the sense of a traditional congregational hymn-tune).

chorale (1) Ger., *Choral*, i.e. type of traditional German metrical hymn-tune for congregational use, e.g. 'A Stronghold Sure' (*Ein' feste Burg*), perhaps composed by Martin Luther; this tune, like many others, was made use of by Bach. So *chorale prelude*, instrumental piece (usually for organ) based on a chorale. (The English word *chorale* is mock-foreign and synthetic, but useful in avoiding 'choral prelude', suggesting a choral work.) For *Passion chorale*, ➤Passion; (2) a choir or choral society – French word, also used in the title of some US (and, more rarely, British) choirs.

Choral Fantasia, the name generally given to Beethoven's Fantasy, op. 80, for piano, chorus and orchestra (the words, by C. Kuffner, in praise of music) – first performed in 1808. It appears to have been used as a kind of study for Beethoven's Ninth Symphony (see next entry).

choral symphony, either (1) a symphony in the normal sense but using a chorus as well, or (2) a work of symphonic dimensions but written for voices alone, e.g. Bantock's *Atlanta in Calydon* (after Swinburne), first performed in 1912. The first of these two senses is much the commoner. 'The Choral Symphony', in common usage, is Beethoven's Symphony no. 9 in D minor, first performed in 1824, having three purely orchestral movements followed by a setting of Schiller's 'Ode to Joy' for four solo singers, chorus and orchestra; among other examples (in the first sense) are

Mahler's ➤*Symphony of a Thousand* and Vaughan Williams's *A* ➤*Sea Symphony*.

chord, any simultaneous combination of notes – but sometimes defined as any simultaneous combination of not less than three notes. (Whether the notes form a ➤concord or discord is irrelevant: the term *chord* is not related to these.) See also following entries.

chording (1) (satisfactory or unsatisfactory) intonation of a chord by several performers, e.g. a choir; (2) in composition, the spacing of the intervals in a chord; (3, US) the provision of chords, e.g. on a guitar, to accompany a melody.

chordophone, term scientifically used to classify an instrument in which a vibrating string produces the musical sound; e.g. harp, violin, piano.

chord-symbol, type of simple harmonic notation used, e.g., in pop music: e.g. C7 means a chord of the minor seventh on C (i.e. C-E-G-B♭). In this form no stipulation is made of which note forms the bass, but it can be additionally indicated. (The classical ➤figured bass has a comparable function.)

choreographic poem, a fanciful label (varying ➤symphonic poem) applied by Ravel to *La Valse* (➤*valse*).

chôro (Port.), an ensemble of serenaders in late 19th-century Brazil. The title was applied also to characteristic pieces; ➤Villa-Lobos.

chorus (1) a substantial body of singers not all singing separate parts; (2) colloquial term for the ➤refrain of a song, in which a chorus (in the first sense) often joins; (3) term figuratively used for a group of instruments, or organ stops, used in the manner of a chorus (i.e. not for solo effect, but as contributing a mass of sound).

Chorus Line, A, musical with text by James Kirkwood and Nicholas Dante; lyrics by Edward Kleban; music by Marvin Hamlisch. Produced in New York, 1975. A chorus dancers' audition proceeds, with autobiographical confessions.

Chou Wen-Chung (b. 1923), Chinese (naturalized American) composer, resident in USA since 1946; pupil (and later executor) of Varèse. Draws on his Chinese heritage in some works and their titles (*Yun* for two pianos, two percussion, wind sextet); other works include *Landscapes* for orchestra.

Christie, William [Lincoln] (b. 1944), American harpsichordist and conductor. Settled in Paris and founded Les Arts Florissants (1979), an ensemble devoted to baroque music, including opera; he revived Lully's *Atys* in Paris and in 1995 conducted Covent Garden's Purcell Tercentenary production of *The Fairy Queen*.

Christmas Carol, A, opera by Musgrave, produced in Norfolk, Virginia, 1979, with libretto (after Dickens) by the composer.

Christmas Concerto, name given to Corelli's Concerto Grosso in G minor, op. 6, no. 8, for strings and continuo, 1712 – intended for church use, inscribed 'made for Christmas night', and having a 'Pastorale' at the end. (The name also applies to Torelli's Concerto Grosso in G minor, op. 8, no. 6, of 1708 and other works.)

Christmas Eve (Rus., *Noch pered rozhdestvom*, 'The Night Before Christmas'), opera by Rimsky-Korsakov, produced in St Petersburg, 1895, with libretto (after Gogol's comic village episode) by the composer. Tchaikovsky's opera *The* ➤*Slippers* ('Cherevichki') is based on the same plot.

Christmas Oratorio (1) work for soloists, chorus, and orchestra by Bach (Ger. *Weihnachts-Oratorium*), 1734 (BWV 248), in the form of six cantatas – the first for performance on Christmas Day and the others to follow on particular days up to Epiphany. Text, the biblical Christmas story, with commentary; (2) short English title often used for the work by Schütz, literally entitled (in German) 'History of the joyful and merciful birth of God's and Mary's Son, Jesus Christ', 1664.

Christmas Symphony (Haydn), ➤*Lamentatione*.

Christoff, Boris (1914–93), Bulgarian bass-baritone who trained in Rome and won intèrnational eminence in opera (Covent Garden, 1949), e.g. in title-role of ➤*Boris Godunov* (which he twice recorded).

Christophe Colomb (Fr., 'Christopher Columbus'), opera by Milhaud, produced (in German) in Berlin, 1930. Libretto (originally in French) by Paul Claudel. The opera uses a cinema screen – e.g. to show images of exotic landscapes when Columbus reads Marco Polo's *Travels*.

Christopher Columbus, opera by Milhaud. ➤*Christophe Colomb*.

Christophers, Harry [originally Richard Henry Tudor Christophers] (b. 1953), British conductor, founder of The ➤Sixteen.

chromatic, pertaining to intervals outside the diatonic (major or minor) scale; so *chromatic scale*, ascending or descending by semitones; *chromatic* ➤*compass*. So also *chromatic progression*, a chord-progression which involves departure from the prevailing diatonic scale; *chromaticism*, tendency of a piece or a composer towards the use of intervals outside the prevailing diatonic scale, and thus often towards a plentiful use of modulation (but the term is not used to cover ➤atonal music, etc.). So also *chromatic* ➤harmonica, *chromatic* ➤harp. And see following entry.

Chromatic Fantasia and Fugue, by Bach for harpsichord, completed in 1730 (BWV 903), the fantasia being notable for ➤chromatic progressions.

Chu Chin Chow, musical comedy with text by Oscar Asche; music by Frederic Norton. Produced in London, 1916. A robber chief is disguised as a Chinese merchant in an Arabian Nights setting.

Chung, Kyung-Wha (b. 1948), Korean violinist; she won the Leventritt competition (jointly with Zukerman) in New York in 1967 and appeared in London with the London Symphony Orchestra, 1970. Has a distinguished international reputation. The pianist-conductor Myung-Whun Chung (see next entry) is her brother; the cellist Myung-Wha Chung is her sister.

Chung, Myung-Whun (b. 1953), Korean pianist and conductor, brother of the foregoing. Appointed in 1989 as music director of the new Paris Opera at the Bastille, he was acrimoniously dismissed in 1994.

church cantata, cantata written for actual performance during church service, though not forming part of the liturgy – e.g. those by Bach.

ciaccona (It., in older spelling *ciacona*), ➤*chaconne*.

Ciccolini, Aldo [Eduardo] (b. 1925), Italian-born pianist who settled in Paris in 1949 and took French nationality in 1971. Though making his New York début in 1950 with Tchaikovsky's concerto no. 1, he specializes in the French repertory and has recorded all Debussy's piano music.

Ciconia, Johannes (*c.* 1373–1411), Flemish composer of church music and author of a musical treatise; also priest. Worked for some time in Italy.

Ciesinski, Kristine [Frances] (b. 1952), American soprano who has appeared in opera with American, British, German and other companies, her roles including the heroines of Berg's *Wozzeck* and Shostakovich's *Lady Macbeth of the Mtsensk District*. Sister of the following.

Ciesinski, Katherine (b. 1950), American mezzo-soprano who made her European début in 1976 at the Aix-en-Provence Festival, and her Metropolitan Opera début in 1988. Has recorded rare operas by Massenet, Dukas, Prokofiev. Sister of the preceding.

Cikker, Jan (1911–89), Czechoslovak composer of *Resurrection* (after Tolstoy), *Mr Scrooge* (after Dickens) and other operas; also orchestral, chamber and piano works.

Cilèa, Francesco (1866–1950), Italian composer chiefly of operas (including ➤*Adriana Lecouvreur*); also of sonata for cello and piano, piano solos, etc.

Cimarosa, Domenico (1749–1801), Italian composer chiefly of operas (more than 60); pupil of Sacchini and Piccinni. Held court posts in St Petersburg and then Vienna, where *Il* ➤*Matrimonio segreto* was produced, 1792, winning wide fame for its combination of dramatic and musical values, in a style near Mozart's. Said to have been condemned to death in Naples for pro-French-Revolutionary sentiment, but reprieved and banished; died in Venice on way back to Russia. Other works include *Il* ➤*maestro di cappella* (comic vocal piece) and church music.

cimbalom (Hung.), large concert ➤*dulcimer* (having horizontal strings struck with hammers and a damping mechanism) used in Hungarian popular music and in certain works indebted to this – e.g. Kodály's opera ➤*Háry János* (and the suite drawn from it).

cimbasso, the term used by Bellini and Verdi for the lowest brass instrument in certain opera scores; it apparently means a valved trombone of bass or double-bass range, though most modern performances employ a tuba.

Cinderella, operas based on Perrault's fairy-tale (1697), e.g. by Massenet (➤*Cendrillon*) and Rossini (➤*Cenerentola*); also a ballet score (with songs) by Prokofiev, produced in Moscow with choreography by R. Zakharov, 1945 (Rus., *Zolushka*, i.e. the Ash-Girl).

cinema organ, ➤theatre organ.

cipher(ing), the continuous sounding, through a mechanical mishap, of a note on the organ.

Cis (Ger.), C sharp; *Cisis*, C double-sharp.

citole, ➤cittern.

cittern (also *cither, cithern*), plucked,

wire-strung instrument (used for popular music, *c.* 1550–1700) with strings in pairs tuned to same note (like lute) but built with flat back (like guitar). An earlier name is 'citole'; but the ➤gittern is a different instrument.

City of Birmingham Symphony Orchestra, orchestra founded in 1920, becoming full-time, 1944; musical director 1980–98, Simon Rattle, whom Sakari Oramo succeeded.

Clair de lune (Fr., Moonlight), piano piece by Debussy (later subjected to multifarious arrangements); ➤bergamasca.

clarabella, ➤claribel.

Clari (opera), ➤Bishop (H.).

claribel, claribel flute (or *clarabella*), an organ stop of flute-like tone.

clarinet, woodwind instrument with single reed and normally a wooden (exceptionally, a metal) body, in use since mid 18th century; constituent of symphony orchestra, military band, dance band, etc. Also favoured as solo instrument and in chamber music – *clarinet trio, clarinet quartet,* trio or quartet incorporating clarinet; *clarinet quintet,* string quartet plus clarinet. Standard orchestral sizes of clarinet are those in B♭ (lowest note, D below middle C) and in A, a semitone lower, both being ➤transposing instruments, with an upward range of more than three octaves. Other instruments found are the *bass clarinet* in B♭, an octave below the standard B♭ (and *bass clarinet* in A; rare); *high clarinet* in E♭, a fourth above the standard B♭ (and *high clarinet* in D; rare); clarinet in C used, e.g., by Beethoven, rarely later; *alto clarinet* (rare; similar to ➤basset-horn); *contra-bass clarinet* (also called *pedal clarinet* and very

rare) an octave below bass clarinet. ➤basset-clarinet.

clarino (It.), name used for high, florid 17th–18th-century trumpet parts or, in usage up to the 18th century, for the (valveless) trumpet itself. The term has been occasionally revived by modern composers (➤Austin (L.), ➤Zwilich).

clarionet, obsolete spelling of ➤clarinet.

Clarke, Jeremiah (*c.*1670–1707), English composer, pupil of Blow; organist, e.g. at St Paul's Cathedral, London. Disappointed in love, he shot himself. Composed church and stage music, choral setting of *Alexander's Feast* (after Dryden), etc., and also harpsichord pieces including *The Prince of Denmark's March* widely known as ➤Trumpet Voluntary (sometimes with a misattribution to Purcell).

Clarke, Rebecca (1886–1979), British viola-player and composer; wrote orchestral and choral music as well as works featuring the viola. Settled in USA, died in New York.

clàrsach (Gael.), ancient small Celtic harp, revived in the 20th century for folk-song accompaniment and very occasionally elsewhere (➤McLeod).

classic(al), classicism, terms commonly used very vaguely, but with three main areas of meaning: (1, as distinct from, e.g., 'popular' or 'folk'), serious, learned, belonging to a sophisticated and written tradition; (2, as opposed to ➤Romantic), aesthetically dependent supposedly more on formal appeal than on emotional stimulation; (3, = *Viennese classic*), belonging to the period and predominant musical style of Haydn, Mozart and Beethoven, *c.* 1770–1830. So also, the *classical* *concerto* (Mozart's); so too (as abstraction), *classicism* and ➤*neo-classic(ism)*.

Classical Symphony, title of Symphony no. 1 by Prokofiev, first performed 1918; its Haydn-sized orchestra and modernized Haydnesque idiom (but with a gavotte instead of the customary minuet of Haydn's period) allude to the first sense given in the preceding entry.

Claudel, Paul (1868–1955), French dramatist and poet. ➤*Christophe Colomb*, ➤*Jeanne d'Arc au bûcher*; ➤Milhaud.

clavecin (Fr.), harpsichord; *clavecinste*, harpsichord-player (term also used for a French composer for the harpsichord in the days of that instrument's pre-eminence, e.g. Couperin).

claves (Sp.), a pair of wooden sticks beaten together to mark the rhythm in Latin-American dance music, and occasionally in the modern concert repertory (➤Birtwistle).

clavicembalo (It.), harpsichord. The term literally means 'keyed dulcimer' and is normally abbreviated to *cembalo*.

clavichord, soft-toned keyboard instrument with strings hit by metal 'tangents'; much used from 16th to 18th centuries as a solo instrument (not loud enough, e.g., for concertos for which a harpsichord was used), and revived in the 20th century for old music. (Since the tangents remain in contact with the string while it is vibrating – unlike the hammers of a piano or the quills of a harpsichord – it is possible by 'shaking' the individual notes of a keyboard to produce a kind of ➤*vibrato* effect; in Ger., *Bebung*.)

clavicytherium, rare 15th–18th-century instrument of harpsichord mechanism with perpendicular strings as in the upright piano.

clavier, term originally French and meaning keyboard, or manual (of an organ); taken into German, where the modern spelling is *Klavier*, and there having its meaning extended to include a piano or any keyboard instrument; used in English for contexts in which a definite choice between different keyboard instruments is not implied – e.g. 'Bach's clavier concertos' (intended for harpsichord, but also performed on piano). So *Das* ➤*Wohltemperirte Clavier*, intended by Bach as suitable for harpsichord or clavichord and likewise in the repertory of pianists. See also following entry.

Clavierübung (Ger., Clavier Exercise), title of a work by Bach (who borrowed the title from Kuhnau) in three sections (1731, 1735, 1739), consisting of works for harpsichord (including the ➤*Italian Concerto*) and organ. The ➤*Goldberg Variations*, 1742, were also headed *Clavierübung* and may be regarded as the fourth section of the work.

Clay, Frederic (1838–89), British composer of 'I'll sing thee songs of Araby' and other favourite Victorian ballads; also of stage music and cantatas.

clef, sign which fixes the location of a particular note on the staff – and hence the location of all other notes; placed normally at the beginning of each line of music and at any point where a new clef cancels the old. The ➤treble clef fixes the note G above middle C; the ➤alto and ➤tenor fix middle C; the ➤bass fixes the F below middle C. Other clefs are obsolete, but the ►soprano lingered well into the 19th century.

Clemens non Papa, nickname given to Jacob Clement (*c.* 1510–*c.*1558), Flemish composer of Latin church music, psalms in Flemish, songs, etc. (The nickname, formerly conjectured to mean 'Clement not the Pope' [i.e. Clement VIII], was probably designed to avoid confusion with a Flemish poet, Clemens Papa, of the composer's home town of Ypres.)

Clementi, Aldo (b. 1925), Italian composer of a series of chamber music pieces called *Ideograms* and another called *Informels*; also *Replica* for harpsichord, concerto for two pianos and wind orchestra, etc.

Clementi, Muzio (1752–1832), Italian composer and pianist who, showing great gifts as a child, was taken to England by Peter Beckford, MP, and thereafter lived mainly there; died at Evesham. Composed mainly for piano, pioneering a new (non-harpsichord) technique. Works include more than 60 sonatas (some with illustrative intent, e.g. one called *Didone abbandonata*, 'The Forsaken Dido') and a famous collection of studies, ►*Gradus ad Parnassum*; in addition to symphonies, chamber music, etc. Also entered the piano-manufacturing trade.

Clemenza di Tito, La (It., 'The Clemency of Titus'), opera by Mozart (K621), produced in Prague, 1791; libretto by C. Mazzolà, after Metastasio – extolling a Roman emperor's sacrifice of his love for his imperial duty.

Cleobury, Nicholas [Randall] (b. 1950), British conductor, active in opera, former cathedral organist; principal opera conductor at Royal College of Music, 1980–87. Brother of the following.

Cleobury, Stephen [John] (b. 1948), British organist and conductor; since 1982, director of music at King's College, Cambridge, with the choir of which he has toured widely and made many recordings. Also chief conductor, BBC Singers, since 1995. His brother is Nicholas Cleobury (preceding).

Clérambault, Louis Nicolas (1676–1749), French composer of cantatas, harpsichord and organ pieces, etc.; church organist in Paris.

Cleveland Orchestra, American orchestra founded in 1918. Its conductor since 1984 (with contract extended to 2000) has been Christoph von Dohnányi.

Cleveland Quartet, American string quartet founded in 1969, all its original members being college teachers in Cleveland, Ohio. Disbanded 1995, its final membership being William Preucil, Peter Salaff, James Dunham, Paul Katz. Recorded Brahms's piano quintet with Ashkenazy. Gave first performance (1995) of Paulus's concerto for string quartet and orchestra.

Cliburn, Van (real forenames Harvey Lavan) (b. 1934), American pianist, winner of International Tchaikovsky Prize in Moscow, 1958. Endowed a piano competition in Texas, 1962. After some years' absence from concerts, he resumed occasional performances in 1989.

Cloak, The, opera by Puccini. ►*Tabarro*.

Clock, The, nickname of Haydn's Symphony no. 101 in D (Hob. I: 101) – from the clock-like ticking at the opening of the slow movement.

close, a ➤cadence; *full close*, perfect cadence; *half-close*, imperfect cadence.

close harmony, a style of harmonizing in which the supporting harmonizing notes keep as near to the melody as possible.

cluster, a group of adjacent notes on the piano keyboard played together, e.g. with the flat of the forearm – demonstrated in public by Cowell (aged 15) in 1912; Ives was independently using the device at the same time (➤Concord Sonata). The usual US term is *tone-cluster*, for which the English would be *note-cluster* (➤tone, 5).

Clustine, Ivan (1862–1941), Russian–French choreographer. *La* ➤*Péri*.

Clutsam, George Howard (1866–1951), Australian-born composer (especially of stage works), pianist and critic who settled in England, 1889; 'edited' (i.e. mauled) Schubert's music for the musical play *Lilac Time*.

Coates, Albert (1882–1953), British composer (operas *Samuel Pepys* and *Pickwick*, etc.), born in Russia of English parents. Also prominent conductor in London, and in Russia both before and after the 1917 Revolution. Settled in South Africa, 1946.

Coates, Eric (1886–1957), British composer of light music including *Knightsbridge* march (part of *London Suite*) and suite *The Three Bears*; also of songs such as 'Bird Songs at Eventide'. In early career was orchestral viola-player.

cobla (Catalan), small band mainly of wind instruments which accompanies the ➤*sardana*.

Cockaigne, concert-overture by Elgar, first performed in 1901. Subtitled 'In London Town', punning on 'Cockaigne' (imaginary land of idle luxury) and 'cockney'.

Cocteau, Jean (1889–1963), French writer. ➤*Antigone*, ➤*Oedipus Rex*, ➤*Voix humaine*; ➤Milhaud.

coda (It., tail), in musical analysis, a section of a movement considered to be added at the end as a rounding-off rather than as a structural necessity. Thus in ➤sonata-form, the coda (if there is one) occurs only after both principal subjects have been recapitulated in the tonic key. (As with all such terms of analysis, the meaning here given is of value only as an approximation: Beethoven's codas, for instance, have great importance in his musical design and do not strike the listener as 'stuck on' at the end.) The diminutive of the term, with a special musical meaning, is ➤codetta.

codetta (It., little tail), in musical analysis, a rounding-off passage which does for a section of a movement what a ➤Coda does for a whole movement.

Coffee Cantata, nickname for a humorous cantata by Bach (BWV 211), composed about 1732 (now sometimes given as comic opera), alluding to the contemporary craze for coffee. Known also by its opening words, 'Schweigt stille, plaudert nicht' (Ger., Be silent, do not chatter).

cogli, ➤*con*.

Cohen, Harriet (1895–1967), British

pianist for whom a number of British composers wrote music expressly – particularly Bax. CBE, 1938.

Coleman, Edward (*c.* 1605–1669), English viol-player and composer of stage music, songs, etc.; wrote part of the music to *The* ➤*Siege of Rhodes* to which his son, Edward (?–1699), also contributed.

Coleridge, Samuel Taylor (1772–1834), British poet. ➤Griffes, ➤Lualdi.

Coleridge-Taylor, Samuel (1875–1912), British composer, born in London of a British mother and West African father; no relation of the poet Samuel Taylor Coleridge. Pupil of Stanford. Wrote works inclining to exotic associations (cantatas ➤*Hiawatha* and *A Tale of Old Japan*; *Symphonic Variations on an African Air*; etc.), as well as a violin concerto, string quartet, many piano solos and songs.

Colette [Sidonie Gabrielle Claudine Colette] (1873–1954), French writer. ➤*Enfant et les sortilèges.*

Colgrass, Michael [Charles] (b. 1932), American composer, also percussionist and inventor of the ➤rototom. He has written several works for percussion; *As Quiet As* for orchestra; *Virgil's Dream* for four actor-singers and four mime-musicians; etc.

coll', colla, colle, ➤*con.*

collegium (Lat.), a learned society; *collegium musicum*, term used in the 18th century for a musical ensemble, and revived in the 20th century mainly for ensembles applying historical knowledge to baroque and older music.

Collingwood, Lawrance [Arthur] (1887–1982), British composer (of operas including *Macbeth*, etc.) and

conductor, especially of opera; CBE, 1948.

coloratura (It.), term applied to an agile, florid style of vocal music or to its performance; *coloratura soprano*, soprano with voice suited to this.

colour (of musical tone), ➤tone-colour; *colour-organ*, term used in English for the light-projecting instrument specified in Skryabin's ➤*Prometheus*, 1911.

Combattimento di Tancredi e Clorinda, Il (It., 'The Combat of Tancred and Clorinda'), work by Monteverdi using three voices (the duellists and a narrator) with strings and *continuo* accompaniment; text from Tasso's poem of the Crusades. Published 1638 as one of the composer's 'warlike' ➤madrigals, not as a stage work.

come (It.), as, like; *come prima*, as at first, as at the opening, etc.; *come sopra*, as above.

comédie-ballet, a type of French theatrical entertainment combining a stage play, songs and dancing, as exemplified by Molière's *Le* ➤*Bourgeois Gentilhomme*, with music by Lully.

commedia (It., comedy), name occasionally used, e.g. by Richard Rodney Bennett, as title of works; *commedia dell'arte* (It., comedy of the profession, i.e. not amateur), type of Italian entertainment originating in the 16th century, using masks, improvisation, and stock types, such as the gullible doctor or boastful soldier, in a parody of social behaviour; of significant influence on Italian comic opera.

commodo, mis-spelling for ➤*comodo*.

common chord, ➤triad.

common metre (in hymns), the metre

of a four-line stanza having eight, six, eight and six syllables per line.

common time, four quarter-notes (crotchets) to the bar, written 4/4 or C. (The latter sign is not a 'C' for common time, but derives from an obsolete way of indicating time-values.)

community singing, singing by the public at a meeting, a sporting event, etc. So *community songs*, those suitable for such occasions.

comodo (It., easy), easily flowing, leisurely.

compass, the range of a voice or instrument from the highest to the lowest note obtainable; *chromatic compass*, the range in which a complete ➤chromatic scale is playable (said of instruments which for part of their compass are not chromatic, e.g. trombone, which has gaps at the lower end of its range).

Compère, Loyset (*c.* 1445–1518), Flemish composer who worked in Milan, then served Charles VIII of France. Works include Masses, motets, chansons.

composition (1) the art of creating original works of music; (2) a piece of music regarded as the result of a deliberate individual creative act – term therefore not usually applied (a) to a folk-tune, which may have reached its present shape through oral tradition and untutored adaptation, and (b) to a musical work not thoroughly original but ➤arranged from some other work. Neither of these senses has any connection with the use of the word in the following entry.

composition pedal, composition piston, foot-operated or hand-operated

lever on the organ bringing into action a pre-selected group of stops simultaneously.

compound time, any musical metre not classifiable as ➤simple time, in which the beat-unit divides into two. Thus 12/8 is a compound time, because the unit of beat is ♩. (the bar having four of these) and this divides not into two but into three sub-units (♫♪). (The term has long been more academic than practical: it is of no use in analysing, say, a score by Boulez, or in classifying a ➤rumba in which the beat occurs at non-uniform intervals.)

comprimario (It., from *con*, 'with', and *primo*, 'first'), a (male) singer of supporting roles in Italian opera, particularly one who has an aria to himself. The feminine form, *comprimaria*, is also encountered.

computer-composed music, type of music in which some post-1950 composers have used a computer program to determine the succession of notes, a succession which may be (as in some works by Xenakis) random at any one point but conforming to an overall statistical pattern.

computer organ, ➤electric organ.

Comte Ory, Le (Fr., 'Count Ory'), opera by Rossini, produced in Paris, 1828. Libretto by E. Scribe and C. G. Delestre-Poirson: the Count is a medieval suitor whose amorous pursuit leads him to disguise himself as a hermit and then as a female pilgrim.

Comus (1) masque with words by Milton, originally produced in 1634 with music by H. Lawes; (2) work in which Milton's words were adapted, and new music was provided by T. Arne, 1738; (3) ballet with choreography by Robert Helpmann, music arranged by Lambert from Purcell, some of Milton's words being spoken; produced in 1942.

con (It.), with; *cogli, coi, col, coll', colla, colle*, with the. (In general, see next word of phrase.) *Con brio*, with spirit: *colla parte*, the tempo and expression of the accompaniment to be accommodated to that of the soloist; *clarinetti coi flauti*, the clarinets to play the same notes as the flutes.

Concentus Musicus Wien, Vienna-based ensemble founded in 1953 by Harnoncourt; its hundreds of recordings on period instruments set a standard in historical treatment of Bach and other baroque composers.

concert, a substantial performance of music before an audience (other than in conjunction with a stage performance, or as part of a religious service or similar ceremony, etc.); a performance given by one or two, however, is not usually called a concert but a ➤recital. An older use denotes a body of performers (as ➤consort). See also following entries.

concertant (Fr.), in a concerted form, with interplay between instruments – term used, e.g., by Stravinsky, *Duo concertant* (1932) for violin and piano, avoiding terms 'sonata' or 'suite'; so also (feminine form) *concertante*, as in F. Martin's *Petite symphonie concertante* for harp, harpsichord, piano and two string orchestras (1945). See also following entry.

concertante (1, Fr.) see preceding entry; (2, It.) in a concerted form; *sinfonia concertante*, term used for a work for solo instrument(s) and orchestra, with the implication that the

form followed is nearer that of the symphony than of the concerto. Similarly *concerto*.

concertato, concertata (It.), concerted (masc., fem. forms). The term *concertato style* is used by some historians for the new style of ensemble writing (vocal or instrumental) of the early 17th century founded on the practice of ➤continuo.

concert band, American type of band of woodwind, brass and percussion instruments (similar to, but not identical with, British ➤military band) for which works have been expressly written by Hindemith, Schoenberg and various American composers.

concerted, pertaining to a performance by several people on more or less equal terms; so a *concerted number* (more usually called 'ensemble') in an opera.

Concertgebouw Orchestra, ➤Royal Concertgebouw Orchestra.

concertina, hexagonal-bodied instrument with bellows, similar to ➤accordion in principle but having only studs (never a piano-like keyboard) for the fingers. Popular for informal occasions (and even sometimes penetrating the concert-hall) in the 19th century, it has now been almost entirely superseded by the accordion.

concertino (1) a little (and usually rather light) ➤concerto, in the first sense given below; (2) in older usage, the smaller group of instruments in a ➤concerto grosso.

concertize (US, chiefly promoters' jargon), to give concerts.

concertmaster (US), the first violinist of an orchestra (following German term *Konzertmeister*) – in British usage, 'leader'.

concerto (It., a concert, a concerted performance), (1. in general modern usage) a work making contrasted use of solo instrument(s) and orchestra – generally in three movements, and generally keeping to certain structural principles of which Mozart is regarded as the classic exponent; (2, earlier use) an orchestral work in several movements, with or without solo instruments (➤*concerto grosso*; ➤*Brandenburg Concertos*); (3) term used apart from this by composers for exceptional reasons of their own – e.g. Bach's ➤*Italian Concerto*, which, though for a single player, employs an effect of instrumental contrast between the two manuals of a harpsichord; Bartók's Concerto for Orchestra (1944), so called because of the solo functions performed by individual orchestral instruments.

concerto grosso (It., great concerto), (1) type of orchestral work prevalent in 17th and 18th centuries, usually (but not always) having an interplay between the larger body of instruments ('concerto' or 'ripieno') and a smaller group ('concertino') each with its own ➤*continuo* – as distinct from the modern concerto, in which only one soloist (rarely more, and anyway not a group) provides the contrast with the orchestra; (2) title used for certain 20th-century ➤neo-classic works based broadly on 17th- and 18th-century models – though Bloch's Concerto Grosso no. 1 has only piano soloist instead of a concertino.

concert-overture, ➤overture.

concierto (Sp.), the Spanish equivalent of ➤concerto, sometimes employed

by Spanish-speaking composers. ➤Aranjuez.

concitato (It.), excited; *stile concitato* (agitated style), a compositional device defined and used by Monteverdi to represent emotional excitement.

concord, a chord which seems harmonically at rest; its opposite, *discord*, seems unsettled, thus requiring a ➤resolution to another chord. What constitutes a concord is not something fixed: throughout history composers have tended to admit more and different chords as concords, and in, e.g., much ➤twelve-note music, the concepts of concord and discord need not have any structural relevance for the composer.

Concord Sonata, Piano Sonata no. 2 by Ives (inscribed 'Concord, Mass., 1840–60'), completed in 1915, first performed in 1939. The movements are I, Emerson; II, Hawthorne; III, The Alcotts; IV, Thoreau; and the music, in Ives's characteristically experimental vein, uses such devices as ➤clusters of notes by laying a strip of wood on the keyboard.

concrete music, ➤*musique concrète*.

conduct, to direct a performance with the motions of a baton or the hands (but formerly, e.g. in early 19th-century Britain, before the advent of the baton, *to conduct* was simply to be in charge of the performance, usually while also playing the piano or organ). So *conductor*, etc.

conductus, in medieval music, a type of secular vocal composition having one 'given' part (➤*cantus firmus*) to which other parts were set in close harmony – the 'given' part being either specially composed or taken from some other secular work, not from plainsong. ➤motet.

conga, a modern Afro-Cuban dance with a pronounced syncopation; *conga drum* (or simply *conga*), a long, finger-played drum, taken from Latin-American bands into post-1950 concert percussion. Such drums usually come in sets of two or more pitches.

conjunct motion, ➤motion.

Conlon, James [Joseph] (b. 1950), American conductor who has appeared with the New York Philharmonic, the Metropolitan Opera (début 1976), etc. Music director at Cologne since 1991; appointed to be principal conductor, Paris Opéra, 1996.

Connell, Elizabeth (b. 1946), Irish soprano, previously mezzo-soprano, of South African birth. As well as leading appearances with British and Australian opera companies, she has performed Wagner at Bayreuth (début 1980), Mozart in Salzburg (1985).

Connolly, Justin [Riveagh] (b. 1933), British composer who also studied law. Teacher at RCM, formerly at Yale University. Compositions include symphony, *Anima* for viola and orchestra, and several works called *Triad* (each for some kind of threesome).

Consecration of the House, The, overture by Beethoven. ➤*Weihe des Hauses*.

consecutive, term applied to harmonic intervals of like kind succeeding one another. E.g. C struck with the E above, and then F struck with the A above (each of these pairs forming the interval of a ➤third) would give *consecutive thirds*. The sounding of *consecutive fifths* was avoided for about five

centuries before 1890 as a musically poor effect – with certain very rare and deliberate exceptions. *Consecutive octaves* come under a similar ban in strict ➤part-writing, since two voices singing consecutive octaves would not be singing two real parts at all, but just the same tune at an octave's distance. But in writing for an orchestra or piano, for instance, consecutive octaves are recognized as valid. 'Hidden fifths' are consecutive fifths not actually present but thought to be implied, and therefore equally liable to academic disapproval.

conservatoire, -torium, -tory, school of musical training – originally in Italian, *conservatorio*, meaning an orphanage where children were 'conserved' and given musical and other training. (*Conservatoire* should be regarded as French; *conservatory* is unexceptionable English; *conservatorium* is the German form and is used also in Australia.)

Consolations, title given (as French word) by Liszt to six nocturne-like pieces for piano, published 1850.

console, the part of an organ actually at the player's command – manuals, pedals, stops, pistons, etc.

consonance, ➤concord.

consort, old English word (16th–17th century) for a group of instrumentalists, e.g. *consort of viols*; term revived as name for post-1950 ensembles devoted to such music, e.g. the (British) *Consort of Musicke* (➤Rooley). The historical meaning of the (rare) terms *broken consort* and *whole consort* is uncertain, but the view that they contrast mixed instruments with instruments of one family is now discredited. See also following entry.

consort song, modern term for the type of old English song (dating from the late 16th and early 17th centuries) in which a consort, generally of viols, accompanies a solo voice or voices.

Constant, Marius (b. 1925), composer and conductor born in Romania who settled in France after World War II. Works include violin concerto, *Three Complexes* for piano and double-bass; ballet *Paradise Lost*. He compiled the version of *Carmen* (called *La Tragédie de Carmen*) used for Peter Brook's touring production, 1981.

Consul, The, opera by Menotti, produced in Philadelphia, 1950. Libretto by the composer: the action takes place in a modern totalitarian state, from which escape to a 'free' country is made impossible by red tape at that country's consulate. (The consul himself never appears.)

Contes d'Hoffmann, Les (Fr., 'The Tales of Hoffmann'), opera by Offenbach, produced in Paris, 1881, after the composer's death. Guiraud completed the scoring and supplied the recitatives which in most productions have replaced the original spoken dialogue. Libretto by J. Barbier and M. Carré. The hero represents the German romantic writer E. T. A. ➤Hoffmann, and the succession of amorous adventures is drawn from his works.

continental fingering, ➤fingering.

continuo (It., abbr. of *basso continuo*), a type of accompaniment (current particularly *c*. 1600–1750) played from a bass-line, most commonly on a keyboard instrument. From the bass-notes, the player worked out the correct harmonies, sometimes aided by numerical shorthand indications provided by the composer (➤figured bass). To *play the continuo*, therefore, is not to play a particular kind of instrument; it is to play on a keyboard instrument (or lute, etc.) a harmonized accompaniment from this type of bass – or to reinforce (e.g. on cello and double-bass) this bass-line without the chords. Hence *continuo group* of such instruments, e.g. in a Monteverdi opera orchestra. The historic English equivalent for *continuo* is 'thorough-bass', i.e. 'through-bass'; but *continuo* has now acquired standard usage in English.

contra-, contre-, Kontra-, Italian, French and German prefixes signifying (of an instrument) 'lower in pitch', usually about an octave lower. So, e.g., *contrebasse, Kontrabass*, French and German terms for ➤double-bass; *contre-basson, Kontrafagott*, French and German terms for double-bassoon (➤bassoon). The Italian terms for these instruments are respectively *contrabbasso* (in older spelling *contrabasso*) and *contrafagotto*. From these come the English-language terms *contrabass* (preferred in USA to 'double-bass') and *contrabassoon* (general in both British and US usage, and colloquially shortened to 'contra'). So also a name indicating the lowest size of a family of instruments, e.g. the rare *contrabass* ➤*clarinet*.

contrabass, contrabasso, contrabassoon, contrabbasso, contrafagotto, see preceding entry.

contralto, lower type of female voice; ➤alto.

contrapunctus (fabricated Lat.), a counterpoint; used by Bach instead of 'fugue' as a heading for movements in his ➤*Kunst der Fuge.*

contrapuntal, pertaining to ➤counterpoint.

contrary motion, ➤motion.

Contrasts, trio by Bartók, 1938, for clarinet, violin and piano – the violinist using two instruments, one of normal tuning (G, D, A, E) and the other tuned G sharp, D, A, E flat. Also title of work by ➤Beecroft.

contre-, ➤contra-.

contredanse, ➤country dance.

Converse, Frederick Shepherd (1871–1940), American composer, pupil of Rheinberger in Munich. Works include four operas, six symphonies and *Flivver 10,000,000* for orchestra (celebrating the manufacture of the 10 millionth Ford car).

Conyngham, Barry [Ernest] (b. 1944), Australian composer who studied with Takemitsu in Japan. Works include *Ice Carving* for violin and four orchestras; *Antipodes* for solo and choral voices, didjeridu and orchestra; theatre music.

Cooke, Arnold [Atkinson] (b. 1906), British composer, pupil of Hindemith. Works include opera *Mary Barton* (after Mrs Gaskell), six symphonies, much chamber and piano music.

Cooke, Benjamin (1734–93), British composer (pupil of Pepusch) and organist; wrote church music, glees and other vocal pieces, organ works, etc.

Cooke, Deryck [Victor] (1919–76), British musicologist who worked extensively for the BBC and who made a completion of Mahler's Symphony no. 10 which has been widely performed.

Cooke, Henry (*c.* 1615–72), English bass singer and composer of church music, songs, part of the music to *The* ➤*Siege of Rhodes* etc.

Cooper, Imogen (b. 1949), British pianist (daughter of the music critic Martin Cooper) who studied at the Paris Conservatoire and made first Proms appearance in 1973; well-known in Mozart, recording concertos for two and three pianos with Brendel and Neville Marriner.

Cooper, James Fenimore (1789–1851), American novelist. ➤*Corsair.*

Cooper, John (*c.* 1575–1626), English composer, player of the viol and other instruments; changed name to Giovanni Coperario (or Coprario) – though there is no evidence that he worked in Italy. Composed music for masques, anthems, songs, fantasies and suites for viols and violins, etc.; author of *Rules how to Compose.* Teacher of the brothers Lawes.

Cooper, Kenneth (b. 1941), American harpsichordist, director of ensembles, editor of Monteverdi's and other works. Has partnered Yo-Yo Ma and others in recordings; performs internationally – also as pianist, including ragtime.

Coperario, ➤Cooper (John).

coperto (It.), covered, e.g. of drums muffled with a cloth to give a muted effect.

Copland, Aaron (1900–1990), American composer, more than anyone else establishing American 'classical' music internationally; also pianist, lecturer and writer, championing American music. Studied in Paris with N. Boulanger. Some of his work calls on American folkish idiom (ballet scores ➤*Billy the Kid,* ➤*Rodeo,*

➤*Appalachian Spring*) or on Latin-American music (*El* ➤*Salón México*, clarinet concerto). Other works include piano variations, piano sonata, opera *The Tender Land*, three symphonies (no. 3 the best-known, incorporating his earlier ➤*Fanfare for the Common Man*); ➤*Quiet City* (orchestral work); ➤*Lincoln Portrait* (with narrator), piano quartet, piano trio ➤*Vitebsk*; film scores.

Coppélia, ballet with music by Delibes, choreography by A. Saint-Léon, produced in Paris, 1870. (Subtitled 'or, The Girl with Enamel Eyes' – a girl deceiving a toy-maker into supposing her a doll come to life.)

Coprario, ➤Cooper (John).

Coq d'or, Le, French title of Rimsky-Korsakov's *The* ➤*Golden Cockerel*; since this is a Russian work, the French title has no claim to usage in English-speaking countries.

cor (Fr.), ➤horn (in general); *cor anglais*, ➤English horn; *cor de chasse* ('hunting-horn'), the original valveless instrument from which the modern orchestral horn developed; and other usages (➤*tenor cor*).

Coralli, Jean (1779–1854), Italian-French choreographer. ➤*Giselle*.

corda (It.; pl. *corde*), a string. So, in piano-playing, *una corda* (one string) – instruction to play with soft pedal, this pedal achieving its effect (on grand pianos) by causing the hammers to hit only one instead of three strings to each note. The terms *tre corde* or *tutte le corde* (three strings, all the strings) cancel this, indicating that the soft pedal is not to be used.

Corelli, Arcangelo (1653–1713), Italian violinist, composer chiefly for his

instrument, of which he was a celebrated exponent (➤*Folía*). In service as musician to a cardinal at Rome. More than anyone else, established the form of the ➤*concerto grosso*; among his examples in this form is the so-called ➤*Christmas Concerto*.

Corelli, Franco (b. 1921), Italian operatic tenor; made first appearances at La Scala, Milan, 1954, and Metropolitan Opera, New York, 1960, and became internationally celebrated in Italian opera roles.

Corigliano, John [Paul] (b. 1938) American composer and university teacher whose works include opera *The* ➤*Ghosts of Versailles*, symphony, concertos for piano, for oboe, for flute and for clarinet.

Coriolan (Ger., 'Coriolanus'), overture by Beethoven, 1807, to a play (not Shakespeare's) by H. von Collin.

Cornelius, Peter (1824–74), German composer (also critic), pupil of Liszt and admirer of Wagner; composed *Der* ➤*Barbier von Bagdad* and other operas, some notable songs and part-songs, etc.

cornemuse (Fr.), ➤bagpipe.

cornet (1) brass wind instrument with three valves, resembling trumpet but squatter in appearance, of wider bore and easier to play; a ➤transposing instrument in B flat, with compass from E below middle C upwards for about two and a half octaves – can be switched to become an instrument in A, half a tone lower. It 'arrived' in 1820s, before the valved trumpet, so found a ready role in being the only brass instrument of its pitch capable of fully chromatic use; but it has now been generally driven out of the symphony orchestra by the valved trumpet (except when called for specially – e.g. by Stravinsky in ➤*Petrushka*, whose score makes use of trumpets as well). It has also been driven out of dance-music, but was used in early jazz. It is still a basic instrument in the brass band (where a smaller, higher *soprano cornet* in E flat is also used) and most military bands. (2) ➤cornett.

Cornet, Pierre (16th–17th century), Netherlands organist and composer of organ music; held court post in Brussels.

cornet-à-pistons (Fr.), ➤cornet (1).

cornett, old wooden or ivory wind instrument having a cup-shaped mouthpiece (like modern brass) but fingerholes (like modern woodwind); used, e.g., in 17th-century ensemble music, and to reinforce choral soprano parts, as trombones would reinforce the lower vocal parts. The ➤ophicleide and ➤serpent are of the same family. (In modern spelling the word would be 'cornet', but the old spelling is kept to distinguish it from ➤cornet above.) Its use has been revived in the 20th century.

Cornish, ➤Cornysh.

corno (It.), ➤horn; *corno inglese*, ➤English horn; *corno di bassetto*, ➤basset-horn. ('Corno di Bassetto' was Bernard Shaw's pseudonym as a music critic.)

cornopean (1) an early form of cornet (brass instrument); (2) organ stop of soft but trumpet-like tone.

Cornysh, William (also Cornish and other spellings) (*c.* 1468–1523), English composer of songs (including a setting of Skelton), church music, etc.; in service as musician, actor and

choirmaster to Henry VII and to Henry VIII, whom he accompanied to the Field of the Cloth of Gold, 1520.

Coronation Concerto, nickname for Mozart's Piano Concerto in D, K537, performed by him at coronation festivities for the Emperor Leopold II at Frankfurt, 1790 (composed 1788).

Coronation Mass (1) nickname for Mozart's Mass in C, K317 (1779), apparently through some association with the annual crowning of a statue of the Virgin; (2) nickname sometimes formerly used for Haydn's Mass in D minor (Hob. XXII: 11), more often called ➤*'Nelson' Mass*.

Coronation of Poppaea, The, opera by Monteverdi. ➤*Incoronazione di Poppea*.

Correa de Araujo (or Arauxo), Francisco (*c.* 1575–1654 or 1655), Spanish organist and composer of organ works (in the forms of ricercar, variations, etc.), also of psalms, etc.

Corrette, Michel (1709–95), French organist and composer of songs for the theatre, keyboard works and church music; author of an instructional method for violin.

Corsaire, Le (Fr., 'The Corsair'), concert-overture by Berlioz, 1831. Not after Byron's poem, but after Fenimore Cooper's novel *The Red Rover* – title of overture having originally been *Le Corsaire rouge*.

Cortot, Alfred [Denis] (1877–1962), Swiss-born pianist resident in France – noted as soloist and as chamber-music partner of Thibaud and Casals, and was also conductor, musical editor and writer.

Così fan tutte, opera by Mozart, produced in Vienna, 1790. Libretto by L. da Ponte, mocking women's vows of fidelity. Title literally means 'So do all women': subtitle is 'or, The School for Lovers' (*La scuola degli amanti*).

Costa, Michael [Andrew Agnellus] (1808–84), Italian-born composer-conductor who settled in London, 1829, and achieved leading position as operatic and concert conductor. Knighted, 1869. Composed operas, oratorios, symphonies, etc.

Costeley, Guillaume (*c.* 1531–1606), French organist and composer, in service to French court; works include chansons, motets, organ pieces.

Cotrubas, Ileana (b. 1939), Romanian soprano who appeared at Glyndebourne from 1969, Covent Garden from 1971 (Tatyana in ➤*Yevgeny Onegin*). After a distinguished career, she retired from opera in 1989.

Cotton, Charles (1630–87), English poet. ➤*Serenade* (song-cycle by Britten).

Coucou, Le (Fr., 'The Cuckoo'), piece for harpsichord by Daquin (published 1735) taking a stylized quotation of the cuckoo's call as its main theme.

Coulthard, Jean (b. 1908), Canadian composer (also university teacher) who studied in London; has written three string quartets, variations for piano on the B-A-C-H theme, and orchestral works, some with Canadian associations.

counterpoint, the simultaneous combination of two or more melodies to make musical sense, one melody then being spoken of as *the counterpoint of* or *in counterpoint to* another. So *double counterpoint*, when two melodies, one above the other, can exchange posi-

tion; similarly *triple, quadruple counterpoint* (etc.), where three, four (etc.) melodies can take up any positions relative to each other – all these being kinds of *invertible counterpoint*, as practised in ➤fugue. A certain academic discipline abstracted from 16th-century practice is called *strict counterpoint; free counterpoint* denotes counterpoint not bound by this.

counter-subject, ➤fugue.

counter-tenor, a rare male voice with range higher than tenor, current in England in Purcell's and Handel's time and revived in the 20th century in concerts and opera; called male ➤alto in, e.g., Anglican cathedral usage. (➤falsetto.)

Count of Luxembourg, The, operetta by Lehár. ➤*Graf von Luxemburg*.

Count Ory, opera by Rossini. ➤*Comte Ory*.

country dance, kind of social dance originating in England (e.g. the 'Sir Roger de Coverley') and cultivated, e.g., by Mozart and Beethoven, who called it *Kontretanz* – based on French *contredanse* (counter-dance), derived by false etymology from the English word.

coup d'archet (Fr.), stroke of the bow, the attack with the bow.

coup de glotte (Fr.), stroke of the glottis; a method of vocal 'attack' counselled by some teachers of singing.

Couperin, French family of musicians (see below). The surname alone is taken to refer to François Couperin.

Couperin, Charles (1638–79), French organist (in Paris) and composer; father of François Couperin.

Couperin, François (1668–1733), called 'Couperin le grand' (the great). French composer, also harpsichordist and organist; pupil of his father (see preceding entry). Held official post under Louis XIV. Composed over 200 harpsichord pieces, some with picturesque titles; chamber music, organ pieces, church and other vocal music. Wrote famous book on harpsichord-playing. Nephew of Louis Couperin.

Couperin, Louis (c. 1626–61), French organist (in Paris) and composer. Brother of Charles Couperin and uncle of François Couperin (see preceding entries).

couple (verb), on the organ, to contrive that the stops normally controlled by one manual are available also on another manual (or on pedals); or that the striking of one note should also cause the sounding of the same note an octave higher or lower. Hence *coupler*, mechanism for this, also sometimes available on a harpsichord and on some electronic keyboard instruments.

coupler, see preceding entry.

couplet (Fr., not the same meaning as in English), (1) stanza of a poem, the music being repeated for each successive stanza – so an operatic song may take the form of *couplets*; (2) forerunner, e.g. in Couperin's works, of what in ➤rondo form is called the 'episode'.

courante (Fr.), dance in triple time occurring in the baroque ➤suite.

course, term used to distinguish a single string from a pair (or more) of strings tuned to the same note (in unison or, rarely, an octave apart). Thus the common form of mandolin

has eight strings in four double courses (a pair tuned to each note); on different forms of lute there may be some courses which are double (two strings tuned to each note), others single (one string to a note).

Covent Garden, the usual name for the London theatre whose official title has been the 'Royal Opera House, Covent Garden' since 1892 (previously the 'Royal Italian Opera House'). It has had its own resident opera and ballet companies since 1946, named Royal Opera and Royal Ballet since 1969 and 1957, respectively. The Opera's musical directors have included Solti (1961), Colin Davis (1971), Haitink (1987).

Coward, Noël [Pierce] (1899–1973), British actor and playwright who wrote the music of many songs in his own musical shows including ➤*Bitter-Sweet* and *Conversation Piece*; also of other songs (which he sang). Knighted, 1970.

cow-bell, the small bell, usually of iron, worn by animals to aid herding; used (more than one) in R. Strauss's ➤*Alpensinfonie* with picturesque intent, by Mahler in Symphonies nos. 6 and 7, etc.

Cowell, Henry [Dixon] (1897–1965), American composer and pianist, pioneer of modern techniques; developed the use of ➤clusters of adjacent notes played, e.g., with forearm on the piano, and extended this to orchestral technique also; co-inventor of the 'Rhythmicon', electrical instrument reproducing predetermined rhythms. Prolific composer for orchestra, band and various instrumental groups; works (some with synthesized titles like *Synchrony*, *Tocanta*) include 20 symphonies, 16 *Hymns and Fuguing Tunes* for various ensembles (after Billings) and many works for piano; also teacher and writer.

Cowen, Frederic Hymen [originally Hyman Frederick] (1852–1935), British composer and conductor, born in Jamaica: works include operas, six symphonies (no. 3, *Scandinavian*) and about 300 songs. Knighted, 1911.

cow-horn, brass instrument (roughly of ➤horn type, but valveless) made to simulate the sound of a rustic horn; used by Wagner as the vassals' instrument in ➤*Götterdämmerung* (where the designation is *Stierhorn*, bull-horn) and by Britten in his ➤*Spring Symphony*.

Cox and Box, or the Long-Lost Brothers, operetta by Sullivan, produced in London, 1866. Libretto by F.C. Burnand. Cox and Box are alternate occupants of the same lodgings.

Crabbe, George (1754–1832), English poet. ➤*Peter Grimes*.

Cranko, John (1927–73), British choreographer. ➤*Pineapple Poll*, ➤*Prince of the Pagodas*.

Crawford Seeger, Ruth [Porter] (also known by her maiden name as Ruth [Porter] Crawford) (1901–53), American composer. Works include a string quartet; three songs with piano, oboe, percussion; *Rissolty Rossolty* for 10 wind instruments, drums and strings. Was also collector and arranger of US folk-songs.

Creation, The, oratorio by Haydn. ➤*Schöpfung*.

Creation Mass, nickname (because of a quotation in it from *The Creation* (➤*Die Schöpfung*)) for Haydn's Mass in B flat, 1801.

Création du monde, La (Fr., 'The Creation of the World'), ballet (a long way after Genesis!) with music by Milhaud, using jazz idiom; produced in Paris (choreography by Jean Börlin), 1923.

Creatures of Prometheus, The, ➤*Geschöpfe des Prometheus*.

Credo, ➤Mass.

crescendo (It., growing), increasing in loudness.

Crespin, Régine (b. 1927), French soprano, internationally noted as Tosca (Puccini), Salome (R. Strauss), etc., and in recital.

Creston, Paul (originally Joseph Guttoveggio) (1906–85), American composer, also organist. Works include six symphonies (no. 3 on Gregorian chant); a saxophone concerto; Concertino for marimba; Fantasia for trombone and orchestra.

Croce, Giovanni (*c.* 1557–1609), Italian composer (and priest), pupil of Zarlino; in charge of music at St Mark's, Venice. Wrote motets, psalms, madrigals, etc.

croche (Fr.), ➤eighth-note, quaver. ('Monsieur Croche' was a pseudonym used by Debussy in writing music criticism.)

Croft, William (1678–1727), English organist (at Westminster Abbey, 1708) and composer of songs, harpsichord pieces, stage music, etc., and much church music including hymntune 'St Anne' ('O God our Help in Ages Past').

crook, detachable section of the tube of horns, trumpets, etc., made in various sizes so as to give a different basic key to the instrument when fitted. (A player in Mozart's time, seeing 'horn in D' specified, would fit a *D crook*, giving a ➤harmonic series with D as the fundamental.) The use of ➤valves, general from about 1850, has almost eliminated the necessity for changing crooks, but on, e.g., an ordinary trumpet in B♭ there is a mechanism which in effect can change the instrument to one having an *A crook*.

croon (particular usage, especially in 1930s), to sing softly and sentimentally into a microphone, as in dance bands.

Cross, Beverley (b. 1931), British playwright. *The ➤Mines of Sulphur*.

Cross, Joan (1900–93), British operatic soprano (also teacher and operatic stage director); created some of Britten's leading opera roles. CBE, 1951.

Crosse, Gordon (b. 1937), British composer, pupil of Wellesz and (in Italy) Petrassi. Works include *Meet my folks!*, and others involving child singers and instrumentalists; two violin concertos; *Wildboy* for clarinet with cimbalom and seven other instruments; vocal settings of poems by Ted Hughes; operas *Purgatory* and *The Story of Vasco*.

cross-fingering, fingering the ascending or descending scale (on woodwind instruments) in a way that goes against the normal order of lifting up and putting down successive fingers.

Crossley, Paul (b. 1944), British pianist, formerly joint artistic director of London Sinfonietta; studied with Messiaen and Loriod in Paris. Tippett's piano sonatas nos. 3 and 4 and Adams' *Eros Piano* were composed for him, and he was the on-stage soloist with English National Opera in Janáček's *Diary of One Who Disappeared*.

crossover, marketing term for the recording of a semi-popular repertory by a classical artist, the sales being aimed at the non-classical public.

cross-relation(s), the relation set up when, for instance, the notes A♮ and A♭ occur simultaneously or in immediate succession in different parts – that is, a special effect of harmony in which the parts are not unanimous in whether they treat a particular note as sharp, natural, or flat. (*Cross-relation*, the standard American term, is clearer than 'false relation', more usual in Britain.)

crotal, type of small bell such as a sleigh-bell; for the French form of the term, with a different meaning, see the following.

crotale (Fr.), the normal modern term for the orchestral percussion instrument formerly known as the ancient cymbal or antique cymbal, used e.g. in Debussy's ➤*Après-midi d'un faune*; such cymbals differ from the larger standard cymbal in being tuned to a definite pitch and in their more delicate tone.

Crotch, William (1775–1847), British composer; child prodigy as organist and composer whose later works (oratorio *Palestine*, church and organ music, etc.) did not fulfil his exceptional early promise. Professor at Oxford, 1797, and first principal of the Royal Academy of Music, 1822.

crotchet, ➤quarter-note.

crowd (string instrument), ➤crwth.

Crown Imperial, march by Walton for coronation of George VI, 1937 (title from William Dunbar's poem 'In Honour of the City', earlier set as cantata by Walton).

Crucifixion, The, oratorio by Stainer (text written, and selected from the Bible, by J. S. Simpson), first performed in 1887.

Crumb, George [Henry] (b. 1929), American composer, pupil of Blacher (in USA and in Berlin). Works include *Echoes of Time and the River* for orchestra; *Ancient Voices of Children*, song-cycle with instrumental ensemble; *Black Angels* for electric string quartet.

crumhorn (Ger., *krumm*, crooked), type of curved, cylindrically bored, double-reed wind instrument current in Europe in 16th–17th centuries; made in at least six sizes of different pitch (a four-part consort was standard); revived in mid 20th century.

Crusell, Bernhard Henrik (1775–1838), Finnish clarinettist and composer who worked mainly in Stockholm. Wrote clarinet concertos, quartets for clarinet or oboe with strings, opera, songs.

crwth (Welsh; equivalent to obsolete English word 'crowd' as musical instrument), medieval and later British stringed instrument shaped like a lyre but played with a bow, surviving longest in Wales; an ancestor of the violin family. (Sometimes misleadingly called a 'bowed harp'.)

csárdás (Hung.), Hungarian dance in sections, *lassú* (slow) and *friss* (quick). See also next entry.

Csárdásfürstin, Die (Ger., literally 'The Csárdás Princess' but known in English as 'The Gipsy Princess'), operetta by Kálmán, produced in Vienna, 1921. The marriage of a prince's son to a mere cabaret singer is permitted when facts about the prince's own wife are discovered.

cuckoo, toy instrument, used e.g. in the ►*Toy Symphony* formerly ascribed to Haydn.

Cuckoo and the Nightingale, The, nickname for an organ concerto in F (1739) by Handel, from its suggestion of these bird-calls.

Cuenod [not Cuénod], Hugues (b. 1902), Swiss tenor of unusually high range; noted in recitals (including medieval music) and in opera. He gave an 86th birthday recital in London.

Cui, César [Antonovich] (1835–1918), Russian composer of French descent; Russian army general; critic, propagandist for 'national' Russian music, and member of the group of composers called the ►*Mighty Handful*. Works include 10 operas, many piano pieces and songs. Completed Dargomizhsky's *The* ►*Stone Guest*.

cuivre, cuivré (Fr.), brass, brassy (the latter term used, e.g., in horn-playing to signify a 'forced', ringing tone); *cuivres*, brass instruments.

cummings, e e [orginally E(dward) E(stlin) Cummings] (1894–1962), American writer and painter. ►Berio, ►Meyerowitz.

Cunning Little Vixen, The (Cz. *Přihody lišky Bystroušky*), opera by Janáček, produced in Brno, 1924; libretto by R. Těsnohlídek, using both human and animal characters.

Cupid and Death, masque with words written by J. Shirley, 1653, with music conjecturally by C. Gibbons; revived, 1659, with music (certainly) by C. Gibbons and M. Locke.

cup mute, ➤mute.

Curlew, The, song-cycle by Warlock, 1923, to four linked poems by Yeats; accompaniment for flute, English horn and string quartet.

Curlew River, dramatic work ('parable for church performance') by Britten, first performed at Orford (Suffolk), 1964. Libretto by William Plomer, based on medieval Japanese Noh play.

Curley, Carlo (b. 1962), American organist, who uses personal showmanship in highly successful 'concerts' (he refuses the term 'recitals'). Touring internationally, he performs on traditional cathedral organs and/or his own very large transportable electronic organ.

curtal, ➤dulcian.

curtal(l), old English name for obsolete family of wind instruments, the bass member surviving longest, transformed in the 18th century into the ➤bassoon.

Curtin, Phyllis (b. 1922), American soprano prominent in opera, creating leading roles in works by Carlisle Floyd; latterly dean of arts, Boston University.

Curzon, Clifford [Michael] (1907–82), British pianist, who made London début at age 16. Developed international career with particular distinction in Schubert. Knighted, 1977.

cut time (US usage), the metre expressed as ₵ , equivalent to 2/2 – two beats to the bar.

Cutting, Francis (active *c.* 1583-*c.* 1603), English lutenist and composer of music for his instrument (including an arrangement of 'Green-sleeves') and for instrumental consort.

cycle (1) name given to a set of works, especially songs, intended to be performed as a group and often linked musically or by other means; (2) name given to certain post-1950 pieces where the performer begins at a point of his own choosing, goes through the written score and concludes at the same point – e.g. Stockhausen's *Zyklus* (*Cycle*) for percussionist, 1959; (3) term used in the expression *cycle of fifths*, the 'chain' by which (given 'equal ➤temperament') a succession of perfect fifths upwards or downwards will lead back to the original note again (at a higher or lower octave) after passing through all the other 11 notes of the chromatic scale. ➤cyclic form.

cyclic form (1) form of a work in which a theme does duty (often in new guise) in more than one movement – e.g. Franck, Symphony in D minor; Elgar, Symphony no. 1; (2, obsolete; ➤cycle, 1) form of any work with more than one movement.

cymbal, percussion instrument consisting of a plate of metal which is usually either struck with drumstick (single stroke or roll) or clashed against another cymbal. Ordinary cymbals are of no definite pitch – but nevertheless one of them may sound higher than another, and modern composers may specify so. *Choke cymbals* are two ordinary cymbals mounted face to face on a rod (e.g. in dance bands) and struck with side-drum stick. The so-called *ancient cymbals* or *antique cymbals* (tuned to definite pitch, as in ➤*Après-midi d'un faune*) are now commonly called ➤*crotales*.

cythern, ➤cittern.

czardas, incorrect spelling of ➤*csárdás*.

Czech Philharmonic Orchestra, Prague-based orchestra becoming independent of its operatic origins in 1901. Gerd Albrecht, conductor 1992–6, was succeeded by Vladimir Válek as interim artistic director.

Czerny, Carl (1791–1857), Austrian pianist and composer of an enormous number of piano studies; also of many other piano works (e.g. fantasies on popular operatic and other tunes of the day) and of church music, etc. Contributor to the ➤*Hexameron*. Pupil of Beethoven and himself a famous teacher – e.g. of Liszt.

D

D, note of the scale. So *D* ➤*flat*, *D* ➤*sharp*, semitonally adjacent notes; *D* ➤*major*, *D* ➤*minor*, keys or chords defined by having D as point of stability (➤tonic). So also *in D*, (1, of a composition or part of it) indication that the music belongs in that key (major unless indicated as minor); (2, of a wind instrument) indication of length of air-column which gives D as the fundamental of its harmonic series: the indication usually but not always implies a ➤transposing instrument. So *trumpet in D* or (colloquially) *D trumpet*.

D, abbr. for (1) *da*, as in *DC, da capo* (➤*da*); (2) abbreviation for 'Deutsch' in numbering the works of ➤Schubert; (3) Doctor, as in D.Mus. or Mus.D., Doctor of Music.

d (lower-case letter), indication of the key of D minor as distinct from capital D for D major – a logical but not universal usage.

d, symbol in ➤*tonic sol-fa* notation for the first degree (tonic) of the scale, pronounced *doh*.

d' (Fr., It), of (before a vowel); see under second word of phrase (except for names such as D'Annunzio).

da (It.), from; *da capo* (abbr. DC), (instruction to) repeat from the beginning.

So also *da capo al fine, da capo al segno,* (repeat) up to the occurrence of the word *fine* (end), or up to the sign indicating this (e.g. ⌒ – ➤pause). Similarly *dal segno,* (repeat) from a specified sign, instead of repeating right from the beginning. So *da capo* ➤aria, one which makes use of this procedure as a formal basis.

da camera, ➤*camera*.

da chiesa, ➤*chiesa*.

da Gagliano, Marco, ➤Gagliano.

Dahl, Ingolf (1912–70), American (German-born) composer, also conductor, writer and teacher. Works include concerto for alto saxophone and wind orchestra; *A Cycle of Sonnets* for voice and piano; *Quodlibet on American Folktunes* for two pianos, eight hands (later orchestrated).

dal, ➤da.

Dalayrac (also spelt d'Alayrac), **Nicolas** (1753–1809), French composer of songs, string quartets and especially operas – over 50 of them, including *Tout pour l'amour* ('All for Love').

Dalcroze, Émile Jaques, ➤Jaques-Dalcroze.

Dale, B. J. [Benjamin James] (1885–1943), British composer and teacher;

won attention with a piano sonata at 17, and later wrote cantata *Before the Paling of the Stars*, music for one or more violas, etc.

Dallapiccola, Luigi (1904–75), Italian composer (born in Pisino – then part of Austria–Hungary, later of Yugoslavia). Was also pianist and noted teacher, e.g. in USA. Works include *Il* ➤*Prigioniero* and other operas; *Canti di Liberazione* (➤*canto*) for chorus and orchestra; a piano concerto; songs (some in German) with various accompaniments.

Dam, José van (originally Joseph Van Damme) (b. 1940), Belgian bass-baritone, internationally prominent in opera; created the title-role in Messiaen's ➤*Saint François d'Assise*.

Damase, Jean-Michel (b. 1928), French pianist and composer of operas, ballet score *La croqueuse des diamants* ('The Diamond-Cruncher'), and several works for harp, including two concertos – his mother being a harpist.

Damnation de Faust, La (Fr., 'The Damnation of Faust'), cantata by Berlioz, 1846; since 1893 also occasionally staged as opera. Words by composer and A. Gandonnière, after Goethe.

Damoiselle élue, La (Fr., 'The Blessed Damozel'), cantata by Debussy, 1887–8, on a French translation of Rossetti's poem.

Dämpfer (Ger.), ➤mute.

damping pedal, soft pedal (of piano).

Damrosch, Walter (1862–1950), German-born conductor who went with his father (Leopold Damrosch, 1832–85, also a conductor) to settle in USA in boyhood; championed

Wagner, and gave many first American performances. He composed operas including *Cyrano* (after Rostand's *Cyrano de Bergerac*), and *The Man Without a Country*; also choral works, etc.

dance band (in modern sense), a band that plays for social dancing; in Europe and North America from the 1920s it generally divided into three – saxophones (some players doubling clarinets), brass (trumpets and trombones) and 'rhythm' (piano, drums, guitar and double-bass usually playing pizzicato). From the 1950s such bands lost their prominence to 'pop groups' based on electrically amplified guitars of differing types, with percussion and later with synthesizers.

Dance of the Hours, ballet music from Act III of Ponchielli's opera *La* ➤*Gioconda*.

dance-poem, description sometimes given by composers (➤*Péri*) to a substantial orchestral work intended for ballet and having narrative interest – on the analogy of ➤symphonic poem.

Dances of Galánta, orchestral suite by Kodály, 1933, based on tunes in a collection of gipsy music from Galánta (a small Hungarian market town).

Dandrieu, Jean-François (*c.* 1682–1738), French organist, composer of works for harpsichord organ, etc.

Daniel, Paul [Wilson] (b. 1958), British conductor who made opera debut with Opera Factory, 1982. On staff of English National Opera 1982–7, music director Opera Factory 1987–90. Music director Opera North 1990–97. Has conducted many world premieres, including *Akhnaten*. In 1997 became music director of ENO.

Dankworth, John [Philip William] (b. 1927), British jazz clarinettist, composer, conductor and festival organizer. Works include piano concerto, film scores and (jointly with Seiber) *Improvisations* for jazz band and orchestra. CBE, 1974.

D'Annunzio, Gabriele (1863–1938), Italian poet and dramatist. ➤*Gioconda*, ➤*Martyre de Saint-Sébastien*, ➤Zandonai.

danse (Fr.), dance; *Danse macabre*, orchestral work by Saint-Saëns, 1874 – inspired by the medieval idea of a skeletons' dance, it quotes the ➤*Dies irae* plainsong tune.

Dante Alighieri (1265–1321), Italian poet. ➤*Dante Sonata*, ➤*Dante Symphony*, ➤*Francesca da Rimini*, ➤*Gianni Schicchi*; ➤Castiglioni, ➤Pacini.

Dante Sonata, usual short name for Liszt's piano work, *Après une lecture du Dante* (Fr., 'After a reading of Dante'), labelled by him as a 'Fantasia, quasi sonata' and included in the ➤*Années de pèlerinage*. Played by Liszt in 1839; given its present form in 1849.

Dante Symphony, orchestral work by Liszt (first performed, 1857) – in two movements, 'Inferno' and 'Purgatorio', ending with the ➤Magnificat sung by a women's chorus. (Liszt wrote two alternative versions of this ending.) ➤Pacini.

danza (It., Sp.), dance.

Danzi, Franz (1763–1826), German composer (son of an Italian), also cellist and conductor. Works include wind quintets and much other chamber music, also operas, oratorio, church music.

Daphnis et Chloé, ballet with music by Ravel (using a chorus), produced in Paris, 1912. (The two orchestral suites drawn from it do not comprise the whole.) Based on an ancient Greek story of pastoral love.

da Ponte, Lorenzo (1749–1838), Italian writer. ➤*Così fan tutte*, ➤*Don Giovanni*, ➤*Nozze di Figaro*.

Daquin (also spelt d'Acquin), **Louis Claude** (1694–1772), French composer of harpsichord pieces, including *Le coucou* (Fr., 'The Cuckoo'), church music, etc.; organist from boyhood, holding post at French Chapel Royal from 1739.

d'Arányi, Jelly, ➤Arányi.

Dargason, English ➤country-dance tune incorporated into Holst's ➤*St Paul's Suite*.

Dargomizhsky, Alexander Sergeyevich (1813–69), Russian composer, 'nationalist' in musical ideas and an inspiration for the younger group known as the ➤*Mighty Handful*. Composed *The* ➤*Rusalka*, *The* ➤*Stone Guest* and other operas; orchestral works; nearly 100 songs, many satirical.

Dart, [Robert] **Thurston** (1921–71), British harpsichordist, organist, conductor and musicologist; professor of music at Cambridge, then (1964) at London University.

Dauberval, Jean (1742–1806), French choreographer. ➤*Fille mal gardée*.

Daudet, Alphonse (1840–97), French writer. L'➤*Arlésienne*.

Daughter of the Regiment, The, opera by Donizetti. ➤*Fille du régiment*.

da Viadana, ➤Viadana.

David, Félicien [César] (1810–76), French composer (also theatre conductor); travelled in Near East, arranged oriental melodies for piano, and won noted success with descriptive orchestral work *Le Désert* ('The Desert'). Also composed operas, four symphonies.

David, Ferdinand (1810–73), German violinist (original performer of Mendelssohn's concerto) and composer – mainly for violin, including five concertos.

David, Johann Nepomuk (1895–1977), Austrian composer, also conservatory director and editor of old music. Works include eight symphonies, many church compositions and organ pieces, etc.

Davidovich, Bella, ➤Sitkovetsky.

Davidovsky, Mario (b. 1934), composer, born in Argentina, naturalized American; has written seven *Synchronisms* for various instrumental or vocal ensembles combined with taped sound, also two string quartets, a cantata with biblical Hebrew text, etc.

Davidsbündler (Ger.), members of Schumann's (imaginary) League of David, opponents of a Philistine attitude to art; hence Schumann's *Davidsbündler-Tänze* ('Dances') for piano, 1837, revised in 1850.

Davie, Cedric Thorpe (1913–83), Scottish composer (pupil of Vaughan Williams and Kodály), also organist and professor at St Andrews University. Composed music for Edinburgh Festival revival (1949) of old Scottish play, *The Thrie Estaites*. OBE, 1955.

Davies, Dennis Russell (b. 1944), American conductor who was musical director of opera and concert seasons in Bonn (1987–90), conducted *Der fliegende Holländer* at Bayreuth, and gave first performances of works by Berio, Carter, Glass and others.

Davies, Hugh [Seymour] (b. 1943), British composer, performer and instrument inventor; assistant to Stockhausen, 1964–6. Besides works for traditional instruments, he has composed others for his own new electroacoustic instruments and 'sound sculptures', e.g. *Strata* for quadrophonic aeolian harp plus tape.

Davies, Peter Maxwell (b. 1934), British composer, very prolific in different styles, winning much success. Directed his own ensemble, 'The Fires of London'; associate conductor/composer, Royal Philharmonic Orchestra, since 1992. Has written operas ➤*Taverner, The* ➤*Martyrdom of St Magnus, The* ➤*Lighthouse, The Doctor of Myddfai* and the semi-staged *Vesalii Icones* (Lat., 'Images from Vesalius', for dancer, cello and ensemble), ➤*Eight Songs for a Mad King*; also six symphonies, a set of ➤*Strathclyde Concertos*, sonatina for violin and cimbalom, etc. His residence in Orkney since the 1970s has involved him in local activity and in such works as *Kirkwall Shopping Songs* for children's voices with accompaniment and ➤*Orkney Wedding with Sunrise*. Knighted, 1987.

Davies, [Henry] **Walford** (1869–1941), British musical educator – professor at University of Wales, and the first widely popular BBC talker on music; also organist (St George's Chapel, Windsor) and composer of church music, etc. Knighted, 1922; Master of the King's Music, 1934.

Davis, Andrew [Frank] (b. 1944), British conductor; music director of the Toronto Symphony Orchestra, then (1989) of the BBC Symphony Orchestra and of Glyndebourne Opera. In 2000, becomes musical director of Chicago Lyric Opera. CBE, 1992.

Davis, Carl (b. 1936), American composer and conductor, resident in Britain; has written *Overture on Australian Themes*, ballet score *A Christmas Carol*, many film scores (some to silent films such as Abel Gance's five-hour *Napoleon* which he conducts 'live' during the film's showing). Collaborator with McCartney in ➤*Liverpool Oratorio*.

Davis, Colin [Rex] (b. 1927), British conductor, formerly clarinettist; conductor, BBC Symphony Orchestra, 1967–71; music director of Royal (Covent Garden) Opera, 1971–86. Principal conductor of Bavarian Radio Symphony Orchestra, 1984–92, of London Symphony Orchestra from 1995. Knighted, 1980.

Davy, John (1763–1824), British composer of song 'The Bay of Biscay', much theatre music, etc.

Davy, Richard (*c.* 1467–*c.* 1516), English composer of a Passion, motets, part-songs, etc.; organist of Magdalen College, Oxford, 1490–92.

Dawson, Peter (1882–1961), Australian bass-baritone who appeared at Covent Garden from 1909 but was more celebrated as concert singer, especially of ballads, some composed by himself as 'J. P. McCall'. Sales of his records are said to have exceeded 13 million.

de (Fr.), of. For names and phrases beginning thus, see next word – except for anglicized or americanized surnames, e.g. 'de la Mare'. (Italian names beginning 'De' are so listed.)

Dead March, any funeral march, especially 'The Dead March in Saul', i.e. from Handel's oratorio *Saul*, 1739.

Death and the Maiden, song by Schubert. ➤*Tod und das Mädchen*.

Death and Transfiguration, symphonic poem by R. Strauss. ➤*Tod und Verklärung*.

Death in Venice, opera by Britten, produced at Aldeburgh, 1973; based on the novel by Thomas Mann about a writer's homosexual passion and his death.

Debussy, Claude-Achille [originally named Achille-Claude] (1862–1918), French composer, with Ravel the outstanding figure of French music of his period. Also noted as critic; worked and died in Paris; visited Russia, 1881. His idiom has been given the name ➤*impressionism*, in token of a supposed kinship with contemporary visual art. Was first pro- then anti-Wagner; his opera ➤*Pelléas et Mélisande* is unlike any predecessor though seemingly indebted to Musorgsky for cultivation of natural speech-inflexions. Achieved first marked success with L'➤*Après-midi d'un faune*, 1894; had already composed cantata *La* ➤*Damoiselle élue*. Also wrote ➤*Iberia*, *La* ➤*Mer*, ➤*Nocturnes* and other works for orchestra; two books of piano preludes (with picturesque titles, including *La* ➤*Fille aux cheveux de lin*) and other piano works including *Suite bergamasque* (➤*bergamasca*) which includes *Clair de lune*, and ➤*Children's Corner*; string quartet, violin sonata, cello sonata, and a trio (which he also called 'sonata') for flute, viola and harp; music to ➤*King Lear* and *Le* ➤*Martyre de St Sébastien*. Unfinished works include an opera on Poe's *The Fall of the House of Usher*; ➤*croche*.

début (Fr., a beginning), in strict usage the very first appearance of an artist before the public: 'She was brought up in London but made her début in New York.' But in practice the term has become shorthand for 'first appearance' (at a variety of events and places) and is so used in this book.

decani (Lat., of the dean), that section of the choir in a cathedral, etc., which is stationed on the south (i.e. dean's) side of the chancel; opposite of ➤*cantoris*.

decibel, the standard unit of measurement (symbol: dB) for the ratio of two intensities of sound. A zero (OdB) is used to represent the threshold of hearing.

Decoration Day, the title of no. 2 of ➤*Holidays* by Ives.

decrescendo (It., lessening), becoming softer.

Deering, ➤Dering.

Defesch, William (1687–?1757), Belgian organist, violinist, cellist and composer who settled in London, 1731; wrote Mass, oratorios, concertos, songs, etc.

degenerate music, ➤*entartete Musik*.

degree, classification of a note with reference to its position in the scale. Thus the notes of the scale of C major (upwards, C-D-E-F-G-A-B-C) are called the first, second (etc.) degrees of the scale, returning eventually to the first degree, i.e. C. The alternative names for the first to seventh degrees (major or minor scale) are ➤tonic, ➤supertonic, ➤mediant, ➤subdomi-nant, ➤dominant, ➤submediant, ➤leading-note. Other names are used in the ➤tonic sol-fa system.

dehors (Fr. outside), sounding prominently – term applied to a melody, etc., which the composer intends should stand out from its surroundings.

de Koven, [Henry Louis] **Reginald** (1859–1920), American composer, educated at Oxford and elsewhere in Europe. Wrote *The Canterbury Pilgrims* (after Chaucer) and other operas – including *Robin Hood*, for a London performance of which he composed the song 'Oh, Promise Me'; also operettas, ballets, piano music, songs, etc.

Delage, Maurice [Charles] (1879–1961), French composer who studied with Ravel and travelled to the Far East; wrote *Quatre poèmes hindous* ('Four Hindu Poems') for voice with instrumental ensemble, a string quartet, etc.

Delalande, Michel Richard, ➤Lalande.

de la Mare, Walter (1873–1956), British poet and novelist. ➤Gibbs.

Delannoy, Marcel [François Georges] (1898–1962), French composer, formerly painter and architect. Works include operas, ballets (*L'Eventail de Jeanne*), two symphonies.

de Lara, Isidore (pen-name of Isidore Cohen) (1858–1935), British singer, concert organizer and composer of operas in English (including *The Light of Asia*, produced in 1892) and in French.

Delden, Lex van (1919–88), Dutch composer of chamber and choral music, *In memoriam* for orchestra (for the 1953 Dutch flood victims), eight symphonies, etc.; also critic.

Delibes (not Délibes), [Clément Philibert] **Léo** (1836–91), French composer, also organist, pupil of Adam. Works include ballet scores ➤*Coppélia* and ➤*Sylvia* (notably full of musical substance); ➤*Lakmé* and other operas; also Mass, songs, etc.

Delius, Frederick (baptized Fritz Albert Theodor) (1862–1934), British composer of German descent, born in Bradford. Beecham's championing (and editing) of his music helped him achieve a considerable following in Britain, little elsewhere. Settled, 1889, in France, dying at his home at Grez-sur-Loing. Had become blind and largely paralysed: ➤Fenby took down some late compositions from dictation. Works include ➤*Koanga*, *A* ➤*Village Romeo and Juliet*, and four other operas; choral-orchestral works *Appalachia*, *A* ➤*Mass of Life*, ➤*Requiem* and ➤*Sea Drift*; for orchestra, two pieces called *Dance Rhapsody* and ➤*On Hearing the First Cuckoo in Spring*, ➤*Brigg Fair*, and *Paris: The Song of a Great City*; also piano concerto, violin concerto, double (violin and cello) concerto; many songs (English, French, German, Danish, Norwegian texts), etc.

Deller, Alfred [George] (1912–79), British counter-tenor, the principal modern reviver of his type of voice, especially in Dowland, Purcell etc. Britten and others wrote specially for him. Also conductor and festival director.

Dello Joio, Norman (b. 1913), American composer (also pianist, organist, and teacher), pupil of B. Wagenaar and Hindemith. Works include *New York Profiles* and *Variations, Chaconne and Finale* for orchestra, opera *The Trial at Rouen* (about Joan of Arc), ballets, a harmonica concerto, three piano sonatas.

Del Mar, Norman [René] (1919–94), British conductor; conductor of BBC Scottish Orchestra, 1960–65. Author of a book on R. Strauss. CBE, 1975.

De los Angeles, Victoria, ➤Los Angeles.

Del Monaco, Mario (1915–82), Italian tenor, internationally known in opera (e.g. in title-role of Verdi's ➤ *Otello*) – at the Metropolitan, New York, from 1950.

Del Tredici, David [Walter] (b. 1937), American composer of *Syzygy* (soprano, horn, tubular bells and chamber orchestra) and other settings of James Joyce; settings of Lewis Carroll including *Final Alice* for amplified soprano, folk group and orchestra, and many others. Also university teacher.

De Luca, Giuseppe (1876–1950), Italian baritone, celebrated in opera, particularly Puccini. He was the first Sharpless in *Madama Butterfly*, 1914.

Delvincourt, Claude (1888–1954), French composer of mime-cantata *Lucifer*; *Pater noster* for chorus and orchestra, a string quartet, etc.; director of the Paris Conservatoire.

Demessieux, Jeanne [-Marie-Madeleine] (1921–68), French organist, pupil of Dupré; noted recitalist, visiting Britain from 1947. Also composer.

Demidenko, Nikolai [Anatolyevich] (b. 1955), Russian pianist who made British début 1985 with Moscow Radio Symphony Orchestra and became resident in Britain, 1990. Performs rarely heard composers, e.g. Alkan, A. Rubinstein. Visiting professor, University of Surrey, 1994.

de Mille, Agnes

de Mille, Agnes (b. 1905), American choreographer. ➤*Rodeo*.

demisemiquaver, ➤thirty-second-note.

Demus, Jörg [Wolfgang] (b. 1928), Austrian pianist, eminent as soloist and song-accompanist (e.g. with Fischer-Dieskau).

Dench, Chris (b.1953), British composer resident in Australia. His works, some using microtones, include *Mentation* for flute, piano and three orchestras; *Tilt* and *Rushes* for piano.

Denisov, Edison [Vasilievich] (1929–96), Russian composer who first trained as mathematician. Much of his music made its initial headway in the West, his opera *L'Écume des jours* ('The Foam of Days') being first produced in Paris in 1986. Has also written various concertos (one for viola later re-worked for alto saxophone), *Canon in memory of Igor Stravinsky* for flute, clarinet and harp, etc.

Dent, Edward Joseph (1876–1957), British musicologist, opera translator, professor of music at Cambridge and composer; made editions of The ➤*Beggar's Opera* and of various works by Purcell.

Denza, Luigi (1846–1922), Italian composer of 'Funiculì, funiculà' and about 500 other songs; also opera, etc. Settled in London, 1879, as a teacher; died there.

de Peyer, Gervase [Alan] (b. 1926), British clarinettist – principal clarinet, London Symphony Orchestra, 1955–71, also prominent as soloist (giving first performances of works by Horovitz, Musgrave and others) and is also occasionally a conductor.

De Quincey, Thomas (1785–1859), British essayist and critic. ➤Dieren.

der (Ger.), (1) the (masc. sing.); (2) of the (fem. sing.).

Dering, Richard (also Deering), (*c*. 1580–1630), English organist, in service to Charles I's queen; composed church music, canzonets, fancies for viols, etc.; previously studied in Italy.

Dernesch, Helga (b. 1939), German soprano, prominent in Wagner's operas, etc. Made Covent Garden début in 1970. Has more recently sung mezzo-soprano roles, e.g. Herodias in *Salome*.

des, of the (Fr. pl.; Ger. masc. and neut. sing.).

De Sabata, Victor (1892–1967), Italian conductor, active in opera (especially at La Scala, Milan) and in concerts, visiting Britain from 1947. Also composer of symphonic poems, operas, ballets, etc.

descant (1) medieval term (➤discant); (2) additional part sung (sometimes improvised) above a given melody, e.g. above a hymn-tune; (3) indication of a high range, as in *descant* ➤*recorder*.

Desert Song, The, musical play with text by Otto Harbach, Oscar Hammerstein II and Frank Mandel; music by Sigmund Romberg. Produced in New York, 1926. The leader of a Moroccan guerrilla band turns out to be the French Governor's son.

desk, an orchestral music-stand; in the strings of an orchestra each desk is shared by two players, so that *first desk only* is an instruction that the particular passage is to be played by the first *two* players only.

Després, Desprez, etc., ➤Josquin.

Dessau, Paul (1894–1979), German composer; works include opera *Die Verurteilung des Lukullus* ('The Trial of Lucullus') (libretto by Brecht), in which a piano with metal-covered hammers is used; also music to Brecht's plays, film music, orchestral works. Also conductor. Lived in France and USA, 1933–45.

Destinn, Emmy (originally Ema Kittlová) (1878–1930), Czech soprano who adopted a teacher's surname, latterly preferring the Czech form 'Destinnová'. Internationally distinguished in opera, especially Puccini.

détaché (Fr.), detached – an instruction to bow the violin, etc., in a particular way. It is the opposite of *lié* (bound) but does not imply ➤*staccato*.

Detroit Symphony Orchestra, American orchestra founded 1914 (but inoperative 1949–52); conductor since 1989, Järvi, succeeding Herbig.

Deuteromelia, a sequel to ➤*Pammelia*.

Deutsch, Otto Erich (1883–1967), Austrian musicologist whose cataloguing of the works of Schubert (1951) gave rise to the now universal 'D.'-numbering of those works.

Deutscher Tanz, ➤German dance.

deutsches Requiem, Ein (Ger., 'A German Requiem'), work for soloists, chorus and orchestra by Brahms; first complete performance 1869. Text from Luther's translation of the Bible into German; title of the work therefore distinguishes it from the traditional (Roman Catholic) Requiem to a liturgical Latin text.

Deutsches Symphonie-Orchester, new name adopted in 1993 by the former Berlin Radio Symphony Orchestra, founded in 1946 during the Allies' occupation of Berlin as the RIAS (Radio in the American Sector) Symphony Orchestra. The conductor since 1989, succeeding R. Chailly, has been Ashkenazy.

Deutschland über Alles, ➤Emperor's Hymn.

deux (Fr.), two.

Deux Pigeons, Les (Fr., 'The Two Pigeons'), ballet with choreography by Louis Mérante, music by Messager, produced in Paris, 1886. Two temporarily separated lovers are the 'pigeons'.

de Valois, Ninette [originally Edris Stannus] (b. 1898), British choreographer. ➤*Haunted Ballroom*, ➤*Job*.

development, the section of a movement (e.g. in ➤sonata-form) between the initial statement of themes and their final recapitulation, during which the themes are 'developed', i.e. expanded, modified, combined, broken up, etc.

Devienne, François (1759–1803), French composer of 12 operas, many concertos for bassoon and for flute (his own instruments), etc. Died insane.

devil in music, ➤*tritone*.

Devil's Trill, The (or, It., *Il trillo del diavolo*), nickname for a violin sonata in G minor by Tartini, composed about 1714, and having a famous trill in the last of four movements; said to be modelled on a sonata played to Tartini by the Devil appearing in a dream.

de Waart, Edo, ➤Waart.

d'Hardelot, Guy (pen-name of Helen

Rhodes, *née* Guy) (1858–1936), born at Hardelot, France – English composer of 'Because' and other sentimental and enormously successful songs.

Diabelli, Anton (1781–1858), Austrian composer (pupil of Haydn) and publisher. Wrote mainly for the piano, including a waltz on which 50 invited composers each wrote one variation, and Beethoven wrote 33 uninvited.

diabolus in musica, ➤*tritone*.

Dialogues des Carmélites, Les (Fr., 'The Dialogues of the Carmelites'), opera by Poulenc, produced (in Italian) in Milan, 1957; libretto, by E. Lavery after a novel by Bernanos, narrates the martyrdom of a group of nuns in the French Revolution.

Diamond, David [Leo] (b. 1915), American composer, pupil of N. Boulanger in Paris. Works include 11 symphonies, Concerto for two solo pianos, quintet (guitar plus string quartet), Jewish liturgical music.

diapason, the 'basic' tone of the organ, 'open' or 'stopped' according to whether the ends of the pipes are clear or plugged, the 'open' being the louder. Normally of eight-➤foot length: *double diapason*, of 16-foot length (➤double, 2). (Other English uses of the term are obsolete, but see following entry.)

diapason normal (Fr.), a standard indication of pitch: A = 435 Hz. The international standard now accepted is different (➤frequency).

diaphony, name sometimes given to simpler types of ➤organum.

Diary of One Who Disappeared, The, usual English title for *Zápisnik zmízeleho* (Cz., 'Diary of a disappeared

[man]'), song-cycle by Janáček for tenor, mezzo-soprano, three other voices and piano, first performed in 1921; occasionally presented as an opera.

diatonic, pertaining to a given major or minor key (opposite of ➤chromatic); so *diatonic scale*, any one of the major or minor scales; *diatonic harmony*, harmony made up predominantly from the resources of the prevailing key, without much use of notes outside its scale; similarly *diatonic discord*, discord arriving from clashes within the key itself. Hence *diatonicism*, a pronounced use of diatonic harmony; so also ➤*pandiatonic(ism)*.

Dibdin, Charles (1745–1814), singer, composer, theatrical manager, publisher, author of novels and other literary works; in 1789 he instituted 'table entertainments' at which he recited, sang and accompanied. Composed 'Tom Bowling' and many other sea-songs, and over 100 stage pieces including *Lionel and Clarissa*.

Dichterliebe (Ger., 'Poet's Love'), song-cycle by Schumann, 1840, to 16 poems by Heine.

Dichtung (Ger.), poem; *symphonische Dichtung*, ➤symphonic poem.

Dickens, Charles (1812–70), British novelist. ➤*Christmas Carol*; ➤Bentzon (J.), ➤Cikker, ➤Goldmark (K.), ➤Hullah, ➤Mackenzie.

Dickinson, Emily [Elizabeth] (1830–86), American poet. ➤Escher, ➤Meyerowitz.

Dickinson, Peter (b. 1934), British composer, from 1991 professor at Goldsmiths' College, University of London; also pianist, collaborating with his sister Meriel (b. 1940), mezzo-soprano. Works include concertos for organ, piano, violin; two string quartets (no. 2 with tape or offstage piano); several works (mainly for piano) based on ragtime and blues; church drama *The Judas Tree*.

diction, correct and clear enunciation in singing. (This is the recognized meaning in musical contexts, though the term primarily refers to literary skill in using words.)

didgeridoo, ➤didjeridu.

didjeridu (the currently preferred spelling), Australian aboriginal wind instrument of trumpet type, made out of a tree trunk up to 180 cm. long.

Dido and Aeneas, opera by Purcell (Z626), usually said to have been first produced at a girls' school in London in 1689; but now thought possibly to have been first given at court, somewhat earlier. Libretto by N. Tate, after Virgil's account of Dido's abandonment by Aeneas and her ensuing suicide. (Purcell's only fully sung stage work.) ➤*chaconne*.

Diepenbrock, Alphons (1862–1921), Dutch composer of incidental music for Goethe's *Faust* and other plays, also of Mass, church music, songs (Dutch, German and French), etc. Also critic.

Dieren, Bernard van (1887–1936), Dutch-born composer and writer on music, resident in Britain from 1909. In a highly idiosyncratic style, wrote many songs, symphony (with voices) on Chinese themes, and a setting for voices and piano of De Quincey's 'On Murder Considered as One of the Fine Arts'.

Dies Irae (Lat., Day of Wrath), a sec-

tion of the Requiem Mass, the plain-song tune of which is quoted, e.g., in Berlioz's ➤*Symphonie fantastique*, Saint-Saëns's ➤*Danse macabre*, and various works of Rakhmaninov including *Rhapsody on a Theme of* ➤*Paganini* for piano and orchestra.

Dies Natalis (Lat., 'Natal day' [of Christ]), setting by Finzi, 1940, of prose and poems by Traherne; for high voice and strings.

diferencia (Sp.), a variation, as in Spanish 16th-century music, for keyboard and for ➤*vihuela*.

differential tone, ➤resultant tone.

Dillon, James (b. 1950), British composer (self-taught), also writer and lecturer on music. Works include *Windows and Canopies* and *Helle Nacht* (Ger., 'Bright Night') for orchestra, *East 11th St NY 10003* for six percussionists, two string quartets.

dim., abbr. for (1) ➤diminished (interval); (2) *diminuendo*, i.e. becoming softer.

diminish (1) to 'lessen' certain intervals which are then referred to as ➤diminished; (2) to subject a melody to ➤diminution.

diminished, term applied to a type of ➤interval regarded as a 'lessened' version of a certain other interval. In practice this is a useful term only for

(1) *diminished fifth*, e.g. one

semitone less than perfect fifth, and

(2) *diminished seventh*, one

semitone less than minor seventh. In effect the latter sounds as i.e.

111

as major sixth; but it is distinctive by the intermediate harmony it is presumed to carry, namely ♪ (and various otherwise ♪ other notations); this chord is the *diminished-seventh chord* on C, elliptically referred to as *C diminished* (abbr. *C dim.*).

diminuendo (It., lessening), becoming gradually softer.

diminution, the treatment of a melody in such a way as to decrease (usually halving) the time-values of its notes (used, e.g. in some fugues).

d'India, Sigismondo, ➤India.

d'Indy, Vincent, ➤Indy.

Dinner Engagement, A, comic opera by Berkeley, produced in Aldeburgh, 1954. Libretto by Paul Dehn, the dinner being given by (relatively) impoverished English nobility.

Dioclesian (properly *The Prophetess, or The History of Dioclesian*), play by T. Betterton for which in 1690 Purcell wrote incidental music (Z627).

director, a term variously used in artistic contexts; *music director* (in older usage *musical director*) indicates an involvement in policy as well as conducting; *stage director* (or just *director*) indicates the person in immediate charge of the action on stage (or film, television, etc.) and is so used in this book with reference to opera – the older British usage being *producer*.

discant, a type of medieval polyphony, notated or improvised, in which all the voices move at the same speed.

discord, opposite of ➤concord, in its technical sense.

disjunct motion, ➤motion.

dissonance, discord (➤concord); *Dissonance Quartet*, nickname for Mozart's String Quartet in C, K465 (1785), opening with a passage in which there is a pronounced use of dissonance.

Di Stefano, Giuseppe, ➤Stefano.

Distler, Hugo (1908–42), German composer of church music, choral works, string quartet, etc. His music was stigmatized by the Nazi authorities as 'degenerate', and he committed suicide.

Dittersdorf [Ditters originally his surname], **Carl Ditters von** (1739–99), Austrian violinist and composer, in service to various noble patrons; friend of Haydn and Mozart. Composed symphonies, string quartets, church music, etc.; also more than 40 operas, including the very successful *Doktor und Apotheker* ('Doctor and Apothecary') and one based on *The Merry Wives of Windsor* (1796).

div., abbr. of ➤*divisi* or 'divided'.

diva (It., 'divine woman', 'goddess'), term of adulation for a female opera-singer, nearly always a soprano. Also title of a film: ➤Fernandez.

divertimento (It., an amusement), a not-too-serious work, usually for a small instrumental group, in several movements (e.g. by Mozart, Stravinsky).

divertissement (Fr., an amusement), (1) a musical paraphrase on familiar tunes, or some similar light instrumental work; (2) a danced entertainment of the type of ➤ballet (1), but being merely a suite of dances not unified by any connecting story.

Divine Poem, The (Rus., *Bozhestvennaya poema*), orchestral work by Skryabin, also called his Symphony no. 3. First performed in Paris, 1905. Illustrates the composer's theosophical ideas and has an explicit literary source. The three movements are entitled 'Struggles', 'Delights', 'Divine Play'.

divisi (It.), divided – term used, e.g., of the first violins or other string group of the orchestra when they temporarily split into two or more smaller bodies playing different parts.

divisions (1) obsolete term for ➤variations, because the splitting of the time-values of notes was formerly a common way of making variations; (2) obsolete term for long, agile vocal runs, whether notated by the composer or introduced by the performer as an embellishment.

division viol, ➤viol.

do, the note C (in Latin countries, and formerly elsewhere); the tonic sol-fa symbol ➤doh is derived from it.

Dobbs, Mattiwilda (b. 1925), American soprano of high range, the first black singer to win international reputation in opera – Covent Garden (1954), Glyndebourne, La Scala (Milan), etc.

dobro, type of guitar with a large circular metal resonator under the bridge. The term is derived from the American inventors, the Dopyera Brothers.

Doctor Faust, opera by Busoni. ➤*Doktor Faust*.

Doctor Gradus ad Parnassum, ➤ *Gradus ad Parnassum*.

Doctor of Music, the highest musical degree (British, Commonwealth and American; not awarded elsewhere). Abbr. *D.Mus.*, *Mus.D.* or *Mus.Doc.*

dodecaphonic (Gk., *dodeka*, 12), a misapplied term: linguistically it should mean (analogously to ➤*monophonic*) 'in 12 strands or parts', but it has been accepted as referring to the ➤twelve-note method of composition. Similarly *dodecaphony, -ist*, etc.

Dodgson, Stephen [Cuthbert Vivian] (b. 1924), British composer. Works include clarinet concerto, piano quintet and (for the guitarist John Williams) two guitar concertos. ➤Peña.

doh, in ➤tonic sol-fa, the spoken name for the first degree (tonic) of the scale, written **d**. Derived from ➤do.

Dohnányi, Christoph von (b. 1929), German conductor, music director of the Cleveland Orchestra since 1984; appointed principal conductor, Philharmonia, 1997. Occasionally stage director for opera. Grandson of the following.

Dohnányi, Ernö [he used the German form, Ernst von] (1877–1960), Hungarian pianist and composer of two piano concertos, *Variations on a Nursery Theme* (same as 'Twinkle, twinkle') for piano and orchestra, two symphonies, three operas, etc. Less nationalist in style than his Hungarian contemporaries, Bartók and Kodály. From 1948 resident in USA.

Doktor Faust (Ger., 'Doctor Faust'), opera by Busoni; completed after Busoni's death by Jarnach and produced in Dresden, 1925. Libretto by composer, on the Faust legend but not based on Goethe's drama.

dolce (It.), sweet(ly); *dolcezza*, sweetness.

dolente (It.), sorrowful(ly).

Doles, Johann Friedrich (1715–97), German composer of church music, songs, etc.; pupil of Bach, and appointed in 1756 as Bach's successor in his Leipzig post.

Dollar Princess, The, operetta by Fall. ➤*Dollarprinzessin*.

Dollarprinzessin, Die (Ger., 'The Dollar Princess'), operetta in three acts by A. M. Willner and Fritz Grünbaum, with music by Leo Fall; produced in Vienna, 1907. (For the New York production in 1909 some additional numbers were contributed by Jerome Kern.) The American millionaire's daughter employs a male secretary.

Dolly, suite of six children's pieces for piano duet by Fauré, 1893; orchestrated for ballet by Rabaud, 1896.

Dolmetsch, surname of a Swiss (anglicized) family famous for the authentic interpretation of old music and for the revived manufacture of old instruments. The most famous members are Arnold Dolmetsch (1858–1940) and his son Carl (1911–97), English (French-born) player chiefly of the recorder but also of violin and viols; CBE, 1954.

Domestic Symphony, ➤symphonia.

Domgraf-Fassbaender, ➤Fassbaender.

dominant, the fifth note of the scale, in relation to the keynote: thus if the key is C (major or minor), the dominant is G. So *dominant seventh*, chord of the (minor) seventh on the dominant (in this case G, B, D, F) resolving normally on the ➤tonic chord (in this case C major or minor). So also *secondary dominant*, term sometimes encountered as translation of Ger. *Wechseldominante* (literally, 'exchange dominant'), meaning 'the dominant of the dominant', e.g. the note D in key C (major or minor).

Domingo, Plácido (b. 1941), Spanish tenor, brought up in Mexico, who made his first appearance at Metropolitan, New York, in 1968 and at Covent Garden in 1971 (in *Tosca*) winning highest international reputation. His very large operatic repertory is chiefly Italian (plus *zarzuelas*) but extends to title-role of *Parsifal* (La Scala, 1991); Menotti wrote ➤*Goya* for him. Is also, occasionally, conductor of opera and concerts.

domra, Russian plucked instrument, usually three-stringed, with convex back like a mandolin; made in several sizes and used for folk-music, etc. often in ensemble with ➤*balalaika*.

Donath [originally Erwin], **Helen** (b. 1940), American soprano resident in Germany. Began her operatic career in 1961, sang at Salzburg under Karajan in 1967, and had long attachment to Vienna State Opera; has recorded a great variety of roles from Gluck to Pfitzner.

Donatoni, Franco (b. 1927), Italian composer of four string quartets, a bassoon concerto, opera *Atem* (Ger., 'Breath'). His *Etwas ruhiger in Ausdruck* (Ger., 'Somewhat more Peaceful in Expression'), for five instruments, pays homage to Schoenberg.

Don Carlo, Italian title often used for Verdi's (originally French) opera *Don Carlos*. It is a mistaken supposition that the composer's abridged version was composed to an Italian text.

Don Carlos, opera by Verdi, produced in Paris, 1867. Libretto (in French) by F. J. Méry and C. du Locle, after Schiller: Don Carlos, the son of Philip II of Spain, is presented as the champion of liberty.

Don Giovanni, opera by Mozart (K527), produced (in Italian) in Prague, 1787. Original title, *Il dissoluto punito, o sia Il Don Giovanni* ('The Rake Punished or, Don Giovanni'). Libretto by L. da Ponte, dealing with some of the loves of the Spanish character better known as Don Juan, who is eventually dragged down to hell by a statue. ➤*Don Juan, The* ➤*Stone Guest,* ➤Gazzaniga.

Donizetti, Gaetano [Domenico Maria] (1797–1848), Italian composer; after 1844 suffered mental illness and paralysis. Composed more than 60 operas in a style of characteristic Italian lyricism but also with humour. Some are in French (e.g. *La* ➤*fille du régiment*) but most in Italian – including ➤*Don Pasquale, L'*➤*Elisir d'amore,* ➤*Lucia di Lammermoor.* The theory that he was the grandson of a Scot named Don(ald) Izett has been declared groundless.

Don Juan (1) ballet with music by Gluck, first performed in 1761; (2) symphonic poem by R. Strauss, first performed in 1889; after a poem by Lenau.

Donne, John (1572–1631), English poet. See ➤Britten, ➤Harris (W.).

Donohoe, Peter [Howard] (b. 1953), British pianist who made London début in 1979 and came joint second at the Moscow Tchaikovsky Competition

in 1982; since 1984 has also been a regular orchestral conductor.

Don Pasquale, comic opera by Donizetti, produced (in Italian) in Paris, 1843. Libretto partly by the composer: Don Pasquale is a foolish old man trapped into a fake marriage.

Don Quichotte, opera by Massenet, produced in Monte Carlo, 1910. Libretto (via a French play) by H. Cain, after Cervantes' Don Quixote, the title-role of the deluded knight-errant being composed for Shalyapin.

Don Quixote, various musical works based on Cervantes' novel, including (1) symphonic poem by R. Strauss, first performed in 1898, styled 'Fantastic Variations on a Theme of Knightly Character'; (2) incidental music by Purcell to a play by D'Urfey, 1694–5; (3) ballet with music by Minkus, choreography by Petipa, 1869; (4) opera by Massenet, ➤*Don Quichotte.*

dopo (It.), after(wards).

Doppel (Ger.), double. So *Doppelschlag,* the ➤turn (musical ornament).

doppio (It.), double; *doppio movimento,* at double the speed (of the preceding section).

Doráti, Antal (1906–88), Hungarian-born, American-naturalized conductor of Minneapolis Symphony Orchestra, 1949–60; later of the BBC Symphony, Stockholm Philharmonic, (US) National Symphony and (1975–8) the Royal Philharmonic Orchestra. Was also a composer, and arranged the music of J. Strauss the younger for the ballet *Graduation Ball.*

Dorian mode, the ➤mode represented by the white keys of the piano beginning on D.

115

'Dorian' Toccata and Fugue, nickname for a certain Toccata and Fugue in D minor (not the familiar one) by Bach, BWV 538; given because, although in fact in D minor, it was originally written without key-signature, as a work in the Dorian mode and ending on D would be.

Dorothy, operetta by Cellier with libretto by B. C. Stephenson. Produced in London, 1886. Title-role is that of a country squire's daughter who is mistaken for a servant and later appears as a potential (male) duellist.

Dostoyevsky, Feodor Mikhailovich (1821–81), Russian novelist. ➤*From a House of the Dead*; ➤Blacher, ➤Jeremiáš (O.), ➤Petrovics, ➤Sutermeister, ➤Tavener.

dot, mark in musical notation (1) placed above note, indicating ➤*staccato*; (2) placed after note, indicating that the time-value of the note is to be extended by half; similarly a *double dot* indicates that the time-value is to be extended by half as much again – e.g.

♩.. = ♩♪♪ (But before the double dot was invented, by Leopold Mozart, the single dot might indicate prolongation by an amount greater than half, even by three-quarters – i.e. as much as the double dot now conveys; the performer deduced from the musical context which interpretation was intended.)

double (1) twofold – so ➤double bar; *double chant*, form of ➤Anglican chant covering two verses of a psalm for each repetition, instead of one; *double choir*, *double chorus*, choir with a twofold multiplicity of voices (usually two choirs of four parts, making eight voice-parts in all); *double concerto*, concerto either with two solo instruments (e.g. Brahms's) or two orchestras (e.g. Martinů's); *double fugue*, ➤fugue with two subjects; ➤double-handed; double ➤horn; *double organ*, obsolete term for an organ with two manuals, or simply with one manual of full range; ➤double-sharp. So also *double octaves*, *double thirds*, etc., octaves or thirds played (on a keyboard) simultaneously in both hands. (2) prefix meaning 'sounding (about) an octave lower'. (This meaning arises because a pipe doubled in length sounds an octave lower: ➤foot.) So ➤double-bass, double ➤bassoon, double ➤diapason; So also *double-bass clarinet*, *double-bass saxophone*, lowest and extremely rare members of the ➤clarinet and ➤saxophone families. (3, verb) term alluding to (a) duplication of a melody by several performers: so, e.g., 'the voice-part is doubled by the clarinet and, an octave lower, by the bassoon'; (b) duplication of instruments by one player: so, e.g., 'Berlioz's *Fantastic Symphony* demands two flutes, the second doubling piccolo', i.e. the second player to play piccolo instead of flute when required. (4, Fr.), a variation, especially in the form of an ornamented version of the theme (corresponding to ➤division). See also the following entries.

doublé (Fr.), the ➤turn (musical ornament).

double bar, double perpendicular line marking the end of a composition or of a major division of it; usually but not always placed coincidentally with the single bar-line, and sometimes equipped with 'repeat' marks.

(➤repeat; ➤bar)

double-bass, the largest and lowest bowed stringed instrument of the orchestra – also used in jazz and dance bands (mainly pizzicato), and occasionally introduced into the military band for concerts; used occasionally in chamber music, very rarely solo. The standard modern instrument has four strings, and a compass from E just over an octave below the bass stave, upwards for nearly three octaves; but on some instruments a mechanism attached to the peg-board allows the lowest string to descend to C sharp; five-string instruments, with an extra string sounding B below bottom E, are also found. Though it belongs to the violin family, some players use under-handed bowing grip (as for viols).

double-flat, indication (notated ♭♭) of the lowering of the pitch of a note by two semitones (➤flat). Its use is necessitated by the 'grammar' of harmony, even though the resultant note, e.g. on the piano, will always have an alternative simpler name – e.g A♭♭ is G♮, i.e. G natural.

double-handed (of an instrumentalist), capable of playing two different instruments. (See ➤double, 3.) But the term does not usually refer to a player skilled merely on different sizes of the 'same' instrument, e.g. flute and piccolo, but to such wider skill as will enable him e.g. to play in a light orchestra on, say, the violin or saxophone as required.

double-sharp, indication (notated 𝄪) of the raising of the pitch of a note by two semitones (➤sharp). Its use is necessitated by the 'grammar' of harmony, even though the resultant note, e.g. on the piano, will always have an alternative simpler name – e.g. F𝄪 is G♮, i.e. G natural.

double-whole-note, the note 𝅜 or ᵓ considered as a time-value. This is standard North American usage and should clearly be preferred to 'breve', still surviving in British use. The corresponding rest is notated ᵓ .

doux, douce(ment) (Fr.), sweet(ly).

Dover Beach, work for voice and string quartet by Barber, 1931, a setting of the poem of the same name by Matthew Arnold.

Dowland, name of two composers; a reference without forename indicates John.

Dowland, John (1563–1626), English lutenist and composer, serving the king of Denmark (1598–1606) and other such patrons; achieved international reputation and had his music published in eight capitals. Became Roman Catholic but later Protestant again. Works are chiefly solo songs with lute, and lute solos; also wrote *Lachrimae* ('seven passionate pavans ... for lute, viols, or violins'), etc. Father of Robert Dowland.

Dowland, Robert (1591–1641), English lutenist (at Charles I's court, succeeding his father, John Dowland), composer, and publisher of an international collection of ➤ayres.

down-beat, the downward motion of the conductor's stick or hand, especially as indicating the first beat of the bar; (term therefore also used for) the first beat of the bar, whether or not the piece is being 'conducted'. The opposite is ➤up-beat.

down-bow, the motion of the bow of a stringed instrument when pulled by

117

the player – the opposite (pushing) motion being an ➤up-bow.

Downes, Edward [Thomas] (b. 1924), British conductor; on staff of Covent Garden, 1952–69, conductor of BBC Northern (later retitled BBC Philharmonic) Orchestra 1980–92. Also translator of Russian opera. Knighted, 1991.

Downes, Ralph [William] (1904–93), British organist and designer of organs, e.g. at the Royal Festival Hall, on which he gave his farewell recital in 1987. CBE, 1969.

D'Oyly Carte Opera Company, style used (not in its earliest years) by the theatrical management of Richard D'Oyly Carte (1844–1901) and his family successors, chiefly in presenting from 1875 the operettas of Sullivan with librettos by W. S. Gilbert (➤Savoy Operas). Though the historic company formally ceased in 1982, a new company with the same name began performing in 1988.

Draghi, Giovanni Battista (1640–1710), Italian harpsichordist, composer of harpsichord pieces, songs, etc.; settled in London, becoming organist to Charles II's wife, and died there.

Dragonetti, Domenico (1763–1846), Italian double-bass player who won exceptional fame as a soloist; was also a composer for his instrument, and a friend of Beethoven; settled in London and died there.

dramatic (soprano, tenor, etc.), having powerful voice and a style suitable for forceful operatic roles.

drame (Fr.), drama; *drame lyrique*, lyric

drama – term used, e.g. by Debussy to classify his opera ➤*Pelléas et Mélisande*.

dramma (It.), drama; *dramma per musica* (drama through music), term frequently used for 'opera' in the 17th and 18th centuries; *dramma giocoso*, comic drama, i.e. (in musical contexts) comic opera which nevertheless has one or more non-comic characters – applied by Mozart to ➤*Don Giovanni*.

Ðrdla, František or **Franz** (1869–1944), Czech violinist and composer chiefly for his instrument, but also of operettas, songs, etc.

Dream of Gerontius, The, oratorio by Elgar, first performed in Birmingham, 1900. Text, Cardinal Newman's poem (abridged) on a vision of the soul's fate after death.

Dreigroschenoper, Die (Ger., 'The Threepenny Opera'), opera by Weill, produced in Berlin, 1928, with libretto by Brecht – a modernization (using jazz) of the idea of The ➤*Beggar's Opera*.

Dresden, Sem (1881–1957), Dutch composer, pupil of Pfitzner. Works include two piano concertos, two violin concertos, cantatas (one with brass band), chamber music. Also writer on music, conductor, and director of The Hague Conservatory.

Dresden State Orchestra (or Dresdner Staatskapelle; ➤Kapelle), German orchestra tracing its origins to the 16th century. Conductor from 1991, Sinopoli.

Drigo, Riccardo (1846–1930), Italian composer of songs, ballet *Les Millions d'Arlequin* (source of popular 'Serenade'), etc.; also conductor, holding posts in St Petersburg and elsewhere.

droit(e) (Fr.), right, right hand; *main droite* or *M.D.*, with the right hand (e.g. in piano music).

drone, pipe(s) sounding note(s) of fixed pitch continuing as a permanent bass on various forms of ➤bagpipe; hence, similar effect (*drone bass*) in other forms of music.

Druckman, Jacob [Raphael] (1928–96), American composer. He was the New York Philharmonic Orchestra's composer-in-residence, 1982–6. Works include several combining taped with 'live' music, also three string quartets, *Windows* for orchestra.

drum, percussion instrument of many varieties, all having a skin or other membrane which is stretched over a hollow space and struck with a stick or (as ➤bongo, ➤tabla) fingers. The ➤*timpani* and some ➤tom-toms are tuned to definite notes; most other drums are not. So *drum-head*, the stretched membrane which is beaten; *drum-roll*, quick succession of strokes on the drum, the instrument's nearest approach to a sustained sound. ➤*bass drum*, ➤*slit-drum*, ➤*snare drum*, and the following entries.

drum kit, ➤kit.

drum machine, an electronic instrument which pre-programmes rhythmic patterns, allotting their constituents to synthesized percussion sounds available via the keyboard of an electronic organ or other controller.

Drum Mass, nickname for Haydn's Mass in C, 1796 (Hob. XXII: 9), in which the timpani are unusually prominent.

drum pad (1) a small block of material on which a drummer, while away

from the normal instrument, can practise the technique of the sticks; (2) a surface which responds to the impact of the drummer's sticks by triggering electronic sounds.

Drum-roll Symphony, nickname for Haydn's Symphony no. 103 in E flat (Hob. I: 103), opening with timpani roll.

Dryden, John (1631–1700), English poet. ➤*Alexander's Feast*, ➤*Indian Queen*, ➤*King Arthur*, ➤*Ode for St Cecilia's Day*; ➤Clarke (J.), ➤Grabu.

dry recitative, ➤recitative.

Drysdale, Learmont (1866–1909), British composer of operas (one on Euripides' *Hippolytus*), cantatas, orchestral works, songs, etc., much of his music having Scottish associations.

du (Fr.), of the.

Dubois, [François Clément] **Théodore** (1837–1924), French composer of operas, church music, orchestral works, etc. Director of Paris Conservatoire, 1896–1905, being obliged to resign after discriminating against the young Ravel.

Ducasse, Jean Jules Aimable Roger-, ➤Roger-Ducasse.

due (It.), two.

Duenna, The, opera (so-called, but more a play with music) with words by Sheridan, music by the elder and younger ➤Linley (with some borrowings from other composers); produced in London, 1775. The play (but not the music) was the basis for two operas entitled *The Duenna*, one by Gerhard (BBC radio, 1949; staged 1992) and one by Prokofiev – libretto (in Russian) by composer and M. Mendelson Prokofiev, produced in Prague, 1946. The latter is known in Russian as *The Betrothal in the Monastery* but Sheridan's title is also sanctioned.

duet, a combination of two performers (sometimes with accompaniment, as is usually implied, e.g., by *vocal duet*), or a work for such a combination; *piano duet*, two performers on one piano. Distinguished from ➤*duo*.

duettino (It.), little duet.

duetto (It.), duet.

Dufay, Guillaume (*c.* 1400–1474), Franco-Flemish composer, also singer – in Papal choir at Rome, 1428–37; also canon of the Church. In 1440s, in service to the court of Burgundy. Noted teacher, e.g. of Ockeghem. Works include Masses (one on *L'*➤*homme armé*), other church music (some with accompanying instruments), and chansons.

Dukas, Paul (1865–1935), French composer – also editor of old music, critic and teacher. Works include opera *Ariane et Barbe-Bleue* ('Ariadne and Bluebeard'), dance-poem *La* ➤*Péri*, descriptive orchestral piece *L'*➤*Apprenti Sorcier*, and many piano works. Is said to have been the first major French composer to write a piano sonata.

Duke, Vernon, ➤Dukelsky.

Duke Bluebeard's Castle (Hung., *A Kékszakállú Herceg Vára*), opera by Bartók, produced in Budapest, 1918. Libretto by Balázs, giving a modern psychological interpretation of the old legend.

Dukelsky, Vladimir (1903–69), Russian-born composer (pupil of Glière) who settled in New York, 1922. Works include three symphonies and a piano concerto; also wrote, as Vernon Duke, 'April in Paris' and other dance-tunes, light theatre music, etc.

dulcian, modern English form of Ger. *dulzian*, a 17th-century forerunner of the bassoon; sizes smaller and larger than the standard were also made. An older English name for it was *curtal*.

dulciana, type of soft organ stop.

dulcimer (1) type of instrument (old, but still in use for traditional music, e.g. in Eastern Europe) in which strings stretched over a sound-board are struck with hammers; the Hungarian kind, sometimes seen in the concert-hall, is the ➤*cimbalom*; (2) name given to an American three-string folk-instrument of zither type (*Appalachian dulcimer*), with strings plucked by player's right hand.

Dumas, Alexandre (junior; 1842–95), French novelist and dramatist. ➤*Traviata*.

Dumbarton Oaks Concerto, Concerto in E♭ for 15 instruments by Stravinsky, 1938 – title taken from the Washington, DC estate of the patron who commissioned it, where it was also first performed. (Title-page of score prints 'Dumbarton Oaks 8-v-38' and then in larger type 'Concerto en mi♭', etc.; 'Concerto' is therefore the real title, 'Dumbarton Oaks' having no more claim to substantive use than has the date.)

dumka (Rus., Cz.; pl. *dumky*), a lament of Ukrainian folk-origin, a movement in which slow and fast tempos alternate – term used by Dvořák, e.g. *dumka* movements in his String Sextet and Piano Quintet. *Dumky Trio*, nickname for Dvořák's Piano Trio, op. 90, 1891, made up of six independent *dumka* movements in different keys.

dumky, see preceding entry.

dump (also *dumpe, dompe,* etc.), English title for a piece for lute or guitar, of which a few survive from around 1700; though the derivation of the word is not known, it apparently signifies a lament.

Dun, Tan ➤ Tan Dun.

Dunayevsky, Isaak [Osipovich] (1900–1955), Russian composer who achieved chief success with popular Soviet songs. Also wrote 12 operettas, etc.

Dunbar, William (*c.* 1460–*c.* 1514), Scottish poet. ➤*Crown Imperial*.

Dunhill, Thomas [Frederick] (1877–1946), British composer (pupil of Stanford), teacher and writer on music. Wrote operetta *Tantivy Towers* (words by A. P. Herbert), many songs, a symphony, chamber music, etc.

Duni, Egidio Romualdo (1708–75), Italian-born composer (pupil of Durante) who settled in France, 1757, and died there. Wrote chiefly opera, in both French and Italian: notable practitioner of the ➤*opéra comique*.

Dunstable (or Dunstaple), **John** (*c.* 1390–1453 or later), English composer of European repute (also mathematician and astrologer); spent some time on the Continent. That more than fifty of his works survive is testimony to his high reputation. Works include motets and other church music, three-part secular songs.

duo (It.), two performers, or a work written for them; *duo-pianist*, member of a duo playing on two pianos (not two people on one piano).

duodecuple scale (Lat., *duodecim,* 12), a scale of 12 notes, i.e. the ordinary European scale considered as having 12 notes all of equal value, as in ➤twelve-note music. (This term avoids the use of ➤chromatic, which has harmonic implications foreign to 12-note practice.)

Duparc, Henri (style of name used by Marie Eugène Henri Foucques-Duparc) (1848–1933), French composer, pupil of Franck, prevented by illness from working after 1885. Noted for his 16 songs, some with optional orchestral accompaniments; wrote little else.

duplet, a pair of notes of equal time-value, written where the number of beats is not capable of simple division by 2 – e.g. two notes occupying a bar of 3/8, written ♫ (One of the notes may, of course, be replaced by a rest.)

duple time, time in which the primary division is into 2 or 4 – e.g. 2/4, 4/4 – as distinct particularly from ➤triple time (primary division into 3). Note especially that 6/4 indicates a bar of two dotted half-notes, i.e. ♩.♩. while 3/2 indicates a bar of three half-notes, i.e. ♩ ♩ ♩ giving different accents although both total six quarter-notes.

Duplex-Coupler piano, ➤Moór.

du Pré, Jacqueline (1945–87), British cellist (married Daniel Barenboim, 1967). Studied with Tortelier and (after her London début, 1961) briefly with Rostropovich in Moscow. Won a devoted following, especially with Elgar's cello concerto, but was incapacitated through multiple sclerosis from 1973. OBE, 1976.

Dupré, Marcel (1886–1971), French organist (pupil of Widor) and composer of many organ works, also two symphonies, etc. Director of the Paris Conservatoire, 1954–6.

Dur (Ger.), ➤major.

Durante, Francesco (1684–1755), Italian composer, mainly of church music; noted as theorist and teacher. Taught Pergolesi, Paisiello and others.

Durchführung (Ger., a through-leading), ➤development.

durchkomponiert (Ger., through-composed), term used of a work, especially a song, composed in a continuous form, not repeating itself in successive stanzas – opposite of ➤strophic. (Term also sometimes used to mean 'fully worked out', 'really composed', etc., as distinct from something that seems to proceed merely in patches.)

Durey, Louis (1888–1979), French composer, influenced by Satie; one of the group of Les ➤Six. Also critic. His works include Fantaisie concertante for cello and orchestra, three string quartets.

D'Urfey, Thomas (1653–1723), English poet and dramatist. ➤Don Quixote (Purcell).

Durkó, Zsolt (1934–97), Hungarian composer, pupil of Petrassi in Rome. Works include opera Moses, wind octet, Movements for tuba and piano.

Dürrenmatt, Friedrich (1921–90), Swiss dramatist. ➤Besuch der alten Dame.

Duruflé, Maurice (1902–86), French organist and composer, pupil of Dukas and others. Works (few in number) include a Requiem, organ pieces and three dances for orchestra.

Dusapin, Pascal (b. 1955), French composer of opera Roméo et Juliette, three string quartets, and many works bearing English titles – If for clarinet, Indeed for trombone, chamber opera entitled To be sung (text adapted from Gertrude Stein).

Dusík, ➤Dussek.

Dussek [form of surname adopted by Jan Ladislav Dusík] (1760–1812), Czech pianist and composer. Wrote chiefly for the piano, but also chamber music, theatre music, etc. Pupil of C.P.E. Bach and friend of Haydn. Lived variously in Paris, Hamburg, London and elsewhere, dying near Paris.

Dutilleux, Henri (b. 1916), French composer of two symphonies, violin concerto L'Arbre des Songes ('The Tree of Dreams'), cello concerto (Tout un monde lointain, 'A whole world far off'), ballets, chamber music, piano solos.

Dutoit, Charles [Édouard] (b. 1936), Swiss conductor, active in Europe before becoming music director of the Montreal Symphony Orchestra, 1977–90, then of Orchestre National de France.

Dvořák, Antonín (1841–1904), Czech composer; 1866–73, viola-player in Czech National Theatre orchestra, conducted by Smetana, who influenced him; 1874, became friend of Brahms. Wrote cantata The ➤Spectre's Bride for use in England, which he visited nine times (Mus.D., Cambridge, 1891). Director of Prague Conservatory, 1891; director of the National Conservatory in New York, 1892–5, composing a string quartet (the ➤American) and the Symphony no. 9 in E minor (➤From the New World) at this time. Until after

World War II this was known as no. 5 and the previous four symphonies were numbered in a chronologically wrong order; in addition there are four earlier symphonies of his which remained unpublished at the composer's death and were not numbered. Current practice is to number all chronologically − 1 in C minor (*The Bells of Zlonice*), 2 in B flat, 3 in E flat, 4 in D minor, 5 in F, 6 in D, 7 in D minor, 8 in G. Wrote also ➤*Slavonic Dances* and ➤*Slavonic Rhapsodies* in a Czech 'national' style which also appears in, but does not dominate, his other works. These include a piano concerto, violin concerto, cello concerto in B minor (and another early cello concerto), cycle of three concert-overtures (➤*Carnival*); 10 operas including ➤*Armida* and *The* ➤*Rusalka*; a Mass and a Requiem; four piano trios; 14 works for string quartet; a piano quintet; piano pieces and many songs and part-songs. ➤*dumka*.

Dykes, John Bacchus (1823–76), British composer of many hymn-tunes and other church music; was also Anglican clergyman.

dynamics, the gradations of loudness and softness in music.

Dyson, George (1883–1964), British composer of *The Canterbury Pilgrims* and other choral works; also of chamber music, church music, etc. Director of the RCM, 1937–52; knighted, 1941.

Dzerzhinsky, Ivan [Ivanovich] (1909–78), Russian composer (also pianist), pupil of Gnesin. Works include *Quiet Flows the Don* and *Virgin Soil Upturned* (from Sholokhov's novels) and other operas; also three piano concertos, orchestral works, theatre and film music, etc.

E

E, note of the scale. So E ➤flat, E ➤sharp, semitonally adjacent notes; E ➤major, E ➤minor, keys or chords defined by having E as point of stability (➤tonic). So also in E flat, (1, of a composition or part of it) indication that the music belongs in that key (major unless indicated as minor); (2, of a wind instrument) indication of length of air-column which gives E flat as the fundamental of its harmonic series: the indication usually but not always implies a ➤transposing instrument. So the small clarinet in E flat or (colloquially) E flat clarinet.

e (It.), and.

e (lower-case letter), indication of the key of E minor as distinct from capital E for E major – a logical but not universal usage.

Eagles, ➤Eccles (S.).

early music, term usually applied to European music from the Middle Ages up to Bach's and Handel's time (mid 18th century) – music supposedly demanding instruments and interpretative conventions different from those of today. Even performances of considerably later music, if associated with the revival of 'obsolete' instruments and 'historical' methods of performance (say, for Elgar, using brass instru-ments of narrower bore than at present current), are said to show 'an early music approach'.

Early Music Consort of London, ➤Munrow.

East, Michael (c. 1580–1648), English composer of madrigals (one in The ➤Triumphs of Oriana), anthems, viol music, etc.

Easter Oratorio (Ger., Oster-Oratorium), work by Bach (BWV 249) for church performance (solo and choral singers with orchestra), composed about 1736 – or rather arranged by him from earlier works to secular texts. It is a short work in 10 numbers, not a full-length work as 'oratorio' usually signifies.

Eaton, John [Charles] (b. 1935), American composer of operas (one based on The Tempest), songs, instrumental music using a syn-ket (type of synthesizer), Blind Man's Cry for soprano and an 'orchestra' of synthesizers.

Eben, Petr (b. 1929), Czechoslovak composer, also pianist, organist and teacher. Has written many works for organ including two concertos; also a string quartet and oratorio The Apologia of Socrates.

Eberlin, Johann Ernst (1702–62),

German organist and composer of church and organ music, etc.

Ebony Concerto, work by Stravinsky for clarinet (slang 'ebony stick') and dance band, augmented by harp; written for Woody Herman's band, and first performed in 1946.

Eccles, John (c. 1668–1735), English composer of masque *The Judgement of Paris* to Congreve's words, also of much other stage music (➤*Semele*), songs, etc. Master of the King's Band, 1700. Of the same family as ➤Solomon Eccles, though the exact relationship is uncertain.

Eccles, Solomon (c. 1617–82), English musician (known also as Solomon Eagles) and shopkeeper who developed a Puritan objection to music and publicly burnt his instruments. A Quaker, he accompanied George Fox to the West Indies in 1671. See preceding entry.

echo (as in 'echo cornet', etc.), term for an instrument which can switch instantaneously from normal to muted tone, suggesting an echo effect.

echo organ, a manual (and the apparatus it controls) found on certain large organs, suitable for echo effects – having soft stops, and sometimes pipes at a distance from the main body of pipes.

écossaise (Fr.), sort of ➤country dance cultivated, e.g., by Beethoven and Schubert. (Although meaning 'Scottish' it is apparently not of Scottish origin, nor identical with ➤Schottische.)

Écurie (Fr., 'stables'), term applied to 17th-century French royal wind-band, La musique de l'Écurie, in contrast with church and chamber

orchestra; revived by the conductor ➤Malgoire for his modern French early music group.

Edwards, Richard (1524–66), English composer, also playwright and poet; wrote words of madrigal 'In going to my naked bed', and probably the music of it – as he certainly did to other verse of his own.

Edwards, Siân (b. 1959), British conductor who studied in Leningrad; made her operatic début in 1986; conducted première of *Greek*, Munich, 1988. Music director, English National Opera, 1993–5. Has conducted concerts in Los Angeles, Sydney, etc.

Egdon Heath, symphonic poem by Holst, first performed in 1928 – after Hardy's description of a Dorset landscape in *The Return of the Native*.

Egge, Klaus (1906–79), Norwegian composer, pupil of Valen and others. Works, sometimes making use of Norwegian folk-music, include two piano concertos, five symphonies, and chamber music.

Egk, Werner (1901–83), German composer of operas, including *Peer Gynt* (after Ibsen), *Der Revisor* (after Gogol's *The Government Inspector*), *Irische Legende* ('Irish Legend') after W. B. Yeats's tale *Cathleen O'Shea* and his play *The Countess Cathleen*, and *Die Verlobung in San Domingo* ('Betrothal in San Domingo'), after Kleist; also orchestral *French Suite* (based on Rameau), a violin concerto, etc.

Egmont, play by Goethe – for a revival of which, in 1810, Beethoven wrote incidental music, comprising overture (in concert performance combined with *Triumph Symphony* from the end of the play), four entr'actes, two songs, music for the heroine's death, and one ➤melodrama (in the technical sense).

Eichendorff, Joseph Karl Benedict, Baron von (1788–1857), German poet. ➤*Liederkranz/Liederkreis*; ➤*Vier letzte Lieder*.

Eichheim, Henry (1870–1942), American composer (also violinist) who travelled in Japan, China, etc., and incorporated the effects of oriental music – and sometimes oriental instruments themselves – into such works as *Nocturnal Impressions of Peking* and *Korean Sketch* for chamber orchestra with oriental instruments.

Eighteen-Twelve (1812), concert-overture by Tchaikovsky, 1880, commemorating Napoleon's retreat from Moscow and incorporating the 'Marseillaise', the Tsarist Russian national anthem, and other material. Scoring includes, optionally, cannon effects and military band.

eight-foot (organ stop, etc.), ➤foot.

eighth-note, the note ♪ considered as a time-value. This term is standard North American usage and, as mathematically corresponding to the element of time-signature represented by /8, should clearly be preferred to 'quaver', still surviving in British use. The corresponding rest is notated 𝄾

Eight Songs for a Mad King, music-theatre piece (for actor-singer and six instrumentalists) by P. M. Davies, 1969; text by Randolph Stow with sayings of King George III.

ein, eine (Ger.), one, a. See next word of phrase and also the following entry.

Eine kleine Nachtmusik (Ger., 'A Little Night Music', i.e. a little ➤serenade), work for strings – quintet or small orchestra – by Mozart, 1787 (K525).

Einem, Gottfried von (1918–96), Swiss-born Austrian composer, pupil of Blacher in Berlin and formerly opera répétiteur. His operas include *Der Prozess* (after Kafka's *The Trial*) and *Der* ➤*Besuch der alten Dame* ('The Visit of the Old Lady'), after Dürrenmatt's play. Other works include four symphonies, Serenade for double string orchestra, chamber music.

Einleitung (Ger.), introduction, prelude, etc.

Einstein on the Beach, opera by Glass with the theatre director Robert Wilson; produced (in English) at Avignon, 1974. Einstein appears as a violinist-onlooker who observes as an abstract action unfolds.

Eisler, Hanns (1898–1962), German composer, pupil of Schoenberg; in USA, 1933–48, then returned to (East) Germany. Works, strongly linked to his Marxist beliefs, include many settings of Brecht such as a choral *Deutsche Sinfonie* ('German Symphony') and a *Lenin-Requiem*; chamber music; film music (and a book on this in English, 1947).

Eisteddfod (Welsh), type of Welsh national music festival, or a local emulation of this – or, as in Australia, any competitive music festival, no connection with Wales being then implied. (Pl. *eisteddfodau* reserved for specifically Welsh contexts.)

Ek, Gunnar (1900–1981), Swedish composer. Works, some with themes from folk-music, include three symphonies, *Swedish Fantasy* for orchestra, choral works, songs, organ music.

el (Sp.), the. See next word of phrase.

Elder, Mark [Philip] (b. 1947), British conductor; musical director of the English National Opera 1979–93; conducted at Bayreuth, 1981. Conductor of the Rochester (NY) Philharmonic Orchestra 1989–94. CBE, 1989.

Electra, ➤*Elektra*.

electric/electronic (instruments), terms not always used with precision to categorize a diversity of instruments conceived as tonal developments (or variants) of original conventional instruments. In general, *electric* signifies only the requirement of electric amplification in order to let the instrument be heard as desired (e.g. electric ➤guitar); *electronic* denotes the actual generation of sound by electronic means as on the ➤Ondes Martenot, ➤theremin, ➤electronic organ, ➤synthesizer.

Electric Phoenix, British vocal group skilled in live-electronic and other modernistic techniques; founder-director (1978) Terry Edwards.

Electrification of the Soviet Union, The, opera by Osborne, produced at Glyndebourne, 1987. Libretto by Craig Raine (on Russian sources by Pasternak), about a young poet's loves and his response to society.

electro-acoustic, the currently preferred classification for what began in the 1950s as ➤electronic music – that is, music assembled on tape from elements either electronically generated (e.g. by synthesizers) or from naturally produced (➤acoustic) sounds which have undergone electronic modification. It may be conveyed to its audience either in unalterable form or with some measure of control or variation in performance (➤live electronics', 1).

electronic, ➤electric/electronic; ➤electro-acoustic; ➤electronic music.

electronic music, music formed from electronically generated (synthesized) sound – in its 'classical' form (Cologne, early 1950s) *wholly* of such sound; but later developments also embraced sounds electronically processed from natural (acoustic) phenomena. The term has now been largely superseded by '➤electro-acoustic music'.

electronic organ, term now applied to virtually any electronic keyboard instrument other than an electronic ➤piano, ➤synthesizer, or ➤sampler; the electronic sound, supposedly modelled on that of the traditional pipe-➤organ, may be supplemented by other electronic devices, e.g. for producing rhythmic patterns. In some classically inclined multi-keyboard models, the organ-like sound is based on digitized ('sampled') recordings of selected acoustic pipes, the term *computer organ* being used by some makers to denote such an instrument.

Electronic Poem, piece by Varèse. ➤*Poème électronique*.

élégie, elegy (Fr., Eng.), a song of lamentation, especially for the dead, or an instrumental work of similar intention or mood.

Elegy for Young Lovers, opera by Henze, produced (in German) in Schwetzingen (Germany), 1961; the libretto (originally in English), by W. H. Auden and Chester Kallman, concerns a self-centred poet, writer of the 'Elegy' of the title.

Elektra, opera by R. Strauss, produced

in Dresden, 1909. Libretto by H. von Hofmannsthal, after Sophocles, concerned with the heroine's part in avenging her murdered father, Agamemnon.

Elgar, Edward (1857–1934), British composer, all but self-taught; Roman Catholic, but was much associated with the Three Choirs Festival (based on Anglican cathedrals). The ➤*Enigma Variations* and *The* ➤*Dream of Gerontius* established him, 1899–1900. Had already written song-cycle ➤*Sea Pictures*. Later wrote oratorios *The* ➤*Apostles* and *The* ➤*Kingdom* (intended as the first two parts of an uncompleted trilogy); cantata *The* ➤*Music Makers*; two symphonies (Anthony Payne completed a third from sketches, 1998), symphonic study ➤*Falstaff*; overtures ➤*Cockaigne* and ➤*In the South*; *Introduction and Allegro for Strings*; a violin concerto, cello concerto, five ➤*Pomp and Circumstance* marches; chamber music, etc. The *Severn Suite* for brass band is one of his few post-1919 works. Knighted, 1904; Order of Merit, 1911; Master of the King's Music, 1924; baronet, 1931. ➤carillon, ➤*chanson*, ➤*pizzicato*.

Elias, German title of Mendelssohn's ➤*Elijah*.

Elias, Brian [David] (b. 1948), British composer, born in Bombay; works include piano concerto, Five Songs to Poems by Irina Ratushinskaya for mezzo-soprano and orchestra (1989), ballet score *The Judas Tree*.

Elijah, oratorio by Mendelssohn, first performed in Birmingham (to English translation of original German text), 1846. Words from the Bible.

Eliot, George (Mary Anne Evans) (1819–80), British novelist. ➤Joubert.

Eliot, T. S. (1888–1965), American, British-naturalized, poet. ➤Adès, ➤Bartolozzi, ➤Pizzetti.

Elisir d'amore, L' (It., 'The Love Potion'), comic opera by Donizetti, produced in Milan, 1832. Libretto by F. Romani; the elixir or love potion is a quack-doctor's dose of cheap wine.

Eller, Heino (1887–1970), Estonian composer; his works include three symphonies and a Sinfonietta, symphonic poems, many short piano pieces.

Ellington, Duke (professional name of Edward Kennedy Ellington) (1899–1974), American pianist, dance-band leader, and composer of dance music and also of concert works in, or indebted to, the jazz idiom.

Ellis, Osian [Gwynn] (b. 1928), British harpist; noted for his association with Britten and for his recitals where he sang Welsh songs to his own accompaniment. CBE, 1971.

Elman, Mischa (German spelling of Russia 'Misha') (1891–1967), violinist born in Russia who visited USA from 1908 and afterwards settled there (US citizen, 1923), maintaining high international reputation.

Eloy, Jean-Claude (b. 1938), French composer, pupil of Milhaud and Boulez, who taught in California, 1966–8. Works include *Equivalences* for 18 instruments; *Polychronies* for wind instruments, piano, harp, percussion; songs; *Shanti* for voices and instruments combined with electronic sound.

Elsner, Joseph [Xaver] (1769–1854), German-Polish composer of 27 operas, etc., and teacher of Chopin at Warsaw Conservatory.

embouchure (Fr., used also in English), the position and application of the lips to the mouthpiece of a wind instrument. (In French the word also means the mouthpiece itself.)

'Emperor' Concerto, nickname (not Beethoven's title) for Beethoven's Piano Concerto no. 5 in E flat, 1808. Origin uncertain.

Emperor Jones, opera by Gruenberg, produced in New York, 1933. Libretto by composer, after O'Neill's play: Jones is a black American railwayman who, after committing murder, becomes 'emperor' of a Caribbean island.

'Emperor' Quartet, nickname (as translation of Ger. *Kaiserquartett*) for Haydn's String Quartet in C (Hob. III: 77, also known as op. 76, no. 3), *c.* 1799, of which the slow movement takes Haydn's own 'Emperor's Hymn' (see next entry) as a theme for variations.

Emperor's Hymn, patriotic hymn by Haydn, 1797 (Hob. XXVIa: 43), adopted as national anthem in Austria and later (to words 'Deutschland über Alles') in Germany. See preceding entry. A similar tune is found in a Telemann suite, so Haydn's may be an adaptation.

empfindsamer Stil; **Empfindsamkeit** (Ger., expressive style; expressiveness), terms characterizing the music of certain German composers of the mid 18th century, e.g. Graun and C. P. E. Bach, with reference to their deliberate cultivation of specified emotions. An alternative translation is 'sensibility', as in Jane Austen's *Sense and Sensibility*.

en (Fr.), in; *En Bateau* ('In a boat'), piece by Debussy for piano duet, 1889, the first number in his *Petite Suite*.

enchaînez (Fr.), link (them) together – i.e. let the next movement follow its predecessor without a break.

Enchanted Lake, The (Rus., *Volshebnoye ozero*), symphonic poem by Lyadov, 1909 – descriptive, but with no explicit story.

Encina, Juan del (1468–1529), Spanish composer, poet and priest. Wrote eclogues (pastoral plays) with songs composed by himself.

encore (Fr., again), term used in English (though the French term is ➤*bis*) to mean 'perform it again', or, loosely, to mean 'perform some more'; hence (noun) a repetition or extra piece in response to such demand.

Endellion String Quartet, British quartet founded 1979, named after the St Endellion Festival in Cornwall; current members Andrew Watkinson, Ralph de Souza, Garfield Jackson, David Waterman. Has recorded quartets by Barber, Bartók, Britten. Quartet-in-residence, Cambridge University, since 1992, and at the Massachusetts Institute of Technology since 1995.

Enescu, George (1881–1955), Romanian violinist and composer (also pianist and conductor) who used a French form of his name, Georges Enesco. Studied in Vienna, and later in Paris with Fauré and Massenet; afterwards mainly resident in France. Distinguished teacher, e.g. of Menuhin. Works include opera *Oedipus*, five symphonies, two *Romanian Rhapsodies* for orchestra, piano and violin solos.

Enfance du Christ, L' (Fr., 'The Childhood of Christ'), oratorio by Berlioz, first performed in 1854. Words by the composer, after the biblical story, including the Flight into Egypt.

Enfant et les sortilèges, L'

Enfant et les sortilèges, L' (Fr., 'The Child and the Spells'), opera by Ravel, produced in Monte Carlo, 1925. Libretto by Colette: fantasy in which objects of furniture, etc., come to life. ➤swanee whistle.

English Chamber Orchestra, a London chamber orchestra which adopted that name in 1960 (earlier the Goldsbrough Orchestra); it had no regular principal conductor until the appointment of Jeffrey Tate in 1985.

English Concert, ➤Pinnock.

English fingering, ➤fingering.

English guitar, ➤guitar.

English horn, woodwind instrument of oboe type, but standing a fifth lower than the oboe, and written as a ➤transposing instrument a fifth higher than sounding; compass from the E below middle C upwards for about two and a half octaves. Used rarely before the 19th-century Romantics but often thereafter in the orchestra – but still rarely in chamber music, as solo instrument, etc. More usually in Britain called 'cor anglais'; but the translated form 'English horn' is more sensible, is accepted American usage, and corresponds also to use in other languages – Italian *corno inglese*, etc. The Italian name was known before the French and the supposed derivation from *anglé* (angled) is wrong: the instrument seems to be called the French 'horn' because of its original curved shape (different from the modern type) and 'English' possibly because of its development in England – Purcell in ➤*Dioclesian* specifies a 'tenor hoboy', i.e. tenor oboe, though this is apparently a different instrument.

English National Opera, London-based opera company performing in English,

adopting this name in 1974 (➤Sadler's Wells). Musical director 1979–93, Mark Elder, then (1993–5) Siân Edwards; from 1997, Paul Daniel.

English Suite, title of six suites for harpsichord by Bach (BWV 806–11), composed in about 1725 – so called, apparently, because, like Purcell's suites and unlike Bach's own ➤*French Suites*, they have preludes for first movements.

enharmonic, description of the difference between, e.g. F♮ and E♯ or D♯ and E♭ – i.e. on the piano and other fixed-note instruments, a difference only of notation, not of pitch; and on other instruments, and voices, possibly a very small change of pitch also, as may be required to adjust to new harmony. Hence *enharmonic change*, the change of a note in a performer's part, e.g. from D♯ to E♭; and similarly, *enharmonic modulation*, involving such a change, as in the two top notes bracketed here:

Enigma Variations, usual name for Elgar's *Variations on an Original Theme, for Orchestra*, first performed in 1899; the word 'enigma' does not occur on the title-page but heads the actual music-type. Each variation 'portrays' a person identified in the score only by initials or a nickname – in one case by three asterisks. No. 9 ('Nimrod', i.e. a hunter; in German, *Jaeger*) depicts Elgar's friend A. J. Jaeger of Novello's, his publishers; no. 14 (finale), 'E.D.U', which quotes some previous variations, represents the composer himself. The naming of the variations is not the only 'enigma': Elgar said that a well-known tune 'goes with' his theme: it has now been plausibly (but not indisputably) identified as 'Auld lang syne'. ➤Potter.

En Saga, ➤*Saga.*

ensemble (Fr., together) (1) the quality of teamwork in performance ('their ensemble was poor'); (2) an item in opera for several soloists, with or without chorus; (3) a group of performers – the term implying a group of no fixed number, and not so numerous and regularly constituted as to deserve the name of orchestra or choir.

entartete Musik (Ger., 'degenerate music'), term used by the Nazi regime in Germany from the 1930s to identify music considered odious – including jazz, music by Jews, and music by modernists such as Hindemith; the term has been used as a kind of honorific for the revival in the 1990s (especially on record) of some works which had been so denounced.

Entführung aus dem Serail, Die (Ger., 'The Abduction from the Seraglio') (K384), opera by Mozart, produced in Vienna, 1782. Libretto by C. F. Bretzner and G. Stephanie, with a non-singing part for the benevolent Pasha who eventually releases his European captives. In 19th-century England this work was given in Italian under the title *Il seraglio.*

entr'acte (Fr.), interval (US, intermission) in a play, opera, etc., or the music to be played in it (➤act tune; ➤*intermezzo*).

entrée (Fr., entry), sub-division of an act, e.g. in 17th–18th-century French ballet, roughly corresponding to a 'scene' in opera.

Entry of the Little Fauns, orchestral piece by Pierné. ➤*Marche des petits faunes.*

Eötvös, Peter (b. 1944), Hungarian conductor and composer, prominent in conducting new works by Boulez, Stockhausen and Birtwistle. Conductor of Ensemble Intercontemporain, Paris, 1979–91.

epicedium (Latinized form of Gk.), dirge; used by Purcell in *The Queen's Epicedium* (Z383), a Latin elegy for Queen Mary, 1695.

episode, a section in a piece of music considered to have a subordinate role; in particular, (1) in a ➤*rondo*, a contrasting section between recurrences of the main theme; (2) in a ➤*fugue*, a section occurring between entries of the subject.

éponge, (Fr.), sponge; *baguettes d'éponge*, drum-sticks with sponge head.

equali (old It. pl., equal), instrumental pieces for instruments of the same kind, especially funeral pieces for four trombones, e.g. by Beethoven (1812).

equal temperament, ➤temperament.

equal voices, voices of the same kind. (Hence a piece of music 'for equal voices', e.g. for three trebles, as in some school music.) ➤*equali.*

Erb, Donald [James] (b. 1927), American composer (pupil of N. Boulanger in Paris) and teacher. Works include *Fallout* for narrator, chorus, string quartet, piano; many concertos including one for double-bassoon; *In no Strange Land* for tape, trombone, double-bass.

Erbse, Heimo (b. 1924), German composer; also conductor and operatic

131

stage director; pupil of Blacher. Works include two symphonies, ballet score *Ruth*, chamber music.

Erkel, Ferenc (1810–93), Hungarian composer, also pianist and conductor. Wrote *Hunyadi László*, *Bánk Bán*, and other nationalistic Hungarian operas; also many songs, etc.

Erl-King, song by Schubert. ➤*Erlkönig*.

Erlkönig (Ger., 'Erl-King'), song by Schubert (D328), composed in 1815, based on a narrative poem by Goethe depicting Death snatching a child. The title appears to mean 'King of the Alders'.

Ermler, Mark (b. 1932), Russian conductor, active at Bolshoi Theatre, Moscow, from 1956 (conducting both opera and ballet); toured with Bolshoi Opera to USA and elsewhere. Guest conductor of ballet at Covent Garden, 1985, of opera (*Carmen*), 1986.

ernst (Ger.), serious. ➤*Vier ernste Gesänge*.

Ernst, Heinrich Wilhelm (1814–65), Moravian violinist; composer of concertos, etc., for his instrument.

Eroica (1) name given by Beethoven to his Symphony no. 3, 1803–4: 'Heroic Symphony to celebrate the memory of a great man', i.e. Napoleon. To him, as a liberator, the work was originally dedicated, the inscription being altered when Beethoven learnt with scorn that Napoleon had taken the title of Emperor; (2) nickname, not Beethoven's, for his set of piano variations, op. 35, the theme (first used in Beethoven's *Die* ➤*Geschöpfe des Prometheus*) being identical with that of the variation-finale of the *Eroica* Symphony.

Erwartung (Ger., 'Expectation'), a 'monodrama' (i.e. stage piece for one character) by Schoenberg, composed in 1909 but not performed till 1924. In it a woman going to meet her lover finds his dead body.

Eschenbach [originally Ringmann], **Christoph** (b. 1940), German pianist and conductor; prizewinner in international contest, Lucerne, 1962. Henze's Piano Concerto no. 2 was written for him. Made début as conductor in 1972; since 1988, music director of Houston Symphony Orchestra.

Escher, Rudolf (1912–80), Dutch composer (also critic, poet and painter). Works include two symphonies; *Summer Rites at Noon* for two orchestras facing each other; *Songs of Love and Eternity* for chamber choir, based on poems of Emily Dickinson.

Eshpay, Andrey [Yakovlevich] (b. 1925), Russian composer, also pianist. Works include four symphonies, a piano concerto, violin concerto, over 30 film scores.

España (Sp., Spain) (1) orchestral rhapsody by Chabrier, first performed in 1883, making exuberant use of Spanish tunes; (2) title of waltz by Waldteufel.

espansiva (It., expansive), title (*Sinfonia espansiva*) of C. Nielsen's Symphony no. 3, composed 1910–11.

Esplá, Oscar (1886–1976), Spanish composer of ballets, symphonic poems, a violin sonata, many piano works, etc. Lived mainly in Belgium, 1936–51, then returned to Spain; active in promoting modern music.

Esposito, Michele (1855–1929), Italian pianist, conductor and composer of *Irish Symphony*, overture to Shakespeare's *Othello*, chamber music, etc.; long resident in Dublin.

estampie (Fr.), an instrumental form (probably of dance origin) current in the 13th–14th centuries, having between four and seven sections (*puncta*, Lat. pl. of *punctum*) each of which is stated twice – with a different ending the second time.

Esther, oratorio by Handel; words by S. Humphreys, after Racine. Originally done as a masque (i.e. with action and costumes) in private, 1720, with the title *Haman and Mordecai*; expanded and given in concert form in London, 1732, thus becoming the first English oratorio.

estinto (It., extinct), as soft and still as possible.

et (Fr., Lat.), and.

ethnomusicology, the study of musical activity in relation to anthropological background – especially that of non-European cultures.

Etler, Alvin [Derald] (1913–73), American composer, pupil of Hindemith; was also oboist. Works include Concerto for brass quintet with string orchestra and percussion; Concerto for string quartet and orchestra.

Étoile, L' (Fr., 'The Star'), opera by Chabrier produced in Paris, 1877. Libretto by Eugène Leterrier and Albert Vanloo. King Ouf I is deterred from executing Lazuli the pedlar on learning that their astrological destinies are linked.

Eton Choirbook, a large manuscript collection (1490–1502) of church music in Latin, including nine settings

of the ➤Magnificat. The collection was made for and is kept at Eton College.

étouffez (Fr.), damp down, stop the tone, etc. – direction used, e.g., when the sound of a cymbal or harp-string is to be cut short.

étude, ➤study.

etwas (Ger.), moderately, somewhat.

Eugene Onegin, opera by Tchaikovsky. ➤*Yevgeny Onegin*.

euphonium, British name for a brass instrument (mainly used in the brass band and military band), equivalent to the tenor ➤tuba; a ➤transposing instrument in B flat.

eurhythmics, a system of expressing the rhythmical aspects of music by bodily movement, invented by ➤Jaques-Dalcroze, who set up an institute for this in Germany in 1910.

Euridice, title of two of the earliest surviving operas, composed by Caccini and by Peri, both presented in Florence – Peri's in 1600 (with *some* music by Caccini incorporated), Caccini's in 1602; libretto of both by O. Rinuccini, after Ovid's retelling of the story of Orpheus and Eurydice.

Euripides (480–406 BC), Greek dramatist. ➤*Alceste*, ➤*Bassarids*, ➤*Iphigénie en Aulide*, ➤*Iphigénie en Tauride*; ➤Buller, ➤Drysdale.

Euryanthe, opera by Weber, produced in Vienna, 1823. Libretto by H. von Chezy: the medieval heroine, whose reputation for chastity is challenged and vindicated, gives her name to the work.

Evangelista, José (b. 1943), Spanish composer resident in Montreal since 1970; works (variously titled in Spanish, French, Latin and English) include

Piano concertant (piano with full orchestra or with 13 instruments), *Alice and Friends* (text from Lewis Carroll) for voice and four instruments, and *O Bali* (with influence of ➤gamelan) for instrumental ensemble.

Evangelisti, Franco (1926–80), Italian composer who broke off studies in engineering to take up music. His works include *4!* (i.e. mathematical 'factorial four') for violin and piano; *Integrated Fields* (tape); and a theatrical piece with mimes, *Die Schachtel* (Ger., 'The Box').

Evans, Anne (b. 1939), British soprano prominent in Wagner – at Bayreuth Festival (1989–92), Welsh National Opera, Covent Garden, Metropolitan Opera (1992), etc.

Evans, Geraint [Llewellyn] (1922–92), British baritone, chiefly noted in opera (Papageno in *Die Zauberflöte*, title-role of *Wozzeck*, etc.); Covent Garden début, 1948. Latterly also operatic stage director. Knighted, 1969.

Evening and Tempest, name given to one of a set of three symphonies by Haydn. ➤*Morning*.

Evita, musical with text by Tim Rice; music by Andrew Lloyd Webber. Produced in London, 1978. On the political career of the actress Eva Perón (1919–52), wife of the Argentinian dictator Juan Perón.

Ewald, Viktor (1860–1935), Russian professor of civil engineering, an amateur cellist, horn-player and composer: among his chamber works, a brass quintet survives in the repertory.

exercise (1) vocal or instrumental study of no artistic value, e.g. a *five-finger exercise* for piano; (2) in the 18th century, a short keyboard work: D. Scarlatti's early sonatas were published under the Italian equivalent of this name, *Essercizi* (plural); (3) the composition which candidates are obliged to write for certain university degrees in music.

Expectation, 'monodrama' by Schoenberg. ➤*Erwartung*.

exposition (1) that part of a ➤sonata-form or similar movement in which the main themes are initially stated before they undergo ➤development; (2) in a ➤fugue, the initial statement of the subject by all the 'voices' in turn.

expressionism, term borrowed from painting and applied to literature, drama and music – involving the expression of the artist's state of mind by means of external symbols not necessarily in normal relation to each other. (The application of the term, e.g. to Schoenberg's music, alludes apparently to an extreme emotionalism and to a 'hard' sound, supposedly opposite to the ➤impressionism of Debussy's muted, more liquid style.)

Exsultate, jubilate (Lat., 'Exult, rejoice'), title of a solo motet by Mozart (K165), 1773, originally for castrato voice with orchestra; contains a celebrated 'Alleluia'.

extemporize, ➤improvise.

extension organ, ➤unit organ.

extravaganza (It., *stravaganza*, Anglicized), 19th-century English type of stage entertainment with music, in the form of farce or burlesque, often harnessing new words to known tunes.

F

F, note of the scale. So *F* ➤*flat*, *F* ➤*sharp*, semitonally adjacent notes; *F* ➤*major*, *F* ➤*minor*, keys or chords defined by having F as point of stability (➤tonic). So also *in F*, (1, of a composition or part of it) indication that the music belongs in that key (major unless indicated as minor); (2, of a wind instrument) indication of length of air-column which gives F as the fundamental of its harmonic series: the indication usually but not always implies a ➤transposing instrument. So *horn in F* or (colloquially) *F horn*. So also *F clef*, clef indicating the position of the F below middle *C* – the ➤bass clef being now the only such clef used.

F, abbr. for Fellow, in musical diplomas or honours, e.g. FRAM (Fellow of the Royal Academy of Music).

f, symbol in ➤tonic sol-fa notation for the fourth degree (subdominant) of the scale, pronounced 'fah'.

f (lower-case letter), indication of the key of F minor as distinct from capital *F* for F major – a logical but not universal usage.

f, abbr. of *forte* (It., loud); hence, as indications of increasingly greater loudness, *ff*, *fff*, etc. – sometimes in even greater aggregations.

fa, the note F (in Latin countries, and formerly elsewhere); the ➤tonic sol-fa symbol ➤*fah* is derived from it.

faburden (Old Eng.; literally 'false bass'), a style of improvised polyphony particularly associated with 15th-century English vocal music, adding an extra voice or voices above and below a given chant. (The cognate French term ➤*fauxbourdon* has a different meaning.)

Façade, a sequence of settings by Walton for reciter and small instrumental ensemble to poems by Edith Sitwell, first performed publicly in 1923. The selection of numbers (Walton wrote a total of more than 40) varied between this and subsequent performances; 21 settings were 'established' from a revival in 1942 and a further eight were given under the title *Façade 2* in 1977. Meanwhile the music had become well known in two orchestral suites and (1931) a ballet under the same title with choreography by Frederick Ashton.

Fach (Ger., compartment), in operatic context, a type of voice – term distinguishing, say, the type of soprano who sings Wagner's heroines from the type allocated to Mimì in *La* ➤*Bohème*.

facile (Fr., It.), easy. So *facilità* (It.), ease, fluency; also a simplified version, e.g. of a solo passage written for

135

virtuoso performers and now brought within more modest capacities.

fado (Port., fate), type of Portuguese urban folksong, sung with traditional small ensemble including Portuguese ➤guitar; often of a melancholy sentiment. A diminutive form of the term is *fadinho*.

Fagott, fagotto (Ger., It.), ➤bassoon.

fah, in ➤tonic sol-fa, the spoken name for the fourth degree (subdominant) of the scale. Derived from ➤*fa*.

Fair at Sorochintsy, The (Rus., *Sorochintskaya yarmarka*), opera by Musorgsky; libretto by composer, after a rustic story (with faked supernatural happenings) by Gogol. Begun 1874, the opera was left unfinished at Musorgsky's death: and is now performed in the completion made by N. Tcherepnin or that made by Shebalin.

Fairfax, Robert, ➤Fayrfax.

Fair Maid of Perth, The, opera by Bizet. ➤*Jolie Fille de Perth*.

Fair Maid of the Mill, The, song-cycle by Schubert. ➤*Schöne Müllerin*.

Fairy Queen, The, an adaptation of Shakespeare's *A Midsummer Night's Dream*, produced in 1692, for which Purcell wrote the music (Z629).

Fall, Leo (1873–1925), Austrian composer of *Die* ➤*Dollarprinzessin* and other operettas.

Falla, Manuel de (1876–1946), Spanish composer, also pianist. Won first major success with opera *La* ➤*vida breve*, produced in 1913; later wrote ballets *El* ➤*sombrero de tres picos* and *El* ➤*amor brujo*. Much influenced by Spanish folk-music in these and other works – e.g. ➤*Noches en los jardines de España*, and *Fantasia Bética* (i.e. Andalusian Fantasy) for piano; but less so in some other works including puppet opera *El* ➤*retablo de maese Pedro*, and a harpsichord concerto. From 1938 resident in Argentina, where he died: his opera *La Atlántida* ('Atlantis') was completed after his death by E. Halffter.

false relation(s), English term of which the American equivalent is the more sensible – ➤cross-relations.

falsetto (It.), type of vocalization in a 'false' (higher than normal) register, as used by the male ➤alto or ➤counter-tenor voice; it is sometimes specified (generally as comic effect, e.g. imitating women) in other male voices.

falsobordone (It., false drone), type of harmonization of a psalm-tune, usually in four-part block chords; a variety is the ➤Anglican chant. (The cognate French term ➤*fauxbourdon* has a different meaning.)

Falstaff, title of works by several composers, after Shakespeare, including (1) opera by Verdi, produced in Milan, 1893 – libretto by A. Boito, based on *The Merry Wives of Windsor*; (2) symphonic study by Elgar, first performed in 1913 – after *King Henry IV* and *King Henry V*. The subject is also treated in Vaughan Williams's opera *Sir John in Love* and in Nicolai's *Die* ➤*lustigen Weiber von Windsor*.

family, term used to group instruments of similar nature and tone-quality – even if there are significant differences in shape (e.g. the saxophone family) or even if they do not all carry the same name (e.g. the 'violin family' of violin, viola, cello and double-bass).

Fanciulla del West, La (It., 'The Girl of the West'), opera by Puccini, produced in New York, 1910. Known in English as 'The Girl of the Golden West', this being the title of the American play by D. Belasco upon which the Italian libretto was based by G. Civinini and C. Zangarini. Set in California at the time of the Gold Rush.

fancy, term used in England in the 16th–17th centuries for ➤fantasy (2).

fandango (Sp.), Spanish dance in triple time, probably of South American origin; accompanied normally by guitar, castanets, etc.

fanfare (1) a flourish for trumpets (or other instruments imitating them), usually by way of a proclamation or introduction; so *fanfare* ➤*trumpet*, instrument designed for such ceremonial purpose; (2) (Fr.), a brass band.

Fanfare for the Common Man, work for brass and percussion by Copland, 1942 (incorporated into his Symphony no. 3, 1946).

Fanshawe, David [Arthur] (b. 1942), British composer and sound archivist whose extensive travels resulted in *African Sanctus* for chorus and orchestra (with extra African percussion) and other works including *Symphony of the Arabian Gulf*.

fantaisie, fantasia, Fantasie (Fr., It., Ger.), ➤fantasy.

Fantasia on a Theme of Thomas Tallis, work for string quartet and double string orchestra by Vaughan Williams, first performed 1910. ➤Tallis.

Fantasia on British Sea Songs, orchestral pot-pourri by Henry J. Wood, made for the centenary (1905) of the Battle of Trafalgar and now performed on the last night of the Proms in an altered version – a sung version of *Rule, Britannia!* replacing Wood's orchestral original.

Fantasía para un gentilhombre (Sp., 'Fantasia for a gentleman'), work for guitar and orchestra (1954) by Rodrigo.

Fantastic Symphony, symphony by Berlioz. ➤*Symphonie fantastique*.

fantasy (or, borrowed from Italian, *fantasia*), term of various musical meanings, but nearly always associated with the idea of the 'free' play of the composer's imagination, as distinct from adherence to 'set' forms. Notable senses are – (1) a mood-piece or character-piece of a 19th-century Romantic kind, e.g. Schumann's *Fantasy Pieces* (Ger., *Fantasie-Stücke*) for piano, 1837; (2) a contrapuntal piece, normally in several sections, for one player (keyboard) or several (e.g. viols) current in the 16th and 17th centuries; an alternative name in this sense was 'fancy', and the spelling 'phantasy' was used when the form was revived in 20th-century English chamber music; (3) a piece compounded of known tunes; so *fantasy on ...* e.g. an opera, i.e. built from tunes contained in the opera; (4) term used in the phrase *free fantasy* or *free fantasia* as a synonym for ➤development, e.g. in ➤sonata-form.

farandole (Fr.), a dance of Provence, accompanied by pipe and tabor – properly in 6/8 time, which the so-called 'Farandole' in Bizet's *L'*➤*Arlésienne* is not, though it is based on an authentic Provençal tune.

Farewell Symphony, nickname of Haydn's Symphony no. 45 (in the unusual key of F sharp minor), 1772 (Hob. I: 45), in which the music of the last movement ends in such a way that the players may leave their stands one after the other, only two violins eventually remaining. (Or perhaps Haydn, as ➤*continuo*-player at the harpsichord, remained?) This is said to have been a hint to Haydn's patron, Prince Esterházy, that the orchestra deserved a holiday.

Farkas, Ferenc (b. 1905), Hungarian composer – and famous teacher of other Hungarian composers such as Ligeti. His works include *A Gentleman in Venice* and other operas, two masses, *Ricordanze* (It., *Remembrances*) for clarinet and string trio.

Farmer, John (*c.* 1560–?), English organist and composer; moved from a Dublin organistship to London in 1599. Noted for madrigals (contributor to *The* ➤*Triumphs of Oriana*); also wrote psalm-tunes, etc.

Farnaby, Giles (*c.* 1565–1640), English composer, living in London. Wrote music for virginals, including pieces with picturesque titles, e.g. *A Toy, Giles Farnaby's Dream*; also canzonets, madrigals, psalm-tunes.

Farncombe, Charles [Frederick] (b. 1919), British conductor conspicuous from the 1950s in the revival of Handel operas; principal conductor at Drottningholm (the Swedish royal theatre where an 18th-century stage survives), 1970–79.

Farrant, Richard (*c.* 1530–1580 or 1581), English organist (St George's Chapel, Windsor) and composer of anthems and other church music; also of songs for plays which he produced with choirboys.

Farrenc [*née* Dumont], [Jeanne-] **Louise** (1804–75), French composer and pianist. One of her works for piano was praised in print by Schumann; her other compositions include a nonet for wind and strings. She was also a pioneer editor of early music.

farruca, energetic Andalusian dance – used, e.g., by Falla for the Miller's Dance in *El* ➤*amor de tres picos*.

Farwell, Arthur (1872–1952), American composer, champion of an American-based music: wrote fantasia *Dawn* on American Indian themes, *Symphonic Song on 'Old Black Joe'*, etc.

Fasch, Johann Friedrich (1688–1758), German composer of church cantatas, concertos (for violin, oboe, etc.) and other works.

Faschingsschwank aus Wien (Ger., 'Carnival Jest from Vienna'), piano work in five sections by Schumann, 1839, described by him as a 'grand Romantic sonata'.

Fassbaender, Brigitte (b. 1939), German mezzo-soprano, daughter and pupil of the baritone Willi Domgraf-Fassbaender (1897–1978). Member of Munich Opera from 1961, she made her Covent Garden début in 1971; made high reputation as recitalist (retired 1995) and is occasional stage director.

Fauré, Gabriel [Urbain] (1845–1924), French composer (also organist); director of the Paris Conservatoire, 1905–20, teacher of Ravel and others. His notable output in smaller forms includes many piano solos, ➤*Dolly* for piano duet, numerous songs, including *La Bonne Chanson* and other song-cycles; also two piano quartets, and other chamber music. Also wrote a

Requiem; orchestral works including ➤*Pavane* (with optional chorus); *Ballade* for piano and orchestra (originally for piano alone); opera *Pénélope*, incidental music to ➤*Pelléas et Mélisande* and other music for the French and English stage.

Faust, opera by Gounod, produced in Paris, 1859. Libretto by J. Barbier and M. Carré, after Goethe's drama of the philosopher who sells his soul to the Devil in return for earthly gratification. Other works on the Faust legend include *La* ➤*Damnation de Faust*, ➤*Doktor Faust*, ➤*Mefistofele* and Schnittke's opera *Historia von D. Johann Fausten*; see also following entries. Incidental music has also been written to Goethe's play itself, e.g. by Diepenbrock.

Faust, opera by Spohr, produced in Prague, 1816. Libretto by J. K. Bernard – without reference to Goethe's *Faust*, at that time not complete.

'Faust', Episodes from Lenau's, two orchestral works by Liszt, first performed, 1861 – the second is the ➤*Mephisto Waltz*, no. 1. After a German poem on Faust by Lenau.

'Faust', Scenes from Goethe's, concert work by Schumann (overture and six other numbers) for soloists, chorus and orchestra, completed in 1853.

Faust Overture, A, by Wagner, 1839, Wagner's revision (1855), in independent concert form, of an overture he originally wrote (1840) for Goethe's drama.

Faust Symphony, A, symphony by Liszt (with choral ending), after Goethe; first performed in 1857, revised in 1880. In three movements respectively on Faust, Gretchen and Mephistopheles, the final chorus however being non-Mephistophelian.

fauxbourdon (old Fr.), a medieval technique of adding one or more lines in counterpoint to a given chant, as in 15th-century French music. (The cognate English and Italian terms (➤*faburden*, ➤*falsobordone*) refer to a similar but not identical practice.)

Favola d'Orfeo, opera by Monteverdi. ➤*Orfeo*.

Fayrfax, Robert (1464–1521), English composer of motets, Masses and songs; organist of St Albans cathedral. As a member of the Chapel Royal, attended Henry VIII to his meeting with Francis I of France on the Field of the Cloth of Gold, 1520, when the English and French choirs sang together.

feierlich (Ger.), solemnly, exaltedly.

Feld, Jindřich (b. 1925), Czechoslovak composer; university teacher in Australia, 1968–9; head of radio music in Prague since 1990. Works include concertos for violin, cello, saxophone, harp; Concerto da camera for two string quartets.

Feldman, Morton (1926–87), American composer, pupil of Riegger and others, and influenced by association with Cage. Works, often in unusual notation allowing much choice to performers, include *The Swallows of Salangan* for chorus and 23 instruments, *The Viola in My Life* for viola with different co-participants.

Feldpart(h)ie, Feldpartita (Ger.), 'field suite', i.e. suite for open-air performance by a wind band (➤*partita*); Haydn wrote 10, using the form *parthie*.

feminine, term formerly used to denote a subordinate or relatively weak position in a musical structure, as with the 'second subject' in ➤sonata-form. So also *feminine cadence, feminine ending*, in which the final chord is reached on a 'weak' beat of the bar – e.g. the end of 'The Vicar of Bray'. (Where the final chord on a weak beat merely repeats a chord first reached on a strong beat, e.g. at the end of 'What shall we do with the drunken sailor?', the ending still remains 'masculine'.)

Fenby, Eric [William] (1906–97), British composer (overture *Rossini on Ilkla Moor*, etc.), who acted as amanuensis to the blind and paralysed Delius from 1928, taking down some of his late works from dictation. OBE, 1962. Also, latterly, conductor of Delius's works.

Ferencsik, János (1907–84), Hungarian conductor, with Budapest Opera from 1927; also principal conductor of Hungarian State Symphony Orchestra. He made his first London appearance in 1957.

Ferguson, Howard (b. 1908), British composer (piano concerto, octet, etc.), pianist and editor of the complete piano works of Schubert and other keyboard works.

fermata (It.), the ➤pause, ⌢

Fernández, Oscar Lorenzo (1897–1948), Brazilian composer and conservatory director. Works include opera *Malazarte* (Master of the Evil Arts), and other music indebted to Brazilian folklore – e.g. *Batuque* (Brazilian dance) for orchestra; also chamber music, piano solos, songs, etc.

Fernandez, Wilhelmenia [original surname Wiggins] (b. 1949), American soprano celebrated for her acted and sung performance in Berneix's film *Diva* (1981); she had already sung at the Paris Opera and as Bess in *Porgy and Bess* on Broadway.

Ferneyhough, Brian (b. 1943), British composer who moved to Switzerland, 1969, and much of whose music (presenting extreme difficulty in performance) has won prior acceptance outside Britain. Works include *Transit* for chamber orchestra and six amplified solo voices; four string quartets; *Bone Alphabet* for solo percussion; a series of works called *Carceri di invenzione* (It., Dungeons of Invention), *Terrain* for solo violin and ensemble.

Ferrabosco, surname of Italo-English musical family, principally the two following.

Ferrabosco, Alfonso (1543–88), Italian composer of motets, madrigals, etc.; intermittently resident in London, for a time court musician to Elizabeth I, but returning finally to Italy, 1578. Father of the following.

Ferrabosco, Alfonso (c. 1572–1628), English composer of Italian descent (son of preceding); court musician to James I, composer of ayres, fantasies for viols, music for masques, etc.

Ferrier, Kathleen (1912–53), British contralto – noted in recital (Bruno Walter accompanied her), oratorio and opera; many works of Britten, including the title-role of The ➤*Rape of Lucretia*, were written for her. CBE, 1953. Achieved unique reputation, particularly in Britain; died of cancer.

Fesch, William, ➤Defesch.

Festa, Costanzo (c. 1480–1545), Italian composer of madrigals (perhaps the first Italian-born composer of them), and of church music; was a singer in the papal chapel.

Festin de l'araignée, Le (Fr., 'The Spider's Banquet'), ballet with choreography by L. Staats, music by Roussel, first produced in Paris, 1913. (Prompted by Fabre's studies of insect life.)

Festing, Michael Christian (c. 1680–1752), English violinist and composer, pupil of Geminiani, member of the King's band and director of the Italian Opera in London. Wrote cantatas, concertos, sonatas, etc.

Fêtes (Debussy), ➤Nocturnes.

Feuermann, Emanuel (1902–42), Austrian-born cellist who settled in Germany and then, after the Nazi advent, in USA; his outstanding career was cut short by his early death.

Février, Henri (1875–1957), French composer of eight operas (including Gismonda, produced in Paris, 1918), songs, etc.; pupil of Massenet and Fauré. Father of the following.

Février, Jacques (1900–1979), French pianist (son of the preceding), associated with many French composers; dedicatee of Poulenc's Concerto for Two Pianos, of which he and Poulenc gave the first performance in 1932.

ƒ-hole, name given to a hole approximately in the shape of an ƒ, of which there are two cut in the belly of a violin, etc., for the sake of the sound.

Fibich, Zdeněk (1850–1900), Czech composer (also conductor and critic) who studied in Leipzig and Paris. Composed operas, including The Tempest (after Shakespeare) and Šarka; also ➤melodramas (in the technical sense); many piano works; symphonic poems; orchestral piece At Twilight, of which the well-known ➤Poem is a movement.

fiddle (1) colloquial term for the violin still preferred in folk-music, etc., (➤ bluegrass); (2) term for the whole range of small, bowed, non-fretted stringed instruments including not only the violin but also its medieval predecessors such as the rebec, and various folk-instruments; (3) term used to identify particular instruments of this range, e.g. the Norwegian Hardanger fiddle, with its ➤sympathetic strings (➤Tveitt). Thus Mahler's direction, in the Scherzo of his Symphony no. 4, that a solo violin with its strings tuned a tone higher than normal is to play 'like a fiddle' – Ger., wie ein Fidel – refers to the imitation of folk idiom. So also (referring to (1) above) bass fiddle, colloquial term for the double-bass.

Fiddle Fugue, nickname for an organ fugue in D minor by Bach (BWV 539), arranged from an earlier (1720) version for violin solo.

Fiddler on the Roof, musical with text by Joseph Stein based on the stories of Sholom Aleichem; lyrics by Sheldon Harnick; music by Jerry Bock. Produced in New York, 1964. In a Jewish community in Russia, 1905, the patriarchal Tevye the Milkman watches the break-up of his family.

Fidel (Ger.), ➤fiddle.

Fidelio, oder Die eheliche Liebe (Ger., 'Fidelio, or Married Love'), Beethoven's only opera, with libretto by J. Sonnleithner. Produced in Vienna, 1805; revised version, 1806; further-revised version, 1814, with new overture now known as Fidelio. The story of a young wife assuming male guise (as 'Fidelio') to rescue her unjustly imprisoned husband is borrowed from a previous operatic plot (➤Gaveaux).

Field, John (1782–1837), Irish pianist and composer, pupil of Clementi in London; settled in St Petersburg in 1803, toured Europe from there, and died in Moscow. Invented the name and style of the ➤nocturne, taken over by Chopin. His work, admired e.g. by Schumann and Liszt, includes 20 nocturnes for piano, seven piano concertos, and chamber music.

Fielding, Henry (1707–54), British novelist. ➤Tom Jones.

Fiery Angel, The (Rus., *Ognenny Angel*), opera by Prokofiev, composed 1919–27, first staged in Venice, 1955; libretto by the composer, after Bryusov's novel, involves witchcraft and religious hysteria in the 16th century. (The opera is also known as *The Flaming Angel, The Angel of Fire*, etc.)

fife, term historically meaning a kind of high-pitched wooden flute, usually without keys; but the modern military 'drum and fife' band includes low-pitched flutes as well as high ones – none, however, identical with the orchestral flute and piccolo.

fifteenth, organ stop of ➤diapason tone sounding two octaves above the note played – i.e. 15 steps (of the diatonic scale) distant, counting both the extreme notes.

fifth, an interval in melody or harmony, reckoned as taking five steps in the (major or minor) scale – counting the bottom and top notes. A *perfect fifth* is the distance, e.g., from C up to G; a semitone less gives the *diminished fifth* (e.g. C up to G♭), and a semitone more gives the *augmented fifth* (e.g. C up to G♯). ➤consecutive.

'Fifths' Quartet, nickname for Haydn's String Quartet in D minor (no. 2 of op. 76, 1797–8; Hob. III: 76), because of the opening melodic leaps of a fifth. The minuet movement is known as the 'Witches' Minuet' (Ger., *Hexenmenuett*) due to its eerie character.

Figaro, ➤*Barbiere di Siviglia, Le* ➤*Nozze di Figaro*.

Figlia del reggimento, La, title given (in Italian usage) to Donizetti's French opera *La* ➤*Fille du régiment*.

figure, a short musical phrase, especially one that is recognizable and repeated.

figured bass, a standardized notation for ➤*continuo* practised especially in the 17th and 18th centuries, and also used today, e.g. in academic training and as a kind of harmonic shorthand. Figures with a bass-note indicate the distance above that bass-note of the other notes in the chords to be sounded. Thus if the key is C major, and the bass-note is C, the figure 5 would indicate G, and 5♯ would indicate G♯: but the choice of the particular octave in which this G or G♯ is to be placed is left to the musicianship of the performer. Various abbreviations and other conventions are also used. (The ➤chord-symbols used in modern pop music, though similar in being a kind of shorthand, are not the same. They are named after chords – major, minor, augmented, etc. – irrespective of which note of these chords come in the bass; *figured-bass symbols* are invariably relative to a particular bass-note.)

Fille aux cheveux de lin, La (Fr., 'The Girl with the Flaxen Hair'), piano piece by Debussy, included in Book 1 of his *Préludes*, published 1910.

Fille du régiment, La (Fr., 'The Daughter of the Regiment'), opera by Donizetti, produced in Paris, 1840.

Libretto by J. H. V. de Saint-Georges and J. F. A. Bayard; the heroine, brought up as a regimental 'mascot', turns out to be of noble (if illegitimate) parentage.

Fille mal gardée, La (Fr., 'The Unchaperoned Daughter'), ballet with choreography by J. Dauberval (Bordeaux, 1789), with later score by Herold, 1828: a rustic love-affair.

fin (Fr.), end.

final (1, Eng.) the note on which the modal scale ends (➤mode), analogous to the keynote of the major or minor scale; (2, Fr.) ➤*finale*.

finale (It., final; but used in English as follows), (1) the last movement of a work in several movements; (2) an ensemble ending an act of an opera – so *first finale*, second finale etc., referring to Acts I, II, etc.

fine (It.), end – term sometimes occurring in the middle of music as notated, in conjunction with some instruction at the end of the music-type to go back to an earlier point and proceed from there to the point where *fine* occurs.

Fine, Irving (1914–62), American composer, pupil of N. Boulanger in Paris; also conductor. Works include Toccata Concertante for orchestra, Partita for wind quintet.

Fingal's Cave, ➤*Hebrides*.

Finger, Gottfried (or Godfrey) (*c.* 1660–1730), Moravian composer who worked in England under James II's patronage until 1702, then in Germany; wrote operas and other stage music, some of it in English, and various instrumental pieces.

fingerboard, the part of a stringed in-

strument over which the strings are stretched, the player's fingers pressing the strings down to select the length of vibrating string required to produce a particular note.

fingering (1) the use of the fingers in playing an instrument; (2) the indication on paper of which fingers are to be used for which notes – so (in piano-playing) *Continental fingering*, numbering the thumb as 1 and the other fingers as 2–5, as opposed to (obsolete) *English fingering*, in which the thumb was signified by + and the other fingers as 1–4.

Finlandia, orchestral work by Sibelius, first performed in 1900 – of patriotic intent but not using folk-music as material.

Finney, Ross Lee (b. 1906), American composer, pupil of N. Boulanger in Paris and Berg in Vienna; also conductor and university teacher. Works include four symphonies, eight string quartets, and *The Nun's Priest's Tale* (Chaucer) for chorus, solo singers (including folk-singer with electric guitar) and small orchestra.

Finnissy, Michael [Peter] (b. 1946), British composer, also an accomplished pianist who has commissioned pieces from Osborne, J. Weir and others. His works include opera *The Undivine Comedy*, many unusually scored vocal works (*Soda Fountain* for four solo singers and two pairs of cymbals), many piano pieces (in one of which, *Kemp's Morris*, the performer wears morris-dancer's bells).

Finta giardiniera, La (It., 'The Pretended Garden-Maid'), opera by Mozart (aged 18), produced in Munich (in Italian), 1775. Libretto ascribed, uncertainly, to G. Petrosellini, the heroine being a disguised marchioness.

Finzi, Gerald (1901–56), British composer, mainly of vocal works including *Let Us Garlands Bring* (song-cycle to poems by Shakespeare) and ➤*Dies natalis*. Also wrote a clarinet concerto, etc.

fioritura (It., a flowering; pl. *-re*), 'decoration' of a melody by ornaments – sometimes added by the performer, e.g. in 17th- and 18th-century Italian opera.

fipple, the obstructive block of wood which canalizes the air in the instrumental species called the *fipple flute* – of which the chief example is the ➤recorder.

Firebird, The (Rus., *Zhar Ptitsa*), ballet (after a Russian fairy-tale) with choreography by Fokin, music by Stravinsky, produced in Paris, 1910; source of orchestral suite of 1911, and of revised versions of this in 1919 and 1945. ➤Lyadov.

Fireworks Music (otherwise *Music for the Royal Fireworks*), suite by Handel for wind band, performed in 1749 at the official London celebration of the Peace of Aix-la-Chapelle. Afterwards Handel added string parts. The orchestral arrangement by Harty represents a selection.

Firsova, Elena (b. 1950), Russian composer whose music first gained prominence outside USSR and who now lives in Britain. Works include four string quartets; Shakespeare settings for voice and organ; chamber opera *A Feast in Time of Plague* (after Pushkin).

first, term implying in an orchestra (e.g. *first trombone*) a position of leadership as well as (usually) a part higher in pitch; but in a choir (e.g. *first basses*) implying only a higher-pitched part, not leadership. See also following entries.

first inversion, ➤inversion.

first-movement form, term sometimes used for ➤sonata-form.

first subject, ➤sonata-form.

Fischer, Edwin (1886–1960), Swiss pianist, also conductor (and simultaneous conductor-pianist, particularly in Bach); noted teacher, and also writer on music.

Fischer, Friedrich Ernst, ➤Fisher (F.E.).

Fischer, Johann Kaspar Ferdinand (1670–1746), German composer of music for organ (including 20 preludes and fugues in 20 different keys – before Bach's ➤*Wohltemperirte Clavier*) and for harpsichord.

Fischer-Dieskau, Dietrich (b. 1925), German baritone, of unsurpassed authority from the 1950s in recitals of German song (retired 1993); had also a very large operatic repertory. From the 1970s he also occasionally appeared as conductor.

Fišer, Luboš (b. 1935), Czechoslovak composer who emigrated to USA, 1971; works include *Fifteen Prints after Dürer's Apocalypse* for orchestra, *Albert Einstein*, a 'portrait' for organ and orchestra, six piano sonatas.

Fisher, F. E. (full name and dates unknown), a possibly British composer, also violinist and cellist, active in London between 1748 and 1773. Works include trio-sonatas (two violins and keyboard continuo). May be identical with Friedrich Ernst Fischer, a German composer known to have worked in Holland.

Fistoulari, Anatole (1907–95), Russian-born conductor ('prodigy' conductor at seven) who has worked much in England and USA, but served in French army in World War II; much associated with ballet. British citizen from 1948.

Fitelberg, Grzegorz (1879–1953), Polish composer (of a symphony, violin sonatas, etc.), and conductor of Polish Radio Symphony Orchestra; father of Jerzy Fitelberg.

Fitelberg, Jerzy (1903–51), Polish composer of two piano concertos, two violin concertos, five string quartets, etc.; from 1940 resident in USA, dying there. Shows influence of Stravinsky.

Fitzgerald, Edward (1808–83), British poet. ➤Lehmann (Liza).

Fitzwilliam Virginal Book, early 17th-century English collection of 297 pieces for keyboard (➤virginal) by various (mainly English) composers in manuscript; named after Viscount Fitzwilliam (1745–1816), into whose hands it came. Published 1899.

Five, The, ➤*Mighty Handful*.

Flagello, Nicolas [Oreste] (1928–94), American composer, pupil of Pizzetti in Rome; also pianist, violinist, viola-player, oboist. Works include *The Passion of Martin Luther King* for soloists, chorus and orchestra; four piano concertos, *Prisma* for seven horns.

flageolet, obsolete high six-holed wind instrument (similar to recorder but with different arrangement of finger-holes and thumb-holes), used e.g. in Handel's ➤*Rinaldo*; so *double flageolet*, instrument of two such pipes side by side, often seen in 'pastoral' illustrations. The terms *flageolet-notes* (Eng.), *flageolets* (Fr.), *Flageolette* (Ger.), meaning ➤harmonics on a stringed instrument, refer to the supposed resemblance of these thin-sounding notes to those of the flageolet.

Flagstad, Kirsten [Malfrid] (1895–1962), Norwegian dramatic soprano internationally celebrated for stage performances of Wagner's heroines and in recital, particularly in German and Norwegian songs.

flam, two-note figure in side-drum playing, in the rhythm ♫. – either *open flam* or *closed flam* according to whether the first or second note falls on the accented beat.

flamenco (Sp.), type of Spanish, particularly Andalusian, song (*cante flamenco*), with various sub-types named after districts – *malagueña, sevillana*, etc.; often danced to. The term is occasionally borrowed by composers; ➤Peña, ➤Surinach. So also *flamenco style* in guitar-playing, indicating a suitably forceful style different (and with different finger technique) from the 'classical' style; the actual instrument used by specialist *flamenco* players differs slightly from the conventional classical model.

Flaming Angel, The, ➤*Fiery Angel*.

Flanagan, William (1923–69), American composer, also critic. Composed songs, *Narrative* for orchestra, music to plays by Albee (who also collaborated on libretto for Flanagan's one-act opera, *Bartleby*); committed suicide.

flat, term indicating a lowering in pitch – either (1) indeterminately, as when a singer is said to sing flat, by mistake; or (2) precisely by a semitone, as represented by the sign ♭; so 'B♭' (B flat), the note a semitone lower than B♮ (B natural); so also, e.g., C♭ –

a notation which is sometimes called for through adherence to the 'grammar' of music, though on, e.g., the piano the note is identical with B♮ (B natural). So ➤double-flat; flat keys, those having flats in their key-signatures; in three flats, in the key of E♭ major or C minor, the key-signature of which is three flats (and similarly with other keys); flattened seventh (US, flatted seventh), the lowering of the seventh degree of the scale by a semitone.

Flatterzunge (Ger.), flutter-tongue (➤tongue).

Flaubert, Gustave (1821–80), French novelist. ➤Hérodiade.

flautando, flautato (It.), direction to player of the violin, etc., to move the bow over the fingerboard in order to produce a thin, special tone supposedly like that of a flute (It., flauto).

flautist (US, flutist), player of the flute.

flauto (It., pl. -i), flute (in the widest sense). Since the period of Haydn this has meant the ordinary side-blown ➤flute, i.e. the transverse flute (flauto traverso); its small size is the flauto piccolo, or little flute – commonly called ➤piccolo. However, in preceding periods flauto alone may indicate the ➤recorder or other end-blown flute – Bach, for instance, writes flauto traverso in full (or just traverso) when he wants not the recorder but the side-blown flute; similarly flauto piccolo in Bach (the word traverso omitted) is thought to mean a flageolet, the piccolo of modern usage having not yet been invented.

flebile (It.), tearful, plaintive.

Flecker, James Elroy (1884–1915), British poet. ➤Hassan.

Fledermaus, Die (Ger., 'The Bat'), operetta by J. Strauss the younger, produced in Vienna, 1874 – Strauss's most successful stage work. Libretto by C. Haffner and R. Genée: the 'bat' has the flimsiest connection with the plot, being merely the fancy-dress costume used by one of the characters on a previous occasion.

Fleisher, Leon (b. 1928), American pianist (first American to win the Queen Elisabeth Competition in Brussels, 1952) whose career was interrupted when he lost the use of his right hand in 1956. Thereafter he played left-hand concertos as well as conducting, and later attempted to resume playing with both hands.

flexatone, instrument which is a kind of superior version of the 'musical ➤saw'; like the saw, it has a steel blade, which is put under varying tension (by thumb-pressure) to produce different notes, but it is shaken (not bowed) to make it vibrate. Rarely used in the concert-hall before World War II (Schoenberg's Variations for Orchestra being exceptional), but not uncommon in modern composers' large groupings of percussion instruments.

flicorno, name of a family of brass instruments similar to ➤saxhorn family, used in Italian military bands.

Fliegende Holländer, Der (Ger., 'The Flying Dutchman'), opera by Wagner, produced in Dresden, 1843; libretto by composer, about the legendary accursed sailor redeemed by love.

Flies, J. Bernhard, ➤Wiegenlied.

Flight of the Bumble-bee, The, orchestral interlude occurring in Rimsky-

Korsakov's opera *The Legend of Tsar Saltan* (1900), in which a prince turns into a bee and stings his villainous aunts. Has been arranged and misarranged as a virtuoso display for various solo instruments.

Flood, The, 'musical play' by Stravinsky for singers, speakers and orchestra, produced on American television, 1962; text from the York and Chester miracle plays.

florid, term descriptive of melody that is full of ➤ornaments – whether such are written in by the composer or, as common e.g. in 17th- and 18th-century Italian opera, intended to be added at the taste of the performer.

Florodora, musical comedy by 'Owen Hall'; lyrics by Ernest Boyd-Jones and Paul Rubens; music by Leslie Stuart. Produced in London, 1899. Title is that of a Philippine island, the source of a unique perfume, the action moving from there to a Welsh castle.

Flothuis, Marius (b. 1914), Dutch composer, also writer on music. Has written concertos for piano, violin, flute, horn; a string quartet, songs, etc.

Flotow, Friedrich von (1812–83), German composer who studied in Paris, and worked there and in Vienna and elsewhere. Wrote operas in French, Italian and German – the German ones including ➤*Martha* and *Alessandro Stradella* (➤Stradella). Composed also ballets, chamber music, etc.

flourish (1) ➤fanfare; (2) decorative musical figuration.

Floyd, Carlisle (b. 1926), American composer, university teacher; works include operas ➤*Susannah*, *Wuthering Heights*, *The Passion of Jonathan Wade*,

Markheim and *Of Mice and Men*; piano pieces, etc.

flue-pipe, organ pipe into which the air is made to enter directly, as into a flute or recorder (not striking a vibrant tongue or ➤reed, as in a reed-pipe).

Flügel (Ger., wing), a grand piano (i.e. a wing-shaped piano) or a harpsichord so shaped.

flugelhorn, type of brass instrument with valves, made in various sizes. (Properly *Flügelhorn*, in German, but in British brass-band usage spelt and pronounced with simple 'u'.) The one used in British brass bands is the alto in B♭, having the same compass as the cornet in B♭; not commonly found in other types of musical combination, but one is used in Stravinsky's ➤*Threni* and in Vaughan Williams's Ninth Symphony.

flute (1) general name for various types of woodwind instruments without reeds, including nose-blown and other primitive instruments; *English flute, German flute*, old English names for the vertical-blown and cross-blown instruments now respectively called ➤recorder and simply 'flute' – see next definition; (2) specifically, the type of cross-blown woodwind instrument (see preceding definition) coming into standard use in the 16th century and mechanically improved since then (now usually made of metal, not wood); used in the orchestra and military band, also occasionally as solo instrument and in chamber music. Compass from middle C upwards for about three octaves. Other sizes of this instrument in current use are (a) the ➤*piccolo*; (b) the various sizes used in a military 'drum and fife' band; (c) the *alto flute*, pitched a fourth or fifth lower than the standard instrument, and sometimes miscalled the *bass flute* – specified in some works by e.g. Ravel and Stravinsky, and functioning as a ➤transposing instrument in G. A true bass flute, an octave below the standard instrument, has also been made since 1910 but is not used in the standard orchestra.

flûte-à-bec (Fr., beaked flute) ➤recorder.

flutter-tongue, ➤tongue.

Flying Dutchman, The, opera by Wagner. ➤*Fliegende Holländer*.

Foerster, Josef Bohuslav (1859–1951), Czech composer who worked for some time in Hamburg and Vienna; also critic. Composed Masses, religious cantatas, a biblical opera; also other operas (one based on *The Merchant of Venice*), five symphonies, songs and choral works.

Fokin(e), Mikhail Mikhailovich (1880–1942), Russian choreographer. ➤*Daphnis et Chloé*, ➤*Firebird*, ➤*Aufforderung zum Tanz*, ➤*Sylphides*.

Folía, La (Sp., also *La follia*, It.), the name originally of a dance ('The Folly') of Portuguese origin, and hence the name of a particular tune used for the dance. This tune enjoyed an extraordinarily wide currency during the 16th–18th centuries, more especially as the subject of variations – e.g. by Corelli, Geminiani, A. Scarlatti.

folk-music, -song, -tune, terms implying that the work concerned has been transmitted aurally among 'the people' from one generation to the next, and can be ascribed to no particular composer. As this definition suggests, (1) a folk-song must be, or

have been, 'popular', but not every 'popular' song is a folk-song; (2) folk-song has special relevance to a 'primitive' population or to a depressed class, where music does not generally take a written form; (3) because of aural transmission, a folk-song is likely to exist in several differing versions. Folk-song, although 'national' in character, has tended to show wide international similarities: in particular it has preserved the ➤modes longer than normal 'composed' music. But it is arguable that certain 'composed' and written-down songs, e.g. Stephen Foster's, have in a sense become folk-songs – i.e. they have been transmitted aurally, they circulate in several versions, and the composer's name is unknown to many who know the songs. Note that (1) the above definition of folk-songs, etc., does not necessarily coincide with the use of parallel words in other languages: e.g. *Volkslied* (Ger.) takes in a wider variety of traditional popular song; (2) the post-1945 revival of what is called 'folk' admits many new songs (in traditional style) by named composers, who are often performers also.

Fontane di Roma (It., 'Fountains of Rome'), an orchestral work by Respighi in four sections each 'depicting' a different fountain; first performed 1917. ➤*Pini di Roma*.

foot, unit of length used to measure the length of a vibrating air-column: hence, a measure of pitch – because, e.g., an air-column eight feet long vibrates twice as fast as an air-column 16 feet long, and so sends out a note one octave higher. So also *eight-foot C*, the C two lines below the bass stave, sounded by a vibrating air-column (e.g. an open organ-pipe) approximately eight feet long; *16-foot C*, the C below this; *four-foot C*, the C above eight-foot C, and onwards in proportion. So organ stops are classified by what sound will issue if the note representing *eight-foot* C is struck. An *eight-foot stop* will sound the note itself; a *16-foot stop* will sound the note an octave below, a *32-foot stop* the note two octaves below; a *four-, two-, one-foot* stop will sound the note one octave, two octaves, three octaves, respectively above eight-foot C. These stops will have similar effects on all other notes, and thus by simultaneous use of several stops the player can sound a melody in various octaves at choice. (This terminology is sometimes used, by analogy, of other instruments, as when a double-bass is said to provide '16-foot tone' to a cello part, i.e. doubling the cello part an octave below.)

Foote, Arthur William (1853–1937), American organist and composer of cantatas (one on Longfellow's *Hiawatha*), orchestral suites, organ and piano works, etc. Also teacher and writer of textbooks.

Force of Destiny, The, opera by Verdi. ➤*Forza del destino*.

Ford, Thomas (*c.* 1580–1648), English lutenist and composer of ayres (with lute), madrigals, anthems, dances, etc.; musician to Charles I.

Forelle, Die (Ger., 'The Trout'), song by Schubert (D550), composed 1817. Hence the nickname ➤*Trout Quintet* for a chamber work in which one movement presents variations on that song.

forlana, forlane (It., Fr.), old Italian dance in 6/8 time.

form, the layout of a piece of music

considered as a succession of sections. A simple song may thus be said to have a *form* consisting of, say, one line, another line, the first line repeated, then another line; while a more involved piece may be said to have a *form* corresponding to one of various basic types – see, e.g., ➤*binary*, ➤*ternary*, ➤*fugue*, ➤*passacaglia*, ➤*rondo*, ➤*sonata-form*, ➤*variations*; or such a piece may be said to be 'free' in form, i.e. unrelated to such a 'set' type. Note that *form* as thus conventionally defined takes in only the 'horizontal' aspects of music and not the 'vertical' (harmony, counterpoint), and does not fully deal with rhythm; it would be better (and more analogous to terminology in, e.g., painting) if *form* were to be defined as taking in these also, i.e. as concerned with the totality of significant relationships between notes.

formalism, a supposed fault in composition for which Russian composers – Prokofiev and Shostakovich, among others – were denounced by Soviet officialdom in 1948; the implication is that the music concerned was deficient in communicative content, over-emphasizing 'form'. There was usually an added implication that the music was over-discordant and uncritically pursued modernity for its own sake.

Forqueray, Antoine (1671–1745). French bass-viol player, chamber musician to Louis XIV, and composer. His son Jean-Baptiste-[Antoine] (1699–1782) was also a bass-viol player and composer.

Forster, E. M. [Edward Morgan] (1879–1970), British novelist. ➤*Billy Budd*.

forte, fortissimo (It.), loud, very loud

(abbr. *f. ff*; quite commonly *fff* and even greater aggregations are used to indicate still greater loudness).

fortepiano, an early Italian name meaning the same as ➤pianoforte; in modern usage arbitrarily restricted to the early types of piano (up to Beethoven's time), wooden-framed and shallower in tone than the modern type. (*Fortepiano* is, however, the standard Russian word for the normal instrument.)

Fortner, Wolfgang (1907–87), German composer (also conductor and teacher). Works include Lutheran church music: *Isaaks Opferung* ('The Sacrifice of Isaac') (for three voices and 40 solo instruments including 'jazz trumpets' and 'jazz trombones'); concertos for various instruments; organ works; opera *Bluthochzeit* (after Lorca's *Blood Wedding*).

'Forty-Eight, The', or *Forty-Eight Preludes and Fugues*, ➤*Wohltemperirte Clavier*.

Forza del destino, La (It., 'The Force of Destiny'), opera by Verdi, produced (in Italian) at St Petersburg, 1862. Libretto by F. M. Piave – a tale of revenge in 18th-century Spain and Italy.

Foss (originally Fuchs) **Lukas** (b. 1922), German-born American composer, also pianist and conductor. Works include opera *The Jumping Frog of Calaveras County* (after Mark Twain), two piano concertos, *Curriculum Vitae with Time Bomb* for accordion and percussion.

Foster, Stephen [Collins] (1826–64), American composer, almost entirely self-taught. Composed mainly songs to his own words, including 'The Old Folks at Home', 'Camptown Races'

and other 'plantation songs' (i.e. of the black-faced minstrel-show type) which became among the world's best-known songs – often with some alteration of the original tunes; also 'drawing-room' songs, e.g. 'Jeanie with the Light Brown Hair'. Died poor and an alcoholic.

Foulds, John [Herbert] (1880–1939), British composer of large vocal-orchestral *World Requiem* (première 1923), many orchestral and piano works, etc.; studied Indian music, in 1939 taking radio music post in Calcutta, and died of cholera there. His music awaits revival.

Fountains of Rome, orchestral work by Respighi. ➤*Fontane di Roma*.

Four Boors, The, opera by Wolf-Ferrari. ➤*Quatro rusteghi*.

four-foot (organ stop, etc.), ➤foot.

Four Last Songs, set of songs by R. Strauss. ➤*Vier letzte Lieder*.

Fournier, Pierre (1906–86), French cellist, internationally prominent as soloist (giving first performances of works by F. Martin and Poulenc) and in chamber music; latterly resident in Switzerland.

Four Saints in Three Acts, opera (in four acts) by V. Thomson, produced in Hartford, Conn., 1934, with an all-black cast. Libretto by Gertrude Stein, with saints (far more than four) and without normal 'plot'.

Four Seasons, The, set of violin concertos by Vivaldi. ➤*Quattro stagioni*.

Four Serious Songs, song-cycle by Brahms. ➤*Vier ernste Gesänge*.

Four Temperaments, The (1) title of Symphony no. 2, 1902, by C. Nielsen

(Dan., *De fire temperamenter*), each of the 'temperaments' having one movement; (2) title of Hindemith's Theme and Variations for piano and strings, 1940, each 'temperament' taking charge for one variation; (3) work for brass band, 1982, by R. Simpson. (The reference is to the types of 'temperament' – choleric, phlegmatic, melancholic, sanguine – thought in medieval times to be the dominant factor in a person's character.)

fourth, an interval in melody or harmony reckoned as taking four steps in the (major or minor) scale, counting the bottom and top notes. Hence *perfect fourth*, the distance, e.g., from C up to F; one semitone more gives the *augmented fourth*, e.g. C up to F♯. The *diminished fourth*, one semitone less than the perfect, is little used, being virtually equivalent – e.g. on the piano – to the major ➤*third*: but it was included, as F♯–B♭, in the so-called 'mystic chord' which Skryabin compounded entirely of various fourths.

Fowler, Jennifer (b. 1939), Australian composer, resident in Britain since 1969. Works for unusual vocal and instrumental combinations include *Lament* for baroque oboe and bass viol and *We call to you, brother* for flute, English horn, cello, two trombones, percussion, didjeridu.

Fox, Virgil [Keel] (1912–80), American organist, whose concerts with lighting effects drew massive audiences to a classical repertory.

fractional tone, ➤microtone.

Fra Diavolo, ou L'Hôtel de Terracine (Fr., 'Fra Diavolo, or The Inn at Terracina'), opera by Auber, produced in Paris, 1830. Fra Diavolo (It., 'Brother Devil') is a character modelled on a celebrated Italian brigand and renegade monk.

Françaix, Jean (b. 1912), French composer (also pianist), pupil of N. Boulanger and others; had a piano suite published at age nine. Works include a piano concertino (1934) and concerto (1936); a symphony for strings; *Beach* and other music for ballet; Serenade for 12 instruments (also used as ballet with title *À la Françaix*, with choreography by Balanchine), chamber music; operas.

Francesca da Rimini (1) 'symphonic fantasy' by Tchaikovsky, first performed in 1877 – after Dante, who narrates her tragic love for Paolo and her fate in hell (Tchaikovsky originally intended an opera on this subject), (2) title of operas on this subject by Goetz, Rakhmaninov, Zandonai and others.

Francescatti, Zino (originally René-Charles) (1902–91), French violinist (father Italian-born); made public appearances from age five, performing in Britain with Ravel as pianist, 1926. Eminent concerto-player and recitalist.

Francis of Assisi, St (?1181–1226), ➤*Saint François d'Assise*; ➤Spies.

Franck, César [Auguste] (1822–90), Belgian composer, son of a German mother; studied at Paris Conservatory and settled in Paris in 1844. Was also organist (eventually at the church of Ste Clotilde, Paris) and noted teacher. Exponent of cyclic form (use of the same theme in more than one movement or section of a work), e.g. in symphony, Symphonic Variations for piano and orchestra, violin sonata. Also composed *Le Chasseur maudit*

('*The Accursed Huntsman*') and other symphonic poems; a piano quintet and other chamber music; piano and organ works; many songs; religious cantatas including *Les Béatitudes*; four operas (not performed in his lifetime).

Franck, Melchior (*c.* 1580–1639), German composer of church music, dance music for instrumental ensembles, etc.

Francœur, François (1698–1787), French violinist, court musician and composer of operas, ballets, violin sonatas, etc.

Frankel, Benjamin (1906–73), British composer whose works include several with Jewish allusions, e.g. violin concerto in memory of 'the six million', i.e. Jews whose deaths were caused by the Nazis; also eight symphonies and a posthumously performed opera *Marching Song*, etc.

Frankenstein!!, work designated a 'pan-daemonium' by H. K. Gruber for 'baritone-chansonnier' (in many performances the composer himself) with orchestra using both normal and toy instruments, with text after children's rhymes by H. C. Artmann; first performed 1978.

Franz, Robert (pen-name of Robert Franz Knauth) (1815–92), German composer, chiefly of more than 250 songs – also of church music, etc. Through deafness and a nervous disease, ceased to compose in 1868.

Fraser-Simson, Harold (1878–1944), British composer of musical comedy *The ➤Maid of the Mountains*, children's songs to A. A. Milne's poems, etc.

Frauenliebe und -leben (Ger., 'Woman's Love and Life'), song-cycle by Schumann, 1840, to eight poems by Chamisso – male poet proclaiming woman's adoring submission.

Frau ohne Schatten, Die (Ger., 'The Woman without a ` Shadow'), opera by R. Strauss, produced in Vienna, 1919. Libretto by H. von Hofmannsthal – legendary tale in which the Empress's lack of shadow symbolizes her barrenness.

Frederick the Great [Friedrich II] (1712–86), King of Prussia, amateur flautist (taught by ➤Quantz) and composer – especially of music with prominent flute parts. While C. P. E. Bach was in his service, J. S. Bach visited him in 1747 and later dedicated to him *Das ➤musikalisches Opfer*.

free-bass accordion, ➤accordion.

free counterpoint, ➤counterpoint.

Freedman, Harry (b. 1922), Polish-born Canadian composer; also oboist and jazz clarinettist. Works include *Tangents* for orchestra, ballet *Rose Latulippe*, and *Rhymes from the Nursery* for children's choir.

free fantasia, name sometimes given to the ➤development section of a movement, e.g. in ➤sonata-form.

Freischütz, Der (Ger., 'The Marksman with Magic Bullets'), opera by Weber, produced in Berlin, 1821, with libretto by F. Kind; the rustic hero is involved in black magic.

French horn, ➤horn.

French overture, ➤overture.

French sixth, type of 'augmented sixth' chord (➤augmented) distinguished by the intermediate intervals of the chord – e.g. (reading upwards) D♭, F, G, B. (The reason for this naming, and similarly with ➤German sixth, ➤Italian sixth, is not known.)

French Suite, title given to each of six suites for harpsichord by Bach, composed about 1722 (BWV 812–17); unlike Bach's ➤*English Suites* they have no preludes, but the supposition that they represent a characteristically French style has not been universally accepted.

Freni, Mirella [surname originally Fregni] (b. 1935), Italian soprano particularly noted in lighter-voiced roles such as Micaela in *Carmen*; made her Glyndebourne début 1966 as Zerlina in *Don Giovanni*. Is now also stage director.

frequency, term in acoustics for the number of complete vibrations undergone by an air-column or a resonating body in one second. The unit of measurement (one cycle per second) is the Hertz, abbreviated Hz. As frequency increases, the pitch of the note sounded is raised, so ➤pitch can be defined by frequency; by international agreement, 1939, the A commonly used for tuning (i.e. that above middle C) is fixed at 440 Hz.

Frescobaldi, Girolamo (1583–1643), Italian composer and organist – at Antwerp, then (1608–28) at St Peter's, Rome, where a presumably over-enthusiastic chronicler reports an audience of 30,000 listening to him. Wrote toccatas, fugues, ricercari, etc., for organ and harpsichord, influencing German and other music; also motets, madrigals, etc.

fret, name given to each of the strips of wood or metal fixed on the fingerboard of, e.g., a guitar, viol, lute (but not the violin family). The player presses the finger against a fret to shorten the length of string vibrating. So *fretted* instruments, those fitted with frets.

fretta (It.), haste; *non in fretta*, not hurrying the pace. Hence ➤*affrettando*.

Frick, Gottlob (1906–94), German bass, well known in Wagner's operas, with international career – Covent Garden 1951, Metropolitan Opera 1962.

Fricker, Peter Racine (1920–90), British composer, from 1964 resident in California as university professor. Works include five symphonies (no. 5 with organ); two violin concertos; four string quartets; a wind quintet; songs and piano works.

friction drum, ➤drum.

Friedman, Ignaz (1882–1948), Polish-born pianist of world-wide celebrity, said to have given 2,800 concerts; settled in Sydney, 1940.

Friml, Rudolf (1879–1972), Czech composer who settled in USA, 1906, and won success with ➤*Rose Marie* and other musical plays; also composer of a piano concerto, etc., and himself a pianist.

Froberger, Johann Jacob (1616–67), German organist and composer for organ and harpsichord; pupil of Frescobaldi; visited England, 1622.

frog, US equivalent of British ➤nut, from Ger. *Frosch*.

'Frog' Quartet, nickname of Haydn's String Quartet in D (Hob. III: 49, also known as op. 50, no. 6), 1787, with a 'croaking' theme in the finale.

From a House of the Dead (Cz., *Z Mrtvého domu*), opera by Janáček, produced in Brno (posthumously), 1930;

text by composer, after Dostoyevsky's novel of a Siberian prison-camp. (Also known as *From the House of the Dead*, the Czech language having no definite or indefinite article.)

From Bohemian Fields and Groves, ➤*My Country*.

From Jewish Folk Poetry (Rus., *Iz evreyskoy narodnoy poezy*), song-cycle by Shostakovich for soprano, contralto, tenor and piano, 1948, on texts translated from Yiddish; barred (because of Stalin's anti-Jewish policies) from performance until 1955. The accompaniment was orchestrated by the composer in 1964.

From My Life (Cz., *Z mého života*), subtitle of the first of Smetana's two string quartets; in E minor, 1876. The high E in the finale depicts 'the fatal whistling in my ear in the highest register which in 1874 announced my deafness'. The quartet has been arranged for full orchestra by G. Szell – first performed in 1941 in this version.

From the New World (Cz., *Z nového svéta*), subtitle of Dvořák's Symphony in E minor, composed in USA and first performed in New York, 1893; no. 9, but formerly called 'no. 5' (as explained under ➤Dvořák). Some of its tunes allude to idioms of US black folk-music, but without any direct quotation.

frottola (It., pl. *-e*), light Italian song for several voices with the melody at the top, flourishing about 1500; set to poems of varying metres, of which successive stanzas were sung to repetitions of the same music.

Frühbeck de Burgos, Rafael (b. 1933). Spanish conductor of German parentage (surname properly Frühbeck; 'de Burgos' an addition from his birthplace). Conductor of Spanish National Orchestra, 1962–78, and (concurrently) of Montreal Symphony Orchestra 1975–7; principal conductor of Vienna Symphony Orchestra since 1991 and of the Deutsche Oper, Berlin, since 1992.

Frumerie, [Per] **Gunnar** [Fredrik] **de** (1908–87), Swedish pianist and composer; works include Symphonic Variations (on a Swedish folk-tune), two piano concertos, two violin concertos, opera *Singoalla*; piano solos. Sometimes wrote in classic dance-forms – saraband, etc.

Fry, Christopher (b. 1907), British poet and playwright. ➤*Paradise Lost*.

Fry, William Henry (1813–64), American composer – opera *Leonora*, 1845, sometimes called the first notable American opera. (It is unconnected with the plot of ➤*Fidelio*.) Also a critic.

Frye, Walter (d. before 1475), English composer active in London from 1457 and then apparently attached to the court of Burgundy; works include Masses and a motet *Ave coelorum regina* quoted by other composers.

fuga, Fuge (It., Ger.), ➤fugue. (The original Italian word means 'flight'.)

fugato (It.), literally 'fugued', i.e. suggestive of the style of ➤fugue though not actually constituting a fugue.

fughetta (It.), a little ➤fugue.

fugue, a type of contrapuntal composition for a given number of ➤parts or 'voices' (so called, whether the work is vocal or instrumental), hence *fugue in three voices, a four-part fugue*, etc. The essential feature of a fugue is the entries of all the voices successively in ➤imitation of each other. The opening entry is in the tonic key and is called the 'subject': the imitative entry of the next voice, in the dominant, is called the ➤'answer'; similarly with the entries of subsequent voices (if any) alternately. Commonly there are several complete entries of all voices (with the order changed) in the course or a fugue; the complete entries are separated by 'episodes'. Commonly also each voice having announced the subject or answer passes to another fixed thematic element called the 'counter-subject' – the counter-subject being heard in the first voice simultaneously with the answer in the second voice, etc. But the great masters of fugue such as Bach (e.g. ➤*Kunst der Fuge*, ➤*Wohltemperirte Clavier*) do not confine the fugue to a strict pattern, though time-wasting academic theorists have done so.

fuguing tune, type of 18th-century American hymn-tune, practised and perhaps originated by Billings – in which there is occasional primitive ➤imitation between parts.

Fuleihan, Anis (1900–1970), Cyprus-born American composer; settled in USA, 1914. Also pianist and conductor. Works include a two-piano concerto; concerto for ➤theremin; *Three Cyprus Serenades* for orchestra; ballet scores; chamber works; songs in English and French. After World War II, became director of the Beirut (Lebanon) Conservatory.

Fulkerson, James [Orville] (b. 1945), American composer, also virtuoso of the trombone who has had more than 150 works written for him. Has written much for modern dance, e.g. *Put your foot down, Charlie* (with speaker). Other works, often with electronics, include *Chord* for any voices or instruments, *Bombs* for bass trombone and piano.

full anthem, anthem (in the Anglican Church) sung by the full choir throughout, without soloists.

full orchestra, an orchestra with the four usual sections (strings, woodwind, brass, percussion) and of normal concert-hall strength.

full organ, direction that the organ should be played at full strength. Owing to the construction of the instrument and of the human ear, this does not necessarily imply the use of all the stops.

full score, ➤score.

fundamental, fundamental note, the primary or 'parent' note of the ➤harmonic series.

funebre, funèbre (It., Fr.), of a funeral. *So marcia funebre, marche funèbre*, funeral march.

Funeral March of a Marionette, humorous piece by Gounod, published (in London under English title) for piano 1872, in orchestral version 1879.

'Funeral March' Sonata, nickname for Chopin's Piano Sonata in B♭ minor, completed in 1839, having a funeral march as its third movement.

fuoco (It.), fire; *con fuoco*, with fire.

für (Ger.), for.

furiant (Cz.), quick dance with changing rhythms – though some of Dvořák's movements so entitled do not change in rhythm. (The word is not connected with 'fury'.)

furniture, type of ➤mixture stop on the organ.

Furtwängler, Wilhelm (1886–1954), German orchestral and operatic conductor, achieving eminence with Berlin Philharmonic and Vienna Philharmonic Orchestras, and making first London appearance in 1924. Accusations of Nazi complicity muted his post-1945 activities. Also composer of three symphonies, etc.

Futurism, attempt, particularly by the Italian poet Marinetti and by Russolo, at 'a great renovation of music through the Art of Noises' – first mooted in 1909 and persisting in Italy at least until the 1920s. Special 'noise instruments' (e.g. exploders, thunderers and whistlers) were invented, composed for, and performed on.

Fux, Johann Joseph (1660–1741), Austrian composer of 18 operas, much church music, etc.; organist; especially known as theorist and author of a highly influential treatise on counterpoint called ➤*Gradus ad Parnassum*.

fz (abbr. of It., *forzando*, forcing), less frequently encountered equivalent of *sf* (➤*sforzando*).

G

G, note of the scale. So *G* ➤*flat*, *G* ➤*sharp*, semitonally adjacent notes; *G* ➤*major*, *G* ➤*minor*, keys or chords defined by having G as point of stability (➤tonic). So also *in G*, (1, of a composition or part of it) indication that the music belongs in that key (major unless indicated as minor); (2, of a wind instrument) indication of length of air-column which gives G as the fundamental of its harmonic series: the indication usually but not always implies a ➤transposing instrument, as in *alto flute in G*. So also *G clef*, clef indicating the position of G above middle C, i.e. the ➤treble clef; *G-string*, string of an instrument tuned to the note G, especially the lowest string of a violin, as in the nicknamed title *Air on the G string* (➤air).

G, abbr. for Graduate (in musical diplomas, e.g. GRSM – Graduate of the Royal Schools of Music).

g (lower-case letter), indication of the key of G minor as distinct from capital G for G major – a logical but not universal usage.

Gabrieli, Andrea (*c.* 1510–86), Italian composer, pupil of Willaert at St Mark's, Venice, where he later became chief organist. Works include motets, madrigals, organ pieces. Pupils included Giovanni Gabrieli (his nephew).

Gabrieli, Giovanni (*c.* 1556–1612), Italian composer, pupil of his uncle (Andrea Gabrieli) whom he succeeded as chief organist of St Mark's, Venice, 1585. Works include *Symphoniae sacrae* (Lat., 'Sacred Symphonies') and other church music for voices with instruments, often using antiphonal groups; music for instrumental ensembles; organ works. Teacher of Schütz.

Gaburo, Kenneth [Louis] (1926–93), American composer who studied in Italy with Petrassi; also teacher (in California, 1968–75) and founder of his own choral group cultivating audience-participation, etc. Works include viola concerto, *Circumcision* for three groups of male voices, *The Flow of E* based on the synthesized sound of the vowel and its electronic transformation.

Gade, Niels Vilhelm (1817–90), Danish composer (opera, choral works, eight symphonies, overture *Echoes from Ossian*, etc.) and conductor. Studied at Leipzig and was much influenced by Mendelssohn.

gagaku (Jap.), the orchestral music traditionally associated (since the eighth century) with the Japanese court, using wind, strings and percussion.

Gagliano, Marco da (1582–1643), Italian composer, also priest. Wrote *Dafne* and other operas, as well as church music, etc.

gaillard (Fr.), ➤galliard.

Gaîté parisienne, ballet for which Manuel Rosenthal arranged music from Offenbach; choreography by Massine, using some characters from *La* ➤*Vie parisienne*.

Gál, Hans (1890–1987), Austrian-born composer and musicologist resident in Scotland from 1938; lecturer at Edinburgh University, 1945. Works include four symphonies and *Lilliburlero: Improvisation on a Martial Melody* for orchestra. OBE, 1964.

galant (Fr.), 'courtly' – term used of a mid-18th-century style distinguished by formal elegance and clarity (rather than by intense feeling), as found e.g. in J. C. Bach, influencing Mozart.

Galantieren, galanteries (Ger., Fr.), in the classical suite, those numbers (e.g. minuet, polonaise) whose inclusion was optional, not obligatory.

Galilei, Vincenzo (*c.* 1520–1591), Italian composer of vocal and instrumental music; lutenist; musical theorist; contributor to the current of ideas from which opera eventually resulted. Father of the astronomer Galileo Galilei.

galliard, lively dance at least as old as the 15th century, usually but not always in 3/2 time; often contrasted with, and sometimes built from the same musical material as, a ➤pavan (which is slower); obsolete, but revived e.g. by Vaughan Williams in ➤*Job*.

Galli-Curci, Amelita (1882–1963), Italian soprano, prominent in opera in Chicago (from 1916) and New York; recordings of her coloratura singing won wide fame.

galop, a 19th-century ballroom dance in quick 2/4 time.

Galuppi, Baldassare (1706–85), Italian composer, chiefly of operas, but also of harpsichord sonatas, etc. Visited London and St Petersburg; in service at St Mark's, Venice, from 1748. (Robert Browning's poem 'A Toccata of Galuppi's' refers to him; but the exact work is unidentified, if not imaginary.)

Galway, James (b. 1939), British flautist, the most celebrated woodwind soloist of his generation; Rodrigo and other composers wrote for him. OBE, 1977.

gamba (It., leg), (1) abbr. for *viola da gamba* (➤viol); (2) organ stop imitating this instrument's tone.

gamelan, Indonesian instrumental ensemble in which sets of tuned gongs, other metallophones and also drums are prominent; according to usage (the Javanese differing from the Balinese), other instruments and voices are also found. Some modern Western composers (➤Harrison, ➤Leeuw) have written works for it.

gamme (Fr.), scale.

gamut (1) compass, range (also metaphorically); (2, various obsolete senses) the G at the bottom of the bass clef; the written system of ➤hexachords; the musical scale.

ganz (Ger.), whole, complete(ly); hence *Ganze*, abbreviation of ➤*Ganzetaktnote*.

Ganzetaktnote (Ger.), ➤whole-note, semibreve – literally meaning a note lasting a whole bar or measure.

gapped, (of a scale) having some intervals of more than a tone's distance, unlike the normal major or minor scales; e.g. the ➤pentatonic scale.

García, Manuel [del Populo Vicente Rodríguez] (1775–1832), Spanish tenor for whom Rossini wrote the role of Almaviva in *Il barbiere di Siviglia*. His opera company toured to USA and Mexico, 1825–8. The singers Maria Malibran and Pauline Viardot-Garcia were his daughters.

Gardelli, Lamberto (b. 1915), Italian-born conductor (also composer) who conducted opera in Sweden, 1946–55, and took Swedish nationality; London appearances from 1966; music director, Budapest Opera since 1961.

Garden, Mary (1874–1967), American (Scottish-born) soprano, famous as the first Mélisande in Debussy's ➤*Pelléas et Mélisande*, 1912; later director of the Chicago Civic Opera.

Gardiner, H. [Henry] **Balfour** (1877–1950), British composer who trained in Germany. Composed little, but works include *Shepherd Fennel's Dance* (after T. Hardy) for orchestra, piano pieces. Noted for promoting and financing performances of music by other British composers. See following entry.

Gardiner, John Eliot (b. 1943), British conductor, great-nephew of the preceding. Founder of the Monteverdi Choir, 1964; of the Orchestre Révolutionnaire et Romantique, 1990. Conductor of the Lyons Opera, 1983–8; of North German Radio Symphony Orchestra, 1991. Knighted 1998.

Gardner, John [Linton] (b. 1917), British composer, formerly teacher at Royal Academy of Music. Works include three symphonies; operas *The Moon and Sixpence* and *The Visitors*; church music. CBE, 1976.

Garrett, Lesley (b. 1955), British soprano, prominent member of English National Opera since 1980 – in *The Mikado*, *The Cunning Little Vixen*, etc.; also appeared at Glyndebourne, 1984. Her solo recordings have won a ➤crossover success.

Gaskell, [Mrs] **Elizabeth** (1810–65), British novelist. ➤Cooke (A.).

Gaspard de la nuit, set of three piano pieces of Ravel, 1908; the title (Gaspard of the Night) was taken from a set of prose-ballads by A. Bertrand, subtitled 'Fantasies in the manner of Rembrandt and Callot'. No. 1 is 'Ondine' (water-nymph seducing young men to their death); no. 2, 'Le Gibet' (The Gibbet); no. 3. 'Scarbo' (name of a diabolic creature).

Gasparini, Francesco (1668–1727), Italian composer of more than 50 operas, also of oratorios, church music, etc.; pupil of Corelli.

Gassmann, Florian Leopold (1729–74), Bohemian composer of operas, chamber and orchestral music; pupil of 'Padre Martini'; worked at court in Vienna.

'Gastein' Symphony, supposedly lost symphony written by Schubert at Gastein (Austria), 1825 (D849); possibly identical to the Symphony no. 9 in C. The Sonata in C for piano duet (➤Grand Duo) was formerly believed to be an arrangement of it.

Gastoldi, Giovanni Giacomo (*c.* 1550–

159

1622), Italian composer of ➤balletts (which influenced those of Morley, etc.) and of madrigals and church music, etc.; was himself singer, then director of music at Milan Cathedral.

Gatti, Daniele (b. 1962), Italian conductor who made his US début with *Madama Butterfly* at Chicago in 1991, his Covent Garden début with *I Puritani* in 1992; music director of Royal Philharmonic Orchestra from 1996.

Gatty, Nicholas Comyn (1874–1946), British composer of six operas (including *The Tempest* and *Macbeth*, after Shakespeare), chamber music, etc.; also critic.

Gaultier, Denis (*c.* 1603–72), French lutenist and composer for the lute, developing a style of ornamentation which influenced others' keyboard style.

Gauntlett, Henry John (1805–76), British lawyer and church musician; composer of 'Once in Royal David's City' and many other hymns (apparently thousands).

Gaveaux, Pierre (1760–1825), French composer (also tenor); wrote about 30 operas including *Léonore, ou L'amour conjugal* ('Léonore, or Wedded Love') to a libretto which was the principal source of the libretto of Beethoven's ➤*Fidelio*.

gavotte, old dance in 4/4 time beginning on the third beat of the bar; sometimes (but not always) a constituent of the baroque ➤suite, and occasionally revived in modern times – e.g. by Prokofiev in his ➤*Classical Symphony*.

Gavrilov, Andrey (b. 1955), Russian pianist who won the Tchaikovsky Competition in Moscow, 1974, and gave a recital at Salzburg that year; London debut (with orchestra) 1976. His recordings include Skryabin's Concerto no. 3.

Gawain, opera by Birtwistle, produced in London, 1991. Libretto by David Harsent, based on *Sir Gawain and the Green Knight* (14th-century poem alluding to King Arthur's court).

Gay, John (1685–1732), English poet and playwright, particularly known for having written the words of *The* ➤*Beggar's Opera* to popular tunes of the day. ➤*Acis and Galatea*.

Gayaneh, ballet with music by Khachaturian, choreography by Nina Anisimova, produced in 1942 – named after its collective-farm heroine, the virtuous wife of a villain. Contains the 'Sabre Dance'.

Gazza ladra, La (It., 'The Thieving Magpie'), opera by Rossini, produced in Milan, 1817. Libretto by G. Gherardini: the magpie is the real perpetrator of the theft for which a maidservant is condemned to death.

Gazzaniga, Giuseppe (1743–1818), Italian composer; his many operas include a *Don Giovanni* (1787), shortly before Mozart's.

Gebrauchsmusik (Ger., 'Utility music'), term used by Hindemith, Weill and others in Germany in the 1920s to indicate music directed to a social or educational purpose and not merely constituting art for art's sake. Hindemith later disowned the term as misleading.

Gedackt, Gedact, end-stopped type of organ pipe of soft tone. (The term means 'covered'; in modern German, *gedeckt*.)

Gedda, Nicolai [originally Nicolai Harry Gustaf Ustinoff] (b. 1925), Swedish-born tenor of Russian and Swedish descent, prominent in opera and operetta in many languages (Covent Garden début, 1954) and on records. Still singing in his 70th year.

Geige (Ger., pl. *-en*), fiddle, violin.

Geisha, The, musical play by 'Owen Hall' (pseudonym of J. Davis); lyrics by Harry Greenbank; music by Sidney Jones. Produced in London, 1896. In 'happy Japan', where geishas are merely singing waitresses, an invasion by British naval officers takes its amorous course.

'Geister' Trio (Ger., 'Ghost Trio'), nickname (from 'mysterious' slow movement) for Beethoven's Piano Trio in D, op. 70, no. 1 (1808).

Geminiani, Francesco (1687–1762), Italian violinist, composer (violin sonatas, trios and works of ➤*concerto grosso* type, etc.), and author of a famous treatise on violin-playing. Pupil of Corelli. After 1714 lived partly in England, and died in Dublin.

gemshorn, soft-toned organ stop usually of four-➤foot pitch.

Genée, [Franz Friedrich] **Richard** (1823–95), German conductor (especially at Vienna), composer of many operettas and librettist of others including *Die* ➤*Fledermaus*.

general pause (abbr. GP), a rest of one or more bars for all performers – i.e. complete silence. Note that this does not correspond to the usual English meaning of ➤pause.

Genzmer, Harald (b. 1909), German composer of three symphonies, concertos for various instruments (two for ➤Trautonium), a septet with harp, and works for organ, etc.

George, Stefan (1868–1933), German poet. ➤Webern.

Gergiev, Valery [Abissalovich] (b. 1953), Russian-Ossetian conductor who made London début in 1988 and became principal conductor of Kirov Theatre (Leningrad/St Petersburg) in that year. Promoted operatic co-productions between the Kirov and Covent Garden and has conducted notable London concert performances of rare Russian operas.

Gerhard, Roberto (1896–1970), Spanish composer, resident in Britain from 1938; pupil of Pedrell and Schoenberg. Composed opera *The* ➤*Duenna* (after Sheridan); four symphonies; a setting of Edward Lear's 'The Akond of Swat' for mezzo-soprano and two percussionists; *Concerto* for eight instruments (including accordion) without orchestra, etc.

German, Edward [originally German Edward Jones] (1862–1936), British composer; also violinist and theatre conductor. Wrote ➤*Merrie England*, ➤*Tom Jones* and other operettas, and music to various plays including Shakespeare's *Henry VIII* and Anthony Hope's *Nell Gwyn* (dances from these becoming popular in their own right). Also composed two symphonies, *Welsh Rhapsody*, etc., and completed Sullivan's *The Emerald Isle*. Knighted, 1928.

German Dance, type of slow waltz, cultivated as Deutscher Tanz e.g. by Mozart and Schubert.

German flute, obsolete name for the

ordinary (cross-blown) flute, as distinct from the ➤recorder, formerly known as the 'English flute'.

Germani, Fernando (b. 1906), Italian organist (also composer); held post at St Peter's, Rome, 1948–59, edited Frescobaldi's organ works, and has been a much-travelled recitalist.

German Requiem, A, work by Brahms. ➤*Deutsches Requiem*.

German sixth, type of 'augmented sixth' chord (➤augmented) distinguished by the intermediate intervals of the chord – e.g. (reading upwards) D♭, F, A♭, B. (If the B is re-named C♭ then the chord becomes also a 'minor seventh' chord, i.e. the dominant seventh in the key of G♭ – an ambiguity useful in modulation.) The reason for this naming (and similarly with ➤*French*, ➤*Italian* sixth) is not known.

German Symphony Orchestra, ➤Deutsches Symphonie-Orchester.

Gershwin, George [originally Jacob Gershvin] (1898–1937), American pianist and composer of many popular songs (including 'Swanee'), and musicals including ➤*Lady, Be Good!, Oh, Kay!, Of thee I sing*. Extended his range (especially in applying jazz idioms to concert works) in ➤*Rhapsody in Blue* (1924), a piano concerto, *Cuban Overture, An* ➤*American in Paris*, opera ➤*Porgy and Bess*, piano preludes. (The orchestration of *Rhapsody in Blue* is by F. Grofé; of the other works, by Gershwin himself.) Died after an unsuccessful brain operation.

Gervaise, Claude (16th century), French viol-player, composer of dance music and chansons; in service to the French court.

Ges (Ger.), G flat.

Gesang (Ger.), song, hymn. So ➤*Lobgesang* (Mendelssohn), known in English as *Hymn of Praise*. Stockhausen's title, *Gesang der Jünglinge*, literally 'Hymn of the Youths' (1956), refers to the book of the Apocrypha traditionally known as the Song of the Three Children.

Geschichten aus dem Wienerwald (Ger., 'Tales from the Vienna Woods'), waltz by Johann Strauss the younger, 1868.

Geschöpfe des Prometheus, Die (Ger., 'The Creatures of Prometheus'), ballet for which Beethoven wrote the music (including overture), 1801, with choreography by S. Vigarò.

gestopft (Ger.), stopped (notes on the horn). ➤stop.

Gesualdo, Carlo (*c*.1560–1613), Italian prince who was also a composer and lutenist; wrote madrigals employing very adventurous and 'prophetic' harmony, and also songs to religious words, etc. Gained notoriety by having his wife and her lover assassinated in 1590. His life is the subject of Schnittke's opera *Gesualdo* (1995).

Geteilt (Ger., in older spelling *getheilt*), divided (➤*divisi*).

Gevaert, François Auguste (1828–1908), Belgian theorist (author of treatises on orchestration, etc.), director of the Brussels Conservatory, composer and musical editor.

Gewaltige Hahnrei, Der (Ger., 'The Magnificent Cuckold'), opera by Goldschmidt, produced in Mannheim, 1932 (but only in 1992 revived and recorded!). Libretto after a play by F. Crommelynck, a sexual farce in which a jealous husband drives his wife to betray him.

Gewandhaus Orchestra, orchestra of Leipzig taking its name from its hall ('Cloth House'); music director from 1998 (succeeding Kurt Masur), Herbert Blomstedt.

Ghedini, Giorgio Federico (1892–1965), Italian composer of operas including ➤*Billy Budd*, *L'Ipocrita felice*, after Beerbohm's 'The Happy Hypocrite'; concertos for string orchestra, church music, etc.; also editor of old Italian music.

Ghelderode, Michel de (1898–1962), Belgian dramatist, writing in French. ➤*Grand Macabre*.

Gheorgiu, Angela [original surname Burlacu] (b. 1965), Romanian soprano who first sang at Covent Garden in 1992 as Zerlina in *Don Giovanni*, and in 1994 sang the heroine of *La Traviata* (under Solti) there. Married ➤*Alagna*.

Ghiaurov, Nicolai (b. 1929), Bulgarian bass who studied in Moscow; noted in Russian and other types of opera – La Scala (Milan) from 1959, Covent Garden from 1962.

Ghosts of Versailles, The, opera by Corigliano, produced at the Metropolitan Opera, New York, 1991. Libretto by William M. Hoffman, after Beaumarchais – who becomes a personage in the story, along with characters from *Le* ➤*Nozze di Figaro*.

'Ghost' Trio, ➤*'Geister'* Trio.

Gianni Schicchi, one-act comic opera by Puccini, produced in New York, 1918 – along with *Il* ➤*Tabarro* and ➤*Suor Angelica*, two other one-act operas which precede it and with which it forms Puccini's *Trittico* (triptych). Libretto by G. Adami: Schicchi, a medieval Florentine rogue mentioned by Dante, is the hero.

Giannini, Vittorio (1903–66), American composer of operas *The Taming of the Shrew* (after Shakespeare) and *Beauty and the Beast*; also symphonies and *Frescobaldiana* for orchestra, based on Frescobaldi's organ works.

'Giant' Fugue, nickname for a fugal chorale prelude in D minor by Bach contained in Part III of the ➤*Clavierübung* (BWV 680) – from the giant-like strides of a figure in the pedals.

Giardini, Felice de (1716–96), Italian violinist, opera manager and composer, long resident in London; collaborated with Avison in oratorio *Ruth*. Died in Moscow.

Giazotto, Remo, ➤Albinoni.

Gibbons, Christopher (1615–76), English composer of fantasies and dances for strings, church music and (with Locke) music for the masque ➤*Cupid and Death*. Private organist to Charles II, organist of Westminister Abbey. Son of Orlando Gibbons.

Gibbons, Orlando (1583–1625), English composer, also virginalist and organist; his father William, brothers Edward, Ellis and Ferdinando, and son Christopher (see preceding entry), were also musicians. Choirboy at King's College, Cambridge; later organist of Chapel Royal and Westminster Abbey. Works include about 40 anthems and other church music; madrigals and part-songs ('The Silver Swan', etc.); works called ➤*In Nomine* and other works for viols; keyboard pieces. ➤*Parthenia*.

Gibbs, [Cecil] **Armstrong** (1889–1960), British composer of songs, many to poems by de la Mare; also of comic opera *The Blue Peter*, waltz *Dusk*, church music, etc.

Gibson, Alexander [Drummond] (1926–95), Scottish conductor – of Scottish National Orchestra, 1959–84; musical director, Scottish Opera, from its foundation, 1962, until 1987. Knighted, 1977.

Gide, André (1869–1951), French writer. ➤*Perséphone*.

Gielen, Michael [Andreas] (b. 1927), German conductor-composer. In Argentina 1940–50; since then has held various conducting posts (music director, Cincinnati Symphony, 1980–86, principal conductor, South-West German Radio Orchestra since 1986). Works include *Un dia sobresale* (Sp., 'One day stood out') for piano, five solo instruments and five groups of five musicians each; *Rückblick* (Ger., 'Retrospect') for three cellos.

Gieseking, Walter [Wilhelm] (1895–1956), German pianist (though born in France). Made début in 1912 and afterwards toured widely; of high international reputation, particularly in French music. Was also composer.

giga (It.), ➤jig.

Gigli, Beniamino (1890–1957), Italian tenor; made début in 1914. Had operatic career but later maintained his exceptional celebrity chiefly by recitals or operatic excerpts, etc., and by records.

Gigout, Eugène (1844–1925), French organist and composer, especially for organ; pupil of Saint-Saëns.

gigue (Fr.), ➤jig.

Gilbert, Anthony (b. 1934), British composer, influential teacher in Manchester at the Royal Northern College of Music. Works include opera *The Scene Machine*, six *Fanfarings* for brass (1983–92), piano music including *Funtoons* for children, and (from a period in Australia) *Begindigendigo* for recorder ensemble.

Gilbert, Henry Franklin Belknap (1868–1928), American composer, pupil of MacDowell; made use of various indigenous American melodies – e.g. Creole in ballet *The Dance in Place Congo*.

Gilbert, W. S. [William Schwenk], Sir (1836–1911), British dramatist. ➤*Gondoliers*, ➤*Grand Duke*, ➤*HMS Pinafore*, ➤*Iolanthe*, ➤*Mikado*, ➤*Patience*, ➤*Pineapple Poll*, ➤*Pirates of Penzance*, ➤*Princess Ida*, ➤*Ruddigore*, ➤*Sorcerer*, ➤*Trial by Jury*, ➤*Utopia Limited*, ➤*Yeomen of the Guard*; ➤Savoy Operas.

Gilels, Emil [Grigoryevich] (1916–85), Russian pianist who won international awards in Vienna (1936) and Brussels (1938) and gained widespread celebrity after World War II.

Giles, Nathaniel (c.1558–1633), English organist (of the Chapel Royal, 1596) and composer of madrigals and much church music.

Gilles, Jean (1668–1705), French composer chiefly of church music, including a famous Requiem; was himself church musician, originally as choirboy.

Gillis, Don (1912–78), American composer (also trumpeter, trombonist, teacher and conductor); works include 10 symphonies and *Symphony No. 5$\frac{1}{2}$* (also called *A Symphony for Fun*).

Gilson, Paul (1865–1942), Belgian composer, also writer on music. Works include *La* ➤*mer* for orchestra, many pieces for wind band, oratorio *Francesca da Rimini*.

gimel, ➤gymel.

Ginastera, Alberto (1916–83), Argentinian composer of music including ballet *Panambí* (based on an American-Indian legend), *Argentinian Concerto* for piano and orchestra; other works include overture to Goethe's *Faust*, operas *Don Rodrigo* and *Bomarzo*. Lived in USA, 1945–6.

Gioconda, La, opera by Ponchielli, produced in Milan, 1876. Libretto by Boito, after Victor Hugo. 'La Gioconda', literally 'the joyful girl', is the name of a street-singer, the heroine. Act III contains the 'Dance of the Hours' (ballet music). The opera is unrelated to da Vinci's portrait or to D'Annunzio's play (1898), similarly named.

giocoso (It.), merry, playful, humorous.

Gioielli della Madonna, I (It., 'The Jewels of the Madonna'), opera by Wolf-Ferrari, produced in Berlin (in German), 1911. Libretto, originally in Italian, by E. Golisciani and C. Zangarini. Blood-and-thunder plot, like ➤*Cavalleria Rusticana*, and likewise containing an orchestral intermezzo which won independent popularity.

Giordanello, see following entry.

Giordani, Giuseppe (1743–98), Italian composer of operas, ballet scores, church music, concertos, songs, etc. – the song 'Caro mio ben' ('My very dear one') is ascribed to him. Never left Italy, but was formerly confused with Tommaso Giordani (no relation). Known also as Giordanello.

Giordani, Tommaso (*c.* 1730–1806), Italian composer (no relation of

Giuseppe Giordani) who worked in Dublin (where he died) and London. Composed or contributed items to more than 50 operas, Italian and English; wrote songs for Sheridan's *The Critic* on its first production.

Giordano, Umberto [Menotti Maria] (1867–1948), Italian composer of ➤*Andrea Chénier*, *Fedora* and other operas of the Italian 'realistic' kind (➤*verismo*).

Giovanni da Cascia (also known as 'da Firenze', of Florence) (14th century), Italian composer of madrigals (in the older sense), *caccie* (➤*caccia*), etc.; held court post at Verona.

Gipsy Baron, The, operetta by J. Strauss the younger. ➤*Zigeunerbaron*.

Gipsy Princess, The, operetta by Kálmán. ➤*Csárdásfürstin*.

Gipsy Rondo, nickname for the final movement of Haydn's Piano Trio (Hob. XV: 25), marked 'In Hungarian style'.

Girl of the Golden West, The, opera by Puccini. ➤*Fanciulla del West*.

Girl with the Flaxen Hair, prelude for piano by Debussy. ➤*Fille aux cheveux de lin*.

Gis, Gisis (Ger.), G sharp, G double-sharp.

Giselle, ou les Wilis (Fr., 'Giselle, or the Wilis'), ballet with music by Adam, choreography by Coralli and Perrot, produced in Paris, 1841. The Wilis are the spirits of maidens who die before their intended marriages.

gittern, old English name for a type of guitar (not the same as ➤cittern).

Giuliani, Mauro [Giuseppe Sergio Pantaleo] (1781–1829), Italian guitarist and composer of three guitar concertos, chamber works with guitar, songs with a choice of guitar or piano accompaniment, etc. Active in Paris, Vienna and elsewhere.

Giulini, Carlo Maria (b. 1914), Italian conductor of great distinction in concerts and opera; music director of La Scala (Milan), 1953–6; first appeared at Covent Garden, 1958. He was music director of the Los Angeles Philharmonic Orchestra, 1978–84.

Giulio Cesare (It., 'Julius Caesar'), opera by Handel, produced in London, 1724 – properly *Giulio Cesare in Egitto*, i.e. in Egypt; libretto, dealing with the relationship between Caesar, Cleopatra, and Ptolemy, by N. Haym. Also an opera by G. F. Malipiero, 1936, after Shakespeare's *Julius Caesar*.

giusto (It.), strict, just, proper; hence such expressions as *allegro giusto*, meaning either (1) *allegro* with a special attention to keeping a strict beat, or (2) a moderate (neither too fast nor too slow) *allegro*.

Glagolitic Mass, Mass by Janáček for chorus, organ and orchestra, 1926. Glagolitic is an obsolete Slav alphabet; the form of Mass associated with it has patriotic Czech associations. A work of this title has also been composed by Hanuš (1985).

Glanville-Hicks, Peggy (1912–90), Australian-born composer who studied in Europe but whose main career was in USA, where she lived 1942–59. Works include a piano concerto, chamber music, operas. Also critic.

Glasser, Stanley (b. 1926), South African composer; teacher at London University. Works include *The Chameleon and the Lizard* (text in Zulu), Sinfonietta Concertante for orchestra.

glass harmonica, obsolete instrument consisting of glass vessels of various sizes, rubbed with damped finger (or operated mechanically) – written for, e.g., by Mozart. Also called the 'musical glasses'. Invented by Benjamin Franklin, 1763. Revived by Crumb in ➤*Black Angels*.

Glass, Philip (b. 1937), American composer, noted exponent of ➤minimalism; studied with N. Boulanger in Paris and also with R. Shankar. Created own ensemble, chiefly amplified electronic music, for performing his concert works (e.g. *Koyaanisquatsi*, American-Indian word for 'life out of balance', which won wider-than-classical popularity). Also well-known for his operas including ➤*Akhnaten*, ➤*Einstein on the Beach*, *The Fall of the House of Usher* (after Poe), *The Making of the Representative for Planet 8* (after Doris Lessing).

Glazunov, Alexander [Konstantinovich] (1865–1936), Russian composer of eight symphonies (all by 1906), plus one (1909) unfinished, first performed in Moscow, 1948; concertos for piano (2), for violin, for saxophone; ➤*Carnival* overture; ballet scores including *The* ➤*Seasons*, piano pieces, songs, etc. Became director of the St Petersburg (later Leningrad) Conservatory but left in 1928 and settled in Paris, where he died.

Glebov, Igor, ➤Asafiev.

glee, short choral composition, properly in several sections and for unaccompanied male voices; flourished in Britain about 1650–1830. Hence *glee club* – term used in US for choir (traditionally all-male) cultivating short works of various types.

Glennie, Evelyn [Elizabeth Anne] (b. 1965), British percussionist, claimed to be the world's first full-time solo percussionist; said to be profoundly deaf yet able to sense musical vibrations; gave London début recital, 1986. Concertos have been dedicated to her by Richard Rodney Bennett (1990), Musgrave, and others. Also composer and pianist. OBE, 1993.

gli (It.), the (masc. pl.).

Glière, Reinhold [Moritzovich] (1875–1956), Russian composer of Belgian descent. Works include *Shah-Senem* (based on folk-music of Azerbaijan) and other operas; *The Red Poppy* and other ballets; three symphonies (no. 3, *Ilya Murometz*); a concerto for coloratura soprano and orchestra; chamber music; many songs and piano pieces.

Glinka, Mikhail Ivanovich (1804–57), Russian composer, the first whose music won general acceptance outside Russia; shows various 'nationalist' traits in his works. Regarded therefore as the 'father' of Russian music. Studied piano with Field; visited Italy and Germany before bringing out operas *A* ➤*Life for the Tsar* (1836) and ➤*Ruslan and Lyudmila*; made other trips abroad later, dying in Berlin. Also composed *Jota aragonesa* and other works in imitation-Spanish style; chamber music for strings and for wind; many piano pieces and songs.

glissando (mock-It. from Fr. *glisser*, to slide), sliding up and down the scale, i.e. making a quick uninterrupted passage up or down the scale, e.g. on the piano, harp, xylophone, trombone. The effect of ➤*portamento* on stringed instruments is not the same, since it implies only the smooth linking of two notes, not the deliberate sounding of the notes in between.

Globokar, Vinko (b. 1934), Yugoslav composer (born in France) who studied in both Yugoslavia and France – and also in Germany with Berio. Is also trombonist, for whom works have been written by Stockhausen, Berio (➤*Sequenza* no. 5), and others. Works include *Traumdeutung* (Ger., 'Explanation of Dreams') for four choruses; *Fluid* for nine brass and three percussion.

Glocke(n) (Ger.), bell(s) – referring, in orchestral scores, to tubular ➤bells.

glockenspiel (Ger., play of bells), percussion instrument of tuned metal bars giving small bell-like sound; played with keyboard or (more usually) small hammers held in hand. The term is also used, though more rarely, for a chime of real bells played mechanically or by hand, i.e. a ➤carillon.

Gloria [in excelsis Deo] (Lat., Glory [to God in the highest]), part of the ➤Mass. A number of composers, e.g. Poulenc, Walton, have set this text separately.

Gloriana, opera by Britten, produced in London, 1953, in honour of the coronation of Queen Elizabeth II. Libretto by W. Plomer; 'Gloriana' is Elizabeth I, the opera concentrating on her relationship with the Earl of Essex.

glotte, coup de, ➤*coup de glotte*.

Glover, Jane [Alison] (b. 1949), British conductor who became known first as a musicologist; conducted at Glyndebourne from 1981, Covent Garden from 1988, and became artistic director of London Mozart Players,

1984–92, and conductor of Huddersfield Choral Society, 1988–96.

Gluck, Christoph Willibald [von] (1714–87), German composer, born in Bavaria but possibly of Bohemian origin; travelled much – London, 1745; Paris, 1773–9, where his followers opposed those of Piccinni; settled and died in Vienna. Was consciously an operatic reformer, stressing importance of subordinating music to dramatic needs – and also dispensing with 'dry ➤recitative'; his ➤*Alceste* (1767) has a famous preface expounding his ideas. This opera, like its predecessor ➤*Orfeo*, was originally in Italian; both were later revised with French texts. Other operas include ➤*Iphigénie en Aulide*, ➤*Iphigénie en Tauride*, ➤*Armide*. Wrote in all more than 45 stage works including ballet *Don Juan*; also instrumental pieces, etc.

Glyndebourne, a small opera house in the Sussex countryside founded by John Christie (1882–1962), owner of the estate in which it stands. International short summer seasons there opened in 1934. A larger theatre, rebuilt on the same site, opened in 1994. Music director from 1989 (succeeding Haitink) until 2000, Andrew Davis. The subsidiary *Glyndebourne Touring Opera* began its activity in 1968: music director since 1992, Ivor Bolton.

Gnecchi, Vittorio (1876–1954), Italian composer of operas, including *La Rosiera*, 1910, with an early use of ➤quarter-tones.

Gnesin [or Gnessin], **Mikhail Fabianovich** (1883–1957), Russian composer, pupil of Rimsky-Korsakov and Lyadov; travelled in Western Europe and Palestine. He composed many works with Jewish associations including operas *The Youth of Abraham* and *The Maccabees*; also symphonic poems, chamber music, etc. The Gnesin Music School in Moscow, famous for its work with gifted child performers, was founded by him and his four sisters, all professional musicians.

Gobbi, Tito (1913–84), Italian baritone who made his first appearance at La Scala, Milan, in 1942, and after the war was internationally acclaimed in such roles as Rigoletto, Scarpia (in *Tosca*) and Falstaff. Also appeared in many films and from 1965 was active as operatic stage director.

Godard, Benjamin Louis Paul (1849–95), French composer, also violinist. Works include *Jocelyn* (from which the well-known 'Berceuse' comes) and seven other operas; also orchestral works, over 100 songs, etc.

Godowsky, Leopold (1870–1938), Polish-born pianist who became American, 1891; made and performed many virtuoso-style transcriptions of famous orchestral and other works. Was also composer, e.g., of the *Triakontameron* (30 piano pieces each composed on a different day).

God save the King (Queen), British national anthem; author and composer unknown, though a keyboard piece by Bull (in the minor key) has some relationship to the tune. Generally adopted in the mid 18th century. (Tune also set to various other words – e.g. US, 'My country, 'tis of thee', 1831.)

Godspell, musical with text by John-Michael Tebelak mainly based on St Matthew's Gospel; music and lyrics by Stephen Schwartz. Produced in New

York, 1971. A celebration of Jesus against a background of modern high-school pupils using clown make-up.

Goedicke, Alexander Fedorovich (1877–1957), Russian pianist, teacher, and composer of operas, three symphonies, etc.

Goehr, [Peter] **Alexander** (b. 1932), British (German-born) composer, pupil in Paris of Messiaen. Professor of music at Cambridge since 1976. Works include operas ➤*Arden muss sterben, Behold the Sun* and *Arianna*; a triptych of 'music-theatre' pieces; various orchestral works including *Colossos or Panic* (after Goya) and a Symphony with Chaconne; choral work *The Death of Moses*. His father was the conductor and composer Walter Goehr (1903–60).

Goethe, Johann Wolfgang von (1749–1832), German poet and novelist. ➤*Damnation de Faust,* ➤*Doktor Faust,* ➤*Erlkönig,* ➤*Faust,* ➤*Mefistofele,* ➤*Mignon,* ➤*Prometheus,* ➤*Werther;* ➤Boulanger (L.), ➤Jelinek, ➤Reutter, ➤Wolf, ➤Zimmermann; also ➤ballad.

Goetz, Hermann (1840–76), German composer of opera *Der* ➤*Widerspänstigen Zähmung* ('The Taming of the Shrew'), a symphony, piano concerto, chamber music, songs, etc.; settled in Switzerland and died there.

Gogol, Nikolay Vasilievich (1809–52), Russian writer. ➤*Christmas Eve,* ➤ *Fair at Sorochintsy,* ➤*Nose,* ➤*Slippers;* ➤Egk, ➤Martinů, ➤Volkónsky.

Goldberg, Szymon (1909–93), Polish-born violinist long resident in Holland (where he directed his own chamber orchestra) and latterly in Britain and USA (where he held leading positions as teacher). ➤Kraus (Lili).

Goldberg Variations, usual name for Bach's 30 variations for harpsichord (with two keyboards) on an original theme, 1742 (BWV 988); written for his pupil, J. G. Goldberg, whose noble patron required music as a solace for insomnia. ➤*quodlibet.*

Golden Age, The, accepted English title (though 'The Gilded Age' gets nearer the meaning) for Rus. *Zolotoy vek* – ballet, with music by Shostakovich, choreography (about virtuous Soviet footballers amid capitalist temptation) by F. Lopukhov; produced in Leningrad, 1930.

Golden Cockerel, The (Rus., *Zolotoy petushok*), Rimsky-Korsakov's last opera; at first banned by censorship, then produced (only after the composer's death) in Moscow, 1909. Libretto by V. I. Bielsky, after Pushkin: title from a magic 'weathercock' which gives warning of danger to the city. The work is a satire on stupid despotism.

Golden Sonata, nickname (not the composer's) for Purcell's Sonata in F for two violins, bass viol and continuo (Z810), no. 9 of a set of 10 so-called *Sonatas of Four Parts* (➤Purcell) published posthumously in 1697.

Goldmark, Karl (1830–1915), Austro-Hungarian composer who trained in Vienna and eventually settled there. Became known for opera *Die Königin von Saba* ('The Queen of Sheba') and orchestral work *Die* ➤ *ländliche Hochzeit* ('The Rustic Wedding'). Also wrote operas based on Shakespeare's *The Winter's Tale* and Dickens's *The Cricket on the Hearth;* two violin concertos; piano music, and songs. Uncle of Rubin Goldmark.

Goldmark, Rubin (1872–1936), American composer, nephew of preceding; pupil of Dvořák, teacher of Gershwin. Wrote orchestral works – one on *Hiawatha* – chamber music, piano pieces, etc.

Goldoni, Carlo (1707–93), Italian dramatist. ➤*Quatro rusteghi*, ➤*Mondo della luna*; Hanuš.

Goldschmidt, Berthold (1903–96), German-born composer (pupil of Schreker) and conductor, resident in Britain since 1935. Works include operas *Der* ➤*gewaltige Hahnrei* and *Beatrice Cenci* (after Shelley); ballet *Chronica*; *Ciaconna Sinfonica* for orchestra. Was still active in his nineties, having won new recognition in Germany and Austria.

Goldsmith, Oliver (1728–74), Irish writer. ➤Lehmann (Liza).

Golliwogg's Cakewalk, ➤*Children's Corner*.

Gombert, Nicolas (*c* 1500–*c* 1556), Flemish (Netherlandish) composer, in service to the (Holy Roman) Emperor Charles V, with whom he travelled widely; he is thought to have been a pupil of Josquin. Wrote more than 70 chansons, also Masses, motets, etc.

Gomes, [Antonio] Carlos (1836–96), Brazilian composer of operas, some in Italian, others in Portuguese; the former include *Il Guarany*, the hero being a member of the American-Indian Guaraní people.

Gomez, Jill (b. 1942), British soprano, born in British Guiana. Has cultivated a wide concert and opera repertory, creating the role of Flora in *The* ➤*Knot Garden*, 1970.

Gondoliers, The, or The King of Barataria, operetta by Sullivan, produced in London, 1889. Libretto by W. S. Gilbert (his last successful collaboration with Sullivan). Title from the heroes, two Venetian boatmen who despite their own egalitarian views find themselves jointly reigning as king. ➤*cachucha*.

gong, circular percussion instrument of bronze, made in various sizes, usually with a turned-down rim; sometimes of definite and sometimes of indefinite pitch. (This is a broad, ethnomusicological definition, but in modern orchestral usage there is a tendency to reserve *gong* for the various-sized instruments with definite pitch and ➤*tam-tam* for those with indefinite.) The gong was possibly first used in the Western orchestra by Gossec in 1791; the earliest known mention is sixth-century Chinese. ➤*gamelan*.

Goodall, Reginald (1901–90), British conductor, celebrated in Wagner, especially for English National Opera productions in London and on recordings. Knighted, 1985.

Good Friday Music, music from Act 3 of Wagner's ➤*Parsifal* (sometimes heard as a separate concert piece), depicting the reverential stillness of Nature on that day.

Goodman, Benny [originally Benjamin David] (1909–86), American clarinettist who became eminent in the jazz sphere (led his own band from 1933) and afterwards became noted soloist with orchestra, chamber-music player, etc.; Copland's Clarinet Concerto and Bartók's ➤*Contrasts* were written for him.

Goossens, [Aynsley] Eugene (1893–1962), British conductor and composer (also violinist), son and grandson of conductors of the same name (of Belgian descent). Active in USA, then (1947–56) conservatory director in Sydney, Australia – left after a conviction for importing pornography. Wrote oratorio *The Apocalypse*, operas *Judith* and *Don Juan de Mañara*, two symphonies, piano pieces, etc. Knighted, 1955. Brother of Sidonie and Marie Goossens, harpists, and of Léon Goossens.

Goossens, Léon [Jean] (1897–1988), British oboist, brother of the foregoing; noted soloist for whom concertos and other works were written by Vaughan Williams and others. CBE, 1950.

gopak, Russian or Ukrainian folkdance in quick 2/4 time. (In English sometimes also written as 'hopak'.)

Górecki, Henryk [Mikołaj] (b. 1933), Polish composer of three symphonies – no. 3, *A Symphony of Sorrowful Songs*, composed in 1977, achieving cult status in the late 1980s; also much chamber music including *Aria* for tuba, piano, tam-tam and bass drum; *Little Requiem for a Polka* for piano and thirteen instruments, Latin church music.

Gore, Walter (1910–79), British choreographer. ➤*Simple Symphony*.

Gossec, François Joseph (1734–1829), Belgian composer, from 1751 living in France (where he died); also musical organizer and teacher. Wrote symphonies, pioneering the form in France; also many operas and ballets, and works for outdoor performance celebrating the French Revolution. Innovator in the massed use of instruments: his *Te Deum* stipulated 1,200 voices and 300 wind instruments.

Gothic, term employed (infrequently) to identify music contemporary with European Gothic architecture (12th–15th centuries). The British ensemble Gothic Voices (founder-director, 1980, Christopher Page) is named in this sense. The *Gothic Symphony* (Symphony no. 1) by Havergal Brian, composed 1919–27, and ending with a 72-minute Te Deum, appears to be named for its cathedral-like vastness.

Gotovac, Jakov (1895–1982), Yugoslav composer of *Ero the Joker* and other operas, choral works, songs with orchestra and with piano, etc. Was also conductor.

Götterdämmerung, ➤*Ring*.

Gottschalk, Louis Moreau (1829–69), American pianist, the first such to win international standing. Also composer of virtuoso-style piano pieces, some in a 'Creole' style foreshadowing ➤ragtime; also of two operas and various orchestral works.

Goudimel, Claude (c. 1510–72), French composer at first of Roman Catholic church music; then, after becoming a Protestant, of psalm-tunes, etc., for Protestant use. Also wrote secular songs. Killed in the aftermath of the 'St Bartholomew' massacre of Protestants.

Gould, Glenn [Herbert] (1932–82), Canadian pianist who made his début with the Toronto Symphony Orchestra at 14, later toured widely (European début with Karajan in Berlin, 1957) – but from mid-1960s very seldom appeared in concerts, preferring only to record. Also composer. Known for idiosyncrasies of performance, wide repertory (including jazz), and taste for controversy.

Gould, Morton (b. 1913), American composer and conductor (also pianist). Associated with 'popular' and film music, but works include three symphonies, ballet score *Fall River Legend* (to Agnes de Mille's choreography), and four *American Symphonettes* (*sic*) from no. 2 of which comes 'Pavanne' (*sic*).

Gounod, Charles [François] (1818–93), French composer, pupil of Halévy and others at the Paris Conservatory, where he won the 'Rome Prize' and so spent three years in Rome; afterwards church organist in Paris. At one time intended to become a priest. In his time was one of the most successful and esteemed of composers, the opera ➤*Faust* being universally performed. Also conductor; first conductor of what is now Royal Choral Society, during the years 1870–75 spent in London. Later concentrated on religious music, e.g. oratorio *The* ➤*Redemption*. Other works include ➤*Roméo et Juliette* and 12 other operas; nine Masses and other church music; many songs; two orchestral symphonies and a *Petite Symphonie* for wind; several miscellaneous pieces including his *Meditation* on the first prelude of Bach's ➤*Wohltemperirte Clavier* (the so-called ➤*Ave Maria*), and the *Funeral march of a marionette*.

Gow, Nathaniel (1763–1831), Scottish musician (son and father of other musicians); was trumpeter, violinist, publisher, song-composer, etc. Wrote tune of song 'Caller Herrin'', the words being fitted later.

Goya, Francisco (1746–1828), Spanish painter; subject of Menotti's opera ➤*Goya*. His paintings also prompted an orchestral work by A. ➤Goehr and Granados's piano pieces and opera, ➤*Goyescas*.

Goya, opera by Menotti (libretto by composer) on the life of the painter; produced in Washington, DC, 1986.

Goyescas (Sp., Goya-esque works), (1) two sets of piano pieces (seven in all) by Granados, suggested by Goya's paintings and first performed in 1914; (2) opera by Granados, produced in New York in 1916, partly based on the preceding and having a plot of love and killing in a Goya-esque setting: libretto (in Spanish) by F. Periquet.

Gozzi, Carlo (1722–1806), Italian dramatist. ➤*Turandot*.

GP, ➤general pause.

Grabu, Louis (d. after 1694), French violinist and composer; Master of the King's Music to Charles II, 1665; composer of music to Dryden's *Albion and Albanius* and other stage works.

grace (verb), to decorate a melody, particularly to add decorations (➤ornament) as an accomplishment in the act of performance; hence *grace* (noun, somewhat obsolete), an ornament. A *grace-note* is a note forming such an addition to a melody, being considered as a decoration even though it may be actually written down by the composer rather than originated by the performer.

Gradual (1) a plainsong chant occurring, in the Roman Catholic Mass, between the lessons of the ➤liturgy; (2) a book containing the chants for the Proper of the Mass, i.e. the part specific to the day.

Graduale (pl. *Gradualia*), Latin for the preceding.

Gradus ad Parnassum (Lat., 'Steps to Parnassus' – the mountain sacred to the Muses), (1) a treatise on counterpoint by Fux, 1725; (2) a collection of piano studies by Clementi, 1817. It is to the latter that Debussy pays humorous homage in *Doctor Gradus ad Parnassum* (➤*Children's Corner*).

Graener, Paul (1872–1944), German composer of operas (one about W. F. Bach), orchestral works, etc.; also conductor. Lived in London 1896–1908.

Gräfin Mariza (Ger., 'Countess Maritza'), operetta by Kálmán with libretto by Julius Brammer and Alfred Grünwald. Produced in Vienna, 1924. The Hungarian countess finds that her estate manager is a prince in disguise.

Graf von Luxemburg, Der (Ger., 'The Count of Luxembourg'), operetta by Lehár with libretto by A. M. Willner and Robert Bodanzky based on Willner's libretto *Die Göttin der Vernunft*. Produced in Vienna, 1909. A wedding ceremony where the parties do not see each other (for the benefit of the impoverished Count) turns out to be a love-match.

Graham, Martha (1894–1991), American choreographer. ➤*Appalachian Spring*; ➤Johnson (H.), ➤Riegger, ➤Surinach.

Grainger, Percy Aldridge (1882–1961), Australian-born composer and pianist; lived 1900–1915 in London and thereafter in USA (naturalized). Pupil in Germany of Busoni; friend of Grieg. Collected and edited English folk-music and based some compositions on it. Also wrote choral works, many short instrumental/orchestral pieces (*Country Gardens*, ➤*Handel in the Strand*, *Mock* ➤*Morris*); usually published his works in several varieties of

scoring. Used deliberately anglicized vocabulary, e.g. 'louden' (crescendo), 'middle-fiddle' (viola), 'bass fiddle' – to mean cello, not double-bass, which term he retained. ➤*Londonderry Air*.

Granados [y Campina], **Enrique** (1867–1916), Spanish composer (pupil of Pedrell), also pianist and conductor; his seven operas include ➤*Goyescas*, partly based on piano works of the same name. Wrote also other piano music, orchestral works and songs, cultivating Spanish 'nationalist' idiom. Died when the ship on which he was returning from New York was torpedoed by a German submarine.

gran cassa (It.), ➤bass drum.

grand chœur (Fr.), ➤full organ.

Grand Duke, The, or **The Statutory Duel**, operetta by Sullivan – his last (unsuccessful) collaboration with W. S. Gilbert as librettist – produced in London, 1896. The Grand Duke appears to lose his title through a type of duel with playing-cards.

Grand Duo, name given to a sonata in C by Schubert (D812; 1824) for piano duet. The theory that this work was the keyboard version of a lost symphony is discredited.

Grande-Duchesse de Gérolstein, La, operetta by Offenbach with libretto by Henri Meilhac and Ludovic Halévy. Produced in Paris, 1867. The ruler of a petty German state loves her army, especially Private (soon to be Captain) Fritz.

Grande Messe des Morts (Fr., Grand Requiem Mass), title given by Berlioz to his setting of the Latin text of the ➤*Requiem*, using an exceptionally large orchestral accompaniment; first performed in 1837.

Grandi, Alessandro (*c.* 1577–1630), Italian composer of madrigals, etc.; also church musician. Died at Bergamo of the plague.

grand jeu (Fr.), ➤full organ.

Grand Macabre, Le (Fr., 'The Great Macabre'), opera by Ligeti, produced in Stockholm, 1978. Libretto, after a play by Ghelderode, is a comic satire on death and sexuality.

grand opera, imprecise term sometimes meaning all-sung opera (without spoken dialogue), sometimes referring specifically to French spectacular opera using historical plots such as ➤*Guillaume Tell* (Rossini) and *Les* ➤*Huguenots* (Meyerbeer); also used by laymen to distinguish 'serious' opera from, e.g., operetta.

grand piano, ➤piano.

graphic notation, term describing certain post-1950 types of musical notation, especially those which pictorialize the action required of the performer, or which represent duration by comparative length of a printed line or other visual symbol.

Grappelli [originally Grappelly], **Stephane** (b. 1908), French violinist famous as a jazz musician and in recordings and performances with Menuhin from the mid-1970s.

Graun, Carl Heinrich (1703/4–59), German composer (also tenor singer), musical director to Frederick II of Prussia from 1740. Earlier influenced by Lotti at Dresden, and later himself visited Italy. Wrote Italian and German operas, chamber music, and church music including notably successful cantata *Der Tod Jesu* ('The Death of Jesus' – ➤*Passion*).

grave (It., heavy, grave), in slow tempo.

gravicembalo (It., corruption of *clavicembalo*), harpsichord.

grazia, grazioso (It.), grace, graceful(ly).

Great, ➤great organ.

Great C-Major Symphony, name for Schubert's Symphony no. 9 in C (D944), in some older editions called no. 7. Probably completed in 1825 (rather than 1828, as previously thought), but never performed in the composer's lifetime. The title distinguishes the symphony from the shorter no. 6 in the same key, and alludes both to its quality and its unusual length: it takes nearly an hour in performance.

Great Fugue, work for string quartet by Beethoven. ➤*Gross Fuge*.

Great Macabre, The, opera by Ligeti. ➤*Grand Macabre*.

great organ (or simply *Great*), chief and most powerful division of an organ (a manual and the equipment controlled by it). No connection with *Great Organ Mass* (see the following).

Great Organ Mass, nickname for Haydn's Mass in E flat, 1774 (Hob. XXII: 4), with an important organ part – distinguished from Haydn's ➤*Little Organ Mass*. Better called *Great Mass with Organ*, avoiding suggestion of a connection with 'great organ'.

Great Service, ➤service.

Grechaninov, Alexander Tikhonovich (1864–1956), Russian composer, resident in France from 1925, in USA from 1939. Works include operas, five symphonies, many songs, music for children, and *Missa oecumenica*, 1944, designed to embrace musically both Eastern and Western Christianity.

Greek, opera by Turnage, produced in Munich, 1988; libretto – adapted from Berkoff's play by the composer and Jonathan Moore – applies the Oedipus legend to modern lower-class city life.

Greek Passion, The, opera by Martinů, produced in Zurich, 1961; libretto (in English) by the composer and N. Kazantzakis, after Kazantzakis's novel *Christ Recrucified*, enacting the Passion in modern times.

Greene, Graham (1904–91), British novelist. ➤*Our Man in Havana*.

Greene, Maurice (1696–1755), English composer of songs, church music, etc.; also organist.

Greensleeves, old English tune mentioned by Shakespeare and found with several sets of words and in several old musical arrangements (➤Cutting); *Fantasia on Greensleeves*, orchestral work by Vaughan Williams adapted (by another hand) from his opera *Sir John in Love*, produced 1929.

Gregorian chant, type of ➤plainsong associated with Pope Gregory I (otherwise St Gregory; *c.* 540–*c.* 604) which became standard in the Roman Catholic Church.

Gregorian tone, name given to each of eight melodies of Gregorian chant (each in a different ➤mode) prescribed by the Roman Catholic Church for the Psalms. The ➤*tonus peregrinus* is additional to these.

Gregson, Edward (b. 1945), British composer whose works include a tuba concerto, a sonata for four trombones, and music for the York Mystery Plays and for Royal Shakespeare Company. Since 1996, Principal of Royal Northern College of Music, Manchester.

Gretchaninov, ➤Grechaninov.

Grétry, André Ernest Modeste (1741–1813), Belgian composer who studied in Italy and in 1767 settled in France (where he died). Was one of the chief composers of ➤*opéra comique*; he wrote dozens of works of this type, including *Zémire et Azor* (based on the tale of Beauty and the Beast) and *Richard Cœur de Lion*. The latter is the source of an aria quoted in Tchaikovsky's The ➤*Queen of Spades* as an evocation of this period.

Grieg, Edvard Hagerup (1843–1907), Norwegian composer whose Scottish great-grandfather's name was Greig; also pianist, particularly as accompanist to his wife (and cousin) Nina, who sang his songs. Encouraged by Ole Bull, went to study in Leipzig; later, pupil of Gade in Copenhagen. Became 'nationalist' in music. At Ibsen's request, wrote music for ➤*Peer Gynt*. Wrote also a celebrated piano concerto, ➤*Holberg Suite* for strings, music to Bjørnson's *Sigurd Jorsalfar* (➤*Homage March*); choral works; *Bergliot* (text by Bjørnson) for reciter and orchestra; three violin sonatas, many songs and piano works, various Norwegian folk-music arrangements. Often visited Britain; Hon. D. Mus., Cambridge, 1894.

Griffes, Charles Tomlinson (1884–1920), American composer – pupil of Humperdinck in Germany, but mainly influenced by French musical ➤impressionism. Overworked, through poverty, and died of pneumonia. Composed

175

The Pleasure Dome of Kubla Khan (after Coleridge) for orchestra; music to a Japanese mime play; *The ➤White Peacock* for piano (later orchestrated) and other piano music.

Grigny, Nicolas de (1672–1703), French organist whose *First Organ Book* (he died young and did not publish another) was copied out in admiration by Bach; it contains music for the Mass, hymns, fugues, etc.

Grimm, Jacob Ludwig Karl (1785–1863) and **Wilhelm Karl** (1786–1859), German folklorists and writers. ➤*Hänsel und Gretel*.

Grisi, Giulia (1811–69), Italian soprano, one of the most famous opera singers of her day in Paris and London. Her sister Giuditta Grisi (1805–40) was a mezzo-soprano.

grosse (Ger.), big; *grosse Trommel*, ➤bass drum; *grosses Orchester*, full ➤orchestra.

grosse caisse (Fr.), ➤bass drum.

Grosse Fuge (Ger., 'Great Fugue'), fugue by Beethoven for string quartet, op. 133 (1825), originally designed as last movement of the Quartet in B flat, op. 130; but Beethoven gave this work a new finale and issued the fugue separately.

Grossi, Carlo (*c*. 1634–1688), Italian composer active in Venice *c*. 1655–*c*. 1680, church singer at St Mark's there; wrote vocal and instrumental music for church use, also operas and chamber music.

ground, ➤ground bass.

ground bass, bass pattern which is persistently repeated while upper parts proceed; hence, e.g. in 17th-century England 'divisions on a ground', i.e. a piece in variation-form constructed by this means. The procedure is related to that of the ➤*chaconne*.

Grove, George (1820–1900), British musical scholar (also engineer, biblical commentator, magazine editor, etc.), first director of the Royal College of Music (1883–94); founder and first editor (1879–89) of *Grove's Dictionary of Music and Musicians*. Knighted, 1883.

Groven, Eivind (1901–77), Norwegian composer of choral music, symphonic poems, etc.; collected more than 1,800 Norwegian folk-tunes. Disliking the use of the 'tempered scale' (➤temperament) he invented an organ 'with automatically controlled non-tempered intervals'.

Groves, Charles [Barnard] (1915–92), British conductor – of Royal Liverpool Philharmonic Orchestra, 1963–77; musical director of English National Opera, 1978–9. Knighted, 1973.

Grovlez, Gabriel [Marie] (1879–1944), French pianist, conductor and composer of songs, two operas, etc.

Gruber, H[ans] **K**[arl] (b. 1943), Austrian composer, additionally styling himself 'actor, singer, chansonnier'. Known for comically outrageous pieces such as ➤*Frankenstein!!* and the opera *Gloria von Jaxtberg*, about a pig; also of violin concerto, *Demilitarized Zones* for brass band, etc.

Gruberová, Edita (b. 1946), Slovak soprano, distinguished as Queen of the Night in *Die Zauberflöte* – her début role at Vienna State Opera (1970), Glyndebourne (1973), and the Metropolitan; also performs varied other (especially coloratura) operatic roles.

Gruenberg, Louis (1884–1964), Russian-born American composer and pianist (brought to USA at age two); piano pupil of Busoni in Vienna. Much influenced by jazz and Afro-American music: his works include ➤*Emperor Jones* and other operas, also a violin concerto, symphonic poems, *Jazzberries* for piano.

Gruenthal, Joseph, ➤Tal.

Grumiaux, Arthur (1921–86), Belgian violinist, pupil of Enescu in Paris, and an internationally celebrated performer (especially in Mozart) from about 1950. Partnered ➤Haskil. He was created a Belgian baron, 1973.

Grümmer, Elisabeth (1911–86), German soprano noted in opera and concerts; at Covent Garden from 1951, Bayreuth from 1957.

gruppetto (It.), ➤turn (type of ornament).

Guadagni, Gaetano (*c.* 1725–1792), Italian male alto (castrato), later soprano. Worked with Handel in London; was the original performer (Vienna, 1762) of title-role of Gluck's ➤*Orfeo.*

Guarneri, Guarnerius, Italian family (the second name is the Latinized form) of 17th- and 18th-century makers of violins, etc. The founder, Andrea Guarneri, was a pupil of Amati. Giuseppe Antonio Guarneri (1698–1744) is known as Giuseppe Guarneri del Gesù.

Guarnieri, [Mozart] Camargo (1907–1993), Brazilian composer, pupil of Koechlin in Paris, also conductor. Works, often making use of Brazilian folk-music, include four symphonies, five piano concertos.

Gubaidulina, Sofia (b. 1931), Russian composer who in the 1980s won marked attention in the West. Compositions include a piano concerto (*Introitus*), violin concerto (*Offertorium*), a symphony entitled *Stimmen . . . verstummen* (Ger., 'Voices . . . Made Dumb'), with one section for conductor alone; four string quartets. ➤*bayan.*

Guerre des Bouffons. ➤War of the Comedians/Buffoons.

Gui, Vittorio (1885–1975), Italian conductor who in 1928 founded in Florence the orchestra from which eventually arose the *Maggio Musicale* (Musical May) Festival there. Noted conductor of opera, e.g. at Glyndebourne from 1952; was also composer.

Guido d'Arezzo (*c.* 992–*c.* 1050), Italian monk (long resident in Arezzo; hence the name) and musical theorist. Inventor of two devices greatly facilitating the practice of music: (1) the names 'ut', 're', 'mi', etc. (ancestors of modern 'do', 're', 'mi') as indication of the relative positions of the notes of the scale – 'ut' to be either G, C or F, bottom notes of the ➤hexachords then used; (2) the 'Guidonian hand', an aid to memory whereby the tips and joints of the fingers are given the names of the various notes.

Guillaume Tell (Fr., 'William Tell'), Rossini's last opera, produced in Paris, 1829. Libretto by V. J. E. de Jouy and H. L. F. Bis – after Schiller's drama about the Swiss national hero.

Guilmant, Félix Alexandre (1837–1911), French organist in Paris and composer of two 'symphonies' for organ and orchestra, many organ solos for recital and church use.

Guion, David [Wendel Fentress]

(1895–1981), American pianist (pupil or Godowsky), composer, and arranger of *Turkey in the Straw* and other traditional American tunes.

Guiraud, Ernest (1837–92), French (American-born) composer (eight operas, one unfinished and completed by Saint-Saëns) and teacher. Wrote recitatives for Bizet's *Carmen*; arranged the second suite from Bizet's L'➤*Arlésienne*; revised the opera *Les* ➤*Contes d'Hoffmann*, left unfinished by Offenbach.

guiro, instrument primarily of Latin-American dance music (Sp. *guira*, calabash tree), originally of an elongated gourd, scraped; commercially made of hardwood. As *râpe* (Fr., rasp), used by Stravinsky in *The Rite of Spring*.

guitar, plucked, fretted string instrument: it exists in various types of which the principal one came to other European countries from Spain and is therefore sometimes called *Spanish guitar*; now normally with six strings, with compass from E below the bass stave upwards for more than three octaves. This type (now also called *classical guitar*) enjoyed revival in the 20th century (➤Segovia having the principal role), calling forth concertos by Villa-Lobos and others; it is also (rarely) used in chamber music (e.g. Schoenberg, *Serenade*). The *electric guitar* and four-stringed *electric bass guitar* (➤electric/electronic) are chiefly used in pop music, etc.; in pop circles *acoustic guitar* (primarily meaning non-electric) is customarily a bulkier instrument than the Spanish guitar. *Baroque guitar*, modern name for a five-string (or five-➤course) instrument of distinct shape, current in 17th century; *English guitar*, a distinct

instrument (of different body and special tuning) popular in the 18th–19th centuries; *Portuguese guitar*, another special type (➤*fado*). Other variants are found (➤*dobro*; ➤*flamenco*; ➤*steel guitar*).

Gulda, Friedrich (b. 1930), Austrian pianist who occasionally added jazz works to the classics in recital; has also composed two piano concertos and works for jazz ensemble, and occasionally plays flute and saxophone.

Gundry, Inglis (b. 1905), British composer, also barrister; works, some with Cornish allusions, include operas *Avon* and (to his own libretto) *Galileo*.

Gung'l, Joseph (1810–89), Austro-Hungarian bandmaster and composer of marches, dances, etc.; visited USA, 1849.

Guridi, Jesús (1886–1961), Spanish (Basque) composer, using Basque themes; studied in Paris and elsewhere. Works include operas, organ music, folk-song arrangements.

Gurlitt, Manfred (1890–1973), German conductor and composer of operas (one on the ➤*Wozzeck* story used by Berg), orchestral and chamber works, etc. Settled in Japan, 1939.

Gurney, Ivor [Bertie] (1890–1937), British composer (also poet) who won distinction for songs, some to his own words. Also composed piano and orchestral music. Became insane, 1922.

Gurrelieder (Ger., 'Songs of Gurre'), work by Schoenberg (1900–1911) for four solo singers, three male choruses, and one mixed chorus and huge orchestra (including eight flutes and a set of iron chains). Text is a German translation from the Danish of J. P. Jacobsen: Gurre is the castle where dwells Tove, beloved of Waldemar IV, a 14th-century Danish king.

gusla (also *gusle*), ancient Slavonic one-string bowed instrument, distinct from the following.

gusli, Russian instrument of zither type used in folk-music; 'played' by Sadko in Rimsky-Korsakov's opera of that name, the effect being simulated in the orchestra.

gut (Ger.), good, well, markedly.

Guy, Barry [John] (b. 1947), British double-bassist and composer, active in jazz and ensembles of modern music. Works include *Incontri* (It., 'Encounters') for cello and orchestra; three string quartets; *Statements II* for amplified double-bass, unaccompanied.

Guy-Ropartz, Joseph, ➤Ropartz.

Guys and Dolls, musical with text by Abe Burrows and Jo Swerling based on a story and characters by Damon Runyon; music and lyrics by Frank Loesser. Produced in New York, 1950. The Salvation Army meets illegal street gamblers.

gymel (from Lat. *gemellus*, twin), type of 13th–15th-century vocal music in two ➤parts, making considerable use of thirds and sixths, and chiefly practised in England.

Gymnopédies, ➤Satie.

Gyrowetz (Germanized form of Czech name 'Jirovec'), **Adalbert** (1763–1850), Bohemian composer, some of whose symphonies (he wrote more than 40) were performed under Haydn's name in Paris. Visited London, 1789–92; court conductor at Vienna from 1804. Composed German and Italian operas, about 45 string quartets, etc.

H

H, German note-symbol. ➤B.

Haas, Pavel (1898–1944), Czech composer of opera *The Charlatan*, three string quartets, etc. Arrested as a Jew by the Nazis, he continued to compose under detention until sent to his death at Auschwitz.

Hába, Alois (1893–1973), Czech composer (pupil of Novák and Schreker), sometimes using quarter-tones with special instruments to play them – and also, less frequently, using sixth-tones; works include opera *The Mother*, orchestral and chamber music, songs with guitar, solos for ordinary piano and for quarter-tone piano. Brother of Karel Hába.

Hába, Karel (1898–1972), Czech violinist, viola-player and composer, pupil of his brother Alois Hába; sometimes used quarter-tones. Works in normal tonal system include a violin concerto, cello concerto, septet.

habanera, Cuban dance with singing introduced into Spain. The word comes from Habana (i.e. Havana), Cuba; whence the French equivalent term, *havanaise*. There is a famous example in Bizet's *Carmen*, borrowed from a Spanish source (➤Yradier). The spelling 'habañera' is mistaken.

Hacker, Alan [Ray] (b. 1938), British clarinettist, also conductor; pioneered the revival of the ➤basset clarinet in Mozart's works.

Hadley, Henry Kimball (1871–1937), American composer and conductor who studied in Vienna; works include operas, four symphonies (no. 2, *The Four Seasons*), choral works, more than 100 songs.

Hadley, Patrick [Arthur Sheldon] (1899–1973), British composer of *La Belle Dame Sans Merci* and other choral works, orchestral and chamber music, incidental music for Sophocles' *Antigone*, etc. Professor at Cambridge, 1946–63.

Haefliger, Ernst (b. 1919), Swiss tenor eminent in oratorio and opera – Salzburg Festival 1949, Glyndebourne 1956, etc. Author of book on singing.

Haendel, Georg Friederich, ➤Handel.

Haendel, Ida (b. 1924), Polish-born British violinist resident in USA; was child prodigy (London, 1937), and has maintained a distinguished career into her seventies. CBE, 1991.

'Haffner' Serenade, nickname of a serenade composed by Mozart, 1776 (K250), for a marriage in the Haffner family of Salzburg. ➤*'Haffner' Symphony*.

'Haffner' Symphony, nickname for Mozart's Symphony no. 35 in D (K385), arranged from a serenade (not that of the preceding entry) written for the Haffner family of Salzburg in 1782.

Hagegård, Håkon (b. 1945), Swedish baritone who sang Papageno in Bergman's film of *Die* ➤*Zauberflöte* (1975), having made his Glyndebourne début in 1973; in 1991 created the role of Beaumarchais in Corigliano's *The* ➤*Ghosts of Versailles* at the Metropolitan Opera, New York.

Hageman, Richard (1882–1966), Dutch-born composer who settled in USA, 1907; also operatic and concert conductor. Works include opera and many songs, such as 'Do not go, my love' (text by Tagore).

Hahn, Reynaldo (1874–1947; the birth-date 1875 is mistaken), French composer, Venezuelan-born, who went to Paris in infancy, entered Conservatory there at 11 (pupil of Massenet and others), and became conductor. Wrote operas (one on *The Merchant of Venice*), operettas, music for plays (including Sacha Guitry's *Mozart*), chamber music, songs (including 'Si mes vers avaient des ailes').

Hair, 'American tribal love-rock musical' with text by Gerome Ragni and James Rado; music by Galt MacDermot. Produced in New York, 1967. Long hair is the emblem of the hippy, Hare-Krishna-chanting tribe.

hairpins, colloquial name for the signs $<$ and $>$ indicating respectively ➤*crescendo* and ➤*diminuendo*.

Haitink, Bernard [Johan Herman] (b. 1929), Dutch conductor, principal conductor of the Concertgebouw Orchestra of Amsterdam, 1961–88, and of the London Philharmonic Orchestra, 1967–79; music director at Glyndebourne, 1978–87, then at Covent Garden. Hon. KBE, 1977.

Halb(e) (Ger.), half: *Halbe, Halbe-note*, ➤half-note, minim.

Hale, ➤La Hale.

Halévy, [original surname Levy] **Jacques François** [Fromental Elias] (1799–1862), French composer; was a pupil of Cherubini in Paris and also studied in Italy. Works include *La* ➤*Juive* ('The Jewess') and more than 30 other operas, usually of a spectacular kind – mostly in French, but one in Italian based on Shakespeare's *The Tempest*. Also composed ballet scores, cantatas, etc. After his death, his daughter married his ex-pupil Bizet.

Half a Sixpence, musical with text by Beverley Cross based on H. G. Wells's novel *Kipps*; music and lyrics by David Heneker. Produced in London, 1963. Shy working-class lad finds and loses wealth.

half-close, imperfect ➤cadence.

Halffter [Escriche], **Ernesto** (1905–89), Spanish composer of partly German descent; also conductor. Works include Sinfonietta, guitar concerto; chamber music. Brother of Rodolfo Halffter. ➤Falla.

Halffter [Escriche], **Rodolfo** (1900–1987), Spanish composer of partly German descent, resident in Mexico; also writer on music. Works include a violin concerto, ballet scores, piano solos. Brother of Ernesto Halffter.

half-note, the note ♩ considered as a time-value. This term is standard

North American usage and, as mathematically corresponding to the element of time-signature represented by /2, should clearly be preferred to 'minim', still surviving in British use. The corresponding rest is noted ▬

Hälfte, die (Ger., the half), direction indicating that a passage is to be played by only half the normal number of instruments, e.g. half the first violins.

Halka, opera by Moniuszko, produced in Vilnius, 1854. Regarded as the chief Polish national opera. Libretto by W. Wolski. Named after the humbly born heroine who drowns herself when her aristocratic lover leaves her with child.

Hall, Richard (1903–80), British composer of five symphonies, organ works, etc. Noted teacher in Manchester, e.g. of P. M. Davies and A. Goehr.

Halle, Adam de la, ➤La Hale.

Hallelujah Chorus, the chorus consisting mostly of the one repeated word 'Hallelujah', at the end of Part II of Handel's ➤*Messiah*. (This is what the term now refers to, though other works have similar choruses.)

'Hallelujah' Concerto, nickname for Handel's Organ Concerto in B flat (no. 3 of his second set, published in 1740), because it contains a phrase also occurring in the 'Hallelujah Chorus'.

Hallé Orchestra, orchestra founded in Manchester in 1858 by the German-born pianist and conductor Carl Halle, 1819–95, who became Sir Charles Hallé. Barbirolli was its conductor, 1943–70; Stanisław Skrowaczewski, 1984–91; Kent Nagano from 1994.

Hallgrímsson, Haflidi (b. 1941), Icelandic composer (also painter, and former orchestral cellist), resident in Britain but maintaining connections with Icelandic culture. Works include *Tristia* for guitar and cello, *Poemi* for violin and string orchestra, *The Flight of Icarus* for flute solo.

halling (Norw.), a Norwegian acrobatic solo dance for men, in 2/4 time, cultivated by Grieg and other Norwegian composers.

Halvorsen, Johan (1864–1935), Norwegian composer, also violinist and conductor; married a niece of Grieg. As a young violinist, worked in Aberdeen. Compositions include two symphonies, a violin concerto, stage music.

Haman and Mordecai, ➤*Esther*.

Hambraeus, Bengt (b. 1928), Swedish composer and organist; till 1972 he worked for Swedish Radio, then took university post in Montreal. Works include *Rota* for three orchestras and tape; *Interferences* for organ; *Symphonia sacra* for five solo voices, choir, wind and percussion.

Hamerik, Asger (1843–1923), Danish composer, pupil of Gade and Berlioz; in USA, 1872–98. Works include seven symphonies (no. 6 *Spirituelle*, i.e. light), four operas, two choral trilogies. Father of Ebbe Hamerik.

Hamerik, Ebbe (1898–1951), Danish composer and conductor. Studied with his father (Asger Hamerik) and abroad. Works include *The Travelling Companion* (after Hans Andersen) and other operas; orchestral *Variations on an Old Danish Folk-Tune*; woodwind quintet.

Hamilton, Iain [Ellis] (b. 1922), British composer, pupil of Alwyn. Originally apprenticed as engineer. Works include four symphonies; a concerto and other works for clarinet; *Sonata notturna* for horn and piano; also operas including *The Catiline Conspiracy, The Royal Hunt of the Sun* (after Peter Shaffer's play) and *Anna Karenina* (after Tolstoy's novel). Professor, Duke University, North Carolina, 1962–71.

Hamlet, title of various works after Shakespeare, including (1) opera by A. Thomas, produced in Paris, 1868 (libretto, J. Barbier and M. Carré); (2) symphonic poem by Liszt, 1858, composed as a prelude to the play; (3) overture-fantasia by Tchaikovsky, 1888; (4) incidental music by Tchaikovsky to the play, 1891 – shortened version of the preceding plus other movements adapted from his earlier works; (5) opera by Searle, produced in Hamburg, 1968.

Hamlisch, Marvin [Frederick] (b. 1944), American composer of the musicals *A* ➤*Chorus Line* and *They're Playing our Song*; also of film scores.

'Hammerklavier' Sonata, nickname for Beethoven's Piano Sonata in B♭, op. 106 (1815–19). The nickname has small justification: the word is merely an ostentatiously German substitute (hammer-keyboard) for the Italian 'pianoforte', and this was not the only sonata to which Beethoven applied it.

Hammond, Joan [Hood] (1912–96), New Zealand-born soprano; spent early years in Australia; made operatic début in Vienna, then appeared (1938) in London, continuing to specialize in operatic music. Created Dame, 1974.

Hammond organ, type of electronic organ (➤electric/electrophonic), usually with two manuals and pedal keyboard; invented in USA, 1934. (Trade name, after its inventor, Laurens Hammond.)

Hampson, Thomas (b. 1955), American baritone who made Metropolitan Opera début in 1986, becoming well known in Mozart and other opera roles; has also recorded songs by Cole Porter, Irving Berlin, etc.

handbell, type of small bell with stiff handle of leather or plastic, assembled in sets for teams of players; mostly in informal amateur use but required in Britten's *Noye's Fludde*.

Handel, George Frideric [originally Georg Friederich Händel or Haendel, adopting new style of name in England] (1685–1759), German-born composer whose success while living (marked by the erection of his statue in Vauxhall Gardens, London) has been universally sustained since. First visited England in 1710, and was naturalized there in 1727. Precocious as a child, at first against his father's wish he became a violinist in Hamburg Opera orchestra, 1703. Visited Italy, 1706–10. Wrote Italian operas for London, including ➤*Rinaldo*, ➤*Alcina*, ➤*Berenice*, ➤*Giulio Cesare*, and ➤*Serse*. 'Invented' English biblical ➤oratorio with ➤*Esther*, 1732; other oratorios include ➤*Saul*, ➤*Israel in Egypt*, ➤*Messiah*, ➤*Samson*, ➤*Judas Maccabaeus*, ➤*Solomon*, ➤*Susanna*, ➤*Theodora* and (last) ➤*Jephtha*. Other vocal works include ➤*Acis and Galatea*, ➤*Semele* and ➤*Alexander's Feast*; ➤*Chandos Anthems* and four coronation anthems including ➤*Zadok the Priest*. Noted harpsichordist and organist; played his organ concertos as intermissions in oratorio. Wrote for orchestra his ➤*Water Music*, ➤*Fireworks Music* and works of ➤*concerto grosso* type (for strings alone and for wind and strings); composed also *The* ➤*Harmonious Blacksmith* (later so called), and other harpsichord pieces. Made some unacknowledged 'borrowings' from other composers (➤Kerll), also reused parts of his own works. Became partially blind, 1751; totally so, 1753. Died in London.

Handel in the Strand, piece by Grainger originally (1912) for instrumental ensemble; the well-known full orchestration is by Henry J. Wood. It alludes to Handel's so-called ➤*Harmonious Blacksmith* and to the Strand as (former) home of musical comedy.

hand-horn, ➤horn.

Handl, Jacob (1550–91), Austrian church musician working finally in Prague; composer of motets, Masses, etc.

Handley, Vernon [George] (b. 1930), British conductor, celebrated for performances and recordings of rare British repertory including several of Robert Simpson's symphonies. Principal conductor, West Australian (Perth) Symphony Orchestra from 1994.

Hänsel und Gretel, opera by Humperdinck, produced in Weimar, 1893. Libretto by A. Wette, the composer's sister, after the brothers Grimm: the two children of the title defeat a witch. (The spelling and pronunciation 'Hansel' without the German *ä* has become standard in English.)

Hans Heiling, opera by Marschner, produced in Berlin, 1833. Libretto by É. Devrient (originally written for Men-

delssohn). Named after a gnome king who unsuccessfully courts a human woman.

Hanslick, Eduard (1825–1914), Austrian music critic, author of influential treatise *The Beautiful in Music*; champion of Brahms and opponent of Wagner, who pilloried him as Beckmesser in *Die* ➤*Meistersinger*.

Hanson, Howard (1896–1981), American composer; worked in Rome, 1921–4, as recipient of an American prize; from 1924, director of the Eastman School of Music, Rochester, NY. Also conductor. Works, some alluding to his Swedish descent, include seven symphonies (no. 1 *Nordic*, no. 4 *Requiem* – in memory of his father; no. 5 *Sinfonia sacra*), a piano concerto, opera, chamber music, songs.

Hanus, Jan (b. 1915), Czech composer of *The Servant of Two Masters* (after Goldoni), *The Torch of Prometheus* and other operas; also of seven symphonies, a wind quintet, etc. ➤*Glagolitic Mass*.

Happy Birthday to You, song by C. F. Summy, first published (in Dallas, Texas) in 1924. The tune (originally wordless) by Mildred J. Hill and Patty S. Hill was published 1893; the authorship of the words is unknown. Used by Stravinsky in *Greeting Prelude*, 1955, and by P. M. Davies in *Birthday Greeting* (for BBC Philharmonic Orchestra), 1994.

Harbison, John [Harris] (b. 1938), American composer. Works include *Ulysses' Raft* for orchestra; *Deep Potomac Bells* for 250 tubas; opera *The Winter's Tale*; *The Great Gatsby* for the Metropolitan Opera, New York.

Hardanger fiddle (Norw., *hardingfele*), ➤fiddle.

Hardenberger, Håkan (b. 1961), Swedish trumpeter and cornetist for whom works have been specially written by Henze (concerto), Birtwistle (*Endless Parade*) and others.

Harding, Daniel (b. 1975), British conductor, made his professional debut in 1994 with the City of Birmingham Symphony Orchestra, where he assisted ➤Rattle. 1995/6 was Assistant to Claudio Abbado at the Berlin Philharmonic, since when has conducted throughout Europe. US debut 1997. From 1998 season, Princ. Cond. of the Trondheim Symphony Orchestra. From 1999, Music Director of the Deutsche Kammerphilharmonie.

Harle, John [Crofton] (b. 1956), British saxophonist, composer and director of his own ensemble (John Harle Band), with predominantly modern repertory extending into jazz. Opera *Angel-Magick*. Works have been written for him by Berio, Torke, Nyman (concerto *Where the Bee Dances*) and others.

Harmonic (adjective), (1) relating to harmony; hence the *harmonic* ➤*minor* scale used in harmonizing; hence also the ➤harmonic series, the series of tones (*harmonic tones*) from which the system of harmony has historically sprung; (2) relating to the harmonic series itself; hence, e.g., the *harmonic flute* stop on an organ, producing four-➤foot tone from an eight-➤foot pipe pierced at half-length – i.e. using the second tone of the ➤harmonic series.

harmonic (noun), = harmonic tone (see preceding entry), i.e. one of the tones of the ➤harmonic series. The lowest such tone, or 'fundamental', is called the *first harmonic*, the next lowest the *second harmonic*, etc. But in such phrases as 'playing in harmonics' on stringed instruments, the allusion

is to harmonics with the exclusion of the first – since the first is the 'normal' sound requiring no special directions. To obtain these harmonics other than the first, it is necessary to set the string vibrating not as a whole length but in fractional parts of its length. A violinist, etc., does this by placing a finger lightly at a given point of a vibrating string: when the string is an open string (i.e. not otherwise fingered) then the result is called a *natural harmonic*, but when the string is a stopped string (one finger used for stopping and another for 'lightly placing') then the result is an *artificial harmonic*. The harmonics obtainable on the harp (also by 'lightly placing' the finger on a vibrating string) are in this sense 'natural' harmonics.

harmonic series, the set of tones (called *harmonic tones* or simply *harmonics*) produced by a vibrating string or air-column, according to whether this is vibrating as a unit through its whole length or in aliquot parts ($\frac{1}{2}$, $\frac{1}{3}$, $\frac{1}{4}$, etc.). Vibration of the whole length gives the lowest ('fundamental') tone, or 'first harmonic'. The other tones, or 'upper partials', i.e. the second, third, fourth, and higher harmonics, are at fixed intervals above the fundamental – an octave above it, then a perfect fifth above that, and so on, decreasingly, ad infinitum. E.g. if the fundamental is the C in the bass stave, the series will begin as shown overleaf. (Not all of these, however, correspond exactly to the notes as tuned in modern European scales.) The importance of the series lies in the following points (among others): (1) the basic technique of brass instruments is to produce the various harmonics by varying the mode of blowing; on, e.g.,

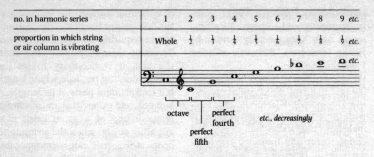

no. in harmonic series	1	2	3	4	5	6	7	8	9 etc.
proportion in which string or air column is vibrating	Whole	$\frac{1}{2}$	$\frac{1}{3}$	$\frac{1}{4}$	$\frac{1}{5}$	$\frac{1}{6}$	$\frac{1}{7}$	$\frac{1}{8}$	$\frac{1}{9}$ etc.

a bugle this one harmonic series yields all the notes available, while on, e.g. a trumpet and trombone the range is made more complete by use of valves and slide respectively; (2) the use of the upper partials also forms an important device in string-playing (see preceding entry); and those tones are used also on woodwind instruments – in the simplest instance, 'blowing harder' on a tin-whistle to produce a higher octave means the use of the second harmonic; (3) every note of normal musical instruments consists not of a 'pure' tone (like that of a tuning-fork) but of a blend of the 'fundamental' and certain upper partials, the precise blend differing between instruments. In fact this difference in blend determines the difference between ➤tone-colours of instruments. A sound in music which does not yield a perceptible pitch (or several pitches, e.g. a bell) is said to have inharmonicity.

harmonica name given to various types of musical instruments – especially, today, to the instrument also called 'mouth-organ', i.e. small wind instrument with metal reeds (one to each note), made in various sizes, most often with range upwards from about middle C, the superior models having chromatic compass. The instrument has mainly been used infor-

mally, e.g. by children, but works by e.g. Milhaud and Vaughan Williams have been written for Larry Adler, its most notable exponent. The name was also given to an instrument consisting of musically tuned glasses (now virtually obsolete: ➤glass harmonica).

harmonie (Fr.), (1) harmony; (2) wind band (not a purely brass band, which in Fr. is fanfare). Also in German, in both senses; hence the two following entries.

Harmoniemesse, German name (see preceding entry) for Haydn's ➤Wind Band Mass.

Harmoniemusik (Ger.), music for wind instruments (➤Harmonie).

Harmonious Blacksmith, The, nickname for a set of variations in Handel's suite for harpsichord in E (1720). Although the regular strokes of the theme may suggest a blacksmith's hammering, the nickname is not Handel's and originated after his death.

harmonium, small portable instrument of the ➤reed-organ family, in which pedals actuate a bellows which drives air through the reeds. Mainly used as a substitute in humble circumstances for the organ as an accompaniment to hymns, etc.; very occasionally elsewhere, e.g. in some *Bagatelles* (with two violins and cello) by Dvořák.

harmony, the simultaneous sounding of notes in a way that is musically significant. (➤Counterpoint is concerned with the simultaneous combination of melodies, not individual notes; but counterpoint and harmony represent overlapping types of relationships between notes, and a composer considers both relationships together.)

Harnoncourt, Nikolaus (b. 1929), German conductor, cellist and musicologist; distinguished in reviving baroque music with authentic instruments, observing historical style (in 1953 founding for this purpose his ➤Concentus Musicus Wien ensemble); he also works with symphony orchestras.

Harold en Italie (Fr., 'Harold in Italy'), work by Berlioz, 1834, for viola and orchestra – but called a 'symphony'. After Byron's *Childe Harold*. Written for Paganini, who wanted a viola work for himself, but rejected by him as giving the soloist too little prominence.

harp, plucked stringed instrument of ancient origin, of which the chief modern development (*double-action harp*, from early 19th century) now has a compass from B below the bass clef upwards for nearly seven octaves. It is much used in orchestral music, less frequently in chamber music, solos and for the accompaniment of voices. Its strings in their basic position give the scale of C♭ major (i.e. for practical purposes, B major) which is modified by the use of seven pedals – one raising all the notes C♭ to either

C♮ or C♯ as desired, the other pedals doing similarly for all the D♭'s, all the E♭'s, etc. Despite the pedal action, the basic tuning of the harp is thus ➤diatonic; a *chromatic harp* (giving a ➤chromatic scale) was also in use in the 19th and early 20th centuries. Earlier types from the medieval, Renaissance and baroque periods (all pedal-less) have been revived. Likewise without pedal are the Welsh *triple harp* with three banks of strings; the large harp used in Latin-American folk-music; and the much smaller varieties which may rest on the knee and are now known as Celtic harp, minstrel harp, troubadour harp, etc.

Harper, Edward [James] (b. 1941), British composer of *Hedda Gabler* (after Ibsen) and other operas; symphony; clarinet concerto. Also Edinburgh University teacher and (1973–91) director of the New Music Group of Scotland.

Harper, Heather [Mary] (b. 1930), British soprano, active in opera (Covent Garden from 1962; Bayreuth from 1967) and in concert (Henry Wood Promenade Concerts for 25 consecutive years from 1957). CBE, 1965.

'Harp' Quartet, nickname for Beethoven's String Quartet in E♭, op. 74 (1809) with harp-like pizzicato arpeggios in the first movement. It is a somewhat absurd nickname, because it might be mistaken for a descriptive name: on the analogy of e.g. 'piano quartet', a 'harp quartet' ought to be a work for harp and three bowed instruments.

harpsichord, keyboard instrument with strings plucked mechanically – as distinct from the piano, in which the strings are struck, and from ►clavichord, where the process is again different. Prominent *c.* 1550–1800 as solo and ensemble instrument and revived after 1900 for new works (e.g. a concerto by Falla) and for performing old music authentically. Two manuals are commonly found, and are actually required sometimes for contrast, e.g. in Bach's ►*Italian Concerto*. On a few modern models there may be a pedal keyboard, as on an organ, but pedals are chiefly provided to help actuate the ►stops and ►couplers. (►spinet, ►virginals.)

harp stop, a contrivance on a harpsichord damping the strings so that the resulting tone resembles the rather thin tone of the harp.

Harrell, Lynn (b. 1944), American cellist who made London début in 1975 and has a distinguished international career. Appointed Principal of the Royal Academy of Music, 1992, but suddenly resigned, 1994.

Harriet: The Woman Called 'Moses', opera by Thea Musgrave, produced in Norfolk, Virginia, 1985. Libretto by composer, about Harriet Tubman, the US abolitionist and rescuer of slaves who was herself a former slave.

Harris, Roy [originally Leroy Ellsworth Harris] (1898–1981), American composer; studied with N. Boulanger in Paris; held various university teaching posts. Works include 13 symphonies of which no. 3 became internationally known; no. 4 (*Folk-Song*) is for chorus and orchestra, incorporating various traditional tunes. Other works include concertos for piano, for two pianos, for accordion; *Elegy and Paean* for viola and orchestra (with electrically amplified piano).

Harris, William Henry (1883–1973), organist of St George's Chapel, Windsor, and composer of church music (including 'Thou hast made me' and 'Bring us, O Lord' on texts by Donne), cantatas, etc. Knighted, 1954.

Harrison, Lou (b. 1917), American composer who studied with Schoenberg and later wrote *Schoenbergiana* for wind sextet. Other works include opera *Rapunzel* (after William Morris), a Mass, three orchestral suites, pieces for classical Korean court orchestra and others using instruments of the Javanese ►gamelan.

Harsányi, Tibor (1898–1954), Hungarian composer, pupil of Kodály, but resident in Paris from 1923 and predominantly French in musical outlook. Works include a symphony, violin concerto, nonet, stage works.

Hartmann, Johan Peter Emilius (1805–1900), Danish composer of operas including *Little Kirsten* (after Hans Andersen), ballet score *A Folk-Tale* (with Gade, his son-in-law), symphonic poems on Nordic subjects, choral works, etc. Director of the Copenhagen Conservatory.

Hartmann, Karl Amadeus (1905–63), German composer. Dissociated himself from the Nazis. Works include eight symphonies, two string quartets, 'pacifist' opera *Simplicius Simplicissimus*. Also organizer of notable concerts of modern music in Munich ('Musica Viva').

Harty, [Herbert] Hamilton (1879–1941), British conductor, born in Northern Ireland; conductor of the Hallé Orchestra, 1920–33, and composer of *Irish Symphony*, a violin concerto, cantata *The Mystic Trumpeter*, many songs, etc. Also pianist and organist. Made orchestral arrangements of excerpts from Handel's ➤*Fireworks Music* and ➤*Water Music* which became standard. Knighted, 1925.

Harvey, Jonathan [Dean] (b. 1939), British composer (also Sussex University professor), pupil in USA of Babbitt. Works include *Persephone Dream* for orchestra; *Timepiece* for orchestra with two conductors; opera *Inquest of Love*; *Round the Star and Back* for piano 'and a few other instruments capable of a reasonable blend'; various works using tape-recorded sound including '*Vivos voco, mortuos plango*' (Lat., 'I call the living, mourn the dead') for computer-modulated real sounds (boy's voice, bells), Percussion Concerto.

Harwood, Basil (1859–1949), British cathedral organist and composer of church music, cantatas, an organ concerto, etc.

Háry János, opera by Kodály, produced in Budapest, 1926; also an orchestral suite drawn from this, first performed in 1927. The opera contains traditional Hungarian tunes, and the libretto (by B. Paulini and Z. Harsányi) concerns the folk-hero whose name forms the title (in Hungarian fashion, i.e. with surname first).

Haskil, Clara (1895–1960), Romanian pianist, naturalized Swiss in 1949; noted in Mozart. A regular partner of ➤Grumiaux; died in Belgium.

Hasler, ➤Hassler.

Hassan, play by Flecker to which Delius wrote incidental music, 1920, including a well-known 'Serenade'.

Hasse, Johann Adolph (1699–1783), German composer, also tenor singer; pupil of Porpora and A. Scarlatti in Italy. Wrote dozens of Italian operas, one on the libretto afterwards used by Mozart in *La* ➤*Clemenza di Tito*; also church music, harpsichord works, etc. Director of the Dresden Court Opera; afterwards lived mainly in Vienna and in Venice, where he died.

Hassler [also Hasler], **Hans Leo.** (1562–1612), German composer, pupil of A. Gabrieli in Venice; also organist at various churches and courts. Wrote church music, organ works, German songs including the original tune made familiar by Bach as the 'Passion Chorale' (➤Passion).

Hatton, John Liptrot (1809–86), British singer, pianist, organist, theatre conductor and composer of 'Simon the Cellarer', 'To Anthea', and about 300 other solo songs; also of part-songs, church music, stage music, etc.

Haubenstock-Ramati, Roman (1919–94), Polish-born composer, resident in Israel 1950–57, later in Paris and Vienna. Works include electronic music; *Interpolation* for flute and recorded tape; *Recitative and Aria* for harpsichord and orchestra; *Credentials* or *Think, Think, Lucky* (text from Beckett's *Waiting for Godot*) for voice and eight instrumentalists – whose written parts are divided into square 'fields' which can be played vertically or horizontally.

Hauer, Josef Matthias (1883–1959), Austrian composer who arrived at a form of ➤twelve-note technique independently of Schoenberg and seemingly a little before him (from 1912; books 1925, 1926); he postulated 44 combinations (called tropes) of the 12 notes of the octave. Works, using this method, include a piano concerto, violin concerto, chamber music, cantata *Des Menschen Weg* ('The Way of Humanity').

Haunted Ballroom, The, ballet with choreography by Ninette de Valois, music by G. Toye, produced in London, 1934.

Haussmann, Valentin (?–*c.* 1612), German composer who assembled a collection of German and Polish dances which he published in 1602 as *Venusgarten* (Ger., 'Garden of Venus'); also composed part-songs, church music, etc.

hautbois (Fr.), oboe – the actual word (literally meaning 'loud wood') from which 'oboe', really an Italian word, is derived.

hautboy, obsolete English term (from preceding entry) for oboe (and, earlier, for the shawm). An alternative spelling was 'hoboy'.

havanaise (Fr.), ➤*habanera*.

Hawaiian guitar, ➤steel guitar.

Haydn, surname of two composers, brothers (below). The surname alone alludes to the first.

Haydn, Franz Joseph (1732–1809), Austrian composer (not, despite some writers, of Croatian descent); with Mozart, the main architect of Viennese-classical style. Born in Rohrau, elder brother of Michael ➤Haydn; cathedral choirboy in Vienna; became pupil of Porpora; married an unappreciative wife, 1760. Took post with Hungarian noble family of Esterházy, 1761–90, first at Eisenstadt (Austria) then at Eszterháza

(Hungary). Achieved European reputation there, especially for his symphonies and string quartets, establishing the now classical concept of both these types: a set of six symphonies was commissioned for a Paris concert series (➤*Paris Symphonies*). Visited Britain in 1791–2 and 1794–5 – presenting in London the last 12 (➤*Salomon*) of his 104 catalogued symphonies, and also other works; received honorary Oxford doctorate. Handel's oratorios heard in London influenced him towards his own *Die* ➤*Schöpfung* and *Die* ➤*Jahreszeiten*, written on his return to Vienna, where he died. Nicknames have been given to many of his symphonies (➤*Bear*, ➤*Clock*, ➤*Drum-roll*, ➤*Farewell*, ➤*Hen*, ➤*Horn Signal*, ➤*Hunt*, ➤*Imperial*, ➤*Lamentatione*, ➤*Laudon*, ➤*London*, ➤*Maria Theresia*, ➤*Military*, ➤*Miracle*, ➤*Morning*, ➤*Mourning*, ➤*Oxford*, ➤*Passion*, ➤*Philosopher*, ➤*Queen*, ➤*Roxolane*, ➤*Schoolmaster*, ➤*Surprise*) and to his Masses (➤*Drum Mass*, ➤*Great Organ Mass*, ➤*Little Organ Mass*, ➤*Nelson Mass*, ➤*Wind Band Mass*). Very prolific throughout a long career, he also wrote two cello concertos (➤Kraft, A.), various other concertos, about 80 string quartets (including ➤*Emperor*, ➤*Fifths*, ➤*Frog*, ➤*Lark*, ➤*Razor*, ➤*Tost*); 125 trios with ➤baryton; more than 20 Italian and German operas (including ➤*Armida, Il* ➤*Mondo della luna, L'*➤*Infedeltà delusa*); songs, some in English; ➤*Emperor's Hymn*; *Die* ➤*sieben Worte des Erlösers am Kreuz*, etc. A ➤*Toy Symphony* is mistakenly ascribed to him; six string quartets listed as Haydn's op. 3 are now thought to be not by him but by Hoffstetter. His works are indexed by 'Hob.' numbers, after the catalogue by

Anthony van Hoboken, first published 1957.

Haydn, [Johann] Michael (1737–1806), Austrian composer of much church music, also of symphonies, chamber music, operas, etc. Also organist. In service to the Archbishops of Salzburg from 1762, dying in Salzburg. Brother of Joseph Haydn.

Head, Michael (1900–1976), British singer, pianist and composer – especially of songs which he sang to his own accompaniment.

head voice, that 'register' of the voice which gives the feeling to the singer of vibrating in the head – i.e. the higher register, contrasted with ➤chest voice.

Heath, Dave [originally David Crispin Heath] (b. 1956), British composer and flautist; his music often aims to break the classical/rock/jazz barriers and includes *Cry from the Wild* (a flute concerto for James Galway), *Alone at the Frontier* (a violin concerto for Nigel Kennedy).

Hebden, John (active 1740–50), British bassoonist, cellist and composer of solos for flute and ➤continuo and of concertos for strings.

Hebrides, The, overture by Mendelssohn, born of his visit there, 1829; later revised, and first performed 1832 in London. (Also called *Fingal's Cave*.)

Heckelclarina, instrument of the clarinet type invented by the German firm of Heckel for the playing of the 'shepherd's pipe' part in Act III of Wagner's ➤*Tristan und Isolde* – now more usually played on the English horn.

Heckelphone, bass instrument of the oboe type (➤oboe) made by the German firm of Heckel; an octave lower in pitch than the oboe; used e.g. by R. Strauss and, under the name 'bass oboe', by Delius.

Heerdenglocken (Ger., herd bells) ➤cow-bells.

Heger, Robert (1886–1978), German composer of opera *Lady Hamilton*, violin concerto, etc. Also conductor, much associated with R. Strauss's operas.

Heifetz, Jascha [originally Yosif] (1901–87), Russian-born violinist, boy prodigy; first appeared in USA, 1917, becoming naturalized there, 1925; continued touring with immense reputation. Commissioned violin concertos from Gruenberg and Walton; made many transcriptions for violin and piano.

Heiller, Anton (1923–79), Austrian composer and organist; works – mainly church music, apart from a chamber symphony – include five Masses, a Te Deum, many motets.

Heine, Heinrich (1797–1856), German poet. ➤*Dichterliebe*; ➤*Liederkranz, Liederkreis*.

Heininen, Paavo (b. 1938), Finnish composer of operas *The Damask Drum* and *The Knife*, also of three piano concertos, a cello concerto, etc.

Heise, Peter Arnold (1830–79), Danish composer of *King and Marshal* and other operas, also songs (some to English texts), chamber music, etc.

Heldenleben, Ein (Ger., 'A Hero's Life'), symphonic poem by R. Strauss, 1898, with autobiographical connotation – the section 'The Hero's Works of Peace' quoting some of Strauss's previous compositions.

Heldentenor (Ger., heroic tenor), tenor capable of 'heavy' dramatic roles in opera, especially those of Wagner.

helicon, form of tuba passing round the player's body, e.g. the ➤*sousaphone*. (Rare in Britain, common in USA.) The name is from its helical (i.e. spiral) shape, not from the ancient Mt Helicon, sacred to the Muses.

Heller, Stephen (1813–88), Hungarian pianist and composer chiefly for the piano – sonatas, fantasies, studies, pieces with 'romantic' titles, etc.

Hello, Dolly!, musical comedy with text by Michael Stewart based on *The Matchmaker* by Thornton Wilder; music and lyrics by Jerry Herman. Produced in New York, 1964. Widow and matchmaker, Dolly Gallagher Levi finds a second marriage with her widowed, half-millionaire client.

Hely-Hutchinson, [Christian] **Victor** (1901–47), South African pianist, conductor, teacher and composer, who worked from 1926 in England; BBC Music Director, 1944–7. Works include *A Carol Symphony* (based on Christmas carols) and chamber music.

hemidemisemiquaver, ➤sixty-fourth note.

hemiola, hemiolia (the former term is commoner, the latter more correct, from Gk., one-and-a-half), term implying the ratio 3:2. In current usage it mainly refers to the rhythmic change resulting when a pulse of 2 × 3 is temporarily replaced by 3 × 2, or vice versa – e.g. when ♩.♩.| is replaced by ♩♩♩|

Hendricks, Barbara (b. 1948), American soprano, resident in Paris since 1977, noted internationally in opera and concert; performed Mimì in the filmed version of *La Bohème*, 1988. Prominent in aiding humanitarian causes such as UNESCO.

Heneker, David (b. 1906), British composer of musicals including ➤*Half a Sixpence*; joint composer of *Charlie Girl* (1965). Also lyricist for the British version of ➤*Irma La Douce*.

Henriques, [Valdemar] **Fini** (1867–1940), Danish composer, pupil of Svendsen; also violinist, pupil of Joachim. Works include operas, ballet *The Little Mermaid* (after Hans Andersen), two symphonies, piano solos.

Henry, Pierre (b. 1927), French composer, pupil of Messiaen and others, active from 1950 in Paris in pioneering ➤*musique concrète*. Several of his taped works, e.g. *Symphonie pour un homme seul* ('Symphony for a Lonely Man'), were choreographed as ballets by Maurice Béjart. Among his later (electronic) works is *La Dixième* ('The Tenth'), described as a gloss on Beethoven's symphonies nos. 1–9.

Henry IV (reigned 1399–1413) and **V** (reigned 1413–22), kings of England, each of whom has been conjecturally credited with vocal works attributed in the ➤*Old Hall Manuscript* to 'Roy Henry' (*roy* being the old French form of *roi*, 'king').

Henry VIII (1491–1547), King of England, amateur composer, some of whose vocal music survives; but the motet 'O Lord, the maker of all things', formerly attributed to him, is really by W. Mundy.

Henschel, George (originally Isidor Georg Henschel) (1850–1934), baritone, pianist, composer and conductor. German-born, he was naturalized British, 1890, and knighted, 1914. Conductor of the newly founded Boston Symphony Orchestra, 1881–4; as singer accompanying himself, broadcast and recorded until his 70s. Composed two operas, songs in German and English, much piano music, etc.

Hensel, Fanny, ➤Mendelssohn [Bartholdy], Fanny.

'Hen' Symphony, nickname for Haydn's symphony no. 83 in G minor (Hob. I: 83), 1786, one of the ➤*Paris* symphonies – the nickname presumably bestowed by someone who eccentrically detected a hen's clucking in the oboe figure of the first movement.

Henze, Hans Werner (b. 1926), German composer (pupil of Fortner) resident in Italy since 1953; also sometimes conductor and stage director of his works. His operas include *Boulevard Solitude* (➤*Manon*), *Der Prinz von Hamburg* (after Kleist), ➤*Elegy for Young Lovers, Der* ➤*junge Lord* and ➤*We Come to the River*. Has also written full-length ballet score *Ondine* (choreography by Ashton, 1958), cantata *Novae de infinito Laudes* (Lat., 'New praises of the infinite') with words by Giordano Bruno; eight symphonies; a secular, non-vocal ➤*Requiem*; secular oratorio *Das Floss der Medusa* ('The Raft of the Medusa'). ➤Seefried.

Herbert, [Sir] **A. P.** [Alan Patrick] (1890–1971), British writer. ➤Dunhill.

Herbert, Victor (1859–1924), Irish-born composer (also cellist, conductor) who settled in New York, 1886, and wrote many successful operettas including ➤*Naughty Marietta* and *Babes in Toyland*; also operas, two cello concertos, etc.

Herbig, Günther (b. 1931), German conductor; held posts in East Germany and elsewhere before becoming music director of the Toronto Symphony Orchestra in 1990.

Her Foster-daughter, ➤Jenůfa.

Herman, Jerry [originally Gerald] (b. 1933), American composer of musicals, also lyricist; in both capacities wrote ➤*Hello, Dolly!* and *La* ➤*Cage aux Folles*.

Hérodiade (Fr., 'Herodias'), opera by Massenet, produced in Brussels, 1881. Libretto by P. Millet and 'Henri Grémont' (i.e. G. Hartmann), after a tale by Flaubert: a variation of the story of Salome, who here begs for John the Baptist's life to be saved and afterwards kills herself. ➤*Salome*.

heroic tenor, ➤*Heldentenor*.

Hérold, [Louis Joseph] **Ferdinand** (1791–1833), French composer of *Zampa, La Pré aux Clercs* (referring to a famous duelling-ground) and many other operas; also two symphonies, etc.

Hero's Life, A, symphonic poem by R. Strauss. ➤*Heldenleben*.

Herrick, Robert (1591–1674), English poet. ➤Lawes (Henry), ➤Meyerowitz.

Herrmann, Bernard (1911–75), American composer, pupil of B. Wagenaar and others; also conductor, especially for radio. Works include a symphony, violin concerto, opera

Wuthering Heights (after E. Brontë), cantata *Moby Dick* (after Melville), a string quartet, and music for *Citizen Kane* and other films.

Hertel, Johann (1727–89), German composer of at least 36 symphonies, also concertos, chamber music, Italian and German opera, church music.

Hervé (pen-name of Florimond Ronger) (1825–92), French composer of operettas, many parodying historical subjects or literary works (one on *The Knights of the Round Table*); also of ballet scores, a symphony with voices *The Ashantee War* (for London), many songs, etc.

Herz, Henri [originally Heinrich] (1803–88), Austrian pianist-composer who settled in Paris and wrote eight piano concertos and other works in brilliant 'virtuoso' style. Contributor to the ➤*Hexameron*.

Heseltine, Philip, ➤Warlock.

Hess, Myra (1890–1965), British pianist, pupil of Matthay, who promoted and directed National Gallery Concerts in London during World War II; created Dame, 1941; celebrated for her piano transcription of a chorale from Bach's church cantata no. 147, under the name 'Jesu, joy of man's desiring'.

Hesse, Hermann (1877–1962), German author. ➤*Vier letzte Lieder*.

Heure espagnole, L' (Fr., 'The Spanish Hour'), opera by Ravel, produced in Paris, 1911. Libretto by Franc-Nohain; in a Spanish clockmaker's shop, the proprietor's wife welcomes customers and finds a gratifying way of passing the time.

hexachord, obsolete (11th–17th centu-

ries) grouping of notes not by octaves (eight notes) but by sixes – Greek *hex*, 6. The 'hard', 'natural' and 'soft' hexachords ascended respectively from G, C, and F, using what are now the white notes of the piano. ➤Guido d'Arezzo.

Hexameron, a set of variations by Liszt, Thalberg, Herz, Pixis, Czerny and Chopin on a march from Bellini's *I* ➤*Puritani*, 1831, with linking passages by Liszt. (From Greek for 'six days' – cf. *Decameron*, 10 days – alluding to the six composers. ➤Godowsky.)

Hexenmenuett, ➤'Fifths' Quartet.

Hiawatha, three cantatas by Coleridge-Taylor, first performed together in 1900: *Hiawatha's Wedding Feast*, *The Death of Minnehaha*, *Hiawatha's Departure*. Words from Longfellow's *Hiawatha*, narrative poem of American-Indian life. The subject was also treated by R. Goldmark.

Hickox, Richard [Sidney] (b. 1948), British conductor, noted choral director. He was artistic director of Northern Sinfonia (Newcastle) 1982–6; has conducted and recorded much opera (Covent Garden 1985), including Monteverdi, Handel, Mozart and Walton.

hidden fifths, ➤consecutive.

Hildegard of Bingen (1098–1179), German abbess, composer and poet. Wrote a cycle of vocal settings of 77 poems arranged according to the liturgical calendar.

Hill, Alfred (1870–1960), Australian composer, also violinist and conductor; studied in Leipzig; spent some time in New Zealand and used Maori folklore for cantata *Hinemoa* and song

'Waiata Pol', etc. Also composed 17 string quartets, *Overture of Welcome* (players of orchestra entering successively), etc.

Hill, Edward Burlingame (1872–1960), American composer and teacher; works include three symphonies, a violin concerto, *Music for English Horn and Orchestra*.

Hiller, Ferdinand (1811–85), German pianist (pupil of Hummel), conductor, teacher and composer – many piano pieces, also operas and three symphonies.

Hiller, Johann Adam (1728–1804), German composer (also flautist and singer) and conductor; cantor at St Thomas's, Leipzig (Bach's old position). Wrote church music, instrumental works and *The Devil is at Large* (*Der Teufel ist los*) – the first of that type of opera known as ➤*Singspiel*.

Hiller, Lejaren [Arthur] (1924–94), American composer (pupil of Sessions and Babbitt) who first worked as research chemist; became a pioneer (in late 1950s) of the application of computers to the techniques of composition. Collaborated with Cage in HPSCHD for 1–7 harpsichords and 1–51 tapes. Also wrote *Machine Music* for piano, percussion and tape, as well as seven string quartets, etc.

Hilliard Ensemble, British male-voice quartet founded 1974, named after the Elizabethan miniaturist painter Nicholas Hilliard (1547–1619). Current members: David James, Rogers Covey-Crump, John Potter, Gordon Jones. Cultivates the Renaissance and baroque repertory with modern excursions.

Hilton, John (*c.* 1560–1608), English organist (of Trinity College, Cambridge) and composer of anthems, madrigals, etc. Contributor to *The* ➤*Triumphs of Oriana*. See also next entry.

Hilton, John (1599–1657), English organist (of St Margaret's, Westminster) and composer of church music, 'Ayres or Fa-Las' (in this case, works of ➤ballett type), etc. Was also compiler and part-composer of *Catch that Catch Can* – a collection of rounds, catches and canons, etc. He was possibly a son of the John Hilton who died in 1608.

Himmel, Friedrich Heinrich (1765–1819), German composer of operas (in German and Italian), church music, piano works, etc.

Hindemith, Paul (1895–1963), German composer – formerly violinist and viola player (soloist in first performance of Walton's Viola Concerto, 1929); teacher in Berlin from 1927. Though not Jewish, banned by Nazis as musically 'degenerate' (➤*entartete Musik*); settled in USA, 1939. Noted teacher and theoretician. Composed for almost every type of musical medium, and (in his earlier period) much music of deliberately functional intent (➤*Gebrauchsmusik*). His earlier work was in a dissonant idiom verging on atonality, e.g. in the works labelled *Kammermusik* (➤chamber music); later he adopted an 'advanced' but strictly tonal idiom. He composed the operas ➤*Mathis der Maler* (on the life of the painter Grünewald) and *Die Harmonie der Welt* (on the life of the astronomer Kepler) and based a symphony on each of these. Other works include operas *Hin und zurück* (➤palindrome) and ➤*Cardillac*; *Nobilissima Visione* and other ballets; *Symphonic Metamorphoses of Themes of*

Weber (➤metamorphosis); a Symphony in E flat and many other orchestral works; *The* ➤*Four Temperaments* for piano and strings; *Funeral Music* (➤*Trauer*) for viola and strings, on the death of George V; six string quartets, many sonatas for various instruments; songs. ➤Requiem.

Hirt auf dem Felsen, Der (Ger., 'The Shepherd on the Rock'), song by Schubert (D.965) with clarinet obbligato, composed 1828.

Histoire du soldat, L' (Fr., 'The Soldier's Tale'), stage work by Stravinsky, produced in Lausanne, 1918. Text by C. F. Ramuz, after a collection of Russian tales: it deals with a soldier, the Devil and a Princess. The work uses speech and dance but no singing, an 'orchestra' of seven, and an idiom indebted to jazz. ➤Muldowney.

HMS Pinafore, or The Lass that Loved a Sailor, operetta by Sullivan, produced in London, 1878. Libretto by W. S. Gilbert, with the action aboard an English warship.

Hob., abbr. for 'Hoboken' in numbering Haydn's works: ➤Haydn.

Hoboken, Anthony van (1887–1983), Dutch musicologist who catalogued the works of ➤Haydn.

hoboy, ➤hautboy.

hocket (Fr., *hoquet*, bump, hiccup), in medieval polyphony, an overlapping stop-and-go effect between two or more parts through the insertion of rests (silences).

Hoddinott, Alun (b. 1929), Welsh composer of nine symphonies, a clarinet concerto, *Four Welsh Dances*, chamber music, operas including *The Beach of*

Falesá and *The Trumpet Major* (based on Hardy's novel), oratorio *Job*, etc. Formerly professor and festival director at Cardiff.

hoe-down, an American folk-dance included in Copland's ballet, ➤*Rodeo*.

Høffding, [Nils] Finn (b. 1899), Danish composer and teacher. Has written opera *The Emperor's New Clothes* and orchestral work *It's a True Story*, both after Hans Andersen; also four symphonies, *Dialogues* for oboe and clarinet, etc.

Hoffmann, Ernst Theodor Amadeus (1776–1822), German Romantic novelist and essayist, influencing e.g. Schumann; also composer of opera *Undine* and other works – and adopting the forename 'Amadeus' in homage to Mozart, replacing 'Wilhelm'. Hero of Offenbach's *Les* ➤*Contes d'Hoffmann*.

Hoffmeister, Franz Anton (1754–1812), Austrian composer of 66 symphonies, much chamber music, nine German operas, etc.; was also important publisher – of Haydn, Beethoven, etc.

Hoffstetter [incorrectly Hofstetter], **Romanus** (1742–1815), Austrian monk and composer who is now believed to have written six string quartets formerly ascribed to Haydn (as op. 3). He also wrote three viola concertos, church music, etc.

Hofhaimer, Paul (1459–1537), Austrian organist (also organ-builder) and composer, in service to the (Austrian) Emperor Maximilian I – based mainly at Innsbruck, but travelling widely. Was given noble rank – exceptional for a musician. His compositions include German part-songs, organ pieces, church music.

Hofmann, Josef [originally Józef Kazimierz Hofmann] (1876–1957), Polish-born pianist, pupil of Anton Rubinstein; composer of symphony, five piano concertos, and other works – some under the name 'Michel Dvorsky'. Public performer from the age of six; first visited USA in 1887, later becoming naturalized and dying there.

Hofmannsthal, Hugo von (1874–1929), Austrian poet, playwright and librettist; long associated with R. Strauss: ➤*Arabella*, ➤*Ariadne auf Naxos*, ➤*Elektra*, ➤*Rosenkavalier*.

Hofstetter, ➤Hoffstetter.

Hogwood, Christopher [Jarvis Haley] (b. 1941), British harpsichordist and conductor, founding director of the Academy of Ancient Music (➤Academy); also director of the St Paul (Minnesota) Chamber Orchestra 1987–92. Author of biography of Handel.

Hohlflöte (Ger., hollow-sounding flute), type of eight-➤foot organ stop in wood or metal.

Hoiby, Lee (b. 1926), American composer and pianist. Works include *Summer and Smoke* and other operas, piano concerto, songs, etc.

Holberg, Ludvig (1684–1754), Norwegian dramatist. ➤*Holberg Suite*, *Maskarade* (➤masquerade).

Holberg Suite, suite composed by Grieg for piano, under title *From Holberg's Time*, then arranged for strings (1884); bicentenary tribute, in the form of a pastiche or old dance-movements, to Ludvig Holberg (above).

Holborne, Anthony (?–1602), English composer who published a book of dances and other music for consort (1599) and composed and arranged other works for lute, etc.

Holbrooke, Joseph (on some scores 'Josef') [Charles] (1878–1958), British composer of operatic trilogy *The Cauldron of Annwen* and other operas; orchestral variations on 'Three Blind Mice'; *Byron* and other symphonic poems. Also pianist, conductor and polemical writer on music.

Hölderlin, Johann Christian Friedrich (1770–1843), German poet. ➤*Antigone*.

Holidays (also known as *New England Holidays*), collective title for four orchestral pieces by Ives, all composed independently: *Washington's Birthday* (1909), ➤*Decoration Day* (1912), *Fourth of July* (1913), *Thanksgiving and/or Forefathers' Day* (with chorus, 1904). The four in this order are sometimes called a symphony.

Höller, Karl (1907–87), German composer of *Variations on a Theme of Sweelinck* and two symphonies, six string quartets, etc.

Höller, York [Georg] (b. 1944), German composer of opera *Der ➤Meister und Margarita*, two piano concertos, electronic music; directs the West German Radio's electronic-music studio in Cologne.

Holliger, Heinz (b. 1939), Swiss oboist and director of chamber-music ensemble. Noted virtuoso in modern works (written for him by Stockhausen, Berio and others). He is also a composer (pupil of Boulez): works include *Pneuma* (Gk., 'breath') for 34 wind instruments, organ, percussion and radio sets: chamber opera *Come and Go*. Wife is Ursula Holliger (b. 1937), harpist.

Hollins, Alfred (1865–1942), British organist (blind from birth) and composer for his instrument; also a pianist, playing concertos, etc.

Holloway, Robin [Greville] (b. 1943), British composer of viola concerto, opera *Clarissa*, song-settings of Housman, Graves, Larkin. A number of works refer musically to older composers, e.g. *Fantasy Pieces* for 13 players on Schumann's *Liederkreis*, op. 24.

Holmboe, Vagn (1909–96), Danish composer, also critic. Pupil of Toch in Berlin. Works include 20 string quartets, 12 symphonies and 13 chamber concertos.

holograph, ➤autograph.

Holst [originally von Holst], **Gustav** [Theodore] (1874–1934), British composer of partly Swedish descent, pupil of Stanford, at various times pianist, trombonist, teacher (especially at Morley College, London), and conductor – of Boston Symphony Orchestra, 1922. Interested in oriental philosophy, and made various settings of the Hindu scriptures in his own translations. Works include operas *At the Boar's Head* (after Shakespeare's *Henry IV*), *The* ➤*Perfect Fool,* ➤*Sāvitri* and also *The* ➤*Planets* for orchestra; ➤*St Paul's Suite* for strings; choral *Hymn of Jesus* and a *First Choral Symphony* (words by Keats; there is no second); music for military and brass band; songs (four for voice and violin), etc. Father of Imogen Holst.

Holst, Imogen (1907–84), British musical educationist, conductor and composer; collaborator with Britten, and author of books on her father (preceding entry).

Holt, Simon (b. 1958), British composer of works for unusual ensembles, his *Icarus Lamentations* using a cimbalom and 14 other instruments. Has also written *Minotaur Games* for chamber orchestra, *Walking with the river's roar* for viola and orchestra, and piano pieces including *Nigredo* (term from alchemy).

homage, hommage (Eng., Fr.), terms used by a composer especially in the expression 'homage to' (or *hommage à*) another composer, usually implying a quotation from that other composer's work or an evocation of his style. Falla used the Spanish form *Homenaje* in his piece for guitar inscribed 'For the grave of Debussy'.

Homage March (1) an item in Grieg's incidental music to Bjørnson's play *Sigurd the Crusader* (Norw., *Sigurd Jorsalfar*), produced 1872; often performed separately in concert; (2) piece by Wagner: ➤*Huldigungsmarsch.*

Homenaje, ➤homage.

Homer (*c.* 700 BC), Greek poet. ➤*King Priam,* ➤*Ritorno di Ulisse in patria*; ➤Logothetis.

Home, Sweet Home, ➤Bishop.

Homme armé, L' (Fr., 'The Armed Man'), title of a popular song (possibly originating in a polyphonic chanson, and possibly composed by Busnois) which was used by Dufay, Palestrina and more than 25 other composers of the 15th, 16th and 17th centuries as a *cantus firmus* in their Masses. Such Masses are accordingly known by this name.

homophony (from Gk. for 'same-sounding'), term used as opposite of ➤polyphony – i.e. signifying that (as for instance in an English hymn-tune) the ➤parts move together, presenting only a top-melody and chords beneath, as distinct from the contrapuntal interplay of different melodies simultaneously. So also *homophonic*.

hondo (Sp., deep), term used in the expression *cante hondo* (deep song), type of sad Andalusian song characteristically using some intervals smaller than a semitone.

Honegger, Arthur (1892–1955), Swiss composer, though born in France and largely resident there. Member of *Les* ➤*Six*. Collaborated with Ibert in opera *L'Aiglon* ('The Eaglet'): other stage works include ➤*Antigone*, ➤*Jeanne d'Arc au bûcher*, *Le* ➤*roi David*. Composed five symphonies – no. 2 for strings plus optional trumpet, no. 3 *Liturgical*, no. 5 *Di tre re* (➤re). Other works include three 'symphonic movements' – ➤*Pacific 231*, *Rugby* and no. 3 (non-programmatic); *Danse de la chèvre* ('Dance of the Goat') for flute; piano solos; French and British film music; *Christmas Cantata* (in English, French, German, and Latin).

Hook, James (1746–1827), British organist and composer – working in both capacities at Marylebone and Vauxhall Gardens, London, 1774–1820; wrote musical plays, concertos, sonatas, cantatas, catches and over 2,000 songs including 'The Lass of Richmond Hill'.

hopak, ➤*gopak*.

Hopkins (surname changed from Reynolds in boyhood), **Antony** (b. 1921),

British composer, pianist, conductor and radio commentator on music. Works include operas *Lady Rohesia* and *Three's Company*; ballet *Café des Sports*. CBE, 1976.

Hopkins, Gerard Manley (1844–89), British poet. ➤Casken, ➤Wellesz.

Hopkinson, Francis (1737–91), American statesman, writer and amateur composer – e.g. of the song 'My Days Have Been So Wondrous Free', the first published composition by a native-born American.

Horenstein, Jascha (1898–1973), Russian-born conductor, naturalized Austrian, later American. Noted interpreter of Bruckner's and Mahler's symphonies; also conducted opera.

horn (1) type of wind instrument descended from primitive use of an animal's horn for blowing through. The term now applies especially to the coiled brass orchestral instrument which was developed (particularly in France, whence the name *French horn*) from the earlier *hunting horn* or *hand-horn*. This earlier instrument, without valves or keys, yielded to the player only the notes of the ➤*harmonic series*, like a bugle, plus a few obtainable by the insertion of the hand in the bell of the instrument. The particular harmonic series sounded depended on the length of the instrument's tube: from about 1700 ➤crooks were inserted into the instrument to vary the length of the tube and thus to make the harmonic series available at various different pitches. But only from about 1850 did the modern horn, with ➤valves to secure a chromatic range of notes, become general. It became standard as a ➤transposing instrument in F, with

199

compass from B below the bass staff upwards for about three and a half octaves. Its more versatile development, in common use today, is the *double horn*, which can be switched from a horn in F (as normal) to a horn in high B♭. Orchestral horn parts assume that the odd-numbered players specialize in the higher notes, the even-numbered in lower: four horns are usually specified in scores, modern orchestral practice often reinforcing them with a fifth (➤bumper); but since Wagner's example, composers have on occasion specified six or eight. The instrument is also standard in the military (not the brass) band; a few concertos have been written for it, e.g. by R. Strauss, or for its valveless predecessor, e.g. by Mozart; (2) term used colloquially in the brass band to mean not the above instrument (not used in the brass band) but the tenor ➤*saxhorn*; and used as jazz slang to mean a trumpet, a trombone, even a saxophone. (Unrelated is the ➤English horn, a woodwind instrument.)

Horn, Charles Edward (1786–1849), British singer and composer of many songs including 'Cherry Ripe'; also of oratorios and music for plays. Settled in USA, 1833, dying there. Son of Karl Friedrich Horn.

Horn, Karl Friedrich (1762–1830), German-born pianist, organist, composer of piano music, etc.; settled in England, 1782, and died there. An early participant in the 19th-century revival of Bach. Father of C. E. Horn.

Horne, Marilyn (b. 1934), American mezzo-soprano active in opera (La Scala, Milan, 1969; Metropolitan, New York, 1970); formerly a celebrated Carmen, she sang (on the sound-track) the title-role in film *Carmen Jones*, 1964. Later she won celebrity in Rossini's coloratura mezzo-soprano roles.

Horneman, Christian Emil (1841–1906), Danish composer of opera *Aladdin*, orchestral and piano music, songs, etc.

hornpipe, lively English dance formerly (e.g. in Purcell) with three beats in the bar, now (as in the well-known 'Sailor's Hornpipe' and as in ➤*Ruddigore*) with two beats in the bar. So named because originally accompanied by pipe made from animal's horn.

Horn Signal, Symphony with the, nickname for Haydn's Symphony no. 31 in D, 1765 (Hob. I: 31) – from the slow movement with its horn calls. Four horns are used instead of the two normal at that period.

Horovitz, Joseph (b. 1926), Austrian-born composer-conductor-pianist resident in England since 1938; pupil of Jacob and N. Boulanger. Works include *Alice in Wonderland* (after L. Carroll) and other ballet scores; one-act operas, clarinet concerto, euphonium concerto (with brass band).

Horowitz, Vladimir (1903–89), pianist, born in Russia; début, 1922. Went to USA, 1928, and settled there, earning highest reputation. Contracted nervous ailment; ceased to give concerts, 1950, though continued to make records; resumed occasional (much-prized) concerts from 1965, continuing into his 80s. Married Toscanini's daughter, Wanda.

Horsley, Charles Edward (1822–76), British pianist, organist and composer especially of oratorios (pupil of Mendelssohn); went to Australia, 1862, and later to USA, where he died.

Horszowski, Mieczyslaw (1892–1993), Polish-born pianist, naturalized American; he studied in Vienna and Paris, performed and recorded with Casals, and gave recitals in London and elsewhere in his hundredth year.

Hotter, Hans (b. 1909), German baritone (formerly church organist) noted in Wagner (e.g. as Sachs in *Die Meistersinger*); stage director of *The ➤Ring*, at Covent Garden, 1962–4. Still performing in his eighties.

Hotteterre, Jacques Martin (1674–1763), French player of the flute (and other instruments), the most famous member of a family of instrumentalists and instrument-makers. Composer of music for flute (and other instruments), and author of a famous instructional treatise, he is regarded as the founder of the French flute tradition.

House of the Dead, ➤*From a House of the Dead.*

Housman, A. E. (1859–1936), British poet. ➤*On Wenlock Edge*, ➤*Butterworth.*

Hovhaness, Alan (b. 1911), American composer of Armenian descent; also conductor and organist. Works, much influenced by ancient Middle Eastern music, mainly have Armenian titles; they include a piano concerto (with strings) entitled *Lousadzak* ('The Coming of Light'), 63 symphonies, *And God Created Great Whales* for humpbacked-whale solo (on tape) and orchestra.

Howarth, Elgar (b. 1935), British conductor, former trumpeter; conducted many first performances of orchestral works and operas (including *Le ➤ Grand Macabre*, Stockholm, 1978, and ➤*Gawain*). Noted brass band conductor, encouraging bands to tackle difficult modern works. Arranged ➤*Pictures at an Exhibition.*

Howell, Gwynne [Richard] (b. 1938), British bass, well known in patriarchal roles at Covent Garden (début 1970), playing Dosifey in *The ➤Khovansky Affair* both there and (1994) at English National Opera; first sang at Metropolitan Opera, New York, in 1985. CBE, 1998.

Howells, Herbert [Norman] (1892–1983), British composer of choral works to religious texts – Requiem, I*Hymnus Paradisi, Missa Sabrinensis* (Lat., Severn Mass), etc.; also orchestral works, a piano concerto, music for brass band, etc. Companion of Honour, 1972.

Hubay, Jenö (1858–1937), Hungarian violinist, also composer. A child prodigy, he became a pupil of Joachim and Vieuxtemps; director of the Budapest Conservatory, 1919–34.

Huber, Klaus (b. 1924), Swiss composer and formerly violinist. Works include *Tempora* for violin and orchestra, *James Joyce Chamber Music* for harp, horn and chamber orchestra; settings of biblical and other religious texts.

Huberman, Bronislav (1882–1947), Polish violinist, internationally noted; in 1936 he organized the Palestine Symphony Orchestra, which became the Israel Philharmonic.

Hucbald (*c.* 840–930), French monk, supposed author of a musical treatise in Latin about the ➤modes, ➤diaphony, etc.

Hudson, George (*c.* 1620–72), English violinist and composer, in service to Charles II; wrote part of the music to *The* ➤*Siege of Rhodes*.

Hughes, Arwel (1909–88), British composer and conductor; works include opera *Menna* (on a Welsh legend) and other works of Welsh inspiration. His son, Owain Arwel Hughes (b. 1942), is also a conductor.

Hughes, Ted (b. 1930), British poet. ➤Crosse.

Hugh the Drover, or Love in the Stocks, opera by Vaughan Williams, produced in London, 1924. Libretto by H. Child: the scene is a Cotswold village at the time of the Napoleonic Wars. Styled 'a Romantic ballad opera' (➤ballad opera).

Hugo, Victor (1802–85), French writer. ➤*Gioconda*, ➤*Mazeppa*, ➤*Rigoletto*, ➤*Ruy Blas*; ➤*pantoum*.

Huguenots, Les (Fr., 'The Huguenots'), Meyerbeer's most successful opera, produced in Paris, 1836. Libretto by E. Scribe and É. Deschamps, culminating in the St Bartholomew Massacre of French Protestants, 1572.

Huldigungsmarsch (Ger., 'Homage March'), ceremonial piece by Wagner, originally for military band, 1864 (for King Ludwig II of Bavaria), later orchestrated.

Hullah, John Pyke (1812–84), British composer of songs including 'O that we two were maying', opera *The Village Coquettes* (libretto by Dickens), etc.; singing-teacher and writer of textbooks.

hum, to vocalize with closed lips – an effect occasionally used in concert works (Lambert's *The* ➤*Rio Grande*) and most famously in the Humming Chorus in Puccini's ➤*Madama Butterfly* – an offstage effect purely for atmosphere.

Hume, Tobias (*c.* 1569–1645), English composer, also professional soldier, known as Captain Hume. Wrote dances and other music for viols; also songs including 'Fain would I change that note'.

Humfrey (or Humphrey), **Pelham** (1647–74), English composer who studied in France and Italy and was in service to Charles II. Wrote music to plays including Shakespeare's *The Tempest*, also church music, vocal solos and duets, etc. One of Purcell's teachers.

Hummel, Johann Nepomuk (1778–1837), Austrian pianist (pupil of Mozart) and composer (pupil of Haydn and others), touring extensively as performer. Wrote concertos and other works for piano, trumpet concerto, mandolin concerto, and also operas, much chamber music, etc.

Humoreske, humoresque (Ger., Fr., the latter also used as Eng.), type of instrumental composition supposedly of a wayward or capricious nature – term used e.g. by Schumann and Dvořák.

Humperdinck, Engelbert (1854–1921), German composer; friend and assistant to Wagner; also teacher (for some time in Spain) and critic. Composed operas including ➤*Hänsel und Gretel* and *Königskinder* ('King's Children'); also incidental music to various plays, choral works, etc.

Humphrey, Pelham, ➤Humfrey.

Hungarian Fantasia, ➤*Hungarian Rhapsody*.

Hungarian Rhapsody, title given by Liszt to each of 19 piano pieces in Hungarian-gipsy style – nos. 1–15 were composed by 1852, the others about 30 years later. Some were afterwards orchestrated, and on no. 14 is based Liszt's *Hungarian Fantasia* (properly *Fantasia on Hungarian Popular Themes*) for piano and orchestra, 1852.

Hunt, The, nickname for Haydn's Symphony no. 73 in D, 1781 (Hob. I: 73) – from the music of the horns and oboes in the finale, a movement originally taken from one of Haydn's operas.

Hunter, Rita [Nellie] (b. 1933), British soprano, noted in Wagner roles from 1970 with the (former) Sadler's Wells Opera, now the English National Opera; first appearance at the Metropolitan, New York, 1972. CBE, 1980. Settled in Australia.

hunting-horn, instrument used for giving signals while hunting, from which evolved the orchestral ➤horn.

'Hunt' Quartet, nickname for Mozart's String Quartet in B flat, K458 (1784), because the opening suggests hunting-horns.

hurdy-gurdy, term applied wrongly to any instrument worked by turning a handle (➤barrel organ, ➤street piano) and correctly only to one such instrument, a kind of portable, mechanical viol called in French *vielle*. One hand turns a handle actuating a rosined wheel which acts as a bow; the other hand stops the strings not directly (as on a viol) but by means of a tiny piano-like keyboard. In addition there are one or two freely vibrating strings, giving a ➤drone bass. Mozart and others wrote for this instrument.

Hurford, Peter [John] (b. 1930), British organist (also composer and editor); eminent recitalist; has recorded complete organ works of Bach, Couperin and Hindemith and held various academic appointments.

Hurlstone, William Yeates (1876–1906), British composer of *Variations on a Swedish Air* for orchestra, also a sonata for clarinet and piano, chamber music, etc.

Husa, Karel (b. 1921), Czech-born composer and conductor, resident in USA since the mid-1950s. Works include *Evocations of Slovakia* for clarinet, viola and cello; concertos for saxophone (with wind band), for trumpet and for organ.

Hvorotovsky [properly Khvorotovsky], **Dmitri** (b. 1962), Russian baritone who won Cardiff 'Singer of the Year' award 1989; is specially noted in Russian opera and song but made American opera début at Chicago, 1993, as Germont in *La* ➤*Traviata*.

hydraulis, hydraulos (Gk., waterpipe), also called water-organ; ancient instrument, cultivated in Greek and Roman eras, precursor of the organ. Water was used to maintain a constant pressure on the air fed to the pipes.

hymn, a song of praise to a deity, saint, etc.; particularly (in Protestant churches) that which has words specially written, not taken directly from the Bible, and is sung congregationally. Also an extended composition to words supposedly of a hymn-like nature – see following entries – or an instrumental composition suggesting a vocal hymn.

Hymn of Praise, symphonic cantata by Mendelssohn. ➤*Lobgesang*.

Hymn to St Cecilia, setting for unaccompanied chorus by Britten (who was born on St Cecilia's Day) of a poem by W. H. Auden, 1942. ➤Cecilia, ➤*Ode for St Cecilia's Day*.

Hymn to the Sun, an aria sung by the Queen of Shemakha in *The* ➤*Golden Cockerel*.

Hymnus Paradisi (Lat., 'Hymn of Paradise'), work for soprano, tenor, chorus and orchestra by Howells, composed 1938 but not brought to performance until 1950; text mainly in English (with some Latin) from biblical and liturgical sources, in the nature of a requiem for the composer's son who had died in boyhood.

I

i (It.), the (pl.) – see next word of phrase.

Iberia (1) four sets each of three piano pieces by Albéniz, representing various parts of Spain; first complete performance in 1909 (five of the pieces were later orchestrated by Arbós): (2) orchestral work by Debussy (properly *Ibéria*), first performed in 1910, being the second part of his ➤*Images* for orchestra. It is in three movements suggestive of aspects of Spain.

Ibert, Jacques [François Antoine] (1890–1962), French composer, pupil of Fauré; director of the French Academy in Rome from 1937. Collaborated with Honegger in opera *L'Aiglon* ('The Eaglet'). Other works include *Angélique* and other operas; symphonic poem after Wilde's *The Ballad of Reading Jail*; orchestral suite *Escales* ('Ports of Call'); *Divertissement*, arranged from his music to the play *Le Chapeau de paille d'Italie* ('The Italian Straw Hat'); *Concertino da camera* for alto saxophone and 11 instruments; *Le petit âne blanc* ('The Little White Donkey') and other piano works.

Ibsen, Henrik Johan (1828–1906), Norwegian dramatist. See ➤*Peer Gynt*; ➤Beecroft, ➤Bibalo, ➤Brunswick, ➤Egk, ➤Grieg, ➤Harper, ➤Saeverud.

idée fixe, term used by Berlioz, e.g. in the ➤*Symphonie fantastique*, for what is usually called ➤motto theme.

idiophone, term used in the scientific classification of instruments to mean 'self-sounding', e.g. cymbals, xylophone, whether hit, rattled, stroked, etc. (But drums, in which a membrane is stretched and an air-space is fully or partly enclosed, are membranophones.)

Idomeneo, re di Creta, ossia Ilia e Idamante (It., 'Idomeneus, King of Crete, or Ilia and Idamantes'), opera by Mozart (K366), produced in Munich (in Italian), 1781. Libretto by G. B. Varesco, after Virgil; a story of love and sacrifice taking place after the Trojan War, Idamante being the son of Idomeneo and the lover of the captive princess Ilia.

idyll, literary term for a peaceful, pastoral work – transferred to music e.g. in Wagner's ➤*Siegfried Idyll*.

il (It.), the (masculine singular).

Illuminations, Les, cycle of nine songs by Britten, 1939, for high voice and strings to French poems by Rimbaud evocative of various sights and sounds.

illustrative music, music describing, evoking, or otherwise alluding to a non-musical source, e.g. a poem, novel, play, picture, landscape, or an explicit emotional experience. (The more usual but confusing term for this is *programme music* or ➤*programmatic music*.)

Images, title given by Debussy to two series of works – (a) two sets each of three piano pieces (1905, 1907), and (b) three orchestral works of which ➤*Ibéria* was completed in 1908, *Rondes de Printemps* ('Spring Rounds') in 1909, and *Gigues* (originally *Gigues tristes*, i.e. 'Sad Jigs') in 1912 – the orchestration of *Gigues* being by Caplet.

Imai, Nobuko (b. 1942), Japanese viola-player who settled in Britain; she took part in the première of Tippett's Triple Concerto, 1980, with Pauk and Kirshbaum.

Imbrie, Andrew Welsh (b. 1921), American composer, pupil of Sessions; has written three symphonies (and a chamber symphony), five string quartets, a violin concerto, opera *Christmas in Peebles Town* (or *Three against Christmas*), etc. Taught at University of California, Berkeley, 1949–91.

imitation, a composers' device in partwriting: one voice repeats (if not literally, then at least recognizably) a figure previously stated by another voice. ➤*Canon* and ➤*fugue* employ imitation according to strict and regular patterns.

Immortal Hour, The, opera by Boughton, produced in Glastonbury, Somerset, 1914. Libretto by composer, based on Celtic legend as drawn from plays and poems of 'Fiona Macleod' (i.e. William Sharp).

Imperial (Fr., *L'Impériale*), nickname for Haydn's Symphony no. 53 in D (Hob. I: 53), about 1780 – presumably named, somewhat arbitrarily, from its 'Largo maestoso' opening.

Imperial Mass, another nickname for Haydn's ➤*Nelson Mass*.

Imperio, Pastora (*c.* 1885–1961), Spanish dancer and choreographer. ➤*Amor brujo*.

Impresario, The, opera by Mozart. ➤*Schauspieldirektor*.

impressionism, term borrowed from painting (applied e.g. to Monet, Degas, Whistler) and used to describe the works e.g. of Debussy and Ravel in so far as they seem to interpret their titles not in a narrative or dramatic way (like the ➤Romantics) but as though an observer were recording the impression conveyed at a given moment. ➤expressionism.

impromptu (Fr., unprompted, but pronounced as English word), short piece of music (usually for piano) seeming to suggest improvisation. Examples by Voříšek antedate those by Schubert and Chopin. Britten called the slow movement of his revised Piano Concerto (1945) an impromptu, and Walton based on it his *Improvisations on an Impromptu by Benjamin Britten* (1970).

improvise (or 'extemporize'), to perform according to spontaneous fancy, not from memory or from written copy – though often a performer improvises 'on' (i.e. round about) a given tune. Hence *improvisation*: this term is sometimes also used as title of an actual written-down piece presumably intended to convey the roving spirit of genuine improvisation (➤impromptu).

in, term with various musical usages

including (1) indication of a conductor's beat – so e.g. *in 2*, meaning that two beats will be actually given to each bar, although the composer may have indicated two or four or six, etc.; (2) indication of the division of forces in an orchestra – so e.g. *in 4*, applied to the violas, would indicate that the viola-players are to be divided into four sections each playing a different ➤part; (3) indication of key, e.g. *symphony in C minor*; (4) indication of (a) the basic key in which a wind instrument is pitched, and sometimes also of (b) the transposition it consequently requires. Only usage can show whether or not the additional meaning (b) is implied. E.g. *horn in F* means not only that the instrument is basically pitched in F (if blown, without depressing any valves, it will produce a ➤harmonic series basically related to the key of F major), but also that it is a ➤transposing instrument sounding a fifth lower than written – the note written as C sounds as F, etc. Thus here both the meanings (a) and (b) are implied. But a bass trombone is sometimes said to be *in G* because of its basic harmonic series, though it is not a transposing instrument, being written at the pitch it sounds.

Inbal, Eliahu (b. 1936), Israeli conductor, pupil of Celibidache (in Italy); conductor of the Frankfurt Radio Symphony Orchestra since 1974. Has recorded all Bruckner's and all Mahler's symphonies.

incidental music, that which is intended to be used intermittently to heighten the performance of a play. (The term is not generally applied to film.)

incipit (Lat., it begins), the first few bars of a musical work, used e.g. in a bibliographical compilation to identify the piece.

Incoronazione di Poppea, L' (It., 'The Coronation of Poppaea'), opera by Monteverdi, produced in Venice, 1642; libretto by G. F. Bussenello, on Nero's expulsion of his wife in favour of his mistress, Poppaea. (*Poppaea* is original Latin form, *Poppea* an italianization of it.)

Incredible Flutist, The, ballet with music by Piston, first performed in 1938, the 'flutist' (US form) being a charmer of snakes and human beings. A concert suite drawn from it was first given in 1940.

indeterminacy, the principle, employed by some composers from the 1950s, of leaving elements of the performance either to pure chance (➤aleatory), or to the decision of the performer.

India, Sigismondo d' (*c.* 1580–1629), Italian composer who held various court positions; wrote 84 airs in monodic style (with adventurous modern harmony) as well as polyphonic motets.

Indian Queen, The, opera by Purcell (Z630), produced in London, 1695 (the last of its five acts is partly by D. Purcell). It was an adaptation, with music, of a play by Dryden and R. Howard on the rivalry of Mexicans and Peruvians – 'Indian' thus meaning American-Indian.

Indy, [Paul Marie Théodore] Vincent d' (1851–1931), French composer, pupil and follower of Franck; enthusiast for Wagner; joint founder of the Schola Cantorum (a Paris musical academy, originally for the study of church music), 1894. Works include *Fervaal* and five other operas; ➤*Symphonie sur un chant montagnard français* and three other symphonies; orchestral variations *Istar* (after a Babylonian epic); a triple concerto for flute, cello, piano and orchestra; much chamber music.

inequality, a modern name for a convention in performing (chiefly) 18th-century music by which a pair of notes printed as of equal duration is sounded long-short. The convention originated in French music (*notes inégales*, unequal notes) and the extent of its proper application to other music is disputed.

Inextinguishable, The, ➤*Unquenchable* (title of symphony by Carl Nielsen).

Infedeltà delusa, L' (It., 'Infidelity Outwitted'), opera by Haydn, produced at Eszterháza, 1773. Libretto by Marco Coltellini: comedy of love and convenience in marriage.

Ingegneri, Marc'Antonio (*c.* 1545–1592), Italian composer, choirmaster of Cremona Cathedral; teacher of Monteverdi. Works include Masses and other church music (some formerly attributed to Palestrina) and madrigals.

Inghelbrecht, Désiré Émile (1880–1965), French conductor and composer of ballet score *El Greco*, chamber music, *La Nursery* for piano duet, etc.

inglese (It.), English. ➤*Corno inglese*, ➤English horn.

inharmonicity, the lack of relationship to the ➤harmonic series.

in modo di (It.), in the manner of.

In Nature's Realm, alternative English name for Dvořák's overture ➤*Amid Nature*.

In nomine, type of 16th- and 17th-century English polyphonic instrumental composition based on a section of the Benedictus of Taverner's Mass *Gloria tibi Trinitas*, at the words 'in nomine'. Transcriptions of this passage were made for viols, lute and keyboard, and later composers up to Purcell gave the name 'In nomine' to works based both on Taverner's composition and directly on the plainsong melody ('Gloria tibi Trinitas') on which Taverner's Mass itself is based.

instrument, musical, an object (other than the organs of the body) used for the production of musical sound by the application of mechanical energy – or, as in ➤electric/electrophonic instruments, by the application of electrical impulses. Non-electrophonic instruments are classified scientifically as ➤*aerophones*, ➤*chordophones*, ➤*idiophones* and ➤*membranophones*, but the usual practical classification is into *wind*, *strings* and *percussion* (in which, respectively, vibrations are set up in an air-column, a string and a membrane or other surface). Wind instruments are divided, e.g. in the orchestra, into ➤woodwind and ➤brass (between which there is a difference in method of sound-production, more important than differences in materials used). Note that this classification is one of practical convenience and is not technically exhaustive: the piano, for instance, uses strings but is also 'percussive' in mechanism – and yet is not normally spoken of as a stringed or percussion instrument. See also next entry.

instrumentation, the writing of music

for particular instruments – term used particularly with reference to a composer's necessary knowledge of what is practicable, and what sounds well, on different instruments. The related term ➤*orchestration* properly applies to scoring for groups and not primarily to the qualities of individual instruments.

Intendant (Ger.), superintendent, administrative director – especially of an opera house or other theatre.

interlude, piece of music inserted between other pieces (e.g. organ passage between the verses of a hymn) or between non-musical events, e.g. between the acts of a play. (Occasionally also used as a musical title without such implications, e.g. the *Four Sea Interludes* extracted from ➤*Peter Grimes* as an orchestral concert item.)

intermède, a French equivalent for ➤*intermezzo*.

intermedio (It.), musical and dramatic entertainment inserted between the acts of plays in Italy in the 16th century and later, leading to the invention of opera. The preferred term from the 18th century onwards was ➤*intermezzo*.

intermezzo (It.), something 'in the middle', hence (specifically musical meanings) – (1) instrumental piece in the middle of an opera, e.g. that which is traditionally performed while the stage is left empty in ➤*Cavalleria rusticana*; (2) short concert-piece – term used e.g. by Brahms for some piano works; (3, obsolete) short comic opera, e.g. Pergolesi's *La* ➤*Serva padrona*, originally played between the acts of an early 18th-century serious opera. See also the following entry.

Intermezzo, opera by R. Strauss, produced in Dresden, 1924. Libretto by composer, based on an episode (i.e. 'intermezzo' in a non-musical sense) in his own life, and having as hero an opera-conductor whose peace is interrupted when his wife suspects him of infidelity.

International(e), socialist anthem composed by P. Degeyter (1848–1932), till 1944 also the national anthem of the USSR; its title refers to an international socialist organization.

interrupted cadence, ➤cadence.

interval, the 'distance' between two notes, in so far as one of them is higher or lower than the other. Thus the interval from C to the G above it is a 'fifth', to the A above it a 'sixth', etc. (These are calculated by counting upwards, and by including in the count the notes at both extreme ends.) The names 'fifth', 'sixth', etc., are themselves further defined – ➤*perfect, major, minor, augmented, diminished*. Intervals above an octave ('eighth') are called *compound intervals*, being 'compounded' of so many octaves plus a smaller interval. Thus the interval from C to the next G above it but one (12 notes, counting the extremes) is called a 12th and is a compound interval made of an octave (C–C) and a fifth (C-G).

In the South, concert-overture by Elgar, subtitled 'Alassio', the Italian town where he composed it (1904). The word 'Moglio' above a clarinet phrase in the score is the name of a nearby village.

In the Steppes of Central Asia, usual English title for the work actually entitled simply 'In Central Asia' (Rus., *V* *srednei Azii*), an 'orchestral picture' by Borodin, 1880, representing the approach and passing of a caravan; composed to accompany a *tableau vivant*.

Intimate Letters (Cz., *Listy důvěrné*), title (referring to a love-affair) of Janáček's Quartet no. 2 (1928).

intonation, tuning (of pitch), either with regard to a system of *temperament* (➤*just intonation*) or, more usually, of performance – a singer's or violinist's intonation is praised if the notes are pitched with a high degree of precision.

intrada (from Sp. *entrada*, entry), a preliminary piece – term used especially *c.* 1600 for the opening number (in pompous, festive style) of a suite of dances.

introduction (1) term often used for the shorter, slower first part of a mainly allegro movement, as in a symphony or in Elgar's *Introduction and Allegro* for strings (1905); (2, from It., *introduzione*), the opening choral number of an act in many 19th-century Italian operas.

invention, name given by Bach to a type of short keyboard work in two-part counterpoint; 15 of these are included in his *Little Clavier Book* (Ger. *Clavierbüchlein*), 1720, for the instruction of his son W. F. Bach. The term has also been applied by Bach's editors to similar pieces in three-part counterpoint in the same collection (called by Bach himself 'symphonies') and has been occasionally used also by later composers.

inversion, ➤invert.

invert, to turn upside-down; thus (1) a chord not in its 'root ➤position' is said to be in one or other *inversion*; (2) two melodies in counterpoint may be mutually *inverted* by the upper becoming the lower and vice versa (counterpoint capable of making sense under this treatment is called *invertible counterpoint* and forms the stuff of, e.g., ➤fugue); (3) a single melody may be *inverted* by being performed 'upside-down', i.e. with all its successive intervals applied in the opposite direction. Thus an upward interval of a major third (say D–F♯) when inverted would be replaced by a downward interval of a major third (D–B♭), or by an upward interval of a minor sixth which would produce the same note (D–B♭) though in a higher octave. A melody so inverted is called the *inversion* of the original – often abbreviated to *I* in the theory of ➤twelve-note technique.

Invisible City of Kitezh, The, opera by Rimsky-Korsakov. ➤*Legend of the Invisible City of Kitezh and of the Maid Fevronia*.

Invitation to the Dance (not 'to the Waltz'), piano piece by Weber. ➤*Aufforderung zum Tanz*.

Iolanta, opera by Tchaikovsky. ➤*Yolanta*.

Iolanthe, or The Peer and the Peri, operetta by Sullivan, produced in London and New York on the same day, 1882. Libretto by W. S. Gilbert, on the interaction of Fairyland and the House of Lords. The term 'Peri', usefully borrowed for the title-pun, is derived from Persian mythology.

Ionian mode, the ➤mode which may be represented by the white keys of the piano from C to C.

Iphigénie en Aulide (Fr., 'Iphigenia in

Aulis'), opera by Gluck, with libretto by M. F. L. G. L. du Roullet, indebted to Racine; produced in Paris, 1774. Among other operas on the plot (after Euripides) is one in Italian by Cherubini. The plot of these operas has its sequel in ➤*Iphigénie en Tauride*.

Iphigénie en Tauride (Fr., 'Iphigenia in Tauris'), operas after Euripides (see also preceding entry) by various composers including (1) Gluck, with libretto by N. F. Guillard; produced in Paris, 1779; (2) Piccinni, with libretto by A. du C. Dubreuil; produced in Paris, 1781. (Supporters of the two composers publicly clashed over the two operas.)

Ippolitov-Ivanov, Mikhail [Mikhailovich] (1859–1935), Russian composer; director of the Moscow Conservatory, 1905–22. Studied folk music, e.g. of Georgia, and wrote orchestral *Caucasian Sketches*, and other regionally titled works – also two symphonies, operas, many songs, etc. Completed Musorgsky's unfinished opera *The Marriage*.

IRCAM, acronym for the Institut de Recherche et de Co-ordination Acoustique/Musique, established in Paris, 1977, under Pierre Boulez, as a laboratory for composition, exploring acoustical and electronic phenomena relating to music.

Ireland, John [Nicholson] (1879–1962), British composer. Published no opera, no ballet, no symphony, but a piano concerto and various orchestral works including *A* ➤*London Overture*; a sonata and many other works for piano; many songs, including 'Sea Fever'; cantata *These Things Shall Be*, etc.

Iris, opera by Mascagni, produced in Rome, 1898. Libretto, set in Japan, by L. Illica – the joint librettist, later, for ➤*Madama Butterfly*.

Irish Symphony, title of works by ➤Esposito, ➤Harty, ➤Stanford, ➤Sullivan.

Irma la Douce, musical play with text by Alexandre Breffort taken from his book; music by Marguerite Monnot. Produced in Paris, 1956 and later in London; ➤Heneker. A law student is transported to Devil's Island for the murder of a fictitious 'Oscar' (himself) but is joyously reunited in Paris with his beloved Irma, lately a prostitute.

Irving, Robert [Augustine] (1913–91), British conductor, especially of ballet; at Covent Garden, then from 1958 with New York City Ballet.

Isaac, Heinrich (c. 1450–1517), Flemish (Germanized) composer, holding posts with the Medici and other noble families, and living in Austria and Italy; died in Florence. Composed church music; instrumental works; songs in French, Italian, German and Latin; the well-known tune 'Innsbruck', which he harmonized, was probably not his own composition.

Islamey, fantasy for piano by Balakirev, evoking an 'oriental' atmosphere and prompted by a visit to the Caucasus; first performed in 1869. Orchestrated by Casella, 1908.

Isle of the Dead, The, a picture by the German painter Arnold Böcklin (1827–1901), which inspired Rakhmaninov's symphonic poem of the same name (1909) and a few other musical works.

isorhythmic (from Gk., equalrhythmed), term applied to certain medieval motets, e.g. by Machaut, of which the rhythms are repeated according to a strict scheme not corresponding to repetition in the melody.

Isouard, Nicolas (or Nicolò) (1775–1818), Maltese-born composer who wrote operas in Italian and, after settling in Paris in 1799, in French – including ➤*Cendrillon* ('Cinderella').

Israel in Egypt, oratorio by Handel, with words from the Bible, first performed in London, 1739; predominantly choral, it includes famous double (i.e. eight-part) choruses. Incorporates unacknowledged 'borrowings' from ➤Kerll.

Israel Philharmonic Orchestra, orchestra based in Tel-Aviv (founded by ➤Huberman in 1936 as the Palestine Symphony Orchestra); music director since 1977, Mehta.

istesso tempo, L' (It.), at the same tempo, i.e. preserving the same pace although the unit of beat may have changed – say from 2/4 to 6/8 in which case the old ♩ and the new ♩. would have the same duration.

Istomin, Eugene [George] (b. 1925), American pianist, noted as trio-partner of Isaac Stern and Leonard Rose. Married Casals' widow, the cellist Marta Casals (née Montañez).

Italiana in Algeri L' (It., 'The Italian Woman in Algiers'), opera by Rossini, produced in Venice, 1813. Libretto by A. Anelli, the heroine easily outwitting her oriental captor.

Italian Caprice, orchestral work by Tchaikovsky. ➤*Capriccio italien*.

Italian Concerto, usual title given to Bach's *Concerto in the Italian Style*

(BWV 971) for harpsichord, published in 1735 as part of the ➤*Clavierübung*. Though for a solo instrument, it maintains the form and style then associated with the term ➤concerto, the necessary element of contrast being available through use of the harpsichord's two manuals.

Italian overture, ➤overture.

Italian Serenade, work by Wolf for string quartet or string orchestra. ➤*Italienische Serenade*.

Italian sixth, type of 'augmented sixth' (➤augmented) chord, distinguished by having a major third (and no other note) between the notes forming the sixth – e.g. (reading upwards) D♭, F, B. The reason for the name, and similarly the ➤French and ➤German sixths, is not known.

Italian Song-book, a set of song-settings by Wolf. ➤*Italienisches Liederbuch*.

Italian Symphony, Mendelssohn's Symphony no. 4 in A major and minor; commemorating a visit to Italy, and first performed in 1833. ➤*saltarello*.

Italian Woman in Algiers, The, comic opera by Rossini. ➤*Italiana in Algeri*.

Italienische Serenade (Ger., 'Italian Serenade'), work by Wolf for string quartet, 1887; he later made an arrangement for orchestra and intended to add two more movements to this.

Italienisches Liederbuch (Ger., 'Italian Song-book'), Wolf's song-settings, 1890–96, of 46 Italian poems in German translation.

Iturbi, José (1895–1980), Spanish conductor and pianist (sometimes simultataneously) who settled in USA; conductor of the Rochester (NY) Philharmonic Orchestra, 1935–44. Made several film appearances.

Ivanhoe, Sullivan's only 'serious' opera, produced in London, 1891. Libretto by J. R. Sturgis, after Scott's novel. The subject was also treated by ➤Marschner.

Ivanov, Lev (1834–1901), Russian choreographer. ➤*Nutcracker.*

Ivan Susanin, ➤*Life for the Tsar.*

Ivan IV, opera by Bizet, with libretto by A. Leroy and H. Trianon about the Russian Tsar; composed in 1865, withdrawn, thought lost, recovered in 1944 and produced in Württemberg, 1946, under the title *Ivan le terrible.*

Ivan the Terrible (see also preceding entry), title sometimes given in the West to Rimsky-Korsakov's opera *The* ➤*Maid of Pskov.*

Ives, Charles [Edward] (1874–1954), American composer of music which, all written before 1920, anticipates later devices, e.g. ➤polytonality, ➤polyrhythm, quarter-tones. Was organist and choirmaster and had business career, his work being little recognized until his ➤*Concord* sonata was played in 1939 and his Symphony no. 3 in 1946. Works include five symphonies. ➤*New England Holidays* and ➤*Three Places in New England* for orchestra, many choral works, and songs.

Ives (or Ive or Ivy), **Simon** (1600–1662), English composer and church organist, more than 100 of whose instrumental and vocal works survive.

Iwaki, Hiroyuki (b. 1932), Japanese conductor, pupil of Karajan: since 1969, principal conductor of NHK Symphony Orchestra (Japan) and, since 1974, of Melbourne Symphony Orchestra.

J

jack, the vertical strip of wood carrying the plectrum that plucks the string or a harpsichord, virginals, etc.; as the finger-key is depressed, the jack moves up and the string is plucked.

Jackson, William (1730–1803), British organist and composer of church music; also of operas, harpsichord pieces, etc. Was organist of Exeter Cathedral and is known as 'Jackson of Exeter'.

Jackson, William (1815–66), British organist and composer (church music, glees, etc.); active in Yorkshire and known as 'Jackson of Masham'.

Jacob, Gordon [Percival Septimus] (1895–1984), British composer, pupil of Stanford and C. Wood; noted also as teacher and as authority on orchestration. Works include *Passacaglia on a Well-known Theme* (Oranges and Lemons) and concertos for various instruments. CBE, 1968.

Jacobi, Frederick (1891–1952), American composer, also conductor; pupil of Bloch and others; studied American-Indian music and wrote a string quartet and other works making use of it; also a symphony, Jewish liturgical music, etc.

Jacobs, René (b. 1946), Belgian counter-tenor, prominent in various early music ensembles including his own Collegium Vocale; has also conducted his own editions of Monteverdi and Cavalli at major festivals.

Jacopo da Bologna (14th century), Italian composer of madrigals (in the earlier sense) and other vocal works; said to have been also a virtuoso of the harp.

Jahreszeiten, Die (Ger., 'The Seasons'), oratorio by Haydn, first performed in Vienna, 1801 (Hob. XXI: 3), to a German text based on an English poem by James Thomson.

Jamaican Rumba, ➤*rumba*.

James, Henry (1843–1916), American novelist. ➤*Turn of the Screw*; ➤ Argento.

jam session, informal improvised performance by jazz musicians; so also *to jam*, etc.

Janáček, Leoš (1854–1928), Czech composer, also choral conductor; visited Britain in 1926; but the high esteem internationally granted to him (especially in opera) has arisen only after World War II. He studied Czech folk-song and speech which greatly influenced his musical idiom. Operas include ➤*Jenůfa*, ➤*Kát'a Kabanová, The* ➤*Cunning Little Vixen, The* ➤*Makropoulous Affair*, ➤*From a House of the Dead*.

Composed also ➤*Glagolitic Mass* and many other choral works; Sinfonietta, *Taras Bulba* and other orchestral works; wind sextet ➤*Mladi* and two string quartets (no. 2, ➤*Intimate Letters*); song cycle *The* ➤*Diary of One Who Disappeared*; folk-song arrangements.

Janequin [also spelt Jannequin], **Clement** (*c.* 1485–1558), French composer of long dramatic ➤*chansons* in four parts with, e.g., representation of bird-song; also of Masses and other church music. Possibly a pupil of ➤Josquin.

janissary music, term for the effect produced by using triangle, cymbals and bass drum, e.g. in Mozart's overture to *Die* ➤*Entführung aus dem Serail* – imitating Turkish music as played by the janissaries (infantry forming the Sultan's bodyguard).

Jannequin, Clement, ➤Janequin.

Janowitz, Gundula (b. 1937), German soprano, noted in opera and in German song; performed at Vienna State Opera from 1960 but not at Covent Garden until 1976.

Janowski, Marek (b. 1939), Polish-born German conductor; music director of Royal Liverpool Philharmonic Orchestra, 1983–6; principal conductor, orchestra of Radio France, since 1984.

Jansons, Mariss (b. 1943), Latvian conductor who trained in Leningrad and, as music director of the Oslo Philharmonic Orchestra since 1979, has raised it to international status. Is also associate conductor of St Petersburg (formerly Leningrad) Philharmonic Orchestra and professor of conducting at that city's conservatory. His father was the conductor Arvid ➤Yansons.

Jaques-Dalcroze, Émile (1865–1950), Swiss (Austrian-born) inventor of ➤eurhythmics; also composer of operas, etc.

Jarnach, Philipp (1892–1982), Spanish (Catalan) composer (French-born) with a German mother. Studied with Busoni and completed Busoni's unfinished ➤*Doktor Faust*. He himself composed *Sinfonia brevis* and other orchestral works, unaccompanied violin sonatas, etc.

Järnefelt, Armas (1869–1958), conductor and composer, Finnish-born, naturalized Swedish in 1910. Introduced Wagner's music to Finland. Works include a *Praeludium* (formerly very well known) and *Berceuse* for orchestra, choral music, songs. His sister married Sibelius.

Järvi, Neeme (b. 1937), Estonian-born conductor, naturalized American; after study in Leningrad, became chief conductor of the Estonian Opera at Tallinn. Emigrated to USA, 1980; principal conductor of Gothenburg (Sweden) Symphony Orchestra since 1982 and of Detroit Symphony Orchestra since 1990.

jazz, term used at least from 1914 for a type of American popular music originating among blacks of New Orleans and taken over also by whites: also applied generally to various types of dance music indebted to this (though purists reserve the term for such music as retains the original flavour and the original basis of improvisation). The jazz idiom, characterized by certain syncopations over strongly reiterated rhythms, influenced e.g. Stravinsky, Walton and Milhaud, as well as many American composers. ➤blue note; ➤blues, ➤ragtime.

Jeanne d'Arc au bûcher (Fr., 'Joan of Arc at the Stake'), play by P. Claudel with some spoken parts (including Joan's) and some sung; music by Honegger – his most widely performed stage work. Produced at Basle, 1938.

Její Pastorkyňa, ➤*Jenůfa*.

Jelinek, Hanns (1901–69), Austrian composer, mainly self-taught but studied briefly with Schoenberg, Berg and Schmidt. Compositions include *Symphonia brevis* (and five other symphonies) for orchestra, *Twelve-note Primer* for piano, song-setting (with orchestra) of Goethe's *Prometheus*.

Jemnitz, Alexander (Hungarian form, 'Sándor') (1890–1963), Hungarian composer, conductor and critic. Works include *Overture for a Peace Festival*; a harp sonata; various piano and organ works.

'Jena' Symphony, name given to symphony found at Jena, Germany, in 1909; wrongly conjectured at the time to be an early work of Beethoven's, it is known to be by J. F. Witt.

Jenkins, John (1592–1678), English composer in service to various noble families. Wrote fantasies for viols, songs and rounds; also sonatas and suites for combinations of violins, viols and continuo.

Jensen, Adolf (1837–79), German pianist and composer, particularly of piano music and songs; also of an opera, cantatas, etc. Pupil of Liszt.

Jenůfa, opera by Janáček, produced in Brno, 1904. Libretto by composer, after a play by G. Preissova; originally titled *Her Foster-daughter* (Cz., *Její Pastorkyňa*). Named after the heroine,

whose illegitimate baby is drowned by Jenůfa's foster-mother.

Jephtha (1) Latin oratorio (originally entitled *Jephthe*) by Carissimi (words from the Bible) for six voices and continuo, composed by 1650; one of the earliest oratorios – each character sings, and there is a narrator; (2) oratorio by Handel, first performed in London, 1752; words by T. Morell, after the Bible.

Jeremiáš, Jaroslav (1889–1919), Czech composer of oratorio *Jan Hus* etc.; pupil of Novák and brother of Otakar Jeremiáš.

Jeremiáš, Otakar (1892–1962), Czech composer, pupil of Novák, brother of preceding. Works include opera *The Brothers Karamazov* (after Dostoyevsky); cantata *Songs of My Country*, Choral Fantasia (with orchestra), etc. Also conductor.

Jeritza (originally Jedlitzka), **Maria** (1887–1982), Czech soprano celebrated in opera in Vienna and, from 1921, at the Metropolitan Opera, New York.

Jerusalem, Siegfried (b. 1940), German tenor, formerly orchestral bassoonist; prominent in Wagner, appearing at Bayreuth Festival from 1977.

Jesu, joy of man's desiring, ➤Hess.

Jesus Christ Superstar, musical with lyrics by Tim Rice, music by Andrew Lloyd Webber. Produced in New York, 1971. The Gospel story, with a principal and sympathetic role for Judas.

Jeux d'enfants (Fr., 'Children's Games'), suite of 12 pieces by Bizet for piano duet, 1871; he afterwards made an orchestral suite of five, and five more were later orchestrated by Karg-Elert.

Jewels of the Madonna, The, opera by Wolf-Ferrari. ➤*Gioielli della Madonna*.

Jewess, The, opera by Halévy. ➤*Juive*.

Jew's harp, primitive instrument held in the mouth, having a strip of metal 'twanged' (i.e. set vibrating) by the finger, the different notes being elicited by altering the shape of the cavity of the mouth. (Reason for the name unknown; apparently not corruption of 'jaw's harp'.)

jig, type of dance usually in 6/8 or 12/8 time, with cognate French and Italian forms *gigue* and *giga*. Under these forms it often constituted the last movement of an 18th-century suite, in which it was usually structured in ➤binary form.

jingling johnny, obsolete military-band percussion instrument shaped like a tree or pavilion (hence other name, 'Chinese pavilion') and hung with bells which were shaken.

Jirák, Karel Boleslav (1891–1972), Czech composer, pupil of Novák; also conductor. Works include six symphonies, *Overture to a Shakespearean Comedy*, seven string quartets, many song-cycles, etc. Resident in USA from 1947.

Jo, Sumi (b. 1962), Korean soprano who studied in Italy, where she made her operatic début in 1985. Specializing in the highest-pitched range (e.g. the Queen of the Night in *Die Zauberflöte*), she first sang at Covent Garden in 1991 and has recorded under Karajan and Solti.

Joachim, Joseph (1831–1907), Hungarian violinist of great distinction; also celebrated as leader of his own string quartet. Lived mainly in Germany; visited Britain aged 13 and many times thereafter. Friend of Brahms, whose Violin Concerto is dedicated to him; himself also a composer of repute, his works including three violin concertos, overtures to *Hamlet* and *King Henry IV*, etc. Made an orchestral version of Schubert's ➤*Grand Duo*.

Joan of Arc at the Stake, play by Claudel with music by Honegger. ➤*Jeanne d'Arc au bûcher*.

Job, works based on the biblical book: oratorio by C. H. H. Parry, first performed 1892; ballet (styled 'a masque for dancing') with music by Vaughan Williams, choreography by N. de Valois after Blake, first staged 1931.

Jocelyn, opera by Godard, produced in Brussels, 1888. Libretto by P. A. Silvestre and V. Capone, after Lamartine: Jocelyn is a seminarist tempted by earthly love. The work is now remembered by the leading tenor's 'Berceuse'.

Jochum, Eugen (1902–87), German conductor celebrated in German and Austrian symphonic music; held posts in Berlin, Munich, Amsterdam; appointed 'conductor laureate' of London Symphony Orchestra, 1975.

jodel, ➤yodel.

Johannespassion, ➤*St John Passion*.

Johnny Strikes Up, opera by Krenek. ➤*Jonny spielt auf*.

John of Fornsete, English 13th-century monk, conjecturally the composer of ➤*Sumer is icumen in*.

John of the Cross, St [Juan de la Cruz] (1542–91), Spanish poet and mystic. ➤Beecroft.

Johnson, Anthony Rolfe, ➤Rolfe Johnson.

Johnson, Graham [Rhodes] (b. 1950), British pianist, born in Rhodesia; prominent as an accompanist to singers, he founded the Songmakers' Almanac (vocal group) in 1976. OBE, 1994.

Johnson, Hunter (b. 1906), American composer of ballet *Letter to the World* (choreography by Martha Graham), a symphony, piano concerto, piano sonata, etc.

Johnson, John (*c.* 1540–1595), English lutenist and composer of songs and lute music; attached to the court of Elizabeth I.

Johnson, Robert (*c.* 1500–1554), Scottish priest and composer who fled to England from religious persecution; wrote Latin motets, English church music, also secular vocal works and music for viol consort.

Johnson, Robert (*c.* 1577–1633), English lutenist, serving Charles I and James I; composed solo songs (including two from *The Tempest*), catches, viol music, etc.

Johnson, Robert Sherlaw (b. 1932), British composer – also pianist, Oxford University lecturer, and author of a book on Messiaen. Works include piano concerto; three piano sonatas, *Asterogenesis* and other works for piano; *Festival Mass of the Resurrection*.

Johnston, Ben [originally Benjamin Burwell Johnston] (b. 1926), American composer (pupil of Milhaud), also pianist. Works include nine string quartets; *Auto Mobile* – a 'sound environment' on tape for a car exhibition; *One Man* for trombonist who also plays percussion (using his feet).

Joio, Norman Dello, ➤Dello Joio.

Jolas, Betsy [originally Elizabeth Illouz] (b. 1926), French-American composer (also pianist and organist), pupil of Messiaen and Milhaud in Paris. Works include opera *Schliemann*, *Points of Dawn* for contralto and 13 wind instruments; *States* for violin and six percussionists; Sonata for 12 solo voices.

Jolie Fille de Perth, La (Fr., 'The Fair Maid of Perth'), opera by Bizet, produced in Paris, 1867. Libretto by J. H. Vernoy de St-Georges and J. Adenis, after Scott's historical novel of 15th-century Scotland.

Jolivet, André (1905–74), French composer, pupil of Varèse and others; one of the former group called 'Young France'. Works include three symphonies (and a symphony for strings); Concertino for piano and trumpet; works for ➤Ondes Martenot; piano solos; oratorio *La vérité de Jeanne* ('The Truth about Joan [of Arc]'. Musical director of the Comédie Française, Paris, 1945–60.

Jomelli, Niccolò (1714–74), Italian composer, pupil of Leo; wrote oratorios, church music, etc., but especially operas – apparently more than 80. Was a pioneer of the use of the orchestral ➤crescendo. Much admired in Germany, and was court music director in Stuttgart, 1753–69.

Jones, Daniel (1912–93), British composer of 12 symphonies (he was apparently the first composer from Wales to have a symphony performed), 9 string quartets, music to *Under Milk Wood* (dramatic poem by his friend Dylan

Thomas); also of a sonata for three timpani. OBE, 1968.

Jones, Della (b. 1946), British mezzo-soprano, well known in Monteverdi's, Handel's and later operas and in a broad concert repertory including modern works; has sung at Covent Garden (Brangaene in *Tristan und Isolde*, 1993), in Los Angeles (in Handel's *Alcina*) and has made many recordings.

Jones, Gwyneth (b. 1936), British soprano (formerly mezzo-soprano); sang at Covent Garden from 1963, and at the Bayreuth Festival from 1966. Created Dame, 1986.

Jones, Philip (b. 1928), British trumpeter, founding director of Philip Jones Brass Ensemble (1951–87), the first such brass group to sustain a long and distinguished reputation.

Jones, Robert (*c.* 1570–after 1615), English lutenist, in service to various patrons; composed songs with lute, madrigals – one in *The* ➤*Triumphs of Oriana*. (An earlier Robert Jones sang in the English Chapel Royal in 1520.)

Jones, [James] **Sidney** (1869–1946), British composer, also theatre conductor, who gained international repute with *The* ➤*Geisha* and whose other London successes included *San Toy* (1899) and *My Lady Molly* (1902).

Jongen, Joseph (1873–1953), Belgian composer of symphonic poems, a piano concerto, a quartet for saxophones, piano and organ works, etc. Director of the Brussels Conservatory, 1920–39. Brother of Léon Jongen.

Jongen, Léon (1885–1969), Belgian composer and pianist; director of the Brussels Conservatory from 1939, suc-

ceeding his brother Joseph Jongen. Works include operas, *Rhapsodia belgica* for violin and orchestra, piano solos.

jongleur (Fr., juggler), medieval wandering minstrel who was singer, instrumentalist (chiefly on a form of fiddle), acrobat, juggler, etc.

Jonny spielt auf (Ger., 'Jonny Strikes Up'), opera by Krenek, in a jazz-influenced style; produced in Leipzig, 1927. Libretto by composer; title-role is that of a black jazz violinist.

Jonson, Ben (1573–1637), English poet and dramatist. ➤Antheil, ➤Burt, ➤Castiglioni.

Joplin, Scott (1868–1917), American composer and pianist whose ragtime compositions for piano had a revived vogue in the 1970s; also composed operas *A Guest of Honour* (lost) and *Treemonisha* (not staged till 1972).

Joseph, opera by Méhul, produced in Paris, 1807; libretto by A. Duval, after the Bible.

Joseph and the Amazing Technicolor Dreamcoat, musical (originally a 15-minute cantata without staging) with text by Tim Rice; music by Andrew Lloyd Webber. First staged performance, Edinburgh 1972. An adaptation from Genesis of the story of Joseph cast out by his brothers.

Josephs, Wilfred (1927–97), British composer of *Requiem* for baritone, chorus and orchestra (text is the ➤*Kaddish*); eleven symphonies, Concerto for brass band, Byrdsong for piano and organ; opera *Rebecca* (after Daphne Du Maurier); etc. He was a dentist before becoming a full-time musician.

Joshua, oratorio by Handel (words by

219

T. Morell, after the Bible), first performed in London, 1748.

Josquin (*c*. 1440–1521), in full Josquin des Prez (and other spellings, 'Josquin' being properly a diminutive forename). Flemish composer, pupil of Ockeghem, and singer at the Papal Church in Rome. Composed Masses, motets (one on the ➤*Stabat Mater* text), chansons, etc. His work is notable for an expressiveness new at that time. ➤*Musica reservata*.

jota, northern Spanish dance in quick triple time, traditionally with castanets.

Joubert, John [Pierre Herman] (b. 1927), South African composer who studied in London and became university teacher at Hull, then Birmingham (1962–86). Works include opera *Silas Marner* (after George Eliot); cycle of Latin unaccompanied motets *Pro Pace* (for peace); two symphonies; songs to poems by Blake, Emily Brontë and others.

Joyce, Eileen (1912–91), Australian pianist who settled in Britain, gaining much popularity in concertos – e.g. at the Proms from 1942.

Joyce, James (1882–1941), Irish writer. ➤*Ulysses*; ➤Cage; ➤Del Tredici; Huber, ➤Mihály, ➤Pisk, ➤Searle, ➤Stevenson, ➤Szymanowski.

Jubilate [Deo], Latin name for Psalm 100, as used in church services (in English, 'O be joyful in the Lord') and as occasionally set for concert and ceremonial purposes, as an expression of rejoicing.

Judas Maccabaeus, oratorio by Handel (words by T. Morell, after the Bible), first performed in London, 1747.

Judenkünig, Hans (*c*. 1450–1526), German lutenist and composer for his instrument, who died in Vienna.

Judith, oratorios based on the Apocryphal book, by (1) T. Arne, 1761, with text by Isaac Bickerstaffe; (2) C. H. H. Parry, 1888, with text direct from the Apocrypha.

juggler, ➤*jongleur*.

Juilliard Quartet, American string quartet founded in 1946 in association with the Juilliard School of Music, New York, with Robert Mann remaining leader through various changes of membership. Has performed more than 600 different works and made celebrated recordings of all Beethoven's, all Bartók's quartets.

Juive, La (Fr., 'The Jewess'), opera by Halévy, produced in Paris, 1835. Libretto by E. Scribe (originally written for Rossini); the 'Jewess', executed by order of a 15th-century Cardinal, turns out to be the Cardinal's own daughter.

Julius Caesar, opera by Handel, ➤*Giulio Cesare*.

Junge Lord, Der (Ger., 'The Young Lord'), opera by Henze, produced in Berlin, 1965; in Ingeborg Bachmann's libretto, the 'English nobleman' is really a dressed-up ape.

Jungfernquartette, ➤*Russian Quartets*.

'Jupiter' Symphony, nickname given in many different countries to Mozart's last symphony, no. 41 in C (K551): the name has no authority, only convenience. The dates of composition of this and the two preceding symphonies span less than seven weeks in 1788.

Jurinac, Sena [short for Srebrenka] (b. 1921), Austrian soprano (born in former Yugoslavia), internationally distinguished in Mozart, R. Strauss, etc., appearing at Glyndebourne 1949–56; member of Vienna State Opera 1944–83.

just intonation, the tuning of an interval in its 'pure' form according to the ➤harmonic series, not a tempered interval (➤temperament); hence a general system of tuning, which must incorporate at least five such 'pure' tunings within the octave. (It is not possible to construct a diatonic scale in which both the major third and the perfect fifth are 'pure'.) Such a tuning is theoretically accessible to voices, bowed string instruments, etc., in which the pitch of the notes is not mechanically fixed. Some twentieth-century composers, e.g. Partch, have had other instruments specially constructed to be tuned to 'pure' intervals.

K

K, abbreviation for (1) ►Köchel in numbering the works of Mozart; (2) ►Kirkpatrick in numbering the works of D. Scarlatti.

Kabalevsky, Dmitri [Borisovich] (1904–87), Russian composer, also pianist and writer on music. Composed operas including *Colas Breugnon* and *The Family of Taras* (based on a story of the Nazi occupation of Russian territory); three piano concertos and other concertos for violin and cello; four symphonies, songs, piano pieces.

Kabeláč, Miloslav (1908–79), Czech composer (also conductor); wrote an *Improvisation on Hamlet*, eight symphonies and other orchestral works; *Ricercari* for 1–6 percussionists; several works for speaker(s) and orchestra; choral music.

Kaddish, Jewish mourners' prayer, in Aramaic (similar to Hebrew); set in Bernstein's Symphony no. 3 and Josephs' *Requiem*.

Kadosa, Pál (1930–83), Hungarian composer and pianist. Works include eight symphonies, four piano concertos, songs.

Kafka, Franz (1883–1924), German-Czech writer. ►Einem.

Kagel, Mauricio (b. 1931), Argentin-ian composer who moved to West Germany in 1957. Works, many including electronics and theatrical elements, include *On Stage* (Fr., *Sur scène*) for speaker, mime, singer and three instrumentalists; *Match* for three players on two cellos with percussion and dice, a *St Bach Passion* and film-collage *Ludwig van*.

Kaiserquartett (Ger.), ►'*Emperor*' *Quartet*.

Kajanus, Robert (1856–1933), Finnish conductor, friend and champion of Sibelius; also composer of symphonic poems, etc.

Kalabis, Viktor (b. 1923), Czech composer, formerly also radio music executive; works include five symphonies, Symphonic Variations, six string quartets, Sonata for violin and harpsichord.

Kalevala, the Finnish national epic poem. ►Sibelius.

Kalinnikov, Vassily Sergeyevich (1866–1901), Russian composer of two symphonies, songs, stage music, etc.

Kalkbrenner, Frédéric [originally Friedrich Wilhelm Michael] (1785–1849), German-born pianist who studied and settled in Paris; noted performer and teacher; also composer of three piano concertos, many studies, etc.

Kalliwoda, Johann Wenzel (or, in Czech, Jan Václav Kalivoda), (1801–66), Bohemian violinist and composer of seven symphonies and other orchestral works formerly often performed; also of opera, string quartets, church music, etc.

Kálmán, Emmerich (1882–1953), Austro-Hungarian composer, particularly of operettas including *Die ➤Csárdásfürstin*, *➤Gräfin Mariza*; latterly lived in France and USA, and died in Paris.

Kalomiris, Manolis (1883–1962), Greek composer, also critic and conservatory director in Athens. Works include operas, three symphonies (two with chorus, one with narrator), songs.

Kaminski, Heinrich (1886–1946), German composer of music to religious texts using modal style; also of opera, Concerto for Orchestra, *Triptych* for voice and organ, etc.

Kaminski, Joseph (1903–72), Polish-born Israeli violinist and composer who emigrated to Palestine, 1936; works include Concertino for trumpet and *Comedy Overture*.

Kammer (Ger.), chamber; hence *Kammermusik*, *Kammersymphonie*, (➤ chamber music, ➤chamber symphony), etc.; also, in the 17th century, *Kammerton* (chamber pitch), denoting a normal lower standard of pitch than *Chorton* (choir pitch), applying to choir and organ.

Kanawa, Kiri Te, ➤Te Kanawa.

Kancheli, Giya (b. 1935), Georgian composer resident in Germany and Belgium (1995), having left Georgia in 1991. Works include seven symphonies, *Light Sorrow* for children's voices and orchestra, *Night Prayers* for string quartet.

Kander, John [Harold] (b. 1927), American composer of musical shows, notably ➤*Cabaret* and *Chicago* (1975).

kantele, traditional Finnish plucked-string instrument, laid flat (on knees or table) to play.

Kantor, ➤cantor.

Kapelle (Ger.), chapel; hence, the musical establishment of a prince's private chapel (➤*cappella*); hence again, any established musical institution, e.g. an orchestra – the director being a ➤*Kapellmeister*.

Kapellmeister (Ger., chapel-master), musical director, originally of a prince's private chapel; term later used also for a 'resident conductor', e.g. of an orchestra. Hence *Kapellmeistermusik*, 'conductor's music', (abusive term for) empty music composed by someone who has a conductor's familiarity with mere technique, but has nothing more.

Karajan, Herbert [originally Heribert] **von** (1908–89), Austrian conductor, also stage and film director for some of his own opera performances. Despite his former Nazi party membership he made his London début in 1947, and in 1955 became conductor of the Berlin Philharmonic Orchestra, resigning only three months before his death. In a career of unsurpassed international fame he recorded all Beethoven's symphonies four times. Equally acclaimed in opera (often his own stage director), he conducted at Bayreuth 1951–2, became artistic director of the Vienna State Opera

1957–64, and then concentrated his operatic work at Salzburg's main (summer) festival and at the Salzburg Easter Festival which he founded in 1967.

Karilia, overture and orchestral suite by Sibelius, 1893; evocative of the province of Karelia in the south of Finland.

Karetnikov, Nikolay [Nikolayevich] (1930–94), Russian composer; Soviet hostility to his modernism impeded performances until his last decade. Wrote opera ➤*Till Eulenspiegel*, four symphonies and a chamber symphony, piano quintet.

Karg-Elert (real name Karg), **Sigfrid** (1877–1933), German composer, also pianist and organist; now known chiefly for his many organ works. Wrote also a symphony, string quartets, many songs, etc.

Karr, Gary [Michael] (b. 1941), American double-bass player, the most celebrated of modern soloists on his instrument; commissioned works from Henze, Schuller and others.

Kastalsky, Alexander Dmitrievich (1856–1926), Russian composer, pupil of Tchaikovsky and Taneyev; active in church music before and after the 1917 Revolution. Also composed patriotic choral works, opera, etc.

Kát'a Kabanová, opera by Janáček, produced in Brno, 1921. Named after the tragic heroine, whose husband is mother-dominated: libretto by composer, after V. Cervinka's translation of Ostrovsky's Russian play *The Storm*.

Katchen, Julius (1926–69), American pianist who, as a child prodigy, with-

drew from career in US, later making European début in Paris, 1946; much admired as a soloist, he also occasionally conducted from 1959. Died in Paris from leukaemia.

Katerina Izmailova, opera by Shostakovich. ➤*Lady Macbeth of the Mtsensk District*.

Katya Kabanova, an alternative spelling of the title of Janáček's opera ➤*Kát'a Kabanová*, reproducing the normal Russian form of the Russian heroine's name.

Kay, Ulysses [Simpson] (1917–95), American composer, pupil of Hanson and Rogers; works include operas, a symphony, a 'Quintet Concerto' for five brass soloists and orchestra.

Kazantzakis, Nikos (*c*.1883–1957), Greek writer. ➤*Greek Passion*.

kazoo, children's musical instrument into which one hums to produce a buzzing sound. Exceptionally brought into concert use (with audience participation) by David ➤Bedford.

Kb., abbr. for Ger. *Kontrabass*, i.e. double-bass.

Keal, Minna (originally Minnie Nirenstein) (b. 1909), British composer who, previously almost unknown, had her Symphony no. 1 (written at the age of 76) performed at the Proms in 1989.

Keats, John (1795–1821), English poet. ➤Castiglioni, ➤Holst.

keen (Ir., *Caoine*), an Irish funeral song accompanied by wailing; to wail thus. ➤Berkeley (M.).

'Kegelstatt' Trio, nickname for trio by Mozart, 1756, for clarinet, viola and piano (a unique combination), K.498, the German nickname ('skittle alley') presumably referring to its place of composition.

(K)ein Sommernachtstraum, orchestral piece by Schnittke, 1985, marked 'not after Shakespeare': title is a pun on *Ein Sommernachtstraum*, the German form of *A Midsummer Night's Dream*, making the first word equivalent to 'not a'.

Keiser, Reinhard (1674–1739), German composer; also director of the Hamburg Opera, and afterwards worked for some time in Copenhagen. Wrote about 50 operas, some with mixed German and Italian words; more than anyone else, established Hamburg as an opera centre. Also composed works to religious texts, including oratio *Der blutige und sterbende Jesus* ('The bleeding and dying Jesus').

Kelemen, Milko (b. 1924), Yugoslav composer, pupil in Paris of Messiaen and Milhaud; settled in Germany, teaching in Düsseldorf and Stuttgart. Works include opera *Der Belagerungszustand* ('The Siege', after Camus's novel *The Plague*), concertos for piano and for violin, and a *Hommage à Heinrich* ➤*Schütz* with biblical text, for unaccompanied solo singers and choir.

Keler-Béla [pen-name of Adalbert von Keler] (1820–82), Hungarian violinist, bandmaster, conductor, and composer chiefly of dances and marches.

Kell, Reginald [Clifford] (1906–81), British clarinettist, noted as soloist and director of his own ensemble; resident mainly in USA, 1948–71.

Kelley, Edgar Stillman (1857–1944), American composer (also organist and critic) who studied in Germany. Studied Chinese music and wrote an orchestral suite on Chinese themes.

Other works include the symphony *Gulliver* (after Swift), operettas, string quartets.

Kelly, Michael (1762–1826), Irish tenor, friend of Mozart; took part in the first performance of *Le* ➤*Nozze di Figaro*; was himself the composer of music for many London stage pieces.

Kelterborn, Rudolf (b. 1931), Swiss composer; works include four symphonies, chamber opera *Julia* (the Romeo and Juliet story in Palestinian/Israeli context) and other operas, *Musik* for six percussionists.

Kempe, Rudolf (1910–76), German conductor; director of the Munich Opera, 1952–4; noted Wagner conductor at Covent Garden; principal conductor, Royal Philharmonic Orchestra, 1961–75.

Kempff, Wilhelm (1895–1991), German pianist, formerly director of a musical academy at Stuttgart; also composer. Continued performing until his 80s.

Kennedy, Nigel [Paul] (b. 1956), British violinist (also viola-player) who performs jazz as well as classical concertos, etc. In 1993 renounced the conventional orchestra circuit returning in 1997. Has won large sales for his recordings of Beethoven, Berg, Elgar and Vivaldi concertos. In 1998 changed name to Kennedy, dropping Nigel.

Kenny, Yvonne (b. 1950), Australian soprano, taking leading operatic roles in London (Covent Garden from 1975), Paris, Berlin, Vienna. Recorded Mozart opera roles under Harnoncourt – sang title-role in first performance (Lyons, 1984) of Bryars' *Medea*.

Kent bugle, ➤ophicleide.

Kentner, Louis [originally Lajos]

Kerl, Johann Caspar

[Philip] (1905–87), pianist born in Karvinna (then in Hungary, now in Czechoslovakia) who studied in Budapest and settled in England, 1935; partner of Menuhin (his brother-in-law) in recitals.

Kerl, Johann Caspar, ➤Kerll.

Kerle, Jacob van (*c*. 1531–91), Flemish composer of church music, long in service to the Bishop of Augsburg; his work was performed with approval at the Council of Trent, 1562–3, when propriety in church music was discussed. Died in Prague.

Kerll [also Kerl], **Johann Caspar** (1627–93), German organist and composer, chiefly in Munich and Vienna. Studied in Italy, wrote Italian operas – also church music, etc. Handel 'borrowed' some of his music: ➤*Israel in Egypt*.

Kern, Jerome [David] (1885–1945), American composer of many popular songs of marked individuality – especially in ➤*Show Boat* and other musical plays, and in films of a similar nature. Composed also a few other works including *Portrait of Mark Twain* for orchestra.

Kertesz, István (1929–73), Hungarian-born, German-naturalized conductor; musical director of Cologne Opera and (1965–8) principal conductor of the London Symphony Orchestra. Drowned while swimming.

Ketèlbey, Albert [William] (1875–1959), British composer of *In a Monastery Garden* and other popular light orchestral pieces; also theatre conductor.

kettledrum, cauldron-shaped drum originally from the Orient, and origin-ally smaller and more delicate-sounding than now; in modern form, tuned to a definite pitch, normally by handles on the rim. Two such drums were normal in the symphony orchestra up to Beethoven, and later composers have used three or more. The drum rests on a stand, the skin facing upwards; the tone-quality may be varied according to the drumsticks used and the point of impact. A cloth on the drum may be used to give the effect of a mute. Mechanically tuned drums, using pedals, and commonly called 'pedal drums', have also come into wide use in the 20th century; they (1) make tuning quicker, allowing rapid, changes in the middle of a movement, and (2) allow the use of glissando (drum struck, then pedal depressed – e.g. in Bartók's Concerto for Orchestra). The kettledrum is standard also in the various types of wind and brass bands including the mounted military band – one slung each side of a horse. For a set of kettledrums the Italian plural *timpani* has become the accepted British and North American usage – the singular *timpano* being awkwardly avoided, though valid in Italian.

Keuris, Tristan (b. 1946), Dutch composer whose visits to USA inspired *To Brooklyn Bridge* for 24 solo voices and instrumental ensemble; also wrote Concerto for saxophone quartet and orchestra, two string quartets, organ concertos, etc.

key (1) a lever, e.g. on piano, organ, or a woodwind instrument, depressed by finger or foot to produce a note; (2) a classification of the notes of a scale, the most important note being called the *keynote* and the others functioning in relation to it. If the keynote is C, then the key may be either C major or C minor, according to whether the ➤major or ➤minor scale is used basically in the music concerned; notes outside the 'basic' scale are said to be foreign to the key. The sharps and flats appertaining to the key are displayed in a ➤key-signature; other sharps, flats and naturals occurring 'casually' in the music are written as ➤ accidentals. The major and minor keys were the only two types of note-ordering generally used in Western music between approximately 1600 and 1900; earlier, the ➤modes prevailed, and later certain composers began to dispense with key altogether, as in ➤atonal music.

keyboard, a continuous arrangement of keys (➤key, 1) either for the fingers, as on the piano, or for the feet, as on the *pedal keyboard* of an organ. So also *keyboard of light*, instrument throwing colours on a screen in Skryabin's ➤*Prometheus*. The term *keyboard* is also used as a general term for *a keyboard instrument* – especially in pop music (where a player may switch between different instruments) and in such contexts as 'Bach's keyboard works' where the works may be suitable for more than one type of keyed instrument.

key-bugle, ➤ophicleide.

keyed bugle, ➤ophicleide.

keyed trumpet, ➤trumpet.

keynote, ➤key, 2.

key-signature, the indication in written music of the number of sharps or flats in the prevailing key, such indication normally being placed at the beginning of each line of music (or at any point when the key-signature is changed). Thus flat-signs on the lines or spaces in the staff denoting B, E and A indicate that these notes are to be played as B♭, E♭ and A♭ – unless an indication to the contrary is given by an ➤accidental. So the key of E♭ major or C minor is indicated, since only these have all these three notes flat (and no others). It is the 'natural' form of the minor scale which is used to determine key-signature.

Khachaturian, Aram [Ilich] (1903–78), Armenian composer, pupil of Gnesin and Myaskovsky. Works, often influenced by Armenian folk-music, include a piano concerto (originally with a part for ➤flexatone, imitating an Armenian folk-instrument), a violin concerto, cello concerto, three symphonies; ballets ➤*Gayaneh* (source of popular *Sabre Dance*) and ➤*Spartacus*; choral, piano and chamber works.

khorovod (Rus.), type of traditional Russian round dance with singing; one of the sections (based on a Russian folk-tune) of Stravinsky's *The* ➤*Firebird* is so named.

Khovanshchina, see following entry.

Khovansky Affair, The (Rus. *Khovanshchina*), unfinished opera by Musorgsky; as completed by Rimsky-Korsakov, it was produced in St Petersburg, 1886. A later completion, more faithful to the composer's harmonic originality, was made by Shostakovich. Libretto, by Musorgsky and V. V. Stasov, about the princes of the Khovansky family at the time of Peter the Great.

Khrennikov, Tikhon [Nikolayevich] (b. 1913), Russian composer, pupil of Shebalin, also pianist; works include three symphonies, two piano concertos, operas. As secretary-general of the

Union of Soviet Composers, he took part in denouncing Prokofiev and other musicians for ➤formalism in 1948, and remained in his post into the 1990s.

Kienzl, Wilhelm (1857–1941), Austrian composer encouraged by Liszt and associated with Wagner; composed operas including *Der Evangelimann* ('The Preacher'), and also many piano pieces and songs.

Kikimora, work by Lyadov styled a 'legend for orchestra' and published in 1910. Kikimora is a malevolent goblin – the name is etymologically related to Fr. *cauchemar*, nightmare.

Kilpinen, Yrjö (1892–1959), Finnish composer enjoying a state grant to enable him to compose; he wrote hundreds of songs in Finnish, Swedish and German, also other works including a suite for bass viol and piano.

Kim, Young-Uck (b. 1947), Korean violinist who studied in USA and settled there; soloist with major orchestras from age 15. Schuller's violin concerto is dedicated to him.

Kinderszenen (in older German *Kinderscenen*: 'Scenes of Childhood'), set of 13 short piano pieces by Schumann, 1838, with titles alluding to childhood life. No. 7 is ➤*Träumerei*.

Kindertotenlieder (Ger., 'Songs on the Death of Children'), cycle of five songs (1901–4) by Mahler, to poems by F. Rückert. There are alternative accompaniments for orchestra and for piano.

King and I, The, musical play with text by Oscar Hammerstein II based on the novel *Anna and the King of Siam* by Margaret Landon; music by Richard Rodgers. Produced in New York, 1951. The governess finds the children easier to manage than her royal employer.

King, Charles (1687–1748), English composer of church music, organist of St Paul's Cathedral, London; pupil of Blow and Clarke.

King, Robert (active 1678–1726), English composer of songs, stage music, etc.; member of Charles II's band, 1680.

King, Robert (b. 1960), British conductor, founder 1979 of The King's Consort (ensemble devoted to baroque music, quickly winning distinction in performances and recordings). Has also conducted symphony orchestras in Madrid and elsewhere, and is the author of book on Purcell (1994).

King, William (1624–80), English organist, priest and composer of church music and songs.

King Arthur, or The British Worthy, opera by Purcell (Z628), with libretto by Dryden, produced in London, 1691. In the convention then prevalent, it is only partly musical: King Arthur and some other leading characters do not sing.

King Christian II, play by A. Paul for which Sibelius wrote incidental music, 1898; concerns the 16th-century Danish king.

King David, 'dramatic psalm' by Honegger. ➤*Roi David*.

Kingdom, The, oratorio by Elgar, first performed in 1906; text from the Bible. ➤*Apostles*.

King Lear, play by Shakespeare, music for which includes overture by Berlioz,

1831; overture and incidental music by Balakirev, 1861; incidental music by Debussy, 1904, only two fragments surviving; opera by Reimann (►Lear, 1978). Verdi also planned, but never completed, an opera based on the play.

'King of Prussia' Quartets, an alternative name for Mozart's set of ►Prussian Quartets.

King Priam, opera by Tippett, produced in Coventry, 1962. Libretto, by the composer, treats the Homeric story of Greek and Trojan leaders.

King Roger (Pol., Król Roger), opera by Szymanowski, produced in Warsaw, 1926. Libretto by composer and J. Iwaskiewicz, about Roger II, 12th-century king of Sicily.

King's Consort, The, ►King (Robert).

Kinsky, Georg (1882–1951), German musicologist whose catalogue of Beethoven's music is used in numbering his works.

Kipnis, Alexander (1891–1978), Russian-born bass resident in USA, with high reputation in Russian and German songs; father of Igor Kipnis (b. 1930), harpsichordist.

Kirbye, George (c.1565–1634), English composer of madrigals (one in The ►Triumphs of Oriana), motets, viol pieces, etc.

Kirche (Ger.), church; so Kirchenmusik (church music), etc.

Kirchner, Leon (b. 1910), American composer, pupil of Bloch, Schoenberg and Sessions; works include two piano concertos, a piano sonata, three string quartets. Is also pianist.

Kirkby, Emma (b. 1949), British soprano who made London début in 1974; became celebrated in Renaissance and baroque music (particularly in partnership with the lutenist Anthony Rooley), cultivating an almost vibrato-less tone which set a new model.

Kirkpatrick, Ralph (1911–84), American harpsichordist (also performer on piano and clavichord) whose biography of D. Scarlatti (1953) incorporated a catalogue of Scarlatti's works which has become standard. Thus these works are referred to by their 'Kirkpatrick' or 'K' or 'Kk' numbers. (This has superseded the ►Longo numbering.)

Kirnberger, Johann Philipp (1721–83), German violinist, composer and important theorist; pupil of Bach.

Kirshbaum, Ralph (b. 1946), American cellist, resident in London since 1971. Prominent in concertos, including première (1980) of Tippett's Triple Concerto.

Kismet, 'musical Arabian Night' with text by Charles Lederer and Luther Davis based on the play by Edward Knoblock; lyrics by Robert Wright and George Forrest; music from the works of Borodin, selected and arranged by Robert Wright and George Forrest. Produced in New York, 1953. The plot involves a Caliph of Baghdad, a prince of beggars, and the historical 11th-century poet Omar Khayyam.

Kissin, Evgeny (b. 1971), Russian pianist who played both Chopin's concertos with the Moscow Philharmonic Orchestra aged 12 and appeared at the BBC Proms, 1988. Rapidly consolidated his reputation, with a speciality in Russian music.

Kiss Me, Kate, musical comedy with

text by Samuel and Bella Spewack; music and lyrics by Cole Porter. Produced in New York, 1947. The plot concerns a Baltimore production of a musical version of Shakespeare's *The Taming of the Shrew*.

kit (1) very small type of violin formerly used by dancing-masters; (2) ➤drum kit.

kitchen department, humorous term for the percussion section of an orchestra.

Kitezh, ➤*Legend of the Invisible City of Kitezh and of the Maid Fevronia*.

kithara, ancient Greek plucked string instrument of lyre type, with a squared-off box resonator at the foot.

Kjerulf, Halfdan (1815–68), Norwegian composer who studied in Leipzig. His works, including choruses, male voice quartets and songs, were among the first to bring the flavour of Norwegian folk-song into the concerthall.

Klang (Ger.), sound; so *Klangfarbenmelodie* (sound-colour melody), a term proposed by Schoenberg, and used by him and by Webern, indicating a succession of notes produced in different instrumental sounds (whether or not at the same pitch); i.e. the change of tone-colour stands for the differentiation which, in normal melody, is effected by a change of pitch.

Klavier (Ger., in older spelling *clavier*), a keyboard, hence a keyboard instrument, particularly harpsichord or piano; so Bach's *Das* ➤*wohltemperirte Klavier* (*Well-Tempered Clavier*). See also following entries.

Klavierauszug (Ger.), a piano 'reduction' – i.e. the score of an orchestral or similar work arranged for piano.

Klavierübung, ➤*Clavierübung*.

Klebe, Giselher [Wolfgang] (b. 1925), German composer, pupil of Blacher and others. Works include five symphonies, one of them for 42 strings; sonatas for viola, for double-bass; operas *Die Räuber* ('The Robbers') (based on Schiller's play), *Alkmene*, *Figaro lässt sich scheiden* ('Figaro seeks a divorce' – sequel to the plot of *Le* ➤*Nozze di Figaro*), *Ein wahrer Held* ('A True Hero') based on Synge's *The Playboy of the Western World*.

Kleiber, Carlos (b. 1930), Germanborn conductor who emigrated in boyhood with his father, Erich Kleiber (below), to Argentina; established European celebrity and became Austrian citizen, 1980. First conducted at Covent Garden, 1974, in *Der Rosenkavalier*.

Kleiber, Erich (1890–1956), conductor, Austrian-born, who rejected the Nazi régime and took Argentinian citizenship, 1938. Noted in opera (at Covent Garden 1950–53; first British stage performance of *Wozzeck*, 1952). Father of Carlos Kleiber (above).

klein (Ger.), little; *kleine Flöte* (little flute), piccolo; *kleine Trommel* (little drum), side drum. ➤*Eine kleine Nachtmusik*.

kleine Nachtmusik, Eine, ➤*Eine kleine Nachtmusik*.

Kleist, Heinrich von (1777–1811), German dramatist and poet. ➤Egk, ➤Henze.

Klemperer, Otto (1885–1973), conductor, German-born (also composer of six symphonies, Mass, etc.), internationally noted in opera and concerts. Expelled by the Nazis (as a Jew), he became an American citizen, then (1970) an Israeli citizen. Became principal conductor of the Philharmonia (later New Philharmonia) Orchestra, London, 1959: named its 'conductor for life', 1964. (He continued despite partial paralysis.) Occasionally, as when conducting *Fidelio* at Covent Garden in 1961, he was his own stage director.

Klenovsky, Nikolai Semenovich (1857–1915), Russian composer of ballets, choral music, etc.; also conductor. Pupil of Tchaikovsky. Not to be confused with the following.

Klenovsky, Paul, the pseudonym under which Henry J. Wood made an orchestral arrangement (1929) of Bach's organ ➤Toccata and Fugue in D minor.

Klien, Walter (1928–91), Austrian pianist who recorded all Mozart's solo piano works, all Schubert's sonatas, etc. Studied composition with Hindemith.

Klopstock, Friedrich Gottlieb (1724–1803), German poet. ➤Resurrection Symphony.

Knaben Wunderhorn, Des (Ger., 'The Youth's Magic Horn'), an anthology of German poetry supposedly of folk origin; Mahler set 13 of these poems to orchestral accompaniment, 1900.

Knappertsbusch, Hans (1888–1965), German conductor with long tenures at the Bavarian State Opera (1922–36) and Vienna State Opera (1936–50).

Knight, Gillian [Rosemary] (b. 1934), British mezzo-soprano who first sang at Covent Garden in 1970 and is particularly known for Gilbert and Sulli-

van performances with D'Oyly Carte company (1959–64) and others.

Knight, Joseph Philip (1812–87), British clergyman who composed 'Rocked in the cradle of the deep' and other songs.

Knipper, Lev [Konstantinovich] (1898–1974), Russian composer, pupil of Glière and, in Berlin, of Jarnach. Works include *The North Wind* and other operas, 14 symphonies and *Turkmenian Suite* for orchestra, a violin concerto, popular songs in Soviet style.

Knorr, Iwan (1853–1916), German composer of operas, chamber music, etc.; teacher in Frankfurt of Quilter, C. Scott and other British composers.

Knot Garden, The, opera by Tippett, first performed in London, 1970. Libretto by composer in contemporary domestic setting but with allusion to Shakespeare's *The Tempest*.

Knussen, [Stuart] Oliver (b. 1952), British composer of three symphonies, horn concerto, operas *Where the Wild Things Are* and *Higglety-Pigglety-Pop*, and *Songs without Voices* for eight instruments; also noted conductor, especially of modern music. CBE, 1994.

Koanga, opera by Delius, produced (in German) in Elberfeld, 1904; revised after Delius's death by Beecham and Edward Agate and produced in London, 1935. Libretto by C. F. Keary, Koanga being an African chief transported as a slave to America. ➤banjo; ➤calinda.

Köchel, Ludwig von (1800–1877), Austrian scholar whose catalogue of Mozart's output, later revised by others, is the basis of the familiar 'K' numeration of Mozart's works.

Kodály, Zoltán (1882–1967), Hungarian composer. Collected and edited Hungarian folk-songs, partly in collaboration with Bartók; developed a strongly national idiom and constructed a system of music education (now internationalized) which bears his name. Works include cantata ►*Psalmus Hungaricus*, opera ►*Háry János* and the orchestral suite drawn from it, Concerto for Orchestra, a symphony, ►*Dances of Galánta*, variations on the Hungarian folk-song 'The Peacock', and other orchestral works, *Dances of Marosszek* for piano (afterwards orchestrated), Missa Brevis and other choral works; sonata for unaccompanied cello, songs, etc.

Koechlin, Charles (1867–1950), French composer, pupil of Massenet and Fauré; also writer of textbooks, etc. Works include a symphony, symphonic poems *La loi de la jungle* and *Les Bandar-Log* (both after Kipling's *The Jungle Book*), and other orchestral pieces; three string quartets, songs, piano solos.

Kogan, Leonid [Borisovich] (1924–82), Russian violinist who won first prize in Brussels international competition, 1951, and thereafter toured widely – British début, 1955; American, 1958.

Köhler, [Christian] **Louis Heinrich** (1820–86), German composer of much educational piano music, and of opera and other works; also pianist and conductor.

Kokkonen, Joonas (1921–96), Finnish composer of four symphonies, a cello concerto, three string quartets, opera *The Last Temptations*, etc.; is also pianist, and was formerly music critic.

Kolisch Quartet, Vienna-based string quartet, 1922–39, led by Rudolf Kolisch (1896–1978), which pioneered works by Schoenberg and Berg.

Kollo (originally Kollodziewski), **René** (b. 1937), German tenor who, after beginning his career in light entertainment, won celebrity in Wagner (at Bayreuth Festival from 1969).

Kol Nidrei (Heb., 'All the vows'), work for cello and orchestra by Bruch, published in 1881, 'after Hebrew melodies'. The title refers to a prayer associated with the annual Jewish Day of Atonement.

Kondrashin, Kirill [Petrovich] (1914–81), Russian conductor of Moscow Philharmonic, 1960–75; left USSR and became conductor of the Concertgebouw Orchestra of Amsterdam, 1979.

Kontarsky, Aloys (b. 1931) and **Alfons** (b. 1932), German pianists, celebrated since late 1950s as piano duo, especially in modern works. They are brothers: a third brother, Bernhard (b. 1937), is a pianist and conductor.

Kontrabass (Ger.), double-bass; similarly *Kontrabassposaune*, double-bass trombone, etc.

Kontrafagott (Ger.), double-bassoon.

Konzertmeister (Ger.), leader of an orchestra, (US) concert-master.

Koopman, Ton [originally Antonius Gerhardus Michael] (b. 1944), Dutch harpsichordist and organist; formed the Amsterdam Baroque Orchestra in 1979, touring widely with it and making many recordings.

kora, plucked stringed instrument of

West Africa with a skin-covered gourd as sound-box, now regularly seen in Western Europe at ➤World Music events, etc.

Korbay, Francis Alexander (really Ferencz Sándor Korbay) (1846–1913), Hungarian singer, also pianist, who settled and taught in London (dying there); arranged Hungarian gipsy songs, with English words.

Korchmarev, Klimenty Arkadievich (1899–1958), Russian composer of operas (including *Ten Days That Shook the World*, based on the 1917 Russian Revolution), piano music, choral symphony *Holland* (on Dutch revolutionary poems), etc.

Korean temple block, ➤temple block.

Kornett (Ger.), ➤cornet, ➤cornett.

Korngold, Erich Wolfgang (1897–1957), Austrian-born composer, naturalized in USA, 1943. Child prodigy: at age 13, wrote piano sonata played by Schnabel. Later works include *Die tote Stadt* ('The Dead City') and other operas, a violin concerto, piano (left-hand) concerto; also much film music – in Hollywood after 1935. Was also conductor.

Kostelanetz, André (1903–80), conductor, Russian-born, who settled in USA, 1922, and, with his own orchestra, won fame chiefly in succulent arrangements of light music. Married the French-American soprano Lily Pons (1898–1976).

koto, a Japanese plucked stringed instrument of the zither type, usually with 13 strings, placed horizontally and played by three plectrums worn on the thumb and two fingers.

Kotzwara (Germanized form of original name Kočžwara), **Franz** (*c.* 1750–91), Czech-born violinist, double-bass-player and composer who settled in London; committed suicide there. His imitative fantasia *The Battle of Prague*, for piano with optional additional instruments, formerly enjoyed great popularity.

Koussevitzky, Serge (form of name used by Sergey Alexandrovich Kusevitsky) (1874–1951), Russian-born conductor (previously double-bass player) who settled in USA; conductor of the Boston Symphony Orchestra, 1924–49. Encouraged young composers, partly by means of the Koussevitzky Music Foundation, which continued after his death. ➤ode.

Kovacevich, Stephen (b. 1940), American pianist (also conductor) of Yugoslav parentage, formerly known as Stephen Bishop or Bishop-Kovacevich. Came to London in 1959 to study with Myra Hess and remained there; gave first performances of concertos by Richard Rodney Bennett and by Tavener. Since 1984, has conducted various major orchestras.

Kozeluch [Germanized form of original name Koželuh], **Leopold** (1747–1818), Czech composer who settled in Vienna; was one of the precursors of the 'classical' symphonic style (i.e. that of Haydn), and one of the first to compose specifically for the piano as distinct from the harpsichord. Wrote also operas, oratorio, arrangements of Scottish, Irish and Welsh folksongs.

Kraft, Anton (1749–1820), Bohemian-Austrian cellist and composer, member of Haydn's orchestra at Eszterháza. Composed chiefly cello music; Haydn's Cello Concerto in D was, for a time, attributed to him.

Kraft, William (b. 1923), American composer, also percussionist and conductor. Works include *Configurations* for four percussionists and jazz orchestra, *A Kennedy Portrait*, for narrator and orchestra, tuba concerto.

Krakowiak, Polish dance in quick 2/4 time from the Cracow region.

Kramář, ➤Krommer.

Kraus, Alfredo (b. 1927), Spanish tenor of Austrian descent; achieved highest distinction in Italian opera repertory at Covent Garden (from 1959), etc.

Kraus, Lili (1903–86), Hungarian pianist who took New Zealand nationality, then American; noted as Mozart soloist and (1935–40) in duo with the violinist Szymon Goldberg. She resumed career after Japanese internment during World War II.

Krause, Tom (b. 1934), Finnish baritone, noted for concert and operatic performances in many languages; sang at Glyndebourne from 1963, at Metropolitan Opera, New York, 1967–73.

Krauss, Clemens (1893–1954), Austrian conductor, director of opera in Vienna, Berlin and Munich successively; friend and noted interpreter of R. Strauss; joint librettist (with the composer) of Strauss's opera ➤*Capriccio*; was married to ➤Ursuleac.

Krebs, Johann Ludwig (1713–80), German organist and composer of church music, keyboard works, etc.; a favourite pupil of Bach.

Krein, Alexander Abramovich (1883–1951), Russian composer of ballet, patriotic cantatas, etc., and also of works with Jewish associations –

e.g. operas *The Youth of Abraham* and *The Maccabees*. Brother of the following.

Krein, Grigory Abramovich (1879–1955), Russian composer, pupil of Glière and (in Leipzig) of Reger. Works include two piano concertos, much chamber music. Brother of the preceding.

Kreisler, Fritz (1875–1962), Austrian violinist of enormous fame; also composer of string quartet, operettas and especially of violin pieces some of which he fathered on various 17th- and 18th-century composers (➤Pugnani) – admitting his hoax in 1935.

Kreisleriana, cycle of piano pieces by Schumann, 1838, dedicated to Chopin – referring to the eccentric musician Kreisler, created in the writings of E. T. A. ➤Hoffmann.

Kreizberg, Yakov (b. 1959), Russian-born conductor who emigrated to USA 1976 and appeared with leading orchestras in USA, Europe, Israel; at Glyndebourne (*Jenůfa*, 1992); conducted BBC Symphony Orchestra at the Proms, 1993 and 1994. Principal conductor of Bournemouth Symphony Orchestra from 1995. His brother is ➤Bychkov, 'Kreizberg' being his mother's maiden name.

Krejčí, Iša (1904–68), Czech composer, pupil of Novák and Jirák; works include opera *The Uproar at Ephesus* (after Shakespeare's *The Comedy of Errors*), Sinfonietta, a nonet and other chamber music.

Kremer, Gidon (b. 1947), Latvian violinist, prominent in new music; mainly resident in the West, he founded the Lockenhaus Festival in

Austria which became established in the late 1980s.

Krenek, Ernst (1900–1991), Austrian-born composer of partly Czech descent, resident in the USA from 1938; US citizen, 1954. Pupil of Schreker; married Mahler's daughter Anna. Discarded the Czech spelling (Křenek) of his name. Showed jazz influence in very successful opera ➤*Jonny spielt auf*, 1927; later operas include *Das Leben des Orest* ('The Life of Orestes'). Also wrote five symphonies, four piano concertos, and various works with specifically American associations – orchestral variations on the folk-tune 'I wonder as I wander', choral *Santa Fé Time-table* (on names of railway stations), etc. Also made use of electronic music and was teacher and writer of textbooks, e.g. on Ockeghem.

Kreutzer, Conradin (1780–1849), German pianist, conductor and composer of *Das Nachtlager von Granada* ('The Night Camp in Granada') and other operas.

Kreutzer, Rodolphe (1766–1831), French violinist and composer of 19 violin concertos, over 40 operas, etc.; friend of Beethoven. ➤*Kreutzer Sonata*.

Kreutzer Sonata, nickname for Beethoven's Sonata in A (1803) for violin and piano, dedicated to Rodolphe Kreutzer.

Krieger, Johann Philipp (1651–1725), German composer, partly trained in Italy. Wrote Masses and other church music, instrumental suites, etc., as did his brother Johann (1652–1734).

Krips, Josef (1902–74), Austrian conductor, prominent in London orches-tral life after World War II; principal conductor, London Symphony Orchestra, 1950–54. His brother Henry (originally Heinrich) Krips (1912–87) was also a conductor.

Krommer, Franz [originally František Vincenc Kramář] (1759–1831), Moravian composer and violinist who held court post in Vienna; composed many concertos and much chamber music for wind instruments.

Kronos Quartet, American string quartet founded 1973 by its first violinist, David Harrington. Other members, from 1978: John Sherba, Hank Dutt and Joan Jeanrenaud. The group almost exclusively plays 20th-century music; it gave the first performance of Reich's *Different Trains* (with tape) in London, 1988.

Kubelík, [Jeronym**] Rafael** (1914–96), Czech conductor; left post-1945 Communist Czechoslovakia; naturalized Swiss, 1973. Music director of Covent Garden Opera, 1955–8; of Metropolitan Opera, New York, 1972–4. Also composer. His father was the violinist Jan Kubelík (1880–1940).

Kubik, Gail [Thompson] (1914–84), American violinist, conductor and composer – pupil of Piston and N. Boulanger. Works include three symphonies, two violin concertos (no. 1 withdrawn), cantata *In Praise of Johnny Appleseed*, music for film cartoon *Gerald McBoing Boing*.

Kuhlau, Friedrich (1786–1832), German flautist and composer who settled in Denmark and wrote Danish operas, keyboard works, etc. Died in Copenhagen.

Kuhnau, Johann (1660–1722), German composer and organist,

Bach's immediate predecessor in Leipzig. Wrote harpsichord works including so-called *Biblical Sonatas*, which are early examples of ➤illustrative music; also motets and other church music.

Kuijken, Sigiswald (b. 1944), Belgian violinist, viol player and conductor; founder of baroque orchestra La Petite Bande, 1972 (touring internationally), and his own string quartet, 1986; has recorded much music from Lully to Mozart. His brothers Wieland Kuijken (b. 1936, viol player) and Barthold Kuijken (b. 1949, flautist) have often performed with him.

Kullak, Theodor (1818–82), German composer of much educational piano music: also of piano concerto, etc.

Kullervo (1) symphony (with voices) by Sibelius, 1902, withheld from performance in his lifetime and first performed 1958; (2) opera by Sallinen to his own libretto, produced in Los Angeles, 1992. Both works are based on the Finnish national epic, the Kalevala, in which Kullervo is a heroic character. *Prelude to Kullervo* is also the title of (3) a work for tuba and orchestra by Wuorinen.

Kunst der Fuge, Die (Ger., 'The Art of Fugue'), work by Bach, a series of fugues and canons all on the same theme; begun in 1748; the final fugue was left incomplete on Bach's death in 1750. It is a demonstration of prodigious resource in contrapuntal technique. No instrument is indicated, but the work was demonstrably intended for keyboard (harpsichord or organ) – though versions with other instrumentation have been made by several 20th-century musicians.

Kurtág, György (b. 1926), Hungarian composer who studied in Paris, 1957–8, and did not start numbering his works (op. 1, etc.) until after that. Works include *Messages of the late Miss R. V. Trusova* (Russian text) for soprano and instrumental ensemble; duos for violin and cimbalom; *The Little Predicament* for piccolo, trombone and guitar; *Samuel Beckett: What is the Word* for reciter, voices and chamber orchestra. See also ➤*Unanswered Question*.

Kvapil, Jaroslav (1892–1958), Czech composer of four symphonies, cantata *The Lion-hearted* (on movement for Czechoslovak independence in World War I), etc., also pianist and organist.

Kyrie eleison (Gk., Lord have mercy [on us]), part of the Mass, often referred to simply as 'Kyrie'.

L

L, abbr. for (1) Licentiate (in musical diplomas, e.g. LRAM – Licentiate of the Royal Academy of Music); (2) London (as in LPO, LSO – London Philharmonic Orchestra, London Symphony Orchestra); (3) ➤Longo.

l, symbol in ➤tonic sol-fa notation for the sixth degree (submediant) of the scale, pronounced *lah*.

l' (Fr., It.), the.

la, the note A (in Latin countries, and formerly elsewhere); the ➤tonic sol-fa symbol ➤lah is derived from it.

la (Fr., It., Sp.), the (feminine singular).

Labèque, Katia (b. 1950) and Marielle (b. 1952), French duo-pianists, sisters, who studied with Pommier in Paris; their duo quickly established its mastery of Messiaen's and other modern music. Katia also partners the guitarist John McLaughlin in jazz.

Lablache, Luigi (1794–1858), Italian bass of French and Irish descent, celebrated in opera, singing in the first performance of *Don Pasquale*, 1843.

Lac des cygnes, Le, ➤*Swan Lake*.

Lachrimae, ➤Dowland.

Ladmirault, Paul Émile (1877–1944), French composer of piano works, operas, church music, etc.; his music often has specifically Breton associations.

Lady, Be Good!, musical play by Guy Bolton and Fred Thompson. Lyrics by Ira Gershwin with additional lyrics by Desmond Carter; music by George Gershwin. Produced in New York, 1924. The lady is good enough to impersonate a Mexican supposedly married to a millionaire – and the millionaire accepts her.

Lady Macbeth of the Mtsensk District, opera by Shostakovich, produced in Leningrad, 1934. Libretto by A. G. Preis and the composer (after a story by Leskov), about a woman who kills her husband and father-in-law. The work was banned under Stalin and brought out in a revised version in Moscow, 1963. The title *Katerina Izmailova* (the heroine's name) had an early usage as an alternative to the original title, but by current convention is applied to the 1963 version only.

Lady Nevill's Book, ➤*My Lady Nevill's Book*.

lah, in ➤tonic sol-fa the spoken name for the sixth degree (submediant) of the scale, written l.

la Hale, Adam de (or Halle) (c. 1230–

c. 1286), French minstrel (➤*trouvère*) known as 'The Hunchback of Arras'. Works include motets, secular songs, and *Le Jeu de Robin et de Marion*, a comic play with music. He died in Naples.

lai, ➤lay.

Lajtha, László (1892–1963), Hungarian composer (also pianist) who worked in France and Switzerland. Followed Bartók in collecting and editing Hungarian folk-music. Works include nine symphonies. 10 string quartets, ballet scores.

Lakmé, opera by Delibes, produced in Paris, 1883. Libretto by E. Gondinet and P. Gille, the title-role being that of the daughter of a Brahmin priest, in love with a British officer.

Lalande, Michel Richard de (1657–1756), French composer and organist; worked at the French court from 1683, becoming master of the French Chapel Royal from 1714; celebrated for church music, he also wrote operas. (The surname is also encountered as Delalande.)

Lalo, [Victor Antoine] **Édouard** (1823–92), French composer, also viola-player; composed little until his 40s. Works include ➤*Symphonie espagnole* and other works for violin and orchestra; opera *Le roi d'Ys* ('The King of Ys'), ballet *Namouna*; chamber music and songs.

Lambert, [Leonard] **Constant** (1905–51), British conductor (particularly of ballet), composer, arranger (➤*Comus*), and author of influential book, *Music Ho!* (1934). Works – influenced by jazz in, e.g., *The* ➤*Rio Grande* and a piano concerto – also include *Summer's Last Will and Testament*

(baritone, chorus and orchestra); *Horoscope* and other ballet scores; songs; film music.

lament, a piece of music signifying grief especially at a death; and, specifically, a type of piece for bagpipes played at Scottish clan funerals.

'Lamentatione' Symphony, nickname (in bastard Latin-plus-Italian form) for Haydn's Symphony no. 26 in D minor, composed about 1767–8 (Hob. I: 26); so called because certain themes resemble plainsong melodies sung in Roman Catholic churches in the week before Easter (see preceding entry).

Lamentations, the biblical Lamentations of the prophet Jeremiah, traditionally sung (in plainsong or to other settings) in Roman Catholic churches in the week before Easter. ➤*Threni*.

Lamoureux Orchestra, a Paris orchestra founded in 1881 by its conductor, Charles Lamoureux (1834–99), and remaining important for some time after his death.

Lampe, John [Frederick] (1703–51), German-born British composer, also bassoonist. Wrote chiefly for the London theatre: his burlesque operas *The Dragon of Wantley* and *Pyramus and Thisbe* (after Shakespeare's *A Midsummer Night's Dream*) have had modern revivals.

lancers, a type of ➤quadrille which became popular in the second half of the 19th century.

Land des Lächelns, Das (Ger., 'The Land of the Smile', usually known as *The Land of Smiles*), operetta by Lehár with libretto by Ludwig Herzer and Fritz Löhner, based on the libretto of an earlier Lehár operetta, *Die gelbe Jacke*. Produced in Berlin, 1929. The 'land of the smile' is China: a young Viennese becomes the wife of its Chief Minister, but he self-sacrificingly permits her to leave.

Landi, Steffano (*c.* 1590–1639), Italian composer of church music and operas; also singer in the Papal choir.

Landini, Francesco [**or** Landino] (*c.* 1335–97), Italian organist, lutenist and composer (also poet); blind from early childhood. Wrote concerted vocal music of various kinds, and was an exponent of ➤*ars nova*. Born, lived and died in Florence. See the following.

Landino sixth, a type of cadence characteristically found in Landini's (Landino's) music. In this the leading-note falls to the submediant before rising from that note to the tonic; i.e. the sixth degree of the scale is inserted between the seventh and the eighth. Thus this term does not refer to 'a sixth' in the harmonic sense but to the melodic insertion of the sixth degree of the scale.

Ländler (sing. or pl.), type of dance in triple time originating in rural Austria and being a slow variant of the waltz. Beethoven and Schubert wrote examples.

Ländliche Hochzeit (Ger., 'Rustic Wedding'), title of symphony by K. Goldmark, 1876; five illustrative movements, no. 1 a wedding march.

Land of Hope and Glory, ➤*Pomp and Circumstance*.

Land of Smiles, The, ➤*Land des Lächelns*.

Landowska, Wanda (1877–1959), Polish-born harpsichordist and scholar, influential in the modern revival of the harpsichord; long resident in France, then from 1941 in USA. Falla's Harpsichord Concerto was written for her.

Landowski, Marcel [François Paul] (b. 1915), French composer of a wide diversity of works – including various concertos (one for the ➤Ondes Martenot), operas (one for child audiences), ballets (one on E. Brontë's *Wuthering Heights*) and a setting of poems by Pope John Paul II, for solo voices, chorus and organ.

Landré, Guillaume [Louis Frédéric] (1905–68), Dutch composer and critic. Works include four symphonies and a *Sinfonia sacra* in memory of his father (also a composer), a violin concerto, much chamber music, opera *Jean Lévecq*, etc. Also critic.

Langlais, Jean [François Hyacinthe] (1907–91), French composer (pupil of Dukas) and organist, blind from infancy; wrote mostly for organ (including three concertos) but also orchestral and other works.

Langridge, Philip [Gordon] (b. 1939), British tenor, distinguished interpreter of Britten at Covent Garden and elsewhere; sang Loge in *Das Rheingold* at the Metropolitan Opera, 1985, and has made more than 50 recordings extending from Monteverdi and Rameau to Berg and Tippett. CBE, 1994.

Lanier [or Laniere], **Nicholas** (1588–1666), English composer, the most prominent of a musical family of that surname. Master of the King's Music to Charles I and Charles II; Italian-influenced, he is said to have introduced the recitative to England. Was also singer and painter. Composed songs, some for masques.

Lanner, Joseph [Franz Karl] (1801–43), Austrian violinist, orchestra-leader, and composer of over 200 waltzes and other light music; the chief rival of Johann Strauss the elder.

Laparra, Raoul (1876–1943), French composer primarily of Spanish-influenced music, e.g. opera *La Habanera*; he was his own librettist. Killed in an air raid near Paris.

Lara, Isidore de, ➤De Lara.

largamente (It.), broadly – a term (derived from ➤*largo*) usually denoting a spacious and deliberate style rather than a clear indication of slow tempo.

large, the note of the largest time-value in the notation which grew up in the Middle Ages and gave rise to the present notation. It was divisible into either two or three ➤longs.

larghetto (It., a little largo), direction indicating a speed not quite as slow as ➤*largo*.

largo (It., broad), slow. 'Handel's Largo' (misnomer), ➤*Serse*.

Lark Ascending, The, 'romance' by Vaughan Williams for violin and orchestra after a poem by Meredith; composed in 1914 but not performed till 1921.

'Lark' Quartet, nickname of Haydn's String Quartet in D, op. 64, no. 5, composed *c*.1790–92 (Hob. III: 63) – named from the high-soaring violin part at the opening.

Larrocha, Alicia de (b. 1923), Spanish pianist who was a child prodigy but became internationally prominent only in the mid-1960s; Spanish music remains prominent in her repertory. Since 1959 she has directed an academy in Barcelona.

Larsson, Lars-Erik (1908–86), Swedish composer, pupil of Berg in Vienna; also conductor and critic. Works include concertos for violin, for cello, for saxophone; piano sonatas; *Missa Brevis* for chorus; opera *The Princess of Cyprus*, etc.

la Rue, Pierre de (*c.* 1460–1518), Flemish (Netherlandish) composer of 36 known Masses, also of chansons, etc.; in service to the court of Burgundy.

Lasso, Orlando di, ➤Lassus.

lassú (Hung.), the slow section of a ➤*csárdás*.

Lassus, Roland de (Italianized form, Orlando di Lasso) (1532–94), Flemish composer. Choirboy in Mons, his birthplace; afterwards choirmaster at the church of St John Lateran, Rome, and then worked in Antwerp before taking service at the Bavarian court in Munich. He settled there (travelling to Italy, however) and died in Munich. His works, all for two or (usually) more voices, number more than 2,000 and include madrigals and similar works to French, German and Italian poetry, as well as much religious music – Masses, motets, miscellaneous biblical settings in Latin, settings of various texts in Italian, etc.

lauda, laude (It.), a song of praise; *lauda spirituale* or *laude spirituale* (pl., *laudi spirituali*), type of Italian religious song for several voices, having its own distinctive poetry and sung (14th–18th centuries) by a religious confraternity called the *laudisti*. This type of work is reckoned a forerunner of ➤*oratorio*.

Lauda Sion (Lat., Praise, O Zion), a Roman Catholic hymn (➤sequence) for the feast of Corpus Christi, sung either to traditional plainsong or to other settings.

laudi, ➤lauda.

'Laudon' Symphony, nickname for Haydn's Symphony no. 69 in C (Hob. 1: 69), 1778–9, composed in honour of the Austrian field-marshal so named.

lavolta, English name for a dance popular in Elizabethan times, featuring a leap (It., *volta*). One is included in Britten's ➤*Gloriana*.

Lawes, Henry (1596–1662), English composer in service at court; celebrated in a sonnet by Milton, having set Milton's ➤*Comus*. Wrote coronation anthem for Charles II, songs (some to poems by Herrick), church music; collaborated in the music to The ➤*Siege of Rhodes*, the first English opera, 1656. Brother of William Lawes.

Lawes, William (1602–45), English composer of masques, songs, music for viols and violins, etc.; pupil of J. Cooper, musician to Charles I; killed while fighting on Royalist side in the Civil War. Brother of Henry Lawes.

lay (English equivalent of Fr. *lai*), 13th-century French narrative poem set to music. The term is also encountered for a purely instrumental work of that period, and in certain more general references (e.g. in Chaucer) it simply means 'a song'.

Lazarev, Alexander (b. 1945), Russian conductor, chief conductor and artistic director of Bolshoi Theatre, Moscow, 1987–95; founder of instrumental ensemble there. Made British début with Royal Liverpool Philhar-

monic Orchestra, 1987; conductor of Royal Scottish National Orchestra from 1997.

Lazarof, Henri (b. 1932), Bulgarian-born American composer and university teacher; pupil of Ben-Haim in Jerusalem and of Petrassi in Rome. Works include a viola concerto, Concerto for piano and 20 instruments, *Spectrum* for trumpet, orchestra and tape, *Asymptotes* for flute and vibraphone.

le (Fr. masc. sing., It. fem. pl.), the.

leader, the directing member of an ensemble, e.g. a string quartet or a pop group. But as applied to an orchestra, *leader* in Britain means the principal violinist (US, concertmaster) as the chief performer, whereas in USA it is an alternative term for conductor. Similarly with 'to lead'.

leading-motive, the equivalent term in English for Ger. *Leitmotiv* (not *motif*) – a musical theme used (particularly in Wagner's operas) recurrently to denote an object, an aspect of character, etc.

leading-note, the seventh degree of the ➤major scale, so called because it seems to lead upwards to the ➤tonic a semitone above it. In the minor scale this note (e.g. B♮ in the key of C minor) is commonly used in ascending but not in descending.

leading seventh, term which is in fact an abbreviation for 'chord of the minor seventh built on the leading-note' – e.g., in C major, the chord B, D, F, A (reading upwards). This is characteristically produced on the harmonica, by sucking.

Lear, opera by Reimann, produced in

Munich, 1978. Libretto by Claus H. Henneberg, based on Shakespeare's *King Lear*; the Fool is a spoken role.

Lear, Edward (1812–88), British writer. ➤Gerhard, ➤Petrassi, ➤Surinach.

Lebègue, Nicolas Antoine (*c.* 1631–1702), French organist and composer of works for organ, for harpsichord, and for voices; in service to Louis XIV.

Leclair, Jean Marie (1697–1764), French violinist and composer – and, in his 20s, a ballet-master. For a time played in the Paris Opéra orchestra, and himself wrote opera *Scylla et Glaucus* and ballets as well as 12 violin concertos and other violin music. Visited Holland to meet Locatelli, and shortly after a second visit there was murdered near his home in Paris.

Lecocq, Alexandre Charles (1832–1918), French composer, also organist. From 1868 successful with dozens of operettas including *Giroflé-Giroflà* and *La Fille de Mme Angot*, from which the ballet *Mam'zelle Angot* (1947) is derived.

ledger line, short line written above or below the staff to accommodate notes outside the staff – as in the following:

(This is the correct spelling, but 'leger line' is also encountered.)

Lees [originally Lysniansky], **Benjamin** (b. 1924), American composer of Russian parentage, born in China. Works include three symphonies; concerto for string quartet and orchestra; cantata *Visions of Poets*.

Leeuw, Ton [originally Antonius Wilhelmus Adrianus] **de** (b. 1926), Dutch composer; pupil of Messiaen (in Paris)

and Badings; also pianist and critic. Works include a piano concerto; two symphonies; orchestral *Funeral Music for Willem Pijper*; television opera *Alceste*, music for ➤gamelan, solo works for accordion, marimba and other instruments.

Lefanu, Nicola [Frances] (b. 1947), British composer, daughter of Maconchy, pupil in Italy of Petrassi; head of music department, University of York, since 1994. Works include opera *The Wildman*; *Columbia Falls* for orchestra; *Antiworld* (based on Russian texts) for dancer, two voices and three instruments; concerto for saxophone and strings.

Lefébure-Wély, Louis James Alfred (1817–69), French organist, performing from age eight, and composer chiefly of organ works.

le Gallienne, Dorian (1915–63), Australian composer who studied in Britain. Works include Sinfonietta, incidental music to plays, piano solos, songs.

legato (It., bound together), smoothly, not ➤*staccato* – as a direction for performance.

Legend of the Invisible City of Kitezh and of the Maid Fevronia, The (Rus. *Skazanie o nevidimom gradie Kitezhe devie Fevronie*), opera by Rimsky-Korsakov, produced in St Petersburg, 1907. Libretto by V. I. Belsky, combining two Russian legends – of the miraculous rescue of Kitezh from the Tartars and of St Fevronia.

léger (Fr., light), *légèrement*, lightly; *musique légère*, light music.

leger line, ➤*ledger line*.

leggero, leggeramente (It.), light

le Jeune, Claude

lightly. (The spellings 'leggiero', 'leggieramente' are obsolete in Italian, though still found in the scores of ill-informed composers and publishers.) So *La Legg(i)erezza* ('lightness'), name sometimes given to the second of Liszt's three *Études de Concert* (*c.* 1848).

leggiero, leggieramente, see preceding.

legno (It.), wood; *bacchetta di legno,* (instruction to drummer to use) wooden-headed drum-stick; *col legno,* with the wood – instruction to string-player to hit the string with the back of the bow instead of with the hair, producing a dry and rather grotesque sound, e.g. in Saint-Saëns's ➤*Danse macabre.*

Lehár, Ferencz (Germanized as Franz, but surname not Léhar) (1870–1948), Hungarian composer, for a time violinist and military band-master; wrote a violin concerto, etc., but mainly many successful Viennese operettas including *Die* ➤*lustige Witwe* ('The Merry Widow'), *Der* ➤*Graf von Luxemburg* ('The Count of Luxembourg'), *Das* ➤*Land des Lächelns* ('The Land of Smiles').

Lehmann, Lilli (1848–1929), German soprano, celebrated in opera (170 roles in 119 works) and in a repertory of more than 600 songs. Prominent in early Salzburg festivals (from 1905).

Lehmann, Liza (form of name used by Elizabetta Nina Mary Frederika Lehmann) (1862–1918), British soprano and composer. Works include *In a Persian Garden* (words from Fitzgerald's translation of Omar Khayyám) and other song-cycles, and opera *The Vicar of Wakefield* (after Goldsmith). ➤Bedford.

Lehmann, Lotte (1888–1976), German operatic and concert soprano who settled in USA (naturalized 1945); celebrated in R. Strauss roles and as teacher in California. Also novelist and autobiographer.

Leibowitz, René (1913–72), French (Polish-born) composer, conductor, and noted theoretician, exponent of Schoenberg and Webern. Works include piano and choral music; Chamber Symphony; *Tourist Death* for soprano and chamber orchestra.

leicht (Ger.), (1) light; (2) easy.

Leiferkus, Sergey [Petrovich] (b. 1946), Russian baritone; after operatic work in Leningrad, developed extensive Western career (Wexford Festival 1982, English National Opera 1987, etc.), proving his worth equally in Russian repertory and in such operas as *Carmen, Il Trovatore, Otello.*

Leigh, Walter (1905–42), British composer of light opera *The Jolly Roger* and other theatre music, Concertino for harpsichord and strings, etc.; pupil of Hindemith. Killed in action.

Leighton, Kenneth (1929–88), British composer, pupil of Petrassi in Rome. Works include three piano concertos; concertos for violin, viola, cello, organ; a piano trio; Mass; opera *Columba.* Also teacher at Edinburgh University, pianist and conductor.

Leinsdorf, Erich (1912–93), American conductor, born and trained in Vienna, conducted opera at the Metropolitan, New York, from 1938; conductor of the Boston Symphony Orchestra, 1962–9.

Leitmotiv, ➤leading-motive.

le Jeune, Claude (*c.* 1530–1600), French composer of Protestant church

243

Lekeu, Guillaume

music (including psalm-settings), chansons, etc.; held court appointment under Henri IV.

Lekeu, Guillaume (1870–94), Belgian composer, pupil of Franck and d'Indy. Works include a piano quartet and cello sonata, both completed by d'Indy after Lekeu's early death from typhoid; also orchestral *Fantaisie sur deux airs populaires angevins*, etc.

Lélio, ou Le Retour à la vie (Fr., 'Lélio, or The Return to Life'), work by Berlioz, called by him a monodrama because it has only one character (spoken role) though three solo singers as well as chorus and orchestra take part. First performed 1832; intended as a sequel to the ➤*Symphonie fantastique*.

Lemare, Edwin Henry (1865–1934), British organist who performed much in USA and died in Los Angeles; composed much organ music including two solo 'symphonies'.

Lemminkäinen's Homecoming, orchestral work by Sibelius referring to one of the heroes of the Kalevala (Finnish national epic); it is no. 4 of four pieces about Lemminkäinen, no. 3 being The ➤*Swan of Tuonela*.

Lenau, Nikolaus (1802–50), Austrian poet. ➤*Don Juan, Episodes from Lenau's* ➤*Faust*.

Léner Quartet, Austro-Hungarian string quartet (active 1918–48) led by Jenö Léner; particularly celebrated in recordings of the 1930s.

Leningrad Philharmonic Orchestra, ➤ St Petersburg Philharmonic Orchestra.

'Leningrad' Symphony, nickname for Shostakovich's Symphony no. 7, glorifying the spirit of besieged Leningrad and partly composed there, 1941.

lent, lento (Fr., It.), slow.

Lenya (also spelt Lenja), **Lotte** [originally Karoline Blamauer] (1898–1981), Austrian-born actress and singer, famous in works by her husband, Kurt Weill, such as *Die Dreigroschenoper*. Refugees from the Nazis, they emigrated to USA.

Lenz, Jakob [Michael Reinhold] (1751–92), German playwright. ➤*Soldaten*.

Leo, Leonardo (1694–1744), Italian composer working in Naples. His comic operas, some in Neapolitan dialect, are considered (with Pergolesi's) pioneers of their type. Wrote, or contributed numbers to, about 70 operas in all; other works include oratorios, church music, harpsichord pieces.

Leoncavallo, Ruggero (1857–1919), Italian composer of ➤*Pagliacci* ('Clowns'), his only successful opera, 1892. Before this worked as café pianist, etc. Was encouraged by Wagner and, acting as his own librettist, wrote various other operas including *La* ➤*Bohème*, which failed where Puccini's on the same subject succeeded. Other works include operettas, symphonic poem *Serafita*.

Leonhardt, Gustav (b. 1928), Dutch organist and harpsichordist, since 1955 director of his own ensemble in historically scrupulous performances of baroque music. Acted the role of Bach in a film, 1967.

Léonin (also Leoninus, Lat.), French composer active about 1163–90 as church musician in Paris: wrote a cycle of two-part organa (➤organum) for all the principal church feasts of the year.

Leonora, a British form of reference to the heroine of Beethoven's opera *Fidelio* – properly ➤Leonore – identifying Beethoven's *Leonora* Overtures nos. 1, 2, and 3 (1804–7). The numbering, formerly thought chronologically deceptive, is now considered correct. Each of these was in its time intended as the overture to the opera, but all were eventually superseded for this purpose by the overture now actually called *Fidelio*. The *Leonora* overtures are now heard as concert pieces; and no. 3, the best-known, is also sometimes performed (without authority from Beethoven) as an orchestral interlude during the opera. ➤Fry (W. H.).

Leonore, name of the heroine of Beethoven's opera ➤*Fidelio* (1814). Some modern revivals of Beethoven's earlier (1805) version of the opera have used *Leonore* as a distinguishing title, but Beethoven adhered to *Fidelio* through all stages. ➤Liebermann.

Leppard, Raymond [John] (b. 1927), British conductor, formerly Cambridge University teacher; prominent in revival of early baroque opera (Monteverdi and Cavalli) in his own editions, especially at Glyndebourne from 1962. Conductor of BBC Northern Symphony Orchestra, 1973–80, though mainly resident in USA from 1977; music director, Indianapolis Symphony Orchestra, since 1987. CBE, 1983.

Leroux, Xavier Napoléon (1863–1919), French composer, also critic. Works include opera *Le Chemineau* ('The Tramp') using French peasant songs; also other operas, church music, songs, etc.

les (Fr.), the (plural form).

Leschetizky, Theodor (Germanized form of Teodor Leszetycki) (1830–1915), Polish piano teacher mainly active in St Petersburg and Vienna; developed a famous 'method', and taught Paderewski and other noted pianists. Also composer of operas, piano solos, etc.

Leskov, Nikolay Semeonovich (1831–95), Russian writer. ➤*Lady Macbeth of the Mtsensk District*.

Lessing, Doris (b. 1919), British writer. ➤Glass.

lesson, English term used in 17th–18th centuries for a short keyboard piece or a set of such pieces, not necessarily implying a teaching purpose.

Lesueur, Jean François (1760–1837), French composer who wrote church music using orchestra and then, when this met with disapproval, wrote spectacular operas and French Revolutionary pieces using enormous forces. In court service to Napoleon and then to Louis XVIII. Taught Berlioz and Gounod.

Lesur, Daniel [Jean Yves] (b. 1908), French composer of orchestral music, *The Inner Life* for organ, piano solos, songs, opera *Andrea del Sarto*, etc. Also pianist and organist. With Baudrier, Jolivet and Messiaen, he formed the 'Young France' group.

Let's Make an Opera!, Britten's 'entertainment for young people' (his own description) produced at Aldeburgh, 1949. It incorporates a miniature opera, *The Little Sweep* – about a maltreated boy chimney-sweep of the mid 19th century – most of the roles in which are for children. This opera is rehearsed in the first section of the 'entertainment' and performed, with the audience's vocal participation, in the second. Libretto by Eric Crozier.

Leveridge, Richard (*c.* 1670–1758), English bass singer and composer chiefly of songs (including 'The Roast Beef of Old England') and stage music, etc.

Levinas, Michaël (b. 1949), French composer, also pianist. Employs electronic transformation of sounds, e.g. in *La Voix des Voix* (Fr., 'The Voice of Voices'), with a microphone for each of nine instrumentalists, plus echo chamber. Other works include *Le Tambour* (Fr., 'The Drum') for Renaissance lute and tape, *Rhythmic Canons* for cello and ➤prepared piano.

Levine, James (b. 1943), American conductor; music director, Metropolitan Opera, since 1975; also pianist, often directing concertos from the keyboard.

Lewis, Anthony [Carey] (1915–83), British composer, conductor and authority on 17th- and 18th-century English music. Professor at Birmingham University, then (1962–83) principal of RAM. Knighted, 1972.

Lewis, Richard (1914–90), British tenor noted in opera (Glyndebourne, Covent Garden, etc.) and oratorio. Created the part of Troilus in Walton's ➤*Troilus and Cressida*. CBE, 1962.

Lewkovitch, Bernhard (b. 1927), Danish composer, also Roman Catholic choirmaster and organist; works include Masses, motets, ➤partitas for brass quintet.

l.h., left hand (e.g. in piano-playing).

Lhévinne, Josef (1874–1944) and **Rosina** (1880–1976), Russian-born American pianists, husband and wife,

who became outstanding teachers e.g. at the Juilliard School, New York.

Liadov, ➤Lyadov.

Liapunov, ➤Lyapunov.

libretto (It., booklet), the text of an opera – or sometimes of an oratorio or other non-stage work. Plural *libretti* (It.) or *librettos*.

licenza (It.), licence, freedom: *con alcuna licenza* (or *con alcune licenze* plural), with some freedom(s) as to performance, or as to the construction of a work (when it is not tied to a 'strict' pattern).

Lidholm, Ingvar [Natanael] (b. 1921), Swedish composer who studied in London with Seiber, 1954; formerly Swedish Radio executive. Works include *Mutanza* (It., 'Mutation') and other works for orchestra; scena *Nausicaa Alone* for soprano, chorus, orchestra; opera *Dream Play* (after Strindberg); Concertino for flute, oboe, English horn and cello (without orchestra).

Lie, Sigurd (1871–1904), Norwegian composer, also violinist and conductor, who before dying of tuberculosis wrote a symphony, many songs, violin sonata, etc.

Liebermann, Rolf (b. 1910), Swiss composer of operas including *Leonore 40/45* (alluding to ➤*Fidelio* in the context of World War II), Concerto for jazz band and symphony orchestra, etc. Administrator of Hamburg State Opera, 1959–72, then of Paris Opera till 1980.

Liebeslieder-Walzer (Ger., 'Love-song Waltzes'), a set of 18 waltzes by Brahms 'for piano duet and [four vocal parts ad lib', 1869; 15 more called *Neue Liebeslieder-Walzer* (1875), were designated as 'for four voices and piano duet'.

Liebestraum (Ger., dream of love; pl. *-träume*), title given by Liszt to his piano arrangements (1850) of three of his songs. No. 3 is the well-known one.

lied (Ger., pl. *Lieder*), song; specifically, in the non-German-speaking world, the type of song with piano composed by, e.g., Schubert, Schumann and Wolf. The term is dubiously applied also to songs not in German but of a similar kind, e.g. by Grieg. For the term *Lieder recital* instead of 'song recital' there is no excuse unless the programme is exclusively German. See also the following entries.

Lieder eines fahrenden Gesellen (Ger., 'Songs of a Wayfarer'), cycle of four songs by Mahler (1883–5); words by composer, expressing the sentiments of a young man scorned by his sweetheart.

Liederkranz, Liederkreis (Ger.), song-➤cycle. *Liederkreis* is used as the actual title of two cycles by Schumann (op. 24, op. 39 – both 1840), to poems by Heine and by Eichendorff.

Lied(er) ohne Worte (Ger., 'Song(s) Without Words'), Mendelssohn's fanciful way of titling his 48 pieces for piano, published at intervals (1832–45) in six books. They resemble song-melodies with accompaniment. Most of the titles (e.g. 'Spring Song' and 'The Bees' Wedding' for nos. 30 and 34) are not Mendelssohn's; but among those he did name are the three 'Venetian Gondola Songs' (nos. 6, 12, 29).

Liedertafel (Ger., song-table – referring to origin in drinking-gatherings),

male-voice choir in German or German-descended communities, e.g. in USA and South Australia.

Lied von der Erde, Das (Ger., 'Song of the Earth'), work by Mahler for mezzo-soprano, tenor and orchestra, 1907–9 (first performed in 1911, after Mahler's death); called by him a symphony, and of symphonic dimensions, but not numbered among his symphonies. Text from German translations of Chinese poems.

Lifar, Serge (1905–86), Russian–French choreographer. ➤*Bacchus et Ariane*.

Life for the Tsar, A (Rus., *Zhizn za Tsarya*), opera by Glinka, produced in St Petersburg, 1836; libretto, by G. F. Rosen, based on a 17th-century patriotic subject. The composer's originally intended title was *Ivan Susanin* (after the peasant hero), a title which was generally adopted under the Soviet régime to 1989, with a new libretto diverting attention from the Tsar; the Bolshoi Theatre re-introduced the original libretto and the 'Tsarist' title in 1989.

Life with an Idiot, opera by Schnittke, produced in Amsterdam, 1991. Libretto (in Russian) by Viktor Yerofeyev about a married couple sharing their flat (and a sexual involvement) with a man who can say only one word.

ligature (1) a symbol in medieval musical notation which combines one or more notes in succession; (2) in standard notation, a slur-mark indicating a group of notes all sung to the same syllable (term sometimes also used in instrumental music when the ➤slur indicates that notes are to be phrased together); (3) on the clarinet, saxophone, etc., the metal band which secures the reed to the mouthpiece.

Ligeti, György (b. 1923), Hungarian composer who left Hungary in 1956, taking Austrian nationality and becoming professor in Hamburg, 1973–89. Works include opera *Le* ➤*Grand Macabre*, music-theatre pieces *Aventures* and *Nouvelles Aventures* ('Adventures/New Adventures'), using a meaningless language; *Atmosphères*, ➤*Lontano*, and other works for orchestra; violin concerto; *Poème symphonique* for 100 metronomes.

light, term applied to music supposedly not requiring the listener's full concentration; *light orchestra*, orchestra providing this. So also *light opera*, imprecise non-technical term sometimes used by laymen in opposition to 'grand opera' (also imprecise), and not clearly distinguishable from 'operetta'.

Lighthouse, The, opera by P. M. Davies, produced in Edinburgh, 1980; libretto, by the composer, deals with a true story of the unexplained disappearance of three lighthouse-keepers.

Lilburn, Douglas [Gordon] (b. 1915), New Zealand composer, partly trained in London. Works include *Aotearoa* (Maori name for New Zealand) for orchestra, three symphonies, electronic music.

Lill, John [Richard] (b. 1944), British pianist, joint winner (with Vladimir Krainev) of the Moscow Tchaikovsky Competition, 1970. He has specialized in Beethoven. OBE, 1978.

Lily of Killarney, The, opera by Benedict, produced in London, 1862; libretto by J. Oxenford and D. Bouci-cault, after the latter's play *The Colleen Bawn*, an Irish adventure of love and menaces.

Lincoln Portrait, work for narrator and orchestra by Copland, on the sayings of Abraham Lincoln; first performed in 1942.

Lind, Jenny [originally Johanna Maria] (1820–87), Swedish soprano who won European fame in opera but gave up opera for concerts at age 29; made celebrated US tour managed by Barnum, 1850–51. Settled in Britain, becoming in her 60s a celebrated teacher at Royal College of Music.

Lindberg, Magnus (b. 1958), Finnish composer whose work has become known in London, Berlin, Moscow, etc., often with the improvisation group, Toimii, founded by himself and ➤Salonen. Works include chamber symphony entitled *Joy*, piano concerto, *Metal Work* for accordion and percussion, *Fresco* and *Feria* for orchestra.

Lindsay String Quartet, British string quartet founded 1966, named after the Principal of Keele University to which it was formerly attached; since 1979 attached to Manchester University. It has recorded all Bartók's and Tippett's quartets. Current members: Peter Cropper, Ronald Birks, Robin Ireland, Bernard Gregor-Smith.

linke Hand (Ger.), left hand.

Linley, Thomas (1733–95), British composer, especially for the stage; composed the song 'Here's to the Maiden' for Sheridan's *The School for Scandal*. Was also singing-teacher and concert-promoter. Father of Elizabeth Ann Linley, singer, who married Sheridan. See also next entry.

Linley, Thomas (1756–78), British composer of opera *The Cady of Baghdad*, etc., and with his father (see preceding entry), of music for Sheridan's *The ➤Duenna*. In boyhood, studied in Italy, met Mozart there and became his firm friend; met early death by drowning.

'Linz' Symphony, nickname for Mozart's Symphony no. 36 in C, K425, composed in Linz and first performed there in 1783.

Lipatti, Dinu (diminutive of Constantin) (1917–50), Romanian pianist, also composer; illness restricted his career, but his recordings continued after his death to win much admiration.

lira (It.), (1) ➤lyre; (2) the ➤vielle in its medieval sense (bowed string instrument, not the hurdy-gurdy); (3) term used in various compound names, e.g. *lira da braccio* (. . . for the arm), type of bowed string instrument developed in the late 15th century, with a less pronounced 'waist' than that of the violin; *lira da gamba* (for the leg), a larger relation of this; *lira organizzata*, superior type of hurdy-gurdy (with organ-like pipes) composed for by Haydn.

Liszt, Ferencz (Germanized as Franz) (1811–86), Hungarian composer whose music was innovatory and influential; also pianist of unsurpassed reputation, and conductor. As child prodigy pianist, visited France and Britain. Lived with the Countess d'Agoult, 1833–44, their daughter Cosima later becoming Bülow's wife and Wagner's mistress (and eventually wife). From 1848 lived with the (married) Princess Sayn-Wittgenstein, then in 1861 separated from her: never married, and in

1865 took minor orders in the Roman Catholic Church and was referred to as 'the Abbé Liszt'. Consistently aided new composers from Berlioz to Grieg, making Weimar a highly important centre when he was court musical director there, 1848–59; revisited London in 1886. His piano works include a sonata (pioneering one-movement form), also ➤*Dante Sonata*, 20 ➤*Hungarian Rhapsodies*, ➤*Mazeppa* (also for orchestra), ➤*Consolations*, and other pieces with allusive titles (➤*Liebestraum*); also many operatic paraphrases, transcriptions of other composers' works, etc.; arranged Schubert's ➤'*Wanderer*' *Fantasy* in a version for piano and orchestra. Also composed *Les* ➤*Préludes*, ➤*Orpheus*, ➤*Hamlet*, ➤*Dante Symphony*, ➤*Faust Symphony*, *Episodes from Lenau's* ➤*Faust*, four ➤*Mephisto Waltzes* etc. for orchestra; ➤*Malediction* for piano and orchestra; ➤*Via Crucis* and other church works; more than 70 songs in French, German, Italian, Hungarian and English (e.g. on Tennyson's 'Go not, happy day'); and much else. Continued to innovate in his very last works. His 'Hungarian' music is chiefly of a gipsy, not an authentically peasant, character.

litany, in Christian worship, a series of petitions – usually with the congregation making a fixed response to each of the parallel invocations (sung to the same syllabic chant, or said) of the celebrant. Polyphonic settings have also been made by Palestrina, Mozart and others.

Litolff, Henry Charles (1818–91), French pianist, composer and publisher; he was born in London of an Alsatian father and settled eventually in Paris. He wrote operas, piano solos and five works for piano and orchestra, each termed a 'symphony-concerto' (*concerto symphonique*), from the fourth of which comes the well-known Scherzo.

Little Barber of Lavapiés, operetta (*zarzuela*) by Barbieri. ➤*Barberillo de Lavapiés*.

Little Night Music, A, musical comedy (the title alluding to Mozart's ➤*Eine kleine Nachtmusik*) with text by Hugh Wheeler suggested by the film *Smiles of a Summer Night* by Ingmar Bergman; music and lyrics by Stephen Sondheim. Produced in New York, 1973. Old loves and new are tangled and resolved in a Swedish country-house weekend.

Little Organ Book, compilation by Bach. ➤*Orgelbüchlein*.

Little Organ Mass, nickname for a Mass in B flat by Haydn, composed in 1778 (Hob. XXII: 7) – short in length and, like the ➤Great Organ Mass, with a solo organ part.

'Little Russian' Symphony, ➤*Ukrainian Symphony*.

Little Sweep, The, ➤*Let's Make an Opera!*

Little, Tasmin (b. 1965), British violinist of wide general repertory including many rarities (concertos by Janáček and Rubbra, sonatas by G. Lloyd); gave first performance of concerto by Saxton (1990; also recorded) and other modern works, and made Proms début in 1990.

Litton, Andrew (b. 1959), American conductor, principal conductor of Bournemouth Symphony Orchestra 1988–94, then music director Dallas (Texas) Symphony Orchestra. Has also conducted at Covent Garden (*Porgy and Bess*, 1992) and the Metropolitan Opera, New York.

liturgy (1) the general fixed structure of religious services of any religious denomination (hence *liturgical music*, setting prescribed texts); (2) in the Eastern Orthodox churches, specifically the service of the Eucharist (corresponding to the Roman Catholic Mass): hence a musical setting of that, e.g. Rakhmaninov's *Liturgy of St John Chrysostom*, 1910.

lituus (Lat.), ancient Roman cavalry trumpet – straight, with small upturned bell. There are various later exceptional uses of the word, Bach in his funeral cantata BWV 118 (*c.* 1737) specifying two *litui*, signifying possibly horns, possibly trumpets.

live (as in 'live recording'), not the opposite of 'dead', but an indication that a recording was made in the presence of a concert or opera audience; the resultant product may actually be compounded from two or more such occasions and even be rounded off with studio material.

live electronics (1) the manipulation of electronic sound as part of its presentation to an audience, so that an element of performer's choice is brought into play; (2) the instant modification, by electronic means other than simple microphoning, of a singer's or instrumentalist's acoustic sound; (3) the integration of taped electronic sound into a performance on conventional instrument(s) or voice(s).

Liverpool Oratorio [actually entitled 'Paul McCartney's Liverpool Oratorio'], work by McCartney and Carl Davis, with words by McCartney, for solo voices, boys' and adults' choir and orchestra, first performed in Liverpool, 1990.

Liverpool Philharmonic Orchestra, ➤Royal Liverpool Philharmonic Orchestra.

Lloyd, Charles Harford (1849–1919), British organist (e.g. of the Chapel Royal) and composer of church and organ music, cantatas, etc.

Lloyd, George (1913–98), British composer of *John Socman* and other operas based on British history or legend; also of 12 symphonies, cantata *The Vigil of Venus*, etc. Also conductor in Britain and USA.

Lloyd, Jonathan (b. 1948), British composer of five symphonies, cantata *Toward the Whitening Dawn*, string quintet for mandolin, lute, guitar, harp and double-bass, etc.

Lloyd, Robert [Andrew] (b. 1940), British bass, particularly well known in opera at Covent Garden from 1972; sang title-role of *Boris Godunov* there and (1990) at Kirov (now Maryinsky) Theatre, St Petersburg.

Lloyd-Jones, David [Mathias] (b. 1934), British conductor and translator from Russian; made Sadler's Wells Opera début conducting first British performance of Prokofiev's *War and Peace*, 1972. Was artistic director of Opera North from its inception, 1978, until 1990. Edited and translated Musorgsky's *Boris Godunov*, 1975 – an edition thenceforth regarded as the most authoritative. Has also conducted in Israel, Canada, etc.

Lloyd Webber, Andrew (b. 1948), British composer who won prodigious international success with such musicals as ➤*Joseph and the Amazing Technicolor Dreamcoat*, ➤*Jesus Christ Superstar*, ➤*Evita*, ➤*Cats*, ➤*Starlight Express*, *The* ➤*Phantom of the Opera*. He also composed a Requiem (1984). Knighted, 1992. Life peerage, 1997. Brother of Julian Lloyd Webber.

Lloyd Webber, Julian (b. 1951), British cellist, brother of Andrew Lloyd Webber. He has commissioned works from many composers including Rodrigo, Arnold, and Richard Rodney Bennett; and made first recording of Sullivan's concerto and other English music including that of his father, William Lloyd Webber.

Lobgesang (Ger., 'Hymn of Praise'), symphonic cantata by Mendelssohn, first performed in 1840. One choral movement (religious text) is preceded by three orchestral ones and the whole is numbered as Mendelssohn's Second Symphony.

Lobo, Duarte (*c.* 1565–1646), Portuguese composer, cathedral organist at Lisbon, favoured by the Portuguese royal family. He published six volumes of polyphonic liturgical music.

Locatelli, Pietro (1695–1764), Italian violinist and composer, pupil of Corelli in Rome, settled in Amsterdam and died there. Works include sonatas, studies and other works for violin; also trios, works of ➤*concerto grosso* type, etc. ➤*Arte del violino*.

Locke (also Lock), **Matthew** (*c.* 1622–77), English composer in service to Charles II, from 1660; also author of pamphlet defending his own 'modern' style. Wrote music for the masque *Cupid and Death* (with C. Gibbons); also opera *The* ➤*Siege of Rhodes* (with others), songs, church music, works for violins and viols. Apparently not the composer of the music to ➤*Macbeth* long attributed to him.

loco (It., place), indication that music

is to be performed at the pitch written, cancelling the instruction *8va sopra* (i.e. *ottava sopra*) or *8va bassa* indicating that music is to be played respectively an octave higher or an octave lower than written.

Locrian mode, the ➤mode that would be represented by the white keys of the piano beginning on B, if it were not rejected as unusable in practice. (Unlike the other modes, it would not include a note a perfect fifth upward from its 'final', B.)

Loder, Edward [James] (1813–65), British composer of operas including *The Night Dancers, Raymond and Agnes*; songs including 'The Brooklet' (translation of the poem set by Schubert as 'Wohin?' in *Die ➤schöne Müllerin*), string quartets, etc.

Loeffler, Charles Martin [Tornow] (1861–1935), Alsatian-born violinist-composer who spent boyhood partly in Russia (his orchestral *Memories of My Childhood* has Russian musical elements) and settled in USA, 1881. Composed other orchestral works including *A Pagan Poem* (after Virgil) with piano, English horn and three trumpets; also cantatas, chamber music, songs, etc.

Lœillet, Jean-Baptiste (1680–1730), Belgian composer, flautist, oboist and harpsichordist, who worked much in London and died there. Wrote music for flute, recorder and other instruments, and helped to popularize the flute (a new instrument compared to the recorder) in Britain.

Loesser, Frank (1910–69), American composer of musicals including ➤*Guys and Dolls* and The ➤*Most Happy Fella*.

Loewe, [Johann] **Carl Gottfried** (1796–1869), German composer, also organist; visited London, 1847. Noted for songs, especially ballads on dramatic poems, e.g. 'Edward' and 'Erlkönig' (➤*ballad*, 2); wrote also operas, oratorios, piano music, etc. Had a six-week trance in 1864 and died after a similar attack.

Loewe, Frederick (1901–88), Austrian (later American) composer who studied piano with Busoni. Settled in USA 1924 and wrote musicals including ➤*Brigadoon*, ➤*Camelot*, ➤*My Fair Lady*.

log drum, name sometimes given to larger forms of ➤slit-drum.

Logothetis, Anestis (b. 1921), Greek (Bulgarian-born) composer, naturalized Austrian. Works include *Labyrinth* for any soloists, any chamber orchestra; *Styx* for orchestra of plucked stringed instruments. Uses his own form of graphic notation.

Logroscino, [Bonifacio] **Nicola** (1698–after 1765), Italian composer active in Naples; wrote dozens of comic operas including *L'inganno per inganno* ('Trick for trick'). Was also organist and composer of church music.

Lohengrin, opera by Wagner, produced in Weimar, 1850; libretto by composer. Lohengrin, Knight of the Holy Grail with personal swan-drawn transport, reveals himself as the son of Parsifal (➤*Parsifal*).

Löhr, Hermann [Frederic] (1872–1943), British composer of 'Where My Caravan Has Rested' and other popular English drawing-room songs.

London Classical Players, an orchestra founded in 1978 by its conductor, Roger ➤Norrington, using appropriate period instruments (and techniques) for a repertory mainly of the early 19th century. Disbanded 1997 and subsumed in ➤OAE.

Londonderry Air, Irish folk-tune which was first brought into print in 1855; it has since been variously arranged (e.g. by Grainger as 'Irish Tune from County Derry') and given various words ('Danny Boy', etc.).

London Mozart Players, a chamber orchestra conducted by its founder, Harry Blech, from 1949 to 1984, with specialization in Haydn and Mozart; the repertory has since expanded. Conductor from 1993, Matthias Bamert.

London Overture, A, orchestral work by Ireland, 1936; has a prominent phrase said to originate from a bus conductor's intonation of 'Piccadilly!'

London Philharmonic Orchestra, an orchestra founded by Beecham in 1932, but becoming self-governing in 1939. Principal conductor, 1990–95, Franz Welser-Möst.

London Sinfonietta, British chamber orchestra founded in 1968, specializing in modern music; it had no fixed conductor until the appointment of Markus Stenz 1994–8.

'London' Symphony, nickname for Haydn's last symphony, no. 104 in D (Hob. I: 104), first performed in 1795 during Haydn's second visit to London. A curious nickname, because all Haydn's last 12 symphonies were written for London and first performed there. See also next entry.

London Symphony, A, title of Vaughan Williams's Symphony no. 2 (but, in conformity with his practice, not numbered by him), first performed in 1914; revised version first performed in 1920. Quotes the Big Ben

chimes and is an evocation of London. ➤*Nocturne.*

London Symphony Orchestra, an orchestra founded in 1904, self-governing from the beginning; principal conductor from 1995 (succeeding Michael Tilson Thomas), Colin Davis.

long, obsolete time-value of a note, in the system of notation which grew up in the Middle Ages and was superseded by the present one; a long could equal either a half or a third of a large and was itself divisible into either two or three breves.

Long, Marguerite (1874–1966), French pianist who championed Debussy and Ravel; duo-partner with Jacques ➤Thibaud. In 1943 they founded an international competition which still bears their names.

Longfellow, Henry Wadsworth (1807–82), American poet; ➤*Hiawatha*; ➤Foote, ➤Luening.

Longo, Alessandro (1864–1945), Italian pianist and composer who supervised the publication of a complete edition of D. Scarlatti's keyboard works, these being referred to as 'Longo No. . . .' or 'L. . . .' (followed by a number). This numbering has been superseded by that of ➤Kirkpatrick.

lontano (It., 'far'), (1) an occasional direction used by composers to indicate the effect of distance; (2) (*Lontano*) piece for orchestra by Ligeti, 1967; (3) name of a London-based ensemble (➤Martinez).

Lopatnikoff, Nikolai [Lvovich] (1903–76), Russian-born composer who lived in Britain, 1933–9, then in USA – naturalized American, 1944. Works include four symphonies, two piano concertos, opera *Danton* (after Büchner).

Lopukhov, Fyodor (1886–1973), Russian choreographer. ➤*Golden Age.*

Lorca, Federico García (1899–1936), Spanish poet and dramatist. ➤Fortner, ➤Nono, ➤Ohana, ➤Szokolay.

Lorengar, Pilar (1921–96), Spanish soprano; sang at Glyndebourne, 1956, then regularly 1958–81 with German Opera, West Berlin, making other appearances at La Scala, Covent Garden, etc.

Loriod, Yvonne (b. 1924), French pianist (also player of the ➤Ondes Martenot) noted especially in performing the works of Messiaen (her husband) and other modern French composers; completed after Messiaen's death his *Concerto à quatre* (four solo instruments) and is also herself a composer.

Lortzing, [Gustav] Albert (1801–51), German composer, almost entirely of operas and operettas, with his own librettos; his ➤*Zar und Zimmermann* became a standard work in Germany. Also conductor and, on occasion, tenor singer.

Los Angeles, Victoria de [originally Victoria Gomez Cima; married surname Magriñá] (b. 1923), Spanish soprano noted in opera (from 1950 at Covent Garden and the Metropolitan, New York) until retirement from the stage in 1969. Equally distinguished as recitalist, occasionally accompanying herself on the guitar in Spanish traditional songs.

Los Angeles Philharmonic Orchestra, orchestra founded 1919; conductor since 1992, Salonen.

Lott, Felicity [Ann] (b. 1947), British soprano with distinguished operatic career at Covent Garden from 1977, also Munich, Paris, Chicago, New York (Metropolitan Opera), Vienna (title-role in R. Strauss's *Arabella*, 1985). Also noted in oratorio, recordings of English song, etc. Created Dame, 1996.

Lotti, Antonio (*c.* 1667–1740), Italian composer of church music, oratorio, etc.; also of opera. Was church singer and organist, becoming chief organist of St Mark's, Venice, from 1704 until his death.

loud pedal, misleading name for the sustaining pedal on the ➤piano.

Loughran, James (b. 1931), British conductor – of Hallé Orchestra, 1971–83. Afterwards conducted in Australia, Japan and elsewhere.

Louise, opera by G. Charpentier, produced in Paris, 1900. Libretto by composer; 'realistic' opera (a French counterpart to Italian ➤*verismo*), which put the slums of Paris on the stage. The heroine is a seamstress.

Louis Ferdinand, Prince (form of name used by Prince Friedrich Christian Ludwig of Prussia) (1772–1806), amateur composer of chamber music, etc.; praised by Beethoven, who dedicated to him his Piano Concerto no. 3.

loure (Fr.), a type of rustic French bagpipe; and hence a French dance, usually in moderate 6/4 time. Hence also *louré* (derived from a technique of bagpipe-playing), a kind of bowing on the violin, etc., in which several notes are taken in one stroke but are slightly detached from one another.

louré, see preceding entry.

Lourié, Arthur Vincent (1892–1966), Russian-born composer who settled first in France (1921), then in USA (1941). Works, some with Roman Catholic allusions, include *Kormchaya* (Rus., 'Helmswoman', i.e. the Virgin Mary) for orchestra; string quartets; settings of poems by Tolstoy and Mayakovsky.

Love for Three Oranges (Rus., *Lyubov k trem apelsinam*), opera by Prokofiev, produced in French in Chicago, 1921. Libretto, in Russian, by composer, after an Italian play by Gozzi: a satirical fable, some of the actors impersonating an audience, the main action being thus 'a play within a play'. The prince who loves the three oranges finds his princess in the third. An orchestral suite drawn from this includes a celebrated march.

Love in a Village, opera with music collected and arranged by T. Arne, produced in London, 1761; the music is by 16 other composers as well as Arne himself, the work being a ►*pasticcio*.

Love Potion, The, opera by Donizetti. ►*Elisir d'amore*.

Love-song Waltzes, works by Brahms. ►*Liebeslieder-Walzer*.

Love, the Sorcerer, ballet score by Falla. *El* ►*Amor brujo*.

Lualdi, Adriano (1885–1971), Italian composer of operas including *La luna dei Caraibi* ('The Moon of the Caribbees', after O'Neill's play) with some unorthodox orchestration – e.g. 'the two lowest strings of a double-bass, untuned'; also a symphonic poem on Coleridge's *The Rime of the Ancient Mariner*, songs, etc. Also music critic.

Lübeck, Vincenz (1654–1740), German organist (latterly in Hamburg), composer of chorale preludes and other works for organ, and of cantatas, etc.

Luca, Giuseppe De, ►De Luca.

Lucas, Leighton (1903–83), British conductor who began his career as a ballet dancer; also composer (film music, a Latin Requiem Mass, orchestral works, etc.).

Lucia di Lammermoor, opera by Donizetti, produced in Naples, 1835. Libretto by S. Cammarano, after Scott's novel *The Bride of Lammermoor*; set in Scotland about 1700. After slaying her husband the heroine has a famous 'mad scene'.

Lucier, Alvin (b. 1931), American composer, particularly for non-standard resources, e.g. *Music for Solo Performer* where three electrodes are attached to the scalp to pick up 10-cycle alpha waves from the brain, this signal being then amplified and used to activate resonances; also of *Composition for Pianist and Mother* (pianist, actress), etc.

Lucrezia Borgia, opera by Donizetti, produced in Milan, 1833. Libretto by Felice Romani, after Victor Hugo's play. It deals principally with the infamous poisoner (1480–1519) and her son.

Ludford, Nicholas (*c.* 1485–*c.* 1587), British composer, church musician in London. His eleven complete and three incomplete Latin Masses identify him as an important composer of his time.

Ludus Tonalis (Lat., 'The Play of Notes'), piano work by Hindemith, first performed in 1943. Intended as studies in both composition and piano technique, it comprises a prelude, 12 fugues separated by 11 interludes, and a postlude which is the ➤inverted (upside-down) version of the prelude.

Ludwig, Christa (b. 1924), German soprano, then mezzo-soprano; sang at Vienna State Opera from 1955, at the Metropolitan, New York, from 1959. Also distinguished exponent of German song. Retired 1994.

Luening, Otto (1900–96), American composer who studied in Munich and in Zurich (pupil of Busoni); was also flautist and conductor. A pioneer in USA (from early 1950s) of electronic music – e.g. *Fantasy in Space* (flute and tape) and, composed jointly with Ussachevsky, *Poem in Cycles and Bells* for tape and orchestra; earlier, wrote three string quartets, Serenade for three horns and strings, opera *Evangeline* (after Longfellow), etc.

Luigini, Alexandre [Clément Léon Joseph] (1850–1906), French violinist, conductor, and composer of orchestral piece called *Ballet Égyptien* and other light orchestral music; also of operas, etc.

Luisa Miller, opera by Verdi, produced in Naples, 1849. Libretto by S. Cammarano, after Schiller: the setting is the Tyrol, and the three acts are respectively headed Love, Intrigue and Poison.

Lully, Jean-Baptiste (originally Giovanni Battista Lulli) (1632–87), Italian-born composer who was taken in boyhood to France and first worked there as a scullion, then as a violinist. Went into service of Louis XIV, 1652;

naturalized French, 1661; achieved the supreme musical position at court, 1662. Himself a dancer, collaborated with Molière in comedy-ballets including *Le* ➤*Bourgeois Gentilhomme*; from 1673 wrote operas including ➤*Alceste* and ➤*Armide*. Wrote also church music, dance music, etc., and established the 'French ➤overture'. A brilliant intriguer; obtained a monopoly of opera production in France; made a fortune by speculation; injured his foot with the long staff he used for beating time on the floor, and died of the resulting abscess.

Lulu, opera by Berg, with libretto by composer; almost completed, but only Acts I and II (of three) published; first staged in Zurich, 1937. Completed by Friedrich Cerha, first performed in Paris, 1979. Its heroine typifies female sexuality and is finally degraded and murdered.

Lumbye, Hans Christian (1810–74), Danish composer of galops and other dance music, etc., and conductor of such works in Copenhagen.

Lumsdaine, David (b. 1931). Australian composer who studied in London and long worked there. His compositions include cantata *Annotations of Auschwitz*, Looking-glass Music for brass quintet and tape, *Kangaroo Hunt* for piano and percussion.

lungo, lunga (It.), long.

Lupo, Thomas (early 17th century), English composer of Italian origin; wrote fantasies and dance-music for viols, anthems, etc.

Lupu, Radu (b. 1945), Romanian pianist who won international competition at Leeds, 1969, and settled in Britain.

Has recorded chamber music as well as concertos.

lur (Dan.), prehistoric large bronze trumpet of which several specimens have been found, chiefly in Denmark.

lusingando, lusinghiero (It.), flatteringly, i.e. alluringly.

lustig (Ger.), cheerful.

Lustigen Weiber von Windsor, Die (Ger., 'The Merry Wives of Windsor'), the most successful opera by Nicolai, produced in Berlin, 1849. Libretto by S. H. Mosenthal, after Shakespeare. (Another German opera so titled, by Dittersdorf, had appeared in 1796.)

Lustige Witwe, Die (Ger., 'The Merry Widow'), first and most popular operetta by Lehár, produced in Vienna, 1905. Libretto by V. Leon and L. Stein, concerning romantic and diplomatic intrigue.

lute, fretted stringed instrument plucked with the fingers (or, in the case of some earlier types, with a plectrum), much in use 1400–1700 for solos, song accompaniment and ensembles; it had isolated orchestral use even as late as Bach's ➤St John Passion, 1723. Since 1950 it has been extensively revived for the playing of old music. The sizes of lutes differed, and also the tuning; but a regular feature was the tuning of strings in pairs (called 'courses') in unison or octaves. Hence *lutenist* (more rarely *lutanist*), a player of the lute. Larger types (➤*archlute*) are particularly used for ➤*continuo*.

luth (Fr.), lute; *luthier*, lute-maker – and hence, today, a maker of stringed instruments in general.

Luther, Martin (1483–1546), German Protestant leader; he was skilled in music (as singer, flautist, and lutenist) and is thought to have written the music to hymns – e.g. 'Ein' feste Burg' ('A stronghold sure'). He certainly wrote the words of hymns and intended a treatise in praise of music. ➤Reformation Symphony.

luthier, ➤*luth*.

Lutosławski, Witold (1913–94), Polish composer, also conductor. Many of his mature works were written for eminent soloists – a cello concerto for Rostropovich, *Paroles Tissées* (Fr., 'Woven Words') for Peter Pears (with 20 solo instruments. Other works include concerto for orchestra, piano concerto; four symphonies; and a series of works each called *Chain*. ➤Paganini.

Lutyens, [Agnes] Elisabeth (1906–83), British composer, daughter of Sir Edwin Lutyens, architect. A lone British disciple of Schoenberg, she composed an unaccompanied motet on German philosophical text by Wittgenstein; a horn concerto; a viola concerto; six Chamber Concertos for various instrumental groups; 12 string quartets; songs in English and French; *Infidelio* and other operas; film music. Also wrote autobiography. CBE, 1969.

Luxon, Benjamin [Matthew] (b. 1937), British baritone, formerly teacher of physical education; prominent in Britten's and other operas (title-role in televised première of Britten's *Owen Wingrave*, 1971); his recitals have had a successfully informal element. Has continued to perform though latterly suffering from tinnitus. CBE, 1986.

Lvov, Alexis Feodorovich (1798–

1870), Russian composer of operas, much church music, and the pre-Revolutionary Russian National Anthem – quoted in Tchaikovsky's overture *1812* (➤*Eighteen-Twelve*).

Lyadov, Anatol Konstantinovich (1855–1914), Russian composer of symphonic poems ➤*Baba Yaga*, *The* ➤*Enchanted Lake*, and ➤*Kikimora*, and other works for orchestra and for piano in Russian nationalist style; also collector and arranger of folk-songs, and conductor. Was originally invited to compose the music for *The* ➤*Firebird* but owing to his characteristic dilatoriness Stravinsky undertook it.

Lyapunov, Sergey Mikhailovich (1859–1924), Russian pianist and composer in 'nationalist' style; friend of Balakirev, and collector of folk-songs. Wrote two symphonies, two piano concertos, piano solos, etc.

Lydian mode, the ➤mode represented by the white keys on the piano beginning on F.

Lympany, Moura [originally Mary Johnstone; mother's surname Limpenny] (b. 1916), British pianist who made her début in 1929 and was still performing in her late 70s. Gave the first performance outside USSR of Khachaturian's piano concerto, 1940. Created Dame, 1992.

lyra, ➤lyre.

lyra glockenspiel. ➤glockenspiel.

lyre (1) general name for a type of plucked stringed instrument in which the strings are fixed to a cross-bar between two arms; (2) ancient Greek instrument (Gk., *lyra*) of this type, rounded off at the foot (distinguished from ➤*kithara*).

lyric (1, strictly) relating to vocal performance with the lyre, i.e. sung; hence *lyric drama*, occasional synonym for opera (especially in French, as *drame lyrique*); hence also *the lyric stage*, i.e. the operatic stage; (2, of a poem) not epic, not dramatic, but fairly short and expressing the writer's own feelings; hence (term taken over from poetry into music) *Lyric Piece* (Grieg), *Lyric Suite* (Berg), etc.; (3, as vocal description, e.g. *lyric soprano*, *lyric tenor*), term indicating intermediate vocal 'weight' between light and 'dramatic' (heavy); (4, *lyrics*, as noun) the words of a song in a musical, etc.; so *lyricist*, writer of such lyrics.

lysarden, the name of a wind instrument found in English sources *c*.1600 – probably the ➤cornett.

M, abbr. for Master (in certain university degrees; e.g. ➤M. Mus., Master of [or 'in'] Music).

m, symbol in ➤tonic sol-fa for the degree (mediant) of the scale, pronounced *me*.

ma (It.), but.

Ma, Yo-Yo (b. 1955), Chinese cellist, born in France, giving public performances from age five; after moving with parents to New York, he performed on television in 1963, studied with Leonard Rose and achieved international eminence as soloist. Gave first performance of H. K. Gruber's cello concerto, 1989.

Maazel, Lorin [Varencove] (b. 1930), American conductor, born in France, also violinist. Music director of the Cleveland Orchestra, 1972–82, of the Vienna State Opera, 1982–4, of the Pittsburgh Symphony Orchestra 1988–95 and of the Bavarian Radio Symphony Orchestra since 1993.

Macbeth, (musical works after Shakespeare, including) (1) opera by Verdi, produced in Florence, 1847, and revised for Paris, 1865; libretto by F. M. Piave and A. Maffei; (2) symphonic poem by R. Strauss, first performed in 1890; (3) opera by E. Bloch, produced in Paris, 1910; libretto by E. Fleg; (4) incidental music (formerly ascribed to Locke) written for a production of the play in a distorted version, 1674; the true composer is unidentified.

McCabe, John (b. 1939), British composer who studied in Manchester and Munich; also pianist and (1983–90) director of the London College of Music. Works include ballet score *Edward II*, four symphonies and *The Chagall Windows* for orchestra; *Postcards* for wind quintet; *Miniconcerto* for organ, percussion and audience ('485 penny-whistles'); piano and organ solos. CBE, 1985.

McCartney, [James] **Paul** (b. 1942), British rock singer and composer, member of the Beatles (dissolved 1970) and afterwards of Wings; also record producer. Collaborated with Carl Davis in ➤*Liverpool Oratorio* using classical performers, also wrote a symphony *Standing Stone*, 1997.

McCormack, John (1884–1945), Irish-born tenor who studied in Italy, made Covent Garden début in 1907, but later appeared chiefly in concert; enormously popular. Became US citizen, 1917; created a papal Count, 1928.

MacCunn, Hamish (1868–1916), British composer, many of whose works are on Scottish subjects including opera *Jeanie Deans*; concert-overtures *Land of the Mountain and the Flood* and *The Ship o' the Fiend*; cantatas, songs, etc. Was also conductor.

MacDermot, Galt (b. 1928), American composer for the musical theatre, notably of ➤*Hair*.

MacDowell, Edward [Alexander] (1860–1908), American composer, also pianist. Trained in France and Germany. Wrote many short piano pieces, which won wide popularity; also two piano concertos, *Hamlet and Ophelia* and other symphonic poems, songs, etc. The MacDowell Colony – a peaceful working-place for composers and other artists, in New Hampshire – was organized in his memory.

McEwen, John Blackwood (1868–1948), British composer of 17 string quartets (no. 6, *Biscay*), orchestral works including *Grey Galloway* (no. 2 of three 'Border Ballads'), a viola concerto, etc. Principal of the RAM, 1924–36; knighted, 1931.

Macfarren, George Alexander (1813–87), British composer of church music, many operas (one on Robin Hood), oratorios, overtures to *Hamlet* and other plays, etc. Principal of the RAM 1876–87; professor at Cambridge, 1875; knighted, 1883. Totally blind in later life.

MacGregor, Joanna (b. 1959), British pianist, also composer; studied with Bolet. Distinguished in modern music, giving first performances of Hugh Wood's piano concerto and (1993) of Birtwistle's *Antiphonies*; has performed in Copenhagen, Paris, etc. Plays occasionally in jazz ensemble.

Mácha, Otmar (b. 1922), Czechoslovak composer of *Lake Ukereve* and other operas, two sinfoniettas, oratorio *The Testament of Comenius*.

Machaut (also Machault), **Guillaume de** (*c.* 1300–77), French composer – also poet and priest, latterly Canon of Rheims. Considered the chief exponent of ➤*ars nova* in France. His Mass for four voices is almost the earliest surviving polyphonic Mass. Composed also other vocal music to religious and secular texts, some to a very intricate scheme of construction (➤isorhythmic).

McIntyre, Donald [Conroy] (b. 1934), New Zealand bass-baritone based in London, making Covent Garden début in 1967; noted in Wagner, he became in 1973 the first British singer to sing Wotan at Bayreuth and sang Sachs in *Die Meistersinger* in Sydney, at Covent Garden, and (1975) the Metropolitan Opera, New York. Knighted (New Zealand honours list), 1992.

Mackenzie, Alexander [Campbell] (1847–1935), British violinist, conductor, principal of the RAM (1888–1924), and composer. Works include *Colomba, The Cricket on the Hearth* and other operas; many vocal works of all types; three orchestral Scottish rhapsodies. Knighted, 1895.

Mackerras, [Alan] Charles [MacLaurin] (b. 1925), Australian conductor (born in USA); resident in Britain since 1947. Conductor of Sydney Symphony Orchestra, 1982–5; musical director of Welsh National Opera 1987–92. Arranger of Sullivan's music for the ballet ➤*Pineapple Poll*. Knighted, 1979. ➤Nathan.

McLaughlin, John, ➤Labèque.

Macleod, Fiona [pseudonym of William Sharp] (1855–95). Scottish poet. ➤*White Peacock*.

McLeod, John (b. 1934), British composer of *The Song of Dionysius* (percussion and piano: for Evelyn Glennie), *The Passage of the Divine Bird* for free-bass accordion; two symphonies, and *Hebridean Prayers* for chorus with ➤clàrsach and organ.

MacMillan, James (b. 1959), British composer of percussion concerto (entitled 'Veni, veni Emmanuel'); opera *Inès de Castro*; overture *Britannia* humorously quoting earlier British composers; works with Scottish nationalist allusion including *The Confession of Isabel Gowdie* for orchestra.

Maconchy, Elizabeth (1907–94), British composer; studied under Vaughan Williams, and also in Prague. Works include *And Death Shall Have No Dominion* for chorus and brass: 12 string quartets and other chamber music; a symphony for double string orchestra; songs, ballets, operas. Created Dame, 1987. ➤Lefanu.

McPhee, Colin [Carhart] (1901–64), American (Canadian-born) composer, pupil of Varèse; lived in Bali, became authority on its music, and composed orchestral work *Tabuh-Tabuhan* based on Balinese musical systems; also piano solos, Concerto for piano and eight wind instruments, etc. Was also writer and teacher.

Madam Butterfly, the usual form of title given in English to Puccini's ➤*Madama Butterfly*.

Madama Butterfly, opera by Puccini, produced in Milan, 1904 (February); successful only in a revised version three months later. Libretto by G. Giacosa and L. Illica, after D. Belasco's (American) play, *Madame Butterfly*: the Japanese heroine is deserted by an American naval lieutenant. ➤samisen.

Maderna, Bruno (1920–73), Italian composer, also a leading conductor of modern music. Works include Concerto for two pianos; and various pieces involving tape and (sometimes) action: in *Giardino religioso* ('Religious Garden') the conductor moves among the orchestra and improvises on some instruments.

madrigal (1) 16th–17th-century type of contrapuntal composition for several voices, originating in Italy but flourishing also in England – mostly self-contained in vocal texture, but some later examples (e.g. by Monteverdi) having independent instrumental accompaniment. The words are usually secular, chiefly amorous, though some *madrigali spirituali* (sacred) exist; (2) term used also for the Italian forerunner of the above type, from the 14th century (after which the term fell out of use until revived as above); (3) term used also in various looser senses – e.g. the so-called madrigals in operettas by Sullivan and German, which pay homage to an older manner without reviving it.

Mad Scene, colloquial description of scenes in opera in which the heroine's (often temporary) insanity is an excuse for coloratura. Donizetti's ➤*Lucia di Lammermoor* provides a celebrated example.

Maelzel, Johann Nepomuk (1772–1838), ➤metronome.

maestoso (It.), majestic, dignified.

maestro (It.), title traditionally given in Italy to recognized conductors and composers (and used, particularly in North America, as a loose honorific for conductors). The *maestro al cembalo* was the musician who in the 18th century and thereabouts directed concerts or operas while playing the harpsichord; so also *maestro di cappella*, the musical director of a chapel of a prince's establishment, etc. (but not used today in such a wide sense as its German equivalent, ➤*Kapellmeister*. See following entry).

Maestro di cappella, Il (It., 'The Musical Director'), short piece by Cimarosa in comic-opera style, composed *c*. 1790, in which a baritone impersonates a conductor guiding an orchestra; it does not appear to have been intended for dramatized stage performance.

Maestro di musica, Il (It., 'The Music Master'), one-act comic opera satirizing the singing-master's profession; the music was formerly ascribed to Pergolesi, but in fact is not by him – apparently it is an altered version of *Orazio*, opera mainly by Auletta, with libretto by A. Palombo, produced in Naples, 1737 or earlier.

maggiore (It.), major.

Magic Flute, The, opera by Mozart. ➤*Zauberflöte*.

Magnard, Albéric (1865–1914), French composer of four symphonies, three operas, etc. Killed resisting the invasion of his home by German troops.

Magnificat, the hymn of the Virgin Mary as given in St Luke (Latin name, from first word of the Vulgate translation); used in Roman Catholic and Anglican services, the musical setting in the latter being often combined with a setting of the ➤*Nunc dimittis*. Hence Vaughan Williams's *Magnificat*, concert-setting of the words of the hymn, plus additional text, first performed in 1932.

Magnificent Cuckold, The, opera by Goldschmidt. ➤*Gewaltige Hahnrei*.

Mahagonny, ➤*Aufstieg und Fall der Stadt Mahagonny*.

Mahler, Gustav (1860–1911), Austrian (Bohemian-born) composer, whose recognition as a major symphonist came after his death; during his lifetime he was best known as conductor, particularly of Vienna Opera, 1897–1907, and then in New York. Jewish by upbringing, but became Roman Catholic. Attended Bruckner's university lectures and admired him, but was never a direct pupil. His Symphony no. 2 is one of the earliest to begin with one key-centre and end with another (➤progressive tonality), and his later music has passages of extreme chromaticism anticipating Schoenberg and ➤atonal music. Most of his works have a literary or other non-musical link. Wrote nine completed symphonies notable for their length, large forces used and highly individual orchestration: nos. 2 (➤*Resurrection*), 3 and 8 (➤*Symphony of a Thousand*) employ vocal soloists and chorus, no. 4 a soprano soloist. No. 5 has famous ➤*Adagietto*. No. 10, left unfinished, was completed by Deryck Cooke and first performed entire in this form in 1964. *Das* ➤*Lied von der Erde*, though formally a song-cycle with orchestra, is also of symphonic dimensions; wrote other orchestrally accompanied song-cycles ➤*Lieder eines fahrenden Gesellen* and ➤*Kindertotenlieder* and other songs (➤*Knaben Wunderhorn*) but little else.

Maid as Mistress, The, comic opera by Pergolesi. ➤*Serva padrona*.

Maiden Quartets, ➤Russian Quartets.

Maid of the Mountains, The, musical comedy with text by Frederick Lonsdale; music by Harold Fraser-Simson with later additions by James Tate. Produced in Manchester, 1916. One of a band of Italian mountain brigands, she survives capture and wins her man.

Maid of Orleans, The (Rus., *Orleanskaya Deva*), opera by Tchaikovsky, produced in St Petersburg, 1881. Libretto by composer after Schiller's play about Joan of Arc.

Maid of Pskov, The (Rus., *Pskovitianka*), opera by Rimsky-Korsakov, produced in St Petersburg, 1873; libretto by composer. Sometimes known in the West as *Ivan the Terrible*, the 16th-century Tsar being one of the chief characters.

maîtrise (Fr.), a choir school attached to a church.

maj., abbr. for major (scale etc.).

major, minor, terms contrasting with one another and having various musical applications – (1) Scales. The *major* ➤scale of C (i.e. treating the note C as its point of repose) is –

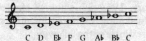

(and the same notes descending). The *minor* scale is divided for theoretical purposes into three types, of which the *natural minor* scale of C is:

(and the same notes descending). The *melodic minor* scale of C differs in its ascending and descending forms:

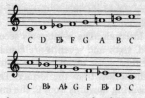

The *harmonic minor* scale of C is

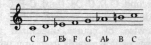

(and the same notes descending). Similarly with scales beginning on the other notes; i.e. all major scales are internally alike, the distances (➤intervals between successive notes being the same, although the note of starting differs. All scales belonging to one of the three types of minor scales are, similarly, alike.

(2) Keys. The ➤key of C *major* is that in which the notes of the scale of C major are treated as 'normal', other notes entering only for special purposes. The key of C *minor* bears a like relation to the scale of C minor; but, though there are three types of minor scale, there is only one type of minor key (the three types of scale corresponding to different aspects of it). The ➤key-signature of a minor key is determined by the *natural minor* scale (above); e.g. for C minor it is three flats (B♭, E♭, A♭)

(3) Chords. A major or minor ➤chord is one which, being built out of the major or minor scale, may serve to identify that scale. More particularly, the *common chord of C major*, or just *chord of C major*, or *C-major triad*, means the notes C, E, G – as contrasted with the *common chord of C*

minor (*chord of C minor, C-minor triad*), C, E♭, G.

(4) Intervals. The ➤intervals second, third, sixth and seventh are classified as either *major* or *minor*, the latter a semitone less than the former. Thus, measuring upwards from C, the major and minor intervals (in that order) are – second, C–D, C–D♭; third, C–E, C–E♭; sixth, C–A, C–A♭, seventh, C–B, C–B♭. Likewise, of course, measured upwards or downwards from any other note.

Makropoulos Affair, The (Cz., *Věc Makropulos*), opera by Janáček, produced in Brno, 1926; libretto by composer, after Čapek's play about an elixir of eternal life administered to a woman called Makropoulos (this is the normal English spelling of such Greek names, though the Czech spelling is different). Also known as *The Makropoulos Case*; but, although the opera is concerned with a lawsuit, no legal 'case' is referred to in the original title.

Maksymiuk, Jerzy (b. 1936), Polish conductor; founder of Polish Chamber Orchestra and principal conductor (1975–7) of Polish National Radio Orchestra. Has been conductor of BBC Scottish Symphony Orchestra, 1984–96 and made first appearance at English National Opera, 1991. Is also composer.

Mal (Ger.), time (in the sense of *1. Mal*, first time, etc.).

malagueña (Sp.), dance originating in Málaga, marked by singing; also instrumental piece of similar nature.

Malcolm, George [John] (1917–97), British harpsichordist, pianist, conductor, church musician and composer of *Variations on a Theme of Mozart* for four harpsichords; 1947–59, Master of the Music at Westminster (Roman Catholic) Cathedral. CBE, 1965.

Malediction, name applied to a Liszt piano concerto, composed apparently in the early 1840s but not published till after his death. In fact Liszt gave the name only to the opening theme of the work.

Malgoire, Jean-Claude (b. 1940), French conductor, known for his performances and recordings (in France and elsewhere) of baroque opera using his own orchestra (➤*Écurie*) of period instruments.

Malibran, Maria [Felicia] (1808–36), Spanish mezzo-soprano, daughter of the Spanish tenor Manuel García; though dying so young, she was internationally celebrated in opera. Sang also soprano roles; e.g. Leonore in *Fidelio* (in English) at Covent Garden, 1835.

maliconia (It.), melancholy.

Malipiero, Gian Francesco (1882–1973), Italian composer of operas including ➤*Giulio Cesare* ('Julius Caesar'); 11 symphonies, and also a 'symphony in one movement' and a *Sinfonia dello Zodiaco*; chamber music including *De profundis* for voice, viola, bass drum and piano; and many songs, etc. Director of the Venice Conservatory, 1939–52; editor of Monteverdi, Vivaldi and other old Italian composers. Uncle of the following.

Malipiero, Riccardo (b. 1914), Italian composer and critic, formerly pianist and cellist; nephew of preceding.

Works include *Concerto breve* for ballerina and orchestra; *Six Poems of Dylan Thomas* for soprano and 10 instruments, operas *Minnie la candida* and *La Donna è mobile* (quotation from *Rigoletto*).

Mallarmé, Stéphane (1842–98), French poet. ➤Boulez; *L'*➤*Après-midi d'un faune*.

mallet instruments, modern generic name for tuned percussion instruments with a piano-like layout of sound-bars struck by mallets in the player's hands: notably, ➤glockenspiel, ➤ marimba, ➤vibraphone, ➤xylophone.

Mallet, David (*c*. 1705–65), Scottish poet and dramatist. ➤*Alfred*.

mambo (Sp.), Afro-Cuban dance in 4/4 time; developed in the 1940s, it became internationally popular.

Mamelles de Tirésias, Les (Fr., 'The Breasts of Tiresias'), opera by Poulenc, produced in Paris, 1947. Libretto by Apollinaire, the male's swelling breasts a symbol in a comic modernization of the Greek myth of transsexuality.

Ma mère l'oye (Fr., 'Mother Goose'), suite by Ravel for piano duet on fairy-tale subjects, 1910; the orchestrated version, first performed 1912, includes additional material.

Mancinelli, Luigi (1848–1921), Italian composer of operas (one in Italian on *A Midsummer Night's Dream*), etc.; noted opera conductor, much at Covent Garden.

Mancini, Henry (1924–94), American composer, conductor, pianist and arranger. Composed more than 70 film scores including *Breakfast at Tiffany's*,

music for television serial *The Thornbirds*, etc.

mandola, mandora, obsolete lute-like stringed instrument, from which the ➤mandolin developed and from which the word mandolin is derived. *Mandola* is also used for a (modern) tenor or bass mandolin.

mandolin (also spelt 'mandoline'), plucked stringed instrument of Italian origin, now usually of eight strings tuned in pairs (to the same four notes as a violin) and played with plectrum. Much used in informal music-making and operatic simulations of this, e.g. in the Serenade in Mozart's *Don Giovanni* and in Verdi's *Otello*; but used also as concerto instrument (Vivaldi), in Mahler's Symphony no. 7, etc.

Manfred, works based on Byron's verse drama – (1) overture and 15 numbers (including background music for speech) by Schumann, composed for stage performance and first given in 1852; (2) symphony by Tchaikovsky, first performed in 1886 – not numbered among his other symphonies.

Manfredini, Francesco [Onofrio] (1684–1762), Italian violinist, church musician and composer of orchestral works (some of ➤*concerto grosso* type), trio-sonatas, etc. Father of the following.

Manfredini, Vincenzo (1737–99), Italian composer who took court post in Russia (and died there); composed operas, ballets, harpsichord sonatas, etc. Pupil of his father (preceding).

Mann, Thomas (1875–1955), German writer. ➤*Death in Venice*; ➤Rosenberg.

mannerism, a term borrowed from art history, identifying a supposed tendency to give more value to a strikingly individual feature of a piece (e.g. a succession of unusual chords) than to an overall direction of form; it is sometimes applied to Gesualdo's music.

Mannheim school, name given by early 20th-century historians to a group of mid-18th-century composers centred at the court of Mannheim (Germany), headed by J. W. ➤Stamitz; held to be historically significant for (1) the cultivation of a type of symphony forerunning the classical (Haydn–Mozart) type; (2) refinement of orchestral technique – the clarinet and the controlled orchestral crescendo supposedly making here their first entry into this type of music.

Manning, Jane [Marian] (b. 1936), British soprano, a champion of the whole range of 20th-century music: more than 300 works have been written for her. Took all eight roles in first performance of J. Weir's ten-minute *King Harald's Saga*, 1979. Formed her own instrumental ensemble, Jane's Minstrels, 1988. OBE, 1990.

Manon, opera by Massenet, produced in Paris, 1884. Libretto by H. Meilhac and P. Gille. Named after the heroine, eventually condemned for prostitution; based on Prévost's novel *Manon Lescaut*, as were also Balfe's opera *The Maid of Artois* (1836), Henze's *Boulevard Solitude*, and the following.

Manon Lescaut, title of various works based on Prévost's novel (see also preceding entry), including (1) ballet with choreography by J. Aumer, music by Halévy, 1830; (2) opera by Auber, produced in Paris, 1856 (libretto by E. Scribe); (3) opera by Puccini, pro-

duced in Turin, 1893 (libretto by M. Praga, D. Oliva and L. Illica – though the process of writing it was so involved that the title-page names no librettist).

manual, a keyboard played with the hands – especially on the organ, as opposed to a pedal-keyboard: hence *manualiter*, bogus-Latin term for 'to be played on the manuals'.

maqam (and variant spellings), term in Arabic music variously translated *mode*, *scale*, *melody*. Camilleri's African-influenced piano concerto no. 2 uses the word as a subtitle.

maraca, Latin-American percussion instrument used in dance bands, etc., and occasionally elsewhere – e.g. in Varèse's *Ionisation*. It is a gourd filled with dried seeds which rustle when the instrument is shaken – or is made of other materials to produce the same effect. Usually as a pair – in plural, *maracas*.

Marais, Marin (1656–1728), French bass-viol player; also composer (pupil or Lully) writing operas, music for viols, a Te Deum, etc.

Marbeck (also Merbecke, etc.), **John** (*c.* 1510–1585), English composer of Mass, motets and (especially) *The Book of Common Prayer Noted*, i.e. the first musical setting of the Anglican prayer-book. Was also organist at St George's, Windsor; compiler of the first biblical concordance in English, and theological writer; condemned to death for heresy in 1543 but pardoned.

marcato (It.), marked; *marcato il basso*, the bass to be played in a prominent manner.

Marcello, Alessandro (1684–1750),

Italian composer of cantatas, concertos, etc. An oboe concerto of his, which Bach transcribed for keyboard, was formerly misattributed to his brother Benedetto Marcello and to Vivaldi.

Marcello, Benedetto (1686–1739), Italian composer, brother of preceding – also violinist, singer, writer, translator and civil servant. Works include operas, oratorios and a setting of Italian paraphrases of the Psalms.

march, a piece for marching, slow (usually 4/4) or quick (usually 2/4 or 6/8); transferred from military to other uses. ➤*marche*, ➤*marcia*.

Marchal, André (1894–1980), French organist, from 1945 at St Eustache, Paris; noted recitalist, touring Europe, USA, Australia; blind from birth.

Marchand, Louis (1669–1732), French organist and composer, chiefly for the organ and harpsichord. Toured in Germany; but the story that he left Dresden rather than face a challenge to compete at the organ with Bach is not authenticated.

marche (Fr.), march: *Marche militaire*, French title used by Schubert for each of three marches for piano duet (D733), composed before 1824 – no. 1 being the famous one.

Marche des petits faunes (Fr., 'Entry of the Little Fauns'), piece by Pierné forming part of his ballet *Cydalise et le chèvre-pied*, produced in 1923.

marcia (It.), march; *alla marcia*, in march-like style – term usually applied to 4/4, 2/4 or 6/8 rhythms (➤march).

Marenzio, Luca (1554–99), Italian composer, wrote more than 200 madrigals, very successful and having much influence in England. Wrote also a Mass and other church music, but, exceptionally for an Italian of that period, never held a church appointment. Worked for a time in Warsaw, but mainly in Rome.

mariache, Mexican dance similar to fandango, hence (in attributive plural) the Latin-American *mariachi band* accompanying this type of music.

'Maria Theresia', nickname for Haydn's symphony no. 48 in C (Hob. I: 48), composed in 1772 – in honour of the Empress of Austria.

marimba, percussion instrument of African origin; the standard Central American form, now well known in concert use, is a sort of large, deeper-toned ➤xylophone (with wooden slabs) played with soft-headed sticks. Milhaud wrote a concerto (1947) for marimba and vibraphone (one player) and it has been extensively cultivated by composers since. The *marimbaphone* (or *steel marimba*) is a patented instrument, similar but with metal instead of wooden slabs (➤xylorimba).

marimbaphone, ➤marimba.

marine trumpet, ➤*tromba*.

Maritana, opera by W. V. Wallace, produced in London, 1845; libretto by E. Fitzball. Named after its Spanish gipsy heroine.

Markevitch, Igor (1912–83), Russian composer and conductor who settled in Paris. Works include Sinfonietta, ballets, a cantata on Milton's *Paradise Lost*. Held conducting posts in Paris, Moscow, and (1973–5) Rome.

Marriage of Figaro, The, opera by Mozart. ➤*Nozze di Figaro.*

Marriner, Neville (b. 1924), British conductor, originally violinist: founder-director of the Academy of St Martin-in-the-Fields (➤Academy); conductor of the Minnesota Orchestra 1979–86, and Stuttgart Radio Symphony Orchestra, 1986–9. Knighted, 1985.

Marsalis, Wynton (b. 1961), American trumpeter, admired both in jazz and the classical repertory, sometimes 'multi-tracking' when recording works for more than one trumpet.

Marschner, Heinrich August (1795–1861), German composer – also conductor, for a time assistant to Weber. Composed German Romantic operas including *Der Vampyr, Der Templar und die Jüdin* (after Scott's *Ivanhoe*), and ➤*Hans Heiling*; also songs, male choruses, orchestral works, etc.

Marseillaise, La, French national anthem of which Rouget de Lisle (1760–1836) wrote both tune and words in 1792; so named because it was associated with the body of volunteers from Marseilles who sang it on entering Paris.

Marsh, Roger (b. 1949), British composer of Serenade for amplified double-bass and 15 strings; *Jesters* (*for sicks*) for six woodwind; music-theatre pieces, *Stepping out* for piano and orchestra.

Marteau sans maître, Le ('The Hammer without a Master'), piece by Boulez for contralto and six instruments, 1957 (text by R. Char); title implies verbal assonance between *marteau* and *maître* (Fr., hammer, master).

martelé, martellato (Fr., It.), hammered, i.e. strongly accented – as applied e.g. to the piano, and to a certain manner of bowing the violin and other stringed instruments.

Martenot, ➤*Ondes Martenot.*

Martha, oder Der Markt von Richmond (Ger., 'Martha, or Richmond Fair'), opera by Flotow, produced in Vienna, 1847. Libretto by F. W. Riese: under the name of Martha, the aristocratic heroine lets herself be bound as a servant (in jest) at the hiring fair at Richmond (presumably Surrey). The opera incorporates 'The Last Rose of Summer' (➤Moore, T.).

Martin, Frank (1890–1974), Swiss composer who worked much in Holland; was also pianist and harpsichordist. In *Le Vin herbé* ('The Drugged Wine') for voices and instruments he used the legend on which also Wagner's *Tristan und Isolde* is based. Other works include *Petite symphonie concertante* for harpsichord, harp, piano and two string orchestras; operas *Der Sturm* (after Shakespeare's *The Tempest*) and *Monsieur de Pourceaugnac*, after Molière; oratorios *Golgotha* and *Le mystère de la nativité*; various orchestral and chamber works.

Martinelli, Giovanni (1885–1969), Italian tenor, celebrated in opera – particularly in the Italian repertory at the Metropolitan, New York (1913–43). Latterly taught in New York.

Martinez, Odaline de la [originally Odaline de la Caridad Martinez] (b. 1949), Cuban–American conductor and composer, resident in Britain. Founder–conductor in 1976 of Lontano, chamber ensemble devoted to modern music; the first woman to conduct a complete programme at the Proms, 1984.

Martini, Giovanni Battista (known as Padre (Father) Martini) (1706–84), Italian priest, mathematician and composer of music for church and stage, etc. Author of learned musical treatises; teacher of Mozart and other distinguished composers.

Martini, Giovanni Paolo (name used by Johann Paul Aegidius Schwartzendorf) (1741–1816), German organist and composer who settled in France. Now remembered for his song 'Plaisir d'amour' (Fr., 'Pleasure of Love'); wrote also operas, church music, works for military band, etc.

Martini, 'Padre', ➤Martini (G. B.).

Martini il Tedesco (It, 'Martini the German'), nickname for G. P. Martini.

Martino, Donald [James] (b. 1931), American composer, pupil of Babbitt, Dallapiccola and others. Works include a piano concerto; triple concerto for clarinet, bass clarinet and double-bass clarinet, *Augenmusik* (Ger., 'Eye-music') for 'actress, *danseuse* or uninhibited percussionist and electronic tape'.

Martinon, Jean (1910–76), French conductor, giving London concerts from 1946; held posts in Chicago, Paris and elsewhere, then from 1974 at The Hague (Residentie Orchestra). Also composer of four symphonies, two violin concertos, etc.

Martinů, Bohuslav (1890–1959), Czech composer, formerly violinist: resident from 1932 chiefly in France, also in USA; pupil of Suk and Roussel. Works include *Comedy on the Bridge*, *Julietta*, *The Marriage* (English libretto by the composer, after Gogol's play), *The* ➤*Greek Passion* and other operas; six symphonies; a 'double concerto' for two string orchestras, piano and timpani; concertos for piano, for two pianos, for violin, for two violins; symphonic poems *La Bagarre* ('Tumult') and *Half-time* (referring to a soccer match); seven string quartets and other chamber music (➤theremin).

Martin y Soler, Vicente (1754–1806), Spanish composer of Italian operas including *Una cosa rara* (It., 'A Rare Thing'), quoted by Mozart in *Don Giovanni*. Also composed Russian operas, church music, etc. Died in St Petersburg, where he held a court post.

Martirano, Salvatore (b. 1927), American composer, pupil of Dallapiccola in Florence. Works include *L's GA* (i.e. Lincoln's Gettysburg Address) for gas-masked politico, helium bomb, three cine projectors and tape – the helium being inhaled by the performer to change the vocal sound; also *Contrasts* for orchestra, *Cocktail Music* for piano, etc.

Martland, Steve (b. 1958), British composer; has written for jazz ensemble (*Remix*, 1986) and, in *Wolfgang*, rearranged six Mozart arias for wind, including instruments unknown to Mozart. Other works include *Drill* for two pianos, ➤*Babi Yar* for orchestra.

Marton [née Heinrich], **Eva** (b. 1943), Hungarian soprano with international career – Metropolitan Opera, New York, from 1976. Noted in 'heavy' roles such as R. Strauss's Elektra.

Martucci, Giuseppe (1856–1909), Italian pianist, composer (two symphonies, two piano concertos, etc.), arranger of old Italian music, conductor, director of Naples Conservatory.

Martyrdom of St Magnus, The, chamber opera by P. M. Davies, produced at Kirkwall, Orkney, 1977; libretto by composer, after George Mackay Brown. Magnus was a 12th-century Viking, Earl of Orkney.

Martyre de Saint-Sébastien (Fr., 'The Martyrdom of St Sebastian'), mystery-play by D'Annunzio for which Debussy wrote incidental music, 1911.

Marx, Joseph (1882–1964), Austrian composer of many songs (some with orchestral accompaniment) in the German Romantic tradition: also of a piano quartet, a 'Romantic Piano Concerto', etc.

marziale (It.), martial.

Masaniello, name often given to Auber's opera, *La Muette de Portici* (Fr., 'The Dumb Woman of Portici'), produced in Paris, 1828. Libretto by E. Scribe and G. Delavigne. Masaniello, a revolutionary leader, is the hero; Auber avoided using his name for the title because another opera of that title (by Carafa) had appeared two months earlier. The other title referred to the principal female character; she is dumb, and the part is traditionally taken by a dancer.

Mascagni, Pietro (1863–1945), Italian composer, pupil of Ponchielli. His ➤*Cavalleria Rusticana* won an operatic competition in 1889 and scored a success which he never afterwards matched in other operas including *L'Amico Fritz* ('Friend Fritz'), ➤*Iris* and *Le Maschere* ('The Masks'). Other works include a symphony and a Requiem;

was also conductor and conservatory director.

mask, old English spelling of ➤masque, now occasionally revived for a work of dramatic or allegorical significance, as in Tippett's *The* ➤*Mask of Time*.

Maskarad, Maskarade, ➤masquerade.

Masked Ball, A, opera by Verdi. ➤*Ballo in maschera*.

Mask of Time, The, concert work for solo singers, chorus and orchestra by Tippett, on texts written and compiled by the composer; first performed in 1984.

Mason, Benedict (b. 1952), British composer of opera *Playing Away* (about football), a 'Concerto for the Viola Section' (the rest of the orchestra accompanying), *Animals and the Origin of the Dance* for four solo synthesizers, wind (including various whistles) and percussion; brass quintet, two string quartets, Sackbut Concerto.

Mason, Daniel Gregory (1873–1953), American composer of three symphonies (no. 3, *A Lincoln Symphony*), piano music, etc.; pupil of d'Indy. Also writer on music. Grandson of the following.

Mason, Lowell (1792–1872), American organist, composer (especially of hymns) and educationalist. Grandfather of the preceding.

masque, type of English stage entertainment (related to opera and ballet), cultivated chiefly in the 17th century (➤*Comus*; ➤*Venus and Adonis*) and intended for aristocratic audiences: it incorporated vocal and instrumental music, dancing and spectacle. Arne's ➤*Alfred* dates from slighty later. Anachronistically and confusingly,

Vaughan Williams's *Job* (ballet) is styled 'a masque for dancing'.

Masquerade, opera by C. Nielsen (Dan., *Maskarade*), produced in Copenhagen, 1906; libretto by V. Andersen after Holberg, involving an 18th-century masked ball.

Mass, form of religious service, which, though occasionally found in other ecclesiastical contexts, is chiefly important as the principal service of the Roman Catholic Church; High Mass is sung, Low Mass said. Traditionally, the musical setting of the 'Proper' of the Mass, varying with the occasion, has been left to the appropriate plainsong – except for the ➤Requiem Mass, to which new settings have been frequently composed. The unvarying part, called the 'Ordinary' or 'Common' of the Mass and consisting of five sections (Kyrie, Gloria, Credo, Sanctus with Benedictus, and Agnus Dei), has been frequently set in the Latin text which was in universal use until the decrees of the Second Vatican Council took effect in the 1970s. Such settings of the Ordinary are usually called simply (e.g.) Mass in C (Beethoven's early setting) – or they may have titles or nicknames (e.g. Haydn's ➤*Nelson Mass*) for ease of identification. The so-called *Mass in B minor* by ➤Bach (➤*Missa*) was not so named by him (nor is it preponderantly in B minor). See also the following entries.

Mass, title of a 'theatre piece for singers, players and dancers' by Bernstein (produced in Washington, 1971) which is *about* a celebration of the Mass and combines the traditional Latin text with other matter by Stephen Schwartz.

Massenet, Jules Émile Frédéric (1842–1912), French composer, pupil of A. Thomas. Wrote 27 operas including ➤*Manon*, ➤*Cendrillon* ('Cinderella'), and ➤*Werther*. Other works include ballet scores, incidental music to plays, orchestral suites, a piano concerto, about 200 songs.

Massine, Leonid, Russian–French choreographer. ➤*Sombrero de tres picos*; ➤Tommasini.

Mass of Life, A, work by Delius for four solo singers, chorus and orchestra; first performed complete in 1909. Text from Nietzsche's *Also sprach Zarathustra*: not a Mass, but a kind of pagan counterpart to one.

Master and Margarita, The, opera by Höller. ➤*Meister und Margarita*.

Master of Music, degree awarded at some universities, ranking between Bachelor and Doctor of Music.

Master of the King's (or Queen's) Music, title of a British court post, dating from Charles I's time, and now carrying a small salary and no fixed duties. It formerly implied the directorship of the sovereign's private band. (The spelling 'musick' has no authority today.) The post has been held since 1975 by Malcolm Williamson (succeeding Bliss).

Master Peter's Puppet Show, opera by Falla. ➤*Retablo de maese Pedro*.

Mastersinger (Ger., *Meistersinger*, sing. and pl.), title given to members of a German guild of musicians, flourishing in the 14th–16th centuries: they were by origin merchants, etc., not aristocrats like the earlier *Minnesingers. The Mastersingers* (or *Die Meistersinger*) is commonly used as a short title for Wagner's opera *Die* ➤*Meistersinger von Nürnberg*.

Mastersingers of Nuremberg, The, opera by Wagner. ➤*Meistersinger von Nürnberg*.

Masterson, [Margaret] Valerie (b. 1937), British soprano, noted in Gilbert and Sullivan with D'Oyly Carte Opera Company, then in Handel and the French repertory with former Sadler's Wells Opera (1972), its successor the English National Opera, and companies abroad.

Masur, Kurt (b. 1927), German conductor who held orchestral and operatic posts in former East Germany. Conductor of the Gewandhaus Orchestra, Leipzig, 1970–96. Made British début in 1973 and became music director, New York Philharmonic Orchestra, 1991.

Mathias, William [James] (1934–92), British composer, also pianist and professor (University of North Wales). Works include some with Welsh connections, also cantata *This Worldes Joie* (and other settings of religious, texts), three string quartets, etc. CBE, 1958.

Mathis, Edith (b. 1938), Swiss soprano, noted in opera: sang at Salzburg from 1960, Glyndebourne from 1965. Sang in premières of works by Henze and others and has recorded Haydn's and other unfamiliar operas.

Mathis der Maler (Ger., 'Mathis the Painter'), (1) opera by Hindemith, produced in Zurich, 1938 (scheduled for Berlin, 1934, but banned by the Nazis); libretto by composer, alluding to the painter Grünewald (early 16th century) and his altar-piece at Isenheim; (2) title of a symphony by Hin-demith, drawn from the opera (the first movement is the overture); first performed in 1934.

Matin, Le, ➤*Morning*.

Matrimonio segreto, Il (It., 'The Secret Marriage'), opera by Cimarosa, produced (in Italian) in Vienna, 1792. Libretto by G. Bertati, a comedy of intrigue based on the English play *The Clandestine Marriage* (1766), by Garrick and Colman.

Matthäuspassion, ➤*St Matthew Passion*.

Matthay, Tobias (1858–1945), British pianist, and famous piano teacher, evolving a method of his own: also composer. His pupils included Myra Hess.

Mattheson, Johann (1681–1764), German organist, harpsichordist, singer, and composer of operas, church cantatas, keyboard music, etc.; also noted writer on music.

Matthews, Colin (b. 1946), British composer. Works include *Fourth Sonata* (orchestral), *Broken Symmetry* for orchestra, cello concerto, three string quartets, *Shadows in the Water* for tenor and piano.

Matthews, David (b. 1943), British composer, brother of preceding; his works include four symphonies, six string quartets, *The Flaying of Marsyas* for oboe, violin and string trio.

Matthews, Denis (1919–88), British pianist, noted in Beethoven, and writer on music; professor at Newcastle University, 1972–84; CBE, 1975. He committed suicide.

mattinata (It.), morning song.

Matton, Roger (b. 1929), Canadian

composer (pupil of N. Boulanger in Paris); also university teacher. Works include *Danse brésilienne* ('Brazilian Dance') for orchestra or two pianos, a saxophone concerto, a *Te Deum*, and a *Suite de Pâques* ('Easter Suite') for organ.

Mauceri, John [Francis Peter] (b. 1945), American conductor, active in new music. Conducted the first European performance of Bernstein's *Mass* (1973); music director, Scottish Opera, 1987–93.

Maupassant, Guy de (1850–93). French novelist. ➤*Albert Herring*.

Maurel, Victor (1848–1923), French baritone, among the most famous of his day; created Iago in Verdi's *Otello*, 1886.

Maw, Nicholas (b. 1935), British composer of operas *One Man Show* and *The Rising of the Moon*; *Scenes and Arias* (concert work for three female singers and orchestra on old French texts); *Odyssey* for orchestra (one movement, 96 mins.); violin concerto; *American Games* for wind ensemble; *Essay* for organ; three string quartets, etc.

Maxwell Davies, Peter, ➤Davies, Peter Maxwell. ('Maxwell' is a middle name, not a surname.)

Mayakovsky, Vladimir (1893–1930), Russian poet. ➤Lourié.

Mayerl, Billy [originally William Joseph] (1902–59), British pianist, the earliest British exponent of 'syncopated novelty' (ragtime) works for piano, broadcasting from 1923; composed theatre music and led his own dance band.

Mayr, Richard (1877–1935), Austrian bass-baritone who took part in the first performances of Mahler's Symphony no. 8 and in early performances of R. Strauss's operas.

Mayr, [Johannes] **Simon** (1763–1845), German-born composer who settled in Italy, writing his first opera *Saffo* ('Sappho') and following it with 67 others including *L'amor coniugale* ('Conjugal Love') – slightly before Beethoven brought out his *Fidelio* on the same plot. Teacher of Donizetti.

Mayuzumi, Toshiro (b. 1929), Japanese composer, trained in Tokyo and Paris. Works include *Bugaku* (alluding to traditional Japanese music) for orchestra, Divertimento for 10 instruments, *Tone-pleromas 55* for five saxophones, musical saw and piano; music for the film *The Bible*.

Mazeppa (1) works by Liszt for piano (final version, 1847) and for orchestra (founded on the former, 1851) – alluding to the story (from Byron and Victor Hugo) that Mazeppa survived his punishment of being lashed naked to a wild horse, and became a Cossack chief; (2) opera by Tchaikovsky, produced in Moscow, 1884, with libretto by composer and V. P. Burenin, after Pushkin – alluding to Mazeppa's later treason to Peter the Great. Mazeppa (1664–1709) is a historical character.

mazurka, Polish country dance in 3/4 or 3/8 time; brought by Chopin (he wrote at least 55) into concert music.

mbira, African instrument otherwise known as thumb piano; it has iron or wooden tongues which are plucked by the thumbs. N. Osborne's work entitled *Mbira* (1985, alluding to this) is for violin and piano.

m.d., right hand (in piano-playing etc.; Fr., *main droite*; It., *mano destra*).

me, in ➤tonic sol-fa, the spoken name for the third degree (mediant) of the scale, written *m* and corresponding to the continental note-name *mi* for E.

Meale, Richard (b. 1932), Australian composer of opera *Voss* (based on Patrick White's novel), orchestral work *Clouds Now and Then*, etc.

mean-tone temperament, ➤temperament.

measure, ➤bar. (Also a term, used poetically, for a dance, etc.).

Medea, opera by Cherubini (➤*Médée*); also operas by other composers including ➤Bryars, and ballet score by Barber.

Médée (Fr., 'Medea'), opera by Cherubini, produced in Paris, 1797. Libretto by F. B. Hoffman, about the sorceress of Greek legend who kills her own children as an act of vengeance.

mediant, name for the third degree of the scale, e.g. E in C major – so called because it stands midway between the tonic (or keynote) and dominant, i.e. between the first and fifth degrees.

Medici Quartet, London-based string quartet (name unexplained; in Italian, accented on first syllable), founded 1974. Current members: Paul Robertson, Cathy Thompson, Ivo-Jan van der Werff, Anthony Lewis.

Medium, The, opera by Menotti, produced in New York, 1946. Libretto by composer, about a fake spiritualistic medium. Also filmed, with the score slightly altered, 1951.

Medtner, Nicolas (properly Nikolay Karlovich Metner) (1880–1951), Russian composer-pianist of German descent. Left Russia, 1921, and in 1936 settled in England, where he died.

Works include three piano concertos, numerous songs in Russian and German, many piano solos (several entitled *Fairy Tales*).

Mefistofele (It., 'Mephistopheles'), opera by Boito, produced in 1868; libretto by the composer, after Goethe's *Faust*.

Mehta, Zubin (b. 1936), Indian conductor (formerly violinist and pianist) who studied in Vienna and won an international conducting competition in Liverpool, 1958. Music director, Los Angeles Philharmonic Orchestra 1962–76; music adviser, Israel Philharmonic Orchestra, since 1968, later music director; music director, New York Philharmonic Orchestra, since 1978.

Méhul, Étienne [Henri Nicolas] (1763–1817), French composer, encouraged by Gluck to write for the stage. Operas include *Joseph* and *Les deux aveugles de Tolédo* ('The Two Blind Men of Toledo'). Also wrote ballets, symphonies, patriotic (French Revolutionary) music etc.

Meier, Jost (b. 1939), Swiss composer, pupil of Frank Martin in Holland; he formerly held opera-house posts as conductor. His works include opera *Dreyfus* (1994), on the celebrated case (1894) of the French captain wrongly convicted of treason through anti-Jewish prejudice.

Meister und Margarita, Der (Ger., 'The Master and Margarita'), opera by Höller (libretto by composer) based on the novel by Bulgakov – the Master is a writer who resists the satanic possession (metaphor for Stalinism) of 1930s Moscow. Produced in Paris, 1989.

Meistersinger von Nürnberg, Die

(Ger., 'The Mastersingers of Nuremberg'), comic opera by Wagner, produced in Munich, 1868. Libretto by composer, dealing with a medieval guild (➤Mastersinger) and serving as a platform for some of Wagner's own views on art.

Melba, Nellie, stage name (from her birthplace, Melbourne) of Helen Porter Mitchell (1861–1931), Australian soprano who settled in Britain and won unsurpassed operatic fame; first sang at Covent Garden in 1888. Created Dame, 1918. Toast Melba and Peach Melba were named after her.

Melchior, Lauritz (originally Lebrecht Hommel) (1890–1973), Danish-born singer who won fame in Wagner; became US citizen, 1947.

melisma (Gk. song, pl. *melismata*), a group of notes sung to a single syllable. (Term also sometimes applied more loosely to any florid vocal passage in the nature of a cadenza.) *Melismata* is also the title of a collection of English vocal pieces published by T. Ravenscroft in 1611.

Mellnäs, Arne (b. 1933), Swedish composer, pupil of Blacher in Berlin. Has produced several electronic works on tape (including *Kaleidovision* for a television ballet) as well as *Capricorn Flakes* for piano, harpsichord and vibraphone, *Aura* for orchestra, etc.

mellophone, American name for the ➤tenor cor.

melodic minor, ➤minor.

Melodica, trade name for an instrument shaped somewhat like a small recorder but using a series of reeds and fingered on a tiny piano-like keyboard.

mélodie (Fr.), (1) melody; (2) a song.

melodrama, term of which the current English sense (a sensational and sentimental play) is a debased meaning. As used in this book, and generally in musical contexts, it refers to the dramatic use of spoken words against a musical background – whether throughout a musical work (as in certain 18th-century examples) or forming part of a work, as in the gravedigging scene in ➤*Fidelio*. But note that the Italian form *melodramma* means simply opera.

melodramma, see preceding entry.

melody, a succession of notes varying in pitch and having a recognizable musical shape. Thus the three 'dimensions' of music are often thought of as (1) melody, (2) rhythm, (3) harmony and counterpoint. The term is also used as title for certain rather simple pieces – e.g. *Melody in F*, the almost sole survivor of Anton Rubinstein's piano solos, being no. 1 of *Two Melodies*, op. 3 (1853).

melos, ancient Greek word (from which 'melody' is derived), sometimes used to indicate a primal musical surge; borrowed for the names of the Melos Ensemble of London, founded 1950, and the following (but note also the leader's name).

Melos Quartet of Stuttgart, German string quartet founded in 1965, with Wilhelm Melcher as leader.

Melville, Herman (1819–91), American novelist. ➤*Billy Budd*; ➤Herrmann, ➤Mennin.

membranophone, term used in the scientific classification of instruments for those in which a stretched skin (or something similar) is set in vibration, by stick or otherwise – drums, etc.

Mendelssohn, name by which the

composer J. L. F. Mendelssohn-Bartholdy and his family (see following two entries) are customarily known. Mendelssohn was their original surname, Bartholdy being added by the composer's father.

Mendelssohn [Bartholdy], **Fanny Cäcilie** (also in the French form, Cécile) (1805–47), German (amateur) pianist and composer, valued consultant of her brother (see next entry). Six of her songs were published as his, and she also wrote part-songs, piano solos, a piano trio. Married W. Hensel, painter, 1829.

Mendelssohn-Bartholdy, [Jacob Ludwig] **Felix** (1809–47), German composer, the surname being normally shortened to Mendelssohn; the enormous esteem he enjoyed in the 19th century has since been a little diminished. A grandson of the Jewish philosopher Moses Mendelssohn, but brought up as a Lutheran (brother of the preceding). Noted pianist and organist; also conductor, head of Leipzig Conservatory (1843), and amateur painter. Born in Hamburg; boy prodigy, composing the overture to *A* ➤*Midsummer Night's Dream* at 17 (the other music to it later). Visited Scotland, 1829 (➤*Scottish Symphony*, ➤*Hebrides*), afterwards revisiting Britain nine times, conducting the first performance of ➤*Elijah* in Birmingham in 1846. Other works include oratorio ➤*St Paul*; five symphonies (no. 2 ➤*Lobgesang*, no. 3 ➤*Scottish*, no. 4 ➤*Italian*, no. 5 ➤*Reformation*); ➤*Ruy Blas* and other overtures; two piano concertos; Violin Concerto in E minor (a youthful concerto in D minor, left in MS, was resuscitated by Menuhin); string octet (the Scherzo later scored for orchestra) and other

chamber music; ➤*Lieder ohne Worte* and other piano solos; organ works; youthful opera *Die Hochzeit des Camacho* ('Camacho's Wedding'), songs. Influential in the revival of Bach, giving in 1829 in Berlin the first performance of the ➤*St Matthew Passion* since Bach's death.

Mengelberg, Willem (1871–1951), Dutch conductor, unique in 50-year conductorship of Concertgebouw Orchestra of Amsterdam, 1895–1945; champion of Mahler and R. Strauss. Disgraced for alleged support of Nazi wartime occupation of Holland, he died in Switzerland.

Mennin, Peter (originally Mennini) (1923–83), American composer, pupil of B. Rogers and Hanson. Wrote seven symphonies, *Concertato* [sic] for orchestra (inspired by Melville's *Moby Dick*), cantata *The Christmas Story*, two string quartets, piano pieces, etc. President of Juilliard School of Music, New York, 1962–83.

meno (It.), less; *meno mosso*, less moved, i.e. slower. Sometimes composers unhelpfully omit *mosso* and write, e.g., *poco meno* (really 'a little less') for a little slower.

Menotti, Gian-Carlo (b. 1911), Italian composer living mainly in USA since 1928; founder of Spoleto Festival, Italy, 1958. Won international success as composer of operas with his own librettos. These include *Amelia Goes to the Ball*, with libretto originally in Italian, and successors in English – including *The Old Maid and the Thief, The* ➤*Medium, The* ➤*Telephone, The* ➤*Consul,* ➤*Amahl and the Night Visitors* (the first opera written for television), and ➤*Goya* (written for Plácido Domingo); also *The Unicorn,* *the Gorgon and the Manticore*, sung off-stage; mimed on-stage; has also written a piano concerto, etc. Regularly the stage director for his operas, he also directed the film of *The Medium*.

mensural notation, i.e. 'measured' or 'proportioned' notation, a system such as that in current use in which relative time-values of notes are mainly indicated by their visual shape. But the term is usually restricted to the early stages of the system (*c.* 1250–1600), with visual shapes not the same as later ones, and a different set of guiding conventions.

menuet, Menuett (Fr., Ger.), ➤minuet.

menuetto, term encountered in the scores of Haydn, Mozart, etc., to mean ➤minuet – probably a hybrid of Fr. *menuet* and It. *minuetto*.

Menuhin, Yehudi (b. 1916), American-born violinist (British citizen, 1985), famous since boyhood; pupil of Enescu and others. Commissioned Bartók's unaccompanied Violin Sonata and in 1952 resuscitated an early concerto by Mendelssohn. Also viola player and conductor, chief musical figure of the Bath Festival and musical director of its chamber orchestra, 1959–68. Hon. KBE, 1965 ('Sir Yehudi' on naturalization); OM, 1987. Life peer (Lord Menuhin), 1993. His sisters are the pianists Hephzibah (1920–81) and Yaltah (b. 1921) Menuhin. Founded a school for musically gifted children, 1963.

Mephisto (abbr. for Mephistopheles), name used by Liszt in four *Mephisto Waltzes* of which no. 1 (➤*Faust*) is the well-known one. Nos. 1 and 2, written for orchestra, were transcribed both for piano solo and for piano duet; no.

3 is for piano; no. 4 (unfinished, not published till 1952) is also for piano.

Mephistopheles, opera by Boito. ➤*Mefistofele*.

Mer, La (Fr., 'The Sea'), 'three symphonic sketches' by Debussy, first performed in 1905: (1) 'From Dawn to Midday on the Sea'; (2) 'Play of the Waves'; (3) 'Dialogue of the Wind and the Sea'. Also title of an orchestral work (1892) by Gilson.

Mérante, Louis (1828–87), French choreographer. ➤*Deux Pigeons*, ➤*Sylvia*.

Merbecke, ➤Marbeck.

Mercadante, [Giuseppe] **Saverio** [Raffaele] (1795–1870), Italian composer of about 60 operas, including *Il Giuramento* ('The Oath') and *Orazi e Curiazi* ('The Horatii and Curiatii'); was also church musician and (1840) director of the Naples Conservatory. Became totally blind in 1862 but continued to compose.

Mercure, Pierre (1927–66), Canadian composer who studied in Paris, active in organizing modern music events in Montreal. (Killed in a car accident.) Works include electronic pieces on tape or for tape-plus-live performance; also *Kaleidoscope* for orchestra, *Dissidence* (three songs) for soprano and piano, etc.

Meredith, George (1828–1909), British poet and novelist. ➤*Lark Ascending*.

Merikanto, Aare (1893–1958), Finnish composer of opera *Juha*, three symphonies, four violin concertos, etc.

Merrie England, operetta by German with libretto by Basil Hood. Produced in London, 1902. Queen Elizabeth I is seen in a relationship of love and jealousy, with May Day and other traditional symbolism.

Merrill, Robert (b. 1919), American baritone who sang with the Metropolitan Opera, New York, in more than 700 performances from 1945; author of autobiography.

Merry Widow, The, operetta by Lehár. ➤*Lustige Witwe*.

Merry Wives of Windsor, The, play by Shakespeare, operatically set by Verdi (➤*Falstaff*), by Vaughan Williams (*Sir John in Love*) and by Nicolai who used a German translation of the title, *Die* ➤*lustigen Weiber von Windsor*.

Merulo [original surname Merlotti], **Claudio** (1533–1604), Italian composer of music for stage and church: noted organist (at St Mark's, Venice) and composer for the organ.

messa (It.), (1) a placing or putting – see next entry; (2) Mass (Lat., ➤*missa*). So *Messa da Requiem*, title used (e.g. by Verdi) for a musical setting of the ➤*Requiem*; *Messa di Gloria*, publisher's title (1951) for Puccini's Mass (1880).

messa di voce (It., placing of the voice), the steady swelling and decreasing of vocal volume in one long-held note.

Messager, André [Charles Prosper] (1853–1929), French composer of *Mirette, Monsieur Beaucaire* (both in English), *Véronique* and other operettas, and of ballets (including *Les* ➤*Deux Pigeons*), piano duets, etc. Also distinguished opera conductor, e.g. of the first performances of Debussy's ➤*Pelléas et Mélisande*, dedicated to him.

Messe (Fr., Ger.), ➤Mass.

Messiaen, Olivier [Eugène Prosper Charles] (1908–92), French composer who through all his years of international celebrity also maintained his position as church organist in Paris; noted teacher of composition. His interest in Indian music emerged in his ➤*Turangalîla Symphonie*; made use of the ➤Ondes Martenot in this and other compositions. Developed an almost literal instrumentation of bird-song in various works including *Le reveil des oiseaux* ('The Birds' Awakening') for piano and orchestra. Also wrote various works with Roman Catholic associations, including *Vingt regards sur l'enfant Jésus* ('Twenty Looks at the Child Jesus') for piano, ➤*Visions de l'Amen* for two pianos; also opera ➤*Saint François d'Assise*, songs, organ works, chamber music including ➤*Quatuor pour la fin du temps*. His wife Yvonne ➤Loriod was among his chief interpreters.

Messiah (not *The Messiah*), oratorio by Handel, first performed in Dublin, 1742. Words selected from the Bible by C. Jennens.

mesto (It.), sad.

metà (It.), half.

Metamorphosen (Ger., 'Metamorphoses'), work for 23 solo strings by R. Strauss, inscribed 'In Memoriam', quoting the funeral march from Beethoven's ➤*Eroica* symphony and being apparently a dirge for lost Germany. First performed in 1946.

metamorphosis, term used to describe the way a composer may change a theme – altering tempo and rhythm, even notes, but preserving something essential and recognizable. This device has its obvious use in ➤illustrative music, and is also used elsewhere, e.g. in some symphonies (Franck's, Elgar's no. 1). Hindemith wrote an orchestral piece called *Symphonic Metamorphoses of* [in English references usually mistranslated as *on*] *Themes of Weber* (1943).

Metastasio, Pietro (1698–1782), Italian poet and dramatist whose opera librettos were repeatedly set by composers. ➤*Clemenza di Tito*.

meter, US spelling of ➤metre.

metre, term used in prosody to cover the relationship between accented and unaccented beats, and sometimes similarly used in music – e.g. 3/8 and 6/8 being described as different kinds of *metres*. Usually the term ➤*rhythm* is so defined as to cover this relationship along with others; but some writers define rhythm and *metre* as mutually exclusive, *metre* concerned with the basic unvarying pulse (as above) and rhythm with the actual time-patterns of notes effected by the composer with reference to this basic pulse. The usage *common metre*, etc., with reference to hymns, alludes to the verse, not to the music.

metrical, of ➤metre, so (referring to the verse, not the music) *metrical psalm*, a psalm translated and versified in a regular syllabic metre, and thus singable to an ordinary hymn-tune.

metronome, apparatus for sounding an adjustable number of beats per minute. The mechanical instrument which was formerly universal is that patented in 1814 by J. N. Maelzel (1772–1838) who stole the invention from D. N. Winkel. Electric/electronic instruments have substantially replaced it. A composer wishing for 60 quarter-note (crochet) beats in one minute writes 'MM [Maelzel's Metronome] ♩ = 60'. Metronome marks for early works are added by some modern editors. The mechanical metronome has jokingly been used as a performing instrument (➤Ligeti, ➤Muldowney).

Metropolitan Opera House (New York), the principal opera house of the United States, opened in 1883, rehoused in 1966. James Levine has been music director since 1975.

Meyer, Kerstin [Margareta] (b. 1928), Swedish mezzo-soprano wellknown in opera; in 1960 first appeared at Covent Garden and at the Metropolitan (New York), in 1962 at the Bayreuth Festival. Hon. CBE, 1985.

Meyerbeer, Giacomo (originally Jakob Liebmann Meyer Beer) (1791–1864), German composer of opera in Italian, German and especially French – including *Robert le diable* ('Robert the Devil'), *Les* ➤*Huguenots*, *Le Prophète*, *L'*➤*Africaine*. These are noted for spectacle and for a striking use of the orchestra. Visited Italy; settled in Paris, 1826, and died there, but was also active in Berlin from 1842 as musical director to the King of Prussia. Wrote also church music, marches, songs, etc.

Meyerowitz, Jan (originally Hans-Hermann) (b. 1913), German-born composer, naturalized American 1951. Works with Jewish allusions include opera *Esther*; other works include flute concerto, settings of Cummings, Emily Dickinson, Herrick.

mezzo, mezza (It.), half. So *mezza voce*, at half voice. i.e. with restricted tone;

mezzo-forte (abbr. *mf*), midway between loud and soft; *mezzo-soprano*, type of female voice halfway between soprano and contralto range. The form *mezzo-contralto* is sometimes encountered, supposedly meaning a little lower than mezzo-soprano.

mf, ➤mezzo.

m.g., left hand (in piano-playing, etc.; Fr., *main gauche*).

mi, the note E (in Latin countries, and formerly elsewhere); the tonic sol-fa symbol ➤me is derived from it. ➤tritone.

Miaskovsky, ➤Myaskovsky.

Michelangeli, Arturo Benedetti (1920–95), Italian pianist, touring widely, first heard in Britain in 1946; noted also as teacher. Greatly esteemed, he made his appearances a rarity. (His surname is really a double one, Benedetti Michelangeli, but in English-speaking use he is commonly referred to only as Michelangeli.).

Michelangelo [Michelagniolo Buonarroti] (1475–1564), Italian poet, sculptor and painter. ➤Britten.

Mickiewicz, Adam (1798–1885), Polish poet. ➤ballade.

microtone, an interval smaller than a semitone. (An alternative name is 'fractional tone'.) ➤Quarter-tones, systematically exploited by A. Hába and others, have also had occasional use in more 'orthodox' contexts, e.g. the string parts of Bloch's chamber music. Third-tone tuning has been used by ➤Ohana.

Midday, name given to one of a set of three symphonies by Haydn: ➤Morning.

middle C, the note C found at approximately the middle of the piano keyboard. It is commonly tuned to 261.6 Hz. (➤frequency).

Midi, Le, title of one of a set of three symphonies by Haydn: ➤Morning.

Midori [her forename; mother's surname Goto] (b. 1971), Japanese violinist; child prodigy, trained by her mother and then at Juilliard School, New York; introduced by Mehta as 'surprise guest' with New York Philharmonic Orchestra, 1982, she now lives in New York, touring internationally (London 1987); has recorded both Bartók's concertos, etc.

Midsummer Marriage, The, opera by Tippett produced in London, 1955. Libretto by composer, applying ancient myth to modern characters (and having parallels to *Die* ➤*Zauberflöte*). A set of *Ritual Dances* for chorus and orchestra is drawn from this.

Midsummer Night's Dream, A, play by Shakespeare which has had various musical treatments. Mendelssohn composed an overture in 1826 (when he was 17), and other incidental music including the celebrated 'Wedding March' in 1842. Incidental music to the play has also been written by Orff (1939). Britten's opera of the same title (produced at Aldeburgh, 1960) has Shakespeare's actual text (abbreviated by the composer and Peter Pears) as its libretto. Among other operas on the play is one by Werle in Swedish (1985). Other works referring to it include *The* ➤*Fairy Queen* (Purcell), ➤*Mignon* (A. Thomas) and, punningly, Schnittke ➤*(K)ein Sommer-nachtstraum*.

Mighty Five, The, an alternative English term for the ➤Mighty Handful.

Mighty Handful, The, English translation of Rus. *moguchaya kuchka*, term invented by the critic Stasov, later applied to Balakirev, Borodin, Cui, Musorgsky and Rimsky-Korsakov. These five Russian composers took up a consciously 'nationalist' standpoint in music, drawing much on Russian history, literature, folk-music and folk-lore generally.

Mignon, opera by A. Thomas, produced in Paris, 1866. Libretto by J. Barbier and M. Carré, after Goethe's *Wilhelm Meister*. The soprano aria 'I am Titania' occurs with reference to a performance (within the action of the opera) of *A Midsummer Night's Dream*.

Mignone, Francisco (1897–1986), Brazilian composer who studied in Italy. Works include opera *O contractador dos diamantes* ('The Diamond Broker'), incorporating a dance called 'Cogada' which is also given as a concert work; a *Sinfonia tropical*; piano solos. Some of his works are indebted to Brazilian folk-lore.

Migot, Georges Elbert (1891–1976), French composer, also writer on music. Works include oratorios, 13 symphonies and *Sinfonia da chiesa* (It., Church Symphony) for 85 wind instruments, solo works for piano and for harpsichord.

Mihalovici, Marcel (1898–1985), Romanian-born composer who settled in Paris in 1919; French citizen 1955. Works include opera *Krapp* (after Beckett's *Krapp's Last Tape*), five symphonies, *Concerto quasi una fantasia* for violin and orchestra, chamber music. Wife was the pianist Monique Haas.

Mihály, András (b. 1917), Hungarian composer, also conductor. Works include three symphonies, opera *To-gether and Alone, Chamber Music* (on texts by James Joyce) for voice and piano.

Mikado, The, or The Town of Titipu, operetta by Sullivan, produced in London, 1885; libretto by W. S. Gilbert. Set in an imaginary Japan, it was its creators' most successful work and has been subjected to various adaptations; filmed versions appeared in 1938 and 1966.

Mikrokosmos (Gk., 'Microcosm'), piano work by Bartók, composed between 1926 and 1937; it consists of 153 small pieces in the nature of technical studies, progressively arranged.

Milán, Luis (*c.* 1500–*c.* 1561), Spanish player of the ➤*vihuela* (Spanish form of lute), and composer of music for it; also composer of songs with vihuela accompaniment in Spanish, Portuguese and Italian – including one of the first published books of songs for a single voice with accompaniment, 1536.

Milhaud, Darius (1892–1974), French composer, one of the group of composers called *Les* ➤*Six*. Associated with various important literary figures, especially Claudel (opera ➤*Christophe Colomb* and other works) and Cocteau (ballets, etc.). Visited Brazil and USA and was influenced by jazz as early as 1922–3 (*La* ➤*Création du monde*) and also by Latin-American music (➤*saudades*; ➤*Scaramouche*). Very prolific, his other works include operas *Bolivar* and *David*; 18 symphonies; 18 string quartets, of which nos. 14–15 can be played separately or together; Jewish liturgical music; many songs. In USA during World War II, and frequently afterwards. ➤*Beggar's Opera*; ➤Zabaleta.

military band, conventional British name for the type of wind-band used in most countries' armed services, consisting of brass and woodwind (not brass alone: ➤brass band) with percussion. The instruments and numbers vary considerably between countries and to a lesser extent within them. A British band of a large late-20th-century type typically uses flute, piccolo, oboe, clarinets, bassoons, saxophones, horns (orchestral), cornets (sometimes trumpets), trombones, euphoniums and tubas, plus percussion, with a double-bass often added when not on the march. ➤concert band; ➤symphonic band.

Military Symphony, nickname for Haydn's Symphony no. 100 in G (Hob. I: 100; first performed in 1794, on Haydn's visit to London), having 'military band' effects from bass drum, cymbals and triangle.

Miller, Arthur (b. 1915), American dramatist. ➤Ward (R.), ➤Rossellini.

Millöcker, Karl (1842–99), Austrian composer of operettas, notably *Der* ➤*Bettelstudent.*

Milne, A. A. [Alan Alexander] (1882–1956), British writer and poet. ➤ Fraser-Simson.

Milner, Anthony [Francis Dominic] (b. 1925), British composer who has written chiefly vocal music including unaccompanied Mass, cantata *The City of Desolation*, and other works with Roman Catholic associations; also works for orchestra, wind band, piano, etc.

Milnes, Sherrill [Eustace] (b. 1935), American baritone, eminent in opera; first appearance at the Metropolitan (New York), 1965, at Covent Garden,

1971. Has also conducted operatic recordings.

Milstein, Nathan [Mironovich] (1904–93), Russian-born American violinist, pupil of Auer and Ysaÿe; eminent soloist, and also arranger of violin pieces.

Milton, John (*c.* 1563–1647), English composer, father of the poet (below). Contributed a madrigal to *The* ➤*Triumphs of Oriana* and wrote other vocal music, fantasies for viols, etc.

Milton, John (1608–74), English poet. ➤*Comus*, ➤*Paradise Lost*, ➤*Schöpfung*, ➤Lawes (H.), ➤Markevich.

mime, acting without speech; a stage piece consisting of such (sometimes given with music).

min., abbr. for minor (scale, etc.).

minacciando (It.), threatening.

Mines of Sulphur, The, opera by Richard Rodney Bennett, produced in London, 1965; libretto, by Beverley Cross, is a ghost-story. The title is metaphorical and a quotation from Shakespeare's *Othello*.

miniature score, ➤score.

minim, ➤half-note.

minimalism, a compositional tendency evolving from the 1960s, particularly evident in the work of such American composers as Riley, Glass and Adams and, among British composers, Michael Nyman; short units of basic harmony and rhythm are cumulated by repetition with little variation.

Minkus, Léon [originally Aloisius Ludwig Minkus] (1826–1917), Austrian-born composer who settled in Russia but died in Vienna; composed mainly for ballet – including the celebrated *Don Quixote* (choreography by Petipa), 1869, and *La* ➤*Bayadère*.

Minnesinger (Ger., sing. and pl.; also as English word), type of minstrel flourishing in guilds in 12th- and 13th-century Germany. By social origin these singers were aristocratic; the ➤Mastersingers who flourished afterwards were of the merchant class.

Minnesota Orchestra, American orchestra founded in 1903 as Minneapolis Symphony Orchestra, taking its present name in 1986; conductors have included Doráti (1949–60), Marriner (1979–86), and currently De Waart.

minor, term opposed to ➤major and applied to scales, keys, chords and intervals.

minore (It.), minor (in the above sense); the word is often used in a 'theme and variations' to label a minor-key variation of a major-key theme.

minstrel (1) general term applied in modern usage to a type of medieval musical performer, usually singing to his own accompaniment, and usually belonging to a guild or other recognized company; in medieval times such performers were classed more particularly (see, e.g., ➤*jongleur*, ➤Mastersinger, ➤*Minnesinger*, ➤*Troubadour*, ➤*Trouvère*; (2) term applied to a black-faced (imitation-Negro) entertainer such as were organized into troupes in USA in the 1830s and later elsewhere. Debussy's *Minstrels*, in his second book of piano preludes, refers to these.

Minton, Yvonne (b. 1938), Australian

mezzo-soprano resident in London, singing Wagner roles at Covent Garden, Bayreuth (Waltraute in *The Ring*, 1976), etc.; also sang Geschwitz in the first complete *Lulu*, Paris, 1979. Her recordings embrace Elgar, Tippett, Boulez.

Mintz, Shlomo (b. 1957), Russian-born Israeli violinist; also viola-player and (1989–93) music director of Israel Chamber Orchestra. Has recorded both Prokofiev's concertos, under Abbado; also many standard concertos and the unaccompanied Bach sonatas.

minuet, minuetto (Eng., It.), dance in triple time of French rustic origin, 'promoted' to court use and becoming widely fashionable in the 18th century. It forms the standard third movement of the 'classical' (Haydn–Mozart) sonata, symphony, string quartet, etc., later developing with Beethoven into the ➤*scherzo*. It is normally in AABA form, the 'B' being in contrast and called 'trio' because of the French custom (long since dropped) of writing it in only three parts. ➤Boccherini.

Minute Waltz, nickname for Chopin's Waltz in D♭, op. 64, no. 1 (published in 1847) – bestowed evidently by someone too insensitive to realize that it can be played in one minute only if taken too fast.

Miracle, The, nickname for Haydn's Symphony no. 96 in D (Hob. I: 96) – because, when Haydn directed its first performance in London in 1791, a chandelier was supposed to have fallen on a vacant space in a crowded hall, hitting no one. This incident is now known to have happened at another concert, so the nickname no longer has a historical basis.

Miraculous Mandarin, The (Hung., *A csodálatos mandarin*), one-act mime-play with music by Bartók (scenario by M. Lengyel), composed 1919; produced in Cologne, 1926; source of a concert suite first performed in 1928. The mandarin, though stabbed and hanged by robbers, refuses to die until the robbers' woman yields herself to him.

Mireille, opera by Gounod, produced in Paris, 1864. Libretto by M. Carré, after a Provençal poem. A rustic tale sauced with the supernatural. The heroine (uniquely in opera!) dies of sunstroke.

mirliton (Fr.), ➤kazoo.

Miroglio, Francis (b. 1924), French composer (also poet and painter), whose works include *Horizons courbes* (Fr., 'Curving Horizons') for instrumental ensemble including sitar, *Ping-Squash* for two percussionists with a third musician as umpire of the 'game'.

Miroirs (Fr., 'Mirrors'), set of five piano pieces by Ravel, 1905; the fourth is the *Alborada del gracioso* (➤*alborada*) which he afterwards orchestrated.

mirror canon, mirror fugue, a canon or fugue in which two or more ➤parts appear on paper simultaneously both the right way up and upside down – i.e. as if a mirror lay between them, making one the reflection of the other. (The use of the term for a piece that can be played backwards – i.e. as if a mirror could be put at the end – is sometimes encountered but is not correct.)

Mirzoyan, Edvard (b. 1921), Armenian composer of cantatas (one called *Soviet Armenia*), *Introduction and Per-* *petuum Mobile* for violin and orchestra, a trombone concerto, etc.

Misa (Sp.), ➤mass; *Misa flamenca*, ➤Peña.

Misérables, Les (Fr., 'The Wretched'), 'musical tragedy' with text by Alain Boublil and Jean-Marc Natel based on the novel by Victor Hugo; music by Claude-Michel Schönberg. Produced in Paris, 1980. With a paroled convict, whores, beggars, student revolutionaries and an avenging police inspector.

Miserere, the name in the Roman Catholic Church for Psalm 50 (51 in the Hebrew and English Bibles), often set by composers, famously by ➤Allegri. A setting is incorporated into *Il* ➤*Trovatore*.

missa (Lat.), Mass. So *Missa brevis*, either (1) a setting of the Mass in unusually concise musical form, or (2) a setting of the Kyrie and Gloria only, in obsolete Lutheran usage, such as Bach composed in the opening two movements of his so-called Mass in B minor; *Missa sine nomine* ('Mass without a name'), Mass of entirely original material, not based on a plainsong or secular tune (term used in the 15th and 16th centuries, when the latter was the common practice, the Mass then taking the name of its source). So also *Missa solemnis*, term sometimes used by composers for a lengthy and exalted setting of the Mass – and now particularly associated with Beethoven's Mass in D (first performance, St Petersburg, 1824), so entitled. ➤parody.

Missa Papae Marcelli, a Mass by Palestrina dedicated to Marcellus II, who became Pope in 1555.

misura (It.), a measure (in various

senses); *senza misura*, not in strict time (e.g. of a passage in which bar-lines are omitted).

mit (Ger.), with.

Mitropoulos, Dmitri (1896–1960), Greek-born American conductor, also pianist and composer; gave premières of works by Hindemith, Copland, Barber (opera *Vanessa*) and other composers. Conductor of New York Philharmonic Orchestra, 1949–57.

mixed chorus, mixed voices, etc., a body comprising both male and female (adult) voices.

Mixolydian mode, the ➤mode represented by the white notes on the piano from G to G.

mixture, type of organ-stop simultaneously sounding two or more of the higher tones (other than octaves) of the ➤harmonic series. A stop sounding two such tones is said to be a mixture of two 'ranks' (and so forth); and the number of ranks is indicated in organ specifications by roman figures. The *mixture* is used in conjunction with 'normal' stops to add richness to the tone.

Mladi (Cz., 'Youth'), title of wind sextet by Janáček, first performed in 1924.

MM, ➤metronome.

M.Mus., abbr. of Master of Music (degree between 'Bachelor' and 'Doctor' of Music, awarded at some universities).

modal, of the ➤modes. See next entry.

mode (1) a way of ordering the notes of a scale; so *major mode, minor mode,* the ➤major and ➤minor scale or key. Most commonly, the term identifies

the so-called *modal system,* classifying the types of scale founded on ➤Gregorian chant and prevalent in west-European art-music before the rise of the major/minor key-system in the late 16th century. Each *mode* may be approximated on the white notes of the piano keyboard, differentiated according to the note on which the melody comes to rest (the *final*). The *Dorian mode* takes D as its final; the *Phrygian,* E; the *Lydian,* F; the *Mixolydian,* G – the names but not the usages being borrowed from Ancient Greek. Two late additions, the *Aeolian* with A as final and the *Ionian* with C as final, anticipate the minor and major respectively. All these are further identified as *authentic* modes with the implication of a melody lying within an octave of the final (e.g. in the range D to D for the Dorian mode); each has a corresponding *plagal* mode denoted by the prefix *hypo-,* with the melodic range spanning both sides of the final – e.g. *Hypodorian,* the final being D as in the Dorian but the melodic range A to A. Thus the modal system links the *kind* of scale with the *pitch* of the scale – though a later composer reviving modal practice may of course transpose by recourse to what would be black notes on the piano keyboard; (2, *rhythmic mode*), a designation of rhythmic pattern (particularly with reference to medieval music), classifying how beats are grouped and subdivided.

moderato (It.), at a moderate pace. It is also used after another tempo-direction, e.g. *allegro moderato,* implying 'a moderate allegro', i.e. that the word 'allegro' is not to be taken in an extreme sense.

modinha, type of Portuguese (and

hence Brazilian) popular song mainly flourishing in the 18th and 19th centuries.

modo (It.), manner; *in modo di*, in the manner of.

modulate (1) to change from one key to another in the course of a composition – such a change being accomplished by 'continuous' musical means (i.e. not simply by starting afresh in another key) and having a definite validity in the structural organization of the music. Hence *modulation* and ➤*style modulation*; (2) in electronic music, to change a characteristic (e.g., frequency, amplitude) of a sound; hence *modulator*, a device to effect this.

modulator, diagram used for instructional purposes in ➤tonic sol-fa for practice in sight-reading and modulation; (2) a device in electronic music; ➤modulate (2).

Moeran, E. J. [Ernest John] (1894–1950), British composer of a symphony, Sinfonietta, violin concerto, cello concerto, chamber music, piano solos, etc.; also a collector of Norfolk folk-songs.

Mohaupt, Richard (1904–57), German-born composer (also conductor), who settled in USA, 1939, but returned to Europe, 1955, and died in Austria. Works include *Die Wirtin von Pinsk* ('The Hostess of Pinsk', based on Napoleon's invasion of Russia) and other operas, symphony, a violin concerto.

Moïse, ➤*Mosè in Egitto*.

Moiseiwitsch (German transliteration of Rus. 'Moiseivich'), **Benno** (1890–1963), Russian-born pianist who set-

tled in Britain during World War I and was naturalized in 1937. Noted interpreter of Rakhmaninov.

Molière [Jean Baptiste Poquelin] (1622–73), French dramatist. ➤ *Ariadne auf Naxos*, ➤*Bourgeois Gentilhomme*, ➤Charpentier (M. A.), ➤Lully.

Molinaro, Simone (*c.* 1565–1615), Italian lutenist and composer of lute music, madrigals and church music; director of music at Genoa Cathedral.

Molique, [Wilhelm] Bernard (1802–69), German violinist and composer of six violin concertos, eight string quartets, and other works including a concerto for the concertina. Lived in London, 1849–66.

moll (Ger.), ➤minor; so *D-moll*, D minor, etc.

Molloy, James Lyman (1837–1909), Irish amateur composer of 'Love's Old Sweet Song' and similar popular Victorian songs; London barrister by profession.

Molter, Johann [Melchior] (1696–1765), German composer of 167 symphonies, and of concertos for clarinet, for one and two trumpets, etc.

molto (It.), much, very; so, e.g., *allegro molto* or (more rarely) *allegro di molto*, very fast.

moment (1) see the following entry; (2) a structural concept in composition devised by Stockhausen; a 'moment' is a normally brief segment of a composition with its own musical characteristic. Occurrences within each 'moment' may be held more important than the succession between moments, and such a succession may indeed be indeterminate, as in Stockhausen's work entitled *Momente* (Ger.

plural form) for soprano, four choirs and 13 instruments, 1964. Hence *moment-form* as description of such a work.

Moment Musical (Fr., pl. *Moments musicaux*), title given by Schubert to each of a set of six short pieces for piano, completed 1828 (D780), and afterwards used similarly by other composers.

Mompou, Federico (1893–1987), Spanish pianist and composer, mainly for the piano but also of songs; he lived at different periods in Barcelona and Paris.

Monaco, Mario Del, ➤Del Monaco.

Monckton, Lionel (1861–1924), British composer of *The Country Girl* and other musical comedies, etc.; collaborated with H. Talbot in *The* ➤*Arcadians*.

Mondo della luna, Il (It., 'The World of the Moon'), opera by Haydn (Hob. XXVIII: 7), produced in Eszterháza, 1777. Libretto by Goldoni, about an astronomer so absorbed in his study of the moon that he allows his daughters to accept 'unsuitable' suitors.

Mondonville, Jean-Joseph Cassanéa de (1711–72), French violinist, composer and court musical director; composed operas, oratorios, violin sonatas, etc.

Moniuszko, Stanisław (1819–72), Polish composer who is regarded as the chief 19th-century composer of his country, after Chopin – especially through his opera ➤*Halka*. Wrote other operas, many songs and much church music. Was also conductor.

Monk, Meredith [Jane] (b. 1942), American composer mainly of vocal works often with extended techniques including operas *Vessel* (1972, for 75 solo voices, electric organ, accordion, two dulcimers) and *Atlas* (1991, with unusual chamber orchestra).

Monk, William Henry (1823–89), English organist and composer of 'Abide with Me' and other hymns, etc.; editor of *Hymns Ancient and Modern*, 1861.

Monn, Georg Matthias (1717–50), Austrian organist, and composer of the first extant symphony in four movements, with a minuet, 1740 (anticipating the Haydn–Mozart type). Also composed concertos, chamber music, church music, etc.

Monnot, Marguerite (1903–61), French composer for the musical theatre: ➤*Irma La Douce*.

monochord, scientific instrument consisting of a single string with a movable bridge, used (since the time of Ancient Egypt) for showing how, by altering the ratios in which the string is vibrating, different notes may be produced. These are the notes of the ➤harmonic series. A musical instrument based on this principle is the ➤*tromba marina*.

monodic, ➤monody.

monodrama, stage piece for one character; e.g. Schoenberg's ➤*Erwartung*. Berlioz's ➤*Lélio* is also so styled because it has only one actor – though many other performers (musicians, not actors).

monody (from Gk. for 'single song'), term used to describe the melody-and-➤continuo style of writing (e.g. in early 17th-century Italian opera) in contrast to the earlier polyphonic style when all parts were held as of equal importance (none simply as accompaniment). So also *monodic*.

monophony (from Gk. for 'single sound'), term used of music with a single line of melody (with neither harmonic support nor other melodies in counterpoint). It is sometimes used also even when a simple accompaniment is present, provided that the melody is self-sufficient. So also *monophonic*, often contrasted with ➤*polyphonic*.

monothematic, having only a single theme.

Monsigny, Pierre Alexandre (1729–1817), French composer, of a noble family. Wrote successful operas of the ➤*opéra-comique* type, including *Rose et Colas* and *Le Déserteur*. Ceased to compose in middle life, with the rise of Grétry.

Montague, Stephen [Rowley] (b. 1943), American composer and pianist who settled in London 1975. His *At the White Edge of Phrygia* exists in versions for chamber orchestra and full orchestra. Also wrote *Strummin'* for piano, strings, lighting and tape, and a series called *Paramell* for various instruments, piano concerto.

Monte, Philippe de (1521–1603), Flemish composer. Visited Italy and (briefly) England. Chapel music director to the Hapsburg emperors at Vienna and at Prague, where he died. Composed madrigals and similar works (more than 1,200 surviving), and also Masses, motets, etc.

Montéclair, Michel Pinolet de (1667–1737), French composer of operas, chamber music, etc.; in early life a church chorister, and afterwards player of double-bass and other stringed instruments in Paris.

Montemezzi, Italo (1875–1952), Italian composer of *L'amore dei tre re* ('The Love of the Three Kings') and other operas; also orchestral works, Elegy for cello and piano, etc.

Monteux, Pierre (1875–1964), French conductor, active in Paris where in 1913 he gave the first (riot-provoking) performance of Stravinsky's *The Rite of Spring*. Later he was conductor of the Boston Symphony Orchestra (1919–24), Paris Symphony Orchestra (1929–35), San Francisco Symphony Orchestra, London Symphony Orchestra (1961–4).

Monteverdi, Claudio (1567–1643), Italian composer, notable in the history of opera, harmony and orchestration. Choirboy at his birthplace, Cremona; afterwards held various state and church musical positions in Mantua and elsewhere — finally in Venice, where he died. Became a priest, 1632. His operas (usually considered history's first major operas) include ➤*Orfeo, Il* ➤*Ritorno di Ulisse* and (when he was 75) *L'*➤*incoronazione di Poppea*. Some other operas are lost. Wrote also more than 250 madrigals (some with independent instrumental parts; ➤madrigal), including a few 'madrigali spirituali' (to religious words); Masses, two settings of the Magnificat, ➤*Vespro della Beata Vergine* and other church music – but no purely instrumental works. ➤*ballo*; ➤*Combattimento di Tancredi e Clorinda*.

Montreal Symphony Orchestra, Canadian orchestra which adopted that title (and its French equivalent) in 1953. Conductor since 1977, Charles Dutoit.

Montsalvatge, Xavier [Bassols] (b. 1912), Spanish (Catalan) composer.

Works include opera *El gato con botas* ('Puss in Boots'), *Poema concertante* for violin and orchestra, songs and piano solos.

Moog, Robert (b. 1934), inventor of ➤synthesizer named after him.

Moonlight Sonata, nickname (not Beethoven's, and fitting only the first movement) for Beethoven's Piano Sonata in C♯ minor, op. 27, no. 2 (1801).

Moór, Emanuel (1863–1931), Hungarian pianist, composer (operas, eight symphonies, etc.), conductor and inventor of what he called the Duplex-Coupler piano (1921) with two keyboards tuned an octave apart. Settled in Switzerland and died there.

Moore, Douglas [Stuart] (1893–1969), American composer; pupil of d'Indy, N. Boulanger and Bloch. Works (several alluding to American history and legend) include operas *The Devil and Daniel Webster* and *The* ➤*Ballad of Baby Doe*; also composed two symphonies, chamber music, works for amateur performers, etc.

Moore, Gerald (1899–1987), British pianist who created a new dignity for the art of the song-accompanist, retiring in 1967 but continuing to write and lecture. CBE, 1954.

Moore, Thomas (1779–1852), Irish poet who wrote (to Irish traditional tunes) the words of 'The Last Rose of Summer' (➤*Martha*) and 'The Minstrel Boy', etc. His poem *Lalla Rookh* also prompted music by such composers as Schumann (➤*Paradies und die Peri*).

Morales, Cristóbal (*c.* 1500–1553), Spanish composer, also priest. For a time was singer in the Papal Chapel in Rome, afterwards holding cathedral music posts in Spain. Composed Masses, motets and other church music; also a few madrigals.

morality, description ('a morality' instead of 'an opera') given by Vaughan Williams to *The* ➤*Pilgrim's Progress*, with allusion to medieval 'morality plays' on religious subjects..

morbido (It.), gentle, delicate (not 'morbid'). So *morbidezza*, delicacy, etc.

morceau (Fr.), a piece (of bread, music, etc.).

mordent, musical ornament which in its standard form consists of a rapid switch from a main note to a subsidiary note a step below, and back again. In this form it is also called a *lower mordent*, having the sign ∿ . Its variant, the *inverted mordent* (also called *upper mordent*), having the sign ∿, has a switch to the note *above*. But the definition of *mordent* and the interpretation of both signs has differed between countries and periods.

Moreau, Jean Baptiste (1656–1733), French composer of church music, stage works, songs, etc. Teacher of both singing and composition, and held a court post under Louis XIV.

morendo (It.), dying – direction aimed not at the performer but at the music, which is to lose force and (if necessary) speed.

Mörike, Eduard Friedrich (1804–75), German poet. *Mörike-Lieder* is the usual name for a set of 53 songs by Wolf (1888) to his verse. Wolf also wrote four earlier settings of Mörike.

Morley, Thomas (1557/8–1602), English composer, pupil of Byrd; organist of St Paul's Cathedral, London, and member of the Chapel Royal. Writer of textbook, *A Plain and Easy Introduction to Practical Music*. His setting of 'It was a lover and his lass' from Shakespeare's *As You Like it* may have been for the original production of the play (1599). He also wrote Latin and English church music, madrigals, ➤balletts (he introduced this form to England), canzonets for two and more voices, solo songs with lute, pieces for viols and for keyboard. Editor of and contributor to *The ➤Triumphs of Oriana*.

Morning; Midday; Evening and Tempest, titles given respectively to Symphonies nos. 6–8 by Haydn, *c.* 1761 (Hob. I: 6–8). The music has illustrative intent, though no explicit clues are given. Haydn affixed the titles in French, the international 'polite' language of the time – *Le Matin*, *Le Midi*, *Le Soir et la tempête*, the last being also known sometimes simply as *Le Soir*.

morris, type of English folk-dance associated with Whitsuntide and historically performed by men, the dancers wearing bells; traditionally accompanied by ➤*pipe* and ➤*tabor*. The supposed derivation from *moresca*/*Moorish* is not proved. ➤Finnissy, ➤Grainger.

Morris, William (1834–96), British poet and artist. ➤Harrison.

Morton, Robert (*c.*1430–*c.*1476), English composer of *chansons*, etc.; in service to the court of Burgundy.

Moscheles, Ignaz (1794–1870), German-Bohemian pianist and composer (eight piano concertos, etc., now hardly ever performed); friend of Beethoven, teacher of Mendelssohn. Resident in England as teacher (and also conductor), 1826–46.

Mosè in Egitto (It., 'Moses in Egypt'), opera by Rossini, originally in Italian,

produced in Naples, 1818, with libretto by A. N. Tottola; revised and enlarged version in French (*Moïse*), produced in Paris, 1827, with libretto by G. L. Balochi and V. J. E. de Jouy. A love-story is added to the biblical narrative, ending with the drowning of the Egyptians in the Red Sea.

Moses, opera by Rossini. ➤*Mosè in Egitto*.

Moses und Aron (Ger., 'Moses and Aaron'), opera by Schoenberg. The libretto, by the composer, exists complete, but he finished the music of only the first two (out of three) acts. The work was first performed posthumously on the Hamburg radio station, 1954, and first staged in Zurich, 1957.

Mosolov, Alexander Vasilievich (1900–1973), Russian composer (also pianist). Won wide notice with orchestral piece *Iron Foundry*, 1928, incorporating a metal sheet, shaken. Other works include six symphonies, a harp concerto, operas.

mosso (It.), moving, animated.

Mossolov, a frequently encountered (but strictly mistaken) spelling for the Russian composer ➤Mosolov.

Most Happy Fella, The, musical with text by Frank Loesser based on *They Knew What They Wanted* by Sidney Howard; music and lyrics by Frank Loesser. Produced in New York, 1956. A middle-aged Italian immigrant to California's fruit-growing area is the hero.

Moszkowski, Moritz (1854–1925), Polish-German pianist and composer, dying in poverty in Paris. Composed sets of Spanish dances for piano duet; also a piano concerto, operas, etc.

motet (1, normal current use) type of church choral composition, usually in Latin, to words not fixed in the liturgy – corresponding in the Roman Catholic service to the ➤anthem (in English) in the Anglican service; (2, exceptionally) type of work related to the preceding but not exactly conforming to it – e.g. Parry's *Songs of Farewell* (designated by the composer as *motets*) which are choral and 'serious' but not ecclesiastical; (3, medieval use) a polyphonic vocal composition based on a 'given' tenor part, over which the upper voice or voices (up to three) moved at a faster rate. In the French secular motet the upper parts commonly had different texts from the Latin tenor and might be in the vernacular (hence *polytextual motet*).

Mother Goose, suite by Ravel. ➤*Ma mère l'oye*.

motif (Fr.), term sometimes used in English for ➤leading-motive and sometimes simply for 'theme', etc.; better avoided because of its ambiguities.

motion, term used to describe the course upwards or downwards of a melody or melodies. A single melody is said to move by *conjunct motion* or *disjunct motion* according to whether a note moves to an adjacent note or to some other note (i.e. by a 'step' or by a 'leap'). Apart from this, two melodies move by *similar motion* (in the same direction, i.e. up or down together), or by *contrary motion* (one up, one down), or by *oblique motion* (one remaining on the same note, the other not). *Parallel motion* is 'similar motion' of such a kind that the parts not only move up and down together, but do so 'in parallel', preserving the same interval between them.

Motiv, motive (Ger., Eng.), a short recognizable melodic or rhythmic figure – term used especially to indicate the smallest possible subdivision in musical analysis, one ➤theme possibly having several *motives*. But the term ➤leading-motive conveys a larger type of unit and a different meaning.

moto (It.), movement; *con moto*, with movement; *moto perpetuo* (perpetual motion), title given to a rapid piece, usually having repetitive note-patterns – also (Lat.), *perpetuum mobile*.

Mottl, Felix [Josef] (1856–1911), Austrian conductor, arranger of orchestral music – e.g. from Gluck's stage works – and composer; one of Wagner's close associates, an early conductor at Bayreuth.

motto, motto theme, theme which, in the course of a piece of music, recurs (perhaps transformed) in the manner of a quotation – e.g. in Berlioz's ➤*Symphonie Fantastique* (where it is called *idée fixe*) and in Tchaikovsky's Symphony no. 5. The device is related to the ➤*metamorphosis* of themes.

Motu Proprio (Lat.), a type of decree issued by the Pope; in musical contexts referring particularly to that of Plus X, 1902, emphasizing the prime value of plainsong and Palestrina-period polyphony for the Roman Catholic Church, and curbing tendencies towards the employment in church of secular-style compositions, orchestral instruments, women's voices, etc.

'Mourning' Symphony, nickname for Haydn's Symphony no. 44 in E minor, *c.* 1772 (Hob. I: 44). Haydn wanted its slow movement to be played at his own funeral service.

Moussorgsky, ►Musorgsky.

mouth music, English equivalent for Gaelic *port á beul*, type of wordless but articulated singing used to accompany Scottish Highland dancing when no instrument is available. The equivalent is known in Ireland as 'lilting'.

mouth-organ, ►harmonica.

Mouton, Charles (1626–after 1700), French lutenist and composer of music for his instrument (and of church music). Held court post at Turin.

Mouton, Jean (*c.*1459–1522), French composer of Masses and other church music, also ►*chansons*; in service at the French court. Pupil of ►Josquin, teacher of Willaert.

mouvement (Fr.), (1) motion, pace; so (paralleling the Italian) *mouvement perpetuel* (►*moto perpetuo*); *au movement* (*a* ►*tempo*); *premier* (1*er*) *mouvement*, ►*tempo primo*; so also *mouvementé*, with movement; (2) a ►movement in the sense below.

movable doh, description of systems of sight-reading, etc., in which (e.g. in ►tonic sol-fa) *doh* represents the keynote, *ray* the note above, etc., whatever the key. (Opposite to systems where, as in Continental ►*solfeggio*, *do* is C, *re* is D, etc., whatever the key.)

movement, the primary self-contained division of a large composition – usually each having a separate indication of speed, hence the name. A large composition without any such division is said to be 'in one movement'. The word is used as a title in Stravinsky's *Movements* for piano and orchestra (short work in five sections, 1958–9).

movimento (It.), motion (not 'movement' in the preceding sense); *doppio movimento*, at double the preceding speed.

Mozart, [Johann Georg] **Leopold** (1719–87), German violinist and author of a famous violin 'method'; composer (►*Toy Symphony*); and father of the following. Settled in Salzburg, Austria.

Mozart, Wolfgang Amadeus (christened Joannes Chrysostomus Wolfgangus Theophilus) (1756–91), Austrian composer, born in Salzburg. With Haydn the chief exemplar of the Viennese-classical style, winning even greater esteem in the 20th century. His father ►Leopold Mozart took him and his sister on tour to Paris, London, etc., chiefly as harpsichord prodigies, in 1763–6. He had already begun to compose (Symphony no. 1, 1764; opera►*Bastien und Bastienne*); by 1773, he had thrice visited Italy and had entered the service of the Prince Archbishop of Salzburg. Disliking it, he left after a quarrel, 1781, settling in Vienna. Visited Prague (where ►*Don Giovanni* and *La* ►*clemenza di Tito* were produced), Berlin and elsewhere; died, poor, in Vienna, of typhus. Other operas include (chronologically) *La* ►*finta giardiniera*, ►*Idomeneo*, *Die* ►*Entführung aus dem Serail*, *Der* ►*Schauspieldirektor*, *Le* ►*nozze di Figaro*, ►*Così fan tutte*, *Die* ►*Zauberflöte*. Wrote also 21 concertos for piano, one for clarinet and various others (►*Symphonie concertante*), more than anyone else establishing classical concerto form. (Four further, juvenile piano concertos are arrangements of others' music.) His symphonies (including those nicknamed ►*Haffner*, ►*Linz*, ►*Prague*, ►*Paris*, ►*Jupiter*) have been numbered up to 41, but some of those so numbered are spurious and some other works of this kind are not so numbered. Composed various serenades (see ➤*Haffner*, ➤*Eine kleine Nachtmusik*); Ein ➤*Musikalische Spass* ('A Musical Joke'); 24 string quartets (some nicknamed, e.g. ➤*Prussian Quartets*), clarinet quintet, six string quintets and other chamber works; sonatas for violin and for harpsichord (or piano); Requiem (unfinished, completed by Süssmayr), 17 Masses, some works for Masonic use, isolated arias with orchestra and songs with piano. Some works are misattributed to him (➤*Wiegenlied*). His compositions are indexed by 'K' numbers, referring to the catalogue made by Ludwig von Köchel, first published in 1862, revised since.

Mozart and Salieri, opera by Rimsky-Korsakov, produced in Moscow, 1898 – a setting of Pushkin's dramatic poem, based on the (false) notion that Salieri poisoned Mozart.

Mozartiana, suite by Tchaikovsky, 1887 – orchestration of three piano works and the motet *Ave Verum Corpus* by Mozart.

Mravinsky, Yevgeny [Alexandrovich] (1903–88), Russian conductor, for 50 years associated with the Leningrad Philharmonic Orchestra; gave premières of five Shostakovich symphonies.

m.s., left hand (in piano-playing, etc.; It., *mano sinistra*).

MS, MSS, manuscript(s).

Mudarra, Alonso de (c. 1510–80), Spanish composer of music for the ➤*vihuela* (Spanish lute) – fantasias, dance music, etc.

Mudge, Richard (1718–63), British clergyman and composer, known for a set of six concertos (of ➤*concerto grosso* type).

Muette de Portici, La, ➤*Masaniello*.

Muffat, Georg (1653–1704), German organist and composer, possibly of Scottish descent. Studied in Paris and Rome; wrote keyboard music, works of ➤*concerto grosso* type, etc. Father of the following.

Muffat, Gottlieb (1690–1770), German composer of suites for harpsichord, fugues and other works for organ; himself an organist, in service to the court at Vienna.

muffle, to cover the surface of a drum with a cloth, producing an effect analogous to that of a ➤mute.

Muldowney, Dominic (b. 1952), British composer (also conductor); since 1976, musical director to (Royal) National Theatre, composing and arranging music for many productions. Other works include opera *Tango*, percussion concerto (the soloist's instruments including ➤boobams), trombone concerto, *Un carnaval cubiste* for ten brass players and metronome, ballet score *The Brontës*.

Mulè, Giuseppe (1885–1951), Italian cellist, and composer of opera, music to Greek plays, symphonic poems, etc.

Mulliner Book, a MS collection of English pieces (mainly for keyboard instrument, but a few for cittern and gittern) made by Thomas Mulliner and apparently dating approximately from 1550 to 1575; published in modern notation in 1951 and reckoned one of the most valuable sources of its period.

Mullova, Viktoria (b. 1959), Russian-born violinist, now Austrian, who made her London début in 1984. Her recordings include Vivaldi concertos with Abbado and Sibelius's with Ozawa, and Beethoven's 'Archduke' Trio with Previn and H. Schiff.

multimedia, term applied to mixtures of musical, visual, poetic and other events as practised by such composers as Berio and Lejaren Hiller, mainly from the early 1960s – often incorporating electronic means and excluding traditional 'mixtures' such as opera and ballet.

multiphonics, the production on an instrument (particularly woodwind instruments or trombone) of two or more notes simultaneously – by means of freak blowing, or by blowing and vocalizing at the same time.

multi-serialism, ➤series.

Mumma, Gordon (b. 1935), American composer who uses the term 'cybersonics' to indicate the use of computer-type electronics in his work – e.g. *Swarm* for violin, concertina, bowed cross-cut saw and cybersonic modification. Other works include *Gestures II* for two pianos.

Munch (originally **Münch**), **Charles** (1891–1968), French conductor who gave many first performances. Conductor of the Boston Symphony Orchestra, 1949–62; founded the Orchestre de Paris, 1967.

Mundy, John (c.1555–1630), English composer of church music, madrigals (one included in *The* ➤*Triumphs of Oriana*), pieces for viols, etc. Organist of St George's Chapel, Windsor. Son of the following.

Mundy, William (c.1529–1591), Eng-

lish composer of anthem 'O Lord, the maker of all things' formerly misattributed to Henry VIII) and other anthems, Latin motets, etc. Singer in the Chapel Royal but perhaps a secret Roman Catholic. Father of the preceding.

Munrow, David [John] (1942–76), British player of the recorder, crumhorn and other medieval (and later) instruments; founder-director of the Early Music Consort of London, 1967. He inspired a wide enthusiasm for ➤early music.

Muradely, Vano [Ilyich] (1908–70), Russian composer, pupil of Shcherbachev and Myaskovsky. Works include two symphonies, choral works, opera *The Great Friendship* (1947) – this work touching off the denunciation by Soviet officialdom in 1948 of Muradely and other composers (including Prokofiev and Shostakovich) for ➤formalism and other alleged faults.

Murail, Tristan (b. 1947), French composer whose works include *Time and Again* (title in English) for orchestra, *Random Access Memory* for electric guitars, percussion, synthesizers, and computers, and *The Seven Words of Christ on the Cross* (choral-orchestral).

murky bass, term of unknown origin, signifying (particularly in 18th-century music) a left-hand keyboard part proceeding in alternating notes an octave apart.

Murray, Ann (b. 1949), British (Irishborn) mezzo-soprano, in particular demand for male (➤*travesti*) roles in opera, playing Cherubino in *Le nozze di Figaro* at her Covent Garden début, 1976, and Sesto in *La clemenza di Tito* at Metropolitan Opera, 1984.

Murrill, Herbert [Henry John] (1909–52), British composer of opera *Man in Cage*, two cello concertos (no. 2 on a Catalan folk-song and dedicated to Casals), etc. Director of music, BBC, from 1950 until his death.

Mus., abbr. for *music* – especially in university degrees, etc.; B.Mus., D.Mus. – bachelor, doctor of music.

Musard, Philippe (1793–1859), French violinist, conductor, composer of quadrilles etc.; gave early successful promenade concerts in Paris and (1840 and afterwards) in London.

musette (1) French type of bagpipe fashionable in Louis XIV's time through the cultivation of 'pastoral' ideal; used in the opera orchestra by Lully; (2) type of gavotte with a drone bass suggesting this instrument.

Musgrave, Thea (b. 1928), British composer, much of whose recent activity has been in USA. Works include *Rainbow* for orchestras, various concerts; *Black Tambourine* for female voices, piano and percussion; operas *The Voice of Ariadne*, *A* ➤Christmas *Carol*, *Mary Queen of Scots*, ➤*Harriet: The Woman Called 'Moses'*.

music (1) 'an arrangement of, or the art of combining or putting together, sounds that please the ear' (*Chambers Essential English Dictionary*, 1968); (2, as in 'Master of the Queen's Music') an old English name for a band of musical performers. See also following entries.

musica ficta (Lat., 'false' or 'feigned' music), the principle, current from *c*.1350 to *c*.1650, by which performers added accidentals to certain notes. The practice was necessary (*causa necessitatis*) to avoid forbidden intervals (such as the augmented fourth or octave), but was also used to create sweeter-sounding intervals (*causa pulchritudinis*). The term is also used today to describe the addition of such accidentals by the editor of a printed edition.

musical (noun, as abbr. for *musical play*), term for the type of light stage entertainment (largely American-influenced) which succeeded the older ➤musical comedy in the 20th century. Not necessarily comedies in dramatic genre, musicals have often come to a near-operatic concentration on the music itself but with almost total dependence on the microphoned voice.

musical box, toy in which pins on a rotating cylinder 'pluck' the teeth of a comb which, being of different lengths, emit different notes; several sets of pins allow several tunes.

musical comedy, type of British and American light entertainment, prominent in later 19th and early 20th centuries – related to ➤operetta, but often less unified musically and using more than one composer. ➤musical.

musical glasses, ➤glass harmonica.

Musical Joke, A, work by Mozart. ➤*Musikalischer Spass*.

Musical Offering, work by Bach. ➤*Musikalisches Opfer*.

musical saw, ➤*saw*.

musica reservata (Lat., 'reserved' music), a term in use approximately 1550–1625, whose meaning is still obscure. It is assumed to refer to a central aspect of the style or performance of music in this period or earlier (particularly that of Josquin and

Lassus). The likelihood is that it involved some musical expression of the verbal text; the use of chromaticism; or some aspect of performing practice, particularly performance by soloists. Or perhaps the music was, by its subtlety, reserved for connoisseurs.

Musica Transalpina, the first printed collection of Italian (i.e. transalpine) madrigals with English words; it had great influence on English music. Edited by Nicholas Yonge in two volumes, 1588 and 1597, the composers including Palestrina, Marenzio and Lassus.

music-drama, term used by Wagner of his operas after *Lohengrin*, the term 'opera' itself being thought to be inadequate or inappropriate to his intended new type of drama set to continuously expressive music based on ➤leading-motives (as distinct from the old division into operatic 'numbers').

Music for Strings, Percussion and Celesta, orchestral work by Bartók, first performed in Basle, 1936 (orchestration also includes piano and harp).

Music for the Royal Fireworks, ➤*Fireworks Music*.

Music Makers, The, work for contralto, chorus, and orchestra, by Elgar, first performed in 1912. Text, A. Shaughnessy's poem. In this score Elgar quotes some of his own earlier works.

Music Master, The, one-act comic opera. ➤*Maestro di musica*.

musicology, musical scholarship – 20th-century word useful in such contexts as 'to study musicology', implying an academic discipline different from that in 'to study music'. So also

musicologist (usually implying someone whose activity is more 'learned' than that of a mere critic), *musicological*, etc.; ➤ethnomusicology.

music-theatre, term of two quite distinct meanings, both post-1950: (1) opera production in a 'realistic' or 'truthful' manner as supposedly distinct from traditional type sacrificing all else to vocal display; (2) a genre of concert works for which a semi-staged presentation is needed, e.g. works by Kagel (*Match*) and P. M. Davies (➤*Eight Songs for a Mad King*).

Musik, musikalisch (Ger.), music, musical; see following entries.

Musikalischer Spass, Ein (Ger., 'A Musical Joke'), work for strings and two horns by Mozart, 1787 (K522), satirizing clumsy composition.

Musikalisches Opfer (Ger., 'Musical Offering'), work by Bach, 1747 (BWV 1079), of 13 pieces in various contrapuntal forms, dedicated to Frederick the Great of Prussia, and all using a theme given by Frederick to Bach on his visit to court that year.

Musikwissenschaft (Ger.), ➤musicology.

musique (Fr.), music.

musique concrète (Fr., 'concrete music'), type of quasi-musical organization of real, 'concrete' sounds (from nature or man-made environment) recorded and arranged on tape – a technique developed chiefly by Pierre Schaeffer at the Paris radio station in 1948–9. The process was soon absorbed in ➤electronic music.

Musorgsky, Modest Petrovich (1839–81), Russian composer; at first army officer, later a civil servant, but studied briefly as a young man with Balakirev (➤Mighty Handful). Evolved, partly from Russian speech-inflexion, a highly individual musical idiom from which he created his masterpiece, ➤*Boris Godunov*. His music was imperfectly appreciated even by admirers, Rimsky-Korsakov 'correcting' (misleadingly) much of his work after his death. (➤*St John's Night on Bald Mountain*). Other works include unfinished operas *The* ➤*Khovansky Affair*, ➤*Fair at Sorochintsy*, *The Marriage*; ➤*Pictures at an Exhibition* for piano (orchestrated by others, notably Ravel); many songs including cycles *The Nursery*, ➤*Songs and Dances of Death*, *Sunless*. Died after alcoholic epileptic fits.

Mussorgsky, a frequently encountered (but strictly less accurate) transliteration of the name Musorgsky.

Mustel organ, keyboard instrument of the ➤American organ type, invented by V. Mustel (1815–90).

muta (It., 'he/she/it changes'), instruction to player that a change has to be made from one tuning to another, or one instrument to another.

mutano (It., 'they change'), term used as the plural of ➤*muta*.

mutation stop, organ stop sounding not the note struck but one of its ➤harmonic series other than the octave – e.g. a stop called '12th' sounding the twelfth note above.

mute, a contrivance to reduce the volume of an instrument and/or modify its tone – on bowed instruments, a prolonged damper placed at the bridge; on brass instruments, an

object of wood, metal, or fibre (there are various types) placed in the bell. To depress the ➤soft pedal of a piano or to ➤muffle a drum is also in effect to apply a mute. (So also *to mute*, as verb.)

Müthel, Johann Gottfried (1718–85), German composer of keyboard works, pupil of J. S. Bach; organist at Lutheran Church in Riga, where he died.

Muti, Riccardo (b. 1941), Italian conductor of (New) Philharmonia Orchestra, 1973, and of Philadelphia Orchestra, 1980–92; also musical director of La Scala, Milan, since 1986 and conductor of opera at other major theatres, and on recordings.

Mutter, Anne-Sophie (b. 1963), German violinist whose youthful gifts were encouraged by Karajan: British début (at Brighton) under Barenboim, 1977; New York recital début, 1988. Her distinguished career has included the first performance of Lutosławski's *Chain 2*, 1986.

Muzio, Claudia [originally Claudina Muzzio] (1889–1936), Italian soprano. Made her opera début 1910 and became celebrated in Italy, New York and Buenos Aires as well as on records; sang at only one Covent Garden season, 1914. At the Metropolitan she created the role of Giorgetta in Puccini's *Il tabarro*, 1918, and was the first to sing Tatyana (Tchaikovsky's *Yevgeny Onegin*) there, 1920.

Myaskovsky, Nikolay [Yakovlevich] (1881–1950), Russian composer, pupil of Glière and Rimsky-Korsakov, and others. One of the most prolific modern composers of symphonies – he wrote 27 (no. 19 is for wind band, no. 27 was performed posthumously). Wrote also symphonic poem *Nevermore* (after Poe), a violin concerto, piano solos, songs, etc. Denounced by Soviet officialdom in 1948 for ➤formalism, etc., along with Prokofiev, Shostakovich and others.

My Country (Cz., *Má Vlast*), cycle of six symphonic poems by Smetana, composed 1874–9 (after he had become deaf): (1) 'Vyšehrad' (an ancient citadel); (2) 'Vltava' (river); (3) 'Šárka' (Bohemian Amazon leader); (4) 'From Bohemian Fields and Groves' (Cz. *Z Českych Luhů a Hájů*); (5) 'Tábor' (city associated with the Hussites); (6) 'Blaník' (legendary sleeping-place of dead Hussite heroes).

My Fair Lady, musical with text by Alan Jay Lerner based on *Pygmalion* by George Bernard Shaw; music by Frederick Loewe. Produced in New York, 1956. The professor of language transforms the speech and manners of a cockney dustman's daughter.

My Lady Nevill's Book, a MS collection of 42 keyboard pieces by Byrd, 1591 (published in 1926).

Mysliveček, Josef (1737–81), Bohemian composer of Italian operas, and also of symphonies, etc.; called *il divino Boemo* (It., the divine Bohemian). Mozart admired him. He died in poverty in Rome.

mystic chord, ➤Skryabin.

N

Nabokov, Nicholas (originally Nikolay) (1903–78), Russian-born composer who lived much in France and died in USA. Works include opera on Shakespeare's *Love's Labour's Lost* and *Sinfonia biblica* for orchestra. Cousin of the writer Vladimir Nabokov.

Nabokov, Vladimir (1899–1977), Russian-born American author. ➤Shchedrin.

Nabucco (It., abbr. of 'Nabucodnosor', i.e. Nebuchadnezzar), opera by Verdi, produced in Milan, 1842. Libretto by T. Solera, after the biblical story of the Israelites' captivity in Babylon.

nach (Ger.), to, after; so, e.g., *E nach G* (instruction to timpanist), 'change the tuning of the drum from E to G'.

Nachez, Tivadar (1859–1930), Hungarian violinist, editor of violin music, composer of a violin concerto, etc. Settled in France and died in Switzerland.

Nachschlag (Ger., after-stroke), (1) the two extra notes which conventionally close a ➤trill; (2) an extra note (printed in small type) coming after a main note and robbing that main note of some of its time-value (➤springer).

Nachtanz (Ger.), 'after-dance', i.e. a quick dance normally used to follow a slow one, e.g. a galliard following a pavan.

Nacht in Venedig, Eine (Ger., 'A Night in Venice'), operetta by Johann Strauss II with libretto by F. Zell and Richard Genée after *Le Château Trompette* by Jules Cormon and Michel Carré; music by Johann Strauss. Produced in Berlin, 1883. Masked intrigue in 18th-century Venice with nobles and gondoliers; the original libretto is commonly modified in performance.

Nachtmusik (Ger.), serenade (literally, 'night music') – not a normal musical term, but used in Mozart's ➤*Eine kleine Nachtmusik*.

Nagano, Kent [George] (b. 1951), American conductor who became music director of the Lyon (France) Opera in 1989, adding music directorship of Hallé Orchestra (Manchester) from 1992. He conducted première of Adams's *The Death of Klinghoffer* (Brussels, 1991); made Metropolitan Opera début, 1994; recorded the rarely heard Busoni operas, *Turandot* and *Arlecchino*.

nail fiddle, nail harmonica, nail violin, alternative names for a freak 18th-century instrument with nails of graduated sizes that were stroked with a violin-bow.

nakers, old English name, deriving from Arabic through French, for the small oriental ➤kettledrum (normally played in pairs) brought to Europe in the 13th century.

Namensfeier (Ger., 'Name-day'), concert-overture by Beethoven, 1814, celebrating the name-day of Francis II, Emperor of Austria.

Nancarrow, Conlon (1912–97), American-born composer; fought for Loyalists in Spanish Civil War, was denied US passport, became Mexican citizen 1956. His String Quartet no. 3, composed 1945, was not performed until 1988; later works, of great rhythmical complexity, are notated only as punched player-piano rolls and performed by activating those rolls.

Nänie, ➤*nenia.*

Nápravník, Eduard (1839–1916), Czech composer of four operas, four symphonies, etc.; settled in Russia, 1861, becoming a leading conductor.

Nardini, Pietro (1722–93), Italian violinist and composer of nine violin concertos, chamber music, etc.; held court posts. A leading pupil of Tartini.

Nares, James (1715–83), British composer of church music, glees, harpsichord pieces, etc.; also organist.

Narvaez, Luis de (*c.*1500–after 1550), Spanish player of ➤*vihuela* (Spanish form of lute) and composer of variations and other works for it; also of church music.

Nash, Peter Paul (b. 1950), British composer, also former radio presenter; works include three symphonies. *Earthquake* for narrator and six players, sextet for piano and wind.

Nathan, Isaac (1790–1864), British singer and composer – of stage works, songs to words by his friend Byron, etc. Settled in Australia, and died there. ➤Mackerras is a descendant.

nationalism, nationalist, terms applied to music which (usually through elements derived from folk-music) suggests supposed national characteristics. The terms are particularly applied to the work of such 19th-century composers as Smetana, Liszt, Balakirev and Grieg, with the implication of national 'emancipation' from the domination of German-Austrian musical concepts.

National Orchestra of Wales, ➤BBC National Orchestra of Wales.

National Symphony Orchestra of Ireland, Dublin-based orchestra supported by state radio, formerly Radio Telefis Eireann Symphony Orchestra; conductor since 1994 (succeeding George Hurst), Kasper de Roo.

Natra, Sergiu (b. 1924), Romanian-born Israeli composer; works include *Song of Deborah* (in Hebrew) for mezzo-soprano and chamber orchestra; sonatinas for trombone, for trumpet and for oboe.

natural (1, of a note or key) not sharp or flat – designated by the sign ♮; (2, of a horn, trumpet, etc.) not having valves, keys, or any other mechanism, and so producing only the notes of the ➤harmonic series as determined by the length of the tube; (3) a type of ➤harmonics in string-playing.

naturale (It., natural), direction that a voice or instrument which has been performing in an 'abnormal' way (e.g. falsetto, muted) should return to its 'natural' manner of performance.

Naughty Marietta, musical comedy with text by Rida Johnson Young; music by Victor Herbert. Produced in New York, 1910. The heroine is Italian but the setting is Louisiana in its era as a French colony; the son of its corrupt governor is the pirate Bras Piqué.

Naumann, Johann Gottlieb (1741–1801), German composer who studied in Italy with Tartini and G. B. Martini, and won wide fame in his day, especially with operas – mostly in Italian (including *La Clemenza di Tito*, 1769), but three in Swedish and one in Danish for Stockholm and Copenhagen. Also wrote symphonies, Masses, oratorios, etc.

Navarra, André [Nicolas] (1911–88), French cellist, internationally prominent; teacher in France, Germany and Italy.

Naylor, Bernard (1907–86), British composer of choral works, *Sonnets from the Portuguese* (E. B. Browning) for voice and string quartet, etc. Pupil of Vaughan Williams, Holst and Ireland; spent two periods as conductor in Canada. Son of Edward Naylor (1867–1934), organist, composer and musicologist.

Neapolitan sixth, a type of chord – in key C, it comprises the notes (reading upwards) F, A♭, D♭; and correspondingly in other keys. The reason for the name is uncertain (as with ➤Italian sixth). But the Neapolitan sixth is always relative to the prevailing key, whereas an ➤Italian sixth is formed irrespective of it. The term *Neapolitan harmony* is sometimes found as indicating (especially in 18th-century music) a pronounced use of this chord.

Neel, [Louis] **Boyd** (1905–81), British conductor. Qualified originally in medicine, but turned to music, founding Boyd Neel String Orchestra in London in 1933. Dean of the Royal Conservatory of Music, Toronto, 1953–71.

Negro Quartet, ➤American Quartet.

Negro spiritual, ➤spiritual.

'Nelson' Mass, nickname for Haydn's Mass in D Minor, 1798 (Hob. XXII: 11), because it is supposed to signalize joy at Nelson's victory in the Battle of the Nile.

nenia (Gk.), a dirge; Brahms used the German form *Nänie* for a choral setting of Schiller, 1881; Birtwistle's *Nenia on the Death of Orpheus* (1970) is for soprano and instrumental ensemble.

neo-, prefix (from Gk. for 'new') used, in classifying musical styles, to indicate the re-adopting (real or supposed) of apparently outmoded characteristics, suitably modified for a new era. So, e.g., ➤neo-classical (see below); *neo-modal*, referring to the 20th-century revival of the old modes; *neo-Romantic*, referring to the inclination of some composers to Romanticism even after the 20th-century reaction against it.

neo-classic(al), **neo-classicism**, misleading terms sometimes applied to the anti-Romantic style of Stravinsky, Hindemith and others in the 1920s, reviving ➤*concerto grosso* textures and counterpoint, avoiding emotional rhetoric. Since the retrospective model was the music of Bach's rather than Mozart's period, the better label would be *neo-baroque* (➤baroque).

Neruda, Pablo (1904–73), Chilean poet. ➤Orrego Salas, ➤Wood (Hugh).

Nesterenko, Evgeny [Evgenyevich] (b.

1938), Russian bass who gave first performances of three of Shostakovich's song-cycles; joined Bolshoi Opera 1971 and became well known in the West (Covent Garden as Basilio in *Il barbiere di Siviglia*, 1978); professor at Tchaikovsky Conservatory, Moscow.

neum(e), generic name for each of the various signs in medieval musical notation (superseded by modern staff notation) showing the note(s) to which a syllable of vocal music was to be sung. As surviving in plainsong notation, the *neums* give precise indication of pitch; but originally, from the seventh century, they were only approximate reminders of the shape of the melody.

Neumann, Vaclav (1920–95), Czech conductor, formerly viola-player; music director of Leipzig Opera, 1964–7; principal conductor, Czech Philharmonic Orchestra, since 1968. Made the first recording of Janáček's opera *The Excursions of Mr Brouček*, 1962.

Neumeier, John (b. 1942), American choreographer. ➤Schnittke.

Neusiedler, Hans (1508–63), German lutenist and composer of lute music – fantasies, dances, song-arrangements, etc.

Nevin, Ethelbert Woodbridge (1862–1901), American composer of 'The Rosary' (sold 6 million copies in 30 years) and other popular sentimental songs; *Narcissus* and other piano pieces, etc. His brother Arthur Finley Nevin (1871–1943) was also a composer and a researcher in American-Indian music.

New England Holidays, alternative name for Charles Ives's ➤*Holidays*.

Newman, John Henry [Cardinal] (1801–90), British writer. ➤*Dream of Gerontius*.

new music, term with two special historical meanings – (1) in the early 17th century, the type of newly expressive Italian music then being pioneered by such composers as Caccini; (2) in the period 1850–1900, the music of Liszt, Wagner and their followers as opposed to that of, e.g., Brahms (supposedly more 'traditional' in outlook).

'New World' Symphony, ➤*From the New World*.

New York Philharmonic Orchestra, orchestra which was called the New York Philharmonic Symphony Orchestra when established in 1928 from a merger of the older New York Philharmonic and New York Symphony Orchestras, but which currently uses the simpler title. Music director 1978–91, Mehta, succeeded by Masur.

Nexus, Canadian/US percussion ensemble founded 1971, retaining original membership (Bob Becker, William Cahn, Robin Engleman, Russell Hartenberger, John Wyre), internationally giving concerts on its own and (➤Takemitsu) with orchestra. Others who have written for it include Bryars (*One Last Bar Then Joe Can Play*), Reich, and members of the group.

Nibelung's Ring, The, ➤*Ring*.

Nicholson, Richard (*c.* 1570–1639), English organist and composer of madrigals (e.g. one in *The* ➤*Triumphs of Oriana*), anthems and songs. The first professor of music at Oxford, 1627.

Nicholson, Sydney [Hugo] (1875–1947), British organist, composer (chiefly of church music), and founder of what is now the Royal School of Church Music; knighted, 1938.

Nicolai, [Carl] **Otto** [Ehrenfried] (1810–49), German composer and conductor; studied in Italy and wrote Italian operas, following with the highly successful *Die* ➤*Lustigen Weiber von Windsor* (on Shakespeare's *The Merry Wives of Windsor*); also choral and orchestral works, etc. Founder-conductor of the Vienna Philharmonic Concerts (i.e. of the present-day Vienna Philharmonic Orchestra), 1842; in 1847 went as director of the court opera and the cathedral choir to Berlin, where he died of a stroke.

Nicolet, Aurèle (b. 1926), Swiss flautist, for whom solo works have been written by Ligeti, Takemitsu and others.

Nielsen, Carl [August] (1865–1931), Danish composer, reckoned his country's greatest; director of the Royal Conservatory, 1930; also conductor, and formerly violinist. In 1891–2 he composed his Symphony no. 1, probably the first ever to begin in one key and end in another (➤progressive tonality) – a principle much evident in his succeeding five symphonies (no. 2 *The* ➤*Four Temperaments*, no. 4 *The* ➤*Unquenchable*). Other works include concertos for flute, for clarinet and for violin; operas *Saul and David* and ➤*Masquerade*; chamber music (➤*serenata*); *Commotio* for organ.

niente (It.), nothing, so *a niente*, to nothing – term used e.g. after sign indicating that the sound is gradually to die away entirely.

Nietzsche, Friedrich Wilhelm (1844–1900), German philosopher. ➤*Also sprach Zarathustra*, ➤*Mass of Life*.

Nigg, Serge (b. 1924), French composer, pupil of Messiaen. Works include symphonic poems, a symphony on Hieronymus Bosch, violin concerto and two piano concertos.

Nigger Quartet, ➤American Quartet.

Night at the Chinese Opera, A, opera by Judith Weir, first produced at Cheltenham, 1987. Libretto by composer after a 13th-century Chinese play; a Chinese collaborator with his country's Mongolian overlords finds that a play (or 'opera') he attends mirrors his own life.

nightingale, imitative toy instrument used in the ➤*Toy Symphony* (Leopold Mozart) and a few other works.

Night in Venice, A, operetta by J. Strauss the younger.➤*Nacht in Venedig*.

Night on Bald Mountain, Night on the Bare Mountain, orchestral work by Musorgsky. ➤*St John's Night on Bald Mountain*.

Nights in the Gardens of Spain, work for piano and orchestra by Falla. ➤*Noches en los jardines de España*.

Nijinsky, Vaslav (1890–1950), Russian choreographer. ➤*Rite of Spring*.

Nikisch, Arthur (1855–1922), Hungarian conductor, pre-eminent in his day; from 1895 he conducted both the Gewandhaus Orchestra (Leipzig) and the Berlin Philharmonic, and was also active in Boston and London.

Nilsson, [Märta] **Birgit** (b. 1918), Swedish soprano, internationally known as Brünnhilde in *The Ring*, in the title-role of *Turandot*, etc. Retired from public performance in 1986.

Nilsson, Bo (b. 1937), Swedish composer, self-taught; works include *Reactions* for four percussionists (and other works with prominent percussion), Mass for Christian Unity, various jazz compositions.

Nilsson, Christine (originally Kristina) (1843–1921), Swedish soprano who established highest operatic fame in Paris (from 1864), London and New York.

Nimrod, a movement (often performed separately, on solemn occasions) in Elgar's ➤*Enigma Variations*.

Nin [y Castellanos], Joaquin (1879–1949), Spanish pianist, editor of old Spanish music, composer of stage works, pieces for violin and for piano, etc. Born and died in Cuba. Father of the following.

Nin-Culmell, Joaquin [Maria] (b. 1908), American composer, born in Berlin, son of preceding. Also pianist, conductor and university teacher. Works include a piano concerto, Mass (in English), incidental music to Shakespeare's *Cymbeline* and other plays.

nineteenth, a ➤mutation stop on the organ producing a note at the interval of a 19th (two octaves and a fifth) above the note touched.

ninth, an interval of nine steps (counting the bottom and top notes), e.g. from C upwards for an octave and a whole-tone to D (*major ninth*) or for an octave and a semitone to Db (*minor ninth*). So, e.g., a *chord of the dominant ninth*: in the key of F major this would be (reading upwards) C, E, G, Bb, D. Since the dominant of F major is C,

the B is flat according to the scale of F major, and the note D indicates the interval of the major ninth from C.

Ninth Symphony (Beethoven), ➤ *Choral Symphony*.

Nixon in China, opera by John Adams, produced in Houston, Texas, 1987. Libretto by Alice Goodman deals with the historic (1972) meeting of the US President with Chairman Mao Tse-Tung.

No, No, Nanette, musical comedy with text by Frank Mandel, Otto Harbach and Irving Caesar and music by Vincent Youmans. Produced in Detroit, 1923. Nanette is the young (and misunderstood) protégée of a Bible-puncher and his wife. (➤*Tahiti Trot*.)

nobile, nobilmente (It.), noble, nobly.

Noble, Thomas Tertius (1867–1953), British organist who lived much in USA, and died there; composer of church music, etc.

Noces, Les, ➤*Wedding*.

Noches en los jardines de España (Sp., 'Nights in the Gardens of Spain'), 'Symphonic impressions' by Falla for piano and orchestra in three movements; first performed in 1916.

nocturne, a night-piece: (1, generally, in Italian, *notturno*) 18th-century composition of ➤serenade type for several instruments in several movements; (2) short lyrical piece, especially for piano, in one movement – a sense originated by Field and adopted by Chopin; (3) term applied at the composer's fancy – e.g. to the third movement of Vaughan Williams's *A* ➤*London Symphony*, which is headed 'Scherzo (Nocturne)', and in Britten's song-cycle with orchestra (1958) entitled *Nocturne*. See also next entry.

Nocturnes, a set of three orchestral pieces by Debussy, first performed complete in 1901 – (1) *Nuages* (Clouds), (2) *Fêtes* (Festivals), (3) *Sirènes* (Sirens), the last employing a wordless female chorus.

node, a stationary point on a vibrating string or air-column – the vibrations taking place in opposite directions on either side of it.

noël (Fr., Christmas), a Christmas carol, or an instrumental piece in the same spirit (often, in the 17th and 18th centuries, for keyboard or instrumental ensemble).

noire (Fr., black), ➤quarter-note, crotchet.

non (Fr., It.), not.

nonet, a composition for nine instruments or nine voices; if the former, it will probably be in some regular several-movement form – as ➤quartet.

non-harmonic note (US, non-harmonic tone), term used in the theory of harmony for a note that is not part of the chord with which it sounds, and therefore needs its own 'explanation' (perhaps as ➤passing-note or ➤*appoggiatura*).

Nono, Luigi (1924–90), Italian composer. Works, often linked to political (Communist) protest, include *Il canto sospeso* ('Song Suspended'), on letters of Resistance fighters, for solo singers, chorus and orchestra; three pieces combined as *Epitaffio* ('Epitaph') for the poet Federico García Lorca; *Canti di vita e amore* ('Songs of Love and Death') subtitled 'On the Bridge at Hiroshima' for singers and orchestra;

opera *Intolleranza* ('Intolerance'); *Incontri* ('Encounters') for 24 instruments. His visit to Moscow in 1962 confronted young Soviet composers with Western modernism.

Norcombe, Daniel (b. 1576, d. before 1626), English lutenist and composer who contributed a madrigal to *The* ➤*Triumphs of Oriana*. (An English viol-player of the same name active in Brussels as late as 1647 is a different person.)

Nordheim, Arne (b. 1931), Norwegian composer (formerly also critic). Works include *Monolith* and other works for orchestra, *Dinosaurus* for accordion with accordion sounds on tape; Partita for viola, harpsichord and percussion. He takes part in 'live electronics' performances as used in several of his own compositions.

Nordraak, Richard (1842–66), Norwegian composer of what is now the Norwegian national anthem; despite his short life, he exerted great influence (e.g. on Grieg) in the direction of a Norwegian national style of music.

Nørgård, Per (b. 1932), Danish composer and teacher. Works include five symphonies, oratorio *Babel* (with four soloists – clown, rock singer, cabaret artist, conductor); *Voyage into the Golden Screen* for chamber ensemble; *Re-percussion* for two percussionists, *Achilles and the Tortoise* for piano.

Norma, opera by Bellini, produced in Milan, 1831. Libretto by F. Romani. Named after the heroine, a young Druid priestess torn between love and duty.

Norman, Jessye (b. 1945), American soprano, with distinguished international career, first appearing at Covent Garden in 1972 and at the

Metropolitan, New York, in 1973 – both as Cassandra in *Les* ➤*Troyens*; equally acclaimed as concert singer.

Norrington, Roger [Arthur Carver] (b. 1934), British conductor, formerly tenor; with his London Classical Players (1978–97) he won fame for performances of Beethoven, Berlioz and Brahms using instruments of the period. Knighted 1997.

Northern Sinfonia (since 1982 Northern Sinfonia of England), chamber orchestra based in Newcastle-on-Tyne, established in 1961. Principal conductor, 1989–96, Heinrich Schiff, then Jean-Bernard Pommier.

Norton, [George] **Frederic** (1875–1940), British composer, also operatic baritone and variety entertainer. His stage works produced in London include *Orpheus in the Underground* [sic] and ➤*Chu Chin Chow*, which set a record with 2,238 performances.

Nose, The (Rus., *Nos*), opera by Shostakovich, with libretto by composer and others, after Gogol, produced in Leningrad, 1930. A human nose is found and its owner located – a satire on St Petersburg society in the 1830s.

nota cambiata (It., exchanged note), a device in counterpoint by which an 'extra' ➤non-harmonic note is used on an accented beat. Instead of (a) below, in which the B is an auxilliary note between the two C's, the use of *nota cambiata* (b) gives the extra note D, which is thought of as a substitute for the B (hence the idea of 'exchange').

(a)   (b)

The leap from B to an accented D, both non-harmonic notes, is the essential feature; or it might have been from D to B. (The North American term is simply *cambiata*.)

notation, the writing down of music – whether by symbols (as in ordinary ➤*staff* notation), by letters (as in ➤*tonic sol-fa*), by a representation of how an instrument should be fingered to produce particular notes (➤tablature), or by diagrammatic means devised by such composers as Feldman and Ligeti (➤graphic notation).

note (1) a single sound of a given pitch and duration; (2) a written sign for the preceding; (3) a lever depressed by the performer on the piano, organ, etc., to produce a sound of particular pitch. The US term for the first of these is ➤*tone*.

note-cluster, ➤cluster.

note-row (in US usage *tone-row*), in ➤*twelve-note* music, the order in which the composer chooses to arrange the 12 notes comprised within the octave, this order serving as the basis for the particular composition.

notes inégales (Fr., unequal notes), ➤inequality.

Notre Dame, school of, modern name for the style of late 12th-century composition represented by Léonin and Pérotin, supposed (not conclusively) to be associated with the recently built cathedral of Notre Dame in Paris.

notturno, ➤*nocturne*.

Novák, Vítězslav (1870–1949), Czechoslovak composer, pupil of Dvořák; director of the Prague Conservatory, 1919–22, and long a professor there. Works include symphonic poems, a piano concerto, three string quartets, cantata *The* ➤*Spectre's Bride*, operas, ballets, Slovak folk-song arrangements.

novelette, Novellette (Eng., Ger.), title for a short instrumental piece supposedly the equivalent of a romantic tale – term apparently first used by Schumann, 1848 (for a piano work).

Novello, Ivor [originally David Ivor Davies] (1893–1951), British playwright, actor and composer of music for his own plays – e.g. *The Dancing Years, King's Rhapsody* – as well as of song 'Keep the home fires burning', etc. Son of the choral conductor Clara Novello-Davies.

Noye's Fludde, work of operatic type (though intended for church performance with participation of the audience in traditional hymns) by Britten, first performed in Orford (Suffolk), 1958. Title is ancient spelling of 'Noah's Flood'; text is adapted from the Chester miracle play.

Nozze di Figaro, Le (It., 'The Marriage of Figaro'), opera by Mozart (K492), produced in Vienna (in Italian), 1786. Libretto by L. da Ponte, based on a comedy by Beaumarchais – sequel to that on which the libretto of Rossini's ➤*Barbiere di Siviglia* is based. Figaro, formerly a barber whose successful intrigues resulted in Count Almaviva's marriage, is now the Count's personal servant. The story is continued in a further Beaumarchais comedy: ➤Klebe.

Nuits d'été, Les, set of songs by Berlioz, composed 1840–41 but not published until 1856; texts by Théophile Gautier.

number, a self-contained item in an opera, a musical, etc. (so called because each such piece is separately numbered 1, 2, etc., in the written score); hence *number-opera*, an opera in which this separation into self-contained items is followed, as distinct from those operas (e.g. Wagner's work from *Tristan und Isolde* onwards) where a whole act is written out without internal divisions and thus without possible pause.

Nunc Dimittis, text from St Luke (named from its opening words, 'Now lettest thou thy servant depart', in Latin translation) forming part of the Roman Catholic and Anglican evening service; for the latter, composers have commonly written a ➤Magnificat and Nunc Dimittis as a unified work.

nut (1) on a stringed instrument, the ridge over which the strings pass between the pegs and the fingerboard; (2) on the bow of, e.g., a violin, the device at the heel by which the tension of the bow-strings can be regulated.

Nutcracker, The (Rus., *Shchelkunchik*), ballet with choreography by L. I. Ivanov, music by Tchaikovsky, produced in St Petersburg, 1892 – some months after the concert suite drawn from it had already been performed. On a fairy-tale, with a battle between the Nutcracker and the King of Mice. ➤celesta.

Nyman, Michael (b. 1944), British composer of opera *The Man Who Mistook His Wife for a Hat*, many scores for films, including *The Draughtsman's Contract, The Piano*; harpsichord concerto; various works for his own band (of amplified instruments), also for ➤gamelan, for saxophone (➤Harle), for ten-piece brass ensemble. ➤minimalism.

Nystroem, Gösta (1890–1966), Swedish composer, pupil of d'Indy in Paris – where, himself a painter, his artistic outlook was influenced by Picasso, Braque, etc. Works include six symphonies (no. 4, *Sinfonia Shakespeareana*), a viola concerto, Sinfonia Concertante for cello and orchestra; songs, some with orchestra.

O

o (It.), or; *o sia,* ➤ossia.

obbligato (It., obligatory), term used of an instrument with a compulsory, unusual and special role – e.g. 'song with flute obbligato' (where *obbligato* is really an adjective qualifying 'flute'). By contrast, 'flute ➤*ad lib*' would imply optional, not compulsory, use of the instrument.

Oberon, or The Elf-King's Oath, opera by Weber, produced in London, 1826; libretto, in English, by J. R. Planché. The story, a romance set in the days of Charlemagne, has nothing to do with the exploits of Oberon in *A Midsummer Night's Dream.*

obligato, mis-spelling for ➤*obbligato.*

oblique motion, ➤motion.

oboe, woodwind instrument, developed from the ➤shawm, blown through a double reed and having a compass from the B♭ below middle C upwards for more than two and a half octaves; standard in the orchestra, and used also in the military band, in chamber music and as solo instrument. *Oboe d'amore*, similar instrument of slightly lower pitch and less pungent tone, specified, e.g., by Bach and exceptionally by 20th-century composers, e.g. Ravel (in *Boléro*) and R. Strauss; *oboe da caccia* – literally 'hunting oboe',

though it is not clear why – a specification by Bach indicating a predecessor of the ➤English horn, the present 'contralto' to the oboe's soprano. The lowest members of the oboe family are two different instruments each with compass approximately an octave below the oboe – the (French) *baritone oboe,* blown through a side tube like the bassoon, and the (German) ➤*Heckelphone,* sometimes called (e.g. in Delius's scores) *bass oboe.*

Obraztsova, Elena [Vasilyevna] (b. 1937), Russian mezzo-soprano; performed in opera at the Bolshoi Theatre while still a student; sang at Metropolitan Opera, New York, 1976. In addition to standard Russian and Italian roles, she has sung the (originally counter-tenor) part of Oberon in Britten's *A Midsummer Night's Dream.*

Obrecht (latinized as Obertus), **Jacob** (*c.* 1450–1505), Netherlandish composer who worked mainly in Flanders, but also visited Italy and died of plague there. Wrote Masses, motets and secular songs; a hidden number-symbolism has been detected in some of his structures.

ocarina, small keyless flute-like instrument (invented *c.* 1860) with holes for fingers; mainly used as a toy, but featured in Irving Berlin's score for the musical ➤*Call Me Madam*. The body is shaped like an egg – or, counting the protruding mouthpiece, rather like a goose, thus possibly suggesting the name (from It. *oca*, goose?).

O'Casey, Sean (1884–1964), Irish dramatist. ➤Siegmeister.

Ockeghem (or Okeghem), **Jean de** (*c.*1410–97), Flemish composer, in service to the French court; also visited Spain. Of great influence; called 'the Prince of Music' in his own day; his pupils included ➤Josquin. Wrote Masses and motets, sometimes choosing a secular tune as ➤*cantus firmus*; wrote also French chansons.

octave, the interval that is considered as having eight (Lat. *octo*) steps, counting both the bottom and top notes; according to standard notation, notes an octave apart from each other have the same letter-names, the note an octave above A being also called A, etc. This naming corresponds to the fact that notes an octave apart seem to the ear like the same note sounded at different pitches, not like entirely different notes. Strictly, the interval from A to the next A above is the *perfect octave*; from A up to A♭ and from A up to A♯ are respectively the *diminished* and *augmented octave*. Thus also *double octave*, two octaves; *at the octave*, (performed) an octave higher than written; *in octaves*, (performed) with each note doubled one or more octaves above or below; *octave coupler*, device on organ or harpsichord whereby the note struck is doubled an octave higher (sometimes called *super-octave coupler*, to distinguish from *sub-octave coupler* doubling at the octave below); *octave key*, finger-lever on

woodwind instruments giving player access to a higher octave. ➤consecutive.

octet, composition for eight instruments or eight voices; if the former, it will probably be in some regular several-movement form – as ➤quartet. Also a group of eight performers.

octobass, a huge, bowed stringed instrument, larger and pitched lower than a double-bass, invented in 1849. It failed to win acceptance.

octuor (Fr.), ➤octet.

ode (1) musical setting of a poem itself called 'ode', such a setting often having a ceremonial nature – see the following entries; (2) term exceptionally used in music with some vaguer significance: Stravinsky's work in memory of Koussevitzky's wife, 1943, is entitled *Ode: Elegiacal Chant*.

Ode for St Cecilia's Day (1) title of four choral works by Purcell, two of 1683 (Z329 and 334), another (Z339) probably of that date, another (Z328) of 1692; Z329 is in Latin, the others in English; (2) title of a setting by Handel of Dryden's poem of the same title, first performed in London. ➤*Hymn to St Cecilia*.

Ode to Napoleon Buonaparte, work by Schoenberg, 1942, for speaker (whose part is rhythmically notated at approximate pitch), strings and piano; text, by Byron, expresses loathing of despotism.

Odo of Cluny (879–942), French monk, appointed Abbot of Cluny in 927; he was a noted composer and teacher, and various writings on music are ascribed to him.

Oedipus Rex (Lat., 'King Oedipus'),

'opera-oratorio' by Stravinsky – intended for stage presentation with restricted movement, but first performed as a concert work in Paris, 1927. The text is a Latin translation by J. Daniélou of a script by Cocteau suggested by Sophocles' Greek tragedy.

Offenbach, Jacques (1819–80), French composer born in Cologne, Germany – the family originally hailing from Offenbach-am-Main; his father's original surname was Eberst (other versions are not substantiated). He was taken to Paris in boyhood and remained there, attaining tremendous success as composer of nearly 90 French operettas including *La ➤Belle Hélène*, ➤*Orphée aux enfers* ('Orpheus in the Underworld'), ➤*Barbe-bleue* ('Bluebeard') and *La ➤Grande-Duchesse de Gérolstein*, satirizing contemporary manners, in a sprightly musical style which became standard for this type of work. Also wrote (but left incomplete at his death) opera *Les ➤Contes d'Hoffmann*. Had early career as cellist, and later managed his own theatres. Visited Britain and USA.

offertoire (Fr.), ➤*offertorium*.

offertorium, offertory (Lat., Eng.), a plainsong or polyphonic setting of biblical works (in Latin) occurring after the Credo in the Mass of the Roman Catholic Church while the Eucharist is being prepared and offered. Organ music supplementing or replacing this is also so called.

Ogdon, John [Andrew Howard] (1937–89), English pianist, joint winner in 1962 of the International Tchaikovsky Competition in Moscow (jointly with Ashkenazy); known for performance of Busoni's Piano Concerto and other unusual, 'heavy-weight' works. Also composer, e.g. of preludes for piano.

Ohana, Maurice (1914–92), French composer (British passport) of Spanish descent, born in Casablanca and resident in Paris; works include choral settings of Spanish verse (some by Lorca) and a guitar concerto. Some other works including *Signes* (flute, two zithers, percussion) use his own invention, a zither with tunings in one third of a tone.

Ohlsson, Garrick (b. 1948), American pianist, the first American to win the Chopin International Competition in Warsaw (1970); his international tours have embraced many returns to Poland.

ohne (Ger.), without.

Oistrakh, David [Fedorovich] (1908–74), Russian violinist to whom Shostakovich's violin concertos are dedicated, and who became among the best-known Soviet artists in the West. Also occasional viola-player and, from the 1960s, conductor. Father of the following.

Oistrakh, Igor [Davidovich] (b. 1931), Russian violinist, pupil of his father (preceding), internationally prominent after winning the Wieniawski Competition in Poland in 1952. Also, since 1968, conductor.

Okeghem, ➤Ockeghem.

Oklahoma!, musical play with text by Oscar Hammerstein II based on *Green Grow the Lilacs* by Lynn Riggs; music by Richard Rodgers. Produced in New York, 1943. The story of rural love and celebration is set during the founding of Oklahoma as a state (1907).

Old Hall Manuscript, a collection of

14th–15th-century church music found at St Edmund's College, Old Hall, Herts, published 1933–9 – and now in the British Library.

oliphant, medieval horn made of elephant's tusk or of gold, a symbol of high dignity (e.g. that of knighthood).

Oliver, Stephen (1950–92), English composer, pupil of Leighton and R. Sherlaw Johnson. Full-length opera ➤*Tom Jones* came after many youthful dramatic pieces including three 'mini-operas' (about 10 minutes each). Also wrote a symphony, etc., and much incidental music for plays, including Royal Shakespeare Co.'s *Nicholas Nickleby*.

Oliver!, musical with text and music by Lionel Bart based on Dickens' *Oliver Twist*. Produced in London, 1960. Orphaned Oliver, expelled from the workhouse, has a happier time in Fagin's criminal gang.

Oliveros, Pauline (b. 1932), American composer making much use of electronics and quasi-theatrical presentations. Works include Trio for flute, piano and page-turner; *To Valerie Solanas and Marilyn Monroe in Recognition of their Desperation* for orchestra, chorus, electronics, lights.

Omar Khayyám (*c.* 1050–1123), Persian poet. ➤Lehmann (Liza).

Ondes Martenot (Fr., 'Martenot Waves'), ➤electronic keyboard instrument named after its French inventor, Maurice Martenot (1898–1980); it sounds only one note at a time. Brought out in 1928, it has achieved occasional, mainly French, usage as a solo and orchestral instrument – e.g. by Honegger in ➤*Jeanne d'Arc au bûcher* and Messiaen in ➤*Turangalîla Sympho-*

nie. Yvonne ➤Loriod is a noted performer.

O'Neill, Dennis (b. 1948), British tenor noted particularly in Italian opera roles; made début at Covent Garden in 1979, San Francisco Opera (Elvino in *La Sonnambula*, 1984), Vienna State Opera (Alfredo in *La Traviata*, 1986); also sang as Caruso in British television documentary.

O'Neill, Eugene (1888–1953), American playwright. ➤*Emperor Jones*; ➤Lualdi.

O'Neill, Norman (1875–1934), British composer of much theatre music, including the incidental music to Barrie's *Mary Rose*: also theatre conductor. In addition he wrote orchestral works, chamber music, etc.

On Hearing the First Cuckoo in Spring, piece by Delius for small orchestra, first performed in 1913; it introduces a Norwegian folk-song, and the cuckoo is discreetly impersonated by a clarinet.

Onslow, George (1784–1853), French composer (mother French, father British); lived for a while in London but settled in France and died there. Wrote 35 string quartets and other chamber music which won fashionable success in England and France; also operas, etc.

On the Town, musical with text by Betty Comden and Adolph Green based on the ballet *Fancy Free*; music and additional lyrics by Leonard Bernstein. Produced in New York, 1944. Three smart sailors explore New York's romantic opportunities.

On Wenlock Edge, song-cycle (named from opening words of first poem) for tenor, string quartet and piano by Vaughan Williams, 1896, to texts from A. E. Housman's *A Shropshire Lad*; the accompaniment was later arranged for orchestra by composer.

On Your Toes, musical comedy with text by Richard Rodgers, Lorenz Hart and George Abbott; music by Richard Rodgers. Produced in New York, 1936. Stage-folk story featuring a jazz ballet score (*Slaughter on Tenth Avenue*).

op., ➤*opus*.

open (1, of a string) allowed to vibrate throughout its full length, not 'stopped' by a finger pressed on it; (2, of a pipe) not stopped at the end – e.g. the *open diapason* of the organ, contrasted with the 'stopped diapason'; (3, of the notes of the orchestral horn) not 'stopped' by the placing of the hand firmly inside the bell.

open form, term used to describe certain compositions (from the 1950s) in which the performer has the option of varying the sequence of component sections or may begin at any point and continue in circular fashion until reaching that point again. ➤cycle (1).

Oper (Ger.), opera – also in the sense of 'opera company'; so *Staatsoper*, State Opera.

opera (1, obsolete) a synonym for ➤*opus*; (2) a company performing opera as defined below; so *Vienna State Opera*, etc.; or an opera house itself, e.g. the 'Opéra' (building) in Paris, opened in 1875; (3, principal meaning) type of drama in which all or most characters sing and in which music constitutes a principal element having its own unity. The first works properly so classified are those arising in Italy about 1600 (➤Caccini; ➤Peri).

Various synonyms or near-synonyms for the term *opera* are to be met (➤music-drama; ➤music-theatre) with precise significance depending on historical context. The apparent subdivisions of opera (see following entries) have seeming inconsistencies which are similarly to be resolved only by their contexts.

opera-ballet, stage work giving approximately equal importance to opera and ballet, especially those written by Lully, Rameau and their contemporaries in 17th- and 18th-century France.

opéra bouffe (Fr.), type of light, often satirical opera or operetta, e.g. the operettas of Offenbach. Term taken from, but historically not identical with, ➤*opera buffa*.

opera buffa (It.), comic opera, particularly the 18th-century Italian kind (in contrast with ➤*opera seria*) as represented by Pergolesi's *La* ➤*serva padrona*, extended up to Rossini's examples.

Opera Cenedlaethol Cymru, alternative (Welsh) name for ➤Welsh National Opera.

opéra comique (Fr.), term literally signifying comic opera, but having two special meanings – (1) in the 18th century, a type of French comic opera with spoken dialogue, e.g. by Philidor and Monsigny, less lofty in ideas and style than the current serious operas (generally on heroic or mythological subjects); (2) in the 19th century, any opera with spoken dialogue, even if not comic – such as *Faust* and *Carmen* in their original versions, without recitatives. (The Paris theatre called the 'Opéra-Comique' originally observed this distinction.)

Opera North, British opera company founded 1975, originally as an off-shoot from English National Opera, taking present name 1981, under David Lloyd-Jones as artistic director to 1990. Music director 1990–97, Paul Daniel. From 1999, the American, Steven Sloane.

opera-oratorio, term applied by Stravinsky to his ➤*Oedipus Rex*, intended to be presented on the stage but in a static manner remote from operatic convention.

opera seria (It.), literally 'serious opera' (as contrasted with ➤*opera buffa*, comic opera); specifically, the type flourishing in Italy in the 18th century with plots taken from ancient history or mythology and with leading roles for ➤*castrato* singers – replaced, in early 19th-century examples such as Rossini's *Semiramide*, by contraltos in heroic male roles.

operetta (It., little opera), term used for an opera of a light type whether full-length or (like some of Offenbach's) in one act. The term is virtually synonymous with 'light opera'; ➤musical comedy.

opérette (Fr.), ➤operetta.

ophicleide, bass instrument made of metal and with keys; used in the orchestra (e.g. by Berlioz, Mendelssohn, early Verdi) as an improvement on the ➤serpent, but superseded about 1850 by the tuba, on which instrument the parts intended for the ophicleide are now normally played. The 'key bugle' (or 'keyed bugle', or 'Kent bugle') was an instrument of related type, but roughly of bugle size and pitch; it had some use in early 19th-century bands before the advent of the cornet.

opus (Lat., a work; abbr. *op.*), term used, with a number, for the enumeration or a composer's works supposedly in the order of their composition: if an 'opus' comprises more than one piece, then a subdivision may be used (e.g. 'opus 40, no. 2'). Occasionally the letters *a* and *b* are used to indicate different but equally valid versions of the same work (➤'St Anthony' Variations). But confusion arises because various composers have (a) failed to number their works, (b) numbered only some and not others, (c) allowed their works to appear with numbers not representing their real order of composition – e.g. Dvořák, to satisfy a publisher's desire to pass off early works as recent ones.

oration, term occasionally used as a musical title, e.g. by Frank ➤Bridge; also, in its Spanish form meaning 'prayer', by ➤Turina.

oratorio (1) type of musical composition (originating about 1600 in performances at the Oratory of St Philip Neri in Rome, hence the name) consisting of an extended setting of a religious text set out in more or less dramatic form – usually for soloists, chorus and orchestra: originally requiring scenery, costumes and action, but later customarily conceived and given in concert form; (2) term used also for a type of work similar to the above but on a non-religious – though usually 'elevated' – subject; e.g. Tippett's *A* ➤*Child of Our Time*.

Orchésographie, title of a French treatise on dancing (an important source in music history), 1589.

Orchester (Ger.), orchestra.

orchestra, a numerous mixed body of

instrumentalists. As a more or less stable institution, the orchestra originated in early 17th-century opera, being afterwards continually modified (obsolete instruments being replaced by new ones), enlarged and re-systematized. So *symphony orchestra*, standard large orchestra of 19th and 20th centuries, able to play symphonies, etc. – as opposed, e.g., to *chamber orchestra* (small size) or *string orchestra* (strings only). The term *theatre orchestra* customarily indicates not an opera orchestra (which is ideally of 'symphonic' size) but a smaller orchestra used for musicals, etc., commonly including saxophones. A combination of wind instruments only, or any combination for dancing to, is commonly called not an orchestra but a band. Note that *philharmonic orchestra*, unlike *symphony orchestra*, does not signify a type of orchestra (➤philharmonic). Although composers may vary both the kind and numbers of instruments used (variety being especially noticeable in the percussion section), the forces standardized by the requirements of symphonic music in the late 19th century and most of the 20th are:

(a) woodwind:
   3 flutes, 1 doubling piccolo
   3 oboes, 1 doubling English horn
   3 clarinets, 1 doubling bass clarinet
   3 bassoons, 1 doubling double-bassoon
(b) brass:
   4 (sometimes 6) horns
   3 trumpets
   3 trombones (2 tenor, 1 bass)
   1 tuba
(c) percussion:
   3 timpani (1 player)
   snare-drum, bass-drum, cymbals, gong, triangle, xylophone, vibra-phone, etc. (2 or more players)
(d) unclassified:
   2 harps
   1 piano
(e) strings:
   first violins (about 14)
   second violins (about 14)
   violas (about 12)
   cellos (about 10)
   double-basses (about 8)

Such works as Tchaikovsky's Symphony no. 6 (1893), Elgar's Symphony no. 1 (1908), Bartók's Concerto for Orchestra (1944) and Shostakovich's Symphony no. 15 (1972) could all be encompassed by these forces. (The order given above is that observed in conventional modern printing of a score, except that there is no standard order in percussion.) Since the 1970s there has been an explosive expansion in the orchestral forces demanded by composers, notably in the range of percussion instruments; but the above remains a basic 'establishment' which the management of a symphony orchestra maintains and budgets for.

Orchestra of the Age of Enlightenment, ➤Age of Enlightenment.

orchestration, the art of writing suitably for an orchestra, band, etc.; or of scoring for these a work originally designed for another medium. So *orchestrate, orchestrator*.

orchestre (Fr.), orchestra.

Orchestre de Paris, French orchestra founded in 1967; Barenboim, conductor from 1975, was succeeded by Bychkov, 1990.

orchestrion, type of large ➤barrel-organ with pipes and percussion, imitating an orchestra.

315

ordre (Fr.), an equivalent of ➤suite, e.g. in Couperin's keyboard works.

Orfeo (properly La favola d'Orfeo, It., 'The Story of Orpheus'), opera by Monteverdi (one of the first of all operas, and the oldest in today's repertory), produced in Mantua, 1607; libretto by A. Striggio. Eurydice dies; her husband Orpheus descends into Hades, rescues her but loses her again.

Orfeo ed Euridice (It., 'Orpheus and Eurydice'), opera by Gluck, produced in Vienna, 1762, with Italian libretto by R. da Calzabigi; revised version in French (Orphée), produced in Paris, 1774. Orpheus's apparent failure to bring his dead wife Eurydice back from Hades is rectified by Cupid's intervention.

Orff, Carl (1895–1982), German composer, chiefly for the stage; also noted musical educator: a specially devised educational range of percussion instruments bears his name and his own music is also conspicuous for its use of percussion (➤stone chimes). Works include operas Die ➤Kluge, Der Mond ('The Moon'), Oedipus der Tyrann, ➤Antigone, Oedipus and others; incidental music to A Midsummer Night's Dream; scenic choral works ➤Carmina Burana (now generally regarded as a concert work), Catulli Carmina (Lat., 'Songs of Catullus'), Trionfo di Afrodite (It., 'Triumph of Aphrodite') – these last three grouped as Trionfi (Triumphs).

organ (1) historically, a keyboard instrument in which wind is blown by a bellows through pipes to sound the notes; made in various sizes down to the medieval 'portative', i.e. portable, carried by the player (as distinct from the ➤positive organ). Tone is varied by the selection and combination of different ➤stops on different keyboards; a pedal keyboard, originating in Germany before 1500, has gradually become standard as well as up to five (very rarely more) manual keyboards. These five are called ➤Choir, ➤Great, ➤Swell, ➤Solo and ➤Echo (reading upwards), but it is common to find only two (Great, Swell) or three (Choir, Great, Swell). The 19th and 20th centuries have brought technical improvements, e.g. electricity to work the bellows, and have also much increased the power and variety of organs – ➤unit organ; ➤theatre organ – but older principles of organ-building are esteemed, and (even in construction of modern instruments) the older 'tracker ➤action' is preferred by soloists to the newer alternatives; (2) term of each tone-producing part of the instrument described above – e.g. the Great Organ, Pedal Organ, meaning the Great and Pedal keyboards plus the pipes controlled by them and the appropriate machinery; (3) a keyboard instrument imitating the traditional organ: ➤electronic organ; (4, extensions of the term) ➤mouth-organ, ➤reed-organ.

organistrum, ➤hurdy-gurdy.

organology, (rare term for) the study of musical instruments in general (not just the organ).

organ-point, ➤pedal-point.

organum (Lat.), a medieval form of ➤part-writing (from the ninth century) based on a plainsong which was harmonized by the addition of one, two, or three (usually parallel) parts.

Orgel (Ger.) = organ; so Bach's ➤Orgelbüchlein.

Orgelbüchlein (Ger., 'Little Organ Book'), a compilation by Bach (1717) of 46 chorale preludes for the organ.

orgue (Fr.) = organ.

Orkney Wedding with Sunrise, orchestral work by P. M. Davies, 1985, with bagpipes in the last part of the score.

Ormandy (original surname Blau), **Eugene** (1899–1985), Hungarian-born conductor (originally violinist). Settled in USA, 1920; succeeded Stokowski as conductor of Philadelphia Orchestra, 1936–80.

Ormindo, opera by Cavalli, produced in Venice, 1644. Libretto by Giovanni Faustini: the title-role is that of a prince of Tunis.

ornament, one or more notes considered as an embellishment of a melody, either – (1) inserted by the performer (e.g. the opera-singer in Handel's time) from his or her knowledge of current conventions, without specific written instructions from the composer (➤*appoggiatura*); (2) conveyed by a sign or abbreviation, e.g. ∿ (➤*turn*), tr ∿ (➤*trill*), or by notes in small type (e.g. ➤*acciaccatura*); or (3) written in full or ordinary notation, even when it could have been conveyed by a sign – as e.g., the turn written out in full by Wagner and Bruckner. Also as verb – to *ornament* a melody in performance, etc.

Ornstein, Leo (b. 1892), Russian-born pianist and composer who settled in USA, 1906. Pioneered Schoenberg's and other new music there; ceased performing in 1920 but continued composing and teaching. Works include *Danse Sauvage* (also known as *Wildman's Dance*) for piano, symphonic poem *The Fog*, and a *Hebraic Fantasy* for violin and piano, in celebration of Albert Einstein's 50th birthday, 1929.

orpharion, plucked, fretted instrument similar to ➤pandora (in its main sense) used in early 17th century

Orphée, opera by Gluck. ➤*Orfeo ed Euridice*.

Orphée aux enfers (Fr., 'Orpheus in the Underworld'), operetta by Offenbach, produced in Paris, 1858 (revised, expanded version, 1874). Libretto by H. Crémieux and L. Halévy, satirizing modern times under cover of guying the old legend. It quotes, satirically, the famous aria 'Che farò' from Gluck's ➤*Orfeo*.

Orpheus, opera by Monteverdi. ➤*Orfeo*.

Orpheus, symphonic poem by Liszt, 1854 – Orpheus, tamer of the beasts, symbolizing the power of art.

Orpheus, ballet with music by Stravinsky, choreography by Balanchine, produced in New York, 1948 – based on story of Orpheus's quest for Eurydice, and his death.

Orpheus and Eurydice, opera by Gluck. ➤*Orfeo ed Euridice*.

Orpheus Britannicus (Lat., the British Orpheus, i.e. Purcell), title of two posthumous volumes of Purcell's songs; a selection of 18 of these was arranged by Britten.

Orpheus in the Underworld, operetta by Offenbach. ➤*Orphée aux enfers*.

Orr, Robin (name used by Robert Kemsley Orr) (b. 1909), British composer. Works include Sinfonia Helvetica, opera *Full Circle*. Professor at Cambridge, 1965–75. CBE, 1972.

Orrego Salas, Juan [Antonio] (b. 1919), Chilean composer of cantata (to words of Neruda) *América, no en vano invocamos tu nombre* ('America, we do not invoke your name in vain'), also of four symphonies, a concerto for piano trio and orchestra, etc. Active in promoting Latin-American music in USA.

Ortiz, Cristina (b. 1950), Brazilian-born pianist, naturalized British 1977; in some concerts and recordings of Mozart concertos, directs orchestra from the keyboard. Has exhibited her wide standard repertory under Ashkenazy, Masur, Mehta, etc., and has recorded Stenhammar's Concerto no. 2.

Ortiz, Diego (*c.* 1510–*c.* 1570), Spanish composer who was in service to the Spanish viceroy in Naples and later to Philip II of Spain; wrote a famous treatise on instrumental variation-technique as well as vocal polyphonic works – Magnificats, motets, etc.

O salutaris hostia (Lat., 'O saving victim'), latter part of a Roman Catholic hymn, sung to its own plainsong melodies or to later composed settings.

Osborne, Nigel (b. 1948), British composer and university teacher; works include *I am Goya* for baritone and instrumental ensemble, opera *The* ➤*Electrification of the Soviet Union* (and other operas), *Hommage à Panufnik* for orchestra. Professor at Edinburgh University since 1990. (➤*mbira*.)

ossia (It., from *o sia,* or it may be), (1) term used to introduce an alternative version of a musical passage, e.g. an editor's correction of an old com-poser's text which appears to be in error, or a composer's own simpler alternative for a passage difficult to perform, (2) term used to introduce an opera's subtitle (➤*Otello*).

ostinato (It., obstinate), a persistently repeated musical figure or rhythm; so *basso ostinato,* a bass having this characteristic – i.e. ➤ground bass. (The term *pizzicato ostinato* in the third movement of Tchaikovsky's Symphony no. 4 exceptionally means only 'persistent pizzicato', not implying repetition.)

Oswald von Wolkenstein (*c.* 1377–1445), German poet, composer and performer of his own songs; member of a knightly family, he was involved in disputes over land and was several times imprisoned. Composed monophonic and polyphonic songs.

Otaka, Tadaaki (b. 1947), Japanese conductor who studied in Vienna; conductor, Tokyo Philharmonic Orchestra 1971–91 (now Conductor Laureate); principal conductor BBC Welsh Orchestra (now National Orchestra of Wales), 1987–96).

Otello, form of name used by Italians for the character called Othello by Shakespeare: title of operas (based on Shakespeare's play) (1) by Rossini, produced in Naples, 1816, with libretto by B. de Salsa (*Otello, ossia Il Moro di Venezia*: 'Othello, or The Moor of Venice'); (2) by Verdi, produced in Milan, 1887, with libretto (*Otello*) by A. Boito.

ôtez (Fr.), take off (imperative); *ôtez les sourdines,* take off the mutes.

Othello, concert-overture by Dvořák (➤*Carnival*) 1892, after Shakespeare. Also Italian operas on the play: ➤*Otello*.

ottava (It., sometimes written 8va.), octave; so *all'ottava*, at the octave (higher); *ottava bassa*, an octave lower.

ottavino (It.), the modern Italian name for the small flute, elsewhere called ➤piccolo (itself signifying 'little' in Italian).

Otter, Anne Sofie von (b. 1955), Swedish mezzo-soprano equally admired in opera (Cherubino in *Le nozze di Figaro* as Covent Garden début, 1985) and concert (American début with Chicago Symphony Orchestra, 1985). Has recorded Swedish songs by Stenhammar.

Otterloo, [Jan] **Willem van** (1907–78), Dutch conductor (and composer of orchestral music); conductor of the Residentie Orchestra of The Hague, 1949–73; he also worked in Sydney and Melbourne.

ottoni (It.), brass instruments.

oud, a French spelling of the Arabic word (in English usage ➤'ud) for the Arab lute.

Our Man in Havana, opera by Malcolm Williamson, produced in London, 1963; libretto by Sidney Gilliat after Graham Greene's novel, bitterly satirizing espionage and 'security'.

Ours, L', ➤*Bear*.

Ouseley, Frederick [Arthur] **Gore** (1825–89), English organist, composer of church music, etc., professor at Oxford, clergyman and baronet (succeeding his father).

Ousset, Cécile (b. 1936), French pianist who achieved international prominence rather later in life than is common; British début, 1980.

ouverture, Ouvertüre (Fr., Ger.), ➤overture.

overblow, to blow a woodwind instrument harder, in such a way that its notes are 'stepped up' from those of its 'basic' pitch. In most such instruments the notes are 'stepped up' first of all by an octave (this representing, in the ➤harmonic series, the distance from the first to the second harmonic), and such instruments are said to *overblow an octave*. In the clarinet, however, the second harmonic is missing and the notes are 'stepped up' not by an octave but by a 12th: it is therefore said to *overblow a twelfth*.

overstrung, description of pianos in which the strings are set at two different levels, crossing – this affording greater length of string for a given size of instrument.

overtone, name for any notes of the ➤harmonic series except the first (fundamental).

overture (1) piece of orchestral music preceding an opera or oratorio – since Gluck, usually musically allusive to what follows; (2) similar piece preceding a play; (3) since the early 19th century, also a type of one-movement orchestral work composed for the concert hall, and usually having a title revealing a literary, pictorial, or emotional clue. (This last type is specifically called *concert-overture*.) So *French overture*, 17th–18th century form of (1) above, in two movements, slow-fast (sometimes with final return to slow tempo); *Italian overture*, in three movements, quick-slow-quick (the form from which the symphony evolved).

Owen, Wilfred (1895–1918), British poet. ➤*War Requiem*.

'Oxford' Symphony, nickname for Haydn's Symphony no. 92 in G (Hob. I: 92), performed when Haydn visited Oxford University in 1791 to receive an honorary doctorate; but composed in 1789 without this purpose in mind.

Ox Minuet (Ger., *Ochsenmenuett*), minuet attributed to Haydn, but really by his pupil, I. X. von Seyfried (1776–1841), who introduced it into an opera of the same name, compiled mainly from Haydn's works. (Haydn was supposed to have received an ox as payment for this minuet.)

Ozawa, Seiji (b. 1935), Japanese conductor, pupil of Karajan in Berlin; music director of Toronto Symphony Orchestra, 1965–70, of San Francisco Symphony Orchestra, 1969–76, of Boston Symphony Orchestra since 1973.

P

p, abbr. of *piano* (It., soft); hence, as indications of increasing degrees of softness, *pp, ppp*, etc. – sometimes in even greater aggregations.

Pachelbel, Johann (1653–1706), German organist and composer of keyboard music (including preludes on Lutheran chorales), church music, chamber music (including the celebrated *Canon and Gigue* in D, originally for three violins and ➤*continuo*), etc. Teacher of Bach's elder brother Johann Christoph.

Pachmann, Vladimir [de] (1848–1933), Russian pianist who specialized in Chopin and was famous for eccentric behaviour at the keyboard.

Pacific 231, 'symphonic movement' by Honegger, first performed in 1924. Named by the composer after an American railway engine – but 'I have not aimed to imitate the noise of an engine, but rather to express in terms of music a visual impression and physical enjoyment'.

Pacini, Giovanni (1796–1867), Italian composer of more than 80 operas including *Maria, regina d'Inghilterra* ('Mary, Queen of England') and several others on English and Scottish history; also of church music, *Dante Symphony* for orchestra with piano, etc.

Paderewski, Ignacy [Jan] (1860–1941), Polish pianist, pupil of Leschetizky in Vienna, and composer of operas, a piano concerto, symphony, piano solos (including Minuet in G), songs, etc. Also statesman: first Prime Minister of the newly created state of Poland, 1919 (he resigned after ten months). Died in New York.

Paer, Ferdinando (1771–1839), Italian composer who became musical director to Napoleon, and settled in Paris, 1807. (In France the spelling 'Paër' is used.) Wrote more than 40 operas including a *Leonora* (in Italian) on the plot which had already served Gaveaux and which was to serve Beethoven in ➤*Fidelio*.

Paganini, Niccolò (1782–1840), Italian violinist, called by Schumann 'the turning-point of virtuosity'; enormously successful – though, with the subsequent advance in the general level of performers' skill, his feats are no longer regarded as freakishly difficult. Was also guitarist (wrote three string quartets with guitar part) and viola-player: he commissioned, but never played, Berlioz's ➤*Harold en Italie*. Compositions include at least six violin concertos (no. 2 has the ➤*Bell Rondo*); a set of variations for violin called *Il* ➤*Carnevale di Venezia* ('The

Carnival of Venice'); and 24 Capricci (i.e. studies) for unaccompanied violin. One of the latter, in A minor, is the source of (1) Brahms's *Studies in Piano Technique: Variations on a Theme of Paganini*, 1866; (2) Rakhmaninov's *Rhapsody on a Theme of Paganini* for piano and orchestra (also in variation-form), 1934; (3) Blacher's orchestral *Variations on a Theme of Paganini*, 1947; (4) Lutosławski's *Variations on a Theme of Paganini* for two pianos, 1941. Liszt, Schumann, Busoni and others also transcribed his works for piano.

Page, Christopher [Howard] (b. 1952), British musical scholar and conductor; founder (1980) of ensemble Gothic Voices (➤Gothic).

Pagliacci (It., 'Clowns'), opera by Leoncavallo, produced in Milan, 1892. Libretto by composer – on the interaction between a play and the real tragic 'drama' lived by the players.

Paik, Nam June (b. 1932), Korean composer who studied in Germany and later worked in New York and Los Angeles. His works include *Étude for Pianoforte* involving among other things 'the destruction of two pianos, cutting John Cage's necktie, and shampooing him without warning'; also other action-pieces, a cello sonata, etc.

Paine, John Knowles (1839–1906), American organist and composer (two symphonies, cantatas, etc.) who studied in Germany and later founded the music faculty at Harvard.

Paisiello, Giovanni (1740–1816), Italian composer who worked in St Petersburg (Catherine the Great's court), Paris (under Napoleon) and Naples, where he died. Wrote more than 100 operas, including a very successful ➤*Barbiere di Siviglia* (before Rossini's); also symphonies, church music, etc.

Palestrina, Giovanni Pierluigi da (1525–94), Italian composer who took the name Palestrina from his native town, near Rome. Was a choirboy, and spent all his musical life in service of the Church; also proved an able businessman. Became choirmaster of the Julian Chapel at St Peter's, Rome, and later held other high positions. After his first wife died he entered the priesthood, but abandoned it and remarried. Apart from a few madrigals his works are all Latin church music for unaccompanied choir – nearly 100 Masses (including ➤*Missa Papae Marcelli* and a Mass on *L'*➤*homme armé*), motets, a Stabat Mater, psalms, etc. Posthumous veneration of him led to various fanciful legends; see next entry.

Palestrina, opera by Pfitzner, produced in Munich, 1917. Libretto by Pfitzner, about the composer – but on the basis of the fiction that Palestrina, by composing his *Missa Papae Marcelli* at direct angelic inspiration, persuaded the ecclesiastical Council of Trent (1545–63) not to ban polyphonic music.

palindrome, a literary name for a word or phrase which reads the same backwards as forwards, e.g. 'Was it a cat I saw?'; hence a similar construction in music, usually involving not note-for-note reversal but a reversed order of sections of a piece, e.g. in Hindemith's opera *Hin und Zurück* ('There and back') (where a revised sequence occurs in both the music and the stage action).

Pallavicino, Carlo (?–1688), Italian

composer, chiefly of opera; worked in Dresden at the Court of Saxony, and died there.

Palmer, Felicity [Joan] (b. 1944), British mezzo-soprano, formerly soprano; her mezzo-soprano roles range from Klytemnestra in *Elektra* (Leipzig and Welsh National Opera, 1991–2) to Katisha in *The Mikado* (English National Opera, 1986). Sang the title-role in the first stage production (Madrid, 1992) of Gerhard's *The Duenna*; recorded Messiaen and Victorian ballads. CBE, 1993.

Palmgren, Selim (1878–1951), Finnish composer who studied in Germany and Italy with Busoni and others; also pianist and conductor; taught in USA, 1923–6. Works include many short piano pieces with 'picturesque' titles (e.g. *Night in May*) and some of Finnish nationalist significance; also five piano concertos, operas, etc.

Pammelia, a collection of English rounds, catches, etc., for voices, published by T. Ravenscroft in 1609. Named from Greek for 'all-honey', and succeeded by *Deuteromelia* (also 1609; Gk., *deutero-*, second).

pan, the name used for the individual metal drums of various sizes in the ➤steel band.

pandiatonic(ism), term coined (from Gk., *pan*, all) by the American musicologist Nicolas Slonimsky to indicate the pronounced use in chord-formation of all seven degrees of the ➤diatonic scale. Examples of such use are the ➤added sixth in jazz and the chord C–E–G–B at the beginning of Delius's ➤*On Hearing the First Cuckoo in Spring*.

pandora (also *bandora*), name given to many varieties of plucked instrument

– especially a type of large, wire-strung ➤cittern used in the 16th–17th centuries as a continuo instrument.

Panis angelicus (Lat., 'Bread of angels'), Roman Catholic text set by Franck as tenor solo accompanied by organ with other instruments, 1872; the setting is also known in various arrangements.

pan-pipes, a series of simple short vertical pipes fixed side by side in order to give a scale when blown – an ancient, medieval and 'folk' instrument. Papageno, as a 'child of Nature', plays one in *Die* ➤*Zauberflöte*.

pantomime (from Gk. for 'all-imitating'), (1) a play in dumb-show, a mime-play – either as a self-contained work or (as in Ravel's ➤*Daphnis et Chloé*, where the story of Pan and Syrinx is mimed) as an episode in a larger work; (2) type of English stage-entertainment presented at Christmas time, loosely founded on a fairy-story or similar traditional source, interspersed with songs and formerly concluding with a harlequinade.

pantonal(ity), ➤atonal.

pantoum (Fr.), type of quatrain of Malayan origin introduced into French verse by Hugo and used by Ravel to describe what is in effect the Scherzo (second of four movements) of his Piano Trio, 1914.

Panufnik, Andrzej (1914–91), Polish composer of ten symphonies (no. 3, *Sinfonia sacra*), *Universal Prayer* for mezzo-soprano, baritone, chorus and orchestra (text by Pope), Polish folk-song settings, etc.; also conductor. Left Poland in protest against political regimentation and came to Britain, 1954 (naturalized 1961); conductor, City of Birmingham Symphony Orchestra, 1957–9. Knighted 1991.

Papillons (Fr., 'Butterflies'), 12 short dance pieces by Schumann, op. 2 (1829–31); thematically connected with Schumann's ➤*Carnaval*.

Papineau-Couture, Jean (b. 1916), Canadian composer and university teacher in Montreal. Works include *Paysage* ('Landscape') for eight narrators, eight singers and instrumental ensemble; a symphony, two string quartets, etc.

Parade, ballet with music by Satie, choreography by Massine, produced in Paris, 1917.

Paradies (or Paradisi), [Pietro] **Domenico** (*c*. 1707–91), Italian harpsichordist, composer of operas, etc., as well as of harpsichord works. Lived for many years as teacher in London.

Paradies und die Peri, Das (Ger., 'Paradise and the Peri'), cantata by Schumann, 1843, with German text translated from part of T. Moore's *Lalla Rookh*. The Peri here is a good spirit of Persian mythology, seeking readmittance to Heaven.

Paradis, Maria Theresia von (1759–1824), Austrian pianist (for whom Mozart wrote a concerto), also organist, singer and composer of three operas and other works; blind from childhood. Performed as pianist in Paris and London.

Paradise Lost, opera by Penderecki, produced in Chicago, 1978; libretto by Christopher Fry, after Milton's poem. Also title of works by ➤Constant; ➤Markevitch.

Paradisi, Domenico, ➤Paradies.

parallel motion, ➤motion.

parameter, vague term (distorted from precise mathematical use) applied from the 1950s to such basic elements of a composition as pitch, loudness, duration and timbre – especially where such elements are subjected to a mathematical order, as in 'total serialism' (➤series).

paraphrase (Fr., Eng.), Liszt's alternative term for 'fantasy' in the sense of a virtuoso solo based on a well-known work – e.g. his *Rigoletto: Concert Paraphrase* for piano, based on Verdi's opera of that name.

parergon (Gk., accessory work), term used by R. Strauss in his *Parergon to the* ➤*Symphonia Domestica* for piano (left hand) and orchestra, 1925, partly based on the other work.

Paris, Orchestre de, French orchestra founded 1967; conductor since 1989 (succeeding Barenboim), Bychkov.

'Paris' Symphonies, a set of six symphonies by Haydn (Hob. I: 82–7) composed in 1785–6, for a series of concerts in Paris: no. 82 is nicknamed *The* ➤*Bear*, no. 83 *The* ➤*Hen*, no. 85 *The* ➤*Queen*.

'Paris' Symphony, nickname for Mozart's Symphony no. 31 in D (K297), composed in Paris for a performance there, 1778.

Park [née Reynolds], **Maria Hester** (1760–1813), British composer, also performing (before her marriage) as pianist and harpsichordist. Her published works include a set of glees as well as a concerto and solo works for harpsichord or piano.

Parker, Horatio [William] (1863–

1919), American composer and organist; pupil of Rheinberger in Germany. Wrote *Hora Novissima* and other oratorios; also two operas, symphony, organ concerto, etc. D.Mus., Cambridge (England), 1902.

parlando, parlante (It., speaking) – either as a literal instruction (e.g. in opera), or as a direction in song indicating a near approach to a speaking tone.

parody, properly (in music as in literature) a work, or part of it, which makes an exaggerated or distorted use of an identifiable model, with humorous intent. But the term is also misleadingly employed to denote a composer's straightforward (non-humorous) imitation or adaptation of his own or someone else's work, e.g. especially the *parody mass* (or, Lat., *missa parodia*) of the 16th–17th centuries, based on a pre-existing motet. This term is a later (musicologists') usage not stemming from the period.

Parrott, Andrew [Haden] (b. 1947), British conductor, also writer on music; sang with the Electric Phoenix group. Founder-director of the Taverner Choir 1973. Conducted Monteverdi's *Vespers* as BBC Proms début 1977 and Salzburg Festival début 1987, and conducted first performance of Weir's *A Night at the Chinese Opera*, 1987.

Parry, [Charles] **Hubert** [Hastings] (1848–1918), British composer of unison song 'Jerusalem', many solo settings of notable English verse, five symphonies, oratorios (➤*Job*, ➤*Judith*), much chamber music, etc. Also writer on music, director of the Royal College of Music (1894–1918), professor at Oxford (1900–1908). Knighted,

1898; baronet, 1903. No relation of the following.

Parry, Joseph (1841–1903), British composer of hymn-tune 'Aberystwyth' (sung to 'Jesu, lover of my soul') and other hymns; also of operas, oratorios, orchestral works, etc. Became professor at Aberystwyth. No relation of the preceding.

Parsifal, opera by Wagner, produced in Bayreuth, 1882; libretto by composer, the hero being the 'simpleton without guile' who restores a sacred spear to the Knight of the Holy Grail. Wagner described the work as a *Bühnenweihfestspiel*, approximately a 'sacred-festival play'. ➤*Lohengrin*.

part (1) the music of a particular performer in an ensemble – the *tenor part*, the *flute part*, etc.; *score and parts*, expression contrasting the score (containing the music of all performers) with the music written separately for individuals; hence – (2) an individual 'strand' of music, whether given to a separate performer or not; a *fugue in four parts* or *four-part fugue*, etc.; so also ➤*part-song*, ➤*part-writing*; (3) a section e.g. of an oratorio (corresponding to an act in opera), a complete evening's work being divided into *parts* so that intervals can be made.

Pärt, Arvo (b. 1935), Estonian composer of a 'St John' Passion, three symphonies, *Cantus in memoriam Benjamin Britten* (➤*cantus*), etc.; emigrated in 1980, settling in West Berlin. His recent compositions, many on religious subjects, include string quartet (entitled *Summa*) and *Sarah was ninety years old* for three voices, percussion and organ.

Partch, Harry (1901–74), American

composer, self-taught, inventor of a series of string and percussion instruments tuned in ➤just intonation and using microtones ('cloud-chamber bowls', 'bamboo marimba', 'quadrangularis reversum', etc.) for which his music is composed – *Windsong, Water, Water* (theatrical work with voices), *And on the Seventh Day Petals Fell in Petaluma*, etc. His other works include a setting of Sophocles' *Oedipus Rex*.

parte (It.), ➤part; *colla parte*, with the (solo) part, i.e. the accompanying instrument(s) accommodating the soloist to allow some licence of tempo.

Parthenia (Gk., maidenhood), fanciful title given to the first book of keyboard music ever printed in England, 1611, containing pieces by Bull, Byrd and O. Gibbons. Full title, *Parthenia, or the Maidenhead of the first music that ever was printed for the virginals*. A succeeding volume was called *Parthenia inviolata* (a pun on 'unviolated' and 'set for viol') – being for keyboard and bass viol.

partial, name given to each of the notes of the ➤*harmonic series*, the lowest or 'fundamental' being the *first partial* and the others (numbered upwards consecutively) *upper partials*.

partie (Fr.), (1) ➤part, (2) ➤partita.

partita (It.), suite or set of variations – term used much in the 18th century, occasionally revived since. ➤*Feldpartie*.

partition, Partitur (Fr., Ger.), ➤score.

Partos, Oedoen (1907–77), Israeli viola-player and composer, Hungarian-born, who settled in Palestine, 1938; works include *In Memoriam* (Heb., *Yizkor*) for viola and orchestra, and a choral fantasy on Yemenite Jewish themes.

Partridge, Ian [Harold] (b. 1938), British tenor who began as piano accompanist. He makes occasional appearances in opera, but has won chief distinction as recitalist in German and English song, with dozens of recordings of Beethoven, Schubert, Britten, Warlock, etc. CBE, 1991.

part-song, (literally) any song written for several vocal ➤parts, without independent accompaniment, as distinct from a solo or unison song; but the term is particularly applied (1) to English songs from the early 16th century onwards, in which the vertical (harmonic) aspect prevails over the horizontal (contrapuntal) one, and the top part most frequently has the melody (unlike the madrigal); (2) to vocal ensemble pieces of similar texture to the above, written in the 19th and 20th centuries.

part-writing, the laying-out of a composition so that each ➤part progresses euphoniously. (The US term is 'voice-leading', introduced as translation of Ger. *Stimmführung* by immigrant musicians unaware of the established English term.)

pas (Fr.), step (in dancing, etc.); *pas d'action*, ballet scene of a dramatic nature; *pas seul, pas de deux*, etc., dance for one person, for two, etc.

pasodoble (Sp., double step), modern Spanish dance in quick 2/4 time – used, in a spirit of parody, in Walton's ➤*Façade*.

Pasquini, Bernardo (1637–1710), Italian organist, harpsichordist and composer of operas, harpsichord sonatas, etc.

passacaglia, passecaille (It., Fr.), instrumental piece (originally a dance) in which a theme stretching over several bars is continually repeated, usually but not necessarily always in the bass. The term is often virtually interchangeable with ➤*chaconne*, except that *passacaglia* seems never to have been applied to a vocal work.

passage, a section of a musical composition – sometimes, not always, with the implication of not having much structural importance (e.g. when a piece is said to contain 'showy passage-work' for a soloist's display).

passaggio (It., 'passage'), the change sensed in a singer's vocal muscles when passing from middle to high register (applied particularly to the tenor voice).

passamezzo (It., also *pass'e mezzo*, i.e. 'pace and a half'), Italian dance, similar to the pavan, known from the 16th century; the music for it often conformed to one of two standardized harmonic patterns.

Passereau, Pierre (active 1509–47), French composer of whom a motet and some chansons survive.

passing-note, in harmony, a note which forms a discord with the chord with which it is heard, but which is 'justified' because it is melodically placed between two notes which are not discordant. E.g. the D in the two examples below: the melody appears merely to be 'passing' on the discordant D between the two notes E and C, both concordant.

Passio (Lat.), ➤Passion.

Passion, a musical setting of the biblical story of the suffering (Lat., *passio*) and death of Jesus, properly to be sung in churches in the week before Easter. Works of this character exist as Latin motets (e.g. by Davy and Rore), but the term is usually reserved for larger works written in the vernacular tongue – notably those in German by Bach (➤*St John Passion*, ➤*St Matthew Passion*) and earlier by Schütz. These have a semi-dramatic form, individual singers taking the parts of Jesus, Judas, etc. The so-called *Passion chorale* (➤chorale) is the hymn 'O Haupt voll Blut und Wunden' (usually translated 'O Sacred Head'), originally by Hassler, which Bach used prominently in both his Passions as part of the (non-biblical) commentary made by soloists and chorus on the story: other hymn-tunes are similarly incorporated. ➤Graun, ➤Pärt, ➤Pepping, ➤Pinkham, ➤Rochberg.

Passion, or (It.) *La Passione*, nickname for Haydn's Symphony no. 49 in F minor, 1768 (Hob. I: 49). The reference is apparently to the Christian Passion (see preceding), perhaps for a performance at Passiontide.

Pasternak, Boris (1890–1960), Russian poet and novelist. ➤*Electrification of the Soviet Union*.

pasticcio (It., a pie), operatic work with music drawn for the purpose from works by different composers – as commonly in the 18th century (➤*Love in a Village*). The term might well be extended to include a piece compiled from different works by the same composer, e.g. ➤*Wiener Blut*.

pastiche (Fr.), (1) ➤*pasticcio*; (2) a piece

composed deliberately in the style of another composer.

pastoral (1) term or nickname for music evoking (e.g. by instrumentation or verbal label) a rustic subject – usually as adjective (see following entries) but also as noun; (2) occasional 18th-century term for a stage entertainment with a rustic setting.

'Pastoral' Sonata, nickname (not the composer's) for Beethoven's Piano Sonata in D, op. 28, 1801: the last movement may seem to suggest a dance to a rustic bagpipe.

Pastoral Symphony (1) Beethoven's own title for his Symphony no. 6 in F, first performed in 1808. Title goes on: '. . . or Memories of Life in the Country (the expression of feeling, rather than painting)' – the five movements having allusive titles (e.g. no. 2, 'By the Brook', incorporating imitations of quail, cuckoo and nightingale); (2) title of an orchestral interlude in Handel's ➤*Messiah*, referring to the shepherds to whom Christ's birth was announced, and said to be based on an Italian folk-melody heard by Handel (➤*piffero*) – this not being a ➤symphony in the modern sense; (3) title (*A Pastoral Symphony*) of Vaughan Williams's Symphony no. 3 (but, in conformity with his practice, not numbered by him – first performed in 1922); it has a wordless high voice in the last movement.

pastourelle (Old Fr., 'shepherdess'), type of poetic dialogue (and the music associated with it) between a shepherdess and a knight aiming to seduce her; current in 13th-century France and earlier. The term was later revived for works making sophisticated allusion to pastoral life.

pathetic, English equivalent to ➤*pathétique*; legitimate but not generally current in such contexts, perhaps because English usage has lost the root-sense of 'pathos'.

Pathétique, title given by Beethoven (*Sonate pathétique*) to his Piano Sonata in C minor, op. 13, composed about 1798; and by Tchaikovsky to his Symphony no. 6, 1893.

Patience, or Bunthorne's Bride, operetta by Sullivan, produced in London, 1881. Libretto by W. S. Gilbert. Patience, the dairymaid heroine of this satire on 'aestheticism', does not become the bride of the poet Bunthorne – nor does anyone.

Patterson, Paul [Leslie] (b. 1947), British composer of Requiem, Mass of the Sea, *Timepiece* for six male voices; *Upside-down-Under Variations* for orchestra, *Cracowian Counterpoints* for 14 instruments. Head of Composition, Royal Academy of Music, 1985.

patter-song, type of comic song (especially in opera) dependent for its effect on the rapid enunciation of syllables – usually a solo, though Sullivan has a patter-trio in ➤*Ruddigore*.

Patti, Adelina [originally Adela Juana Maria] (1843–1919), Spanish-born Italian soprano who made her operatic début at 16 in New York, later settling in Britain; one of the most famous performers of her period.

Pau, Maria de la, ➤Tortelier.

Pauk, György (b. 1936), Hungarian-born violinist, naturalized British in 1967; recital partner with Peter Frankl; performs major modern works (➤Imai).

Pauke(n) (Ger.), kettledrum(s); *Pauken-messe*, ➤Drum Mass; *Sinfonie mit dem Paukenschlag* ('Symphony with the Drum-stroke'), ➤*Surprise Symphony*; *Sinfonie mit dem Paukenwirbel*, ➤Drum-Roll Symphony.

Paul Bunyan, operetta by Britten, with text by W. H. Auden, on the subject of an American legendary lumber-man hero; first performed, New York, 1941, then suppressed by the composer until 1976 (when publication and radio and stage performances took place).

Paulus, ➤*St Paul*.

Paulus, Stephen [Harrison] (b. 1949), American composer of operas *The Postman Always Rings Twice* (after James Cain's novel) and *The Woodlanders* (after Hardy's); also of Symphony in Three Movements, concerto for string quartet and orchestra, etc.

pausa (It.), Italian term equivalent to the English ➤rest, not to the English ➤pause (It., *fermata*).

pause (Eng.), (1) the sign ◠ meaning that the note or rest so marked must be held longer than normally. How long is determined by the performer's discretion, though the composer may add the words 'short' or 'long' in various languages as an additional indication; (2) ➤general pause.

Pause (Ger.), (1) a ➤*pause* (as in English, above); (2) a ➤*rest*; (3) an interval (in a concert, etc.).

pavan, pavane (Eng., Fr.), slow, stately dance dating at least from the 16th century, and mentioned in Shakespeare; it was often followed by the quicker ➤*galliard*. Fauré's work so entitled (1887) is for orchestra and op-

tional chorus; Ravel's *Pavane pour une Infante défunte* ('Pavane for a deceased Infanta') was composed for piano in 1899 and later orchestrated. (Note that *pavan*, accented on first syllable, is the authentic English form.) ➤*passa-mezzo*; ➤Gould (M.).

Pavarotti, Luciano (b. 1936), Italian tenor, eminent in opera: Covent Garden from 1963; La Scala, Milan, from 1966. Continued into the 1990s as major star in the operatic repertory and conquered non-classical public with soccer World Cup 'anthem' (1990), 'Nessun dorma' from *Turandot*.

pavillon (Fr.), the 'bell' (extremity opposite to the mouthpiece) of a horn, trumpet, etc. (Named from its pavilion-like shape.) So, as direction to brass-players, *pavillons en l'air*, with the bells held high up so as to increase the volume. *Pavillon Chinois* ('Chinese pavilion'), ➤*jingling johnny*.

Pearl-Fishers, The, opera by Bizet. ➤*Pêcheurs de perles*.

Pears, Peter [Neville Luard] (1910–86), British tenor, devoted interpreter (and homosexual companion) of Britten, who wrote for him the leading tenor parts in his operas and other works (e.g. ➤*Peter Grimes*, ➤*Serenade*, ➤*War Requiem*). Internationally distinguished also in Bach, etc.; also writer on musical subjects, editor, etc. Knighted, 1978.

Pearsall, Robert Lucas (calling himself de Pearsall) (1795–1856), British composer, chiefly of vocal music – madrigals in 16th-century style, part-songs, Anglican and Roman Catholic church music, etc. Settled in Switzerland and died there.

Pearson, Henry Hugo, ➤Pierson.

Pêcheurs de perles, Les (Fr., 'The Pearl-Fishers'), opera by Bizet, produced in Paris, 1863. Libretto by E. Cormon and M. Carré; the scene is set in Ceylon, though the characters are called Indians.

ped., abbr. for ➤*pedal*: (1, in piano music) instruction that the sustaining pedal is to be depressed until a point when its release is indicated; (2, in organ music) indication of music to be played on the pedal keyboard.

pedal (1, in harmony) a note sustained below (i.e. at the foot of) changing harmonies: this is called a *pedal* or *pedal point* or *pedal bass*. If it is thus sustained but not in the bass it is an *inverted pedal*; (2) the lowest ('fundamental') note of the harmonic series; (3) a foot-operated lever – as on ➤harp, ➤harpsichord, ➤kettledrum, ➤organ, ➤piano.

pedal-board, a keyboard played with the feet – such as is normally found on the organ, rarely on other keyboard instruments.

pedal clarinet, ➤clarinet.

pédalier (Fr.), (1) ➤pedal-board, (2) ➤pedal-piano.

pedal-piano, a piano fitted with a pedal keyboard in addition to its ordinary one – used by organists for home practice, but also written for expressly, e.g. by Schumann and Alkan.

pedal point, ➤pedal (1).

Pedrell, Felipe (1841–1922), Spanish musicologist, editor of old Spanish music; teacher of Falla, Granados and others, and composer of operas, church music, symphonic poems, etc.

Pedrotti, Carlo (1817–93), Italian composer of *Tutti in maschera* ('Everyone Masked') and many other operas; also conductor of a much admired orchestral concert series (1868–82) in Turin. He committed suicide.

Peer Gynt, play by Ibsen (named after its boasting folk-hero) for which Grieg wrote incidental music for the original production, 1876: two orchestral suites aré drawn from this. An opera by Egk (1938) is also based on the play, as is a ballet with music by Schnittke (1989). Incidental music to the play has also been written by Saeverud (1948).

Peerson, Martin (*c.* 1571–1651), English composer of church music and other vocal music and also works for viols and for keyboard, etc.: master of the choristers at St Paul's, London.

Peeters, Flor (1903–86), Belgian organist, pianist, composer of an organ concerto, songs, etc.; was created a Belgian baron in 1971.

Pelléas et Mélisande (Fr., 'Pelléas and Mélisande'), play by Maeterlinck, 1892 (named from its ill-fated medieval lovers) – source of (1) opera by Debussy, almost a word-for-word setting of the play, produced in Paris, 1902; (2) incidental music to the play composed by Fauré, 1898, and by Sibelius, 1905; (3) symphonic poem by Schoenberg, composed 1902–3, first performed in 1905.

Peña, Paco (b. 1942), Spanish guitarist, exponent of ➤flamenco style; professor in Rotterdam since 1985. With choral cooperation from S. Dodgson, composed a Mass (*Misa flamenca*), 1990.

Peñalosa, Francisco de (*c.* 1470–1528), Spanish composer, court and cathedral musician; wrote Masses, motets and other vocal works.

Penderecki, Krzysztof (b. 1933), Polish composer who has travelled widely to supervise (and sometimes conduct) his own music. His compositions include *Threnody for the Victims of Hiroshima* for 52 string instruments, *De natura sonoris* (Lat., 'Of the Nature of Sound') for orchestra, operas *The Devils of Loudun* and ➤*Paradise Lost*; also various works for voices and orchestra on religious texts – Stabat Mater, 'St Luke' Passion, etc.

penillion (Welsh, pl.), a type of traditional Welsh singing, in which verses (either given or improvised) are sung in counterpoint to a well-known melody played on the harp. Term used also as title of an orchestral work by Grace Williams, 1955, based on the musical ideas of traditional penillion.

penny-whistle, ➤tin-whistle.

pentatonic (from Gk., *pente*, five), term used of a scale comprising only five notes – particularly that represented by the five black keys of the piano (or other notes in the same position relative to each other). This form of pentatonic scale is widely used in folk-music of many countries – Scottish, Chinese, Afro-American (e.g. 'Swing Low, Sweet Chariot'), etc.

Pentland, Barbara [Lally] (b. 1912), Canadian composer, pupil of Copland and others; formerly university teacher. Works include four symphonies, three string quartets, piano pieces.

Pépin, [Jean-Joséphat] Clermont (b. 1926), Canadian composer, pupil of Honegger, Jolivet and Messiaen in Paris. Works include ballet scores, five symphonies and symphonic poem *Guernica*; five string quartets.

Pepping, Ernst (1901–81), German composer, chiefly of Protestant church music – unaccompanied motets, a *St Matthew* ➤*Passion*, etc.; also of works for orchestra, for piano and for organ.

Pepusch, Johann Christoph (also known as John Christopher) (1667–1752), German-born composer (also organist) who settled in London about 1700, and died there. Arranged the music for the original production of *The* ➤*Beggar's Opera*; also composed other stage music, church music, concertos, etc., and wrote theoretical treatises.

per (It.), by, through, for, etc.; *per archi*, for strings; *dramma per musica*, drama through music, i.e. opera.

Perahia, Murray (b. 1947), American pianist who won the Leeds Piano Competition in 1972 and settled in London; became a co-director of the Aldeburgh Festival 1982–9. He directs Mozart concertos from the keyboard.

percussion, collective name for instruments in which (usually) a resonating surface is struck by the player – in most cases directly by hand or stick, but sometimes through leverage as in the type of bass-drum used in dance bands, operated by a pedal. The piano and celesta come technically within this definition of percussion instruments but are not conventionally so classified: however, the piano is sometimes said to be 'employed as a percussion instrument' (i.e. for percussive rather than melodic effect) in such works as Stravinsky's *The* ➤*Wedding* and various works of Orff. Percussion instruments as used today in the symphony orchestra, dance band, etc., may be tuned to a definite pitch (e.g., ➤kettledrum, tubular ➤bell, ➤glockenspiel, ➤xylophone, ➤vibraphone, ➤marimba) or may be of indefinite pitch, e.g. ➤triangle, ➤gong, ➤castanets, ➤whip, ➤rattle, ➤anvil and the following drums – ➤snare-drum, ➤tenor drum, ➤bass drum, ➤tabor, ➤tambourine, ➤bongo; the ➤tom-tom may be of definite or indefinite pitch: the normal ➤cymbals are of indefinite pitch but the 'ancient cymbal' or ➤crotale is not. Instruments that are shaken rather than struck, e.g. ➤maraca, ➤rattle, are also placed within the percussion section of an orchestra, as are certain freak instruments, e.g. motor-horn, iron chains, when (exceptionally) employed. In listing the members of an orchestra, a common but absurd British practice gives 'timpani [i.e. kettledrums] and percussion' as though these were mutually exclusive; the reason is that the timpanist counts as the senior player, the other players taking any other instruments specified.

perdendosi (It., losing itself; accent on second syllable), direction for performance indicating 'softer and softer until dying away'.

perfect (1) term used to describe the intervals of a fourth, fifth and eighth (octave) in their 'standard' dimensions – e.g. C up to F, to G, and to C respectively. They become ➤diminished if lessened by a semitone and ➤augmented if enlarged by a semitone; (2) type of ➤cadence; (3) term used in the phrase *perfect time*, meaning (in medieval music) triple time; (4) term used in the phrase *perfect ➤pitch*.

Perfect Fool, The, opera by Holst, produced in London, 1923. Libretto by composer. The work parodies the operatic manner of other composers; the title refers not to any of them, however, but to the simpleton hero.

performance practice, 20th-century term (translated literally from Ger. *Aufführungspraxis*) for the body of conventions and historical knowledge needed to interpret a composer's notation and instructions.

Pergolesi, Giovanni Battista (1710–36), Italian composer, also violinist and church organist. Among his comic operas *La ➤serva padrona* won enormous success: brought to France, it provoked a quarrel between supporters of French and Italian opera – the so-called ➤War of the Comedians. After his early death, many works not his were ascribed to him and sometimes still are – among them the opera *Il ➤maestro di musica*, concertinos for strings, the songs 'Se tu m'ami' (used by Stravinsky in ➤*Pulcinella*) and 'Tre giorni son che Nina'. Authentic works include a ➤*Stabat Mater* for (male) soprano and alto with orchestral accompaniment.

Peri, Jacopo (1561–1633), Italian composer who wrote the first real operas to be staged, *Dafne* (conjecturally 1598; lost) and *Euridice* (1600); also composed other operas (some in collaboration with other composers), ballets, madrigals, etc. Was a priest in service to the Medici family. ➤*Camerata*.

Péri, La (Fr., 'The Peri'), ballet with choreography by Clustine, music by Dukas – the score being described as a *poème dansé* – produced in Paris, 1912.

The Peri is here a good female spirit of Persian mythology.

Perlman, Itzhak (b. 1945), Israeli violinist, son of Polish émigré parents; contracted polio at age four and so plays seated. Trained in New York (US citizen; 1974) and made début there in 1963; appeared in London from 1968 and has continued to sustain highest reputation.

Perosi, Lorenzo (1872–1956), Italian priest and composer who won short-lived success (especially in Italy) with a series of New Testament oratorios, more than 30 Masses, etc. Suffered from mental illness.

Pérotin [Latinized as Perotinus], French composer active in the early 13th century; composed liturgical music showing a high degree of structural organization, in the style later known as ➤*ars antiqua.*

perpetual canon, ➤canon.

perpetuum mobile, ➤*moto.*

Perrault, Charles (1628–1703), French writer. ➤*Cinderella.*

Perrot, Jules Joseph (1810–82), French choreographer. ➤*Giselle.*

Perséphone, stage work by Stravinsky for speaker, singers and orchestra; produced in Paris, 1934. Libretto in French, based on the Greek myth, by A. Gide.

Persichetti, Vincent (1915–87), American composer, pupil of Roy Harris; also pianist, conductor, writer on music, and music publishing executive. Works include nine symphonies (no. 6 is for wind-band); Concerto for piano duet and orchestra; ballet score *King Lear*; sonatas for violin alone and for cello alone.

Perti, Giacomo [Antonio] (1661–1756), Italian composer of operas, oratorios, Masses, etc.; for 60 years director of music at the church of San Petronio in Bologna.

pesante (It.), heavily.

Pešek, Libor (b. 1933), Czech conductor; music director of Czech State Chamber Orchestra 1969–77, principal conductor Royal Liverpool Philharmonic Orchestra since 1987 (BBC Proms 1991). His recordings include the complete symphonies of Dvořák.

Peter and the Wolf (Rus., *Petya i volk*), 'musical tale for children' by Prokofiev, first performed in 1936; a narrator's words are illustrated by the orchestra.

Peter Grimes, opera by Britten, produced in London, 1945. Libretto by M. Slater, after Crabbe's poem, 'The Borough'; named after its misanthropic fisherman hero.

Petipa, Marius (1818–1910), French-Russian choreographer. ➤*Don Quixote,* ➤*Seasons,* ➤*Sleeping Beauty.*

petit(e) (Fr.), little; *petite flûte,* ➤piccolo.

Petite Messe Solennelle (Fr. 'Little Solemn Mass', the 'little' apparently in self-deprecation), Mass-setting by Rossini, 1863, for soloists, small choir, two pianos, harmonium; arranged for full orchestra 1867.

Petrarch [Francesco Petrarca] (1303–74), Italian poet. ➤Victory.

Petrassi, Goffredo (b. 1904), Italian composer of operas *Il Cordovano* ('The Spanish Screen') and *Morte dell'aria* ('Death in the Air'), eight concertos for orchestra; *Coro di morti* ('Chorus of the Dead') for male voices, 3 pianos, bass and percussion, and other choral works including *Nonsense* (title in English) on poems by Edward Lear in Italian translation; piano works, songs, etc.

Petri, Michala (b. 1958), Danish recorder player who played on Danish Radio aged five, and now performs internationally. Malcolm Arnold (*Fantasy*, 1987) and other composers have composed specially for her, and she has extensively recorded Vivaldi, Albinoni, etc.

Petrovics, Emil (b. 1930), Yugoslav-born composer who studied in Hungary and lives there; conservatory teacher and operatic administrator in Budapest. Works include operas *C'est la guerre* (Fr., 'That's War' – text in Hungarian), and *Crime and Punishment* (after Dostoyevsky); also a flute concerto, Sinfonia for strings, etc.

Petrushka, ballet with choreography by Fokin, music by Stravinsky, produced in Paris, 1911. The suite drawn from it was revised in 1947. Petrushka (the French form is 'Pétrouchka') is a traditional Russian puppet figure.

Pettersson, [Gustaf] **Allan** (1911–80), Swedish composer, also orchestral viola-player. Studied with Honegger in Paris; composed 15 symphonies, songs, etc.

petto, voce di, ➤chest voice.

Petzold (also Pezel), Johann Christoph (1639–94), trumpeter and violinist, employed as municipal musician at Leipzig and Bautzen; composer and publisher of suites and other works for wind ensemble.

Peyer, Gervase de, ➤De Peyer.

Pezel, ➤Petzold.

pezzo (It., pl. *-i*), a piece, a play, a musical work, etc.

Pfitzner, Hans [Erich] (1869–1949), German composer, born in Moscow; also pianist, conductor and polemical writer – attacking Busoni and modernism generally. Works include ➤*Palestrina* and other operas, a piano concerto, violin concerto, chamber music, songs (some with orchestra).

Phantasie, phantasy (Ger., Eng.), ➤fantasy.

Phantom of the Opera, The, musical with text by composer, Richard Stilgoe, and Charles Hart, based on the novel by Gaston Leroux; lyrics by Charles Hart; music by Andrew Lloyd Webber. Produced in London, 1986. The deformed creature who lurks in the Paris Opéra terrorizes its personnel until a chaste kiss softens him.

Philadelphia Orchestra, American orchestra established in 1900; Stokowski, whose conductorship (1912–38) made it famous, was succeeded by Eugene Ormandy, followed by Riccardo Muti (1980–92), then Wolfgang Sawallisch.

Philharmonia Orchestra, British orchestra founded in 1945 under private management; it was succeeded in 1964 by the self-governing New Philharmonia Orchestra, which itself dropped the 'New' in 1977. Sinopoli was principal conductor 1984–94, from 1997, Christoph von Dohnányi.

philharmonic (from Gk., 'friendly to harmony'), term used as title of various orchestras and other musical bodies. Note that *philharmonic orchestra* merely identifies a particular orchestra; it does not also stand for a type of orchestra, as 'symphony orchestra' does (➤orchestra).

Philidor, surname of a French musical family of whom the most important is François André [Danican] Philidor (1726–95), composer especially of operas (➤opéra comique) including ➤*Tom Jones*; also of a Requiem for Rameau, etc. He was also noted as a chess-player. Died in London.

Philips, Peter (*c.* 1561–1628), English composer of madrigals, motets, pieces for virginals, etc.; also organist. A Roman Catholic, he worked mainly in the Low Countries (then under Spanish rule) and died probably in Brussels.

Phillips, Montague [Fawcett] (1885–1969), English composer best known for his light music (operetta *The Rebel Maid*, many songs); also wrote a symphony, two piano concertos, etc.

Philosopher, The, nickname for Haydn's Symphony no. 22 in E flat, 1764 (Hob. I: 22), perhaps because it has a grave first movement instead of the customary lively one.

phrase, a small group of notes forming what is recognized as a unit of melody; so *to phrase* and *phrasing*, terms used in regard to a performer's correctly observing the division of a melody into phrases. So also *phrase-mark*, a line linking written notes and indicating that they belong to one phrase.

Phrygian cadence, ➤cadence.

Phrygian mode, the ➤mode represented by the white keys of the piano beginning on E.

piacere, a (It.), at pleasure, i.e. (in performance) at the performer's discretion, especially as meaning that strict time need not be observed.

piacevole (It.), agreeably, pleasantly, easily.

piangendo (It. weeping), plaintive(ly).

pianino, a small upright piano.

pianissimo (abbr. *pp*), very softly, (➤piano, 1).

piano (It.), (1) soft, abbr. *p*; so *pianissimo* or *pp*, very soft. (2) common English word for the keyboard instrument called in Italian *pianoforte* (literally soft-loud) – the shorter term being more convenient than the longer, and no worse English. The instrument, distinguished e.g. from harpsichord and clavichord by having its strings struck with hammers, was invented shortly after 1700 and by the early 19th century (➤*fortepiano*) had displaced the harpsichord in private and public use. The modern piano is iron-framed and normally has 88 keys: it is either 'upright' (i.e. the strings are vertical) or 'grand' (i.e. they are horizontal). It has a 'sustaining pedal' (wrongly called 'loud pedal') operated by the right foot to prolong the sound by holding off the dampers; and a 'soft pedal' (left foot) lessening the volume by causing fewer than the normal number of strings to be struck or by bringing the hammers nearer the strings before they start their movement. On a minority of pianos, there is also a centre pedal enabling selected notes to be sustained independently of others. An early form of piano was the *square piano* (oblong, box-like in shape, horizontally strung) sometimes miscalled ➤spinet. Used universally as a solo, accompanying and chamber-music instrument, it has been increasingly used in the 20th century as an ordinary member of the orchestra and

pianoforte

as a repository of differing sounds –
the strings being 'doctored' (➤ prepared piano), plucked by hand, or used
(e.g. by Xenakis) as resonators for the
sounds of brass instruments played
over them. Pianos have also been
constructed with double keyboards
(➤Moór), with quarter-tone tuning,
etc., but none of these have become
standard. So also *electric piano*,
without strings (➤electric/electro-
phonic), ➤ *pedal-piano*, ➤*street piano*
and (from its type of keyboard) *piano
➤accordion*.

pianoforte, Italian name for the instrument more commonly called ➤piano in
English. The name literally means
'soft-loud', alluding to the much
greater possibilities of grading volume
than on the harpsichord; an early
variation of the name was ➤*fortepiano*.

pianola, ➤player-piano.

piano organ, ➤street piano.

piano quartet, ➤quartet.

piano quintet, ➤quintet.

piano score, ➤score.

piano trio, ➤trio.

Piatigorsky, Gregor (1903–76), cellist,
Russian-born, who settled in USA, becoming naturalized in 1942; internationally noted as soloist and teacher.
Gave first performances of Hindemith's and Walton's cello concertos,
composed and arranged works for the
instrument.

pibroch (Gael., *piobaireachd*), type of
Scottish Highland bagpipe music, in a
kind of elaborate variation-form.

Picardy third or (Fr.) *tierce de Picardie*,
the major third used at the end of a
piece otherwise in the minor key, con-

verting the expected minor chord into
a major one. The effect was common
up to the mid-18th century; its occasional subsequent use tends to sound
deliberately old-fashioned.

Piccaver [orginally Peckover], **Alfred**
(1884–1958), British tenor. Had a
long and distinguished career at
Vienna Court Opera (later State
Opera), 1910–37. Also performed at
Covent Garden and later taught in
London; in 1955 returned to Vienna,
where he died.

Piccinni (or Piccini), Nicola (1728–
1800), Italian composer of more than
100 operas including *La buona figliuola*
('The Good Girl'), after Richardson's
Pamela; also of oratorios, church
music, etc. Lived partly in Paris, and
died there. His Paris supporters
clashed with those of Gluck: both composers wrote an opera on ➤*Iphigénie en
Tauride*.

piccolo (It. small), small flute pitched
an octave above the standard flute,
used in the orchestra and military
band. (The name is from It. *flauto piccolo*, small flute, but the current It.
term is *ottavino*, from the word for
octave.) The word is occasionally borrowed to indicate other instruments
of smaller size and higher pitch than
standard: *piccolo* ➤*trumpet*, ➤*violino
piccolo*.

Pickett, Philip (b. 1950), British performer on early wind instruments (including crumhorn and shawm);
founder-director of New London Consort, 1977, which tours internationally. Has recorded much medieval,
Renaissance and baroque music, vocal
and instrumental.

Pick-Mangiagalli, Riccardo (1882–
1949), Bohemian-born composer

partly of Italian descent; naturalized Italian. Became director of Milan Conservatory. Works include operas, ballets, piano pieces.

Pictures at an Exhibition (Rus. *Kartinki s vistavki*, literally 'Pictures *from* an exhibition'), piano work by Musorgsky, 1874, giving a musical impression of 10 pictures by the Russian artist Victor Hartmann; a 'Promenade' is used as an introduction and linking passage. Of orchestral versions of the work, the standard one is by Ravel (1922).

Pie Jesu (Lat., 'O, good Jesus'), opening words of a section of the Latin ➤*Requiem* as used in Roman Catholic worship; music set to this section has occasionally been published separately.

Pierné, [Henri Constant] **Gabriel** (1863–1937), French organist, conductor, and composer of *La croisade des enfants* ('The Children's Crusade') for children's choir and orchestra, orchestral suites, operas, ballets – including *Cydalise et le Chèvre-pied* (satyr), from which comes the ➤*Marche des petits faunes*, known in English as *The Entry of the Little Fauns*.

Pierrot Lunaire (Fr., 'Moonstruck Pierrot'), cycle of 'three times seven' songs by Schoenberg for voice (using ➤*Sprechgesang*), flute (also piccolo), clarinet (also bass-clarinet), violin (also viola), cello and piano, to poems translated into German from the French of Albert Giraud – first performed in 1912.

Pierson [originally Pearson], **Henry Hugo** (1815–73), British composer who, after resigning from his Edinburgh professorship, settled in Germany in the mid-1840s. Died there.

Wrote notable songs and part-songs (including 'Ye Mariners of England'), also German operas, English oratorio *Jerusalem*, etc.

pifa, ➤*piffero*.

pifferaro, a player on the ➤*piffero*.

piffero, rustic Italian wind instrument of the ➤shawm family, to whose characteristic music Handel apparently alludes in writing the word *pifa* above the music of the ➤*Pastoral Symphony* in *Messiah*.

Pijper, Willem (1894–1947), Dutch composer (the most prominent of his generation), also writer on music. Works include three symphonies and the piece called *Six Symphonic Epigrams*; five string quartets (no. 5 unfinished) and other chamber music; opera *Halewijn*, music to plays, piano pieces, Dutch folk-song arrangements.

Pilgrim's Progress, The, opera (but, instead, styled 'A Morality') by Vaughan Williams, produced in London, 1951. Libretto by composer, after Bunyan. It incorporates the composer's earlier one-act opera, *The Shepherds of the Delectable Mountains* (London, 1922).

Pilkington, Francis (*c.* 1565–1638), English composer, also clergyman. Composed madrigals (one in *The* ➤*Triumphs of Oriana*), songs with lute, lute solos, etc.

Pineapple Poll, ballet with choreography by John Cranko, music adapted by Mackerras from the Gilbert and Sullivan operettas, produced in London, 1951. The story is based on one of Gilbert's 'Bab Ballads'.

Pini di Roma (It., 'Pines of Rome'),

orchestral work by Respighi, in four linked movements, referring to the pines of four Roman sites; first performed in 1924. The score includes a nightingale (on a gramophone record). ➤*Fontane di Roma.*

Pinkham, Daniel (b. 1923), American composer, pupil of Piston, Copland, and others; also organist, harpsichordist and church musician. Works include four symphonies, concertos for trumpet, violin, organ, piano, piccolo; St Mark Passion.

Pinnock, Trevor [David] (b. 1946), British harpsichordist and conductor who founded the English Concert in 1973 as his personal ensemble; it won admiration for performances of music from the Bach–Handel period. He has also conducted opera, e.g. Handel's *Giulio Cesare* at the Metropolitan, New York. Artistic director, National Symphony Orchestra of Canada (Ottawa) since 1991. CBE, 1992.

Pinto, George Frederick [original surname Saunders or Sanders; Pinto his mother's surname] (1785–1806), British composer of songs, five piano sonatas, duets for two violins, etc.; also pianist and violinist.

Pinza, Ezio [Fortunato] (1892–1957), Italian bass who settled in USA; after noted operatic career (Metropolitan Opera, New York, from 1926), appeared in films, Broadway musicals, etc.

pipa (pronounced *piba*), a Chinese lute; the name is related to Japanese ➤*biwa.*

pipe, a hollow cylinder or cone in which air vibrates, e.g. in an organ or a blown wind instrument; (term also used for) type of simple wind instrument itself composed only of such a cylinder or cone without mechanism – e.g. the three-holed pipe used in English folk-dancing with the ➤tabor.

Pipkov, Lubomir [Panayatov] (1904–74), Bulgarian composer, pupil in Paris of N. Boulanger and Dukas; works include four symphonies. Also pianist and conductor (music director of the Sofia Opera, 1944–7).

Pique Dame, German translation (not French, which would be *La Dame de Pique*) of the original title of Tchaikovsky's opera *The* ➤*Queen of Spades*. It has no claim to use in English-speaking countries.

Pirandello, Luigi (1867–1936), Italian dramatist and novelist. ➤Weisgall.

Pirates of Penzance, The, or The Slave of Duty, operetta by Sullivan, produced in New York, 1879 (preceded by partial performance in Paignton, Devon, to establish British copyright). Libretto by W. S. Gilbert: the pirates are all 'noblemen who have gone wrong'.

Pisador, Diego (*c.* 1508–after 1557), Spanish player of the ➤*vihuela* and composer of music for his instrument; he took minor orders in the Church but did not become a priest.

Pisk, Paul Amadeus (1893–1990), Austrian composer (pupil of Schoenberg) who settled in USA as university teacher; also musicologist. Works include *Three Ceremonial Rites* for orchestra, song-settings with words by James Joyce and others.

piston, ➤valve (on brass instruments). Hence in French *piston* is also used as an abbreviation for *cornet-à-pistons*, i.e. the ordinary cornet.

Piston, Walter [Hamor] (1894–1976),

American composer, pupil of N. Boulanger in Paris; professor at Harvard, author of important textbooks. Works include eight symphonies, a violin concerto, five string quartets, ballet *The* ➤*Incredible Flutist*.

pitch, the property according to which notes appear to be (in the conventional phrase) 'high' or 'low' in relation to each other – a property scientifically determined by the ➤*frequency* of vibrations of the sound-producing agent. So *concert pitch* is the standard of pitch to which instruments are normally tuned for performance. By international agreement of 1939, the tuning-note A (directly above middle C) was fixed at a frequency of 440 Hz; this makes middle C 261.6 Hz, and the C higher 523.2 Hz (i.e. twice the frequency of the octave below, as is the invariable rule). But in scientific investigation it is found mathematically convenient to suppose this C to have a frequency of 512 Hz (i.e. 2^9). In former centuries, pitch had wide variations according to period and place. *Absolute pitch* or *perfect pitch*, term for the faculty possessed by those who on hearing a note can identify it by name: it would be better to call this not *absolute pitch* but *an absolute sense of pitch*, etc. – though in fact such a faculty of identification is really not absolute but relative (to the nearest whole-tone, semitone, etc.). See also the following entries.

pitch-class, theorists' term, consequent on the practice of serial composition (➤series), for all notes of the same name in whatever octave – e.g. the *pitch-class* C includes middle C and all other notes called C.

pitch-pipe, small wind instrument employed to give correct starting pitch to singers or by which to tune instruments.

più (It.), more; *più lento*, slower.

piuttosto (It.), rather, somewhat.

Pixis, Johann Peter (1788–1874), German pianist, composer of piano music, operas, etc., contributor to the ➤*Hexameron*.

Pizarro, Artur [in full: Artur Manoel Pinto Pizarro de Brito Subtil] (b. 1968), Portuguese pianist; made London solo début in 1989 and won the Leeds International Piano Competition in 1990. Toured Australia with Royal Philharmonic Orchestra, 1992. Has recorded solo works by Liszt and Skryabin.

pizz., abbr. for ➤*pizzicato*.

Pizzetti, Ildebrando (1880–1968), Italian composer of *Dèbora e Jaele* (on biblical story of Deborah), *Assassinio nella cattedrale* (on T. S. Eliot's *Murder in the Cathedral*) and other operas; also of incidental music for plays, a piano concerto, cello concerto, and other orchestral works, choral works, chamber music, etc.

pizzicato (It., pinched), direction that notes on bowed string instrument are to be plucked, not bowed; abbr. *pizz.* So *pizzicato tremolando*, direction used by Elgar in his Violin Concerto to make the orchestral string-players 'thrum' rapidly with the fingers across the strings. Bartók sometimes required a *pizzicato* so forcible as to cause the string to snap back against the fingerboard, e.g. in his String Quartet no. 4. ➤*ostinato*.

plagal cadence, ➤cadence.

plagal modes, ➤mode.

plainchant, plainsong, type of medieval church music which in its developed form called ➤*Gregorian chant* became standard in Roman Catholic use. It consists of a single line of vocal melody (properly unaccompanied) in 'free' rhythm, not divided into regular bar-lengths; it has its own system of notation. (The ritual music of the Greek church – called 'Byzantine music' – and of the Jewish synagogue, though of a somewhat similar type, is not called plainsong.)

Planets, The, orchestral suite by Holst, first performed complete in 1920. Its seven movements treat their subjects from an astrological viewpoint; the last, 'Neptune, the Mystic', uses two three-part female choruses, wordless and unseen.

Planquette, Robert (1848–1903), French composer of *Les Cloches de Corneville* ('The Bells of Corneville') and other operettas.

plainsong, ➤plainchant.

Plath, Sylvia (1932–63), American poet and novelist. ➤Turnage.

Plato (*c.* 427–347 BC), Athenian philosopher. ➤*Socrate*.

player-piano, general name for a piano fitted with the type of mechanism usually known by such trade names as 'Pianola'. By this mechanism the keys are depressed not by the fingers but by air-pressure supplied by bellows and pedals, or electrically: the air-pressure is applied through perforations on an unwinding paper roll, such perforations being arranged so that a composition is played. There is, of course, no need for the perforations to be restricted to the normal number of notes playable by two (or four) hands. Sometimes the perforations are made mechanically from an actual performance by an eminent pianist, the player-piano then reproducing (within limits) this actual performance: for this reason the alternative name *reproducing piano* is sometimes used. ➤Nancarrow.

plectrum, small piece of wood, metal, or other material used to pluck the strings of a lute, mandolin, banjo, etc.; also the part of the mechanism of the harpsichord which performs an analogous function.

plein(e) (Fr.), full; *plein jeu* (full play), either (1) a type of ➤*mixture* stop on the organ, or (2) ➤*full organ*.

Pletnev, Mikhail (b. 1957), Russian pianist and conductor, also composer. At 21, won the Moscow Tchaikovsky Competition; has recorded the original *Pictures at an Exhibition*. Founder-conductor (1990) of the Russian National Orchestra. Made London début as conductor (with Philharmonia Orchestra), 1993.

Pleyel, Ignaz Joseph (1757–1831), Austrian pianist, violinist, composer (29 symphonies, chamber music, etc.), pupil of Haydn and founder of the piano-making firm of Pleyel in Paris.

pneuma (Gk., breath), a type of florid passage sung to a single vowel in plainsong.

pochette (Fr., pocket), small-size violin (small enough to be kept in a long pocket) formerly used by dancing-masters: same as ➤kit (1).

pochetto, pochettino (It.), very slightly. (Diminutives of ➤*poco*.)

pochissimo (It.), the least possible. (Superlative of ➤*poco*.)

poco (It.), slightly. In correct Italian *un poco crescendo* (with a little increase in volume) differs from *poco crescendo* (with little increase in volume) – the difference between 'a little' and just 'little' (with its negative sense) in English. But in musical contexts the sense is usually 'a little', even without the *un*.

Poe, Edgar Allan (1809–49), American writer. ➤Debussy, ➤Glass, ➤Myaskovsky, ➤Rakhmaninov, ➤Sitsky.

poem, poema, poème (Eng., It., Fr.), term which was brought into music by Liszt in the expression ➤symphonic poem and which has since been somewhat extended, as in the following entries.

Poem, title of a movement from Fibich's orchestral piece, *At Twilight* (Cz., *V. Podvečer*), 1893.

Poème (Fr., 'Poem'), work for violin and orchestra, in one movement, by Chausson, 1896.

Poème électronique (Fr., 'Electronic Poem'), title of electronic piece (recorded and assembled from 'real' rather than synthesized sounds) by Varèse, composed for the Brussels International Exhibition, 1958, where it was distributed over 425 loudspeakers.

Poem of Ecstasy, The (Rus., *Poema ekstasa*), orchestral work by Skryabin (on 'joy in creative activity') first performed in New York, 1908. ➤*Divine Poem*, ➤*Prometheus*.

Poem of Fire, ➤*Prometheus*.

Poet's Love, song-cycle by Schumann. ➤*Dichterliebe*.

Pogorelich, Ivo (b. 1958), Yugoslav pianist who trained in Moscow (and married his teacher); noted for individualistic interpretation. Settled in London. Named as Ambassador of Goodwill by UNESCO, 1987.

poi (It.), then; *scherzo da capo, e poi la coda*, repeat the scherzo and then go on to the coda.

point (1) the end of the bow opposite to that held by the hand; (2) ➤pedal, (1); (3) ➤pointing.

point d'orgue (Fr., organ-point), (1) pedal-point (➤pedal, 1); (2) the ➤pause, ⌢; (3) the place in the music – generally a pause on the second inversion of the tonic chord – at which a cadenza in the classical concerto begins.

pointillist(e), term borrowed from painting (where it refers to the use of separate dots of pure colour instead of mixed pigments) and applied to music where the notes seem to be disposed in isolated 'dots' rather than in normal melodic curve, as in certain music of Webern.

pointing, in Anglican chant, the allotting of syllables to the notes on which they are to be sung.

polacca (It.), ➤polonaise.

'Polish' Symphony, nickname for Tchaikovsky's Symphony no. 3, 1875; it has a finale in ➤polonaise rhythm but has no other claim to the name.

polka, a dance in 2/4 time for couples, originating in the 19th century in Bohemia.

Pollini, Maurizio (b. 1942), Italian pianist, pupil of Michelangeli; winner of International Chopin competition in Warsaw, 1960; known for modern as well as classical-virtuoso repertory. Has also occasionally conducted.

Polly, ballad opera with words by John Gay and musical arrangements by Pepusch – a sequel to *The Beggar's Opera*. Published in 1729, but banned from the London stage as subversive of authority and not produced till 1777.

polo, type of southern Spanish dance, with song.

polonaise (Fr., Polish), a stately Polish dance in 3/4 time, dating from the 16th century, if not earlier – its use for concert pieces goes back at least to Bach. Among Chopin's examples are some of an ardent, even martial, nature, apparently expressing patriotic sentiments.

Polovtsian dances, ➤*Prince Igor*.

polymetre, polymetrical, terms which may refer to a composer's simultaneous use of different types of ➤metre or simply to the use of different metres successively in the course of a single movement.

polyphonic (1) of ➤polyphony, indicating counterpoint; (2 of synthesizers, etc.), able to sound several notes simultaneously.

polyphony, term literally meaning (from Gk.) any simultaneous sounding of different notes – but commonly referring to techniques of composing for several different voices (➤parts) in counterpoint; opposite to ➤homophony, where melodic interest is virtually confined to one 'line' of music, the other sounds acting as accompaniment. Hence historical references to the *polyphonic period*, imprecise term usually indicating a period from about the 13th to the 16th or early 17th centuries, ending

with (e.g.) Palestrina, Lassus and Byrd. (The style of such a later composer as Bach is also polyphonic, but there the polyphony is governed by the harmonic scheme, whereas in the earlier period the polyphony supposedly 'comes first' and gives rise to the harmony.)

polyrhythm, the systematic exploitation of several rhythms performed simultaneously – especially in African music and in European music of the 20th century. But there are earlier European examples, notably Mozart's three different simultaneous dance-rhythms in ➤*Don Giovanni*.

polytonal, ➤polytonality.

polytonality, the simultaneous use of more than one key (an effect used systematically e.g. by Holst, Milhaud). Where only two keys are involved the more precise term is 'bitonality'.

pommer, ➤shawm.

Pommier, Jean-Bernard (b. 1944), French pianist, prominent in festival and similar appearances from early 1960s, soloist with American orchestras from 1973–4. Partnered L. Rose in Brahms's cello sonatas; also conductor of Northern Sinfonia since 1996.

Pomp and Circumstance, title of five military marches by Elgar: nos. 1–4 composed in 1901–7, no. 5 in 1930. Title is a quotation from Shakespeare's *Othello*. Elgar adopted part of no. 1 in his *Coronation Ode* (1902) with the words 'Land of Hope and Glory'.

Ponce, Manuel (1882–1948), Mexican composer of *Concierto del sur* (Sp., 'Concerto of the South'), for guitar and chamber orchestra; a violin concerto (using in the second movement his own well-known song 'Estrellita'); orchestral and piano works, etc.

Ponchielli, Amilcare (1834–86), Italian composer of *La* ➤*Gioconda* (from which the 'Dance of the Hours' comes) and other operas; also cantatas (one in memory of Garibaldi), etc. Was also church musician.

Pons, José (*c.* 1768–1818), Spanish composer, choirmaster at Valencia Cathedral; composed Masses, Lamentations and other church music.

Ponselle [originally Ponzillo], **Rosa** (1897–1981), American mezzo-soprano. Sang opposite Caruso in the first operatic performance of her life (1918), which was also the first production at the Metropolitan of Verdi's *La forza del destino*. She subsequently sang 21 other roles there, and also appeared at Covent Garden (début as Norma, 1929). In retirement she became a noted teacher.

ponticello (It.), the bridge of a violin or other stringed instrument; *sul ponticello* (literally, 'on the bridge'), instructions to play with the bow as close to the bridge as possible, for the production of a special kind of 'nasal' or 'metallic' tone-quality.

Poot, Marcel (1901–88), Belgian composer of operas, three symphonies, symphonic poem *Charlot* (i.e. Charlie Chaplin), chamber music, etc. Director of the Brussels Conservatory, 1949–66. Pupil of Dukas and others.

pop, abbr. for 'popular' (originally adjective, hence noun). In older usage it carries the straightforward meaning of 'appealing to a wide audience' – e.g. as in the Monday Popular Concerts (abbr. 'Monday Pops'), chamber music series in Victorian London (➤Boston Pops Orchestra). Since the 1950s, however, it has usually referred to a non-classical, commercially promoted type of mainly American-derived song, whether delivered by solo or group vocalists, assuming the role of a popular alternative to the classical tradition of composition and performance. Hence *pop groups* (performers, usually comprising singers, guitars, keyboards, percussion), *pop festivals*, etc. Differentiated from ➤jazz (now an older, less commercialized tradition); ➤rock.

Pope, Alexander (1688–1744), English poet. ➤Panufnik, ➤Walond.

Popp, Lucia (1939–93), Czech-born Austrian soprano, active in opera – Salzburg Festival from 1963, Covent Garden from 1966, etc.

Popper, David (1843–1913), Austrian cellist, born in Prague, composer of many works for his instrument including a celebrated *Elfentanz* ('Dance of the Elves').

popular, ➤pop.

Porgy and Bess, the only full-length opera by Gershwin, produced in Boston, 1935. Libretto by D. Heyward and I. Gershwin (the composer's brother). Written for a black cast on a story about blacks – Porgy (crippled) and Bess are lovers.

Porpora, Niccolò Antonio (1686–1768), Italian composer; in London, his operas rivalled Handel's in popularity. Was also church musician and, especially, singing-teacher; one of the most famous ever. Haydn, as a young man, was for a time his pupil, accompanist and valet.

port á beul, ➤mouth music.

Porta, Costanzo (1528/9–1601), Italian composer and Franciscan monk; working at Padua, Ferrara and elsewhere, he wrote in a contrapuntal style that was much admired. A distinguished teacher of other composers.

portamento (It.), the 'carrying' of a sound – e.g., on a voice or a stringed instrument, the transition from one note to another higher or lower without any break in the sound.

portando (It.), carrying; *portando la voce*, indication of a vocal ➤*portamento*.

portative, a portable organ, especially that which in medieval and Renaissance times could be placed on a table or carried in procession.

port de voix (Fr., carrying of the voice), a vocal ➤*portamento*. The term is also used for certain 'ornaments' in French music from the 17th century and later.

Porter, Cole (1891–1964), American composer of popular songs – many for musical plays (e.g. *The Gay Divorce*, ➤*Kiss Me Kate*, etc.), and films. Pupil of d'Indy. Also writer of words to his own songs.

Porter, [William] Quincy (1897–1966), American composer, pupil of d'Indy (in Paris), Bloch and others; also viola-player, and professor at Yale. Works include a viola concerto, a two-piano concerto, two symphonies, 10 string quartets.

Porter, Walter (*c.* 1588–1659), English composer of motets, madrigals, etc.; also lutenist and singer (boy chorister at Westminster Abbey, then tenor). May have been a pupil of Monteverdi.

Portsmouth Point, concert-overture by Walton, 1925, after a drawing by Rowlandson of a cheerful quayside scene.

Portuguese guitar, ➤guitar.

Posaune (Ger.), trombone (in standard musical use: but also 'trumpet', e.g. in the biblical phrase 'the last trumpet').

positif (Fr.), ➤choir-organ.

position (1, in string-playing) term used to specify how far along the finger-board the left hand should rest in order to play a given passage – *first position* being that nearest the pegs; *second*, etc., progressively further away; (2, in trombone-playing) term specifying how far the slide should be pushed out (*first position* the least extended); (3, in harmony) the 'layout' of a chord, determining which note comes at the bottom. E.g., with the chord consisting of the notes, C, E, G, B♭ (i.e. the dominant-seventh chord in key F) – if the note C (regarded as the 'root' of the chord) is at the bottom, then the chord is in *root position*; if E is at the bottom then it is in the 'first inversion'; if G is at the bottom, the 'second inversion'; if B♭, the 'third inversion'. It is solely what note is at the bottom that determines these 'positions'; the order of the upper notes is irrelevant.

positive, type of small organ with a single manual (usually without pedal), in use from 10th to 17th century (and revived in mid 20th); too large to be carried (in contrast to the ➤portative), it was 'positioned' (hence its name) on the floor or on a table.

possibile (It.), possible; term used elliptically, e.g. *dim. possibile* or even $>$ *possibile* – meaning that the sound is to be diminished to the faintest possible (not 'diminish as rapidly as possible').

post-horn, brass instrument of simple design – a long tube, made without valves or keys, and so able to produce only the notes of one ➤harmonic series. Built in various shapes (often, however, in a straight unbent tube) and formerly used by postillions for signalling. The well-known *Post-Horn Galop* (composed by the cornettist Koenig, 1844), for post-horn solo with accompaniment, skilfully uses the instrument's limited range of notes.

postlude, a final piece – opposite of ➤prelude, and an equally imprecise term, but much less commonly found.

Postnikova, Viktoria [Valentinovna] (b. 1944), Russian pianist, noted from the mid-1960s (BBC Proms début 1967). She has recorded all Janáček's piano music and her repertory extends from Bach to Schnittke. Married to Rozhdestvensky, with whom (as pianist) she occasionally plays duos.

post-Romantic(ism), terms applied to 20th-century musical styles seeming to continue (or revive) ➤Romantic traits long after the original 'wave' of Romanticism in music apparently reached its climax in Wagner.

pot-pourri (Fr.), term used in a musical sense for a medley of tunes with little formal cohesion between them.

Potter, [Philip] **Cipriani** [Hambly] (1792–1871), English composer of nine symphonies, piano works including a set of variations entitled *The Enigma* ('in the style of five eminent artists') etc.; as a student he was advised by Beethoven in Vienna. Principal of the Royal Academy of Music, 1832–59.

Poule, La, ➤*Hen*.

Poulenc, Francis (1899–1963), French composer, member of the group of *Les* ➤*Six*; also pianist, noted particularly as accompanist to Pierre Bernac. Works include a piano concerto, two-piano concerto; Concerto for organ with strings and timpani; piano solos, songs; operas ➤*Les* ➤*Dialogues des Carmélites, Les* ➤*Mamelles de Tirésias* and *La* ➤*Voix humaine*; ballets, incidental music to plays and films, and works with Roman Catholic associations: ➤*Gloria*, ➤*Stabat Mater, Litanies à la vierge noire* ('Litanies to the Black Virgin'), etc.

Pousseur, Henri (b. 1929), Belgian composer of electronic music and other works including *Votre Faust* ('Your Faust', an opera where the audience chooses the ending) and smaller works arising from this; also a quintet (clarinet, bass clarinet, piano, violin, cello) in memory of Webern, *Mobile* for two pianos, etc.

Powell, Mel [originally Melvin Epstein] (b. 1923), American composer, also pianist, university teacher and writer on music; formerly active in jazz. Works include *Analogs 1–4* (tape), *Stanzas* for orchestra, *Filigree Setting* for string quartet.

Power, Leonel (*c.* 1375–1445), English composer serving the Duke of Clarence, brother of Henry V. Composed church music and, with Dunstable, was one of the best-known English composers on the Continent.

Powers, Anthony (b. 1953), British composer of orchestral works including *Stone, Water, Stars*; horn concerto, *Nymphéas* (after Monet's paintings) for 12 instruments, a piano sonata, etc.

Praeludium (Lat.), prelude; the well-known orchestral work so entitled is by Järnefelt, first heard in Britain in 1909. ➤Pugnani

Praetorius, Latinized name of several German musicians, before 1700. The most important is Michael Praetorius (*c.* 1571–1621), composer, organist, writer on music.

'Prague' Symphony, nickname for Mozart's Symphony no. 38 in D (K504), first performed in Prague, 1787.

Pralltriller, a musical ornament related to upper ➤mordent but of differing significance at different periods.

Pré, Jacqueline du, ➤du Pré.

precentor, ecclesiastical musical dignitary – in an Anglican cathedral, the cleric in charge of the vocal music, to whom the organist is technically subordinate.

Preciosa, German play on a gipsy subject by P. A. Wolff (produced in 1821), to which Weber wrote the overture and other music.

precipitato, precipitoso (It.), impetuously.

pre-classic(al), term used of composers (e.g. C. P. E. Bach, J. C. Bach) whose style is considered later than baroque and leading to the 'Viennese ➤classical' style of Haydn and Mozart.

prelude, properly a piece preceding something – e.g. preceding a fugue, or forming the first number of a suite, or forming the orchestral introduction to an act of an opera; but the term is also used for a short self-contained piece, for piano – whether quite abstract, e.g. Chopin's and Rakhmaninov's, or illustrative, e.g. Debussy's. See also following entries.

Prélude à l'après-midi d'un faune, orchestral work by Debussy; ➤*Après-midi d'un faune.*

Préludes, Les (Fr., 'The Preludes'), symphonic poem by Liszt, taking its title from a poem by Lamartine, but originally the overture to an unpublished choral work and having no connection with the poem. Composed in 1848, revised several times, given final form in 1854. Liszt's prefatory note suggests that life is a series of preludes to the hereafter. (Thus 'prelude' is not used here in its musical sense.)

preparation, a device in harmony by which the impact of a discord is softened: the actual note which, in a chord, causes that chord to be discordant, is sounded first in the preceding chord where it does not form a discordant element. Thus a discord is said to be *prepared* – or, if the impact is not 'softened' in this way, *unprepared.*

prepare (1, in harmony) see preceding entry; (2) to 'set' an instrument ready to produce a particular effect, e.g. double-basses in an orchestra may be instructed to *prepare low* E flat, i.e. to let down to E flat their lowest string which is normally tuned to E natural: see also the following entry.

prepared piano, a piano in which the strings are 'doctored' with various objects in order to produce tone-qualities other than normal, sometimes with the addition of unusual techniques of playing – e.g. reaching over the keyboard and plucking the strings by hand. The term originated with ➤Cage but the practice had been initiated in 1914 by ➤Cowell.

pressez (Fr.), increase speed.

prestissimo (It.), very fast. (Superlative of ➤*presto*.)

presto (It.), fast. In the period of Mozart, this approximates to the meaning 'as fast as possible'; later composers have tended to convey this meaning by *prestissimo*.

Preston, Simon [John] (b. 1938), British organist and university teacher (Christ Church, Oxford, 1970–81, then Westminster Abbey till 1987); also harpsichordist and conductor.

Prêtre, Georges (b. 1924), French conductor; conducted at Covent Garden (*Tosca* with Callas), 1965; music director of Paris Opera, 1970–71.

Previn, André (originally Andreas Ludwig Priwin) (b. 1929), German-born conductor and pianist who was brought up in Los Angeles and acquired American nationality in 1943. Principal conductor of Houston (Texas) Symphony Orchestra, 1967–9; of London Symphony Orchestra, 1968–79; music director, Royal Philharmonic Orchestra, 1985–7, afterwards styled principal conductor, to 1991. Also composer of guitar concerto, piano pieces, opera, *A Streetcar Named Desire*, etc. Honorary KBE, 1996.

Prévost, Abbé [Antoine François Prévost d'Exiles] (1697–1753), French writer. ➤*Manon*, ➤*Manon Lescaut*.

Prey, Claude (b. 1925), French composer chiefly of operas including *Les Liaisons Dangereuses* and *Le Rouge et le Noir* (1989, after Stendhal's novel).

Prey, Hermann (1929–98), German baritone, active in opera (Metropolitan, New York, 1960 and continuing into the 1990s); distinguished recitalist in German song. In 1976 he founded an annual Schubert festival at Hohenems, Austria.

Price [Mary Violet] **Leontyne** (b. 1927), American soprano, eminent in opera: sang in USA and Europe as Bess in Gershwin's *Porgy and Bess*, 1952–5; first appeared at Covent Garden, 1958; Metropolitan, New York, from 1961 until she retired from opera in 1985.

Price, Margaret [Berenice] (b. 1941), British soprano who made her début in 1962 with the Welsh National Opera; later appeared at Covent Garden (from 1963), in German opera-houses, etc., with a speciality in Mozart. Created Dame, 1983.

prick-song, old English term for music that was 'pricked', i.e. written down, as distinct from traditional or improvised music.

Priestley, J. B. [John Boynton] (1894–1984), English novelist and dramatist. ➤Bliss.

Prigioniero, Il (It., 'The Prisoner'), opera by Dallapiccola, produced in Florence, 1950 (previously on Turin radio); libretto by the composer, after a short story by Villiers de l'Isle Adam, 'Torture by Hope'.

primo, prima (It., masc., fem.), first. So *primo*, the top part in piano duets: *prima donna*, the chief woman singer in the cast of an opera, etc. (over-use of this term giving rise to *prima donna assoluta*, the 'absolutely chief' woman); *primo uomo*, the chief male singer in an opera, etc.; *prima vista*, first sight (as in sight-reading); *tempo primo*, with the same tempo as at first; *come prima*, as at first; *prima volta*, first time.

Primrose, William (1903–82), British viola-player (originally violinist), resident in USA from 1937. Various works were written for him, including Bartók's Viola Concerto. CBE, 1953.

Prince Igor (Rus., *Knyaz Igor*), opera by Borodin, produced in St Petersburg, 1890. Libretto by composer. The work was left unfinished, and after Borodin's death was brought to a completion (now questioned) by Rimsky-Korsakov and Glazunov. Named after its 12th-century Russian warrior hero, captured by the Polovtsians – whose dances occur in Act II.

Prince of Denmark's March, The, ►*Trumpet Voluntary*.

Prince of the Pagodas, The, ballet (on a fairy-tale subject) with choreography by John Cranko, music by Britten; produced in London, 1957.

Princess Ida, or Castle Adamant, operetta by Sullivan, produced in London, 1884. Libretto by W. S. Gilbert. Styled 'a respectful operatic per-version of Tennyson's *Princess*' – to which poem the libretto alludes by quotation and parody. The Princess heads a women's university.

principal (1) leading player of a particular instrument (e.g. *principal horn*) in an orchestral section; (2) a singer who takes main parts in an opera company – thus *principal tenor* does not mean the chief tenor, but any tenor who has attained the standing of a 'principal'; (3) an organ stop of the open ►diapason type but sounding an octave higher.

Prisoner, The, opera by Dallapiccola. ►*Prigioniero*.

Pritchard, John [Michael] (1921–89), British conductor active in opera at Glyndebourne (musical director, 1969–77), Covent Garden and abroad; was conductor of the Royal Liverpool · Philharmonic Orchestra, then (1962–6) of the London Philharmonic Orchestra. Chief conductor BBC Symphony Orchestra, 1982–9. Knighted, 1983.

Prodaná Nevěsta, ►*Bartered Bride*.

programmatic music, programme music, music interpreting a story, picture etc. A better term – because self-explanatory, and avoiding the confusion with 'concert programmes' etc. – is ►illustrative music.

progression, motion from one note or chord to the next, in accordance with a musically logical plan.

progressive tonality, a musicologists' (rather than composers') term for the systematic plan of beginning a movement in one key and ending it in another, as in certain works by, e.g., Mahler and C. Nielsen.

Prokina, Elena [Nikolayevna] (b. 1964), Russian soprano, a member of the Kirov Opera (Leningrad/St Petersburg) till 1992. Her much-praised appearances in the West have included title-role of *Katya Kabanova* at Covent Garden and Tatyana in *Yevgeny Onegin* at Glyndebourne, both 1994.

Prokofiev, Sergey [Sergeyevich] (1891–1953), Russian composer with a commanding place in 20th-century music; also pianist. Pupil of Rimsky-Korsakov and others. Lived much abroad from 1918, but settled again in Russia in 1934; his style then became more straightforward and 'popular' as in ►*Peter and the Wolf* and

Violin Concerto no. 2. Some of his later works nevertheless fell under the Soviet attack on ➤formalism in 1948, and his last opera, *The Story of a Real Man*, was publicly produced only after his death, 1960. His previous operas include ➤*Love for Three Oranges*, *The* ➤*Fiery Angel*, *The* ➤*Duenna* and ➤*War and Peace*. Also composed seven symphonies (no. 1, ➤*Classical Symphony*), five piano concertos, concerto and other works for cello and orchestra; ➤*Cinderella*, ➤*Romeo and Juliet* and other ballets; songs, patriotic cantatas (e.g. ➤*Alexander Nevsky*); nine piano sonatas, ➤*Visions fugitives* and other works for piano, two violin sonatas; film music. Died on the same day as Stalin.

prolation, in medieval musical notation, the division of the whole-note (semibreve) into either three smaller time-units (*major prolation*) or two (*minor prolation*).

Promenade concert, the accepted British misnomer (since the audience do not now walk about) for a concert at which some members of the audience stand. Henry J. Wood's London series of Promenade Concerts began in 1895, more than 50 years after the first British examples of this type, and are now (under BBC management) known as the Henry Wood Promenade Concerts.

Prometheus, Greek legendary figure alluded to in various musical works, including song-settings of Goethe's poem 'Prometheus', by Schubert (1819) and Wolf (1889), Beethoven's ballet score *Die* ➤*Geschöpfe des Prometheus*, and Skryabin's ➤*Prometheus – The Poem of Fire*. ➤*Eroica*, ➤Jelinek.

Prometheus – The Poem of Fire (Rus.,

'Prometei – Poema Ognya'), symphonic poem by Skryabin, with chorus ad lib and properly with a ➤keyboard of light; first performed, without this, in 1911.

prompt (in operatic performance), to supply cues to a singer – not merely, as in a play, when the performer forgets, but often supplying verbal and musical cues in anticipation throughout a performance.

Proms, the, abbreviation for ➤*promenade concerts*, specifically (and as used in this book) the BBC's annual Henry Wood Promenade Concerts.

Prophetess, The, ➤*Dioclesian*.

proportional notation, proportionate notation, ➤graphic notation.

Prout, Ebenezer (1835–1909), British composer, professor and critic; writer of musical textbooks which are ridiculed as pedantic by those ignorant of them.

'Prussian' Quartets, name (not the composer's) for a set of string quartets by Mozart, intended for the use of Friedrich Wilhelm II, King of Prussia, who was a good cellist; only three were actually written (K575, 589, 590), 1789–90.

psalm, properly (from Gk.) a hymn sung to a harp; applied almost exclusively to the contents of the Old Testament Book of Psalms, for which various settings (➤metrical psalms) exist for religious use – also a number of concert settings.

psalmody, the study, etc., of the psalms; or an arrangement of psalms for singing.

Psalmus Hungaricus (Lat., 'Hungarian Psalm'), work for tenor, chorus and orchestra by Kodály, 1923, based on Psalm 55 in a 16th-century Hungarian translation.

psalter, volume containing the Book of Psalms, often with music.

psaltery, ancient and medieval stringed instrument, plucked like a lyre and of similar shape, but with a soundboard at the back of the strings.

Pskovitianka, ➤*Maid of Pskov*.

Psota, Ivo Váňa (1908–52), Czech choreographer. ➤*Romeo and Juliet* (Prokofiev).

Puccini, Giacomo [Antonio Domenico Michele Secondo Maria] (1858–1924), Italian composer, the dominant creator of Italian opera of his period. In youth a church musician; among his very few non-operatic works are a youthful Mass (➤Messa) and a string quartet entitled *Crisantemi* ('Chrysanthemums'). His operas include (in this order) ➤*Manon Lescaut* (1893), *La* ➤*Bohème*, ➤*Tosca*, ➤*Madama Butterfly*, *La* ➤*Fanciulla del West*; a *trittico* (It., 'triptych', intended to form a single evening) consisting of *Il* ➤*tabarro*, ➤*Suor Angelica*, ➤*Gianni Schicchi*; ➤*Turandot* (1924, unfinished). For the realism and/or violence of some of his plots the term ➤*verismo* is appropriate.

Pugnani, Gaetano (1731–98), Italian violinist and composer of violin sonatas, operas, etc.; the *Praeludium and Allegro*, formerly said to be arranged from Pugnani by Kreisler, was admitted by Kreisler in 1935 to be entirely the latter's own work.

Pugno, [Stéphane] **Raoul** (1852–1914), French pianist, organist, composer of operas, ballets, etc. Died in Moscow.

Pulcinella, ballet with music by Stravinsky (including songs), produced in Paris, 1920. Based on music supposed to be by Pergolesi, but now known not to be. ➤Pergolesi.

Pult (Ger.), desk – in the sense of an orchestral music-stand shared e.g. by two string-players; so *1. Pult*, first desk, i.e. instruction that a passage is to be played only by the first two players of that section.

Punch and Judy, opera by Birtwistle, produced in Aldeburgh, 1968. Libretto by S. Pruslin reinterprets the traditional puppet-play.

punta (It.), point; *punta d'arco*, (with the) point of the bow.

punteado (Sp., plucked), indication of normal classical technique in playing the guitar, in contrast with ➤*rasgueado*.

Purcell, the surname alone indicates Henry Purcell – below.

Purcell, Daniel (*c.* 1663–1717), English composer of much stage music (➤*Indian Queen*), also cantatas, etc. Also organist. Brother of Henry Purcell.

Purcell, Henry (1659–95), English composer, recognized as among his country's greatest. Was boy chorister; pupil of Humfrey and of Blow, whom he succeeded as organist of Westminster Abbey in 1679. Said to have died through a cold caused by being locked out of his own house at night. Wrote short opera ➤*Dido and Aeneas*, also what are now called semi-operas (music not altogether predominant) including *The* ➤*Fairy Queen*, ➤*King Arthur*, ➤*Dioclesian*, *The* ➤*Indian Queen*, and music for various plays including *Abdelazer* (tune used in

Britten's ➤*Young Person's Guide*). Other works include ➤*Odes for St Cecilia's Day* and other cantatas; songs (➤*Orpheus Britannicus* and ➤*Epicedium*); keyboard works; ➤trio-sonatas (some described as in three parts and some as in four, but identical in scoring), including the ➤*Golden Sonata*; anthems (including ➤*Bell Anthem*) and other church music. Notably influenced such 20th-century composers as Holst, Tippett, Britten. A so-called ➤*Trumpet Voluntary* is misattributed to him. His work is indexed by 'Z' numbers, referring to the thematic catalogue made by Franklin Zimmerman in 1963.

Purcell Quartet, British quartet founded 1984 (currently Catherine Mackintosh, Catherine Weiss, violins; Richard Boothby, cello/bass viol; Robert Woolley, harpsichord/organ) formed to play 17th–18th-century ➤trio-sonatas and similar works. Has recorded not only all Purcell's output of this type but works by Corelli, Leclair, etc. Expands to larger consort under name Purcell Simfony (*sic*).

Puritani, I (It., *The Puritans*), Bellini's last opera, produced in Paris (in Italian), 1835. Libretto by C. Pepoli on the 17th-century conflict of Royalists and Cromwellians, based ultimately on Scott's *Old Mortality*. ➤*Hexameron*.

Pushkin, Alexander (1799–1837), Russian writer. ➤*Aleko*, ➤*Boris Godunov*, ➤*Golden Cockerel*, ➤*Mazeppa*, ➤*Mozart and Salieri*, ➤*Queen of Spades*, ➤*Rusalka*, ➤*Ruslan and Lyudmila*, ➤*Yevgeny Onegin*; ➤Britten, ➤Firsova.

Puyana, Rafael (b. 1931), Colombian harpsichordist, pupil of Wanda Landowska in USA. Resident in Spain; has had international career since mid-1950s, with works written for him by Thompson, McCabe and others.

puzzle canon, ➤canon.

Pycard (late 14th, early 15th century), French composer who served John of Gaunt, fourth son of Edward III of England; composed church music in a notably complex technique.

Q

quadrille, type of square-dance very popular in the 19th century – in four sections of 32 bars each, plus a final section. Operatic and other popular tunes were commonly adapted for the music. The 'lancers' is a type of quadrille.

quadruple counterpoint, ➤counterpoint.

quadruplet, a group of four notes (or notes and rests) of equal time-value, written where a group of three, five, or some other number of notes is suggested by the time-signature. E.g. a four-note group occupying a bar of 3/4 time, written

quail, toy instrument imitating a quail used e.g. in the ➤Toy Symphony formerly ascribed to Haydn.

Quantz, Johann Joachim (1697–1773), German composer and flautist; taught Frederick the Great to play the flute, and remained in his service from 1741 until death. Wrote about 300 concertos for one or two flutes, many flute solos; also hymns, songs, etc. Author of a treatise on flute-playing.

quarter-note, the note ♩ considered as a time-value. This is standard North American usage and, as mathematically corresponding to the element of time-signature represented by /4, should clearly be preferred to 'crotchet' still surviving in British use. The corresponding rest is notated ↿ or ↾

quarter-tone, half a semitone – an interval not used in Western music until the 20th century, and then only exceptionally, e.g. by Gnecchi, by Hába and other Czech composers (making use of special quarter-tone pianos) and by Bloch as an occasional melodic subtlety in string-writing. ➤microtone.

quartet (1) a performing group of four instrumentalists or singers. If instrumental, then with rare exceptions (➤Purcell Quartet), where the instruments are unspecified (e.g. Juilliard Quartet) a string quartet is assumed – two violins, viola, cello. A *piano quartet* consists of piano, violin, viola, cello; (2) a piece for four performers; if instrumental, and actually entitled 'Quartet', it will probably have the character of a ➤sonata for four performers, in several movements. See following entries.

Quartet for the End of Time, work by Messiaen. ➤*Quatuor pour la fin du temps*.

Quartet Movement, ➤*Quartettsatz*.

Quartetto Italiano, an Italian quartet founded in 1945 (known as the

Nuovo Quartetto Italiano until 1951), led by Paolo Borciani and (rare at the time) having a female violinist, Elisa Pegreffi, alongside three men. Played an extensive repertory from memory; disbanded in 1981.

Quartettsatz (Ger., 'Quartet Movement'), name used for a movement by Schubert (D703), in C minor (1820), intended for a string quartet that was never completed.

quasi (It.), almost, as if, approximating to.

Quatro rusteghi, I (It. or rather Venetian dialect, 'The Four Boors', but known in Britain as 'School for Fathers'), comic opera by Wolf-Ferrari, produced (in German) in Munich, 1906. Libretto by G. Pizzolato, after the play by Goldoni: heavy fathers are outwitted by love and commonsense.

Quattro stagioni, Le (It., 'The Four Seasons'), a set of four concertos by Vivaldi (op. 8, nos. 1–4; RV 269, 315, 293, 297), published in 1725, for violin and orchestra, 'depicting' birds, storms, falls on the ice, etc., as indicated on score.

quatuor (Fr.), ➤quartet.

Quatuor pour la fin du temps (Fr., 'Quartet for the End of Time'), work by Messiaen (composed in a German prisoner-of-war camp and first performed there, 1941) for violin, clarinet, cello and piano.

quaver, ➤eighth-note.

Queen, The (Fr. *La Reine*), nickname of Haydn's Symphony no. 85 in B flat (one of the ➤'Paris' Symphonies), composed in 1785–6 (Hob. I: 85) and so called perhaps because Queen Marie

Antoinette liked it. Its slow movement consists of variations on a French song.

Queen of Spades, The (Rus., *Pikovaya Dama*), opera by Tchaikovsky, produced in St Petersburg, 1890. Libretto by Modest Tchaikovsky (the composer's brother) after Pushkin. *The Queen of Spades* is the nickname of an old Countess, with allusion to her former uncanny luck at cards. ➤Grétry.

Querflöte (Ger., cross-flute), the normal (transverse) flute.

Quiet City, orchestral work by Copland for trumpet, English horn and strings, first performed in 1941; taken from incidental music to a play so named.

Quiet Place, A, opera by Bernstein, produced in Houston, Texas, 1983, with libretto by Stephen Wadsworth; originally written as a sequel to *Trouble in Tahiti* (1952, libretto by the composer), it was later adapted to incorporate the earlier piece (in two flashbacks). Mocks modern urban domesticity: 'Tahiti' figures only as part of the title of a film which the heroine describes.

Quilter, Roger (1877–1953), British composer, trained in Germany. Wrote chiefly song-settings of Shakespeare, Herrick and other distinguished poets.

quint, organ stop sounding a note a fifth (Lat., *quintus*) higher than the key depressed. It is with the aid of this stop on the pedals that the effect of a 32-ft stop is produced even without 32-ft pipes (➤acoustic bass).

quintadena, quintaton, types of organ stop which sound not only the note of the key depressed, but also the note a 12th (i.e. an octave plus a fifth) higher.

quintet (1) a performing group of five instrumentalists or singers; a *string quintet* adds an extra viola or cello to the standard string ➤quartet, and a *piano quintet* usually adds a piano to this standard string quartet – the ➤'Trout' Quintet forming an exception; (2) a piece for five performers; if instrumental, and actually entitled 'Quintet', it will probably have the character of a ➤sonata for five performers; in several movements.

quintuor (Fr.), ➤quintet.

quintuplet, group of five notes (or notes and rests) of equal time-value, written where a group of three, four or some other number of notes is suggested by the time-signature. E.g. a five-note group occupying a bar of 4/4 time, written

quodlibet (Lat., *quod libet*, what is desired), piece containing several popular tunes put together in unusual and (usually) ingenious fashion – such as that which ends Bach's ➤*Goldberg Variations*, incorporating two well-known tunes of his day.

R

R, abbr. for (1) as in *r.h.*, right hand (in piano music, etc.); (2) Royal, as in names of some British institutions, e.g. RAM (Academy of Music), RCM (College of Music), RCO (College of Organists), RNCM (Northern College of Music), RPO (➤Royal Philharmonic Orchestra); (3) Ryom, especially in the form RV (Ger., *Verzeichnis*, i.e. index), in numbering the compositions of ➤Vivaldi.

r, symbol in ➤tonic sol-fa for the second degree (supertonic) of the scale, pronounced *ray*.

rabab (Arabic), the short-necked fiddle of classical North African music; Chaucer's *rubible* may be related to the term. ➤rebec.

Rabaud, Henri [Benjamin] (1873–1949), French composer, pupil of Massenet and others; also conductor, and (1920–41) director of the Paris Conservatory. Works include *Mârouf, le savetier du Caire* ('Mârouf, the Cobbler of Cairo') and other operas (one based on Synge's *Riders to the Sea*), symphonic poems, songs, film music. He orchestrated Fauré's ➤*Dolly*.

Rachmaninov, ➤Rakhmaninov (the spelling which is consistent with the standard transliteration of other Russian names).

Racine, Jean (1639–99), French poet and dramatist. ➤*Esther*, ➤*Iphigénie en Aulide*; ➤Auric, ➤Charpentier (M.A.).

racket(t), double-reed wind instrument of various sizes cultivated in the 16th–18th centuries; a late variety was sometimes called the 'sausage bassoon'. (The name is of uncertain derivation but does not mean 'noise'.)

Rácóczy March, ➤*Rákóczi March* (correct spelling).

Radetzky March, march by Johann Strauss the elder, 1848, named after an Austrian field-marshal and coming to symbolize the Hapsburg monarchy.

Radio Telefís Eireann (orchestra of), ➤National Symphony Orchestra of Ireland.

Raff, [Joseph] **Joachim** (1822–82), Swiss composer, disciple of Liszt, some of whose works he scored for orchestra. Prolific composer of 11 symphonies with allusive titles (no. 1 *To the Fatherland*, no. 3 *In the Forest*, etc.), chamber music, operas, etc.; best known for a ➤*Cavatina* (violin and piano).

rag, a piece in the syncopated style called ➤ragtime (most such original pieces being for piano).

rãg (Hindi), the approximate equivalent in Indian music of a scale – but the term also has connotations of mode, melodic shape and even ornamentation.

ragtime, name given to a forerunner of jazz, particularly associated with piano-playing, with characteristic syncopations; e.g. *Maple Leaf Rag* (Joplin). In vogue *c*.1890–1920, revived in 1970s. Stravinsky's *Ragtime for 11 instruments* and *Piano-Rag Music* (alluding to this type of work) date from 1918 and 1919 respectively.

Raimondi, Pietro (1786–1853), Italian composer, also opera director and church musician (at St Peter's, Rome, 1851). Works include three oratorios (on the Old Testament subject of Joseph) which could be, and in 1852 were, performed simultaneously.

Raimondi, Ruggero (b. 1941), Italian bass, celebrated in opera, particularly as Mozart's Don Giovanni (on stage and in 1979 film version).

'Raindrop' Prelude, nickname for Chopin's Prelude in D flat, op. 28, no. 15 (1839), on the fanciful supposition that the repeated note A♭ (G♯) represents persistent raindrops.

Rainier, Priaulx (1903–86), South African composer, resident in Britain; she studied with N. Boulanger in Paris. Works include a cello concerto, string quartet, *Barbaric Dance Suite* for piano, *Cycle for Declamation* (unaccompanied high voice, on a text by Donne).

Rake's Progress, The, opera by Stravinsky, produced in Venice, 1951; libretto by W. H. Auden and C. Kallman derived from Hogarth's series of paintings (1735) and moralistically showing the downfall of an offender.

Rakhmaninov, Sergey Vassilievich (1873–1943), Russian composer, also pianist, maintaining throughout his career his position as travelling virtuoso performer. (The spellings 'Rachmaninoff', etc., are inconsistent with the now standard system of transliteration from Russian.) Wrote his Piano Prelude in C sharp minor at age 20. Left Russia, 1918, disliking the Soviet régime, and lived mainly in Switzerland and in USA, where he died. Nevertheless he always maintained a Russian outlook which permeated his style. Works include four piano concertos, *Rhapsody on a Theme of Paganini* for piano and orchestra (➤Paganini), many piano solos (including transcriptions from other composers) and some two-piano works; also three symphonies, symphonic poem *The ➤Isle of the Dead*, ➤*Aleko* and two other operas, choral work *The ➤Bells* (after Poe), songs (➤*vocalise*).

Rákóczi March, a Hungarian march dating from the early 19th century (composer unknown), named after prince Ferenc Rákóczi II, leader of a Hungarian revolt against the Austrians, 1703–11; has Hungarian patriotic associations. Best known from the orchestral arrangement by Berlioz included in his ➤*Damnation de Faust*; it also enters into Johann Strauss's *Der* ➤*Zigeunerbaron*.

rallentando (It.), slowing down.

Rameau, Jean Philippe (1683–1764), French composer – also organist, harpsichordist and writer of an important *Treatise on Harmony* and other theoretical works. At 50, he began his succession of more than 20 operas and opera-ballets, including *Les Indes Galantes* ('The Courtly Indies') and *Castor* *et Pollux*. His champions and those of Pergolesi clashed in the so-called ➤'War of the Buffoons' (Fr., *Guerre des bouffons*). Other works include chamber music; dance-music and other pieces for harpsichord; cantatas and church music.

Ramey, Samuel (b. 1940), American bass-baritone; has ranged from Handel (Metropolitan Opera début 1984, in *Rinaldo*) to all four 'villain' roles in *Les Contes d'Hoffmann*; sings Mephistopheles in both Gounod's *Faust* and Boito's *Mefistofele*.

Rampal, Jean-Pierre [Louis] (b. 1922), French flautist, well known as soloist in 18th-century chamber music, etc.; Poulenc, Jolivet and others have written works for him.

Ramsay, Allan (1686–1758), Scottish poet. ➤*Gentle Shepherd*.

Randegger, Alberto (1832–1911), Trieste-born conductor, composer (operas, Masses, etc.), and singing-master who in 1854 settled in London; died there.

Rands, Bernard (b. 1935), British composer, professor at University of California, San Diego, from 1976. Works include *Canti del Sole* (Songs of the Sun) for tenor and orchestra, *Ology* for 17-piece jazz orchestra, *Hiraeth* (Welsh, 'yearning') for cello and orchestra, and a series of pieces each called *Espressione* for piano(s).

Rangström, Ture (1884–1947), Swedish composer, largely self-taught; several of his works are associated with Strindberg, whom he knew. Works include four symphonies (no. 1 *In Memoriam August Strindberg*), three operas, more than 50 songs with orchestra.

rank, a set of organ pipes – term used particularly of ➤mixture stops.

Rankl, Karl (1898–1968), Austrian-born composer (pupil of Schoenberg) and conductor, resident in Britain from 1939. Musical director of Covent Garden Opera, 1946–51; works include eight symphonies, opera *Deirdre of the Sorrows* after J. M. Synge's play (not produced).

rant, term applied to a wide range of 17th-century English dances.

ranz des vaches, type of Swiss tune (name means 'cow-rank') sounded vocally or on an alphorn to call the cows; incorporated e.g. into Rossini's overture to ➤*Guillaume Tell*, Beethoven's *Pastoral Symphony* (last movement), and (satirically) Walton's ➤*Façade*.

râpe, ➤*guiro*.

Rape of Lucretia, The, opera by Britten, produced at Glyndebourne, 1946. Libretto by R. Duncan. The main tragedy, set in Rome, is commented on by a male and female 'chorus' (one performer each) standing outside the temporal dimension of the plot.

rappresentazione (It.), a representation, a staged action; hence *rappresentativo*, of the stage, in stage style; so ➤*stile rappresentativo*.

Rappresentazione di anima e di corpo, La (It., 'The Representation of the Soul and the Body'), musical and dramatic work composed by Cavalieri, staged in Rome, 1600 – regarded both as an early example of opera and (because it is a narrative work of a religious and allegorical nature) a progenitor of oratorio.

Rapsodie (Fr., variant of the spelling now more usual, *Rhapsodie*). So

357

Rapsodie espagnole ('Spanish Rhapsody'), orchestral work by Ravel, 1907, using themes of Spanish national character.

rasch (Ger.), quick.

Rascher, Sigurd (b. 1907), German saxophonist, whose concert performances from the 1930s established the alto saxophone as a solo instrument. Glazunov was among the composers who wrote concertos for him.

rasgueado (Sp. strummed), a mode of playing the guitar, distinct from the *punteado* (plucked) of normal classical technique.

Rasiermesser Quartet, ➤*Razor Quartet*.

Rasoumoffsky, Rasumovsky, variant spellings of ➤Razumovsky, the standard transliteration of this Russian name into English.

rasp, ➤guiro.

Rathaus, Karol (1895–1954), Polish-born composer who studied in Vienna, taught in Berlin, and in 1934 settled in London and afterwards in USA. Works include three symphonies, five string quartets.

Ratsche (Ger.), ➤rattle.

Rattle, Simon [Denis] (b. 1955), British conductor; worked at Glyndebourne (from 1977) and with London Sinfonietta (from 1976); principal conductor, 1980–98, City of Birmingham Symphony Orchestra, vastly enhancing its prestige. Made US opera début with *Wozzeck* at Los Angeles, 1988. Knighted, 1994.

rattle, ratchet-toothed noise-making device which is occasionally used as an orchestral percussion instrument, e.g. in R. Strauss's ➤*Till Eulenspiegel*.

Ratushinskaya, Irina (b. 1954), Russian poet. ➤Elias (Brian).

Rauschpfeiffe (Ger., 'pipe making a rushing sound'), German name for a double-reed 16th–17th century instrument similar to the shawm.

Rauzzini, Venanzio (1746–1810), Italian castrato singer and composer of vocal works in Italian and English, etc.; settled in London and then (1780) in Bath; died there. Noted teacher.

Ravel, [Joseph] **Maurice** (1875–1937), French composer, the outstanding figure (with Debussy) in French music of his period. Pupil of Fauré and others at the Paris Conservatoire. His work, often described as ➤impressionist, exploits piano technique and sonorities in a sonatina, suites ➤*Gaspard de la nuit* and ➤*Miroirs* (including ➤*Alborada del gracioso*), ➤*Pavane pour une Infante défunte*, ➤*Valses nobles et sentimentales*, Le ➤*Tombeau de Couperin* and (for piano duet) ➤*Ma mère l'oye*; most of these he later transcribed for orchestra. Other orchestral works include two piano concertos (one for left hand), ➤*Boléro*, ➤*Rapsodie espagnole* and La ➤*Valse*. Also composed ballet ➤*Daphnis et Chloé* and operas L'➤*Heure espagnole* and L'➤*Enfant et les sortilèges*; a septet including harp (also called *Introduction and Allegro*) and piano trio; ➤*Tzigane* for violin with piano or orchestra; songs, some with orchestra (➤*chanson*, ➤*Shéhérazade*). He orchestrated Musorgsky's ➤*Pictures at an Exhibition*. Visited England (Hon. D.Mus., Oxford, 1928) and USA.

Ravenscroft, Thomas (*c.* 1582–*c.* 1635), English composer of psalm-tunes, etc.; collector and editor of popular songs and rounds, published in

➤*Pammelia* (with sequel *Deuteromelia*) and ➤*Melismata*; author of a musical treatise.

ravvivando (It.), reviving, i.e. returning gradually to a previous faster tempo.

Rawsthorne, Alan (1905–71), British composer – mainly self-taught, having studied dentistry first; also studied piano. Works, almost entirely instrumental, include three symphonies, Symphonic Studies, two piano concertos, three string quartets, ballet *Madame Chrysanthème*, film music.

ray, in ➤tonic sol-fa, the spoken name for the second degree (supertonic) of the scale, written r. Derived from ➤*re*.

Razor Quartet, name for Haydn's String Quartet in F minor, op. 55, no. 2 (Hob. III: 61). When Haydn was visited in 1787 by the English publisher Bland, he is said to have exclaimed that he would 'give his best quartet for a good razor', and (Bland having supplied the razor) this is it.

Razumovsky Quartets, name for Beethoven's three String Quartets, op. 59 (in F, E minor, and C), 1806–7, dedicated to Count Andreas Razumovsky, Russian ambassador in Vienna – and, in compliment to him, using a traditional Russian tune in the first two, and perhaps (though it is not identifiable) in no. 3.

re, the note D (in Latin countries, and formerly elsewhere); the ➤tonic sol-fa symbol ➤*ray* is derived from it. Honegger's Symphony no. 5, first performed in 1951, is subtitled *Di tre re* – of the three D's – referring to the quietly emphatic note D ending each of the three movements.

Read, Gardner (b. 1913), American composer; works include four symphonies, opera *Villon*, piano and organ music. Also teacher, radio commentator, and writer on music.

Reading Rota, ➤*Sumer is icumen in*.

real, term used in opposition to 'tonal' in special senses; ➤answer; ➤sequence.

realism, stylistic term with at least two meanings – (1) the use in opera of characterization and stories based on contemporary life as it is actually observed (not forgetting 'life in the raw'), as distinct from 'remote' subjects and 'refined' treatment: in this sense the term indicates a correspondence with the literary outlook e.g. of Zola, and is used e.g. of Italian opera of the Puccini–Mascagni type – more usually called by its Italian equivalent, ➤*verismo*; (2) ('socialist realism'), the stance considered 'correct' for creative artists under Soviet officialdom up to the 1980s – showing optimism, sympathy with 'the people', a desire to be comprehensible, an avoidance of such deviations as ➤formalism, etc.

realize, to work out in full and artistically such music as was originally left by its composer in a sparsely notated condition. E.g. a 17th- or 18th-century piece might originally have a ➤continuo bass-line, might require ornaments (originally left to performers' taste), and might need written directions to assist a modern performer. Such a phrase as 'Britten's realizations of Purcell' covers all these functions and does not carry (as ➤arrange does) the implication of arbitrary alteration.

rebec(k), a bowed instrument of Arab origin, current in Europe in the

13th–16th centuries; generally pear-shaped with three strings; regarded as a forerunner of the violin and later surviving as a folk-instrument.

Rebel, Jean-Féry (1661–1747), French composer and violinist, pupil of Lully, chamber-composer to Louis XIV. Wrote works for violin. His son was the composer François Rebel (1701–75).

Rebikov, Vladimir Ivanovich (1866–1920), Russian composer of *The Christmas Tree* and other operas, and many works for piano and for piano and voice. Made use of ➤whole-tone scale and other harmonic novelties.

recapitulation, a section of a composition which repeats (in something like their original shape) themes which were originally presented in an earlier section but have interveningly undergone 'development'. The term is particularly used in the scheme of construction called ➤sonata-form, and variants of it.

recit., abbr. of ➤recitative.

récit (Fr.), ➤swell (organ).

recital, a musical performance, usually by soloists or duettists, rarely by larger combinations.

recitative, type of speech-like singing which is written in ordinary notation but in which a certain freedom in rhythm (and sometimes also in pitch) is allowed in performance; used particularly in opera, oratorio, etc. up to mid 19th century as preliminary to a song (so *recitative and air*, etc.). In Italian music (and styles related to it, e.g. Handel's oratorios), it is either *accompanied recitative* (It., *recitativo accompagnato* or *stromentato*) with

normal orchestral accompaniment, or *dry recitative* (*recitativo secco*), accompanied only by 'punctuating' chords on the harpsichord and/or other continuo instruments. (The word is commonly pronounced to rhyme with 'thieve', probably on the mistaken supposition that it is French; as it is only English, it might well be made as English-sounding as 'narrative'.)

recitativo, see preceding entry.

recorder, type of woodwind instrument, without reed, much used in 16th–18th centuries but ousted by the more powerfully toned 'ordinary' flute, which it resembles except for being blown at the end and held downwards instead of crosswise. The recorder itself was formerly known as the 'English flute'; and in the usage of Bach's period the term 'flute' actually meant 'recorder' unless some such word as 'transverse' was added to indicate the other instrument. The recorder has been extensively revived in the 20th century, (a) to play the old music written for it; (b) as an inexpensive and relatively easy instrument for schoolchildren, etc. Some later composers, e.g. Rubbra and Berio, have also written for it. It is currently employed chiefly in five sizes named as follows – sopranino; descant (English) or soprano (Continental); treble (English) or alto (Continental); tenor; and bass. Two sizes of still lower pitch, the great bass and the double-bass (or contrabass), are also found. The size most often encountered is the descant, though nearly all old solo music is for the treble.

recte et retro (Lat., right way and backwards), the use of a theme performed normally, in counterpoint with that same theme performed backwards.

Redemption, The, oratorio by Gounod (words, in English, compiled from the Bible by the composer) first performed in Birmingham, 1882.

Redford, John (?–1547), English composer, organist (St Paul's Cathedral, London), poet and playwright; works include motets and organ music.

reduction, an edition enabling music to be played by fewer performers – particularly *piano reduction* (of an orchestral score).

reed, a vibrating 'tongue' of thin cane or metal, used to set the air-column vibrating in certain types of mouth-blown wind instruments, certain organ pipes, etc. The reed may beat freely (e.g. in the harmonica, i.e. mouth-organ), or against a surface, as does the single reed of a clarinet; or two reeds may beat against each other, e.g. the double reed of an oboe. So *reed stop* on an organ, controlling pipes which have reeds.

reed-organ (1) general name for types of keyboard instrument using free-beating ➤reeds (one for each note) and no pipes, e.g. ➤harmonium, ➤American organ; (2) name sometimes also used (by extension from the preceding) to cover various other instruments working on the same principle but not organ-like in appearance – e.g. ➤accordion, ➤harmonica (mouth-organ).

reel, quick dance for two or more couples – found chiefly in Scotland, Ireland, Scandinavia and North America.

Refice, Licinio (1883–1954), Italian composer, priest, and choirmaster in

Rome. Wrote Masses and other religious music; also symphonic poems with chorus, and operas.

'Reformation' Symphony, descriptive name given by Mendelssohn to his Symphony no. 5, 1830. The first and fourth (last) movements respectively quote the 'Dresden Amen' and the chorale 'A Stronghold Sure' (*Ein' feste Burg*), respectively of Roman Catholic and Lutheran associations. ➤Luther.

refrain, part of a song that recurs (both words and music) at the end of each stanza.

regal, type of small portable keyboard instrument of ➤reed-organ type (15th–17th centuries); in church it was employed to regulate the singing (Lat., *regolare* – hence the name). Some models could be folded shut like a book and so were named *bible-regal*. In some later models, short pipes were added, taking the instrument strictly out of the reed-organ class.

Reger, [Johann Baptist Joseph] **Max** [imilian] (1873–1916), German composer – also pianist, organist, conductor and teacher. Works include *Variations on a Theme of Mozart* and other orchestral works; much chamber music; piano and organ pieces; songs.

register (1) a set of organ pipes controlled by one particular stop; so *to register* a piece for the organ is to select the stops appropriate to it; (2) part of an instrument's compass appearing to have a distinct tone-quality of its own, e.g. the ➤chalumeau register of the clarinet; (3) a part of the compass of the voice giving its own distinctive sensation to the singer (➤chest voice, ➤head voice).

Regondi, Giulio (*c.* 1822–72), Italian

guitarist and concertina player, and composer for both instruments. A child prodigy on the guitar, he came to London and won further fame in taking up the English concertina (➤Molique).

Reich, Steve (b. 1936), American composer, director of his own unique ensemble comprising mainly percussion and electronic keyboards. Studied African drumming, Javanese gamelan music and Jewish cantillation, and evolved a repetitively patterned music of his own, now called ➤minimalism. Works include *Drumming* (for drums and other instruments), *Different Trains* for string quartet and tape, *Vermont Counterpoint* for 11 flutes, mixed-media theatre pieces, *The Cave*, *Hindenberg*.

Reicha, Antonín (1770–1836), Bohemian composer and teacher, friend of Beethoven; settled in Paris, becoming professor at the Conservatory in 1818. Himself a flautist, he composed 24 wind quintets as well as operas, symphonies, piano works, etc.

Reichardt, Johann Friedrich (1752–1814), German composer, musical director at the Prussian court; also writer on music. Wrote some notable German songs; also operas, incidental music to plays, etc.

Reimann, Aribert (b. 1936), German composer (pupil of Blacher and Pepping), also well known as piano accompanist to singers. Works include operas *Ein Traumspiel* and *Die Gespenstersonate* (respectively after Strindberg's *A Dream Play* and *Ghost Sonata*) and *Lear* (after Shakespeare's *King Lear*); songs and choral settings; a cello concerto.

Reine, La, ➤Queen.

Reinecke, Carl [Heinrich Carsten] (1824–1910), German composer, pianist, conductor, writer on music; works include operas, four piano concertos, wind octet.

Reiner, Fritz (in Hungarian form, Frigyes) (1888–1963), Hungarian-born conductor, naturalized American in 1928; held important European and US posts, including conductorship of the Chicago Symphony Orchestra 1953–63.

Reinken, Johann Adam [or Jan Adams] (1623–1722), German organist and composer; Bach several times walked long distances to hear him in Hamburg. Said to have been still active as an organist in his 90s.

Reisinger, Václav (1928–92), Bohemian choreographer. ➤*Swan Lake*.

Reizenstein, Franz (1911–68), German-born composer and pianist who settled in Britain 1934 – pupil of Hindemith (in Germany) and Vaughan Williams. Works include cantata *Voices of Night*, a cello concerto, two piano concertos and many piano solos.

Rejoice in the Lord Alway, anthem by Purcell (➤Bell Anthem).

related, term used as a measure of one key's harmonic nearness to (or distance from) another. Hence, e.g., G major is more nearly related to D major (a difference of only one sharp in the key-signature, meaning that the modulation between them is of the simplest kind) than either is to A♭ major. The use of the term categorically (as when two keys are spoken of as *related*, and another two as *not related*) is inadvisable, since all keys are related at a greater or lesser remove, and the historical evolution of harmony has been to lessen the difficulty of transition between them.

relative, term used to indicate the fact that a common key-signature is shared by one major and one minor key: e.g. E minor is termed the *relative minor* of G major, and G major as the *relative major* of E minor, both having a key-signature of one sharp, and modulations between them being accordingly of a simple kind.

Reményi, Ede (originally Eduard Hoffmann) (1828–98), Hungarian violinist who toured with Brahms as his pianist-partner in 1885; also composer.

reminiscence motive, a recurring theme in an opera, identified with a character or emotion, etc. (but not necessarily subject to musical transformation as a Wagnerian ➤leading-motive may be).

Renaissance (Fr., rebirth), term used by historians of visual arts to identify the rediscovery and reapplication of 'classical' (ancient Greek and Roman as opposed to Christian) images and values in the 14th–16th centuries and the emergence of a more individualistic and worldly art; analogously used by music historians to denote a period of style between 'medieval' and ➤baroque – from early 15th century (e.g. Dunstable, Dufay) to early 17th (Byrd).

repeat (noun), a section of a composition consisting of a repetition of a previous section. To save the space of writing out the passage again, such a repetition is indicated by pairs of dots (called *repeat marks*) and a double bar.

On reaching these the per-

former repeats from the previous pair of dots or (if there is none) from the beginning.

répétiteur (Fr., also used in Eng.), the member of the musical staff of an opera company who coaches the singers and may also be employed to ➤prompt a performance.

répétition (Fr.), rehearsal; *répétition générale*, final (dress) rehearsal.

repiano, ➤ripieno.

Representation of the Soul and the Body, The, dramatic work by Cavalieri. ➤*Rappresentazione di anima e di corpo*.

reprise (Fr., also used in Eng.), a 'retaking-up', particularly a return to the first section of a composition after an intervening and contrasting section, or (in an operetta or musical, etc.) the further occurrence of a song which has already been heard.

reproducing piano, ➤player-piano.

Requiem (1, also *Requiem Mass*) the Roman Catholic Mass for the dead, in Latin, beginning with the word *requiem* ('repose'); sung to plainsong or in settings by various composers – many appropriate to concert rather than liturgical use, e.g. Berlioz's (➤*Grande Messe des Morts*) and Verdi's (1874, in memory of the writer Alessandro Manzoni, 1785–1873); (2) a choral work similarly appropriate to the commemoration of the dead but with a different text – e.g. Brahms's (1866–8), based on biblical texts, called *Ein* ➤*deutsches Requiem* (German as opposed to Latin), and Delius's (1914–16) on a pantheistic, non-biblical text by H. Simon; (3) term occasionally used allusively in other musical contexts – e.g. Britten's

➤*Sinfonia da Requiem*. Hindemith's choral work *When Lilacs Last in the Dooryard Bloom'd* (1946, on a text by Whitman) is subtitled 'Requiem for those we loved'. Henze's Requiem (1993) is for piano, trumpet and orchestra, with distant allusion to the R. C. text.

resolution, the progression from a discord to a concord or to a less acute discord; so *to resolve* a discord.

Respighi, Ottorino (1879–1936), Italian composer, pupil of Rimsky-Korsakov in Russia; also conductor, teacher, and editor of old Italian music. Works include orchestral suites *Gli* ➤*Uccelli* ('The Birds'), ➤*Fontane di Roma*, ➤*Pini di Roma*; nine operas. ➤*Soirées musicales*.

responsory/respond, type of plainsong piece in which solo voice alternates with a choral refrain; also a 16th-century polyphonic development of this.

rest, the notation of an absence of sound in a performer's part for a length of time corresponding to a given number of beats or bars. So *eighth-note (quaver) rest, two bars' rest*, etc.

resultant tone, name given to either of two acoustical phenomena: (a) when two loud notes are sounded, another note may sometimes also be heard, lower in pitch, which corresponds to the difference in vibration between the original two and is called 'differential tone'; (b) another note, higher than the original two, may also be heard corresponding to the sum of their vibrations ('summational tone'). (➤acoustic bass.)

'Resurrection' Symphony, nickname for Mahler's Symphony no. 2 (1894): its final movement, with soprano and alto soloists and choir, is a setting of German words by Klopstock (1724–1803) on the subject of (Christian) resurrection.

Retablo de maese Pedro, El (Sp., 'Master Peter's Puppet Show'), opera by Falla, first staged in Paris, 1923 (after an earlier performance in Seville in concert version). Libretto by composer, after an episode from *Don Quixote*. Uses three human characters plus marionettes.

retardation, ➤suspension.

retenu (Fr.), held back (as to speed).

Rethberg, Elisabeth (originally Lisbeth Sattler) (1894–1976), German-born soprano who settled in USA and sang 30 roles at the New York Metropolitan Opera from 1922, retiring in 1942.

retrograde, term used of a theme when performed backwards – a device prominently used e.g. in the 15th century, in Bach's *Die* ➤*Kunst der Fuge*, and in ➤twelve-note technique. In this last, both *retrograde* and *retrograde inversion* are standard procedures, the latter meaning that the theme is turned upside-down as well as played backwards. ➤invert.

Return of Lemminkäinen, The, ➤*Lemminkäinen's Homecoming*.

Return of Ulysses, The, opera by Monteverdi. ➤*Ritorno di Ulisse in patria*.

Reubke, Julius (1834–58), German pianist and composer, pupil of Liszt. Compositions, published after his early death, include an organ sonata on Psalm 94 (alluding to the psalm's call for vengeance).

Reutter, Hermann (1900–1985),

German composer – also pianist, particularly song-accompanist. Works include operas (one based on Thornton Wilder's *The Bridge of San Luis Rey*), choral works (texts by Goethe and others), four piano concertos.

'Revolutionary' Study, nickname for Chopin's Study in C minor, op. 10, no. 12 (1831) supposedly expressing his patriotic anger at the news of the fall of Warsaw to the Russians.

Revueltas, Silvestre (1899–1940), Mexican violinist, conductor and composer of symphonic poems on Mexican subjects for orchestra, three string quartets, songs, etc. Studied partly in USA; worked in Spain on the Republican side in the Civil War.

Reyer, Ernest (pen-name of Louis Étienne Ernest Rey) (1823–1909), French composer (operas, cantatas, etc.) and critic, follower and champion of Wagner.

Reynolds, Roger [Lee] (b. 1934), American composer who has worked in Paris, Cologne and Tokyo; works include *Ping* for flute, piano, harmonium, bowed cymbal, tam-tam, film, slides, tape and electronic equipment; *Masks* for chorus and orchestra.

Rezniček, Emil Nikolaus von (1860–1945), Austrian composer and conductor who settled in Germany and died there. Works, mainly before 1920, include *Donna Diana* and other operas (one based on the ➤'Till Eulenspiegel' tale used by R. Strauss), four symphonies, Mass, Requiem.

rfz., abbr. for ➤*rinforzando*.

rhapsody, title (not in itself denoting a particular musical form) used in the 19th and 20th centuries for a work

generally in one continuous movement and usually suggestive of some kind of romantic 'inspiration'. Thus the basis may be some already existing theme(s): e.g. Liszt's ➤*Hungarian Rhapsodies*, Delius's *Brigg Fair* (using an English folk-tune), Rakhmaninov's *Rhapsody on a Theme of Paganini*. Or no such allusiveness may be implied – e.g. Brahms's Rhapsodies for piano, his ➤*Alto Rhapsody* (voices and orchestra), and the following.

Rhapsody in Blue, work for piano and dance-band orchestra by Gershwin (the first notable concert work by a jazz composer in the jazz idiom), first performed in 1924, later arranged for piano and symphony orchestra. Orchestration for both versions was by Grofé.

Rheinberger, Josef [Gabriel] (1839–1901), German organist – child prodigy, holding church post at age seven – pianist, conductor and composer of many organ works. Also composed operas, Masses, chamber music, etc. Distinguished teacher of organ and composition.

Rheingold, Das, ➤*Ring*.

'Rhenish' Symphony, name given to Schumann's Symphony no. 3 in E♭ (1850): the fourth of its five movements was prompted by the composer's witnessing the installation of a cardinal in Cologne (on the Rhine).

Rhinegold, The, ➤*Ring*.

rhythm, that aspect of music concerned not with pitch but with the distribution of notes in time and their accentuation – related to the concept of ➤metre. Hence such phrases as a *strongly marked rhythm* or (by ellipsis) a *strong rhythm; two-beat rhythm* (accent on every other beat); a *five-bar rhythm* (each five bars making a regular rhythmic unit); *waltz rhythm* (accent on the first of every three beats, at waltz pace); *free rhythm*, rhythm not determined by the regular incidence of bar-lines but arrived at by the performer according to the natural or conventional flow of the notes (as in plainsong). So also *a sense of rhythm*, implying a performer's ability to convey the rhythmic element of a composition intelligibly; *rhythm section* of a dance band of the 1930s, collective term for those instruments more concerned with giving the beat than with melody – e.g. piano, drums and other percussion, guitar(s), double-bass.

rhythm machine, ➤drum machine.

rhythmic mode, ➤mode (2).

Ricci, Ruggiero (b. 1918), American violinist who made first tour of Europe in 1932; eminent as solo performer (e.g. in Paganini's works) and in concertos – giving first performances of those by von Einem and Ginastera.

Ricciarelli, Katia (b. 1946), Italian soprano eminent in Italian operatic roles. US début at Chicago, 1972; Covent Garden début, 1974.

Rice, Elmer (1892–1967), American playwright. ➤*Street Scene*.

ricercar(e) (It., to search), type of contrapuntal instrumental composition current in the 16th–18th centuries, usually in the strictest style of ➤imitation.

Richards, [Henry] Brinley (1817–75), British pianist and composer of song 'God Bless the Prince of Wales', etc.

Richardson, Samuel (1689–1761), English novelist. ➤Piccinni.

Richter, Franz Xaver (1709–89), Bohemian composer, a leading figure of the ➤Mannheim school; composed about 70 symphonies and was also bass singer and violinist.

Richter, Syvatoslav [Teofilovich] (1915–97), Russian pianist, formerly opera coach. Played in USA 1960, Britain 1961, and has sustained highest international reputation; Prokofiev's Piano Sonata no. 9 was dedicated to him.

riddle canon, ➤canon.

Riders to the Sea, opera by Vaughan Williams, produced in London, 1937: almost a word-for-word setting of Synge's play about an Irish fishing family. ➤Rabaud.

Riegger, Wallingford (1885–1961), American composer who studied and conducted in Germany. Wrote many works for Martha Graham's and other dance companies; also three symphonies, Concerto for piano and wind, three string quartets, *Study in Sonority* for 10 violins (or any multiple of 10), *Music for Brass Choir* (in 26 independent parts).

Rienzi, oder Der Letzte der Tribunen (Ger., 'Rienzi, or The Last of the Tribunes'), opera by Wagner, produced in Dresden, 1842. Libretto by composer, after Bulwer-Lytton's novel: the hero is a historical 14th-century Italian patriot.

Ries, German family of musicians, the most important being Ferdinand Ries (1784–1838), friend of Beethoven, pianist, violinist, conductor, and composer of three operas, six symphonies, etc.

Rieti, Vittorio (1898–1994), Egyptian-born Italian composer; settled in USA 1940. Works include operas, ballets, five symphonies, triple concerto (piano, violin, cello).

riff, in jazz and its derivatives, a short, tuneful phrase subjected to repetition and possible harmonic variation; hence Bernstein's orchestral *Prelude, Fugue and Riffs*, 1955.

Rifkin, Joshua (b. 1944), American pianist, also university professor, Bach scholar and conductor. In the 1970s he became well known as a pianist for his revival of Scott Joplin's ragtime music.

rigadoon, rigaudon (Eng., Fr.), old French dance of a lively nature in 2/4 or 4/4 time.

Rigoletto, opera by Verdi, produced in Venice, 1851. Libretto by F. M. Piave, after Hugo's *Le Roi s'amuse*: title taken not from its romantic tenor role but from its baritone hero, a tragic court jester. 'La donna è mobile' ('Woman is Fickle'), its most famous aria, has itself been taken as an opera title by R. Malipiero.

Rihm, Wolfgang (b. 1952), German composer of *Jacob Lenz* and other operas, also of three symphonies (no. 3 with soprano and baritone soloists); *Départ* for singing chorus, speaking chorus and 22 players including six percussionists (text by Rimbaud), five string quartets.

Riley, Terry [Mitchell] (b. 1935), American composer (also pianist and saxophonist) whose works prominently use keyboards, electronics and indeterminate structures. They include *In C* for any number of instruments; *A Rainbow in Curved Air* for electronic

keyboard instruments; *Cactus Rosary* for instrumental ensemble.

Rimbaud, Arthur (1854–91), French poet. ➤*Illuminations*; ➤Rihm.

Rimsky-Korsakov, Nikolay Andreyevich (1844–1908), Russian composer, also conductor; the most prolific and successful member of the 'nationalist' group of composers called the ➤Mighty Handful. In early life was naval officer, and picked up much of his musical technique after being appointed professor at the St Petersburg Conservatory, 1871. Author of a textbook on orchestration with examples entirely from his own work. Wrote operas including *The* ➤*Maid of Pskov, Mlada, The* ➤*Snow-Maiden*, ➤*Sadko*, ➤*Mozart and Salieri, The Legend of Tsar Saltan, The* ➤*Legend of The Invisible City of Kitezh and of the Maid Fevroniya* and *The* ➤*Golden Cockerel* (this last banned for its 'seditious' satire until after his death). Other works include three symphonies (no. 2, Antar), ➤*Russian Easter Festival* overture, suite ➤*Sheherazade*, ➤*Capriccio espagnol*, a piano concerto, folksong arrangements. His orchestrations and revisions of other composers' works, though some have now yielded to more faithful editions, were of historical importance: ➤*Boris Godunov, The* ➤*Khovansky Affair*, ➤*Prince Igor*, ➤*St John's Night on Bald Mountain, The* ➤*Stone Guest*.

Rinaldo, the first opera written by Handel for London; produced there in 1711. Libretto, in Italian, by G. Rossi, ultimately after Tasso's *Jerusalem Delivered*, of which epic of the Crusades Rinaldo is a hero. The opera has a famous march 'borrowed' in *The* ➤*Beggar's Opera*.

rinforzando (It., reinforcing), direction

that volume is to be suddenly increased on a particular note or chord or a small series of these; abbr. *rinf.*, *rfz*.

Ring, The, usual short title in English for *Der Ring des Nibelungen* (Ger., 'The Nibelung's Ring'), series of four operas by Wagner – called by him a trilogy 'with a preliminary evening'. The complete cycle of four was first performed complete in Bayreuth, 1876, but the first two parts had already been given separately – *Das Rheingold* ('The Rhinegold'), Munich, 1869; *Die Walküre* ('The Valkyrie'), Munich, 1870; *Siegfried*; *Götterdämmerung* ('Twilight of the Gods'). These form a single developing musical structure and unfold a continuous plot: libretto by composer, after old German legends. The 'Nibelung' of the title (member of a race of dwarfs) is Alberich, the first possessor of the magic ring.

Rio Grande, The, work by Lambert for chorus, orchestra and piano solo, first performed in 1928; it uses jazz idioms and jazz percussion instruments. Setting of a poem by Sacheverell Sitwell.

ripieno (It., replenished), term indicating (e.g. in the baroque *concerto grosso*) the full body of performers as distinct from the solo group; so also indicating an additional 'filling-in' part. In the brass band the *ripieno cornets* (usually corrupted in writing and speech to *repiano cornets*) are those used to supplement the 'solo' (i.e. first) cornets.

Rise and Fall of the City of Mahagonny, opera by Weill. ➤*Aufstieg und Fall der Stadt Mahagonny*.

rit., abbr. for ➤*ritardando* or ➤*ritenuto*.

ritardando (It.), becoming slower.

ritenuto (It.). held back (as to tempo) – effectively the same as ➤*ritardando*.

Rite of Spring, The (Rus., *Vesni svyashchenni* – literally *Spring, the Sacred*), ballet with choreography by Nijinsky, music by Stravinsky, produced in Paris, 1913 – and occasioning a riot between its champions and its opponents. The French title then used, *Le sacre du printemps*, is the source of the common English form of the title.

ritmo (It.), rhythm; *ritmo di tre battute*, in a rhythm of three bars (i.e. three bars are treated as forming a rhythmical unit).

ritornello (It., little return), a recurring passage, e.g. an instrumental passage always occurring between the verses of a song; so also a passage for full orchestra (without soloist) in a baroque or later concerto, thought of as 'coming round again' even though the material may not all be literally repeated. Hence *ritornello form*, as of a movement based on such recurrences (in various keys), e.g. the opening movement of the classical concerto.

Ritorno di Ulisse in patria, Il (It., 'The Return of Ulysses to his Country'), opera by Monteverdi, produced in Venice, 1640; libretto by G. Badoaro, after Homer's *Odyssey*.

Ritual Dances, ➤*Midsummer Marriage*.

Ritual Fire Dance, ➤*Amor brujo*.

Rizzi, Carlo (b. 1960), Italian conductor; conducted opera in Italy, then for the Australian Opera (1989–90), for Opera North, etc.; also orchestral conductor. Music director of Welsh National Opera since 1992.

Robbins, Jerome (b. 1918), American choreographer. ➤*Age of Anxiety*.

Roberton, Hugh [Stevenson] (1874–1952), British choral conductor – founder and conductor of Glasgow Orpheus Choir, 1906–51; also composer and arranger of vocal music.

Robeson, Paul [Leroy] (1898–1976), American bass of international repute, the most famous black performer of his day; specialized in spirituals and was also stage and film actor.

Robles, Marisa (b. 1937), Spanish-born harpist, resident in Britain (naturalized 1960), becoming noted television performer. Also composer of *Basque Suite* for flute and harp, and other works; director of World Harp Festivals, Cardiff, from 1991.

Robson, Christopher (b. 1953), British counter-tenor noted in baroque opera (Cavalli, Handel); also in modern works, including the title-role of *Akhnaten* in the first American performance (1984) and first British performance (English National Opera, 1985). Has recorded Schütz, Vivaldi, Britten, etc.

Rochberg, George (b. 1918), American composer. Works include several with Jewish references, e.g. choral psalm-settings in Hebrew; six symphonies (no. 3, *A 20th-century Passion* with voices); a violin concerto (first performed, and recorded, by Isaac Stern), 7 string quartets no. 7 with baritone; *Nach Bach* ('After Bach') for harpsichord or piano.

rock, type of popular music (originating from *rock 'n' roll*) which from US roots has spread over the Western world since about 1950 – based on solo voice and guitars (mainly electric), and mainly diffused by sound-recording. *Rock 'n' roll* is now applied only to a sub-type, with particular rhythmic and other features. Fusions with other popular music are indicated by such terms as *folk-rock* and *jazz-rock*. The term ➤pop overlaps but is not used synonymously, 'pop' denoting a more commercialized, more juvenile and more easily assimilable product than 'rock'.

rock 'n' roll (i.e. *rock and roll*, bodily movement of response), see preceding.

rococo, term originally alluding to fancy rock-work (Fr., *rocaille*) and applied in visual art to the predominantly diverting – rather than elevating – style of e.g. Watteau (1684–1721) and to related styles in architecture. It has been borrowed by writers on music and applied e.g. to F. Couperin (1668–1733): in all cases the allusion is to a decorative and light art-style succeeding the massiveness and constructive ingenuity of ➤baroque.

Rodeo, or The Courting at Burnt Ranch, ballet with choreography by Agnes de Mille, music by Copland, produced in 1942. Set in the Wild West and musically alluding to some traditional American songs.

Rodgers, Richard (1902–79), American composer of light music, especially of musicals in collaboration with the writer Oscar Hammerstein – including ➤*Carousel, The* ➤*King and I*, ➤*Oklahoma!* ➤*On Your Toes, The* ➤*Sound of Music*.

Rodrigo, Joaquin (b. 1901), Spanish (blind) composer, pupil of Dukas in Paris. Works include ➤*Concierto de Aranjuez* and ➤*Fantasia para un gentil-hombre* ('Fantasia for a Gentleman'), both for guitar and orchestra; other concertos for piano, violin, cello, harp; songs.

Rogé, Pascal (b. 1951), French pianist who made début at 11 in Paris, has toured widely in Europe and North America, and has recorded all Saint-Saëns' five concertos, all Debussy's solo piano music.

Roger-Ducasse, Jean Jules Aimable (1873–1954), French composer, pupil of Fauré. Works include mime-drama *Orphée* ('Orpheus'), three motets, symphonic poems, piano solos. Completed and orchestrated the Rhapsody for saxophone and orchestra which Debussy left unfinished at his death.

Rogers, Benjamin (1614–98), English organist and composer of church music – including the Latin hymn still sung at dawn on May Day from the tower of Magdalen College, Oxford, where he was organist – and also chamber and keyboard music.

Rogers, Bernard (1893–1968), American composer who studied with Frank Bridge in London and N. Boulanger in Paris. Composer of opera *The Warrior*, five symphonies and other orchestral works, religious choral works, *Pastorale* for 11 instruments.

Rogg, Lionel (b. 1936), Swiss organist and harpsichordist famous for his Bach recordings, who has toured widely; also composer and professor at Geneva Conservatory.

Rohrflöte, Rohr flute (Ger., Eng.), type of organ stop, the pipes being plugged at the end but having a thin tube (Ger. *rohr*, reed) through the plug.

Roi David, Le (Fr., 'King David'), 'dramatic psalm' by Honegger – basically an oratorio with spoken narration. Words by R. Morax, after the Bible. First performed, as a stage work, in Mézières, Switzerland, 1921.

Roldán, Amadeo (1900–1939), Cuban composer (born in Paris of Cuban parents), also conductor in Havana. Works include ballet *La Rebambaramba* with orchestra including indigenous Cuban instruments; *Danza negra* for voice, two clarinets, two violas, percussion.

Rolfe Johnson, Anthony (b. 1940), British tenor, widely known in Handel oratorio and in opera; début at Covent Garden 1988, at Salzburg in concert 1987. CBE, 1992.

roll, a very rapid succession of notes on a drum, approximating to a continuous sound. The technique varies between types of drum: on the snaredrum each hand gives a double stroke.

Roman, Johan Helmich (1694–1758), Swedish composer of church music, 21 symphonies, etc.; studied in London and was influenced by Handel.

Roman Carnival, overture by Berlioz. ➤*Carnaval romain.*

romance, romanza, Romanze, respectively the French (and English), Italian and German forms of a term used with wide and vague musical significance. The slow middle movement of Mozart's Piano Concerto in D minor, K466 (1785), is headed 'Romanze' (an early use); Mendelssohn's *Songs without Words* are called in French *Romances sans paroles* (*romance* in French, like its parallel in Russian, may simply signify any solo song); Vaughan Williams frequently employed *romance* and *romanza* as the titles of slow movements, and his single-movement work (1951) for harmonica with strings and piano is called Romance. A quality of intimacy and tenderness is often implied. The term now bears no direct relation to the following entry, despite the common origin of the words.

Romantic(ism), terms alluding to an artistic outlook discernible in European literature towards the end of the 18th century, and taken over to describe a supposedly similar outlook in music, principally in the 19th century. One of its literary aspects, that of harking back to the Middle Ages, is rarely found in musical contexts – apart from Bruckner's 'Romantic' Symphony (no. 4 in E flat, 1874), a nickname bestowed after the composer's description of the opening in terms of a scene of medieval chivalry. Another literary aspect, that of cultivation of the supernatural, is evident e.g. in Weber but not in other composers supposedly no less typed as Romantic, e.g. Chopin. The main musical implication is that the composer is more concerned with the vivid depiction of an emotional state (often linked with a narrative or some other extra-musical element) than with the creation of aesthetically pleasing structures. (Such structures must, however, be the result if not the aim of any successful method of composition.) The attempt at more and more 'vividness' led to (a) a trend to the evocation of 'extreme' emotions, (b) an expansion of orchestral resources for this purpose. Romanticism is thus contrasted with ➤classicism; it is also, less clearly, differentiated from ➤impressionism. The term ➤post-Romantic is applied to a late blooming in this style.

romanza, Romanze, ➤*romance*.

Romberg, Andreas Jakob (1767–1821), German violinist, conductor, and composer of violin concertos, string quartets, etc.; also of a *Toy Symphony* (not the famous one). Cousin of the following.

Romberg, Bernhard (1767–1841), German cellist and composer of ten cello concertos, also of operas, symphonies, etc.; cousin of the preceding.

Romberg, Sigmund (1887–1951), Hungarian-born composer of operettas (*New Moon, The* ➤*Student Prince, The* ➤*Desert Song*, etc.) and other music, resident in USA from 1909.

Romeo and Juliet, play by Shakespeare, source of many operas and other musical works, the best-known including (1) opera by Gounod – ➤*Roméo et Juliette*; (2) ballet with music by Prokofiev, choreography by I. V. Psota, produced in Brno, 1938 (two orchestral suites have been drawn from it); (3) 'dramatic symphony' by Berlioz, with solo singers and chorus, 1839; (4) overture-fantasy by Tchaikovsky, 1869–70. Also operas by Sutermeister, 1940 (*Romeo und Julia*), by Zingarelli in 1796 and Zandonai in 1921 (both *Giulietta e Romeo*).

Roméo et Juliette, opera by Gounod, produced in Paris, 1867; libretto J. Barbier and M. Carré, after Shakespeare's play.

Ronald, Landon [form of name used by Landon Ronald Russell] (1873–1938), British pianist (accompanist to Melba), composer (song 'Down in the Forest', etc.), and conductor, noted in early orchestral recordings. Son of Henry Russell. Knighted, 1922.

rondeau (Fr.), a musical (and/or poetic) form suggestive of a circle or of recurrence; in particular (1) a 13th–15th-century vocal form where certain sections of both verse and music recur; (2) a 17th-century and later instrumental form in which the opening section recurs at intervals – in which sense, the term was taken into Italian (and wider) usage as ➤*rondo*.

rondel (Fr.), variant spelling of ➤*rondeau* (1).

rondo (properly spelt, in It., *rondò*, itself an Italianized form of Fr. *rondeau*), a form of composition, especially an instrumental movement, in which one section recurs intermittently (the French spelling *rondeau* was used e.g. by Bach). By Mozart's time the rondo had evolved into a standard pattern and was much used, e.g., for the last movement of a sonata or concerto. A simple rondo is built up in the pattern of ABACADA ... (etc.), where A represents the recurring section (called *rondo-theme*) and B, C, D ... represent contrasting sections called 'episodes'. (The rondo-theme can undergo some variation in its reappearances.) A combination of this with ➤sonata-form led to what is called the *sonata-rondo* (used e.g. by Mozart, Beethoven) in which the first episode (B) is originally in a key other than the tonic but later reappears in the tonic key (like the 'second subject' in sonata-form). Occasionally in Italian opera (e.g. Mozart, Rossini), rondò is used to designate an aria in which a slow section is succeeded by a faster one (without an implication of recurrence); the reason for this is obscure.

Rooley, Anthony (b. 1944), British lutenist, joint founder (1969) and later sole director of the Consort of Musicke, one of the most successful early-music ensembles.

root, the lowest note of a chord when that chord is in what is regarded as its 'basic' position – e.g. for the chord of C major (C, E, G) the root is C, which is regarded as the basic note of the chord (the other notes being built up from it by thirds). In the case of complex chords, analysis may indicate a root which is not actually sounded. (➤position (3).)

Ropartz, Guy (form of name used by Joseph Marie Guy-Ropartz) (1864–1955), French composer of operas, five symphonies, organ and piano music, etc.; pupil of Massenet, Franck and others.

Rore, Cyprian (or Cipriano) **de** (1516–65), Flemish composer who worked in Italy (and died there); pupil of Willaert in Venice, then held various church and court posts. Wrote notable madrigals; also church music, instrumental fantasies, a *St John* ➤*Passion*, etc.

Rorem, Ned (b. 1923), American composer of many songs and song-cycles; *Miss Julie* (after Strindberg) and other operas; three symphonies, *Diversions* for brass quintet, church music. Lived in Paris, 1949–55. Also noted as writer, not only on music.

rosalia, name sometimes given to a 'real ➤sequence' (because it occurred at the beginning of an old Italian popular song, 'Rosalia mia cara').

Rosamunde, Fürstin von Cypern (Ger., 'Rosamond, Princess of Cyprus'), play by Helmine von Chézy, 1823, for which Schubert wrote three entr'actes, two ballet pieces and various vocal numbers. The piece now known as the overture to *Rosamunde* was originally written for an earlier stage piece, *Die Zauberharfe* ('The Magic Harp'); the overture actually used at the first performance of *Rosamunde* was that already written for ➤*Alfonso und Estrella* and is still known by that name.

rose, ➤sound-hole.

Rose, Leonard (1918–84), American cellist, principal cellist of New York Philharmonic, 1943–51, thereafter prominent as soloist and teacher.

Roseingrave, English family of musicians, the most important of whom is Thomas Roseingrave (1688–1766), organist and composer of an opera, Italian cantatas, English church music, organ and harpsichord pieces, etc.; in Italy he became acquainted with A. and D. Scarlatti. Latterly lived in Ireland and died there.

Rose Marie, musical play with text by Otto Harbach and Oscar Hammerstein II; music by Rudolf Friml and Herbert Stothart. Produced in New York, 1924. The French-Canadian heroine and her gold-miner sweetheart are linked by the 'Indian Love Call'.

Rosen aus dem Süden (Ger., 'Roses from the South'), waltz by Johann Strauss the younger – from his operetta *Das Spitzentuch der Königin* ('The Queen's Lace Handkerchief'), 1880.

Rosen, Charles (b. 1927), American pianist, pupil of Moriz Rosenthal; New York début, 1951. Also writer of books on the Vienna classics and on Schoenberg, etc.

Rosenberg, Hilding [Constantin] (1892–1985), Swedish composer, also conductor; studied in Germany and France. Works include eight symphonies – no. 4, *The Revelation of St John*, with chorus; concertos for violin, viola, cello, trumpet; ballet *Orpheus in Town*; tetralogy of stage oratorios after Thomas Mann's *Joseph and his Brethren*; 12 string quartets, piano solos, etc.

Rosenkavalier, Der, opera by R. Strauss, produced in Dresden, 1911. Libretto by H. von Hofmannsthal. The 'Cavalier of the Rose', bearer of an older man's betrothal gift, makes the bride-to-be his own.

Rosenmüller, Johann (*c*. 1620–84), German composer who worked for nearly 20 years in Paris. Wrote Masses and other church music, suites of instrumental dances, etc.

Rosenthal, Manuel (b. 1904), French composer, pupil of Ravel; also conductor, especially in France and (1946–51) in USA. Works include symphonic suite *Jeanne d'Arc* ('Joan of Arc'), operettas. He orchestrated some of Ravel's piano music and arranged the music for the ballet *Gaîté parisienne* (➤Offenbach).

Roses from the South, waltz by Johann Strauss the younger. ➤*Rosen aus dem Süden*.

Rosetti, Francesco, ➤Rössler.

Roslavetz, Nikolay [Andreyevich] (1881–1944), Russian composer of violin concerto, piano solos including preludes in all the keys. A notable harmonic innovator, arriving independently at a system akin to Schoenberg's, he died in total obscurity.

Rossellini, Renzo (1908–82). Italian composer of *Uno sguardo dal ponte* (after Arthur Miller's play *A View from the*

Bridge) and other operas, orchestral works, and music to films directed by his brother Roberto Rossellini, etc.

Rosseter, Philip (*c.* 1568–1623), lutenist and composer of ayres with lute and other accompaniment, music for broken consort, etc. Active at Queen Elizabeth's court.

Rossetti, Dante Gabriel (1828–82), British poet. ➤*Blessed Damozel*.

Rossi, Luigi (1598–1653), Italian singer, organist and composer – e.g. of opera *Orfeo* ('Orpheus'), said to be the first Italian opera to be heard in Paris, 1647; also of solo cantatas, etc.

Rossi, Salomone (*c.* 1570–*c.* 1630), Italian composer – Jewish, but exempted from the stigma of wearing the yellow badge otherwise then compulsory for Jews in Italy; colleague of Monteverdi at the court of Mantua. Wrote Italian madrigals, Hebrew psalms, etc.; pioneered the form of ➤trio-sonata.

Rossi-Lemeni, Nicola (1920–91), Italian bass singer. Turkish-born (mother Russian, father Italian); began operatic career (specializing in Russian opera) in Italy; later sang in New York (1951), London, etc. From 1965 also operatic stage director.

Rossini, Gioachino (in modern spelling Gioacchino) **Antonio** (1792–1868), Italian composer, born in Pesaro; master of opera in different genres; exploiter of the orchestral crescendo, and noted in his day for noisy effects. Visited England in 1823–4, and after 1829 lived mostly in Paris, where he died. Successful in opera from 1810, although *Il* ➤*barbiere di Siviglia* (1816) was at first a failure. Other Italian operas include *La* ➤*scala di seta*, ➤*Tancredi*, *L'*➤*Italiana in Algeri*, ➤*Otello*, *La* ➤*Cenerentola*, *La* ➤*gazza*

ladra, ➤*Armida*, ➤*Mosè in Egitto*, ➤*Semiramide*; wrote for Paris, in French, *Le* ➤*Siège de Corinthe*, *Le* ➤*Comte Ory*, and ➤*Guillaume Tell* (1829) – after which he lived for nearly 40 more years but wrote no more operas. Other works include ➤*Stabat Mater* and ➤*Petite Messe solennelle* and a few songs and duets (among them the collection ➤*Soirées musicales*) and piano pieces, etc. The so-called ➤*Cat Duet* is misattributed to him.

Rössler (or **Rösler**), **Franz Anton** (1750–92), German (Bohemian-born) composer of a Requiem, two oratorios, more than 30 symphonies, etc. He Italianized his name (presumably for reasons of fashion) as Antonio Rosetti and on modern programmes is sometimes designated 'Rös[s]ler-Rosetti.'

Rostand, Edmond (1868–1918), French dramatist. ➤Alfano, ➤Damrosch.

Rostropovich, Mstislav [Leopoldovich] (b. 1927), Russian cellist held in highest international esteem; also pianist (accompanist to his wife, Galina Vishnevskaya, soprano), composer and conductor. He was much associated with Prokofiev, whose Cello Concertino he completed after the composer's death. Gave first performances of both cello concertos by Shostakovich (1959, 1966). Left USSR and was deprived of citizenship (later restored), 1975; music director of National Symphony Orchestra, Washington, DC, 1977–94. Holds over 30 honorary doctorates. Hon. KBE, 1987.

rota (Lat., wheel), term sometimes used for ➤round; particularly the famous ➤*Sumer is icumen in*, sometimes called the 'Reading Rota', because its conjectural composer John of Fornsete, was a monk of Reading Abbey.

Rota, Nino (1911–79), Italian composer of operas including *I due timidi* ('The Two Shy People') originally for radio; also of three symphonies; chamber music, songs (some to texts by Tagore), film music for Fellini, Visconti and other noted directors.

Rothenberger, Anneliese (b. 1924), German soprano, member of Hamburg State Opera 1946–72. Noted in Mozart and in Viennese operetta.

Rothwell, Evelyn, ➤Barbirolli.

rototom, type of tunable drum invented by the percussionist-composer Michael ➤Colgrass; rotation by hand within a frame enables the pitch to be altered throughout an octave's range.

roulade (Fr., a 'rolling'), non-technical term often applied to an extravagant display of notes, especially in operatic singing.

round, type of short vocal 'perpetual ➤canon' in which the voices, entering in turn, all sing the same melody at the same pitch (or at the octave). 'London's Burning' is a familiar example. ➤*rota*.

Rousseau, Jean-Jacques (1712–78), Swiss philosopher resident in France: he wrote on various aspects of music. Championed Italian, as against French, opera (in the 'War of the Buffoons') and himself composed opera *Le Devin du village* ('The Village Soothsayer') in demonstration of his views; also composed songs.

Roussel, Albert (1869–1937), French composer; had naval career until 1893. After visiting India wrote some

works in an Eastern-influenced style, including opera-ballet *Padmâvatî*. His later works include four symphonies, an orchestral suite in F, comic opera *Le Testament de Tante Caroline* ('Aunt Caroline's Will'), ballets ➤*Bacchus et Ariane* and *Le* ➤*Festin de l'araignée*; also chamber works, piano pieces, songs, etc.

rovescio, al (It.), in reverse. This may refer to either (1) a passage that can be performed backwards, or (2) a type of ➤canon in which an upward interval in the original voice becomes a downward interval (of the same distance) in the imitating voice, and vice versa.

Roxolane, La, nickname for Haydn's Symphony no. 63 in C, composed about 1777 (Hob. I: 63), named after a French song which is used in it as the subject of variations.

Royal Concertgebouw Orchestra, Dutch orchestra named from its concert-hall (Du., 'concert-building') in Amsterdam, opened in 1888, and of its resident orchestra. Conductor, 1961–88, Bernard Haitink (at first jointly with Eugen Jochum); from 1988, Riccardo Chailly. Title 'Royal' conferred 1989.

Royal Danish Orchestra, orchestra based in Copenhagen, tracing its descent from the 16th-century royal establishment. Principal conductor since 1993, Paavo Berglund.

Royal Liverpool Philharmonic Orchestra, an orchestra which became fulltime in 1943; its parent society dates from 1849. The title 'Royal' was granted in 1956. Conductor 1987–97, Libor Pešek, then Petr Altrichter.

Royal Opera House, ➤Covent Garden.

Royal Philharmonic Orchestra, a London orchestra founded by Beecham in 1946. It has no present link with the Royal Philharmonic Society (founded 1813). Music director from 1996 (succeeding Vladimir Ashkenazy), Daniele Gatti.

Royal Scottish National Orchestra (title 'Royal' granted 1990), Glasgow-based orchestra founded in 1891 as Scottish Orchestra. Conductor 1992–96, Walter Weller, then Alexander Lazarev.

Rozhdestvensky, Gennady [Nikolayevich] (b. 1931), Russian conductor who took his mother's surname (father was the conductor Nikolai Anosov, 1900–1962). Principal conductor, Bolshoi Theatre, Moscow, 1965–70; 1978–81, conductor of BBC Symphony Orchestra.

Rózsa, Miklós (1907–95), Hungarian composer who studied in Leipzig, then resided in Paris, London and (from 1940) USA, later becoming naturalized there. Composed much film music (including *The Lost Weekend*, *Double Indemnity*, *Ben Hur*) and also violin concerto, cello concerto, etc.

rubato (It., robbed), to be performed with a certain freedom as to time, for the purpose of giving the music suitable expression. As a noun ('he played with too much *rubato*') it is really short for *tempo rubato*.

Rubbra, Edmund [Charles] (1901–86), British composer, pupil of Vaughan Williams, Holst and others; also pianist. Works include 11 symphonies; two Masses – one Anglican, one for the Roman Catholic Church, which Rubbra entered in 1948. CBE, 1960.

rubible, ▸rabab.

Rubini, Giovanni Battista (1794–1854), Italian tenor celebrated in operas by Bellini and Donizetti, setting a model of style.

Rubinstein, Anton Grigorevich (1829–94), Russian pianist of great distinction, and composer of *The Demon* and other operas, six symphonies, five piano concertos, etc. Now hardly known except for a few songs and piano pieces including *Melody in F*. Brother of N. Rubinstein, below; no relation of Arthur Rubinstein.

Rubinstein, Arthur (1886–1982), Polish-born pianist, naturalized American 1946; internationally known virtuoso of very wide repertory, with speciality in Spanish music as well as in Chopin. Revisited Poland and Russia (but, as a Jew, declined to revisit Germany) after World War II. Author of two volumes of autobiography. No relation of the other Rubinsteins. (The spelling Arthur, not Artur, was preferred by him.) Hon. KBE, 1977.

Rubinstein, Nikolay Grigorevich (1835–81), Russian pianist, founder and principal of Moscow Conservatory, and composer of piano music, etc. Brother of the more famous Anton Rubinstein (above).

Ruddigore, or The Witch's Curse, operetta by Sullivan, produced in London, 1887. Libretto by W. S. Gilbert: the plot, with 'Ruddigore' as the name of a family of 'bad baronets', parodies Victorian melodrama. The original spelling was 'Ruddygore', soon changed because thought offensive.

Ruders, Poul (b. 1949), Danish composer (also organist) whose music has achieved the recognition of recordings by London Sinfonietta, Ensemble Inter-contemporain (Paris), etc. Works include viola concerto, *glOriA* for chorus and brass, and *Vox in Rama* for clarinet, electric violin and piano.

Rudhyar, Dane (pen-name of Daniel Chennevière) (1895–1985), French-born composer who settled in USA, 1917; also writer and painter. His musical works, mostly linked to occultist beliefs, include symphonic poems (*To the Real*, *The Surge of Fire*, etc.), piano pieces, songs.

Rue, Pierre de la, ➤La Rue.

Ruffo, Titta (originally Ruffo Cafiero Titta) (1877–1953), Italian baritone with a long European and American career in opera 1898–1931.

Ruggles, Carl [originally Charles Sprague Ruggles] (1876–1971), American composer, also painter. He completed only a few works – of a pioneering modern nature including *Angels* for six trumpets, symphonic poems *Men and Mountains* and *Sun-Treader*, and *Organum* for orchestra.

Rührtrommel (Ger., rolling drum), ➤tenor drum.

Rule, Britannia!, ➤*Alfred*.

rumba, Cuban dance in 8/8 time (3 + 3 + 2) which became established in ballroom dancing in USA and Europe about 1930. Occasional use in concert music, Arthur Benjamin's *Jamaican Rumba* (originally for two pianos, 1938) achieving popularity in various arrangements.

Runnicles, Donald [Cameron] (b. 1954), British conductor who developed operatic career in Germany; made Glyndebourne début in 1991; début at Bayreuth with *Tannhäuser*,

1993; music director of San Francisco Opera since 1992. Has conducted Chicago Symphony and other major orchestras.

Rusalka, a water-sprite in Slavonic legend. *The Rusalka* is thus the title of operas by (1) Dargomizhsky, produced in St Petersburg, 1856; libretto by composer, after Pushkin; (2) Dvořák, produced in Prague, 1901; libretto by J. Kvapil.

Ruslan and Lyudmila, opera by Glinka, produced in St Petersburg, 1842. Libretto by V. Shirkov and others, after Pushkin: named after the two lovers, eventually united despite the powers of magic.

Russell, Henry (1812–1900), British singer, organist, and composer of 'A Life on the Ocean Wave' and other songs: father of Landon Ronald.

Russian bassoon, ➤serpent.

Russian Easter Festival Overture (Rus., *Voskresenaya uvertyura*, i.e. Resurrection Overture), work by Rimsky-Korsakov, 1888, based on Russian Orthodox Church melodies and showing finally 'the unbridled pagan-religious merry-making on the morn of Easter Sunday'.

Russian Quartets, name for Haydn's six String Quartets, op. 33, of 1783 (Hob. III: 33); they are dedicated to the Grand Duke Paul of Russia. They are also known as 'Gli Scherzi' from the character of their minuet movements (➤scherzo), or the 'Maiden Quartets' (Ger. *Jungfernquartette*) for a reason unknown.

Russolo, Luigi (1855–1947), Italian composer (also painter) who in 1913–14 demonstrated his own invention of 'noise-instruments' in compositions of his own (now lost). ➤Futurism.

'Rustic Wedding', symphony by Goldmark. ➤*Ländliche Hochzeit*.

Rute (Ger., rod), indication in German-language scores that a drummer is to use a (birch or wire) brush instead of the normal stick.

Rutter, John [Milford] (b. 1945), British composer, also conductor; director of music, Clare College, Cambridge, founder-director of Cambridge Singers. Has reached a broad audience with his Requiem, carols, and other music of Christian context; other works include *Partita* for orchestra.

Ruy Blas, play by Victor Hugo for which Mendelssohn wrote an overture and a chorus for a production in Leipzig, 1839.

Ryom, Peter (b. 1937), Danish musicologist, cataloguer of the works of ➤Vivaldi.

Rysanek, Leonie (1926–97), Austrian soprano who won distinction in R. Strauss's and other roles at the Vienna State Opera; appeared also at the Bayreuth Festival (1951–68) and at the New York Metropolitan Opera, etc.

Rzewski, Frederic [Anthony] (b. 1938), American composer and pianist (took part in Stockhausen premières), whose own music sometimes expounds a socialist message, e.g. in 36 variations for piano entitled *The People United will Never be Defeated*. Other works include *Satyrica* for jazz band, *Una breve storia d'estate* (It., 'A Short Story of Summer'), for three flutes and small orchestra.

s, symbol in ➤tonic sol-fa for the fifth degree (dominant) of the scale, pronounced *soh*.

Saariaho, Kaija [Anneli] (b. 1952), Finnish composer, in some cases of computer-assisted music (*Jardin secret* I, for tape); she has also written *Nymphea*, otherwise *Jardin secret* III, for live electronics with string quartet; score for ballet *Maa* (Finnish, 'world').

Sabata, Victor De, ➤De Sabata.

Sabre Dance, ➤*Gayaneh*.

Sacchini, Antonio [Maria Gasparo] (1730–86), Italian composer who lived in London, 1773–81, and later in Paris, where he died. Wrote about 40 operas in Italian and French. Also composed church music, two symphonies, etc.

Sacher, Paul (b. 1906), Swiss conductor, founder in 1926 of the Basle Chamber Orchestra, subsequently commissioning about 200 works for it, the composers ranging from Stravinsky and Bartók (*Music for Strings, Percussion and Celesta*) to Henze, Carter and Birtwistle; also founded (1933) Schola Cantorum Basiliensis for research and performance of early music on period instruments, and has conducted in Britain, USA and elsewhere.

sackbut, an early form of trombone, revived in mid-20th-century reconstructions of early music. (The name is also used in older biblical translations for an instrument which is not identified with the trombone.)

Sacred Service, title usual in English for E. Bloch's setting of a Jewish Sabbath morning service (1933) for baritone, chorus and orchestra. The Hebrew title is *Avodath hakodesh*, and the text follows a US 'Reformed' Jewish use.

Sacre du printemps, Le, ➤*Rite of Spring*.

Sadko, opera by Rimsky-Korsakov, produced in Moscow, 1898 – partly based on a symphonic poem of the same name by the composer, 1867. Libretto by the composer and V. I. Belsky: Sadko is a minstrel-turned-merchant, the setting is 10th-century, and the story is legendary in character. The work is styled an *opera-bylina* (from a type of old Russian saga).

Sadler's Wells, a London theatre dating from the late 17th century; reopened 1931 for a repertory of plays and operas, plays being shortly dropped and ballet added. Sadler's Wells Opera at first retained its name on moving to the London Coliseum in 1968, then became the ➤English National Opera.

Saeverud, Harald [Sigurd Johan]

(1897–1992), Norwegian composer of nine symphonies, 50 *Little Variations* (on a theme three bars long) and other works for orchestra; incidental music to Ibsen's *Peer Gynt*; many piano pieces, including *Ballad of Revolt* (also orchestrated).

Saga, A (Swe., *En Saga*), symphonic poem by Sibelius, 1892, revised in 1901. It alludes to the nature of the Scandinavian sagas in general.

Saint ... (Titles beginning 'Saint' or 'St' are all listed here, but saints as people are listed by their commonly used names, e.g. Cecilia under C.)

St Anne, English hymn-tune, probably by Croft, published in 1708; now usually sung to the words 'O God, our help in ages past'. By mere coincidence an organ fugue in E flat by Bach opens with the same notes; this is therefore known in Britain as the 'St Anne' Fugue.

'St Anthony' Variations, work by Brahms for orchestra, 1873, also issued by the composer for two pianos. Brahms took the theme from a ➤*Feldparthie* by Haydn, and called it *Variations on a Theme of Haydn*; but it has since been found that the theme itself (called the 'St Anthony' Chorale) was not Haydn's own but was borrowed by him for the occasion. The present name is thus now preferred.

Saint François d'Assise (Fr., 'St Francis of Assisi'), opera by Messiaen (libretto by composer), produced in Paris, 1984.

'St John' Passion, or *The Passion According to St John* (Ger., *Johannespassion*), a setting by Bach (BWV 245) for solo voices, chorus and orchestra of the ➤Passion narrative from St John's

Gospel, with interpolations; first performed in 1723.

St John's Night on Bald Mountain (Rus., *Ivanova noch na lisoi gore*), orchestral work by Musorgsky, alluding to a 'witches' sabbath'; it took various forms, originating in 1867, and eventually was used as an introduction to Act III of the opera *The* ➤*Fair at Sorochintsy*. This last version was revised and altered by Rimsky-Korsakov, and it is his version (1908, usually called *Night on the Bare Mountain* or *Night on Bald Mountain*) that has been generally performed. The North American styling of *Bald Mountain* (rather than 'the bare mountain') is apparently closer to the Russian.

Saint-Léon, Arthur (1821–70), French choreographer. ➤*Coppélia*.

'St Matthew' Passion, or *The Passion According to St Matthew* (Ger., *Matthäuspassion*), a setting by Bach (BWV 244) for solo voices, chorus and orchestra of the Passion narrative from St Matthew's Gospel, with interpolations; first performed in 1729.

St Paul, oratorio by Mendelssohn (Ger., *Paulus*), first performed in Düsseldorf, 1836; text from the Bible.

St Paul's Suite, work for string orchestra by Holst, 1913 – written for the orchestra of St Paul's Girls' School, Hammersmith (London), where he taught. Incorporates the ➤Dargason in the last movement.

St Petersburg Philharmonic Orchestra, Russian orchestra founded in 1921, which changed its name in 1991 from that of Leningrad Philharmonic Orchestra; principal conductor since 1988, Temirkanov.

Saint-Saëns, [Charles] Camille (1835–

1921), French composer, also pianist and organist. Works include ➤*Samson et Dalila* and other operas; three symphonies (no. 3 with organ), ➤*Danse macabre* and other works for orchestra; five piano concertos, three violin concertos, two cello concertos, *Le* ➤*carnaval des animaux* for two pianos and orchestra; chamber music, church music, many songs. Frequently visited Britain in his exceptionally long and prolific career. Hon. Mus.D., Cambridge, 1893.

Salad Days, musical entertainment with text by Julian Slade and Dorothy Reynolds; music by Julian Slade. Produced in London, 1954. With a magic piano that makes everyone dance.

Salas, Juan Orrego, ➤Orrego Salas.

Salieri, Antonio (1750–1825), Italian composer who lived mainly in Vienna, and died there: Beethoven and Schubert were among his pupils. He intrigued against Mozart, but history gives no backing for the supposition (as in Pushkin's play, *Mozart and Salieri*, and in Peter Shaffer's play, *Amadeus*) that he contrived Mozart's death. Wrote mainly Italian operas including *Prima la musica e poi le parole* ('First the music and then the words') and a *Falstaff*, after Shakespeare's *The Merry Wives of Windsor*; also symphonic and church music.

Sallinen, Aulis [Heikki] (b. 1935), Finnish composer (and formerly manager of the Finnish Radio Symphony Orchestra). Works include operas *The Red Line*, ➤*Kullervo*, *The King Goes Forth to France* and *The Palace*; violin concerto, cello concerto, four symphonies, five string quartets.

Salminen, Matti (b. 1945), Finnish

bass who studied in Italy and Germany; member of Cologne Opera 1972–9, later noted in Wagner roles at Covent Garden (from 1974), Bayreuth (from 1976), etc.

salmo (It., pl. *-i*), psalm.

Salome, opera by R. Strauss, produced in Dresden, 1905. Libretto a German translation of Oscar Wilde's French play – after the New Testament, plus the medieval idea that Salome was in love with John the Baptist.

Salomon, Johann Peter (1745–1815), German-born violinist and concert organizer who settled in London (dying there); brought Haydn to England and commissioned what are now called the ➤*Salomon Symphonies*.

Salomon Symphonies, the 12 symphonies (Hob. I: 93–104) commissioned from Haydn by J. P. Salomon (above) for Haydn's visits to England, 1791–2 and 1794–5. They were Haydn's last symphonies including those nicknamed ➤*Clock*, ➤*Drum-roll*, ➤*London*, ➤*Miracle*, ➤*Surprise*.

Salón México, El, work by Copland, first performed in Mexico City, 1937; based on the composer's impressions of a Mexican dance-hall, and incorporating traditional Mexican tunes.

Salonen, Esa-Pekka (b. 1958), Finnish conductor, also composer of a saxophone concerto and other works. Principal conductor of Swedish Radio Symphony Orchestra since 1985, additionally music director of Los Angeles Philharmonic Orchestra since 1992.

saltarello, salterello, type of Italian dance: in its most common meaning, a lively dance incorporating jumps, the music similar to ➤*tarantella* but not so smoothly flowing. The finale of Mendelssohn's ➤*Italian Symphony* is so styled. The preferred modern Italian spelling is *salterello*, but Mendelssohn wrote *saltarello*, as did older Italian composers.

Salzédo, Carlos (1885–1961), French-born harpist who settled in USA (naturalized 1923); innovator in harp technique and composer of works for his instrument.

Salzman, Eric (b. 1933), American composer; also critic and organizer of concerts. Works, many incorporating electronics, visual images, etc., include *The Nude Paper Sermon*, described as 'Tropes for actor, Renaissance consort, chorus and electronics'.

Samazeuilh, Gustave [Marie Victor Fernand] (1877–1967), French composer of symphonic poems, chamber works, Serenade for guitar, etc.; also critic.

Saminsky, Lazare (1882–1959), Russian-born composer and conductor resident in USA from 1920. Works include five symphonies, music for Jewish worship, opera-ballet *Jephtha's Daughter*. Was also writer and synagogue music director.

samisen, Japanese lute-like, plucked-string instrument: the application of this term to a gong-like percussion instrument in Puccini's ➤*Madama Butterfly* is an error.

Sammartini, Giovanni Battista (*c.* 1700–1775), Italian composer and organist (brother of the following); teacher of Gluck, and pioneer of ➤sonata form in composition. Among his works (said to number 2,000) are operas, string quartets, more than 70 symphonies.

Sammartini, Giuseppe (1695–1750), Italian oboist and composer (brother of preceding) who settled in London, taking a post with the Prince of Wales.

sampler, a device used in electronic music: by converting sound from an analog representation into a digital code, it enables digitally altered sound to be delivered instantly (in 'real time') from a keyboard or other controller.

Samson, oratorio by Handel (text from poems by Milton, based on the Bible), first performed in London, 1743.

Samson and Delilah, usual English form of title for Saint-Saëns' opera ➤*Samson et Dalila*.

Samson et Dalila (Fr., *Samson and Delilah*), opera by Saint-Saëns, produced (in German) in Weimar, 1877. Libretto by F. Lemaire. At first barred, because of its biblical subject, from stage presentation in Britain and performed only in concert.

Sanctus (Lat., holy), part of the Mass, beginning with a threefold assertion of that word.

Sand, George [Aurore Dudevant] (1804–76), French writer. ➤Chopin.

Sanderling, Kurt (b. 1912), German conductor who moved to Russia in 1936, becoming joint principal conductor (1942–60) of Leningrad Philharmonic Orchestra with Mravinsky; then returned to (East) Germany, taking posts in Berlin and Leipzig. Made British début 1970, later recording all Beethoven's symphonies with Philharmonia Orchestra. His son Thomas Sanderling (b. 1942) is also a conductor.

San Francisco Symphony Orchestra, American orchestra founded in 1911; Michael Tilson Thomas became music director in 1994.

Sanz, Gaspar (1640–1710), Spanish guitarist whose manual of instruction for the instrument (1674) is the source of many pieces favoured by later players.

saraband, sarabande (Eng., Fr.), dance coming to the rest of Europe from Spain, and forming a regular constituent of the old ➤suite; it is slow and in 3/2 time.

sarangi, traditional Indian stringed instrument with ➤sympathetic strings, played with a curved bow.

Sarasate [y Navascues], Pablo Martin Melitón (1844–1908), Spanish violinist (among the most famous virtuosos of his time), who toured widely; composed many works for his instrument, including a fantasy (with orchestra) in gipsy style called *Zigeunerweisen* (➤*Zigeuner*.)

Saraste, Jukka-Pekka (b. 1956), Finnish conductor; principal conductor of Scottish Chamber Orchestra 1987–91, of Finnish Radio Symphony Orchestra since 1987 and additionally of Toronto Symphony Orchestra since 1994. Has also conducted other North American and European orchestras.

sardana (Sp.), a national dance of Catalonia, properly to characteristic accompaniment (➤*cobla*).

Sardou, Victorien (1831–1908), French dramatist. ➤*Tosca*.

Sargent, [Harold] Malcolm [Watts] (1895–1967), British conductor; also

composer, arranger, pianist and organist. Conductor of BBC Symphony Orchestra, 1950–57, of the Royal Choral Society, 1928–67; chief conductor of the Proms, 1948–66. Knighted, 1947.

Šárka, ➤*My Country*.

sarod, Indian plucked instrument; it generally has 4–5 melody strings, 3–5 drone strings and 11 or more ➤sympathetic strings.

sarrusophone, double-reed instrument, classified as woodwind though made of brass; named after, but not invented by, a mid-19th-century French bandmaster, Sarrus, and made in various sizes. The largest or second largest has been stipulated in the orchestra to replace the double-bassoon, e.g. by Saint-Saëns and Delius (although the parts are now usually given back to double-bassoon).

Sarti, Giuseppe (1729–1802), Italian composer who travelled much, wrote more than 70 operas (in Italian, French, Danish and Russian), and died in Berlin. Other works include church music and harpsichord sonatas. In ➤*Don Giovanni* Mozart uses an air from Sarti's *Fra due litiganti* ('Between Two Litigants') as part of the hero's supper-music.

Satie, Erik [Alfred Leslie] (1866–1925), French composer; for a time worked as café pianist, etc. Influenced younger composers (*Les* ➤*Six*) towards a cool, clear style represented by his piano solos and duets, many with eccentric titles, e.g. *Gymnopédies* (name derived from an ancient Greek festival) and *Trois Morceaux en forme de poire* ('Three Pear-Shaped Pieces'); several of these were orchestrated by

Poulenc and others. Wrote also ballets, including ➤*Parade* and *Relâche* (the word displayed by French theatres when they are closed), symphonic drama ➤*Socrate*, etc.

Satz (Ger., a setting), term of several different musical applications in German, including (1) a musical setting; so *Tonsatz* (note-setting), a composition; (2) a movement; so Schubert's isolated movement for string quartet is called ➤*Quartettsatz*; (3) a theme or subject – so *Hauptsatz*, main theme; *Nebensatz*, subsidiary theme.

saudades, Portuguese (plural) word of uncertain origin, but carrying the implication of wistful remembrance of things past; it has been used for two sets of piano pieces by Milhaud, *Saudades do Brasil* (. . . of Brazil), and for a set of songs by Warlock.

Sauguet, Henri [originally Jean Pierre Poupard] (1901–89), French composer, also critic. Works, many in a light vein, include opera *Les caprices de Marianne*; ballet *Les Forains* ('The Strolling Players'), song-cycle with orchestra *La Voyante* ('The Fortune-Teller'); three piano concertos, two string quartets.

Saul, oratorio by Handel, first performed in London, 1739. Text, based on the Bible, by C. Jennens. Contains a famous 'Dead March'.

Sauret, Émile (1852–1920), French violinist who taught in London (where he died), Chicago and elsewhere; composer of two violin concertos, etc.

sausage bassoon, an alternative and more informal name for the ➤racket(t).

sautillé (Fr., springing), type of bowing

on the violin, etc., in which the bow rebounds off the string.

Savile, Jeremy (17th century), English composer known only for a few songs (including 'Here's a Health unto His Majesty') and part-songs.

Sāvitri, one-act opera by G. Holst, produced in London, 1916. Libretto by composer, after an episode in the Hindu scriptures; Sāvitri is the devoted wife of a woodman.

Savoy Operas, name given to those operettas (or light operas) presented under the management of Richard D'Oyly Carte, either at the Savoy Theatre, London, from 1881 or at other London theatres previously; primarily those by Sullivan with librettos by W. S. Gilbert. The name is also extended to cover ➤*Cox and Box* (libretto by F. C. Burnand, not by Gilbert) since this was later absorbed into the ➤D'Oyly Carte company's repertory.

saw, musical, a hand-saw used as a musical instrument for purposes of novel entertainment – very rare in serious composition (➤Boyd); it is held by the knees and played with a violin bow, the left hand altering the tension (and thus the pitch of the note produced) by bending the saw.

Sawallisch, Wolfgang (b. 1923), German conductor, also well known as piano accompanist to leading singers. Since 1971, music director (later, general director) of the Bavarian State Opera, Munich; principal conductor of Philadelphia Orchestra since 1992.

Sax, Adolphe (real first names Antoine Joseph) (1814–94), Belgian inventor of the ➤saxhorn and ➤saxophone families of instruments.

saxhorn, type of brass instrument with valves invented by A. Sax in 1845. As to nomenclature, there is a great difference between authorities and between various countries. The instruments used in brass bands in Britain, which are ➤transposing instruments, are the *tenor saxhorn* in E flat and the *baritone saxhorn* in B flat, known simply as 'tenor horn' (or 'E flat horn') and 'baritone': the former is also used in military bands but neither is used in the orchestra. The series of instruments may be regarded as being continued downwards in pitch by the ➤tuba family, including ➤euphonium.

saxophone, name of a family of wind instruments having a reed resembling a clarinet's – and therefore classified among the ➤woodwind (not 'brass') despite a metal body. Invented by A. Sax about 1840. Made in various sizes, the lower-pitched ones in S-shape or with additional curves (the *alto saxophone* exists in both S-shaped and straight forms). The most common are the *alto* (➤transposing instrument in E♭) with compass from the D♭ below middle C upwards for about two and a half octaves, and the *tenor saxophone* in B♭ a fifth lower. Both these are occasionally used in the symphony orchestra, and regularly in dance bands and military bands (not brass bands). Less frequently used are the *baritone* (below the tenor, in E♭) and *soprano* (above the alto, in B♭); still rarer are the *bass* (lower than the baritone, in B♭) and the *sopranino* (higher than the soprano, in E♭). The saxophones are thus alternately in B♭ and E♭. Most solo music heard in the concert-hall (e.g. concertos by Glazunov and Schuller) is for the alto.

Saxton, Robert (b. 1953), British composer of opera *Caritas* (libretto by Arnold Wesker); *Elijah's Violin* for orchestra; cello concerto (for Rostropovich); *A Song of Ascents* (trumpet concerto); settings of Auden, Hölderlin, Rimbaud and others.

Scala, La, the common form of reference to the Teatro alla Scala in Milan, erected in 1788, and now ranking as Italy's main opera-house. It is so named because it was built on the former site of a church, Santa Maria alla Scala. Musical director since 1986, Ricardo Muti.

Scala di seta, La (It., 'The Silken Ladder'), comic opera by Rossini, produced in Venice, 1812. Libretto by G. Rossi; the ladder conveys a lover to his lady's room.

scale, a progression of single notes upwards or downwards in 'steps'. (Cf. It. *scala*, stairway.) So *scalic* – e.g. 'a scalic figure', progressing upwards or downwards in steps. So ➤*major* and ➤*minor* scales. See also ➤chromatic, ➤diatonic,➤pentatonic,➤whole-tone, ➤mode, ➤twelve-note.

Scaramouche, title of suite for two pianos by Milhaud: so called because it is based on music by Milhaud for a play, *The Flying Doctor*, produced in Paris, 1937, at the Théâtre Scaramouche.

Scarlatti, [Pietro] **Alessandro** [Gaspare] (1660–1725), Italian composer who worked chiefly in Naples; pioneered the type of Italian opera which conquered all Europe in the 18th century. More than 60 of his operas survive in whole or in part, including *Mitridate Eupatore, Griselda* (his last, 1721) and his only comic opera, *Il trionfo dell'onore* ('The

Triumph of Honour'). Wrote also hundreds of ➤cantatas for one or more voices, chamber music, church music. Father of Domenico Scarlatti.

Scarlatti, [Giuseppe] **Domenico** (1685–1757), Italian composer; at first wrote Italian opera, etc., on the model of his father (see preceding entry), and was known also as a harpsichord virtuoso; but went in 1720 to Portugal and later to Spain (dying in Madrid) and there wrote the greater number of his single-movement harpsichord sonatas. These, numbering over 550 (➤'Cat's Fugue') and in their time also called 'exercises' (It., *essercizi*), exploit the resources of the instrument and of ➤binary form in great variety. Other works include a *Stabat Mater* and other church music. The keyboard works are numbered as K. or Kk. (➤Kirkpatrick), superseding the older L. (Longo) numbering.

Scelsi, Giacinto (1905–88), Italian composer whose titles indicate the eclecticism of his music – *Kong-Om-Pax* ('three aspects of sound') for choir and orchestra; *Aiôn* ('four episodes in a day of Brahma') for timpani, six other percussionists, and orchestra without violins or violas; *Coelocanth* for unaccompanied viola.

scena (It., stage, scene), (1) a 'scene' (subdivision of an act); (2) in 19th-century operatic scores, a musical unit incorporating recitative, and leading to an aria, a duet, etc.; so *scena ed* [and] *aria*; (3) term sometimes meaning the double unit of recitative *plus* aria, etc.; (4) a concert item corresponding to this (third) dramatic form. Spohr gave the designation 'in the form of a song-scena' to his Violin Concerto no. 8.

Scenes of Childhood, set of piano pieces by Schumann. ➤*Kinderszenen.*

Sch-, German spelling for Russian names now conventionally spelt in English 'Sh-'; e.g. Shebalin. An exception is the Russian name of German origin, Schnittke.

Schaeffer, Bogusław [Julian] (b. 1929), Polish composer, pioneer in Poland of specifically modern (12-note, etc.) style. Works include *Non-Stop* (eight hours of music for piano), *Kwaiwa* for violin and computer, concertos for various instruments including accordion, *Tentative Music* for 159 instruments. Is also playwright.

Schaeffer, Pierre [Henri Marie] (b. 1910), French composer and author. Pioneer in 1948–9 of ➤*musique concrète* exemplified in his *Études de bruit* ('Studies in Noise') and (in collaboration with Pierre Henry) *Symphonie pour un homme seul* ('Symphony for a Lonely Man').

Schafer, R. [Raymond] **Murray** (b. 1933), Canadian composer; at Simon Fraser University, Vancouver, he promoted much musical activity and researched 'acoustic ecology'. Works include *Requiems for the Party Girl* for soprano and nine instruments; *From the Tibetan Book of the Dead* (text in Tibetan) for soprano, instruments, chorus, tape.

Scharwenka, [Franz] **Xaver** (1850–1924), German pianist and celebrated teacher (in Berlin, and in 1891–8 in New York); composer of piano solos (including *Polish Dances*), four piano concertos, opera *Mataswintha*, etc. His brother Philipp Scharwenka (1847–1917) was also a composer.

Schat, Peter (b. 1935), Dutch composer, pupil of Seiber in London. Works include opera *Reconstruction* (jointly composed with Jan van Vlijmen, Louis Andriessen, Reinbert de Leeuw, Misha Mengelberg); *First Essay on Electrocution* for violin, guitar and metal percussion; *Improvisations and Symphonies* for wind quartet.

Schauspieldirektor, Der (Ger., 'The Impresario'), stage work with overture and other music by Mozart: in essence a spoken play with music, but sometimes classed as one of Mozart's operas. Produced in Vienna, 1786 (K486). Libretto by G. Stephanie, satirizing the relationships of impresario and female singers.

Scheherazade, ➤*Sheherazade*.

Scheidemann, Heinrich (*c*. 1596–1663), German organist who held a church post in Hamburg, having studied with Sweelinck in Amsterdam. Composer of organ music, etc.

Scheidt, Samuel (1587–1654), German organist and composer, especially of organ works (including hymn-tune harmonizations); church music, dance music, etc. His *Tabulatura nova* (1624) advocated staff notation for organ, in place of ➤tablature.

Schein, Johann Hermann (1586–1630), German composer, church musician in Leipzig. Works include hymns (some to his own words), instrumental dances, madrigals.

Schelle (Ger.), small bell, e.g. the ➤sleigh-bell.

Schelomo (Heb., 'Solomon'), rhapsody for cello and orchestra by E. Bloch, first performed in 1917; the reference is to Solomon as depicted in the Bible. The title represents a German spelling of the Hebrew name.

Schemelli Hymn-book, usual name for the *Musical Song-book* published in 1736 by Georg Christian Schemelli (*c*. 1678–1762); its musical editor was Bach, who afterwards wrote chorale preludes on some of its hymn-tunes.

Schenker, Heinrich (1868–1935), Austrian composer (pupil of Bruckner) and highly influential theorist. He claimed that a single type of basic music structure underlies all the masterpieces written in the period from Bach to Brahms. His analytical method has been applied to music outside this range.

scherzando (➤*scherzo*), direction that an impression of light-heartedness is to be given.

Scherzi, Gli (It., 'The Jokes'; ➤*scherzo*), another name for Haydn's ➤Russian Quartets. Alludes to the character of the 'minuet' movements.

scherzo (It., joke), a type of lively movement which historically – chiefly through Haydn, and, especially, Beethoven – developed from the minuet as used in symphonies, string quartets, etc. Usually therefore it is in the characteristic minuet form, AABA; and the B section is called the ➤trio (as in the minuet). Usually also it is in 3/4 time. The original implication of humour is by no means always maintained, but fast tempo is obligatory and sentimentality is avoided. Examples exist also of the scherzo not as a movement of a larger work, but as an independent work of its own – notably Chopin's four for piano.

scherzoso, same as ➤*scherzando*.

Schicksalslied (Ger., 'Song of Destiny'), work by Brahms for chorus and orchestra, 1871, to a poem by Hölderlin.

Schiff, András (b. 1953), Hungarian pianist who made his London début in 1976; noted in Bach but has also recorded all Mozart's concertos, Tchaikovsky, etc.

Schiff, Heinrich (b. 1951), Austrian cellist who made his London début in 1973; also conductor, musical director of Northern Sinfonia from 1990.

Schiller, Johann Christoph Friedrich von (1759–1805), German poet and dramatist. ➤*Choral Symphony*, ➤*Don Carlos*, ➤*Guillaume Tell*, ➤*Luisa Miller*, ➤*Maid of Orleans*, ➤*Turandot*; ➤Klebe.

Schipa, Tito [originally Raffaele Attilio Amadeo] (1888–1965), Italian tenor with prominent operatic career in Chicago (1919–32) and New York; also well known for concert performances.

Schlaginstrument(e) (Ger.), percussion instrument(s).

schleppend (Ger.), dragging; *nicht schleppend*, direction that the pace is not to be allowed to drag.

Schlick, Arnolt (before 1460– c. 1525), German composer (born blind); author of an influential treatise on the organ. Works include song-arrangements for organ or lute.

Schluss (Ger.), end; *Schluss-Satz*, final section (➤*Satz*).

Schlüssel (Ger.), clef. (Not 'key', though in German *Schlüssel* literally means 'key', as *clef* [or *clé*] does in French.)

Schmelzer, Johann Heinrich (c. 1623–

80), Austrian composer (also violinist) in service at the Austrian court. Composed trio-sonatas and other chamber works, ballet music for court spectacles, Masses and other church music.

Schmidt, Franz (1874–1939), Austrian composer of oratorio *Das Buch mit sieben Siegeln* ('The Book with Seven Seals') (after Revelation); four symphonies, etc.; also pianist, organist and cellist.

Schmidt-Isserstedt, Hans (1900–1973), German conductor; founder-conductor of the Hamburg Radio Symphony Orchestra, 1945–71; composer of opera and orchestral works.

Schmieder, Wolfgang (b. 1901), German musicologist. ➤Bach.

Schmitt, Florent (1870–1958), French composer, also pianist and writer on music. Works include *La tragédie de Salomé* (written for ballet, revised as symphonic poem), *Symphonie concertante* for piano and orchestra, choral setting of Psalm 47 (46 in RC Bible); quartet for three trombones and tuba; many piano solos.

Schnabel, Artur (1882–1951), Austrian pianist and noted teacher; driven from Germany by the Nazis, settled in USA, died in Geneva. Composer of three symphonies, etc.

Schnebel, Dieter (b. 1930), German composer (also Lutheran minister) whose works use non-musical and non-sound effects. Works include *Nostalgia* (*Visible Music II*) for conductor alone; *Concert sans orchestre* for piano and audience.

schnell (Ger.), fast; *schneller*, faster. See also following entry.

Schneller (Ger.), an ornament classified as a variety of ➤mordent, the main note moving quickly to the note above (only once) and back again: often designated by a small wavy line above the written note.

Schnittke, Alfred [Garyevich] (1934–98), Russian composer of part-German descent who spent boyhood years in Vienna. Taught at Moscow Conservatory but won notice chiefly abroad for music often boldly radical including operas ➤*Life with an Idiot* and ➤*Gesualdo*; eight symphonies (no. 4 with solo voices), ➤*(K)ein Sommernachtstraum* for orchestra; ballet score *Peer Gynt*, after Ibsen (choreography by John Neumeier, 1984), *Moz-Art à la Mozart* for 8 flutes and harp; also more than 60 scores for Russian films. ➤Faust.

Schobert, Johann (*c.* 1740–67), German harpsichordist and composer who lived in Paris from 1760 and died there (of eating toadstools mistaken for mushrooms). Wrote harpsichord solos and concertos, etc.; influenced Mozart, whose first four numbered keyboard concertos were arrangements of Schobert and other composers.

Schoeck, Othmar (1886–1957), Swiss composer and conductor, pupil of Reger. Works include a violin concerto, operas and many songs – with accompaniments for piano, for chamber groups and for orchestra.

Schoenberg, Arnold (1874–1951), Austrian-born composer who worked in Germany and then (driven out by the Nazis as a Jew and a composer of 'decadent' music) from 1933 in USA, thereafter changing the spelling of his name from the original 'Schönberg'. A chief figure in 20th-century music,

more by influence on other composers than by his share of performances. After works in post-Romantic style (➤*Verklärte Nacht*, ➤*Gurrelieder*), developed a technique of ➤atonality or keylessness (as in ➤*Pierrot Lunaire*); then from about 1923 systematized this into ➤twelve-note technique. He later relaxed his adherence to this technique, re-admitting the idea of key, e.g. in his late ➤*Ode to Napoleon Buonaparte*. Several works use ➤*Sprechgesang*, invented by him (and also influential). Other works include opera ➤*Moses und Aron*, monodrama ➤*Erwartung*, cantata *A* ➤*Survivor from Warsaw*, a piano concerto, violin concerto, symphonic poem ➤*Pelléas und Mélisande*, two ➤Chamber Symphonies, four string quartets (no. 2 with soprano solo), various songs and piano pieces. Also writer of textbooks on music, etc.

schola cantorum (Lat., 'School of Singers'), (1) originally, the body of singers at the papal court, perhaps dating from around 600; (2) name assumed by certain choirs (especially for the performance of Roman Catholic church music) and by wider-ranging educational institutions – notably that founded in 1894 in Paris by d'Indy and colleagues, and in 1933 in Basle as the *Schola Cantorum Basiliensis* (➤Sacher).

Schönberg, Arnold, ➤Schoenberg.

Schönberg, Claude-Michel (b. 1944), French composer of Les ➤*Misérables*, *Miss Saigon*, and other works for the musical theatre.

Schöne Müllerin, Die (Ger., 'The Fair Maid of the Mill'), song-cycle by Schubert, 1823, to 20 poems by W. Müller about a young man's disappointed love.

School for Fathers, opera by Wolf-Ferrari. ➤*Quatro rusteghi*.

Schoolmaster, The, nickname for Haydn's Symphony no. 55 in E flat, 1774 (Hob. I: 55), perhaps from the grave character of its second movement.

Schöpfung, Die (Ger., 'The Creation'), oratorio by Haydn (Hob. XXI: 2), first performed in Vienna, 1798. Composed to an unidentified German translation of an English text indebted to Genesis and Milton's *Paradise Lost*.

Schöpfungsmesse (Ger., 'Creation Mass'), nickname (because of a quotation in it from *Die* ➤*Schöpfung*) for Haydn's Mass in B flat, 1801.

Schottische (Ger. pl., Scottish), type of ballroom dance similar to polka, popular in the 19th century. The origin of the name is unknown; the dance is not the same as the ➤*écossaise*, despite the name.

Schrammel quartet, type of Austrian light-music combination of two violins, guitar and accordion (named after Joseph Schrammel, 1850–93, leader of such a quartet).

Schreier, Peter [Max] (b. 1935), German tenor, celebrated in Mozart at Salzburg Festival, etc.; former member of (East) Berlin State Opera. Also, since 1969, occasional conductor.

Schreker, Franz (1878–1934), Austrian composer of *Der ferne Klang* ('The Distant Sound') and eight other operas, ballet after Oscar Wilde's *The Birthday of the Infanta*, songs with orchestra; also a ➤chamber symphony (1916, in notable contrast to the 'outsize' orchestrations then in vogue).

Schubert, Franz [Peter] (1797–1828), Austrian composer who was born and died (aged 31) in Vienna, and hardly ever left the city, but who won posthumous international recognition among the greatest composers. Wrote song 'Gretchen am Spinnrade' ('Gretchen at the Spinning-wheel') at 17. Often worked very fast, once producing eight songs in a day; composed more than 600 songs (➤*Lieder*) of great range (➤*Erlkönig*, ➤*Hirt auf dem Felsen*, ➤*Schöne Müllerin*, ➤*Schwanengesang*, ➤*Winterreise*) and many piano works including sonatas, dances, ➤*Wanderer Fantasy*, ➤*Impromptus*, ➤*Moments musicaux*; also works for piano duet (➤*Marche militaire*). Of his nine symphonies he never heard a performance of no. 8 (➤*Unfinished*) or of no. 9 (the ➤*Great C major*; no. 4 is entitled ➤*Tragic Symphony*. Showed his admiration for Rossini in his *Overture in the Italian Style*; for Beethoven, in his string quartets: he wrote 15 (➤*Tod und das Mädchen*), and an isolated movement (➤*Quartettsatz*), also a piano quintet (➤*Forelle*), string quintet and other chamber music (➤*Arpeggione*). Other works include ➤*Alfonso und Estrella* and other unsuccessful operas; music to the play ➤*Rosamunde, Fürstin von Cypern*; six Latin Masses. Unmarried. Died supposedly of typhus. His works are indexed by 'D' numbers, after the thematic catalogue published by O. E. Deutsch in 1951.

Schulhoff, Erwin (1894–1942), Czech composer and pianist, who studied with Reger and became an exponent of quarter-tone music. Composed a setting of the original Communist Manifesto of 1848. As a Jew, was arrested and died in a Nazi concentration camp.

Schuller, Gunther [Alexander] (b. 1925), American composer (formerly horn-player), also conductor; president of the New England Conservatory (Boston), 1967–77. Several of his works use jazz performers (e.g. *Variants* for jazz quartet; *Conversations* for jazz quartet and string quartet). Other works include opera *The Visitation*; *Concerto festivo* for brass quintet and orchestra; *Museum Piece* for Renaissance instruments and orchestra.

Schuman, William [Howard] (1910–92), American composer. President of the Juilliard School of Music, New York, 1945–61. Works include 10 symphonies (no. 5 *Symphony for Strings*); *American Festival Overture*; *William Billings Overture* and *New England Triptych* (both with reference to themes by ➤Billings); *A Free Song* and other cantatas; opera *The Mighty Casey* (about baseball; revised as *Casey at the Bat*), ballet *Undertow* (and a suite drawn from it), a piano concerto, violin concerto, chamber music.

Schumann, Clara [Josephine] (born Wieck; 1819–96), German pianist and composer, chiefly for piano; daughter of the composer Friedrich Wieck (1788–1873) and wife of R. Schumann (below). Made many visits to Britain; internationally noted as a performer of her husband's and other works, and also as a teacher.

Schumann, Elisabeth (1888–1952), German-born soprano, admired in operas by Mozart and R. Strauss. Toured USA with Strauss as her piano accompanist, 1921. Left Austria for USA, 1938; naturalized American, 1944.

Schumann, Robert [Alexander] (1810–56), German composer, a major figure of Romanticism in music; was also pianist, conductor and influential critic with wide sympathies. Married Clara Wieck (➤Schumann, C.), 1840. Developed mental instability, in 1854 throwing himself into the Rhine; afterwards was in a mental asylum, where he died. Many of his piano works have fanciful titles (some given after composition, however): ➤*Abegg Variations*, ➤*Carnaval*, ➤*Faschingsschwank aus Wien*, ➤*Kreisleriana*, ➤*Papillons*, ➤*Kinderszenen*; note also ➤*Davidsbündler*. Other works include many songs, some in cycles (➤*Dichterliebe*, ➤*Frauenliebe und leben*, ➤*Liederkreis*); three string quartets, a piano concerto, cello concerto, violin concerto (not heard till 1937, being suppressed by Clara Schumann and Joachim as unworthy); four symphonies (no. 1 ➤*Spring Symphony*, no. 3 ➤*Rhenish*, no. 4 originally written directly after no. 1, later re-scored); cantata *Das* ➤*Paradies und die Peri*, opera *Genoveva*, *Scenes from Goethe's Faust* (➤*Faust*), incidental music to Byron's ➤*Manfred*.

Schumann-Heink (née Rössler), **Ernestine** (1861–1936), Austrian-born contralto who became a favourite singer at the New York Metropolitan Opera and was naturalized American in 1908.

Schurmann, Gerard (b. 1928), Dutch composer, Indonesian-born, resident in England; also conductor. Works include *Six Studies of Francis Bacon* for orchestra, a piano concerto, violin concerto; *Chuench'i* (song-cycle based on English translations of Chinese texts) – optionally with piano or with orchestra.

Schütz, Heinrich (1585–1672), German composer; studied under G.

Gabrieli in Venice and worked mainly as court composer in Dresden, introducing Italian musical ideas to Germany. Works include the earliest German opera, *Dafne* (music now lost); Italian madrigals; *Symphoniae sacrae* (Lat., 'sacred ➤symphonies') etc., for voices and instruments; three ➤Passions (Matthew, Luke, John), 'Resurrection' and ➤Christmas Oratorios.

Schwanda the Bagpiper, ➤*Švanda the Bagpiper*.

Schwanengesang (Ger., 'Swan Song'), name given – by the publisher, not by Schubert – to a collection of 14 songs by Schubert, published in 1828 (after his death). They were not grouped by Schubert and do not form a unity like his genuine song-cycles.

Schwartz, Stephen (b. 1948), American composer and lyricist of the musical ➤*Godspell*; also co-librettist with Bernstein of Bernstein's ➤*Mass*.

Schwartzendorf, ➤Martini (G.P.).

Schwarz, Gerard [Ralph] (b. 1947), American trumpeter, active in modern music and since 1978 also well known as conductor; music director of Seattle Symphony Orchestra since 1986.

Schwarzkopf, [Olga Maria] **Elisabeth** [Friederike] (b. 1915), German (British-naturalized) soprano. Began operatic career in Berlin, 1938; first appeared at Covent Garden in the Vienna State Opera's visit, 1947. Sang Anne in première of Stravinsky's *The* ➤*Rake's Progress*. Noted in Mozart's and Strauss's operas, and also as recitalist and, latterly, teacher. Hon. D.Mus., Cambridge, 1976. Created Dame, 1992.

Schweitzer, Albert (1875–1965), French (Alsatian) theologian, medical missionary, and musician – organist, and writer on Bach. Awarded the Nobel Prize, 1952.

Schwertsik, Kurt (b. 1935), Austrian composer (also pianist and formerly orchestral horn player). Works include fairy-tale opera *Fanferlizzy Sunnyfeet* (authorized English translation!); Concerto for alphorn and chamber orchestra; *Moment musical* for clarinet and piano.

Sciutti, Graziella (b. 1927), Italian soprano, eminent in opera; sang at La Scala, Milan, from 1955, at Covent Garden from 1956. Noted in light ('soubrette') roles such as Despina in *Così fan tutte*. Her recent operatic work in Britain and USA has been as stage director.

scoop, colloquial term for a fault in singing – to glide up to a note disagreeably from below instead of attacking it cleanly.

scordatura (It., mis-tuning), the tuning of a stringed instrument to notes other than the normal, for special effects – much used in the 17th century and revived in later times; e.g. in Mahler's Symphony no. 4, a solo violinist has to tune all his/her strings up a tone to represent the unearthly fiddling of a 'dance of death'. ➤*Contrasts*.

score, a music-copy combining in ordered form all the different ➤*parts* allotted to various performers of a piece; so (e.g. in an orchestral library) *score and parts*, meaning both the combined music-copy (for the conductor) and the separate copies containing just the music for particular instruments. So also *full score*, a score displaying every different participating voice and instrument; *short score*, a compressed version of the preceding, such as a composer may write out at first, when the outlines of his instrumentation are decided on but not the details; *open score*, a score displaying every part on a separate line – particularly for study or academic exercise, in cases when normal reasons of economy and convenience would suggest compression on to fewer staves; *miniature score* or *pocket score* or *study score*, one which reproduces all the details of a full score but is of a size more suitable for study than for a conductor's desk; *vocal score* (or, US, *piano-vocal score*), one giving all the voice-parts of a work but having the orchestral parts reduced to a piano part; *piano score*, one in which not only the orchestral parts but also the vocal parts (if any) are all reduced to a piano part. So also *to score*, to arrange a work for a particular combination of voices and/or instruments (whether this is part of the composing process, or an arrangement of an already existing work).

scorrevole (It.), scurrying, with rapid fluency.

Scots snap, name for a rhythmic figure consisting of a short note on the beat followed by a longer one held until the next beat, e.g. Found in Scottish folk-music, but also elsewhere, e.g. in Hungarian folk-music, and in Purcell (as in the setting of English words like 'ruin'd').

Scott, Cyril [Meir] (1879–1970), British composer who trained mainly in Germany and won considerable suc-

cess there and in England up to about 1930 – particularly with songs and piano pieces; nicknamed 'the English Debussy'. Also composed three operas (only one produced, in Germany); a piano concerto; choral works; two string trios and other chamber music. Writer on music and also on occultism, food reform, etc.

Scott, Francis George (1880–1958), British composer mainly of songs to Scottish verse, but also orchestral works, songs to French and German verse, etc.

Scott, John [Gavin] (b. 1956), British organist; as director of music at St Paul's Cathedral, London, since 1990, has toured internationally with its choir. Appears widely also as organ recitalist (USA, continental Europe, Hong Kong), and with major orchestras. Has recorded complete organ works of Duruflé.

Scott, [Sir] **Walter** (1771–1832), British novelist and poet. ➤*Ivanhoe*, ➤*Lucia di Lammermoor*, ➤*Puritani*, ➤Boïeldieu, ➤Marschner.

Scottish National Orchestra, ➤Royal Scottish National Orchestra.

'Scottish' (in former use 'Scotch') **Symphony**, nickname for Mendelssohn's Symphony no. 3, completed in 1842, dedicated to Queen Victoria, and inspired originally by the composer's visit to Scotland, 1829. No detailed scheme of allusions, however, has been discovered to be behind the music.

Scotto, Renata (b. 1933), Italian soprano, eminent in opera; at La Scala, Milan, from 1954. Recorded more than 30 operas and has recently been operatic stage director.

Scriabin(e), Alexander, ➤Skryabin.

Sculthorpe, Peter [Joshua] (b. 1929), Australian composer and university teacher. Often makes Australian allusions, as in mainly orchestral series called *Sun Music*; *Nourlangie* for guitar, percussion and strings; *The Songs of Talitnama* for high voice, six cellos and percussion. Has also written 11 string quartets, film scores, etc. OBE, 1977.

Sea, The, 'three symphonic sketches' by Debussy. ➤*Mer*.

Sea Drift, choral and orchestral work (with baritone solo) by Delius, on text by Walt Whitman, first performed (in Germany and in German), 1906.

Sea Pictures, cycle of five songs by Elgar for contralto and orchestra, 1899 – poems by various writers including (no. 2) Elgar's wife.

Searle, Humphrey (1915–82), British composer, pupil of Webern. Works include a trilogy using speakers and orchestra – *Gold Coast Customs* (text, Edith Sitwell), *The Riverrun* (James Joyce), *The Shadow of Cain* (Edith Sitwell); *Hamlet* (after Shakespeare) and other operas; five symphonies. CBE, 1968. Author of book on Liszt.

Seasons, The (1) oratorio by Haydn (➤*Jahreszeiten*); (2) ballet with music by Glazunov, choreography by Petipa, produced in 1900. Vivaldi's work of nearly the same title is *I* ➤*quattro stagioni* ('The Four Seasons').

Sea Symphony, A, title of Vaughan Williams's Symphony no. 1 – which, however, was (in conformity with his practice) given no number by him. In four movements, it is a setting, for soprano, baritone, chorus, and orchestra, of verse by Whitman. First performed in 1910.

sec (Fr., dry), direction that a note or chord is to be struck and released sharply.

secco, ➤recitative.

Sechter, Simon (1788–1867), Austrian organist, composer, and noted theorist and teacher of counterpoint. Bruckner studied with him and Schubert intended to do so (dying before he could).

second (noun), an interval in melody or harmony, reckoned as taking two steps in the (major or minor) scale, counting the bottom and top notes: either a *minor second* (one semitone, e.g. C up to D♭), or *major second* (two semitones, e.g. C up to D), or *augmented second* (three semitones, e.g. C up to D♯). The last gives what is equivalent in practice to the minor third, e.g. C up to E♭, but the terms imply different harmonic contexts. See also following entries.

second (adjective), term implying the performance of a lower-pitched part (*second tenor, second trombone, second violins*, etc.) and usually – but not in choirs – also implying an inferiority in rank to the 'first' of the kind.

secondary dominant, ➤dominant.

Second Mrs Kong, The, opera by Birtwistle, first performed at Glyndebourne, 1994. Libretto by Russell Hoban introduces not only the film monster King Kong but Orpheus and Eurydice and the painter Vermeer.

secondo (It., second), the lower of the two parts in a piano duet.

Secret Marriage, The, opera by Cimarosa. ➤*Matrimonio segreto*.

Secret of Susanna, The, opera by Wolf-Ferrari. ➤*Segreto di Susanna*.

Seefried, Irmgard (1919–88), German soprano resident in Austria, active 1943–77 at the Vienna State Opera, and internationally noted also as recitalist. Her husband was Wolfgang Schneiderhan (b. 1915), Austrian violinist: Henze's *Ariosi* (1963, on poems by Tasso) for soprano, violin and orchestra was written for them.

Seeger, Ruth Crawford, ➤Crawford.

segno (It.), sign; *dal segno* (or *DS*), from the sign, i.e. repeat the preceding passage beginning at the appropriate sign (usually 𝄋).

Segovia, Andrés (1893–1987), Spanish guitarist, for whom many works (e.g. by Castelnuovo-Tedesco and Rodrigo) were specially written and who transcribed many works (notably Bach's) for his instrument. His artistry was chiefly responsible for the 20th-century revival of the guitar as a 'classical' instrument.

segue (It., [it] follows), term used as a direction to the performer to proceed with the next section without a break.

seguidilla, type of quick Spanish dance in triple time, often accompanied by castanets.

Seiber, Mátyás [György] (1905–60), Hungarian-born composer, resident in England from 1935; also conductor and noted teacher. Works include cantata ➤*Ulysses* (text from James Joyce), three string quartets, a violin concerto, clarinet concertino, folksong arrangements, etc.

Seidl, Anton (1858–98), Austro-Hungarian conductor, assistant to Wagner at Bayreuth; from 1885 in New York as outstanding conductor of opera and concerts.

Seixas, José (1704–42), Portuguese organist and composer of sonatas and dances, etc., for harpsichord; also choral works, etc.

Semele, work by Handel, first performed in 1744: of oratorio type, though not biblical, about Semele's love for Jupiter. Text adapted from the libretto written by Congreve for John Eccles's opera *Semele*, intended for performance about 1705, but not then given.

semibreve, ➤whole-note.

semi-chorus, a section of a choral body – not necessarily exactly half of the full chorus.

semidemisemiquaver, an unusual equivalent of hemidemisemiquaver: ➤sixty-fourth-note.

semi-opera, modern term for certain 17th- and 18th-century English stage works (particularly Purcell's, e.g. ➤*King Arthur*) in which music is not so pervasive as to justify the title of 'opera' as now understood. In Purcell's own time, however, the word 'opera' was freely used for such.

semiquaver, ➤sixteenth-note.

Semiramide, opera by Rossini, produced in Venice, 1823. Libretto by G. Rossi (after Voltaire) about the ancient queen of Nineveh. Semiramis is the accepted historical form.

semitone, the smallest interval commonly used in European music – on the piano, the interval between any note and the next note, higher or lower (whether this next note happens to be white or black). ➤tone (3).

semplice (It.), simple, simply.

sempre (It.), always; *sempre più mosso*, always getting faster, i.e. getting faster and faster.

Senaillé [or Senallié], **Jean Baptiste** (1687–1730), French violinist and composer, member of the orchestra at the French court. Wrote many sonatas for violin – from one of which comes an 'Allegro spiritoso' now heard in various arrangements.

Senesino (i.e. 'the man from Siena'), professional name of Francesco Bernardi (*c.* 1680–1759), Italian castrato who sang in 13 of Handel's operas, under the composer's direction.

Senfl, Ludwig (*c.* 1490–1543), Swiss-born composer who, after studying with Isaac, took service with the (Austrian) imperial court and then with the Bavarian court at Munich. Composed choral song-settings, more than 300 of which survive; also motets, Masses, etc.

senza (It.), without.

septet (1) a performing group of seven instrumentalists or singers; (2) a composition for such; instrumental, and actually entitled 'Septet', it will probably have the character of a ➤sonata for seven performers, in several movements.

septimole, septolet, ➤septuplet.

septuplet, a group of seven notes (or notes and rests) of equal time-value, written where a group of three, four or some other number of notes is suggested by the time-signature, e.g. a

seven-note group occupying a bar of 3/4 time, written

sequence (1) the repetition of a phrase at a higher or lower pitch than the original: if the intervals within it are slightly altered in the repetition so as to avoid moving out of key, it is a *tonal sequence*, if they are unaltered, it is a *real sequence*; (2) hymn-like composition with non-biblical Latin text, sung during the Roman Catholic High Mass or Requiem Mass; some sequences have been set by various composers, notably that known as ➤*Stabat Mater*; (3) term used by Berio (It., ➤*sequenza*) as title of a series of works for different solo instruments, unaccompanied.

sequenza, term used by Berio for a series of works (12 so far) for different solo instruments including trombone (no. 5) or voice (no. 3).

Seraglio, The, workably short English title for Mozart's comic opera *Die* ➤*Entführung aus dem Serail*.

Serebrier, José (b. 1938), Uruguayan composer of orchestral *Variations on a Theme from Childhood*, saxophone quartet and other works; also conductor in USA, Europe, Australia.

serenade, properly a piece of open-air evening music, e.g. a lover's song outside his mistress's window, but now a term of the widest and vaguest significance. The classical (18th-century) use of the term indicates a piece for several instruments (often wind instruments only) written in several movements of which the first is in ➤sonata-form and one at least of the others is a minuet. A German equivalent is *Nachtmusik* (as in ➤*Eine kleine Nacht-*

musik), or, for the song-type, *Ständchen.* ➤*Hassan* and the following entries.

Serenade, title of a song-cycle by Britten for tenor with accompaniment of horn and string orchestra, first performed in 1943. The words, by various poets (Blake, Cotton, Jonson, Tennyson, Anon.), have a general association with evening or night.

'Serenade' Quartet, nickname for a famous string quartet in F, long known as Haydn's op. 3, no. 5, but now thought to be by a contemporary of his, R. Hoffstetter: its slow movement (violin melody, plucked-string accompaniment) is reminiscent of a song sung as a serenade with guitar.

Serenade to Music, work by Vaughan Williams for 16 solo voices and orchestra, written in honour of Henry J. Wood's jubilee as a conductor and first performed in 1938. Words adapted from Shakespeare's *The Merchant of Venice.*

serenata (It.), (1) a serenade, e.g. the popular piece by Braga so entitled, or Mozart's *Serenata notturna* (1776) for two orchestras (K239), or C. Nielsen's *Serenata in vano* (It., 'Serenade in Vain') for five instruments, 1914; (2) 18th-century English term for a type of cantata approaching operatic form, such as Handel's ➤*Acis and Galatea.*

seria, ➤*opera seria.*

serialism, ➤series.

series, a set of notes treated in composition not mainly as a recognizable theme, but as a kind of plastic material from which the composition is made. The order of the notes in the series is considered its main characteristic: though the series can be turned upside-down, backwards etc., a relationship to this order must be preserved. The 'note-row' in ➤twelve-note technique is the main example of such a series, but other serial techniques are possible. Hence *serialism*, usually referring to the practice of 12-note technique. The term *multi-serialism* or *total serialism* is applied to composition in which not only pitch is treated serially, but also other dimensions ('parameters') of music – e.g. time-values, volume, force of attack – these being similarly placed in a given mathematical order (e.g. certain works of Boulez, Berio, Nono in the 1950s).

Serious Songs, ➤*Vier ernste Gesänge.*

Serkin, Peter [Adolf] (b. 1947). American pianist with public career from age 12. Founder of ensemble 'Tashi' (1973), devoted to modern music. Son of the following.

Serkin, Rudolf (1903–91), Austrian pianist of Russian origin, naturalized American, 1939. Noted as soloist and as partner of Adolf Busch, violinist (1891–1952), whose daughter he married. Father of preceding.

Sermisy, Claude (or Claudin) **de** (*c.* 1490–1562), French composer (and priest); wrote more than 200 chansons, also Masses, motets, etc. As a singer of the French Chapel Royal he attended François I at his meeting with Henry VIII at the Field of the Cloth of Gold, 1520.

Serocki, Kazimierz (1922–81), Polish composer (also pianist), active in promoting modern music. Works include *Forte e piano* for two pianos and orchestra, *Niobe* for two narrators, chorus and orchestra; also song-cycles, some with orchestral accompaniment.

Serov, Alexander Nikolayevich (1820–71), Russian composer of operas (including *Judith* and *The Power of Evil*), orchestral works, a Stabat Mater, etc.

serpent, obsolete large S-shaped bass wind instrument (related to the ➤cornett) with finger-holes and sometimes keys; usually made of wood but sometimes of metal. It was used e.g. in military bands and in churches up to the mid 19th century. Modified versions were the so-called Russian bassoon and the (English) 'bass horn' from which developed the ➤ophicleide which ousted the serpent from concert use.

serré (Fr., tightened), with increasing speed and tension (It., *stringendo*).

Serse (It., 'Xerxes'), opera by Handel, produced in London, 1738. Libretto by N. Minato about the ancient Persian warrior-king. Contains the famous aria 'Ombra mai fù' ('in praise of a tree's shade') known as 'Handel's Largo' – though Handel actually headed it 'Larghetto'.

Serva padrona, La (It., 'The Maid as Mistress'), comic opera by Pergolesi, produced in Naples, 1733 (as 'intermezzo' between the acts of a serious opera). Libretto by G. A. Frederico. A fighting comedy for master and maidservant. Prodigiously successful – in Paris set off the ➤War of the Comedians.

service, term used for a musically unified setting of the Anglican canticles for morning or evening prayer, or for the Communion service; *short service* and *great service*, terms used in the 16th and early 17th centuries to distinguish between less and more elaborate settings. Note the antithesis between *service* (setting of prescribed liturgical text) and ➤*anthem* (to the composer's own choice of text).

sesquialtera, a type of ➤mixture stop on the organ. (From Latin, expressing the ratio of 3:2 between certain lengths of pipes.)

Sessions, Roger [Huntington] (1896–1985). American composer, pupil of Bloch and others; lived for several years in Europe; noted teacher. Works include nine symphonies, a violin concerto (with orchestra including five clarinets and no violins), operas *The Trial of Lucullus* and *Montezuma*, cantata *Turn O Libertad* (Whitman), three piano sonatas.

sestet, obsolete equivalent of ➤sextet.

Seter, Mordecai (b. 1916), Russian-born Israeli composer who studied in Paris. Works include *Ricercar* for strings, four string quartets, symphony *Jerusalem* (with chorus).

Ševčík, Otakar (1852–1934), Czech violinist, famous as teacher in Prague, London and various US cities.

Seven Last Words of our Saviour on the Cross, The, orchestral work by Haydn. ➤*Sieben Worte des Erlösers am Kreuz*. Also a setting by Murail.

seventh, an interval in melody or harmony, reckoned as taking seven steps in the (major or minor) scale, counting bottom and top notes. The *major seventh* is the distance e.g. from A up to the next G♯; one semitone less gives the *minor seventh* (e.g. A up to G♮), and one further semitone less gives the *diminished seventh* (e.g. A up to G♭). This last is virtually equivalent in practice to the major sixth (e.g. A up to F♯), but is used in a different harmonic context, especially when the *diminished seventh chord* (e.g. A, C, E♭, G♭), is sounded or implied (➤diminished).

Sévérac, [Joseph Marie] Déodat de (1872–1921), French composer, pupil of Magnard and d'Indy. Works include three operas, orchestral and chamber works, songs (some in the old Provençal language), many piano pieces.

sextet (1) a performing group of six instrumentalists or singers; (2) a piece for six performers; if instrumental, and actually entitled 'Sextet', it will probably have the character of a ➤sonata for six performers, in several movements.

sextolet, ➤sextuplet.

sextuplet, a group of six notes (or notes and rests) of equal time-value, written where a group of four, five or some other number of notes would be suggested by the time-signature, e.g. a group of six notes occupying a bar of 4/4, written

sf., abbr. of ➤*sforzando*.

sfogato (It., evaporated), direction used e.g. by Chopin to indicate an airy, delicate manner of performance.

sforzando, sforzato (It., reinforced), direction that a note or chord is to be played in a 'forced' manner, i.e. with special emphasis.

sfp., abbr. signifying that a ➤*sforzando* is to be followed by a (sudden) softness of tone.

Sgambati, Giovanni (1841–1914), Italian pianist (pupil of Liszt) and composer or two symphonies, various piano works, etc.

Shaffer, Peter (b. 1926), British playwright. ➤Hamilton.

shahnai, a north Indian reed instrument; the word is related to ➤shawm.

shake, ➤trill.

Shakespeare, William (1564–1616), English poet and dramatist. ➤Béatrice et Bénédict, ➤Coriolanus, ➤Fairy Queen, ➤Falstaff, ➤Greensleeves, ➤Giulio Cesare, ➤Hamlet, ➤King Lear, ➤Knot Garden, Die ➤lustigen Weiber von Windsor, ➤Macbeth, ➤Midsummer Night's Dream, ➤Mignon, ➤Mines of Sulphur, ➤Oberon, ➤Otello, ➤Othello, ➤Pomp and Circumstance, ➤Romeo and Juliet, ➤Taming of the Shrew, ➤Tempest; ➤Berlioz, ➤Castiglioni, ➤Dittersdorf, ➤Eaton, ➤Elgar, ➤Esposito, ➤Fibich, ➤Finzi, ➤Foerster, ➤Gatty, ➤German (Edward), ➤Giannini, ➤Goetz, ➤Goldmark (Karl), ➤Gounod, ➤Hahn, ➤Halévy, ➤Harbison, ➤Holst, ➤Humfrey, ➤Joachim, ➤Johnson (Robert, 2), ➤Kabeláč, ➤Krejči, ➤Locke, ➤MacDowell, ➤Macfarren, ➤Mancinelli, ➤Martin, ➤Mendelssohn, ➤Morley, ➤Nin-Culmell, ➤Nystroem, ➤Orff, ➤Persichetti, ➤Prokofiev, ➤Salieri, ➤Searle, ➤Shebalin, ➤Sibelius, ➤Storace, ➤Strauss (Richard), ➤Sutermeister, ➤Sviridov, ➤Tchaikovsky, ➤Veracini, ➤Wilson, ➤Zandonai, ➤Zingarelli.

shakuhachi, type of Japanese end-blown bamboo flute, used by Takemitsu as solo instrument with Western orchestra.

Shalyapin, Feodor Ivanovich (1873–1938), Russian bass singer noted in Russian opera – brought to London and Paris by Diaghilev, 1913 – and more widely in recital. After the 1917

Russian Revolution he was at first treated as a distinguished artist of the Soviet régime, but afterwards he settled abroad and died in Paris. (The form 'Chaliapin(e)' is a French spelling of his surname, which takes its stress on the 'ya'.)

shamisen, variant spelling of ➤*samisen*.

Shamus O'Brien, opera by Stanford, produced in London 1896. Libretto by G. H. Jessop, the title-role being that of an Irish rebel against British occupation in 1798.

Shankar, Ravi (b. 1920), Indian sitarist, composer and lecturer. Works include a concerto for sitar and orchestra, music for *Pather Panchali* and other films; largely responsible for the new vogue in the West for Indian music arising in the 1950s and still performing in the 1990s.

shanty, type of sailors' work-song, dating from the era of sail-power and unmechanized ships, suitable for aiding such rhythmical movements as pulling together on a rope. The spelling 'chanty' is a 'literary' form introduced to emphasize the probable derivation from the French imperative *chantez* (sing).

Shao, En (b. 1954), Chinese conductor who, after early career in China, studied in Britain from 1988, won a Hungarian competition for conductors in 1989, and has been principal conductor of the Ulster Orchestra since 1993.

Shapero, Harold [Samuel] (b. 1920), American composer of a symphony, *Nine-minute Overture*, *Hebrew Cantata*, *Three Studies* for piano and synthesizer; also university teacher.

Shapey, Ralph (b. 1921), American composer, also university teacher. Works include Concertante for trumpet and 10 players, Concertante for saxophone and 14 players, *Incantations* for wordless soprano and seven players; also seven string quartets.

Shaporin, Yury [Alexandrovich] (1887–1966), Russian composer, pupil of Glazunov, N. Tcherepnin and others. Works include a symphony, patriotic cantatas, opera *The Decembrists* (alluding to a Russian political conspiracy of December 1825), piano sonatas, songs, etc.

sharp, term indicating a raising in pitch – either (1) indeterminately as when a singer is said to sing sharp, by mistake; or (2) precisely by a semitone, as represented by the sign ♯: so G♯ (G sharp), the note a semitone higher than G♮ (G natural); so also, e.g., B♯ – a notation which is sometimes required by the 'grammar' of music, though on e.g. the piano the note is identical with C♮ (C natural). So ➤double-sharp; *sharp keys*, those having sharps in their key-signatures; *in four sharps*, in the key of E major or C♯ minor, the key-signature of which is four sharps (and similarly with other keys); *sharpened fourth* (US, *sharped . . .*), the raising of the fourth degree of the scale by a semitone.

Sharp, Cecil [James] (1859–1924), British musician who, after holding an organist's and other posts, concentrated on reviving English folk-songs and folk-dances – collecting, editing, performing and writing about them; regarded as the leader of the English folk-music revival in the late 19th century.

Shaw, George Bernard (1856–1950), Irish dramatist (also music critic).

➤*My Fair Lady*, ➤*Tapfere Soldat*; ➤corno.

Shaw, Martin [Fallas] (1875–1958), British composer (church music, songs, etc.), organist and editor of hymn-books, etc.

shawm, double-reed woodwind instrument, forerunner of the oboe much used in the 16th–17th centuries, some varieties still surviving in folk-music, e.g. in Catalonia; made in several sizes, the larger (lower-pitched) ones being called ➤*bombarde* or pommer. (Shawm and ➤*chalumeau* are cognate words.)

Shchedrin, Rodion [Konstantinovich] (b. 1932), Russian composer of ballet *The Little Hump-backed Horse*, operas *Not Only Love* and *Lolita* (after Nabokov's novel), two piano concertos, *Cryptogram* for vibraphone, *Poco misterioso* for ➤bayan; also of *Carmen Suite* (for ballet, transcribed from Bizet's ➤*Carmen*).

Shcherbachev, Vladimir [Vassilevich] (1889–1952), Russian composer, born in Warsaw; pupil of Lyadov and others; noted teacher. Works include five symphonies, a piano suite on poems by Alexander Blok, opera, film music.

Shebalin, Vissarion [Yakovlevich] (1902–63), Russian composer of five symphonies and a 'dramatic symphony' with singers entitled *Lenin*; opera *The* ➤*Taming of the Shrew*; nine string quartets; piano sonatas; music to plays and films. Made a completion of Musorgsky's ➤*Fair at Sorochintsy*.

Sheep may safely graze, familiar English title for an aria by Bach from secular cantata (*c.* 1713) BWV 208, originally with obbligato for two recorders, now heard in various arrangements. Original Ger. words begin 'Schäfe können sicher weiden'.

Sheherazade (1) symphonic suite by Rimsky-Korsakov, 1888 – Sheherazade being a sultan's wife (in the *Arabian Nights*) who tells stories to stave off her execution (the ballet set to this music, 1910, is on a scenario quite distinct from Rimsky-Korsakov's); (2) a set of three songs with orchestra, 1903, by Ravel; the poems, by Tristan Klingsor, are on oriental subjects, but despite the title (in French 'Shéhérazade') there is no direct allusion in the songs to the *Arabian Nights* character. (The form *Scheherazade*, common in references to Rimsky-Korsakov's work, represents the German spelling of the Russian title.)

Shelley, Percy Bysshe (1792–1822), British poet. ➤Goldschmidt.

sheng, a Chinese form of mouth-organ with free reeds and upward-pointing pipes.

Shepherd, Arthur (1880–1958), American composer of two symphonies (no. 1 originally called *Horizons* and incorporating some traditional cowboy songs), five string quartets, cantatas, etc. Also conductor and university teacher.

Shepherd, John, ➤Sheppard.

Shepherd on the Rock, The, ➤*Hirt auf dem Felsen*.

Shepherd's Hey, British morris-dance tune known through Percy Grainger's composition (1909) of that name.

Sheppard, John (*c.* 1515–1558), English composer of Latin and English church music; organist of Magdalen College, Oxford, and a member of the Chapel Royal.

Sheridan, Richard Brinsley (1751–1816), Irish dramatist. ➤*Duenna*; ➤Giordani, ➤Linley.

Sheriff, Noam (b. 1935), Israeli composer born in Palestine, but studied with Blacher in Berlin. Works include *Metamorphoses on a Galliard* and *La* ➤*Folía* variations for orchestra; electronic score for ballet *Cain;* a viola sonata.

Shield, William (1748–1829), British composer, also violinist and viola-player. Master of the King's Music, 1817, and composer to Covent Garden Theatre. Wrote *Rosina* and other operas, often incorporating (as was then customary) items by other composers; also songs, string quartets, string trios (with some movements in 5/4 time). Among his songs is *The Plough Boy*, often supposed (in Britten's arrangement) to be a folksong.

Shifrin, Seymour (1926–79), American composer, pupil of Milhaud (in Paris) and others; also university teacher. Works include *Satires of Circumstance* (after Hardy) for mezzo-soprano and six instruments; five string quartets; a chamber symphony.

Shirley, James (1596–1666), English dramatist. ➤*Cupid and Death.*

Shirley-Quirk, John [Stanton] (b. 1931), British baritone, creating many roles in Britten's operas including the sevenfold baritone role in ➤*Death in Venice* (the work in which he also first appeared, 1974, at the Metropolitan, New York). Is also noted in concert. CBE, 1975.

Shnitke, Alfred, ➤Schnittke. (He prefers the ancestral German form of his Russian name.)

sho, a variant name for the ➤sheng.

shofar (Heb.), wind instrument made of a ram's horn, stipulated in the Old Testament for religious ritual and still used on the most solemn occasions in the synagogue. Simulated, with reference to this, in Elgar's oratorio *The* ➤*Apostles.*

Sholokhov, Mikhail Alexandrovich (1905–84), Russian writer. ➤Dzerzhinsky.

short score, ➤score.

Shostakovich, Dmitry [Dmitrievich] (1906–75), Russian composer, also pianist, the dominant figure (and rebel) of the Soviet musical scene of his time. Pupil of Glazunov; at 19, wrote very successful Symphony no. 1; 14 others followed, including no. 7, ➤*Leningrad* Symphony; no. 13, ➤*Babi Yar;* no. 14 for soprano and bass soloists with chamber orchestra. Denounced by Soviet officialdom for unmelodiousness, freakishness, etc. in 1936 (after his opera ➤*Lady Macbeth of the Mtsensk District*, later called *Katerina Izmailova*); again denounced, for ➤formalism and other disapproved traits, in 1948. In each case admitted 'errors' and endeavoured to find a reconciliation; in 1962, joined the Communist party. Composed other operas including *The* ➤*Nose;* musical comedy *Moscow-Cheryomushki*, ballets including *The* ➤*Golden Age; Song of the Forests* and other cantatas to patriotic Soviet texts; songs and piano pieces (including three sets of preludes and fugues); concerto for piano, trumpet, and orchestra; two violin concertos; 15 string quartets, a piano quintet; songs including cycle ➤*From Jewish Folk Poetry;* film music, etc. Re-orchestrated Musorgsky's ➤*Boris Godunov* and made a completion and orchestration of Musorgsky's ➤*Khovanshchina.* His son Maxim (b. 1938) is a pianist and conductor.

Show Boat, musical play with text by Oscar Hammerstein II based on the novel by Edna Ferber; music by Jerome Kern. Produced in New York, 1927. Mississippi entertainers encounter racial and other problems.

si, the note B (in Latin countries and formerly elsewhere); the ►tonic sol-fa system avoided it as having the same initial as *soh*, and adopted *te* instead for the seventh degree of the scale.

Sibelius, Jean (original forenames Johan Julian Christian) (1865–1957), Finnish composer who studied in Berlin and Vienna. Was enabled by a Finnish government grant to give up teaching and concentrate on composing from 1897, becoming a major 20th-century symphonist. Much of his work has Finnish national associations often relating to the Kalevala (Finnish national epic poem) – e.g. *A* ►*Saga*, ►*Karelia* (overture and suite), *The* ►*Swan of Tuonela*, ►*Lemminkaïnen's Homecoming*, ►*Finlandia*, ►*Tapiola*. In his last 30 years he published almost nothing. Of his seven numbered symphonies, the last is in one movement only. Other works include ►*Kullervo* symphony, a violin concerto; small orchestral pieces including *Valse triste* (►*Valse*); an unpublished opera; many songs in Finnish and Swedish; incidental music to A. Paul's ►*King Christian II*, Maeterlinck's ►*Pélleas et Mélisande*, H. Procope's ►*Belshazzar's Feast*, Shakespeare's *The* ►*Tempest*, and other plays. Married a sister of Järnefelt.

siciliana (It.), type of song or instrumental piece (also *siciliano* and in French *sicilienne*) derived presumably from some Sicilian dance: much cultivated in the 18th century, it is in slow 6/8 (or sometimes 12/8) time, usually in a minor key.

Sicilian Vespers, The, opera by Verdi; ►*Vêpres siciliennes*.

side-drum, ►snare-drum.

Sieben Worte des Erlösers am Kreuz, Die (Ger., 'The Seven Last Words of the Saviour on the Cross'), orchestral work by Haydn (Hob. XX: 2) in the form of seven slow movements for performance in Cadiz Cathedral (1785) as 'incidental music' to a Lenten service when the 'Words' (actually sentences) were read and preached on. Haydn arranged the music later for string quartet and for piano, and later still as a cantata, the text including the 'Words' themselves.

Siège de Corinthe, Le (Fr., 'The Siege of Corinth'), opera by Rossini, produced in Paris, 1826. It was a revised French version of Rossini's earlier Italian opera *Maometto II*, produced in Naples, 1820, with libretto by C. della Valle. The plot concerns the love of an 18th-century Muslim conqueror for the daughter of the Christian Governor of Corinth.

Siege of Rhodes, The, opera produced in London (1656) and reckoned the first English opera. The music (now lost) was contributed by Locke, H. Lawes, H. Cooke, Coleman and Hudson. Libretto by W. Davenant, referring to the Turkish siege (1480–81) of the last Christian outpost then surviving in the Mediterranean.

Siegfried, opera by Wagner. ►*Ring*; ►*Siegfred Idyll*.

Siegfried Idyll, work by Wagner, 1870, for small orchestra, celebrating the birth of his son Siegfried, and

403

using themes from his opera of that name (not yet produced).

Siegmeister, Elie (1909–91), American composer, also writer on music; pupil of Riegger and N. Boulanger. Works include eight symphonies; *The Plough and the Stars* (on O'Casey's play) and other operas; sextet for brass and percussion.

Siepi, Cesare (b. 1923), Italian bass, eminent in such operatic roles as Don Giovanni, particularly at the New York Metropolitan for 23 seasons from 1950.

sight-reading, sight-singing, the playing or singing of music at first sight.

signature, ➤key-signature, ➤time signature; *signature-tune*, a piece (whether or not specially written) used by a radio or TV programme, etc., at each performance as a means of identification.

Silja, Anja (b. 1935), German soprano, associated with the stage director Wieland Wagner in the 'new Bayreuth' approach to Wagner (his grandfather); her leading roles at Bayreuth began 1960 (Senta in *Der fliegende Holländer*). Continued in strongly dramatic roles elsewhere, making Glyndebourne début, 1989, as the Kostelnička in *Jenůfa*.

Silken Ladder, The, opera by Rossini. ➤*Scala di seta*.

Sills, Beverly [originally Belle Miriam Silverman] (b. 1929), American soprano, celebrated chiefly in coloratura roles of Italian opera; at New York City Opera from 1955, at Metropolitan from 1975; Covent Garden, 1970. Director, New York City Opera, 1979–88.

Siloti, Alexander, ➤Ziloti; the form 'Siloti' to represent this Russian name,

though common in Western references, assumes the German sound of 's' (= English 'z').

similar motion, ➤motion.

simile (It., similar), term indicating that a phrase, etc., is to be performed in the same manner as a parallel phrase preceding it.

Simionato, Giulietta (b. 1910), Italian mezzo-soprano whose distinguished career included many appearances with Callas, e.g. at Covent Garden and on recordings of operas by Bellini and Donizetti. Retired in 1966.

Simon Boccanegra, opera by Verdi, produced in Venice, 1857 (libretto by F. M. Piave); new version, with libretto altered by A. Boito, produced in Milan, 1881. Named after the historical 14th-century Doge of Venice, its hero.

Simonov, Yuri [Ivanovich] (b. 1941), Russian conductor, principal conductor at Bolshoi Theatre, Moscow, 1970–85. Toured internationally with that company; made first appearance with a Western company at Covent Garden, 1982 (*Yevgeny Onegin*); music director of Belgian National Orchestra from 1994.

simphony, old English variant of *symphony*; ➤Purcell Quartet.

simple interval, an ➤interval of an eighth (octave) or less.

Simple Symphony, a symphony for string orchestra by Britten, 1934, 'entirely based on material from works which the composer wrote between the ages of nine and 12'. Used for a ballet (choreography by Walter Gore), 1944.

simple time, a scheme of time-division (distinguished from ➤compound time) in which the beat-unit is divisible by 2

– e.g. 4/4, in which the beat-time is the quarter-note (crotchet) divided into two eighth-notes (quavers).

Simpson (or **Sympson**), **Christopher** (c. 1605–1669), English player of the bass viol, author of musical treatises, composer of various works for his instrument and for groups of strings.

Simpson, Robert [Wilfred Levick] (1921–97), British composer of 11 symphonies, 15 string quartets, *The ➤Four Temperaments* and other works for bass band. Author of book on C. Nielsen, and former member of BBC music staff.

Simpson, Thomas (1582–after 1630), English viol-player and composer (dances, songs, etc.) who held various posts in Germany and Denmark.

Sinding, Christian (1856–1941), Norwegian composer (also pianist) who studied in Germany and in 1921–2 taught in USA. Besides *Frühlingsrauschen* ('Rustle of Spring') and other piano pieces, wrote three symphonies, two concertos for violin and one for piano, etc.

sinfonia (It.), ➤symphony; *sinfonia concertante*, term applied to orchestral works of the Haydn–Mozart period with more than one solo instrument (➤*symphonie concertante*) and used by Walton and some other 20th-century composers for works with only one solo instrument (perhaps because it does not seem to emphasize, as 'concerto' does, the element of display). The term has occasionally been used by non-Italian composers simply wanting a variant of *symphony*; and as title of an orchestra (➤Northern Sinfonia).

Sinfonia Antartica (It., 'Antarctic Symphony'), title given by Vaughan Williams to his Symphony no. 7 (but, in conformity with his practice, not numbered by him), first performed in 1953. It is based on Vaughan Williams's music to the film *Scott of the Antarctic* (1949); each of the five movements is prefaced by a literary quotation, the last one from Scott's Journal.

Sinfonia da Requiem (It., 'Requiem Symphony'), orchestral work by Britten, 1940, in three movements headed 'Lacrymosa', 'Dies Irae' and 'Requiem Aeternam' (titles of sections of the ➤Requiem Mass).

sinfonietta (term formed as a diminutive from *sinfonia*, but not an authentic Italian word), a small (and probably rather light) symphony; also a performing name for a small orchestra.

Singakademie (Ger., singing-academy), title used by certain choirs in German-speaking countries.

Singspiel (Ger., song-play), a type of opera. Although the term was more freely applied in the 18th century, modern usage confines it to the historical type of German opera popular in Germany and Austria in Mozart's time. Mozart's *Die* ➤*Entführung aus dem Serail* and *Die* ➤*Zauberflöte* are of this type – having spoken dialogue instead of recitative, and being in the vernacular tongue instead of Italian.

Sinigaglia, Leone (1868–1944), Italian composer who, untypically, wrote no opera. Works include overture to Goldoni's comedy *Le baruffe chiozzotte* ('The Row at Chioggia'), Variations on a Theme of Brahms for string quartet. Was a pupil of Dvořák in Prague.

Sinopoli, Giuseppe (b. 1946), Italian conductor, also composer, who formerly practised as surgeon and psychiatrist; conductor of the Philharmonia Orchestra since 1984. Conductor, Dresden State Orchestra, 1991.

Sirmen, Maddalena Laura Lombardini (Sirmen her married name; 1745–1818), Italian violinist, singer and composer of six string quartets sufficiently esteemed to be published in Paris, 1769.

Sister Angelica, opera by Puccini. ➤*Suor Angelica*.

sistrum, ancient rattle-like percussion instrument with rings which jangled on a metal frame when the instrument was shaken.

sitar, an Indian long-necked lute with movable frets, and originally with three strings, now with 4–7, and sometimes sympathetic strings also. It is played with a plectrum worn on the right forefinger. One of the few Western concert works to use it is by ➤Miroglio.

Sitkovetsky, Dmitry (b. 1954), Russian-born violinist who emigrated to USA 1977, developing a repertory of more than 40 concertos and partnering his mother, the pianist Bella Davidovich, in recital: conductor of Ulster Orchestra since 1996.

Sitsky, Larry (b. 1934), Australian composer, born in China of Russian descent; university teacher in Canberra. His works include three violin concertos, opera *The Fall of the House of Usher* (after Poe), *Three Scenes from Aboriginal Life* (short theatre pieces using children's voices).

Sitwell, Edith (1887–1964), British poet. ➤*Façade*; ➤*Searle*.

Sitwell, Osbert (1892–1969), British writer. ➤*Belshazzar's Feast*.

Sitwell, Sacheverell (1897–1988), British poet. ➤*Rio Grande*.

Six, Les (Fr., 'The Six'), name given to the French composers Auric, Durey, Honegger, Milhaud, Poulenc and Tailleferre. It was invented in 1920 by the French critic Henri Collet (after these composers had together published an album of pieces) on the analogy of the Russian 'five' composers (➤Mighty Handful). They did not remain a group, and only Honegger, Milhaud and Poulenc achieved wide fame.

Sixteen, The, British vocal group (now often augmented beyond the original number) founded in 1977 by its director, Harry Christophers, known for many performances and recordings of Renaissance, baroque and (less frequently) later music.

sixteen-foot (as measurement of organ pipes, etc.), ➤foot.

sixteenth-note, the note ♪ considered as a time-value. This term is standard North American usage and, as mathematically corresponding to the element of time-signature represented by /16, should clearly be preferred to 'semiquaver', still surviving in British use. The corresponding rest is notated ♪

sixth (1) an interval in melody or harmony, reckoned as taking six steps in the (major or minor) scale, counting the bottom and top notes. The *major sixth* is the distance e.g. from C up to A, *a minor sixth* (one semitone less) from C up to A♭, an *augmented sixth* (one semitone more) from C up to A♯. The last gives an interval which in practice is virtually the same as the 'diminished seventh' (C up to B♭) but the harmonic context implied is different; (2) term used in the phrase *Landino sixth* (➤Landino), referring to the sixth degree of the scale, not the interval of six notes as described above.

sixty-fourth-note, the note ♪ considered as a time-value. This term is standard North American usage and, as mathematically corresponding to the element of time-signature represented by /64, should clearly be preferred to 'hemidemisemiquaver', still surviving in British use. The corresponding rest is notated ♪

Skalkottas, Nikos (1904–49), Greek composer (also orchestral violinist), pupil of Schoenberg; also made use of Greek folk-music. Works (little known in his lifetime) include *Greek Dances* for orchestra, three piano concertos, four string quartets.

Skelton, John (*c.* 1460–1529), English poet. ➤Cornysh.

Skempton, Howard (b. 1947), British composer who sometimes uses unbarred notation and has written many works for the accordion (which he plays) with or without other instruments; also *A Humming Song* for pianist who hums to prolong certain notes; and *Lento* (BBC commission, 1991) for orchestra.

sketch (1) a rough draft of a composition, or a musical jotting made by a composer as a 'germ' or reminder; so Beethoven's *Sketch-books*; (2) a short piece usually interpreting pictorial or other extra-musical ideas.

Skilton, Charles Sanford (1868–1941), American composer who studied American-Indian music and made use of it in many of his works – including radio opera *The Sun Bride*, and

Shawnee Indian Hunting Dance for orchestra.

Skriabin, ➤Skryabin.

Skrowaczewski, Stanisław (b. 1923), Polish conductor who worked in USA (naturalized in 1966) and was conductor of the Hallé Orchestra, 1984–92. Also composer of violin concerto, film music, etc.

Skryabin, Alexander [Nikolayevich] (1872–1915), Russian composer, pupil of Taneyev and others; also virtuoso pianist, touring greatly. Composer of early Chopin-like piano pieces, then of larger-scale works using a highly chromatic new type of harmonic style designed to express theosophic beliefs. Invented the so-called 'mystic chord' of ascending fourths, C–F♯–B♭–E–A–D, as a replacement for ordinary major and minor chords. Works include orchestral ➤*Divine Poem,* ➤*Poem of Ecstasy,* ➤*Prometheus – The Poem of Fire,* 10 piano sonatas and many other piano works.

Slaatt(er), ➤Slått.

Slade, Julian [Penkivil] (b. 1930), British composer of shows for the musical theatre including *Follow that Girl* and ➤*Salad Days.*

Slatkin, Leonard [Edward] (b. 1944), American conductor, music director of St Louis Symphony Orchestra 1979–96, then music director of National Symphony Orchestra (Washington, DC). At BBC Proms, 1991, conducted the movements of Musorgsky's ➤*Pictures at an Exhibition* in several different orchestrations; is also opera conductor (début at Metropolitan, New York, 1991).

slått

slått (Norw., pl. *slåtter*), type of composition (originally a march, but afterwards more broadly treated) played by Norwegian folk-musicians on the Hardanger ➤fiddle; Grieg transcribed several examples, and other Norwegian composers have also written works of this kind. (The spellings *slaatt* and *slaatter* were formerly current in Norwegian.)

Slavonic Dances, two sets each of eight dances by Dvořák – in folk-music vein, but all original – for piano duet, 1878 and 1886; also orchestrated by the composer.

Slavonic Rhapsodies, three orchestral works by Dvořák (1878) in the vein of Czech folk-music, but all original.

Sleeping Beauty, The (Rus. *Spyashchaya krasavitsa*), ballet with choreography by Petipa, music by Tchaikovsky, produced in St Petersburg, 1890. (*The Sleeping Princess* was the title adopted by Diaghilev for his London presentation of it, 1921, to avoid possible confusion with a Christmas pantomime.)

sleigh-bell, conventional name for small bell with slit-like mouth, a set of such bells traditionally attached to horses, carriage-harness, etc. Used in no. 13 of Mozart's German Dances, K. 506, known as *The Sleigh Ride*, requiring the bells to be tuned to definite notes; also (with the same signification) in Mahler's Symphony no. 4, with pitch indeterminate.

slentando (It.), becoming slower.

slide, a device on some brass instruments (notably the ➤trombone) for altering the length of the tube (and thus the notes produced). So *slide-*➤*trumpet*.

Slippers, The (Rus., from Ukrainian, *Cherevichki*), opera by Tchaikovsky, produced in Moscow, 1887. Libretto by Y. P. Polonsky (a revision of the composer's earlier *Vakula the Smith*), based on Gogol's comic plot of village life to which Rimsky-Korsakov also turned in ➤*Christmas Eve*.

slit-drum, percussion instrument of many tropical peoples – a log with one or more slits along the side.

Slonimsky, Sergey [Mikhailovich] (b. 1932), Russian composer of symphony; opera *Maria Stuart; Antiphones* for string quartet in which the performers walk about the platform and hall, etc. He is the nephew of the Russian-born American musicologist Nicolas Slonimsky (1894–1996).

slur, in musical notation, a curved line grouping notes together and indicating that in performance they are to be joined smoothly together – sung in one breath, played with one stroke of the bow, etc.

Smalley, Dennis [Arthur] (b. 1946), New Zealand composer, head of music department at City University (London) since 1994. Directed concert of electro-acoustic music during the Proms, 1989, including his own *Pentes*. His other works include *Pneuma* for amplified voices and percussion, *Clarinet Threads* for amplified clarinet with electro-acoustic sounds.

Smalley, Roger (b. 1943), British composer, also pianist. Works include *Beat Music* for 55 players; *Gloria tibi Trinitatis I* for orchestra; electronic music; *Strung Out* for 13 solo strings. Resident in Australia as university teacher since 1976.

Smetana, Bedřich (1824–84), Czech

composer, also conductor and pianist; encouraged by Liszt. Took part in the unsuccessful Czech revolt against Austria, 1848, and afterwards worked for some years in Sweden; but from 1861 settled again in Prague. Became totally deaf in 1874 but continued to compose – e.g. cycle of symphonic poems ➤*My Country*, two string quartets (no. 1, ➤*From My Life*), opera *The Kiss* and others. Previous works include operas *The* ➤*Bartered Bride* and *Dalibor*, choral works, many piano pieces. Developed a Czech national style influenced by folk-music.

Smirnov, Dmitry [Nikolayevich] (b. 1948), Russian composer, pupil of Denisov in Moscow, now resident in Britain (he and his wife Elena ➤Firsova are jointly professors at the University of Keele). Has based many works on William Blake (whom he first encountered in Russian translation); including opera *Tiriel*, *Six Poems by William Blake* for voice and organ and *The Seven Angels of William Blake* for piano; also two symphonies, concerto for violin and 13 strings.

Smith, John Stafford (1750–1836), British organist, musical antiquarian, and composer of catches, glees, etc. His song, 'To Anacreon in Heaven' furnished the tune to which the words of *The* ➤*Star-Spangled Banner* were later set.

Smith, Ronald (b. 1929), British pianist (also composer) who has specialized in performing and recording the works of Alkan and has written extensively on that composer.

Smith Brindle, Reginald (b. 1917), British composer of two symphonies, *Tubal Cain's Legacy* for trombone and piano, pieces for one and for more guitars, etc. Professor, University of Surrey, 1970–85.

Smyth, Ethel [Mary] (1858–1944), British composer who studied in Germany and had operas and other works performed there. Joined militant agitation for women's vote in Britain and was jailed, 1911; created Dame, 1922. In late years suffered from deafness and distorted hearing. Works include *The* ➤*Wreckers*, *The Boatswain's Mate* and other operas; Mass; a concerto for violin, horn and orchestra; chamber music. Also autobiographer.

snare, ➤snare-drum.

snare-drum, small drum (slung slightly to one side when marching – hence alternative British [not US] name, 'side-drum'); used in the orchestra, military band, dance band, etc. It has a skin at either end of a shallow cylinder, the upper skin being struck with a pair of wooden sticks and the lower one being in contact with gut strings or wires (called snares) which add a rattling effect to the tone and can be disengaged at will.

Snegurochka, ➤*Snow Maiden*.

Snow Maiden, The (Rus., *Snegurochka*), opera by Rimsky-Korsakov, produced in St Petersburg, 1882. Libretto by composer, after a play by Ostrovsky: the Snow Maiden, daughter of Fairy Spring and King Frost, is wooed in vain by the Sun-God.

Snowman, The, work by Howard Blake for narrator, boy soprano and orchestra, 1982; text by the composer after the children's story by Raymond Briggs.

soap opera, not an opera but a radio or television serial of a sentimental type – in USA designed to sell the sponsor's product, e.g. soap.

soave (It.), sweet(ly), tender(ly).

Socrate (Fr., 'Socrates'), work for voices and orchestra by Satie, first performed in 1920; called a 'symphonic drama' but not intended for the stage. Texts translated from Plato's dialogues.

Söderström, [Anna] **Elisabeth** (b. 1927), Swedish soprano, eminent in a wide range of operas; at Glyndebourne 1957–79, at Metropolitan, New York, 1959–87. Artistic director of Drottningholm Court Theatre, 1993.

soft pedal, ➤piano(2).

soh, in ➤tonic sol-fa the spoken name for the fifth degree (dominant) of the scale, written s.

Sohal, Naresh (b. 1939), Indian composer,· pupil in England of Goehr. Works with Indian titles include *Asht Prahar* (Sanskrit: *asht* = eight, *prahar* is a division of the day) for orchestra and *Gitanjali* ('Song Offering', used by Tagore for a collection of poems). Other works include harmonica concerto, two brass quintets.

Soir (et la tempête), Le, title of one of a set of three symphonies by Haydn: ➤Morning.

Soirées musicales (Fr., musical evenings), a collection of songs and duets by Rossini, published in 1835; an orchestral arrangement by Britten (1936) of five of its numbers bears the same title. Other arrangements include Respighi's in the ballet *La Boutique fantasque*.

sol, the note G (in Latin countries, and formerly elsewhere); the➤tonic sol-fa symbol ➤*soh* is derived from it.

Soldaten, Die (Ger., 'The Soldiers'), opera by Zimmermann, produced in Cologne, 1965, with libretto after J. Lenz's play; the heroine ends as a soldiers' prostitute.

Soldier's Tale, The, stage work by Stravinsky. ➤*Histoire du soldat*.

Soler, Antonio (1729–83), Spanish friar and composer of harpsichord sonatas, church music, incidental music to plays, etc.

sol-fa, ➤tonic sol-fa.

solfège, solfeggio, French and Italian terms for a method of ear-training and sight-reading by which the pupil names each note of a melody (*do* for C, *sol* for G, etc.) by singing it. The Italian is the original term; the French, derived from it, is also used in a broader sense to take in the whole system of rudimentary musical instruction in which the above is a prime element. The name *solfeggio* is also given to a vocal exercise written for the above method of study.

solmization, the designation of musical notes by a system of syllabic names – as applied to a nomenclature devised by Guido of Arezzo in the 11th century and now to a development of this. Such a development is represented by the current Italian *do, re, mi, fa, sol, la, si* (representing the notes from C up to B), paralleled in British ➤tonic sol-fa by doh, ray, me, fah, soh, lah, te. But these are not fixed in pitch but relative, doh representing C in C major, D in D major, etc., the other notes ascending from it.

solo (It., alone), a piece or passage performed by one performer – either alone or with others in a subordinate, accompanying role. So *solo song* normally denotes a song for one singer with piano accompaniment. Plural in Italian, *soli*; in English, *solos*. The *solo organ* is a manual on some organs, having mainly stops suitable for the solo treatment of melodies. *Soloistic*, in musicologists' jargon, refers to the use of instruments in the orchestra not as contributing to massed effects but for their individual qualities.

Solomon, oratorio by Handel, produced in London, 1749. Text (based on the Bible) by someone now unknown.

Solomon (professional name used by Solomon Cutner) (1902–88), British pianist who appeared from age eight, and became internationally noted. CBE, 1946. Incapacitated after a stroke, 1956.

Solti, Georg (1912–97), Hungarian-born conductor (also pianist); from 1939 resident in Switzerland and later in Germany; music director of the Frankfurt Opera, 1952; of Covent Garden Opera, 1961–71; of Chicago Symphony Orchestra, 1969–91; of London Philharmonic Orchestra, 1979–83. Celebrated also for massive output of recorded operas (including the first complete recording of the ➤*Ring*, 1958–65) and symphonic works. Naturalized British, 1972; his previous honorary KBE (1971) became a regular knighthood.

Sombrero de tres picos, El (Sp., 'The Three-Cornered Hat'), ballet with choreography by Massine, music by Falla, first produced in London, 1919.

Somers, Harry [Stewart] (b. 1925), Canadian composer, pupil of Milhaud in Paris. Works include opera *Louis Riel*; five *Concepts* for orchestra; three string quartets; *Voiceplay* for singer-actor (any voice, any range).

Somervell, Arthur (1863–1937), British composer of choral works, songs, etc., and musical educationist. Knighted, 1929.

sommo, somma (It.), highest: *con somma passione*, with the utmost passion.

son (Fr.), sound; *musique de douze sons*, ➤twelve-note music; *sons bouchés*, ➤'stopped' notes on the horn.

sonata (It., a piece sounded, as distinct from 'cantata', a piece sung), originally (in Italy, *c.* 1600) any instrumental piece not in a prevailing form such as ➤*canzona*, ➤*ricercar*, or a dance-form. Later, since the Haydn–Mozart era (regarded as the 'classic' era for this type of work), usually a work in three or four movements – or, following the example of Liszt's Piano Sonata (1852–3), in one movement deliberately conceived as equal to (and about as long as) several 'normal' movements combined. Only a work for one or two players is now normally called a sonata; a work of this type for three is called a trio, for four a quartet, etc., and for an orchestra a symphony. Such terms as *violin sonata, cello sonata* normally assume the participation also of a piano. Characteristic of the sonata at least up to 1914 is the use (normally in the first movement and often in others too) of what is called ➤sonata-form or a modification of it. Among the notable forerunners of this now standard type are D. Scarlatti's short one-movement keyboard works, now usually also called sonatas. In the 17th and early 18th centuries the application of the term was wider, the *chamber sonata* (It., *sonata da camera*) representing virtually a suite (mainly in the form of dance-movements) for two or more stringed instruments with keyboard accompaniment. The *church sonata* (It., *sonata da chiesa*) was similar but of a 'graver' type, avoiding dance-movements. This pre-Haydn usage of *sonata* as applied to a work for orchestra or smaller ensemble has occasionally been revived, e.g. by Colin Matthews. The ➤sonatina is a derivative.

sonata-form, term used to describe a certain type of musical construction normally used in the first movement of a ➤sonata and of a symphony (which is in effect a sonata for orchestra) and similar works. An alternative name is 'first-movement form' – but the form is also found in movements other than first movements, just as it is also found in works not called sonatas. It may also be called 'compound binary form' (➤binary). The essential is the division of a movement (sometimes after an introduction) into three parts – exposition, development, recapitulation. The exposition, having its first theme in the 'home' key of the movement, moves into another key normally presenting a fresh (second) subject in that key, and ends in that key; the next section 'develops' or expands the material already presented; the last section is basically a varied repetition of the first, but ending in the home key, normally by bringing the second subject into that key. Afterwards may follow a further section, called coda ('finishing off' the movement). The key into which the

first section moves is normally the dominant (if the piece is in the major key) or the relative major (if the piece is in the minor key). Thus sonata-form consists basically in a relationship of keys: if the term is applied to keyless (➤atonal) music, then it must be with an altered significance.

sonate (Fr., Ger.), ➤sonata.

sonatina, sonatine (It., Fr.), a 'little sonata', usually shorter, lighter, or easier than most sonatas; *sonatina* is used in English.

Sondheim, Stephen [Joshua] (b. 1930), American composer of musicals, including *A ➤Little Night Music* and ➤*Sweeney Todd, the Demon Barber of Fleet Street*, also lyricist for his own works and for Bernstein's ➤*West Side Story*.

song, any short vocal composition, accompanied or not – usually for one principal performer, unless a ➤*part-song*. The word has no precise meaning, but is effectively defined in various contexts by contrast with other terms – e.g. *songs and duets* (implying vocal solos and vocal duets). In opera the word 'aria' or 'air' is more usual. When, as normally, a song repeats the same tune for successive stanzas of a poem, it is said to be ➤'strophic'; if not, then the clumsy term 'through-composed' (from Ger. *durchkomponiert*) is sometimes applied to it. So also *song-➤scena; song-cycle*, a set of songs grouped by the composer in a particular order (usually with reference to the sense of the words) and intended to be so performed. The term *song* or its German equivalent ➤*Lied* is also applied in a generalized sense to certain large-scale works – e.g. Brahms's ➤*Schicksalslied*.

song-form, name sometimes given to ordinary ➤ternary form as used in an instrumental slow-movement.

Song of Destiny, choral work by Brahms. ➤*Schicksalslied*.

Song of the Earth, vocal-orchestral work by Mahler. ➤*Lied von der Erde*.

Song of the Three Holy Children, a text from the Apocrypha related to the Book of Daniel, used for an electronic composition by Stockhausen (➤*Gesang*).

Songs and Dances of Death (Rus., *Pesni i plyaski smerti*), cycle of four songs by Musorgsky, 1875–7, to poems by Golenishchev-Gutuzov evoking different aspects of death.

Songs for a Mad King, work by P. M. Davies. ➤*Eight Songs for a Mad King*.

Songs of a Wayfarer, song-cycle by Mahler. ➤*Lieder eines fahrenden Gesellen*.

Songs of Gurre, work by Schoenberg. ➤*Gurrelieder*.

Songs on the Death of Children, song-cycle by Mahler. ➤*Kindertotenlieder*.

Songs Without Words, piano works by Mendelssohn. ➤*Lieder ohne Worte*.

sonic, (in general) of sound; *sonic composition*, composition not confined to conventionally agreed notes and a chosen set of instruments and/or voices, but electronically manipulating the basic (micro-) elements of the ➤spectrum, as in ➤electro-acoustic music.

Sonnambula, La (It., 'The Sleepwalker'), opera by Bellini, produced in Milan, 1831. Libretto by F. Romani, the heroine's sleepwalking habit leading her into a compromising situation.

sonore (Fr., 'sonorous'), direction for performance used e.g. by Debussy; non-French composers have also incorporated it into their scores, apparently under the impression that it is an Italian word (properly *sonoramente*).

sop., abbr. of ➤soprano.

Sophocles (495–406 BC), Greek dramatist. ➤*Antigone*, ➤*Elektra*, ➤*Oedipus Rex*; ➤Hadley (P.), ➤Partch.

sopranino (It., diminutive of ➤soprano), name for a size of instrument higher than the soprano size – e.g. sopranino ➤recorder, sopranino ➤saxophone.

soprano (It., upper), (1) the highest type of female voice, with approximate normal range from middle C upwards for two octaves; or a child's high voice (➤treble, 1); (2, *male soprano*) type of male adult voice of similar range, produced by castration, as used for some operatic and church singers, e.g. in the 17th and 18th centuries; (3, *soprano clef*) name of a clef (now obsolete) having middle C on the bottom line of the staff: ; (4) name given, in a 'family' of instruments (i.e. a group of different sizes), to the one with a range approximating to the soprano voice – and usually also carrying the implication of being higher than the 'normal'-sized instrument. E.g. *soprano* ➤*cornet*, *soprano* ➤*recorder*, *soprano* ➤*saxophone*; the small clarinet in E♭ is occasionally (though not commonly) called a *soprano clarinet* for the same reason.

Sor [also Sors], [Joseph] **Fernando** [Macari] (1778–1839), Spanish guitarist; teacher of his instrument in Paris, London, and elsewhere; composer of many highly regarded pieces for his instrument, but was also

413

admired for his songs and ballet music (especially for *Cendrillon*, 1822).

Sorabji, Kaikhosru Shapurji (1892–1988), British composer (originally Leon Dudley Sorabji), son of a Parsi father and a Spanish-Sicilian mother, also pianist and polemical writer on music. Works (for orchestra, piano, organ, etc.) include the two-hour *Opus clavicembalisticum* for piano. Until the mid-1970s he discouraged public performances of his works.

Sorcerer, The, operetta by Sullivan, produced in London, 1877. Libretto by W. S. Gilbert. A representative of a respectable firm of 'family sorcerers' administers a love-potion to an English village.

Sorcerer's Apprentice, The, orchestral work by Dukas. ➤*Apprenti sorcier*.

sord., abbr. of ➤*sordino*.

sordina, an occasionally found alternative to ➤*sordino*.

sordino (It., pl. -*i*), a mute; abbr. *sord*. So *con sordini*, with mutes, put on mutes; *senza sordini*, without mutes, take off mutes. As applied to the piano, *sordini* refers to the dampers which remain in operation unless the sustaining pedal (right-hand side) is depressed; *senza sordini*, i.e. without dampers, means that this pedal is to be brought into use.

Sorochintsy Fair, opera by Musorgsky. ➤*Fair at Sorochintsy*.

Sors, ➤*Sor*.

sostenuto (It.), sustained, i.e. in a smooth manner.

Soto de Langa, Francisco (1534–1619), Spanish priest, castrato singer (active for 49 years) and composer; settled in Rome and composed *Laude*

spirituali for the oratory church of Filippo Neri. ➤*Lauda*.

sotto voce (It., under the voice), whispered, barely audible – term used of instrumental as well as vocal music.

soubrette (Fr.), type of pert female character (often a servant) sung by a light soprano voice in opera or operetta – e.g. Despina in ➤*Così fan tutte*, Adèle in *Die* ➤*Fledermaus*.

sound-board, a wooden board on the piano and other keyboard instruments, located close to the strings, vibrating when they are struck, and serving to amplify the volume of their sound.

sound-hole, hole cut out of the upper surface of stringed instruments to assist resonance – the violin and related instruments having two holes shaped like an *f* and called *f*-holes, the lute and some guitars having one hole cut in an ornamented manner somewhat like a flower and called 'rose'.

Sound of Music, The, musical with text by Howard Lindsay and Russel Crouse; lyrics by Oscar Hammerstein II; music by Richard Rodgers. Produced in New York, 1959. Maria leaves an Austrian convent to be governess to the children of a widowed Captain and later marries him; their Nazi pursuers are foiled.

sound-post, piece of wood connecting vertically the upper and lower surfaces of the body of a violin and other stringed instruments. It helps to support the pressure of the strings on the bridge (and hence on the upper surface) and serves to distribute the vibrations of the strings over the body of the instrument.

sourdine (Fr.), a mute (as ➤*sordino*); *mettez, ôtez, les sourdines*, put on, take off, mutes.

Sousa, John Philip (1854–1932), American band-conductor and composer of marches ('The Washington Post', 'The Stars and Stripes Forever', etc.); also of *El capitán* and other operettas. The story that his name was a fabrication to include the letters USA is itself a fabrication. The ➤*sousaphone* is associated with, but was not invented by, him.

sousaphone, type of ➤tuba made in a shape circling the player's body and ending in a big bell facing forward. It was associated with the band conducted by Sousa (above) and is still used in American bands; it was also used in some early manifestations of jazz.

Souster, Tim [Timothy Andrew James] (1943–94), British composer, also writer on music. His compositions mostly involve electronics, including trumpet concerto and *The Transistor Radio of St Narcissus* (with flugelhorn), *Curtain of Light* for percussion and tape.

soutenu (Fr.), sustained, smoothly flowing (the French equivalent of ➤*sostenuto*).

South Pacific, musical play with text by Oscar Hammerstein II and Joshua Logan adapted from *Tales of the South Pacific* by James Michener; music by Richard Rodgers. Produced in New York, 1949. Racial prejudice is overcome by island romance, with US Navy involved.

Souzay, Gérard [originally Gérard Marcel Tisserand] (b. 1928), French baritone, with European and American reputation in performances of French and German songs; also opera singer (Metropolitan, New York, 1965).

Sowerby, Leo (1895–1968), American organist, and composer of works for organ alone, and for organ with orchestra; also of two piano concertos, chamber music, etc.

Spanisches Liederbuch (Ger., 'Spanish Song-book'), Wolf's song-settings, 1890, of 44 Spanish poems in German translation.

Spanish Caprice, orchestral work by Rimsky-Korsakov. ➤*Capriccio espagnol*.

Spanish Hour, The, opera by Ravel. ➤*Heure espagnole*.

Spanish Rhapsody, orchestral work by Ravel. ➤*Rapsodie espagnole*.

Spanish Song-book, song-settings by Wolf. ➤*Spanisches Liederbuch*.

Spanish Symphony, orchestral work by Lalo. ➤*Symphonie espagnole*.

Spartacus [Rus. *Spartak*], ballet with music by Khachaturian, produced in Leningrad, 1966. Choreography by Leonid Yakobson, the hero being the leader of the historical slave revolt in ancient Rome.

species, name given to each of five types of academic 'strict ➤counterpoint', progressively more complex (called *first species*, *second species*, etc.).

spectral composition, ➤spectrum.

Spectre de la rose, Le, ➤*Aufforderung zum Tanz*; also title of a song by Berlioz in *Nuits d'été*.

Spectre's Bride, The, usual English title for *Svatebni košile* (Cz., 'The Wedding Shift'), cantatas written to a text of K. J. Erben by – (1) Dvořák, first performed (in English) in Birmingham, 1885; (2) Novák, 1913 (called by composer 'A symphony of horror').

spectrum, late-20th-century term (on the analogy of the optical spectrum) for the totality of perceptible frequencies within a defined sound. Hence, the *spectral analysis* of a defined sound to determine its component frequencies; *spectral composition*, a procedure (usually in ➤electro-acoustic music) in which the analysed components of a note are treated as raw material by the composer.

speech-song, ➤*Sprechgesang*.

Speer, Daniel (1636–1707), German musician, in municipal service at Göttingen as wind-player; composed songs (including collection of a whimsical nature), chamber music, etc.

Spelman, Timothy Mather (1891–1970), American composer who studied in Germany. Works include symphonic poem *Christ and the Blind Man*, a symphony, chamber music, piano works, many songs.

spianato (It.), smoothed out, smooth.

spiccato (It., separated), a certain method of playing rapid detached notes on the violin and related instruments, the bow rebounding off the strings.

Spider's Banquet, The, ballet score by Roussel. ➤*Festin de l'araignée*.

Spies, Claudio (b. 1925), Chilean-born composer, who studied in USA and was naturalized there in 1966. Works include *Ensembles* for orchestra, *Times 2* for two horns, *Viopiacem* for viola with harpsichord/piano; also vocal settings from the Bible, from St Francis of Assisi, etc.

spinet (1) wing-shaped keyboard instrument of harpsichord type, but more compact and of different shape – current in 16th–18th centuries, revived in the 20th for old music; (2) incorrect name for the 'square ➤piano'.

spinto (It.), pushed, urged on – especially in voice-classification; *lirico spinto*, a ➤lyric voice (tenor or soprano) which has been 'pushed' into more forceful singing.

spirito, spiritoso (It.), spirit, spirited.

spiritual, name given to a type of religious folk-song of the American blacks, usually of solo-and-refrain design. Authorities also use the term *white spirituals* for similar songs among certain whites in the Southern States.

Spofforth, Reginald (1770–1827), British organist and composer, especially of glees such as 'Hail, smiling morn'.

Spohr, Louis (1784–1859), German violinist, conductor and composer of 17 violin concertos (no. 8 'in the form of a song-scena'); also of operas (including a ➤*Faust*, before Gounod's), oratorios, symphonies, much chamber music (including four 'double string quartets' and a nonet), songs, including a set of six with clarinet and piano. Was one of the first orchestral conductors to use a baton – but his own autobiographical claim to have used one in London as early as 1820 is unsupported by evidence.

Spontini, Gaspare [Luigi Pacifico] (1774–1851), Italian composer, in the main of operas of a heroic and historical kind, such as *La Vestale*, composed for Paris where he had settled in 1803. As musical director to the court in Berlin, 1820–41, continued to compose operas (e.g. *Agnes von Hohenstaufen*, in German) and made notable reputation as opera conductor. Became deaf, 1848; died at his birthplace, near Ancona.

Sprechgesang (Ger., 'speech-song'), type of vocal utterance midway between speech and song, originated by Schoenberg and used in ➤*Gurrelieder*, ➤*Pierrot Lunaire* and later works; the voice touches the note (usually notated in a special way, e.g. ♩) but does not sustain it. A voice-part employing *Sprechgesang* is designated *Sprechstimme*.

springar (Norw.), Norwegian folkdance in 3/4 time, cultivated e.g. by Grieg and Svendsen.

springer, a musical ornament (used e.g. by Chopin) in which an extra note, notated in smaller type, robs the preceding note of part of its time-value. Thus: [musical notation] played [musical notation] The German equivalent is *Nachschlag* (literally 'afterstroke').

'Spring' Sonata, nickname (not the composer's) for Beethoven's notably cheerful Sonata in F for violin and piano, op. 24 (1801).

Spring Song, ➤*Lieder ohne Worte*.

'Spring' Symphony (1) nickname, authorized by the composer, for Schumann's Symphony no. 1 in B♭, 1841; (2) title of a work by Britten, 1949, for three solo singers, mixed chorus, boys' chorus and orchestra (on poems on or near the subject of spring). The final section introduces the tune and words of ➤*Sumer is icumen in*.

square piano, ➤piano.

Staats, Leo (1877–1952), French choreographer. ➤*Festin de l'araignée*.

Staatsoper (Ger.), State Opera (house or company).

Stabat Mater, a devotional poem in medieval Latin about the vigil of Mary by the Cross; used as an authorized hymn (➤sequence, 2) in the Roman Catholic Church since 1727, and even before then set by Josquin, Palestrina and other composers. There are also later settings, e.g. by Szymanowski – as well as a traditional plainsong melody.

stabile (It.), stable, firm; term used of an orchestra to denote 'permanent', 'regular', 'resident', etc.

staccato (It., detached), a method of performance denoted by a dot over the note, and signifying that the note is to be made short – and thus detached from its successor – by being held for less than its full length; so the superlative *staccatissimo*.

Stadler, Anton (1753–1812), Austrian clarinettist and basset-horn player, for whom Mozart wrote the Clarinet Quintet and Clarinet Concerto. He invented a specially extended clarinet capable of reaching lower notes: modern reproductions of it have taken the name ➤basset-clarinet.

Städtische Oper (Ger.), Municipal Opera (house or company).

staff, the framework of lines and spaces on which music is ordinarily written; so *treble staff*, *bass staff*, the five-line framework respectively carrying the treble and bass clefs. So also *staff notation*, ordinary notation as distinct e.g. from ➤tonic sol-fa notation; *Great Staff*, fictitious academic construction of 11 lines to include both the treble staff and bass staff with middle C in between. (An alternative name is *stave*, and the plural is always *staves*.)

Stainer, John (1840–1901), British organist, editor of old music, professor at Oxford, writer on music, and composer of oratorio *The* ➤*Crucifixion* and of church music in mid-Victorian English idiom. Knighted, 1888.

Stamic, ➤Stamitz.

Stamitz, German form of Czech surname Stamic, adopted by a Czech family of musicians whose chief members were (1) Jan Václav Stamic (or Johann Wenzel Stamitz) (1717–57), violinist and composer of violin concertos, symphonies, harpsichord sonatas, etc., who became musical director at the court of Mannheim, 1745, and is regarded as the founder of the ➤Mannheim school; (2) his son Karel Stamic (or Karl Stamitz) (1745–1801), violinist and composer of symphonies, operas, etc.

Ständchen (Ger.), ➤serenade.

Stanford, Charles Villiers (1852–1924), Irish composer, also organist, conductor, professor at Cambridge, teacher at RCM. Works include seven operas (including *Shamus O'Brien*, *The Critic*, *The Travelling Companion*); seven symphonies (no. 3, 'Irish') and five orchestral *Irish Rhapsodies*; *The Revenge* and other cantatas; church music; many songs, including Irish folk-song settings. Knighted, 1901.

Stanley, [Charles] **John** (1712–86), British composer and noted organist, though blind from the age of two. Wrote organ music, concertos for strings, various vocal settings, etc.

Starer, Robert (b. 1924), Austrian composer, also pianist, who emigrated to Palestine and since 1949 has worked in USA. Compositions include several to Hebrew texts; violin concerto (for Itzhak Perlman), Serenade for trombone, vibraphone and strings.

stark (Ger.), loud, strong.

Starker, János (b. 1924), Hungarian cellist who settled in USA (naturalized, 1954); he achieved high distinction as soloist, teacher and musical editor.

Starlight Express (1, correctly *The Starlight Express*), play by Violet Pearn, produced 1915, to which Elgar wrote incidental music; (2) musical with text by Richard Stilgoe, music by Andrew Lloyd Webber. Produced in London, 1984. Story of railway locomotives and carriages, with powerful diesel-driven Greaseball cheating in a race.

Starokadomsky, Mikhail (1901–54), Russian composer of an organ concerto (rare in Soviet music), Concerto for orchestra, string quartets, operettas, etc.

Star-Spangled Banner, The, the national anthem of the USA, not officially adopted until 1931, although the words were written in 1814 to the tune composed earlier by John Stafford ➤Smith.

stave, ➤staff.

steel band, ensemble of a type developed in the West Indies from the 1940s, the instruments ('pans') made from the tops of oil drums, which are hammered into segments to sound at various pitches.

steel guitar (or Hawaiian guitar), instrument of guitar-like shape but held horizontally, the strings not 'stopped' with the fingers but with a small metal bar (called a 'steel') forming a movable ►nut going right across all the strings. The particular intervals of the tuning can therefore be reproduced at any pitch by sliding the steel, making possible the sliding thirds characteristic of the instrument (e.g. in commercialized 'Hawaiian'-style dance music, popular before World War II). Modern examples are often electronic and placed on a stand, further reducing kinship to the traditional guitar.

Stefano, Giuseppe di (b. 1921), Italian tenor, prominent at La Scala, Milan (from 1947) and elsewhere; he partnered Callas on her final recital tour, 1973–4.

Steffani, Agostino (1654–1728), Italian composer, also priest and diplomat; became court musical director in Hanover (Handel afterwards succeeding him). Wrote notable vocal duets, some in his Italian operas; also church music, chamber music, etc. Died in Frankfurt on a diplomatic visit.

Steg (Ger.), bridge (of a stringed instrument); *am Steg*, on the bridge; ►*ponticello*.

Steibelt, Daniel (1765–1823), German pianist, composer (much piano music, also operas, etc.), and fashionable teacher in Paris and London. In 1808 he took a court musical post in Russia, where he died.

Stein, Gertrude (1874–1946), American writer. ►*Four Saints in Three Acts*; ►Berners, ►Thomson (V.).

Steinberg, Maximilian [Osseyevich] (1883–1946), Russian composer, pupil and son-in-law of Rimsky-Korsakov, director of the Leningrad Conservatory where his students included Shostakovich. Works include five symphonies – no. 4 called *Turksib* (Turkestan–Siberia Railway), ballet music, string quartets, etc.

Steinberg, William (originally Hans Wilhelm) (1899–1978), German-born conductor who after a period in Palestine settled in USA, became musical director of the London Philharmonic Orchestra, 1958–60; 1969–72, of Boston Symphony Orchestra.

Steinspiel, ►stone chimes.

Stendhal [pseudonym of Marie Henri Beyle] (1783–1842), French novelist. ►Prey (Claude).

Stenhammar, Vilhelm Eugen (1871–1927), Swedish composer, also concert and operatic conductor in Stockholm and Gothenburg. His works include two operas, two symphonies, two piano concertos, six string quartets.

Stenz, Markus (b. 1965), German conductor noted in other modern music; since 1994–8 principal conductor of London Sinfonietta. Also guest conductor of English National Opera (1995), etc.

Stern, Isaac (b. 1920), Russian-born American violinist, brought to USA in infancy, making his recital début in San Francisco in 1935. He has toured widely, achieving the highest distinction. Gave first performance of concertos by Rochberg (1975), Dutilleux (1985) and P. M. Davies (1986). In 1960 his was the initiative that saved Carnegie Hall, New York, from demolition. Formed notable chamber-music trio with Istomin and Rose, 1960–84.

stessa, stesso (It.), same.

Stevens, Wallace (1879–1955), American poet. ➤Wuorinen.

Stevenson, Ronald (b. 1928), British composer and pianist whose work makes use of Scottish literary and musical sources; also writer on music. Compositions for piano include Prelude, Fugue and Fantasy for piano after Busoni's *Doktor Faust*, and *Passacaglia on DSCH* – representing Dmitri Shostakovich's name in German spelling. Other works include *Voces Vagabundae* (Lat., 'Wandering Voices') for string quartet; song-settings of Chaucer, Tennyson, Joyce and others.

stile rappresentativo (It.), a 'style aimed at representation, theatrical style' – term used by early 17th-century Italian composers of opera and oratorio, alluding to the theatre and to their newly invented device of ➤recitative, based on the natural spoken inflexions of the voice.

Still, William Grant (1895–1978), American composer, reputedly the first black musician to compose a symphony (1931) and to conduct a major symphony orchestra. Works include *Afro-American Symphony*, *Lenox Avenue* (for speaker, chorus and orchestra, later as ballet) alluding to Harlem; opera *Troubled Island*.

Stimme (Ger., pl. *-en*), voice, instrumental ➤part; etc. So *Stimmführung*, ➤part-writing.

Stimmung (Ger.), (1) tuning; (2) atmosphere (in sense of 'prevailing mood'); (3) work by Stockhausen (1968), presumably drawing on both these senses, for six singers unaccompanied who vocalize without words.

stochastic (from Gk.), governed by the mathematical laws of probability – term applied by ➤Xenakis to procedures whereby, having determined a total massive sound, a composer makes a mathematical calculation (worked out by himself or by computer) to decide the distribution of its component sounds among the participating forces. This is Xenakis's own procedure in *Metastaseis* and other works for large numbers of individual players.

Stockhausen, Karlheinz (b. 1928), German composer, pupil of F. Martin and (in Paris) of Messiaen. Innovative and influential in concepts of form, range of sound, use of electronics: he was the first composer to have an electronic 'score' (or rather diagram) published, 1956 (➤*Gesang*; ➤moment). Exploited spatial possibilities and a measure of free choice by performers – e.g. in *Gruppen* ('Groups') for three orchestras (and three conductors); ➤*Zyklus* ('Cycle') for one percussion-player who may begin on any page. Other works include ➤*Stimmung* for vocal ensemble; cycle of operas (in progress) entitled *Licht* (Ger., 'Light'), each part being named after a day, e.g. *Donnerstag* (Thursday); *Kurzwellen* ('Short Waves') for electronics and four radio sets; *Mantra* for two pianos, wood-block and two ring-modulators.

Stokowski, Leopold (1882–1977), British-born conductor (surname *not* originally Stokes; father Polish), naturalized American, 1915. Won huge following, not only through highly visual magnetism (dispensing with baton), especially as conductor of Philadelphia Orchestra, 1912–36. Gave more than 2,000 first performances (or first American performances) of works ranging from Mahler and Rakhmaninov to Ives and Varèse.

One of the first conductors to take positive role in recording studio. Appeared in Disney's *Fantasia* and other films; transcribed for orchestra Bach's organ Toccata and Fugue in D minor and other works. Continued to record until the year of his death (in Britain, where he had come to live) at the age of 95.

Stolz, Robert (1880–1975), Austrian composer and conductor who lived in USA, 1940–46; wrote over 50 operettas including *Wenn die kleinen Veilchen Blühen* ('Wild Violets'); part-composer of *Im weissen Rössl* ('White Horse Inn'). Active as conductor into his nineties.

stone chimes (Ger., *Steinspiel*, i.e. 'stone-play' on the analogy of *glockenspiel*), percussion instrument prescribed by (and specially made for) Orff's operas *Antigone* and *Oedipus der Tyrann*, etc.; it has a short, keyboard-like arrangement of different-sized stone bars, struck by beaters held in the hand.

Stone Guest, The (Rus., *Kamenny Gost*), opera by Dargomizhsky, begun in 1866, left not quite finished at his death; completed by Cui, orchestrated by Rimsky-Korsakov, and produced in St Petersburg, 1872. It is a setting of Pushkin's play, on the same story as ➤*Don Giovanni*.

stop (noun), (1) a row of pipes on an organ all put in or out of operation by one lever; or the lever itself; (2) by analogy, the mechanism used in the harpsichord for similar purpose – e.g. *sixteen-foot stop* (➤foot) for adding tone an octave lower, *harp stop* for simulating harp tone.

stop (verb), (1, stringed instruments) to place the finger on a string, thus deter-

mining the length of the portion of the string which is to vibrate; so *double-stopping*, *triple-stopping*, this action on 2–3 strings at once. The opposite of a *stopped string* is an 'open string', i.e. one vibrating its full length without being shortened by the placing of a finger. Note that the phrase *double-stopping* is loosely used for 'playing on two strings', whether or not both strings are actually stopped or open (and *triple-stopping* similarly); (2, horn-playing) to insert the hand into the bell of the instrument, altering the pitch and tone-quality of the note; (3, acoustics, organ-building, etc.) to block the passage of air through one end of a pipe (thus creating a *stopped pipe* or *end-stopped pipe* as distinct from an 'open pipe'), producing a note an octave lower than would otherwise sound.

Storace, Stephen (1762–96), British composer whose training in Italy served him in Italian and English operas, including *Gli equivoci* ('The Errors', based on Shakespeare's *The Comedy of Errors*) and *No Song, No Supper*. Also wrote chamber music, etc. Friend and presumed pupil of Mozart in Vienna.

Stothart, Herbert (1885–1949), composer for the musical theatre, collaborating with Friml in *Rose Marie*.

Strad, colloquial name for an instrument made by the ➤Stradivari family.

Stradella, Alessandro (1644–82), Italian composer of operas and cantatas with notable choral writing; also of church music, sinfonias for strings, etc. Was murdered, for reasons unknown – fictionally treated in Flotow's opera of 1844, *Alessandro Stradella*.

Stradivari, Stradivarius, Italian and Latinized names of a family of Italian violin-makers at Cremona – principally Antonio Stradivari (1644–1737).

strascinando (It.), dragging – direction referring not so much to tempo as to one note's 'dragging' the next behind it, e.g. in singing ➤*portamento.*

Stratas, Teresa (originally Anastasi Stratakis) (b. 1938), Canadian soprano of Greek descent; well known in opera (Covert Garden début 1961), she sang the title-role in Berg's *Lulu* in Paris when it belatedly received its first full-length performance, 1979.

Strathclyde Concertos, a series of ten concertos for various instruments, commissioned from P. M. Davies for the Scottish Chamber Orchestra (resident in Glasgow, in the region of Strathclyde); nine completed by 1995.

Straus, Oscar (not 'Strauss'; 1870–1954), Austrian composer (originally surnamed Strauss; from which he dropped an 'S' to separate himself from the other composers). Wrote Viennese operettas including *Der* ➤*tapfere Soldat* ('The Chocolate Soldier') and *Ein* ➤*Walzertraum.* Also conductor into his eighties. Naturalized French, 1939.

Strauss, surname of a family of Austrian musicians – Johann the elder, Johann the younger, Josef and Eduard (separately below); also of Richard Strauss (below), no relation.

Strauss, Eduard (1835–1916), Austrian composer of dance music, etc., and conductor; son of Johann Strauss the elder.

Strauss, Johann (the elder; 1804–49), Austrian violinist, conductor and composer who toured much – was in Britain in 1838 for celebrations of Victória's coronation. Wrote waltzes, polkas, etc., and the celebrated ➤*Radetzky March.* Father of Eduard Strauss (above) and Johann and Josef Strauss (below).

Strauss, Johann (the younger; 1825–99), Austrian violinist, conductor, and composer of *The* ➤*Blue Danube* and other enormously successful waltzes in noticeably artistic style – including ➤*Rosen aus dem Süden,* and ➤*Geschichten aus dem Wienerwald,* called 'the Waltz King'. Wrote also polkas including *Tritsch-Tratsch* and other dances; and 16 operettas including *Die* ➤*Fledermaus* and *Der* ➤*Zigeunerbaron.* Other operettas, e.g. ➤*Wiener Blut,* have been made by others from his music. Toured much (London, 1869; USA, 1872). Son of Johann Strauss (above). Collaborated in a few works with his brother Josef Strauss.

Strauss, Josef (1827–70), Austrian composer of *Dorfschwalben aus Oesterreich* ('Village Swallows from Austria'), *Sphärenklänge* ('Music of the Spheres') etc. and other waltzes; also other orchestral dance-music, piano pieces, etc. Collaborated with his brother Johann in a *Pizzicato Polka* and two other works.

Strauss, Richard [Georg] (1864–1949), German composer, the most celebrated of his generation; also conductor; no relation to the other Strausses. Born in Munich, later settling in Garmisch (also in Bavaria) where he died. After early work in traditional forms, took up and developed the ➤symphonic poem – ➤*Mac-*

beth, ➤*Don Juan*, ➤*Tod und Ver-klärung*, ➤*Till Eulenspiegel*, ➤*Also sprach Zarathustra* ('Thus Spake Zarathustra'), ➤*Don Quixote*, *Ein* ➤*Heldenleben*. Also of the character of symphonic poems are his ➤*Symphonia Domestica* (with its ➤parergon) and *Eine* ➤*Alpensinfonie* (1915, his last work of this illustrative type). Collaborated with the writer Hugo von Hofmannsthal in operas ➤*Salome*, ➤*Elektra*, *Der* ➤*Rosenkavalier* (all sensationally successful) and later in ➤*Ariadne auf Naxos*, *Die* ➤*Frau ohne Schatten*, *Die Aegyptische Helena*, ➤*Arabella*; other operas include ➤*Intermezzo*, ➤*Capriccio*. Wrote also ballet *Josephslegende*, incidental music to Molière's *Le* ➤*Bourgeois gentilhomme*; two horn concertos, symphony for wind; ➤*Metamorphosen* for strings; many songs, several with his own orchestral accompaniments (among them ➤*Vier letzte Lieder*). The degree of culpability in his relations with the Nazis is disputed.

Stravinsky, Igor [Fedorovich] (1882–1971), Russian-born composer, a prodigiously successful figure of 20th-century music in many genres; also pianist, conductor, and author of autobiographical and other writings. Pupil of Rimsky-Korsakov; left Russia in 1914; lived mainly in Paris, naturalized French, 1934; settled in USA, 1939, naturalized there, 1945. Won initial fame with pre-1914 ballets *The* ➤*Firebird*, ➤*Petrushka* and (using enormous orchestra and 'savage' dynamic elements), *The* ➤*Rite of Spring*. Later developed ➤neo-classical tendency (compact forms, small forces, avoidance of 'emotion'). Showed interest in ➤ragtime and jazz (e.g. in *L'*➤*Histoire du Soldat*); based ballet

➤*Pulcinella* on music supposedly by Pergolesi; adopted a deliberate back-to-Mozart style in opera *The* ➤*Rake's Progress* (1951). Other works include ➤*Symphony of Psalms* (with chorus), ➤*Dumbarton Oaks Concerto*, ➤*Ebony Concerto* (for dance band); hybrid stage pieces ➤*Oedipus Rex* and ➤*Persé-phone*; ➤*Ode* in memory of Natalie Koussevitzky; ballets ➤*Apollo Mus-agetes*, ➤*Orpheus*, ➤*Agon*; Mass. Long adhered to tonality, but from the choral-and-orchestral *Canticum sacrum* ('Holy Canticle', in Latin, for St Mark's, Venice), 1955, he adopted a 12-note technique indebted to Webern's. Late works included ➤*Movements* for piano and orchestra; ➤*Threni*; *The* ➤*Flood*; *Sacred Ballad* (in Hebrew, based on the biblical story of Abraham and Isaac) for baritone and small orchestra; *Elegy for J. F. K[ennedy]* on text by Auden, for baritone, two clarinets and basset-horn.

street piano, type of instrument used by itinerant musicians, being basically a mechanical form of piano: a selection of tunes is available, played by the turning of a handle which operates a barrel-and-pin mechanism similar to that of a musical box. An alternative name (because the turning of the handle is similar to that of a ➤barrel-organ) is 'piano-organ'.

Street Scene, opera by Weill, with libretto (based on his own book) by Elmer Rice; lyrics by Langston Hughes; produced in New York, 1947. A multiracial tenement block in New York is the scene of hope, despair, marital infidelity and murder.

stretta (It., drawn together; fem. form of following), term used in some Italian operatic scores for the section towards the end of a long ensemble when a quicker tempo succeeds a slower one.

stretto (It., drawn together), (1) direction that the pace is to become faster; (2) term used of the overlapping of entries in certain examples of ➤fugue or similar composition, the subject beginning in one voice before the preceding voice has finished uttering it. A *stretto maestrale* (magisterial) occurs when the full length of the subject, and not just the first part of it, is subjected to overlapping.

strict counterpoint, ➤counterpoint.

Strindberg, August (1849–1912), Swedish writer. ➤Alwyn, ➤Bogusławski, ➤Lidholm, ➤Rangström, ➤Reimann, ➤Rorem, ➤Weisgall.

string(s), name given to the thin strands of wire or gut which are set in vibration, e.g. on the piano (by hammers), violin (by the bow), harp and guitar (by plucking); hence the word *strings* is used for 'stringed instruments'. But in normal use *the strings* or *the string section* of an orchestra means only the violins (divided into first and second), violas, cellos and double-basses – not the harp and piano which, if used, are classified separately. Similarly a *string orchestra* normally implies violins (first and second), violas, cellos and double-basses only. The standard *string quartet* is two violins, viola, cello; *string trio*, violin, viola, cello.

stringendo (It., tightening), direction to a performer to increase the 'tension' of the music – in effect, to increase speed, often as preparation for a new section of basically faster tempo than the old one.

stromento, ➤*strumento*.

strophic, term used of a song in which the same music is repeated (exactly or almost exactly) for each successive stanza of a poem. The opposite type, in which the music progresses continually, has usually been called in English a 'through-composed song' (from Ger., *durchkomponiert*); it would be less ugly and less awkward to say 'non-strophic' or 'non-repeating'.

Strozzi, Barbara (1619–64 or later), Italian singer and composer active in Venice, who composed madrigals, cantatas, etc. She was the adopted daughter of the poet Giulio Strozzi and the pupil of Cavalli.

strumento (It., pl. *-i*), instrument. The old form *stromento* is also encountered.

Stuart, Leslie [originally Thomas Augustine Barrett] (1864–1928), British composer (also organist) chiefly successful in the musical comedy ➤*Florodora*; also wrote 'Lily of Laguna' and other popular songs.

Student Prince, The, musical play with text by Dorothy Donnelly based on *Old Heidelberg* by Rudolf Bleichman, a version of *Alt Heidelberg* by Wilhelm Meyer-Forster; music by Sigmund Romberg. Produced in New York, 1924. The hero gives up the love of his student days (with her agreement) for reasons of state.

Studer, Cheryl (b. 1955), American soprano who also studied piano and viola; made early operatic career in Germany. First sang at Bayreuth in 1985, having appeared with Chicago Opera (Micaela in *Carmen*), in 1984. Also noted in R. Strauss operas at Vienna, Berlin, etc.

study, an instrumental piece (usually solo) written to train or demonstrate the facility of the performer in certain points of technique – but sometimes having artistic value as well, e.g. the three sets (27 in all) by Chopin for piano. (The word translates the French *étude*, which is also, needlessly, used in English.) ➤symphonic study.

Sturm, Der, *The* ➤*Tempest* (play by Shakespeare).

style, term used in different senses to differentiate the usages of a period, nationality or individual, in composition or performance. So *Monteverdi's style*, the *classical style* (often implying the Haydn–Mozart period), a *bravura style* (of performance). So also *style modulation*, name applied to a composer's deliberate, temporary adoption of another composer's work or manner.

su (It.), on; *sul, sulla*, on the; *sul G*, on the G-string; *sul ponticello* (on, i.e. near, the bridge), *sul tasto* or *sulla tastiera* (on the fingerboard) – special methods of bowing the violin and related instruments.

subdominant, name for the fourth degree of the scale, e.g. F in key C (major or minor). It is so called because it dominates the scale to an extent subordinate to the ➤dominant or fifth degree.

subito (It.), immediately; *attacca subito*, go on (to the next section) without a break.

subject, term used in musical analysis to define a group of notes which appears to form a basic element in a composition and which is given prominence by its position, by being re-

peated or developed, etc. In ➤sonata-form the main musical ideas (usually two) announced in the 'exposition' and then developed are called subjects; in ➤fugue the term is more narrowly restricted.

submediant, the sixth degree of the scale, e.g. A in the key of C major, A♭ in the key of C minor. So called because it is halfway between the keynote and the subdominant (working downwards), whereas the ➤mediant (third degree of the scale) is halfway between the keynote and the dominant (working upwards).

Subotnick, Morton (b. 1933), American composer, active in electronic music (his *Silver Apples of the Moon*, 1967, is thought to be the first electronic work composed for issue as a recording). Has also written a series of works (for different performing groups) each called *Play!*; a *Ritual Game Room* with tape, lights, dancer, four game-players and no audience, etc.

Suchoň, Eugen (1908–93), Slovak composer of operas *The Whirlpool* and *Svätopluk*; cantata *Psalm of the Carpathian Land*; *Pictures of Slovakia* for piano, etc.

suite (Fr., a sequence), the most common name for an instrumental piece in several movements, usually (in older use) a sequence of dances. Its characteristic in the 17th and 18th centuries was the inclusion of the dance-forms 'allemande', 'courante', 'sarabande', and 'gigue' (these French names were widely used) with optional additions. With the later rise of the ➤sonata, the suite has lost a strict specification, and in the 19th and 20th centuries has often been used for a work rather lighter or more loosely connected than a work of sonata type: it may describe a set of movements assembled from an opera or ballet score, etc. Its use by ➤Shostakovich for a sequence of songs is exceptional.

Suk, Josef (1874–1935), Bohemian composer – also violinist, for 40 years in the Bohemian String Quartet. Pupil and son-in-law of Dvořák; his music carries on Dvořák's ideas with some modernization. Works (nearly all instrumental) include symphony *Asrael*; *Prague* and other symphonic poems; cycle of piano pieces *Things Lived and Dreamed* (Cz., *Životem snem*) and other piano works.

Suk, Josef (b. 1929), Czech violinist, grandson of the preceding. Made his British début (at the Proms) in 1964, and performed in trio with Katchen and Starker, 1967–9.

sul, sulla, ➤*su*.

Sullivan, Arthur [Seymour] (1842–1900), British composer, the most prominent of the Victorian age; also conductor. Studied in Leipzig. Wrote music of many types, including symphony, *Overtura di ballo* (➤*ballo*), religious cantatas such as *The Golden Legend*, opera ➤*Ivanhoe* – but made his lasting reputation in a long series of successful operettas. Those written with W. S. Gilbert as librettist are *Thespis* (lost, unpublished), ➤*Trial By Jury, The* ➤*Sorcerer*, ➤*HMS Pinafore, The* ➤*Pirates of Penzance*, ➤*Patience*, ➤*Iolanthe*, ➤*Princess Ida, The* ➤*Mikado*, ➤*Ruddigore, The* ➤*Yeomen of the Guard, The* ➤*Gondoliers* and, finally and unsuccessfully, ➤*Utopia Limited* and *The* ➤*Grand Duke*. Operettas without Gilbert include ➤*Cox and Box* and (unfinished) *The*

Emerald Isle, completed by German. Wrote also ballet scores including *Victoria and Merrie England*; songs of almost Schubertian kind such as 'Orpheus with his Lute' as well as popular ballads ('The Lost Chord') and many hymn-tunes ('Onward Christian Soldiers'). Knighted, 1883. A compilation from his scores is ➤*Pineapple Poll*.

Sumer is icumen in, English mid-13th-century work, the oldest known canon and the oldest-known six-➤part composition. It has alternative words in Latin for church use. Known also as the 'Reading ➤Rota' because its conjectural composer was John of Fornsete, monk of Reading Abbey. It is quoted in Britten's ➤*Spring Symphony*.

summational tone, ➤resultant tone.

Suor Angelica (It., 'Sister Angelica'), one-act opera by Puccini, produced in New York, 1918, along with two others – *Il* ➤*tabarro* preceding it and ➤*Gianni Schicchi* following, making a *trittico* (It., 'triptych'). Libretto by G. Forzano: Sister Angelica is a nun and the setting is a convent.

supertonic, the second degree of the scale, e.g. the note D in the key C (major or minor) – lying immediately above the ➤tonic (first degree).

Supervia, Conchita (1895–1936), Spanish mezzo-soprano; at 15 she sang Octavian in the first Rome performance of *Der Rosenkavalier*, but won chief fame in the mid-1920s for the coloratura roles, e.g. of *L'Italiana in Algeri* and *La Cenerentola*. Sang at Covent Garden 1934–5; died aged 41 after childbirth.

Suppé, Franz von (Germanized form

of name used by Francesco Ermenegildo Ezechiele Suppé-Demelli) (1819–95), Austrian (Dalmatian-born) composer of Belgian descent. Wrote succession of popular operettas including *Die schöne Galathee* ('The Beautiful Galatea') and ➤*Boccaccio*; overtures to plays including *Dichter und Bauer* ('Poet and Peasant'), a Mass, etc.

sur (Fr.), on; *sur la touche, sur le chevalet*, on the fingerboard, on (i.e. near) the bridge – special methods of bowing a violin and related instruments.

Surinach, Carlos (b. 1915), Spanish-born composer, naturalized American 1959; also concert and operatic conductor. Works include a *Sinfonietta flamenca*, violin concerto, ballets including *The Owl and the Pussycat* (after Edward Lear, with choreography by Martha Graham).

'Surprise' Symphony, nickname for Haydn's Symphony no. 94 in G (Hob. I: 94), composed in 1791 – so called because of the sudden loud chord in the slow movement.

Survivor from Warsaw, A, work by Schoenberg (first performed in 1948) for speaker, men's chorus and orchestra; text by the composer (in English, apart from German interpolations and a Hebrew prayer) alluding to the Nazis' murder of Jews.

Susanna, oratorio by Handel, first performed in 1749; text after the Apocrypha by author now unknown.

Susanna's Secret, opera by Wolf-Ferrari. ➤*Segreto di Susanna*.

Susannah, opera by Floyd, produced in Tallahassee, Florida, 1955. Libretto by composer based on the tale (of hypocritical moral accusation) of Susannah and the Elders in the Apocrypha but transferred to a Tennessee mountain valley.

Susato, Tielman (*?–c*. 1561), German music publisher and composer; from 1529 town trumpeter in Antwerp, where he died. Composed songs, dances, etc.

suspension, a device in harmony by which a note in a chord is kept sounding when that chord has been succeeded by another in which the prolonged note forms a discord. This discord is then normally resolved when the prolonged note falls to a note forming part of the new chord. If it rises instead of falling, then the process is in some textbooks called 'retardation', presumably on the pedantic ground that a thing 'suspended' must fall. The reverse process to both of these, when the note precedes the chord of which it forms a part, is called ➤anticipation.

Süssmayr, Franz Xaver (1766–1803), Austrian composer of operas, church music, etc., and conductor. A pupil of Mozart, he made a completion (usually but not invariably followed in modern performances) of the Requiem which Mozart left unfinished at his death.

sustaining pedal, ➤piano (2).

Sutermeister, Heinrich [Paul] (1910–95), Swiss composer of operas, including *Romeo und Julia*, *Die Zauberinsel* ('The Magic Island') after Shakespeare's *The Tempest*, and *Raskolnikov* (after Dostoyevsky's *Crime and Punishment*); also three piano concertos, a two-piano concerto, etc.

Sutherland, Joan (b. 1926), Australian soprano; joined Covent Garden Opera Company, 1952; attained international celebrity in Donizetti's *Lucia* *di Lammermoor* (Covent Garden, 1959) and continued to enjoy operatic prominence into her mid-60s. Created Dame, 1979; retired in 1990. Married to Richard ➤Bonynge.

Suzuki, Shin'ichi (1898–1998), Japanese violinist who evolved a technique of teaching very young children the violin (and other instruments) which won worldwide success from the 1950s.

Švanda the Bagpiper (Cz., *Švanda dudák*), opera by Weinberger, produced in Prague, 1927. Libretto by M. Kares, on a Czech folk-tale of which Švanda is the hero. (The spelling 'Schwanda' is inappropriate in English, being only the German representation of the sound of the Czech name.)

Svendsen, Johan [Severin] (1840–1911), Norwegian composer, also conductor and pianist who studied in Leipzig. Composed four *Norwegian Rhapsodies* and other works of Norwegian associations; *Carnival in Paris* for orchestra: four symphonies, chamber music, etc.

Sviridov, Georgy [Vasilyevich] (b. 1915), Russian composer of many songs (some translated into Russian from Shakespeare and Burns), *Miniature Triptych* for orchestra, *Pathetic Oratorio*, etc.

swanee whistle, crude woodwind instrument, mainly used as a toy; at one end is a recorder-type mouthpiece, at the other a slide which is worked backwards and forwards to vary the length of the tube and so produce different notes. Continued accuracy of pitch is almost impossible and a sliding effect is characteristic; but it has been occasionally used in the orchestra –

e.g. in Ravel's opera *L'*➤*Enfant et les sortilèges*.

Swan Lake (Rus., *Lebedino ozero*), ballet with music by Tchaikovsky, produced in St Petersburg, 1895. The original choreography by V. Reisinger was replaced by that of Petipa and Ivanov. The swans are maidens transformed by a wicked magician.

Swann, Donald [Ibrahim] (1923–94), British pianist, singer and composer noted for his comic duo with the writer-performer Michael Flanders (1922–75).

Swan of Tuonela, The, 'symphonic legend' by Sibelius, 1893 – originally written as a prelude to an opera, but published as one of four pieces on Finnish legendary subjects (➤*Lemminkäinen's Homecoming*). Tuonela is the land of death surrounded by waters on which the swan floats, singing.

Swan Song, ➤*Schwanengesang*.

Swayne, Giles (b. 1946), British composer. Works include *Cry* (75 minutes, wordless) for 28 solo voices, amplified; *God-Song* for mezzo-soprano, flute, trombone, cello, piano, on text from the York Mystery Plays, and *The Song of Leviathan* for orchestra.

Swedish Rhapsody, ➤Alfvén.

Sweelinck, Jan Pieterszoon (1562–1621), Dutch composer – also organist and harpsichordist. Wrote organ works, notable for their development of the fugue, and for their pioneering of an independent part for the pedals; taught many German organist-composers. Wrote also various vocal Italian madrigals and other vocal works in French and Latin, including all the Psalms.

Sweeney Todd, the Demon Barber of Fleet Street, 'musical thriller' by Hugh Wheeler based on a play by Chris Bond. Music and lyrics by Stephen Sondheim. Produced in New York, 1979. The eponymous Todd is the Victorian horror-figure who slit the throats of his clients, their flesh being minced to make pies.

swell, a device for increasing and diminishing the volume of sound on an organ, or on certain 18th-century harpsichords. So ➤swell organ.

swell organ (or simply *swell*), name given to a section of the organ in which the pipes are set in an enclosed space; the player can consequently regulate the volume of sound through a pedal (*swell pedal*) which opens and closes a shutter. The manual controlling this (placed directly above the ➤Great) is called the *swell manual*. The *swell effect* (of being able to increase and decrease volume) can usually be obtained also on the 'Choir' and 'Solo' manuals of the modern organ.

Swift, Jonathan (1667–1745), English writer. ➤Kelley.

Swinburne, Algernon Charles (1837–1909), English poet. ➤*Choral symphony*.

Sylphides, Les, ballet with music arranged from piano works by Chopin; produced in Paris, 1909, with choreography by Fokin. Various orchestrations are used. (Title is merely French for 'The Sylphs'.)

Sylvia, ballet with music by Delibes, choreography by L. Mérante, produced in Paris, 1876; the heroine is a mythical huntress.

sympathetic, term used in allusion to the capacity of strings and other bodies to vibrate (and thus give a note) when this note is sounded near them by some other agent. So *sympathetic strings*, e.g. on the ➤viola d'amore, not touched by the bow but vibrating by their proximity to the bowed strings lying above them.

symphonia, Greek word taken into Latin and used in certain modern contexts as equivalent to 'symphony' – e.g. in R. Strauss's *Symphonia Domestica* ('Domestic Symphony'), 1904, describing with semi-realistic touches the composer's home life.

symphonic band, alternative (originally US) to 'concert band', intended to make a parallel with ➤symphony orchestra and to eliminate military and similar associations.

symphonic poem, term introduced by Liszt for an orchestral work which is approximately of the size and seriousness customarily associated with a symphony, but which is meant as an interpretation of something non-musical, e.g. a work of literature. A not quite satisfactory synonym is ➤tone-poem.

symphonic study, term not in standard use, but used by Elgar (as a variant of ➤*symphonic poem*) for his ➤*Falstaff*. Schumann's *Symphonic Studies* (1836, revised 1852) are a set of variations for piano solo. ➤study.

symphonie (Fr.), symphony – sometimes with a qualifying word (➤*symphonie concertante*; ➤*Symphonie espagnole*; ➤*Symphonie fantastique*).

symphonie concertante, the French equivalent (and the original form) of what is now more often called the *sinfonia concertante* (Ital.), i.e. a concerto-type work featuring more than one solo instrument, such as

Mozart's Sinfonia Concertante for violin and viola, K364.

Symphonie espagnole (Fr., 'Spanish Symphony'), work by Lalo for violin and orchestra – really a violin concerto in five movements – first performed in 1875 and written for the Spanish violinist Sarasate. Has themes of Spanish national character.

Symphonie fantastique (Fr., 'Fantastic Symphony'), symphony by Berlioz, 1830, subtitled 'Épisode de la vie d'un artiste' ('Episode in the life of an artist') – with a programmatic basis derived from Berlioz's own despairing love for the actress Harriet Smithson.

Symphonie sur un chant montagnard français (Fr., 'Symphony on a French Mountaineer's Song'), work for piano and orchestra by d'Indy, first performed in 1887.

symphony, term literally meaning 'a sounding-together', formerly indicating (1) an overture, e.g. to an opera; (2) the instrumental section introducing, or between the verses of, a vocal work. Occasionally such archaic meanings are revived, e.g. in Stravinsky's work entitled *Symphonies for Wind Instruments* (1920). But, in general, since the mid 18th century, the word has ordinarily indicated (3) an orchestral work of a serious nature and a substantial size, in the shape of a ➤sonata for orchestra. Most such works are in four movements; some are in three; some are in one ('telescoping' a larger number of movements together) or five: other numbers are very rare. Symphonies may have a name (e.g. Beethoven's ➤*Pastoral Symphony*), or may include vocal parts (since Beethoven's ➤*Choral Symphony*); but such remain the

minority. A *symphony orchestra* (or, in North America, just 'a symphony') is an orchestra large enough to play symphonies and having a repertory of 'serious' music; a *symphony concert* is one including a symphony or other work of similar type. ➤*Choral Symphony*.

Symphony of a Thousand, nickname for Mahler's Symphony no. 8, first performed in 1910 – because of the huge forces employed (large orchestra, an extra brass group, seven vocal soloists, boys' choir, two mixed choirs).

Symphony of Psalms, work for chorus and orchestra by Stravinsky, 1930, 'composed to the glory of God, dedicated to the Boston Symphony Orchestra'. In three movements; text from Psalms, in Latin.

Symphony on a French Mountaineer's Song, work for piano and orchestra by d'Indy. ➤*Symphonie sur un chant montagnard français*.

syncopation, a displacement of accent on to a beat that is normally unaccented.

Synge, John Millington (1871–1909), Irish poet and dramatist. ➤*Riders to the Sea*; ➤Klebe, ➤Rabaud.

synthesizer, general word for an electronic apparatus by which any one of a number of musical sounds can be put together (by analog or digital process) from its physical components (harmonic constituents, characteristics of attack and decay, etc.) at such a speed and with such convenience as to make possible the performance of a piece from a musical score; generally controlled from a piano-like keyboard.

system, a grouping of staves in a score (with a vertical left-hand line joining the staves) to show a group of instruments and/or voices performing together; thus, where a composer writes for four voices (each on a separate stave) on 12-stave printed paper, the page will accommodate three systems each of four lines.

Szabó, Ferenc (1902–69), Hungarian composer, resident in USSR 1932–45; works include political (Communist) cantatas, Sinfonietta and Moldavian Rhapsody for orchestra, etc.

Szell, Georg (originally György Széll) (1897–1970), Hungarian-born conductor who grew up in Vienna, naturalized American in 1946; won particular fame as conductor of the Cleveland Orchestra, 1946–70. ➤*From My Life.*

Szervánszky, Endre (1911–77), Hungarian composer, also critic and academic teacher. Works include serenade for clarinet and orchestra, flute concerto, pieces for two violins, Hungarian folk-song arrangements.

Szeryng, Henryk (1918–88), Polish-born violinist who settled in Mexico (naturalized, 1946); eminent in concertos, etc.; touring internationally from the mid-1950s.

Szigeti, Joseph (originally József) (1892–1973), Hungarian-born violinist, naturalized American in 1951; made London début in 1907 and pioneered many new works including (1938) E. Bloch's concerto.

Szokolay, Sándor (b. 1931), Hungarian composer of opera *Blood Wedding* (based on Lorca's play); *Déploration* (Fr., 'Lament'), in memory of Poulenc, for chorus and orchestra; a trumpet concerto, etc.

Szymanowski, Karol (1882–1937), Polish composer (also pianist) born in the Russian Ukraine. Works include operas *Hagith* and ➤*King Roger*; two violin concertos; three *Myths* for violin and piano (no. 1, 'The Fountain of Arethusa'); four symphonies; a ➤*Stabat Mater*; song-settings of James Joyce, Tagore and other poets. Died in a Swiss sanatorium.

T

t, symbol in ➤tonic sol-fa for the seventh degree (leading-note) of the scale, pronounced *te* (varied from ➤*si*, the Continental name for the note B).

Tabarro, Il (It., 'The Cloak'), one-act opera by Puccini, produced in New York, 1918, with the other two one-act operas (➤*Suor Angelica* and ➤ *Gianni Schicchi*) that follow it to form what Puccini called his *Trittico* (Triptych). It is under a cloak that a husband reveals to his wife the body of her lover whom he has killed.

tabla, the paired drums of North India, played with the fingers and other parts of the hand.

tablature, a system of writing down music by symbols which represent not the pitch (as in ordinary modern notation) but the position of the performer's fingers. Such a system was formerly used for the lute, and another one for keyboard (➤Scheidt). The diagrammatic notation used in popular music for guitar, ukelele, etc., is a tablature.

Tábor, ➤*My Country*.

tabor, small drum used e.g. to accompany folk-dancing – the player beating the drum with one hand while the other hand plays a three-holed pipe.

tacet (Lat., is silent), indication that a particular performer or instrument has no part for considerable time, e.g. for a whole movement.

Taddei, Giuseppe (b. 1916), Italian baritone; sang Scarpia in *Tosca* as his London début, 1947, and at the Vienna State Opera to celebrate his 70th birthday. Noted also in comic roles.

Tafelmusik (Ger., table-music), music suited to convivial gatherings, e.g. for performance at or after dinner: title of actual collections of such pieces by ➤Telemann.

Tagore, [Sir] Rabindranath (1861–1941), Indian poet. ➤Hageman, ➤Rota (N.), ➤Sohal, ➤Szymanowski.

Tahiti Trot, name given to Shostakovich's orchestration (1928) of the song 'Tea for Two' from ➤*No, No, Nanette* by Youmans.

Tailleferre, Germaine [Marcelle] (1892–1983), French composer (also pianist), the only female member of *Les* ➤*Six*. Works include a piano concerto, a harp concertino, *Hommage à Rameau* for percussion and two pianos; operas, ballets.

Takacs Quartet, string quartet of Hungarian origin, founded in 1975, resident since 1983 at the University of Colorado. Current members Edward

John Dusinberre, Karoly Schranz, Roger Tapping, András Fejér.

Takemitsu, Toru (1930–96), Japanese composer, mainly self-taught, very prolific. Works, often using idiosyncratic English titles, include *A flock descends into the pentagonal Garden* for orchestra, *A Way a Lone* for string quartet, *From me flows what you call Time* for percussion (➤Nexus) and orchestra; also *November Steps No. 1* for shakuhachi, biwa (Japanese instruments) and orchestra; electronic music; more than 100 scores for Japanese films.

Tal (originally Gruenthal), **Josef** (b. 1910), Polish-born Israeli composer who studied in Germany. Works on Hebrew texts include operas *Ashmedai* and *The Temptation*, cantata *Call of the Fallen Soldiers*; has also written six piano concertos (no. 4 with tape).

Talbot, Howard [original surname Munkittrick] (1865–1928), British composer (born in USA, but came to Britain as a child) whose musical comedies successfully produced in London included *A Chinese Honeymoon* (1899) and (with Monckton) *The* ➤*Arcadians*. Was also theatre conductor.

Tales from the Vienna Woods, waltz by J. Strauss the younger. ➤*Geschichten aus dem Wienerwald*.

Tales of Hoffmann, The, opera by Offenbach. ➤*Contes d'Hoffmann*.

Talich, Václav (1883–1961), Czechoslovak conductor, one of his country's most prominent musicians; a leading orchestral and operatic conductor in Prague.

Tallis, Thomas (*c.* 1505–85), English composer and organist; from 1572 joint organist with Byrd at the Chapel Royal, and from 1575 joint holder with Byrd of a State monopoly of music-printing in England. His contrapuntal ingenuity is shown in his Latin motet 'Spem in alium' in 40 parts, i.e. for eight choirs each of five voices. Wrote mainly church music, in Latin (➤*Cantiones Sacrae*) and then in English; also some pieces for keyboard, viols, etc. The so-called 'Tallis's Canon' is an adaptation from one of a set of psalm-tunes, 1567; Vaughan Williams's ➤*Fantasia on a Theme of Tallis* is based on another of the same set.

talon (Fr.), heel (of the bow of a stringed instrument), i.e. the end of the bow which is held by the player.

Talvela, Martti (1935–89), Finnish bass, prominent in opera – Bayreuth Festival, 1962; La Scala, Milan, from 1964. Appointed director of Finnish National Opera, but died before taking up the post.

Tamagno, Francesco (1850–1905), Italian tenor, noted in opera; chosen by Verdi to sing the title-role of ➤*Otello* at its première.

Tamberlik, Enrico (1820–89), Italian tenor for whom Verdi wrote the principal tenor role in *La* ➤*forza del destino*; prominent performer in Paris and London.

tambour (Fr.), drum; *tambour de Basque*, ➤tambourine; *tambour militaire*, ➤snare-drum.

tambourin (Fr., originally diminutive of *tambour*, drum), a dance-movement, e.g. in the works of Rameau, simulating the combination of a rustic drum-beat with a pipe-melody, a Provençal equivalent to the English pipe and ➤tabor.

tambourine, type of small drum struck with the fingers and rattled with the hand; it has little jingles inserted into its wooden frame. It is of Arab origin but was known in Europe before 1300; brought into the modern orchestra by Weber, Berlioz and later composers mainly to evoke revelry, gipsies, exotic scenes, etc.

tambura (also *tanbura, tanpura*), a long-necked Indian lute having four wire strings and no frets; plucked with the fingers, it is used only to provide a drone.

tamburo (It.), drum; *tamburo piccolo* (literally, little drum), ➤snare-drum.

Taming of the Shrew, The, title of operas (after Shakespeare's play) by several composers including Shebalin (Moscow, 1955) and Goetz: ➤*Widerspänstigen Zähmung*.

tam-tam, ➤gong. (Not the same as ➤tom-tom.)

Tancred, 12th-century Norman crusader; the story in Tasso's *Gerusalemme liberata* ('Jerusalem Liberated', 1581) of Tancred's love for a woman on the enemy side is the source of the following operas, and of Monteverdi's *Il* ➤*Combattimento di Tancredi e Clorinda*.

Tancrède, opera by Campra, produced in Paris, 1702, with a libretto by A. Danchet. ➤Tancred.

Tancredi, opera by Rossini, produced in Venice, 1813, with a libretto by R. Rossi. ➤Tancred.

Tan Dun (b. 1957), Chinese composer, the first such to show (c. 1980) alignment with Western avant-garde. Compositions include opera *Marco Polo, Death and Fire: Dialogue with Paul Klee* for orchestra and *In Distance* for piccolo, harp and bass drum, Symphony 1997 (Heaven, Earth, Mankind) to mark the handover of Hong Kong to China. Resident in USA.

Taneyev, Alexander Sergeyevich (1850–1918), Russian composer of operas, orchestral works, etc.; pupil of Rimsky-Korsakov.

Taneyev, Sergey Ivanovich (1856–1915), Russian pianist and composer of four symphonies, songs and choral works, etc.; pupil and friend of Tchaikovsky. Noted teacher.

tangent, the metal 'tongue' which, on the clavichord, touches a string when a key is struck and so sounds that string. It remains in contact with the string for as long as the note sounds, unlike the hammers of the piano. (From Lat. *tangere*, touch.)

tango, Argentinian dance supposed to have been imported by African slaves into the American continent; taken into general use in ballroom dancing about the time of World War I.

Tann, Hilary (b. 1947), British composer, resident in USA as college teacher; works include *The Open Field* for orchestra, *Look little low heavens* for unaccompanied trumpet, *Arachne* for unaccompanied soprano.

Tannhäuser und der Sängerkrieg auf der Wartburg (Ger., 'Tannhäuser and the Singing Contest on the Wartburg'), usually shortened to *Tannhäuser*, opera by Wagner, produced in Dresden, 1845. What is called the 'Paris version' refers to the revision made by Wagner for the Paris production of 1861. Libretto by composer: Tannhäuser is a medieval minstrel torn between 'sacred' and 'profane' love.

Tansman, Alexandre (1897–1986), Polish-born composer and pianist who settled in Paris 1919 and was naturalized French in 1938; in USA 1940–46. Works include seven symphonies, eight string quartets, operas, ballets, pieces for one and two pianos.

tanto (It.), so much; *allegro ma non tanto*, fast but not too fast.

Tantum ergo, name for part of a Latin hymn by St Thomas Aquinas, which is used in Roman Catholic services; it has its own plainsong melodies and has also been set afresh by various composers.

Tanz (Ger., pl. *Tänze*), dance.

tape, term which in musical references stands for electronic-recording audiotape, particularly where the composer has assembled sound-material (whether from 'natural' or electronic sources), and recorded it. The playback of this tape then constitutes the performance or is further modified ('live electronics') and may be combined with conventional vocal or instrumental performance. So music 'for piano and tape', etc.

Tapfere Soldat, Der (Ger., 'The Valiant Soldier'; known in English as *The Chocolate Soldier*), operetta by Oscar Straus with libretto by Rudolf Bernauer and Leopold Jacobson after George Bernard Shaw's *Arms and the Man*. Produced in Vienna, 1908. Swiss mercenary soldier escaping from duty (fighting the Bulgarians) arrives in the bedroom of a Bulgarian colonel's daughter.

Tapiola, symphonic poem by Sibelius,

1926 – named after Tapio, the forest god of Finnish mythology.

tarantella, fast Italian dance in 6/8 time with alternating major-key and minor-key sections, named from the South Italian town of Taranto, habitat of the tarantula: superstition declared the tarantula poisonous, and the dance was said to be the result of (or sometimes the cure for) this poison.

tárogató, Hungarian single-reed woodwind instrument, related to the clarinet and saxophone; it has sometimes been used to perform part of the shepherd's piping in Act III of Wagner's ➤*Tristan und Isolde*.

Tárrega, Francisco (1852–1909), Spanish guitarist, and composer and arranger of many works for his instrument.

Tartini, Giuseppe (1692–1770), Italian violinist and composer, founder of a famous school for violin-playing. Travelled much in Italy, and for three years worked in Prague. Wrote concertos and sonatas (➤*Devil's Trill*) for violin; also trio sonatas, church music, etc. Improved the violin-bow. Also author of theoretical writings on music, and discoverer of what are now known as ➤resultant tones.

Tasso, Torquato (1544–95), Italian poet. ➤*Armida*, ➤*Rinaldo*, ➤*Tancred* (➤*Tancrède*, ➤*Tancredi*); ➤Seefried.

tasto (It.), (1) the fingerboard of a keyboard instrument; *sul tasto*, on the fingerboard; (2) the finger-key of a keyboard instrument: *tasto solo*, finger-key only – i.e. (in music which has a ➤*continuo* part) instruction to play only the single bass-note written, and not the supporting chords which a continuo-player would normally add.

Tate, Jeffrey (b. 1943), British conductor who trained first as a doctor; internationally active in opera (principal conductor, Covent Garden, 1986–91; principal conductor, English Chamber Orchestra, since 1985). He suffers from curvature of the spine and conducts seated.

Tate, Nahum (1652–1715), English poet. ➤*Dido and Aeneas*.

Tate, Phyllis [Margaret Duncan] (1911–87), British composer; works include opera *The Lodger*, songs, a saxophone concerto, *A Secular Requiem* for voices, organ and orchestra.

Tauber [originally Denemy], **Richard** (1892–1948), Austrian tenor, naturalized British, 1940. Well known in opera, recital and (especially) Lehár's operettas. Also composer and conductor.

Tausig, Carl (1841–71), Polish pianist who settled in Germany, becoming pupil of Liszt; made arrangements for the piano of some organ works of Bach, orchestral pieces by various composers, etc. Also composer. Died of typhoid.

Tavener, John [Kenneth] (b. 1944), British composer, whose works on religious subjects (both before and after his conversion to Russian Orthodoxy) include cantata *Ultimos ritos* (Sp., 'Last Rites'), and *The Protecting Veil* for cello and orchestra; operas including *A Gentle Spirit* (after Dostoyevsky), oratorio *The Apocalypse* (on gigantic scale) with text from Revelation.

Taverner, opera by Peter Maxwell Davies, produced in London, 1972;

libretto by composer, about the 16th-century musician – see following.

Taverner, John (*c.* 1490–1545), English composer and organist: wrote chiefly church music in Latin, including eight Masses – one based on the then popular song. 'The Western Wind'. His mass *Gloria tibi Trinitas* was the starting-point of the musical form known as ➤*In nomine*. The oft-retailed story that in later life he became an active agent in the political suppression of the monasteries is now held to be a fiction.

Taylor, [Joseph] **Deems** (1885–1966), American composer of operas (including *The King's Henchman* and *Peter Ibbetson*), orchestral works (including suite *Through the Looking-Glass*, after Lewis Carroll, originally for chamber-music group), etc.; also writer and radio commentator on music.

Taylor, Samuel Coleridge-, ➤Coleridge-Taylor.

Tchaikovsky, Pyotr Ilyich (1840–93), Russian composer, outstanding for his orchestral music including concertos and ballet scores; aloof from the overt nationalism of the ➤Mighty Handful group, he nevertheless wrote in a distinctively Russian style. A homosexual, left his wife a few weeks after marriage (1877); 1876–90, carried on an extensive correspondence with Nadezhda von Meck, a wealthy widow who made him a monetary allowance – but they hardly met. Visited USA, 1892; England, 1893 (D.Mus., Cambridge). The circumstances of his death (usually attributed to cholera after drinking unboiled water) are still disputed. Died in St Petersburg a few days after the first performance of his last symphony, the ➤*Pathétique*.

His Second Symphony is nicknamed ➤*Ukrainian* (or Little Russian), and his Third Symphony ➤*Polish*; his ➤*Manfred* Symphony is unnumbered. Composed Piano Concerto no. 1 (famously rejected by its intended dedicatee, N. Rubinstein, but then hugely popular), followed by two more (no. 3 unfinished); also a violin concerto, ➤*Variations on a Rococo Theme* for cello and orchestra and much other orchestral music including ➤*Mozartiana* and descriptive works *The* ➤*Tempest*, ➤ *Romeo and Juliet*, ➤*Hamlet*, ➤*Francesca da Rimini*, ➤*Eighteen-Twelve*; 11 operas including ➤*Yevgeny Onegin*, *The* ➤*Queen of Spades*, ➤*Yolanta*, ➤*Mazeppa*; full-length ballet scores ➤*Swan Lake*, *The* ➤*Sleeping Beauty*, *The* ➤*Nutcracker*; chamber works, songs.

Tcherepnin, Alexander [Nikolayevich] (1899–1977), Russian-born composer and pianist, settled in Paris, 1921; university teacher in Chicago, 1949–64. Works include three operas, four symphonies, six piano concertos. Son of Nikolay Tcherepnin (below).

Tcherepnin, Nikolay [Nikolayevich] (1873–1945), Russian composer of ballets, symphonic poems, a piano concerto, etc.; also pianist and conductor, conducting for Diaghilev Ballet 1909–14. Made a completion of Musorgsky's ➤*Sorochintsy Fair*. Settled in Paris, 1921, with his son (above).

te, in ➤tonic sol-fa, the spoken name for the seventh degree (leading-note) of the scale, written t. The initial letter *t* was adopted because *s* (to correspond with Continental ➤*si*) might be confused with *soh* (fifth degree).

Tear, Robert (b. 1939), British tenor, prominent in opera (creating the role

of Dov in Tippett's *The* ➤*Knot Garden*) and noted in varied concert repertory including Russian and Polish songs. Also since 1985 occasional conductor of concerts. CBE, 1984.

Tebaldi, Renata (b. 1922), Italian soprano, distinguished in opera – at La Scala, Milan, from 1946; first sang in Britain (with La Scala company at Covent Garden), 1950. Retired in 1976.

tedesco (It., fem. *-a*), German; *alla tedesca*, in German fashion – usually meaning 'in the manner of a ➤German Dance', but Vaughan Williams's 'Rondo alla tedesca' in his Tuba Concerto (1954) apparently indicates merely a rondo as in a symphonic work by such German composers as Beethoven.

Te Deum, a Latin hymn of thanksgiving to God, used in the Roman Catholic Church and as 'We praise thee, O God' in the Anglican Church, etc. There is a traditional plainsong melody for it, and other settings for liturgical use; also settings by Handel and other later composers for concert or ceremonial use. Walton's was written for the coronation of Queen Elizabeth II, 1953.

Teil (Ger.), part, section (not in the sense of a voice-➤*part*, etc.).

Te Kanawa, Kiri (b. 1944), New Zealand soprano, of mixed Maori and European origin, resident in Britain since 1966; internationally celebrated in opera (Covent Garden from 1970). Sang at the Prince of Wales's wedding, 1981. Recorded ➤*West Side Story* with Bernstein conducting and has made many ➤crossover recordings. Created Dame, 1982.

Telemann, Georg Philipp (1681–

1767), German composer of 40 operas, many oratorios, church cantatas, about 100 concertos and other vocal and instrumental works. His chamber music includes instrumental suites published as *Musique de table* (➤*Tafelmusik*). Friend of Bach. Held a leading church music post in Hamburg from 1721 until his death.

Telephone, The, one-act comic opera by Menotti, produced in New York, 1947. Libretto by composer. For two characters only (lovers) – plus the distracting telephone.

tema (It.), theme.

Temirkanov, Yuri [Khatuevich] (b. 1938), Russian conductor; principal conductor of the Kirov Opera 1977–88, then music director of the Leningrad (from 1991 St Petersburg) Philharmonic Orchestra; also from 1992 principal conductor of the Royal Philharmonic Orchestra. Has also conducted Boston Symphony and other leading US orchestras.

temper(ed), ➤temperament.

temperament, the 'tempering' (i.e. slight lessening or enlarging) of musical intervals away from the 'natural' scale deducible by physical laws. In particular the piano, the modern organ, and other fixed-pitch modern instruments are tuned to *equal temperament*, meaning that each semitone is made an equal interval. In this way the notes D♯ and E♭ are made identical, and other pairs similarly (though by physical laws they differ slightly); it is therefore equally easy to play in any key or, having started in one key, to modulate to any other. (Bach's 48 Preludes and Fugues, called ➤*Wohltemperirte Clavier*, were among the first

works to require some such system as this, being set in all the major and minor keys.) An earlier system was *mean-tone temperament*, which gave a nearer approximation to 'natural' tuning than does equal temperament for C major and keys nearly related to it; but it was so far out for keys remote from C major that playing in them was virtually impossible, unless such devices as separate notes for D♯ and E♭ were adopted (as they were on some old organs). Instruments where the notes are not 'pre-set' (e.g. the violin family) can have no 'system' of temperament, since the player alone determines the pitch of the note and checks it by ear, approaching a ➤just intonation.

Tempest, The, play by Shakespeare, to which Sibelius wrote incidental music (1926), and on which Tchaikovsky based his orchestral fantasy, *The Tempest* (1873); it is the source also of Frank Martin's opera of the same name (Ger., *Der Sturm*), an almost literal setting of the text, produced in Vienna, 1956, and of works by ➤Sutermeister and ➤Weldon.

temple block (or Korean temple block), type of hollowed-out wooden vessel, approximately in the shape of a human head, struck with a stick as a percussion instrument. Formerly a 'novelty' sound in dance-bands, etc., it is now increasingly found in modern composers' large arrays of percussion – in several sizes, giving different pitches though not tuned to any one clear note.

tempo (It.), time, pace (pl. *tempi* or, as naturalized Eng. word, *tempos*). So *tempo primo* or *a tempo*, direction to return to the original pace; *tempo di*

..., at the pace of (a specified dance-movement, for instance); *tempo* ➤*giusto*.

ten., abbr. of (1) tenor; (2) *tenuto*.

tenero (It.), tender; *teneramente, tenerezza*, tenderly, tenderness.

Tennstedt, Klaus (1926–98), German conductor who made North American début 1974 with Toronto Symphony Orchestra and Boston Symphony Orchestra and was music director of the London Philharmonic Orchestra 1983–7. Distinguished in the classical repertory and has recorded all Mahler symphonies. Cancer compelled a severe curtailment of his concerts from mid-1987, and he retired in 1994.

Tennyson, Alfred [Lord] (1809–92), British poet. ➤*Princess Ida*; ➤*Serenade* (Britten); ➤Bridge (Frank), ➤Liszt, ➤Stevenson.

tenor (1) the highest normal male voice, apart from ➤*alto* or ➤*countertenor* (which uses falsetto) – so named because, when polyphonic music emerged in the late Middle Ages, its function was to hold (Lat., *tenere*) the plainsong or other 'given' tune while the other voices proceeded in counterpoint to it; (2) name given, in 'families' of instruments, to that instrument considered to have a position parallel to that which the tenor voice has among voices – so *tenor* ➤*recorder*, ➤*saxhorn*, ➤*saxophone*, *trombone*, ➤*viol*; (3) abbreviation for *tenor saxophone*; (4) obsolete English usage for ➤viola; (5) *tenor clef*, type of clef (now little used, but sometimes encountered for cello, bassoon, tenor trombone) written ♯ , in which the note middle C is indicated on the top line but one

of the staff; (6, *tenor horn*), common brass band usage for tenor saxhorn. See also following entries.

tenor cor, an instrument similar to the standard (French) ➤horn but manufactured so as to be easier to play, at the cost of richness of tone.

tenor drum, percussion instrument of similar type to snare-drum (and capable of similar rolls, etc.) but deeper in pitch, bigger and without snares. Occasionally used in the orchestra, from the 19th century; also in the military band.

tenor tuba, ➤tuba.

tenuto (It., held), direction that a note is to be fully sustained, up to (and sometimes even over) its full written time value.

Terfel, Bryn [originally Bryn Terfel Jones] (b. 1965), British bass-baritone, winner of the *Lieder* prize at Cardiff Singer of the World competition 1989, immediately proceeding to major operatic engagements; Covent Garden début as Masetto in *Don Giovanni*, 1992. Took part in Abbado's recording of Mahler's Symphony no. 8; at the BBC's Last Night of the Proms, 1994, was soloist in *Belshazzar's Feast* and (displacing customary female voice) in *Rule, Britannia!*.

Termen, Lev Sergeyevich, ➤theremin.

ternary, in three sections; *ternary* (as distinct from ➤*binary*) *form*, classification used of a movement in three sections of which the third is a repetition (exact or near) of the first – i.e., a movement which may be represented as ABA or ABA'. The term is also used even if the first section is initially stated twice (AABA or AABA') as in the conventional 'minuet and trio', in which the 'minuet' section is given twice on its first statement but only once on its return.

Tertis, Lionel (1876–1975), British viola-player who raised his instrument to a new importance, many (chiefly British) composers writing new works specially for him; he himself introduced new technical specifications for the making of the instrument.

tessitura (It., texture), the compass of notes to which a particular singer's voice naturally inclines ('he has a high *tessitura*') though exceptional notes may be produced outside it; similarly, the general compass (not counting exceptional notes) of a vocal part.

tetrachord, an obsolete scale-pattern (ancient Greek, also medieval) grouping four adjacent notes a whole-tone or semitone apart. (Originally from *tetrachordon*, Greek four-stringed instrument.)

Tetrazzini, Luisa (originally Luigia) (1871–1940), Italian soprano who won great success after operatic débuts in London, 1905, and New York, 1908, but devoted her later career (1918–34) to the concert-hall, becoming one of the earliest singers to become a household name mainly on the basis of recordings.

texture, the relative density of sound as perceived in a composition or orchestration; hence 'Brahms's orchestral texture is thicker than Bizet's', etc. (The literal Italian equivalent, ➤*tessitura*, has a quite different meaning.)

Teyte, Maggie (originally Margaret Tate) (1888–1976), British soprano who became famous on the French opera stage (studying the role of Mélisande with Debussy) and in recitals, especially in French song. Created Dame, 1958.

Thaïs, opera by Massenet, produced in Paris, 1894. Libretto by L. Gallet. Named after its heroine, a fourth-century courtesan who becomes a nun. The well-known orchestral *Meditation* is an intermezzo between the second and last acts.

Thalben-Ball, George [Thomas] (1896–1987), Australian-born organist (also composer) resident in Britain; well-known recitalist, from 1923 to 1981 organist of the Temple Church in London, and from 1949 to 1982 Birmingham City Organist. Knighted, 1982.

Thalberg, Sigismond (1812–71), Austrian (Swiss-born) virtuoso pianist (pupil of Hummel) and composer of a piano concerto and many solos exploiting piano technique; contributor to the ➤*Hexameron*. Wrote also operas, songs, etc.

theatre organ (also called *cinema organ*), type of ➤organ in vogue particularly 1925–50 for use in intermissions at cinema performances, etc., featuring some 'freak' stops, e.g. piano, motor-horn.

theme, a group of notes constituting (by repetition, recurrence, development, etc.) an important element in the construction of a piece. In some types of musical analysis it is broadly equated with ➤subject; but it often indicates separately recognizable elements within a subject. In the phrase *theme and variations* it refers to the whole musical statement on which the variations are based (i.e. something much longer than *theme* in most other senses). So *metamorphosis of themes*, the process by which a theme can be altered in character (e.g. by changing its rhythm) to suit the dramatic progress of a ➤symphonic poem or such work while retaining its essence. So also *representative theme*, a theme which carries some extra-musical indication (e.g. a person or object or emotion) for dramatic or narrative purpose – e.g. the Wagnerian ➤*leading-motive*. In the term *theme-song* (recurring in a musical play, etc., in association with a particular character) the word *theme* is used in a general and not a technical musical sense.

theme-song, see preceding.

Theodora, oratorio by Handel, first performed in London, 1750. Libretto by T. Morell: the heroine is a Christian martyr.

theorbo, type of archlute (bass lute) with long, off-the-fingerboard extra strings and an extra (S-shaped) neck; used in 16th–18th centuries to accompany singing and generally as a continuo instrument.

theremin (or *thereminovox*), instrument having an upright sensitive 'pole' which produces sound from the motion of the hand in space round it; invented in Russia, 1920, by Lev Sergeyevich Termen (1896–1993) who adopted 'Theremin' as the Western form of his name and patented an improved version of the instrument in USA, 1928. Composers using it in ensemble have included Varèse (*Equatorial*, 1934) and Martinů (*Phantasy* with string quartet, oboe, piano, 1945). Sounding only one note at a time, it has a range of five octaves and a diversity of tone-colour.

Thibaud, Jacques (1880–1953), French violinist, noted as a soloist and as a trio-partner of ➤Cortot and ➤Casals, duo-partner of ➤Long; he never retired, performing when over 70, and was killed in an air crash.

Thieving Magpie, The, opera by Rossini. ➤*Gazza ladra*.

third (noun), an interval in melody or harmony, reckoned as taking three steps in the (major or minor) scale, counting the bottom and top notes: either a *major third* (four semitones, e.g. C up to E) or *minor third* (three semitones, e.g. C up to E♭) or *diminished third* (two semitones, e.g. C♯ up to E♭).

third inversion, ➤position.

third sound, Tartini's name (It., *terzo suono*) for the acoustical phenomenon he discovered (➤resultant tone).

third stream, hopeful term originated about 1957 by Gunther Schuller for music which should be neither jazz nor classical but should absorb both traditions.

thirty-second-note, the note ♪ considered as a time-value. This term is standard North American usage and, as mathematically corresponding to the element of time-signature represented by /32, should clearly be preferred to 'demisemiquaver', still surviving in British use. The corresponding rest is notated ♪

Thomas, [Charles Louis] **Ambroise** (1811–96), French composer – also pianist, and director of the Paris Conservatory. Wrote ➤*Hamlet*, ➤*Mignon*, also ballets, church music, instrumental pieces, songs, etc.

Thomas, Arthur Goring (1850–92),

British composer, pupil of Sullivan and Bruch. Works include operas *Esmeralda* and *Nadeshda*, cantata *The Sun Worshippers*, songs. Became insane, 1891.

Thomas, Dylan (1914–53), British poet. ➤Jones (Daniel).

Thomas, Michael Tilson (b. 1944), American conductor and pianist, also composer and television presenter; principal conductor of the London Symphony Orchestra 1988–95, then of San Francisco Symphony Orchestra.

Thomas, Theodore [Christian Friedrich] (1835–1905), German-born American conductor, a major activator of orchestral life in New York and Chicago; founder of the Chicago Symphony Orchestra (1891).

Thomé, Francis (original forenames Joseph François Luc) (1850–1909), French (Mauritius-born) composer of *Simple Aveu* ('Simple Avowal'), piano piece later subject to multitudinous arrangements; also of operas, operettas, etc.

Thompson, Randall (1899–1984), American composer, pupil of Bloch and others; also university teacher. Wrote three symphonies, *The Peaceable Kingdom* and other choral works, opera *Solomon and Balkis*, etc.

Thomson, James (1700–1748), Scottish poet. ➤*Alfred*, ➤*Jahreszeiten*.

Thomson, Virgil [Garnett] (1896–1989), American composer, pupil of N. Boulanger in Paris; also organist and noted critic in New York. Works include operas ➤*Four Saints in Three Acts*, *The Mother of Us All* (both to librettos of Gertrude Stein), and *Lord Byron*; also *Symphony on a Hymn-tune*, a cello concerto, *Portraits* of various named people (some for orchestra, some for piano, some for unaccompanied violin), songs in English and French, stage and film music.

thorough-bass, ➤*continuo*.

Three-Cornered Hat, The, ballet score by Falla. ➤*Sombrero de tres picos*.

Three Places in New England, orchestral work in three movements by Ives, composed 1906–14, first performed 1931.

Three Screaming Popes, orchestral work by Turnage, 1989, based on the painting by Francis Bacon.

Threepenny Opera, stage work by Weill. ➤ *Dreigroschenoper*.

threni, term from Greek, used as equivalent of ➤*Lamentations* and hence employed by Stravinsky as title of his (Latin) setting of part of this ecclesiastical text, 1958.

through-composed (of a song), not ➤strophic.

thumb piano, ➤mbira.

thunder-machine, a piece of theatre machinery imitating thunder; brought into a few orchestral scores, e.g. R. Strauss's ➤*Alpensinfonie*.

Thus Spake Zarathustra, symphonic poem by R. Strauss. ➤*Also sprach Zarathustra*.

tie, a line in musical notation joining two adjacent notes of the same pitch indicating that the sound of the first is to be prolonged continuously into the second, instead of the latter's being struck afresh. So also *to tie*, *tied note*.

tief (Ger.), deep, low-pitched.

tierce de Picardie, ➤Picardy third.

Till Eulenspiegel, usual abbreviated title for *Till Eulenspiegels lustige Streiche* (Ger., 'The Merry Tricks of Till Eulenspiegel'), symphonic poem by R. Strauss, first performed in 1895. The hero, whose name is sometimes rendered as Tyll Owlglass in English, is a traditional rogue of German folklore, dating at least from the 15th century; other composers who have also written works based on his exploits include Karetnikov and Rezniček.

timbale (Fr.), ➤kettledrum.

timbral, ➤timbre.

timbre (Fr., a stamp, an individual mark), an individual quality of sound – term usually referring to the characteristic difference between the ➤tone-colours of different instruments; but in ➤electro-acoustic music it applies to the (analysable) property of a particular ➤spectrum. Hence (adjective, in both senses) *timbral*, pronounced as English.

timbrel, old English name for ➤*tambourine*; it is also used in biblical translation for a Hebrew instrument thought to be of this type.

time, term used in music to classify basic rhythmical patterns: thus a movement is said to be in *six-eight time* (6/8 time), having six eighth-notes (quavers) to the bar. So also, e.g., *common time* (4/4); *waltz time* (3/4, with a characteristic lilt); *march time* (usually 4/4 or 6/8); in *free time*, without any regular accent. So also *duple*, ➤*triple time*, and looser usages such as *in quick time*.

time-signature, sign at the beginning of a composition or movement (and thereafter when a change has to be indicated) conveying by means of figures the kind of beats in the bar and (above it) the number of such beats, E.g. $\frac{3}{2}$ indicates three half-notes (minims) to the bar, $\frac{3}{8}$ indicates three eighth-notes (quavers).

timpani (It., not *tympani*) ➤kettledrums. (The singular *timpano* is not generally used in English, though it is standard Italian.)

tin-whistle, rudimentary, six-holed, keyless wind instrument of ➤recorder type but made of metal. Also called *penny-whistle*.

Tippett, [Sir] **Michael** [Kemp] (1905–98), British composer of long-sustained output of orchestral works and operas; he announced on the eve of his 90th birthday that *The Rose Lake* for orchestra would be his last such work. Always his own librettist for operas; they are *The Midsummer Marriage* (from which come the choral and orchestral 'Ritual Dances'), ➤*King Priam*, *The* ➤*Knot Garden*, *The Ice Break* and *New Year*. Other works include four symphonies, a concerto for double string orchestra and Concerto for Orchestra, *Fantasia Concertante on a Theme of Corelli*, piano concerto and four piano sonatas, five string quartets, song-cycles *Boyhood's End* and *The Heart's Assurance*; oratorio *A* ➤*Child of Our Time*, cantatas *The Vision of St Augustine* and *The* ➤*Mask of Time*. Imprisoned as conscientious objector during World War II. Published his autobiography, 1991. Knighted, 1966; CH, 1979; OM, 1993.

Tishchenko, Boris (b. 1939), Russian composer, pupil and friend of Shostakovich (some of whose song-accompaniments he orchestrated). Works include six symphonies (no. 6 with vocal soloists), harp concerto, five string quartets, nine piano sonatas, *Twelve Inventions* for organ.

Titan, name given by Mahler to his Symphony no. 1 when he conducted its second performance (1893); the label was later discarded by him but is sometimes retained as a nickname.

toccata (It.), (1), a solo instrumental piece, usually for keyboard, exhibiting rapid display of the player's touch (It., *toccare*, to touch) – as in many baroque examples (see next entry) and some later usages e.g. by Debussy (for piano) and by Widor, whose celebrated Toccata comes from the fifth of his 'symphonies' for organ alone (*c.* 1880); (2) a fanfare-like ceremonial flourish, such as opens Monteverdi's opera ➤*Orfeo*.

Toccata and Fugue in D minor, work for organ usually ascribed to Bach (BWV 565), though this attribution is now questioned; well known in orchestral arrangements by Stokowski (1926) and by Henry J. Wood (1929), initially under the pseudonym Paul Klenovsky. To be distinguished from Bach's so-called ➤'Dorian' Toccata and Fugue.

Toch, Ernst (1887–1964), Austrian-born composer (also pianist) naturalized in USA, 1940. As well as Hollywood film scores, composed four operas, seven symphonies, orchestral fantasy *Big Ben* (on the Westminster chimes), chamber music, and a *Geographical Fugue* (separate editions in German and English) for speaking chorus on a text of exotic place-names.

Tod und das Mädchen, Der (Ger., 'Death and the Maiden'), title of song by Schubert (D531), 1817; hence nickname of Schubert's String Quartet in D minor, 1824, the second movement of which uses part of the song as a theme for variations.

Tod und Verklärung (Ger., 'Death and Transfiguration'), symphonic poem by R. Strauss, first performed in 1890.

Tokyo Quartet, American string quartet founded 1969, originally of Japanese players from the Juilliard School, New York; associated with Yale University since 1978. Peter Haig Oundjian (Canadian) and Kikue Ikeda are now first and second violinists, with two of the original members: Kazuhide Isomura, Sadao Harada. It commissioned and gave first performance of Takemitsu's Quartet no. 1, 1980.

Tolstoy, Leo Nikolayevich [Count] (1828–1910), Russian writer. ➤*War and Peace*; ➤Cikker, ➤Hamilton, ➤Lourié.

Tomaschek, Wenzel Johann, a Germanized form of the following name.

Tomášek, Václav Jan (1774–1850), Bohemian composer, also pianist and organist. Composed three symphonies, operas, church music, and innovative piano works and songs.

Tomasi, Henri Frédien (1901–71), French composer of operas including *La silence de la mer* ('The Silence of the Sea', after Vercors), concertos for 13 different instruments, choral works, etc. Was also conductor.

tombeau (Fr., tomb, tombstone), term used by French 17th-century composers for memorial works – a usage revived by Ravel in *Le Tombeau de Couperin*, for piano, 1917, four of the six movements being later orchestrated.

Tom Jones (1) operetta by German with libretto by Alexander M. Thompson and Robert Courtneidge and with lyrics by Charles H. Taylor, after the novel by Henry Fielding. Produced in London, 1907. The dashing Tom, a foundling, discovers his identity and finally wins his true love. Also operas on the same source composed by (2) Philidor, 1765, and (3) Oliver, 1976.

Tomkins, name of an English family of musicians of whom the most important was Thomas Tomkins (1572–1656), pupil of Byrd, organist of the Chapel Royal, composer of much church music including about 100 surviving anthems, also of madrigals (one in *The* ➤*Triumphs of Oriana*) and music for keyboard and for viols.

Tomlinson, John (b. 1946), British bass of operatic distinction; made Covent Garden début in 1976 and has sung at Bayreuth (Wotan in *The Ring*, etc.) every year since 1988. Sang title-role, and was also stage director, in rare production of Verdi's first opera, *Oberto* (Opera North, 1995). CBE, 1997.

Tommasini, Vincenzo (1878–1950), Italian composer; arranged D. Scarlatti's music for the ballet *The Good-humoured Ladies* (choreography by Massine), and wrote operas, orchestral works, chamber and choral music, etc.

Tomowa-Sintow, Anna (b. 1941), Bulgarian soprano; began her operatic career in East Germany, was 'discovered' by Karajan and rose to international prominence in Mozart, R. Strauss, etc.

tom-tom, type of high-pitched drum (imitation of African drum) used in Western dance-bands since the 1920s, and occasionally from the 1950s in the orchestra – often in sets of two or more, either tuned to definite notes or otherwise. (Not the same as ➤tam-tam.)

ton (Fr.), term which as used in various contexts may mean 'note', 'tone' (interval or two semitones), or 'key'.

Ton (Ger., pl. *Töne*), note, sound (not the interval of a 'tone', i.e. two semitones). So *Tonreihe*, note-row (as in ➤twelve-note composition); *Tondichtung*, symphonic poem (this German word in fact providing the origin of the unsatisfactory English term ➤tone poem; *Tonkunst*, music (literally, 'sound-art'); *Tonkünstler*, musician(s).

tonada (Sp.), tune, air. (Used e.g. as title of some works by Allende.)

tonadilla (Sp.), type of Spanish stage entertainment employing a few singers.

tonal (1) of notes in the most general sense ('a sound of tonal splendour'); (2) of tonality, as distinct from ➤atonality (so *a tonal composition*); (3) opposite to 'real' in certain technical contexts of formal composition (➤answer, ➤sequence).

tonality (1) key: 'C major is the prevailing tonality'; (2) a general adherence to the key-system, distinguished from ➤atonality.

Tondichtung, ➤*Ton* (Ger.).

tone (1) quality of musical sound ('he plays with a pleasing tone'); (2) a musical sound consisting of a 'pure' note, as in acoustical analysis ('a note on the violin may be analysed as containing several different tones'); (3) the interval consisting of two semitones, e.g. from C up to D (also ➤whole-tone); (4) one of the plainsong melodies

(➤Gregorian tone) used for the singing of psalms in the Roman Catholic Church; (5, US) a note (in such usages as 'a chord consisting of four tones'). It is because of this last use, derived from German ➤Ton and needlessly confusing, that there have arisen such American compounds as *tone-row* and *twelve-tone* (Eng., note-row, twelve-note).

tone-cluster, ➤cluster.

tone-colour, the quality which distinguishes a note as performed on one instrument from the same note as performed on other instruments (or voices). The French word *timbre* is also used in English in this sense. On analysis the differences between tone-colours of instruments are found to correspond with differences in the ➤harmonic series represented in the sound.

tone poem, a translation of Ger. *Tondichtung* (➤Ton), i.e., a ➤symphonic poem.·

tongue, to articulate a note on a wind instrument with a certain use of the tongue; so *single-*, *double-* and *triple-tonguing*, making for progressively faster articulation; *flutter-tonguing*, the articulation of sound as if trilling an *r* (e.g. on the flute, where the resulting tone sounds pigeon-like, and on the trumpet).

tonic, the first degree, or keynote, of the scale, e.g. F in the keys of F major and F minor. So ➤tonic sol-fa.

tonic sol-fa, English system of notation and sight-reading introduced in the 1840s by J. S. Curwen (1816–80), though partly anticipated by others. It is based on naming the notes in relation to the ➤tonic, not by their absolute positions as in ➤*solfeggio*, where *do* is C whatever the tonic, etc. In Curwen's system the notes of the major scale are named (ascending) *doh, ray, me, fah, soh, lah, te* – where *doh* is the keynote (tonic), the other notes being thus related to the keynote of the moment. Time-values are indicated by bar-lines and dots, and there is other symbolization. Formerly much used in amateur choral music, now moribund.

Tonkunst, Tonkünstler, ➤*Ton* (Ger.).

tonus (Lat.), (1) Gregorian tone (➤tone, 4); (2) ➤*mode*, in such uses as ➤*tonus peregrinus*.

tonus peregrinus (Lat., foreign tone), (1) medieval term for what is now called an irregular scale, not 'recognized' in the modal system then prevalent; (2) the plainsong sung in the Roman Catholic Church to Psalm 114, being in the above scale.

Toovey, Andrew (b. 1962), British composer of *Ubu* (after Jarry's play *Ubu Roi*), string quartet, *Cantec* for viola and piano. Directs his own Ixion Ensemble.

Torelli, Giuseppe (1658–1709), Italian violinist and composer who worked largely in Bologna; pioneer practitioner of the *concerto grosso* (➤Christmas Concerto), he also wrote many works for one or more trumpets with string orchestra.

Torke, Michael (b. 1961), American composer, also pianist. Works include piano concerto, *Adjustable Wrench* for chamber ensemble, Mass (with chamber orchestra), songs, television opera *King of Hearts*.

Toronto Symphony Orchestra, Canadian orchestra which took that name in 1926; principal conductor from 1990, Günther Herbig.

Torroba (actually Moreno-Torroba), **Federico** (1891–1982), Spanish composer of music for guitar (including a concerto) and of ➤zarzuelas (Spanish operettas), etc.

Tortelier, Paul (1914–90), French cellist, also conductor and composer of three violin concertos, Concerto for two cellos and orchestra, *Israel Symphony*. Lived in Israel 1955–6. His widow, Maud Martin Tortelier (b. 1926), is a cellist and their daughter, Maria de la Pau (b. 1950), a pianist. Their son is Yan Pascal Tortelier.

Tortelier, Yan Pascal (b. 1947), French conductor and violinist (son of preceding). Principal conductor of Ulster Orchestra 1989–92, then of BBC Philharmonic (Manchester). Has also conducted opera at Wexford Festival, English National Opera, and elsewhere. He made an orchestral version of Ravel's piano trio.

Tosca, opera by Puccini, produced in Rome, 1900. Libretto by G. Giacosa and L. Illica, after Sardou's French play *La Tosca*. The title-role is that of an operatic prima donna moved in desperation to kill.

Toscanini, Arturo (1867–1957), Italian conductor (formerly cellist), eminent in concert and opera; his many important 'first performances' included that of Puccini's ➤*Turandot*. Refused to perform under German or Italian fascism and settled in New York, where the National Broadcasting Company's orchestra was specially created for him (1937). Conducted always from memory, being too shortsighted to read a score from the rostrum. His daughter Wanda married ➤Horowitz.

Toselli, Enrico (1883–1920), Italian composer of songs, including a famous 'Serenata', and also of operettas, chamber music, etc.

Tosti, [Francesco] **Paolo** (1846–1916), Italian composer and singing-master who settled in London, taught the British royal family, and was knighted (1908). Wrote 'Good-bye' and other songs in English, also songs in French and Italian.

Tost Quartets, name given to 12 string quartets by Haydn, 1789–90, Hob. III: 57–68 (op. 54 nos. 1–3, op. 55 nos. 1–3, op. 64 nos. 1–6), dedicated to a violinist named Johann Tost.

total serialism, ➤series.

touche (Fr.), fingerboard (of stringed instruments); *sur la touche*, direction to play 'on the fingerboard' (a special method of bowing).

toujours (Fr.), always, still.

Tournemire, Charles Arnould (1870–1939), French organist and composer of many organ works (also of operas, chamber music, etc.); noted recitalist. His *L'Orgue Mystique* ('The Mystical Organ') is a collection of 253 pieces to span the liturgical year.

tourte bow, ➤bow.

Tovey, Donald Francis (1875–1940), British pianist, composer (opera *The Bride of Dionysus*, a cello concerto, etc.), conductor, professor at Edinburgh University; celebrated for his programme-notes, collected as *Essays in Musical Analysis*, and other writings on music. Made, with great technical skill, a conjectural completion of the final unfinished fugue in

Bach's *Die ➤Kunst der Fuge*. Knighted 1935.

Tower, Joan [Peabody] (b. 1938), American composer of *Fanfare for the Uncommon Woman* (brass and percussion), also of *Petrouschkates* (flute, clarinet, violin, cello, piano), a piano concerto, etc. Also pianist, who founded and performed with the Da Capo Chamber Players.

toy(e), old English term sometimes used for a light piece for the keyboard or lute.

toy symphony, a symphony of a simple kind in which toy instruments are employed. The best-known example, formerly ascribed to Joseph Haydn, is now considered to be the work of Leopold Mozart. Another was written by Malcolm Arnold (1957).

tr., abbr. of (1) ➤trill, (2) ➤trumpet.

tracker action, ➤action.

Traetta, Tommaso [Michele Francesco Saverio] (1727–79), Italian composer of more than 40 operas written for Parma, Venice, Mannheim, Vienna, St Petersburg, London and elsewhere. Worked for a time in St Petersburg and London.

tragédie lyrique (Fr., 'sung' tragedy), the usual term for French serious opera in the period of Lully and Rameau (17th–18th centuries).

Tragic Overture, concert-overture by Brahms. ➤*Tragische Ouvertüre*.

'Tragic' Symphony, nickname given (by the composer) to Schubert's Symphony no. 4 in C minor, 1816 (D417).

Tragische Ouvertüre (Ger., 'Tragic Overture'), concert-overture by Brahms, first performed in 1881; it does not refer to any particular tragedy.

Traherne, Thomas (c. 1636–74), English poet. ➤*Dies Natalis*; ➤Butterley.

transcribe (1) to arrange a piece of music for a performing medium other than the original – or for the same medium but in a more elaborate style. The term usually implies a freer treatment than the simple verb 'to arrange' by itself; (2) to convert a piece from one system of notation to another, e.g. from medieval notation to the modern. So also *transcription*.

Transfigured Night, work for string sextet by Schoenberg. ➤*Verklärte Nacht*.

transition (1, in analysis) a passage serving mainly to join two passages more important than itself; (2) a change of key, particularly one of a sudden kind, not going through the regularly ordered process called 'modulation' (➤modulate).

transpose, to write down or perform music at a pitch other than the original. So certain instruments on which the player produces a note different from the written note are called ➤transposing instruments; e.g. an English horn, playing a perfect fifth below the written note, is said to *transpose down a fifth*. A song is often *transposed* to a higher or lower key to suit a singer's convenience. So also a piece written in one of the old ➤modes may be said to be in, e.g., the *Dorian mode transposed*, meaning with the same intervals as the Dorian mode but ending elsewhere than D on which the Dorian ends. So also *transposing keyboard*, one on which the performer can transpose by mechanical aid – he or she strikes the keys as usual, but the sideways shifting of the keyboard causes strings higher or lower than normal to be struck. See also the following.

transposing instrument (see preceding entry), an instrument on which the player produces a sound at a fixed interval above or below the note written. The chief reason for this is the convenience of a player changing between different sizes of instrument. A player of e.g. the clarinet knows that when seeing the note middle C in the printed music, he or she always puts down the same fingers in the same way. On the 'clarinet in C' the note sounded is the note written, i.e. middle C; other clarinets' names indicate the note each produces instead of C. E.g. on the 'clarinet in B♭', the note written C sounds as B♭ – the instrument transposing the C (and all other notes) one tone lower; the 'clarinet in A' transposes one and a half tones below the written note; the 'clarinet in E♭', one and a half tones higher; the 'bass clarinet in B♭' an octave and one tone lower. The horn and trumpet usually work as transposing instruments (e.g. 'horn in F', 'trumpet in B♭'), as do saxhorns and saxophones.

transverse flute, name for the ordinary flute, to distinguish it (as held cross-wise) from the recorder (of the same basic instrumental type, but held downwards).

trascinando (It.), dragging.

Traubel, Helen [Francesca] (1899–1972), American soprano, noted in Wagner at the New York Metropolitan Opera from 1939 – leaving in 1953 when Rudolf Bing, its director, objected to her also performing in nightclubs. Also novelist (author of *The Metropolitan Murders*) and autobiographer.

Trauer (Ger.), mourning. So *Trauermarsch*, funeral march; Haydn's *Trauersymphonie* (➤'Mourning' Symphony); Mozart's *Maurerische Trauermusik* (Masonic Funeral Music). Hindemith used the title *Trauermusik* ('Music of Mourning') for a piece for viola and strings, 1936, written in a few hours for a concert next day, two days after the death of George V.

Träume (Ger., 'Dreams'), song by Wagner. ➤*Wesendonck-Lieder*.

Träumerei (Ger., 'Reverie'), piano piece by Schumann, 1838, no. 7 of the ➤*Kinderszenen*.

Trautonium, trade name (after its inventor, F. Trautwein, 1930) for a type of electronic instrument (➤electric/electronic); invented in Germany in 1930; it produced only one note at a time. It could be fixed to a piano, one hand playing each instrument. R. Strauss and Hindemith wrote for it.

traversa, name occasionally found instead of ➤*traverso*.

traverso, name sometimes used in old scores as abbreviation of *flauto traverso* (It.), i.e. the transverse flute – to distinguish this instrument (the ordinary flute, held cross-wise) from the recorder, held downwards.

Traviata, La (It. 'The Woman Gone Astray'), opera by Verdi, produced in Venice, 1853. Libretto by F. M. Piave, after the younger Dumas's *The Lady of the Camellias* – the heroine being a self-sacrificing courtesan who eventually dies.

treble (1) type of high voice – the term usually being kept today to children's voices, the adult female equivalent being 'soprano'; (2) the upper part of a composition, or the upper regions of pitch generally – especially in antithesis to ➤*bass*; (3) name given to high-pitched members of certain 'families' of instruments: e.g. *treble* ➤*recorder, treble* ➤*viol*; (4, *treble clef*) clef written 𝄞 indicating the G above middle C as the next-to-bottom line of the staff. It is normally used for high-pitched instruments and for women's and children's voices; also for right-hand piano parts. It is moreover used for the tenor voice, by a convention according to which the notes are sounded an octave lower than written: occasionally, to indicate this, a figure 8 is written below the clef-sign.

Tremblay, Gilles. (b. 1932), Canadian composer, pupil in Paris of Messiaen and others; also university teacher in Montreal. Works include *Sonorisation* – electronic sounds on 24 tape-channels; *Kekoba* for three voices with ➤Ondes Martenot and percussion; a series of works called *Champs* (Fr., 'Fields') for different instrumental ensembles.

tremolando (It., trembling), having the effect of a ➤*tremolo*.

tremolo (It., a shaking, a trembling) (1, in string-playing) the rapid reiteration of a single note by back-and-forth strokes of the bow; (2, in string-playing, and on other instruments) the alternation between two notes as rapidly as possible. Not properly applied to vocal wobble – an excess of ➤*vibrato* (fluctuation of pitch), whereas *tremolo* gives a fluctuation of intensity, i.e. of volume.

tremulant, device on the organ im-

parting a wobbling effect to the note through variation of the wind-pressure: an element both of ➤*tremolo* and ➤*vibrato* is involved.

trepak, lively Russian dance in 2/4 time.

triad, a three-note chord consisting of a particular note plus its third and fifth above – e.g. C-E-G, which is called the 'common chord' of C major, no matter whether C remains the bass-note or is replaced by one of the other notes. Similarly C-Eb-G is the 'common chord' of C minor. So also *augmented triad*, containing the augmented fifth (e.g. C, E, G♯); *diminished triad*, containing the diminished fifth (e.g. C, Eb, Gb).

Trial by Jury, operetta (but styled a 'dramatic cantata') by Sullivan, produced in London, 1875. Libretto by W. S. Gilbert, burlesquing an action for breach of promise. (It is the only Gilbert-and-Sullivan stage piece that is sung throughout, with no spoken dialogue.)

triangle, three-cornered metal-framed percussion instrument, struck with a metal stick; its tinkling sound is without definite pitch.

trill, a musical ornament (usually designated by *tr* 〰 over the note) also called 'shake', consisting of the rapid alternation of the written note and the note above. Whether this note is a whole-tone or a semitone above depends on which of these notes occurs in the scale in use at the moment – unless the composer directs otherwise.

trillo (It.), (1) trill; *Trillo del Diavolo*, ➤*Devil's Trill*; (2) a 17th-century vocal ornament in which a single note was repeated, the repetitions getting ever faster – it has been revived in modern performances, e.g. of Monteverdi's operas.

trio (1) a combination of three performers; *string trio*, violin, viola, cello; *piano trio*, piano, violin, cello; (2) a work for three performers – if instrumental and actually called a 'trio', it will probably have the character of a ➤sonata for three performers, in several movements; (3) the central section of a ➤minuet, so called because formerly it was conventionally written in three-part harmony only, as for a 'trio' in the normal sense; so also when a scherzo or a march is constructed in minuet form (AABA), the 'B' section may be called a trio; (4) name given also to certain works by Bach for organ (or for harpsichord with two manuals and pedals) having three melodic ➤parts but played by one performer; these are more reasonably called ➤trio-sonatas or sonatas.

trio-sonata, type of composition favoured in the late 17th and early 18th centuries, usually for two violins and a cello (or bass viol), with a keyboard instrument also playing the bass-line and supporting it with harmonies worked out by the player (➤continuo). Also a modern name for a certain type of work by Bach: ➤trio (4).

triple concerto, concerto with three soloists, e.g. Beethoven's (piano, violin, cello), 1805, or Tippett's (violin, viola, cello), 1979.

triple counterpoint, ➤counterpoint.

triplet, a group of three notes (or notes and rests) of equal time-value, written where a group of two, four or some other number of notes is suggested by the time-signatures. E.g. a three-note group occupying a bar of 2/4 time, written ♩♩♩

triple time, time in which the primary division is into three beats, as distinct particularly from ➤duple time (primary division into two), normally indicated by the figure 3 or 9 as the upper digit of a time-signature: thus $\frac{3}{4}$ indicates three quarter-notes (crotchets) to the bar, $\frac{9}{8}$ indicates nine eighth-notes (quavers), split into three groups of three. (The upper digits 6 and 12 do not denote triple time: $\frac{6}{4}$ indicates two pulses each of three quarter-notes, $\frac{12}{8}$ four pulses of three eighth-notes, etc.)

Triptych, ➤*Trittico*.

Tristan und Isolde, opera by Wagner, produced in Munich, 1865. Libretto by composer, after the Arthurian legend. The two lovers (also known in English forms as Tristram and Yseult) drink a love-potion in mistake for poison, but eventually die just the same.

tritone, the interval of three whole-tones (➤tone, 3), e.g. from F up or down to B. This is a relatively awkward interval to sing, and its use in composition was formerly (in medievial and later practice) hedged round with various prohibitions. Hence the jingle, 'Mi contra fa diabolus est in musica' (*Mi* against *fa* [the old names for these notes according to the system of ➤hexachords] is the devil in music).

Trittico (It., Triptych), Puccini's name for the three contrasted one-act operas produced in a single evening in New York in 1918: *Il* ➤*Tabarro*, ➤*Suor Angelica*, ➤*Gianni Schicchi*.

Triumphs of Oriana, The, English

collection of madrigals by various composers, edited by Morley and published in 1601: in the form (modelled on an Italian collection) of tributes, each poem ending 'Long live fair Oriana'. It is generally believed that 'Oriana' was Elizabeth I. Among the 23 English composers represented in the first edition were J. Bennet, Hilton (the elder), Kirbye, Milton, Morley, J. Mundy, Norcombe, Tomkins, Weelkes, Wilbye; an Italian madrigal (translated into English) by Croce was also included. Works by Bateson and Pilkington were added in later editions.

Troilus and Cressida, opera by Walton, produced in London, 1954. Libretto by C. Hassall, principally after Chaucer's (not Shakespeare's) version of the story of the lovers in ancient Troy, besieged by the Greeks.

Trojans, The, opera by Berlioz. ➤*Troyens*.

tromba (It.), ➤trumpet; *tromba da tirarsi* (to be pulled), slide-➤trumpet. The term *tromba marina* (literally 'marine trumpet') refers to an obsolete bowed instrument (sometimes six feet long), one end of which rested on the floor. By the pressing of a finger at correct points on its single string, notes of the ➤harmonic series could be obtained. This reliance on harmonics perhaps explains the name 'trumpet', though 'marine' remains baffling.

Tromboncino, Bartolomeo (*c.* 1470– after 1534), Italian composer, singer, and lutenist. Works include madrigals, canzonets, church music.

trombone (from It., literally 'large trumpet'), type of brass instrument, generally possessing a slide which serves to vary the effective length of the tube. (But see *valve-trombone*,

below.) In any one position of the slide, the notes of the ➤harmonic series can be produced; and there are seven recognized positions of the slide, producing harmonic series a semitone apart. A combination of moving the slide (i.e. picking a particular series) and controlling the breath (i.e. picking a note within a series) yields a chromatic range – *tenor trombone*, from E below the bass stave upwards for about two and a half octaves; *bass trombone*, from the B lower. (Below this, a few isolated 'pedal notes' can be produced: they are actually the first tones of the harmonic series in various positions, and are not usually called for.) Two tenor and one bass trombones are regarded as the standard within the orchestra, but the (generally obsolete) *alto trombone* has been revived, e.g. by Britten (*The Burning Fiery Furnace*), and the lower *double-bass trombone* (or *contrabass trombone*) was occasionally used by Wagner and a few others. The *tenor-bass trombone* is basically a tenor with a mechanism permitting access to an extra length of tubing for conversion to bass. (The *valve-trombone*, with valves instead of slide, is rarely met with but exists in both tenor and bass sizes: ➤*cimbasso*.) The trombones, previously confined largely to church music, entered the opera orchestra in the late 18th century and the symphony orchestra shortly afterwards; now standard also in military, brass and dance bands, etc. Among rare examples of their solo use is Muldowney's concerto for tenor trombone and orchestra.

Trommel (Ger.), drum; *grosse Trommel*, bass drum.

tronco, tronca (It.), broken off short

(of a note, especially in vocal music).

trope (1) type of musical interpolation into traditional liturgical plainsong, from about the ninth to the 15th century – the ecclesiastical ➤*sequence* being a survival of this; hence *Troper*, a medieval book containing tropes; (2) term used, in quite a different sense from the above, of the form of 12-note technique invented by ➤Hauer.

troppo (It.), too much; *allegro non troppo*, or *allegro ma non troppo*, fast but not too fast.

troubadour (Provençal, 'inventor'), type of itinerant poet-musician of southern France flourishing in the 11th–13th centuries, writing and singing songs in the old Provençal language (as distinct from the northern French ➤*trouvère*; the form *trovatore*, as in Verdi's opera, is a translation into Italian).

Trouble in Tahiti, ➤*Quiet Place*.

'Trout' Quintet, name for Schubert's Quintet (D667), 1819, for piano, violin, viola, cello and double-bass; the fourth of its five movements comprises variations on Schubert's song 'The Trout' (Ger., *Die Forelle*).

trouvère, the northern French counterpart of the ➤troubadour, writing and singing his songs in Old French, not in Provençal.

Trovatore, Il (It., 'The Troubadour'), opera by Verdi, produced in Rome, 1853. Libretto by S. Cammarano: the hero, though eventually revealed as a nobleman's son, has been brought up by a gipsy and has become a troubadour.

Troyens, Les (Fr., 'The Trojans'), opera by Berlioz with libretto by composer, after Virgil's *Aeneid*. In two parts – (1) *La Prise de Troie* ('The Taking of Troy'), produced (in German) in Karlsruhe, 1890, after Berlioz's death; (2) *Les Troyens à Carthage* ('The Trojans at Carthage'), produced in Paris, 1863.

trumpet, metal wind instrument, cylindrically bored, used for signalling, etc., from ancient times, and regularly appearing in the orchestra from the 17th century. The standard modern form (from mid 19th century) has three valves. The trumpet in most common use is either a ➤transposing instrument in B♭ with compass from E below middle C upwards for nearly three octaves, or a non-transposing instrument in C (one tone higher). Trumpets in D and in E♭ (higher, smaller) are in increasing use. The trumpet is found in dance bands and other popular formations as well as in the orchestra; in the brass band and some military bands it is replaced by the cornet. The *bass trumpet* (rare) is similar, but in C an octave lower. The so-called *piccolo trumpet* is pitched an octave higher than the standard instrument (and sometimes has four valves). The so-called *Bach trumpet* is a late-19th-century type of high-pitched trumpet (sometimes made in long, straight form), suitable for playing high-pitched trumpet parts as written by Bach – but having valves, so not being a historical reconstruction. *Fanfare trumpets* are a set in various sizes for ceremonial purposes, made in long, straight form on which banners can be hung. Before the modern valve trumpet the normal instrument was a 'natural' (valveless, keyless) trumpet producing one ➤harmonic series only, like a bugle; but the use of different instruments and of changeable ➤crooks (altering the instrument's total length of tube) went some way to allow a choice of different harmonic series as the music required it. Attempts before the valve-trumpet to enlarge the number of notes available led to the invention of various types of *slide-trumpet* (having a slide like a trombone's) and of the *keyed trumpet* for which Haydn wrote his concerto.

trumpet marine, ➤*tromba*.

Trumpet Voluntary, not a ➤voluntary in the usual sense, but a title affixed by Henry J. Wood to a keyboard piece which he arranged for a combination of organ, brass and timpani (later for full orchestra) and which he followed another editor in mistakenly attributing to Purcell. Now known to have been composed by J. ➤Clarke, it was originally entitled *The Prince of Denmark's March*.

Tsar and Carpenter, or The Two Peters, opera by Lortzing. ➤*Zar und Zimmermann, oder Die Zwei Peter*.

Tschaikowski, German spelling of the name ➤Tchaikovsky.

tuba (1) type of bass brass valved instrument made in several sizes and shapes – when circular, called 'helicon', of which the ➤sousaphone is a variety. The standard orchestral tuba (or *bass tuba*) was formerly in F, with compass from the F an octave below the bass clef, upwards for about three octaves, but today's preferred instrument is in E♭, a tone lower. Since its invention (1835) it has become the normal lowest brass instrument of the orchestra: very rarely used as soloist, though Vaughan Williams has composed a concerto for it. *Double-bass tuba* signifies a lower and rarer instrument, used e.g. by Wagner in

The ➤*Ring* in conjunction with the ➤Wagner tubas, of which it is not one. *Tenor tuba* signifies an instrument higher than the bass tuba – in Britain equated with the euphonium. The lowest and therefore largest instruments of the brass and military band are tubas (often called just 'basses'): they are the E♭ (same as standard tuba) and the B♭ (same as double-bass tuba) – the latter often in band usage called BB♭ bass (spoken as 'double B flat'); (2) trumpet-like organ stop; (3) ancient Roman straight trumpet.

Tubin, Eduard (1905–82), Soviet-Estonian composer who settled in Sweden; works include 10 symphonies (plus another unfinished), a balalaika concerto, two operas.

tubular bell, ➤bell.

Tucker, Richard (originally Reuben Ticker) (1913–75), American tenor, famous chiefly for his performances (more than 600) at the New York Metropolitan Opera.

tucket, obsolete English word (found in Shakespeare) for a fanfare, sometimes supposed to be related to ➤*toccata* (2).

Tuckwell, Barry [Emmanuel] (b. 1931), Australian horn-player active in Britain since 1951; internationally eminent soloist, leader of his own wind quintet and also a conductor. Concertos have been written for him by Musgrave and others. OBE, 1965.

Tudor, David [Eugene] (1926–96), American pianist who gave first performances of works by Cage, Stockhausen, etc., and is also composer, mainly of pieces using theatrical and lighting effects – 4 *Pepsi Pieces* for sound-and-light resources of Pepsi-

Cola Pavilion at Expo '70, Osaka (Japan), etc. Collaborated with Cage in joint compositions. Is also player of the ➤bandoneon, performing music written for that instrument by Kagel.

Tudway, Thomas (*c.* 1650–1726), English composer of church music, organist, processor at Cambridge, and compiler of a collection of English cathedral music.

Tunder, Franz (1614–67), German organist, composer of organ works, choral cantatas, etc. Buxtehude was his son-in-law and successor in church post in Lübeck.

tune (1) melody, especially the upper part of a simple composition; (2) term (noun and verb) referring to correct intonation – so *in tune, out of tune, to tune a piano*, etc. ('Dancers dancing in tune' is a phenomenon observed only by Tennyson.)

tuning-fork, a two-pronged metal object set in vibration to produce a sound which serves to check the pitch of instruments and to give the pitch to voices. Its note is virtually a 'pure' tone – lacking the upper harmonics (see ➤harmonic series) which enter into the tone of normal instruments. Other devices (mechanical, electrical, electronic) for giving a tuning note have gone far to supplant it.

Turandot (1) opera by Puccini, produced in Milan, 1926; completed by Alfano, Puccini having died; libretto by G. Adami and P. Simone; (2) opera by Busoni, produced in Zurich, 1917; libretto (in German) by composer; (3) play by Schiller for which Weber wrote incidental music, 1809. The source of all these is an Italian play by Gozzi: Turandot is a cruel Chinese

princess eventually conquered by love.

Turangalîla Symphonie, title of a 10-movement work for orchestra (three movements being entitled *Turangalîla*) by Messiaen, with prominent parts for piano and for ➤Ondes Martenot; first performed 1949. Title supposedly indicates, in Sanskrit, both love and divine action.

turba (Lat.) crowd; so, in musical settings of the Passion, e.g. Bach's, a passage allotted to the bystanders, collectively.

turca, alla (It.), in the Turkish style – in effect using, or simulating, the percussion instruments brought to Austria (and so introduced to Western Europe) by Turkish military bands in the 18th century (➤janissary music). So the *Rondo alla turca* forming the last movement of Mozart's Piano Sonata in A (K331), 1778 – arranged by others for various combinations.

Turchi, Guido (b. 1916), Italian composer and music administrator. Works include opera on Hašek's novel *The Good Soldier Švejk*; a *Piccolo concerto notturno* ('little night concerto') for orchestra, *Concerto breve* (in memory of Bartók) for string quartet or string orchestra.

Tureck, Rosalyn (b. 1914), American pianist, her Bach performances and recordings in the 1950s defying the fashionable view that Bach's music was unfitted for the modern grand piano (the harpsichord being preferred). Also lecturer, writer, and occasional conductor.

Turina [y Pérez], **Joaquín** (1882–1949), Spanish composer, pupil of d'Indy in Paris. Works include symphonic poem *La procesión del Rocío* ('The procession of the Virgin of the Dew'); *La oración del torero* ('The Bullfighter's Prayer') for string quartet or string orchestra, piano solos and songs.

turn, musical ornament normally indicated by a special mark, as follows:

played

Turnage, Mark-Anthony (b. 1960), British composer of operas *Greeks* (after Berkoff's play), *Twice Through the Heart*, *Country of the Blind*, *The Silver Tassie*, *Night Dances* for orchestra, *Lament for a Hanging Man* (text from the Bible and Sylvia Plath).

Turner, Eva (1892–1990), British soprano who sang at La Scala, Milan, from 1924; noted as Turandot (Puccini). Later taught in USA and London. Created Dame, 1962.

Turn of the Screw, The, opera by Britten, produced in Venice, 1954. Libretto by M. Piper, after Henry James's story about the ghostly possession of children.

tutti, ➤*tutto*.

tutto (It., fem., *-a*, pl. *tutti*, *tutte*), all. So, in piano works, *tutte le corde*, all the strings, i.e. not with soft pedal (➤*corda*). The word *tutti*, meaning 'all the performers', is loosely used e.g. in a concerto as signifying a passage for the orchestra without the soloist – whether or not every member of the orchestra is actually playing. In choral works *tutti* can mean chorus as opposed to soloists, or full chorus as opposed to semi-chorus.

Tveitt, [Nils] Geirr (1908–81), Norwegian composer; also pianist and writer on music. Works include six piano concertos; two concertos for Hardanger ➤fiddle, operas, choral works, chamber music.

Twain, Mark (real name Samuel Langhorne Clemens) (1835–1910), American writer. ➤Foss, ➤Kern.

twelfth, on the organ, a mutation stop sounding a 12th (i.e. an octave plus a fifth) above the note depressed.

twelve-note, term used to describe a technique of composition in which all 12 notes within the octave (i.e. the seven white and five black notes of the piano) are treated as 'equal' – i.e. are subjected to an ordered relationship which (unlike that of the major-minor key system) establishes no 'hierarchy' of notes (but see below). Although one such technique was invented by ➤Hauer, the term is now virtually confined to the technique invented by Schoenberg, described by him as a 'method of composing with 12 notes which are related only to one another'. This method works through the 'note-row' (US 'tone-row') or ➤series, in which all the 12 notes are placed in a particular order as the basis of a work. No note is repeated within a row, which accordingly consists of 12 different notes and no others: it may be used as it stands, or transformed (➤invert; ➤retrograde) or transposed; it does not necessarily form a theme or part of one, but forms a reservoir of patterns for the whole composition. Originally 12-note technique developed as a standardization of ➤atonal music; but certain composers (e.g. Alban Berg, Dallapiccola), while using 12-note methods of construction, allowed the resultant music to present an implied relation to the major-minor key system.

Twilight of the Gods, opera by Wagner. ➤*Ring des Nibelungen*.

Tye, Christopher (*c.* 1505–1573), English composer who became a clergyman in the newly reformed Church of England. Wrote notable church music in Latin and English, including settings of the Acts of the Apostles in metrical rhymed English translation. Also wrote works of the ➤*In nomine* type, for viols.

tzigane (Fr.), gipsy (both sexes), equivalent to Ger. *Zigeuner*, etc.; used by Ravel as title of an extended virtuoso piece for solo violin with piano or orchestral accompaniment (1924).

U

Uccelli, Gli (It., 'The Birds'), orchestral suite by Respighi, first performed in 1927; based on pieces by composers of the 17th and 18th centuries.

Uchida, Mitsuko (b. 1948), Japanese pianist who trained in Vienna; well known in Mozart, she often directs the piano concertos from the keyboard, performing the entire cycle in London, 1985–6. Made New York début in 1987.

'ud (Arabic), the original lute of Arab culture, from which the European lute developed.

Uhr, Die, German nickname ('The Clock') for Haydn's ➤*Clock Symphony*.

Uillean pipes, ➤bagpipes.

'Ukrainian' Symphony, nickname for Tchaikovsky's Symphony no. 2 in C minor, first performed in 1873; so called from the use of folk-tunes in the first and fourth movements. More often called 'Little Russian' Symphony (meaning the same, from a Russian nationalist viewpoint); but 'Ukrainian', as the more intelligible term nowadays, is preferable.

ukulele (or *ukelele*), small guitar-like four-stringed instrument from the South Pacific islands (but of Portuguese origin); having some vogue since the 1920s in the USA and Europe, being cheap and easily learnt. A special notation is used (➤tablature).

Ulisse (It., 'Ulysses'), opera by Dallapiccola, produced in Berlin, 1968; libretto by the composer, freely restructuring the narration of the hero's adventures in Homer's *Odyssey*.

Ullmann, Viktor (1898–1944), Austrian composer (also conductor) who, as a Jew, died at Auschwitz concentration camp. His works include piano concerto, three string quartets, and unfinished opera *Der Kaiser von Atlantis* ('The Emperor of Atlantis') – first performed, in a version completed by the British conductor Kerry Woodward, in Holland, 1975.

Ulster Orchestra, Belfast-based orchestra founded 1966; music director since 1996 (succeeding En Shao), D. Sitkovetsky.

Ulysses, cantata by Seiber, first performed in 1949; text (philosophically speculative) from James Joyce's novel, which takes its name from the parallel with Ulysses, otherwise Odysseus, hero of Homer's *Odyssey*. The Homeric subject was directly treated by Monteverdi in *Il* ➤*ritorno di Ulisse* and by Dallapiccola in ➤*Ulisse*.

un, una, uno (It.), a. (For entries beginning thus, see under second word.)

un, une (Fr.), a. (For entries beginning thus, see under second word.)

unaccompanied, term often used in place of ➤*solo* to emphasize the absence of an expected accompanying instrument, as in Bach's ➤*chaconne* (for violin alone, not with harpsichord).

Unanswered Question, The, orchestral work by Ives, composed 1906, later revised, not published until 1953. A work by Kurtág (*Ligatura – Message to Frances-Marie*) for solo cello has the subtitle *The Answered-Unanswered Question*.

und (Ger.), and.

unda maris (Lat., 'wave of the sea'), organ stop similar to 'voix céleste' (➤*voix*).

'Unfinished' Symphony, name given to Schubert's Symphony no. 8 in B minor, 1822 (D759); not performed until 1865, long after the composer's death. It has only two completed movements, though sketches exist for a third (Scherzo). Schubert presumably either intended to complete the work later; or abandoned it, possibly re-using the intended finale as part of the music to ➤*Rosamunde*.

Union pipes, ➤bagpipes.

unison, a united sounding of the same note: thus *unison song*, a song for several people all singing the same tune (not harmonizing). Expressions such as *singing in unison* are generally (but loosely) also applied to the singing of the same tune by men and women an octave apart – where 'singing in octaves' would be more strictly accurate.

unit organ (also called *extension organ*), type of organ which saves expense in construction, and also saves space, by having various stops 'borrow' pipes from each other. Thus an eight-➤foot stop and a four-foot stop will share pipes for the part of their range that overlaps, instead of having completely separate sets of pipes as on a 'normal' organ. ➤theatre organ.

unprepared (discord), ➤preparation.

Unquenchable, The (Dan., *Det Uudslukkelige*), title of Symphony no. 4 by C. Nielsen, 1916. The title – more usually and more awkwardly translated as 'The Inextinguishable' – comes from the composer's dictum, 'Music is life, and as such is unquenchable'.

up-beat, the upward motion of the conductor's stick or hand, especially as indicating the beat preceding the bar-line, i.e. the beat preceding the main accent (a ➤down-beat); term therefore also used for the beat preceding such an accent, whether or not the piece is being 'conducted'.

up-bow, the motion of the bow of a stringed instrument when pushed by the player – the opposite (pulling) motion being a ➤down-bow.

upper partial, ➤harmonic series.

upright piano, ➤piano.

Upshaw, Dawn (b. 1960), American soprano who performed in the first American performance of Hindemith's opera *Sancta Susanna* (New York, 1983); début at Metropolitan Opera, 1985. Sang the solo in the recording which made a cult-work of Górecki's Symphony no. 3, 1992.

Ursuleac, Viorica (1894–1985), Romanian soprano who settled in Vienna, gave more than 500 performances of roles in R. Strauss's operas, and was married to Clemens Krauss.

Urtext (Ger., original text), an edition purporting to present a composition exactly as written down by the composer, without changes, additions or aids (such as tempo directions) supplied by an editor.

Ussachevsky, Vladimir [Alexis], (1911–90), Manchurian-born composer of Russian parents, resident in the US from 1930; innovator in electronic music. Works include *Creation-Prologue* for four choruses and electronic sounds; *We* (computer-synthesized tape score for radio-dramatic production).

ut, French name for the note *C* in ►solmization.

Ustvolskaya, Galina [Ivanovna] (b. 1919), Russian composer of five symphonies (no. 3 subtitled 'Jesus Messiah, Save Us!', nos. 4 and 5 for less-than-orchestral forces); six piano sonatas, a clarinet concerto from which Shostakovich (her teacher) quoted in two of his own works, etc.

utility music, English equivalent for the original German form ►*Gebrauchsmusik*.

Utopia Limited, or The Flowers of Progress, operetta by Sullivan, produced in London, 1893. Libretto by W. S. Gilbert, postulating a Utopia run on the lines of a British limited-liability company.

V

va., abbr. of ➤viola.

Vagabond King, The, musical play with text by W. H. Post and Brian Hooker, based on *If I Were King* by Justin McCarthy; music by Rudolf Friml. Produced in New York, 1925. The (historical) 15th-century French poet and brawler François Villon is given viceregal power for a day.

Valen, Fartein [Olav] (1887–1952), Norwegian composer who spent his early years in Madagascar and then studied in Berlin; stimulated by Schoenberg's music, evolved his own ➤atonal idiom. Works include five symphonies (no. 5 unfinished), a violin concerto, two string quartets.

Valkyrie, The, opera by Wagner. ➤ *Ring des Nibelungen*.

valse, the French dance-term corresponding to ➤waltz, in wide use (not only by French composers). So *La Valse*, 'choreographic poem' by Ravel for orchestra, 1920; *Valses nobles et sentimentales*, a set by Ravel for piano, 1911, afterwards orchestrated (Ravel intended homage to Schubert, who composed for piano some 'Valses nobles' and some 'Valses sentimentales'). So also *Valse triste* ('sad'), by Sibelius – originally for strings and occurring in the incidental music to the play *Death* by Arvid Järnefelt, afterwards scored for full orchestra and in this version first performed in 1904.

valve, mechanism on brass instruments whereby, at the pressure of the player's finger, the current of air is diverted round an additional length of tubing. Thus the vibrating air-column becomes longer, giving a different ➤harmonic series from that of the unlengthened tube. By means of three valves, each giving a different additional length of tubing, and usable singly or in combination, the modern trumpet (and other instruments) can produce a complete chromatic scale; whereas the valveless trumpet of e.g. Bach's day, like a modern bugle, could produce only one harmonic series, leaving large gaps in the scale. All the brass instruments now normally used in the orchestra, military band, brass band and dance band have valves varying the length of tube for this purpose – except the (normal) trombones, which have slides. A valve is also used (e.g. on a horn in F/B♭ or a cornet in B♭/A) to convert the instrument's basic length to another, thus saving the player the necessity of changing between two instruments.

valve-trombone, ➤*cimbasso*; ➤trombone.

Valverde, Joaquin (1846–1910),

Spanish composer of songs including 'Clavelitos' (Sp., 'Carnations'), etc.

vamp, to improvise an instrumental accompaniment or introduction. e.g. to a song.

van, van den, van der, prefixes to names – see next word of the name, and the following entry.

Van Allan, Richard [originally Alan Philip Jones] (b. 1935), British bass-baritone, active from 1969 in Sadler's Wells (later English National) Opera, his roles ranging from Boris Godunov to Pooh-Bah (in *The Mikado*); has also sung at Covent Garden (since 1971), and at the Metropolitan Opera. Director of the National Opera Studio (training school) since 1986.

Vaňhal, Vanhall, ➤Wanhal.

Varèse, Edgard (1883–1965), French-born composer who settled in USA, 1915, and cultivated music involving extremes of dissonance, unusual instrumentation, and (often) 'scientific' titles – e.g. *Ionisation* (percussion instruments only), *Density 21.5* (flute solo, referring to specific gravity of platinum), *Octandre* (Fr., form of Lat. *octandria*, plant with eight stamens). Was also an influential pioneer in the use of taped and electronic music (➤*poème électronique*).

variation, a passage of music intended as a varied version of some 'given' passage. So *Variations on ... a tune* (whether or not the tune has been specially composed by the composer of the variations), the tune being called the 'theme' of the variations. Such variations may diverge only slightly from the theme, mainly by melodic ornamentation (as in Mozart), but usage since the mid 19th century has tended to a looser type allowing a much freer form of composition, e.g. Elgar's ➤*Enigma Variations*. Other forms implying variations include ➤*chaconne*, ➤ground bass, ➤*passacaglia*.

Variations and Fugue on a Theme of Purcell (Britten), ➤*Young Person's Guide to the Orchestra*.

Variations on a Rococo Theme, work by Tchaikóvsky for cello and orchestra, first performed in 1877 in a version now regarded as unauthentic; original version first heard in 1941. The theme, in olden style (➤rococo), is the composer's own.

Variations on a Theme of Haydn, ➤*St Anthony Variations*.

Varnay, Astrid [Ibolyka Maria] (b. 1918), Swedish-born American soprano of Hungarian parentage; distinguished in Wagner at the New York Metropolitan Opera (from 1941) and elsewhere. In later career sang mezzo-soprano roles.

Varviso, Silvio (b. 1924), Swiss conductor, eminent in opera; first appeared at the Metropolitan Opera, New York, 1961, at Covent Garden and Glyndebourne, 1962. Musical director of the Paris Opera, 1980–85.

Vásáry, Tamás (b. 1933), Hungarian pianist who gave a full evening's recital at age nine; left Hungary in 1956; made London and New York débuts in 1961. Also conductor – music director, Northern Sinfonia, 1979–82; principal, Bournemouth Sinfonietta, 1989–97, Conductor Laureate, Bournemouth Sinfonietta.

vaudeville, French theatrical term of varying meanings, among them that of a song with verses sung by different characters in turn, each verse followed by the same refrain – as in the final number of Mozart's *Die* ➤*Entführung aus dem Serail*.

Vaughan Williams, Ralph (1872–1958), British composer, the representative national figure of his generation; studied briefly with Ravel in Paris. Close associate of Holst; collected English folk-music and drew on it forming his own style. Based his ➤*Sinfonia Antartica* (Symphony no. 7) on his score for film *Scott of the Antarctic*, and brought out his last (ninth) symphony at the age of 85. He numbered only no. 9, identifying the others by key or by name (➤*Sea Symphony* with solo singers and chorus, ➤*London Symphony*, ➤*Pastoral Symphony*). Other works include operas ➤*Hugh the Drover*, ➤*Riders to the Sea, The* ➤*Pilgrim's Progress, Sir John in Love* (➤*Greensleeves*); ballet ➤ *Job*; many choral works (➤*Magnificat*); ➤*Serenade to Music*, originally for 16 solo voices and orchestra; orchestral works with solo instruments including *The* ➤*Lark Ascending*, ➤*Romance* (for harmonica), a tuba concerto (➤*tedesco*); ➤*Fantasia on a Theme of Tallis* for strings; songs, including 'Linden Lea' and cycle ➤*On Wenlock Edge*. Also conductor, especially choral, and hymn-book editor. OM, 1935.

Vautor, Thomas (*c.* 1580–*c.* 1620?), English composer of 'Sweet Suffolk Owl' and other distinctive madrigals in a collection published in 1619. (He was one of the last of the English madrigal school.)

Vecchi, Orazio (1550–1605), Italian composer, also priest; holder of church and court musical posts. Celebrated for *L'*➤*Amfiparnaso*, a sequence of

madrigals forming a comedy; composed many other madrigals and other secular vocal pieces, also Masses and other church music.

Végh, Sándor (1905–97), Hungarian violinist, who studied composition with Kodály, emigrated to Switzerland, then naturalized French in 1953; with Casals at Prades Festival; eminent quartet-leader and teacher. Hon. CBE, 1988.

Vejvanovský, Pavel [Josef] (1633/9–1693), Moravian composer (also trumpeter), who served for 30 years at the court of the prince-bishops at Kroměříž, latterly as musical director. Works include Masses, other church music, chamber music.

veloce (It.), quickly – normally a direction to give an impression of uninterrupted swiftness, rather than to increase actual speed.

Venetian Gondola Song, title used by Mendelssohn for some of the pieces in his ➤*Lieder ohne Worte*.

vent (Fr.), wind: *instruments à vent*, wind instruments.

Ventadorn, Bernart de, ➤Bernart.

Venus and Adonis, masque with music by Blow, produced in London about 1684; librettist unknown.

Vêpres siciliennes, Les (Fr., 'The Sicilian Vespers'), opera by Verdi with libretto by C. Duveyrier and E. Scribe concerning the historic massacre in 1282; first performed in Paris, 1855.

Veracini, Francesco Maria (1690–1768), Italian violinist, composer of more than 50 violin sonatas, various concertos, church music, etc.; three times visited London as performer and composer, and wrote for London (1744) his Italian opera *Rosalinda* (after Shakespeare's *As You Like It*).

Verbunkos (Hung., from Ger. *Werbung*, recruiting), a lively Hungarian dance evoked in the music of Liszt and other Hungarian composers; originally associated with the recruitment of Hungarian soldiers for the Austrian army before 1850, the music being provided by gipsy bands.

Vercors, pseudonym of Jean Bruller (1902–91), French writer. ➤Tomasi.

Verdelot, Philippe (?–before 1552), Flemish composer who held church musical posts in Italy. Was one of the first madrigal-composers (➤madrigal, 1) and wrote also Masses, motets, etc.

Verdi, Giuseppe [Fortunino Francesco] (1813–1901), Italian composer, a commanding figure in opera. Was organist and composer in boyhood, but was rejected by Milan Conservatory as over-age and insufficiently gifted. First opera was *Oberto*, 1839, but first success came with ➤*Nabucco* (1842). There followed (among others) ➤*Macbeth*, ➤*Rigoletto*, *Il* ➤*Trovatore*, *La* ➤*Traviata*, *Les* ➤*Vêpres siciliennes*, ➤*Simon Boccanegra*, *Un* ➤*ballo in maschera*, *La* ➤*forza del destino*, ➤*Don Carlos*, ➤*Luisa Miller*, ➤*Aida*, ➤*Otello* and ➤*Falstaff* (the last two composed in his seventies, in a markedly new style). He also planned a setting of Shakespeare's *King Lear*. Wrote also ➤*Requiem* and a few other works to religious texts, though not himself a churchman; also a string quartet – little else. Through the plots of some of his earlier operas he became the symbol of resurgent Italian nationalism, and frequently clashed with censorships suspecting revolutionary im-

plications: in 1861–5, sat as member of parliament in that part of Italy already unified. Founded a home for aged musicians in Milan. After early death of his first wife he lived with and then married the singer Giuseppina Strepponi. Died in Milan.

Veress, Sándor (1907–92), Hungarian composer (also pianist, writer on music, and collaborator with Bartók in folk-music research); resident mainly in Switzerland from 1950 (naturalized 1975). Works include a concerto for two trombones and orchestra; *Hommage à Paul Klee* (one movement for each of seven pictures) for two pianos and strings; *Sinfonia Minneapolitana* (for what is now the Minnesota Orchestra); trio for ➤baryton, viola and cello.

verismo (It.), realism – term applied particularly to Italian opera of about 1900 (e.g. Mascagni, Puccini) with reference to its 'contemporary' and often violent plots, sometimes amid sordid surroundings – e.g. Puccini's *Il* ➤*tabarro*, aboard a canal barge.

Verklärte Nacht (Ger., 'Transfigured Night'), work by Schoenberg (op. 4, composed in 1899) for string sextet – in effect a 'symphonic poem' for this combination, after a poem by R. Dehmel about a moonlit walk by a man and a woman. The composer's arrangement for string orchestra appeared in 1917.

Véronique, operetta by Messager with libretto by Albert Vanloo and Georges Duval. Produced in Paris, 1898. Pretending to be Véronique, a florist's assistant, the well-to-do Hélène wins a viscount for a husband.

Verrett, Shirley (b. 1931), American mezzo-soprano (also singing some soprano roles) who performed with the New York City Opera from 1958, then internationally; sang Dido in Berlioz's *Les Troyens* at the opening of the Bastille Opera in Paris, 1990.

Verschiebung (Ger., a displacing), use of the soft pedal of the piano.

verse (1) term used in Gregorian chant in the sense of a biblical verse, i.e. a sentence from the Psalms or other text; (2) term indicating, in Anglican church music, the use of solo voice as contrasted with full choir; *verse anthem*, one using such a contrast; (3, as equivalent to Fr. ➤*verset*) a short organ piece replacing a 'verse' in the first sense.

verset (Fr.), a short organ piece, originally as an instrumental replacement for the verse of a psalm in Roman Catholic church usage.

Vespers (Lat., *ad vesperas*, 'in the evening'), the evening service of the Roman Catholic Church (corresponding to Evensong in the Anglican); term also used in the Orthodox churches (➤Vigil). For the 'Monteverdi *Vespers*', ➤*Vespro della Beata Vergine*.

Vespri siciliani, I, Italian title sometimes used for Verdi's (originally French) opera *Les* ➤*Vêpres siciliennes*.

Vespro della Beata Vergine (Lat., 'Vespers of the Blessed Virgin'), designation of a work by Monteverdi published in 1610. It contains more items than would be required for any one service (e.g., two settings of the Mass), and its rationale is debated.

Vestale, La (Fr., 'The Vestal Virgin'), opera by Spontini, produced in Paris, 1807. Libretto by V. J. E. de Jouy. The heroine's religious vows conflict with human love.

via (It.), away with; *via sordini*, take off mutes.

Via Crucis (Lat., 'The Way of the Cross'), work by Liszt for solo singers, chorus and organ, completed in 1879; text, partly biblical, on the Stations of the Cross. Not performed until 40 years after Liszt's death.

Viadana, Lodovico Grosso da (*c.* 1560–1627), Italian composer who took the name Viadana from his birthplace; was also monk. Wrote some madrigals, canzonas, etc., but mainly church music: his *Concerti ecclesiastici* of 1602 are vocal settings printed with an instrumental bass-line below – an early foreshadowing of ➤continuo practice.

Viardot-Garcia, [Michelle Ferdinande] **Pauline** (1821–1910), French mezzo-soprano, daughter of Manuel Garcia the elder, and sister of Maria Malibran. Outstanding in opera, she was much admired by composers: sang the title-role of Gluck's *Orphée* more than 150 times in the edition which Berlioz made for her.

vibraharp, a lesser-used name for the ➤vibraphone.

vibraphone, percussion instrument on which tuned metal bars (laid out on the pattern of a piano keyboard) are struck with small padded beaters held in both hands; beneath the bars are resonators which, constantly opened and closed electronically, impart a vibrating sound to the tone. Compass most commonly from F below middle C, upwards for three octaves. Invented *c.* 1916; thereafter used occasionally in symphonic and operatic music (e.g.

by Berg in ➤*Lulu*) and also in jazz, etc.

vibration, the side-to-side motion of a string, a struck surface, or air-column, by which musical sounds are produced. ➤*frequency*.

vibrato (It., vibrated), a rapid regular fluctuation in pitch – whether tasteful (e.g. as imparted by the oscillatory motion of a violinist's left hand) or exaggerated to a fault, as in a singer's 'wobble'. Not the same as ➤*tremolo*, a fluctuation of intensity, i.e. loudness, not of pitch.

Vickers, Jon [originally Jonathan] [Stewart] (b. 1926), Canadian tenor, eminent in such 'heavy' operatic roles as Verdi's Otello and Wagner's Tristan – at Covent Garden 1957–84, Bayreuth Festival from 1958, etc.

Victoria, Tomás Luis de (1548–1611), Spanish composer (also poet) who worked in Rome for nearly 20 years (hence 'Vittoria', the sometimes encountered Italian form of his name). Then took up a church choirmaster's post in Madrid and died there. Composed only church music, including settings of all the hymns of the Roman Catholic liturgical year and 19 Masses.

Victory, Gerard (form of name used by Alan Loraine) (b. 1921), Irish conductor and composer, music director of Irish Radio and Television, 1967–82. Works include 15 operas (in Gaelic and in English); two symphonies; *Homage to Petrarch* for strings.

Vida breve, La (Sp., 'Brief Life'), opera by Falla, produced in Nice, 1913 (but composed 1904). Libretto by Carlos Fernandez Shaw, the heroine dying of love when her seducer marries another.

vide (Lat., 'See!'), instruction in a written score to make a cut in performance, usually indicated by putting the letters 'vi–' at the point of cut and '–de' at the point of resumption.

vielle (Fr.), term normally meaning a ➤hurdy-gurdy, but also used for the medieval fiddle (➤fiddle, 1).

Vienna Blood, operetta with music by J. Strauss the younger. ➤*Wiener Blut*.

Vienna Boys' Choir, usual English appellation for the Wiener Sängerknaben (Ger., Viennese Singing Boys), descending from the chapel establishment of the former Austrian imperial court, and performing on their own or with adult males.

Vienna Philharmonic Orchestra, a self-governing orchestra tracing its history to the Philharmonic Concerts begun in Vienna by Otto Nicolai in 1842. The orchestra also plays for the Vienna State Opera. Conductors associated with it since World War II have included ➤Karajan, ➤Solti, ➤Böhm, ➤Bernstein, ➤Abbado.

Vie Parisienne, La, operetta by Offenbach with libretto by Henri Meilhac and Ludovic Halévy. Produced in Paris, 1866. A Brazilian, a Swedish couple and other visitors to Paris are happily bamboozled by enterprising young men-about-town.

Vier ernste Gesänge (Ger., 'Four Serious Songs'), song-cycle for bass and piano, based on biblical texts, by Brahms, 1896, his last work but one. The piano accompaniment has been orchestrated, e.g. by Sargent.

Vier letzte Lieder (Ger., 'Four Last Songs'), title bestowed by R. Strauss on his set of songs with orchestra,

1948, to texts by Eichendorff and Hesse.

Vierne, Louis (1870–1937), French organist and composer, pupil of Franck and Widor; born blind, but gained limited sight after operation in childhood, losing it again in his mid-forties. Organist of Notre Dame, Paris; died while playing there. Noted international recitalist. Composer of six 'symphonies' and other solo pieces for organ; also of a Mass, string quartet, etc.

Viertel (Ger., quarter), ➤quarter-note, crotchet.

Vieuxtemps, Henri [Joseph François] (1820–81), Belgian violinist (touring from age seven) and composer of seven violin concertos and other works for his instrument. For a time taught in Russia. Died while visiting Algeria.

vif (Fr.), lively.

Vigarò, Salvatore (1769–1821), Italian choreographer, ➤*Geschöpfe des Prometheus*.

Vigil, alternatively *All Night Vigil*, in the Russian Orthodox Church a long (two or three hour) service combining ➤Vespers and ➤Matins.

vihuela, Spanish plucked instrument of the Renaissance period, shaped like the guitar of that period but strung like the lute; though it was largely superseded by the guitar, music written for it (e.g. by Luis ➤Milán) has been revived by guitarists and lutenists.

Village Romeo and Juliet, A, opera by Delius, produced in Berlin, 1907. Libretto (after a story by G. Keller) by composer, in German (*Romeo und Julia auf dem Dorfe*), though no librettist's name is given in the printed score. The two lovers are the children of quarrelling landowners, and eventually commit suicide together.

Villa-Lobos, Heitor (1887–1959), Brazilian composer, the first South American composer to become world-famous; was also pianist and teacher. Prolific output, including operas, ballets, 12 symphonies, 17 string quartets, songs, etc., in varied styles but frequently with pronounced 'national' flavour. Composed nine ➤*Bachianas Brasileiras* (pieces supposedly both Bach-like and Brazilian) for various ensembles; also 14 works characterized as '*chôros*' (➤*chôro*), for various combinations (some including Brazilian native instruments, explaining the title as synthesizing 'the different modalities of Brazilian, South-American Indian and popular music'. Wrote also *New York Skyline Melody* (on melodic 'shape' suggested by skyline) for piano or orchestra.

villancico (1) a Spanish poetical and musical song-form usually to amorous or devotional words, current in the 16th century: (2) a Spanish 17th-century term for an extended cantata with instrumental accompaniment.

villanella, villanelle (It., Fr.), a countrified or rustic song (or an instrumental piece suggestive of such); especially a type of 16th-century Italian part-song of less complexity than the madrigal.

Villiers de l'Isle Adam, Auguste (1840–89), French writer. ➤*Prigioniero*.

Vinay, Ramón (b. 1912), Chilean tenor famous in 'heavy' operatic roles such as Verdi's Otello and Wagner's Tristan; previously sang baritone, and reverted to baritone in later career

(1962–9), when he also directed operas.

Vinci, Leonardo (*c.* 1690–1730), Italian composer and church musician; wrote operas, some in Neapolitan dialet. No relation of da Vinci the artist.

Viñes, Ricardo (1875–1943), Spanish pianist who settled in Paris, giving early performances of Debussy, Ravel and Falla.

viol, type of bowed stringed instrument of various sizes, current up to about 1700 and thereafter superseded by instruments of the violin type; resuscitated in the 20th century, however, for old music. The viols differ from the violin family in shape, in having frets, and in the kind of bow and style of bowing used. The three principal sizes (often encountered in ensemble) were the *treble viol, tenor viol* and *bass viol*. All, being rested on or between the legs, are properly called *viola da gamba* (. . . for the leg) though that term most commonly indicates the bass viol (approximately cello size). By contrast with *da gamba*, a *viola da braccio* ('viol for the arm') indicated in Renaissance terminology *not* a viol but a violin. The *division viol* was a small bass viol suitable for solos (such as the playing of ➤divisions, i.e. variations); the term ➤*violone* may, but does not always, indicate a deeper-than-bass viol corresponding to modern double-bass.

viola (1) bowed stringed instrument, a lower-pitched relative of the violin, invariably present in the orchestra and the string quartet (and used also as a solo instrument); its compass is from the C below middle C, upwards for more than three octaves. The *viola pomposa* was a rare 18th-century viola with an extra (fifth) higher string; (2) Italian for ➤viol.

viola da braccio, not a viola, nor a viol, but (in Renaissance terminology) a violin. ➤viol.

viola d'amore (It., love-viol), bowed stringed instrument related primarily not to the modern viola but to the ➤viol family – but, unlike them, having no frets, and played under the chin. It has (usually) seven strings touched by the bow, and seven ➤sympathetic strings beneath them (hence the instrument's name) whose vibration is induced by the sounding of the upper set. The instrument is occasionally encountered in music of the 17th–18th centuries and there are some later exceptional uses (e.g. in Meyerbeer's *Les* ➤*Huguenots*).

violin, bowed four-stringed instrument, the principal (and highest) member of the family of instruments (called 'the violin family') which superseded the ➤viols from the late 17th century. The other members are the viola, cello and double-bass. But an early *bass violin*, before the cello was standardized, was used e.g. in Purcell's music as the bass of ensemble, with no double-bass. The violin is prominently used in the orchestra (where the players normally divide into first and second violinists, a division usually corresponding to higher- and lower-pitched parts) and in solo and chamber music. Its compass is from the G below middle C, upwards for three and a half octaves and more.

violino (It.), violin; *violino piccolo*, small-sized, higher-pitched violin occasionally used in 16th–18th centuries, e.g. in Bach's Brandenburg Concerto no. 1.

violoncello, ➤cello.

violone (It., literally 'big viol'), a lower-pitched stringed instrument, with a varying significance according to historical context – a 'double-bass' size of viol, an ordinary double-bass, or even (in Italian baroque music) a cello.

Viotti, Giovanni Battista (1755–1824), Italian violinist and composer (pupil of Pugnani) who came to London in 1792, and afterwards had varied career including the directorship of the Italian Opera in Paris. Died, impoverished, in London. Wrote 29 violin concertos and other violin works; also 10 piano concertos, songs, etc.

virelai, type of medieval French song.

Virgil [Publius Vergilius Maro] (70–19 BC), Roman poet. ➤*Dido and Aeneas*, ➤*Idomeneo*, ➤*Troyens*; ➤Colgrass, ➤Loeffler.

virginal(s) (1) term in English 16th-century sources for all types of keyboard instruments, including the *virginal* proper (see (2) below), the harpsichord, and even the organ; (2) 16th- and 17th-century keyboard instrument of harpsichord type (i.e. the strings being plucked), but smaller and of different shape – oblong, and with its one keyboard along the longer side of the soundboard (not at the end). Its name may be derived from Lat. *virga* (rod or jack) or *virgo* (maiden or virgin), possibly because it used to be played by maidens (or because some analogous instrument had been so played), but certainly not because

of the Virgin Queen, as the instrument was known before her time. The Italian term *spinetto* is used both for this and for the wing-shaped but otherwise similar instrument; but the best English practice is to confine the term ➤spinet to the latter type. Hence *virginalist*, a player on or composer for the virginals.

virtuoso (It.; correct feminine form, *virtuosa*), a performer of exceptional skill, especially in the technical aspects of performance.

Vishnevskaya, Galina [Pavlovna] (b. 1926), Russian soprano who sang at the Bolshoi Theatre, Moscow, from 1953 and became internationally eminent. Sang in first performance of Shostakovich's Symphony no. 14. Married to Rostropovich, she went into forced emigration with him. Retired 1982; published her autobiography in 1984.

Visions fugitives (Fr., 'Fleeting Visions'), collective title for 20 pieces for piano by Prokofiev, first performed (by the composer) 1918.

Visit of the Old Lady, opera by von Einem. ➤*Besuch der alten Dame*.

Vitali, Giovanni Battista (1632–92), Italian violinist and composer who held church and court posts; wrote dance music, sonatas for two and more instruments, psalm-settings, etc. Father of Tommaso Antonio Vitali (below).

Vitali, Tommaso Antonio (1663–1745), Italian violinist and composer of sonatas for two violins with *continuo*, etc. The attribution to him of a famous Chaconne for violin with keyboard accompaniment is now considered unreliable.

Vitebsk, title of a piano trio by Copland (1929), subtitled *Study on a Jewish Theme*, on a melody hailing from that Russian town. (The only overtly Jewish work by this Jewish composer.)

Vitry, Philippe de (1291–1361), French composer – also poet, priest and French court official. Much esteemed in his day, but only a few of his motets survive. Exponent of ➤*ars nova* and author of a treatise on it; thought to have originated the ➤isorhythmic motet.

Vittoria, ➤Victoria, Tomás Luis de.

vivace (It.), lively.

Vivaldi, Antonio (1678–1741), Italian violinist and composer; also priest, nicknamed 'the red priest' (*il prete rosso*) from the colour of his hair. Long in charge of music at an orphanage-conservatory in Venice, but died in obscure circumstances in Vienna. Wrote more than 450 concertos (broadly conforming to the ➤*concerto grosso* type) with various solo instruments, many with illustrative titles, e.g. 'The Four Seasons' (➤*Quattro stagioni*); also operas, church music, oratorios, including *Juditha triumphans*. Bach admired him and transcribed many of his works (e.g. Bach's Concerto for four harpsichords and strings is a transcription of Vivaldi's Concerto for four violins and strings); and there has been a notable revival of interest in his works in the mid 20th century. The currently accepted numbering of his works (superseding various others) follows the thematic catalogue made in 1974 by Peter Ryom: numbers are prefaced RV = *Ryom-Verzeichnis* (Ger., 'index').

Vivier, Claude (1948–83), Canadian composer who studied with Stockhausen; his stay in Bali resulted in *Pulau dewata* for percussion ensemble, and other works; wrote also opera *Copernicus*, choral and piano works. Was murdered.

vivo (It.), lively.

Vlad, Roman (b. 1919), Romanian-born Italian composer, writer on music and festival administrator. Works include *Variations on a 12-note Theme from Mozart's 'Don Giovanni'* for piano and orchestra; Serenata for 12 instruments, operas, ballets, more than 100 film scores.

Vladigerov, Pancho (1899–1978), Bulgarian composer (also pianist) who studied in Berlin; works include opera *Tsar Kaloyan*, a violin concerto, and five piano concertos.

Vltava, ➤*My Country*.

vocal cords (not 'chords'), ➤voice (1).

vocalise (Fr., noun), a wordless composition for solo voice, whether for training purposes or for concert performance. Rakhmaninov's work of this name, though most commonly heard in the purely orchestral version, was originally for voice and piano (1912, revised in 1915).

vocal score, ➤score.

voce (It.), voice: *colla voce*, direction to play 'with the voice' (i.e the accompaniment accommodating the singer on matters of tempo); *sotto voce*, 'under the voice', i.e. in a subdued tone; *voce di petto*, ➤chest voice; *voce di testa*, ➤head voice.

Voces intimae (Lat., 'innermost

voices'), subtitle of Sibelius's only string quartet, 1909.

Vogel, Vladimir [Rudolfovich] (1896–1984), Russian-born composer who studied in Berlin (under Busoni) and settled in Switzerland in 1939, becoming naturalized in 1954. Works include memorial works to Busoni (for orchestra) and to Berg (for piano); secular oratorios *Thyl Claes*, about the 16th-century revolt of the Netherlands); and *Gli spaziali* ('The Spacemen') on text including words of US astronauts.

Vogelhändler, Der (Ger., 'The Bird-Seller'), operetta by Zeller with libretto by Moritz West and Ludwig Held after the comedy *Ce que deviennent les Roses* by Varin and Biéville. Produced in Vienna, 1891. The Tyrolean birdseller nearly loses his intended bride, the village postmistress.

Vogelweide, Walther von der (*c.* 1170–*c.* 1230), German singer and composer of the ➤*Minnesinger* variety), mentioned by Wagner in *Die ➤Meistersinger*.

Vogler, Georg Joseph (1749–1814), German pianist, organist and composer who travelled much and taught many, including Meyerbeer and Liszt; was also priest, and known as the Abbé Vogler ('Abt Vogler' in Robert Browning's poem).

voice (1) the human (and animal) means of sound-production using the two vibrating agents called the vocal cords (not 'chords'); hence (2) a separate 'strand' of music in harmony or counterpoint, whether intended to be sung or played. Thus a fugue is said to be in, say, four voices (for four ➤parts), whether its four 'strands' are sung by individual voices, sung by

several voices each, played by instruments, or all played on one instrument (e.g. piano); (3, verb) to adjust a wind instrument or organ-pipe in the process of construction so that it exactly fits the required standards of pitch, tone-colour, etc.

voice-leading, US term for ➤part-writing.

voix (Fr.), ➤voice (1, 2); so *voix céleste* ('heavenly voice'), a type of organ stop with two pipes to each note, tuned slightly apart and producing a wavering effect.

Voix humaine, La (Fr., 'The Human Voice'), opera (for one woman, desperately telephoning) by Poulenc, produced in Paris, 1959. On the play by Cocteau.

Volans, Kevin (b. 1949), South African composer who studied with Stockhausen; some works have South African associations including *Mbira* (➤mbira) for two harpsichords and rattles. Has also composed *White Man Sleeps* for two harpsichords, bass viol and percussion (with alternative string quartet version requested by Kronos Quartet), chamber opera *The Man with Footsoles of Wind*.

Volkmann, [Friedrich] Robert (1815–83), German composer encouraged by Schumann; works include two symphonies, cello concerto, much chamber music.

Volkonsky, Andrey [Mikhailovich] (b. 1933), Russian (Swiss-born) composer, also pianist; pupil of N. Boulanger in Paris. In Moscow, directed an early-music ensemble. Works include cantata *Dead Souls* (after Gogol); *Serenade to an Insect* for chamber orchestra; a piano quintet, string quartet. Emigrated to Israel in 1973.

Volkslied, ➤folk-song (the two terms not being quite identical).

Volles Werk (Ger., 'full apparatus'), ➤full organ.

volta (It.), time (in the sense of *prima*, *seconda volta*: (first, second time).

Voltaire, François Marie Arouet de (1694–1778), French writer. ➤*Candide*.

volti (It.), turn (imperative); *volti subito* (abbr. VS), turn over the page immediately – direction used especially in old music to prevent a performer's ending or making a break in the music at the bottom of a page, or to warn, after 'rests' at the bottom of a page, that notes begin immediately overleaf.

voluntary, historically (from mid 16th century) a piece suggesting improvisation, but currently signifying an organ piece of the kind used chiefly at the beginning and end of a church service. Some 18th-century English examples using a 'cornet stop' on the organ were known as 'Cornet Voluntary'; but the title ➤*Trumpet Voluntary* is unique – and misleading.

von, von der, prefixes to names – see under next word of the name.

Voříšek, Jan [Hugo] (1791–1825),

Czech composer (also organist and pianist); works include symphonies, ➤impromptus and other works for piano solo, a piano concerto.

Vorspiel (Ger.), prelude. (Term used also e.g. by Wagner in the sense of overture, e.g. that to *Die* ➤*Meistersinger*.)

vox (Lat.), voice; *vox humana*, a reed-stop on the organ supposedly reminiscent of the human voice.

Vranický, Antonín (1761–1820), Moravian violinist and composer of 15 violin concertos, chamber music, etc., who worked from 1783 in Vienna and died there. Brother of the following.

Vranický, Pavel (1756–1808), Moravian violinist and composer of *Oberon* and other operas, 51 symphonies, etc. He worked in Vienna from 1785 and died there. Brother of the preceding.

VS (1) abbr. for 'vocal ➤score'; (2) abbr. for ➤*volti subito*.

vuoto, vuota (It.), empty – applied e.g. to a bar of music in which all performers' parts have a 'rest' (i.e. a ➤general pause); *corda vuota*, open string.

Vyšehrad, ➤*My Country*.

W

W, abbr. for *Werk[e]*, i.e. work(s) (Ger.); equivalent to ➤opus.

Waart, Edo [abbreviation of Eduard] **de** (b. 1941), Dutch conductor, formerly orchestral oboist; musical director of the Rotterdam Philharmonic, 1973–9, of the San Francisco Symphony Orchestra, 1977–85, of the Minnesota Orchestra 1986–95, and chief conductor of Sydney Symphony Orchestra since 1993, chief conductor, Netherlands Opera from 1999–2000.

Waechter, Eberhard (1929–92), Austrian baritone who performed at Bayreuth from 1958 and whose recordings include *Die Fledermaus* under Karajan; became administrator of the Volksoper in Vienna, 1987, and later of the Vienna State Opera also.

Wagenaar, Bernard (1894–1971), Dutch-born composer who settled in USA, 1921, as orchestral violinist and then college teacher. Composed opera *Pieces of Eight*, Triple Concerto (flute, cello, harp), four symphonies, songs, etc. Pupil of his father, Johan Wagenaar (1862–1941).

Wagenseil, Georg Christoph (1715–77), Austrian composer, pupil of Fux; also harpsichordist and organist. Composed at least 30 symphonies (of 'pre-classical') type and 16 operas, also church music, keyboard works, etc.

Wagner, [Wilhelm] **Richard** (1813–83), German composer, profound innovator of opera; for musical and other reasons the most-discussed as well as one of the most-performed of composers. Writer of his own librettos, and of essays on music, theatre, politics, 'race' (violently anti-semitic) and other topics; also conductor, in which function he earned his early living. Born in Leipzig, travelled greatly, met much opposition. Visited London in 1855 and 1877. From ➤*Rienzi* (1842) proceeded to successful operas *Der* ➤*fliegende Holländer*, ➤*Tannhäuser* and ➤*Lohengrin*; then, propounding new relation of music and drama, composed ➤*Tristan und Isolde*, *Der* ➤*Ring des Nibelungen* (cycle of four operas), and ➤*Parsifal*, using a quasi-symphonic construction with ➤leading-motives (i.e. themes), not through the contrast of set 'numbers'. Aimed at the *Gesamtkunstwerk*, the work of art uniting all the arts, towards which end the Festival Theatre at Bayreuth (opened 1876) was built to his own revolutionary design. His only mature comic opera is *Die* ➤*Meistersinger von Nürnberg*. Other compositions include *A* ➤*Faust Overture*, ➤*Huldigungmarsch*, ➤*Siegfried Idyll*, and five ➤*Wesendonck-Lieder*, song-settings (with piano) of poems by Mathilde Wesendonck, at that time his mistress; later lived with Cosima, wife of Bülow and daughter of Liszt, and married her after her divorce from Bülow. He died in Venice. His expansion of the orchestra, especially in *Der* ➤*Ring*, involved the ➤Wagner tuba, constructed to his specification. ➤Baermann.

Wagner-Régeny, Rudolf (1903–69), Romanian-born composer (German citizen from 1933), noted principally for operas including *Die Bürger von Calais* ('The Burghers of Calais') and *Das Bergwerk zu Falun* ('The Mine at Falun').

Wagner tuba, type of instrument (more like a modified orchestral ➤horn than the usual ➤tuba), made in two sizes (tenor and bass), designed to Wagner's specification and used by him (two of each) in *The* ➤*Ring*. The compass of the tenor is from the B♭ in the bass stave upwards for about two and a half octaves; the bass has a compass an octave lower. The instruments have been used also by Bruckner, R. Strauss, and a few others. (Note that the 'double-bass tuba', which Wagner uses with these instruments in *Der Ring*, is not of this family: it is a 'real' tuba of the largest size.)

wait (1) a salaried musician acting as town watchman, or as a member of a court band, etc., in medieval England (hence the modern application of the title to street-singers at Christmastime); (2) old English name for ➤shawm, an instrument much used by the medieval waits.

Walcha, [Arthur Emil] **Helmut** (1907–91), German organist, noted in recitals, almost exclusively of Bach (Royal Festival Hall, London, from 1955); became blind at age 16.

Wald flute, Waldflöte (Ger., forest flute), organ stop of flute-like tone.

Waldhorn (Ger., forest horn), hunting-horn, i.e. a 'natural' ➤horn having no valves.

'Waldstein' Sonata, nickname for Beethoven's Piano Sonato in C, op. 53 (1804), dedicated to Count Waldstein, a musical amateur who was one of Beethoven's patrons.

Waldteufel, Emil (1837–1915), French (Alsatian) pianist and composer of waltzes including the well-known *Les Patineurs* ('The Skaters') and ➤*España*; also other dance-music. Was pianist to the Empress Eugénie of France.

Walker, Sarah (b. 1943), British mezzo-soprano who also studied violin and cello; active in opera, notably in Handel (sang in *Samson* at the Metropolitan, New York, 1986); also soloist in the ritual Last Night of the Proms, etc.

Walküre, Die, opera by Wagner. ➤*Ring*.

Wallace, Ian [Bryce] (b. 1919), British bass who trained as a lawyer; sang at Sadler's Wells Opera and at Glyndebourne, 1948–56. The title of his autobiography, *Promise Me You'll Sing Mud*, 1975, marks his association in light entertainment with Michael Flanders and Donald ➤Swann.

Wallace, John (b. 1949), British trumpeter, well known as soloist on modern and baroque trumpets. Founder (1986) and leader of his own ensemble, the Wallace Collection.

Wallace, William (1860–1940), British composer of *The Passing of Beatrice* (1892), thought to be the first symphonic poem by a British composer; also of other symphonic poems, songs, etc. Was also writer on music, and ophthalmologist. No relation of William Vincent Wallace.

Wallace, William Vincent (1812–65), Irish composer of the formerly very popular opera ►*Maritana* and of other operas, a violin concerto, piano solos, etc. Originally violinist. Visited Australia and New Zealand as a young man, and North and South America later. Died in France.

Wallfisch, Raphael (b. 1953), British cellist, prominent as recitalist and in concertos – has recorded those by Barber, Bax, Delius as well as the standard works. Was often partnered by his father, the pianist Peter Wallfisch (1924–93).

Wally, La (name of heroine; the *La* is superfluous), opera by Catalani, produced in Milan, 1892, with libretto by L. Illica: an Alpine drama in which the heroine and her lover are finally engulfed in an avalanche.

Walmisley, Thomas Attwood (1814–56), British organist, professor of music at Cambridge, and composer chiefly of church and organ music.

Walond, William (*c.* 1725–1770), British composer of keyboard pieces, an *Ode on St Cecilia's Day* to Pope's words, etc.; also organist. Another composer of the same name (?–1836) was probably his son.

Walter, Bruno [originally Bruno Walter Schlesinger] (1876–1962), German-born conductor, also pianist; settled in Austria, then (penalized as a Jew under the Nazis) took French (1938) and later US (1946) nationality. Disciple and advocate of Mahler;

noted also in opera (at Covent Garden 1924–31).

Walther, Johann (1496–1570), German composer and publisher, adviser to Luther; he issued in 1524 the first Protestant hymn-collection. Composed also secular songs and instrumental music.

Walton, William [Turner] (1902–83), British composer, largely self-taught. Showed early influence of jazz and Stravinsky, e.g. in ►*Façade* (reciter and instruments; later arranged for ballet). Other works include two symphonies, concertos for viola (►Hindemith), violin and cello; *Improvisations on an Impromptu by Benjamin Britten* for orchestra (►impromptu); overture ► *Portsmouth Point*; march ►*Crown Imperial*; ►*Belshazzar's Feast* and smaller choral works (►*TeDeum*); operas ►*Troilus and Cressida* and *The* ►*Bear*; film music (including *Henry V*); two string quartets, a violin sonata (►twelvenote). Knighted, 1951. OM, 1968. Lived from 1948 in Ischia (Italy).

waltz, dance in triple time becoming universally known in the 19th century, the French form ►*valse* being often used; characteristically harmonized with only one chord to each bar.

Waltz Dream, A, operetta by Oscar Straus. ►*Walzertraum.*

Walzer (Ger.), ►waltz.

Walzertraum, Ein (Ger., 'A Waltz Dream'), operetta by Oscar Straus, produced in Vienna, 1907. Libretto by F. Dörmann and L. Jacobson; a waltz is treated as the symbol of a nostalgic longing for Vienna.

Wand, Günter (b. 1912), German

conductor, principal conductor of North German Radio since 1982; has toured widely, making London début in 1951. Is also composer.

'Wanderer' Fantasy, nickname given to Schubert's Fantasy for piano in C, 1822 (D760), because it makes use of material found also in his song 'Der Wanderer' (1816). Best known as arranged by Liszt for piano and orchestra.

Wanhal(l), Johann Baptist (German form of Jan Křtitel Vaňhal) (1739–1813), Bohemian composer; his name was sometimes (e.g. on English editions) spelt 'Vanhall', and he has thus been erroneously said to be of Dutch descent. Visited Italy but worked mainly in Vienna, where he died. Friend of Haydn and Mozart: composed more than 70 symphonies, about 100 string quartets, much church music, etc.

War and Peace (Rus., *Voyna i mir*), opera by Prokofiev; libretto, after Tolstoy's novel, by the composer and M. Mendelson. The first version was heard in a partial concert performance with piano in Moscow, 1944, and first staged in Prague, 1948; after that what is regarded as the first substantially complete performance took place in Moscow, 1959.

War of the Comedians/Buffoons, name given (in French as *Guerre des Bouffons*) to the literary quarrel in Paris between the champions of the Italian style, as evidenced by Pergolesi's opera *La* ➤*Serva padrona*, and of the French.

Ward, John (1571–1638), English composer; published a set of madrigals – the type of work for which he is noted – in 1613; wrote also music for viols and for keyboard, church music, etc.

Ward, Robert [Eugene] (b. 1917), American composer of operas *He Who Gets Slapped* and *The Crucible* (after Arthur Miller); also of six symphonies, choral works, etc.

Warlock, Peter, pseudonym used (as composer) by Philip [Arnold] Heseltine (1894–1930), who also wrote about music (e.g. a book on Delius) under his own name. Works include song-cycle *The* ➤*Curlew* and many other songs; also suite ➤*Capriol*, choral works, orchestral serenade for Delius's 60th birthday, etc. Also transcribed old English music, e.g. by Dowland. His sudden death is often presumed to have been a suicide.

War Requiem, A, work by Britten for soprano, tenor, baritone, chorus and orchestra, first performed in Coventry, 1962; text – from Roman Catholic Requiem (in Latin) and Wilfred Owen's poems – carries an anti-war message.

Water Music, name commonly used to designate a set of orchestral pieces by Handel, composed for a royal procession on the Thames (1715, 1717?) – the exact circumstances being uncertain. Published later as set of 20 pieces, of which six were arranged by Harty in a celebrated suite (1920) using modern orchestration.

water-organ, ➤hydraulis.

Watkins, Michael Blake (b. 1948), British composer (also guitarist). Works include trumpet concerto, double concerto (oboe, guitar, orchestra), various solo and ensemble pieces for guitar(s).

Watts, André (b. 1946), American pianist of Hungarian and black American parentage, born in Germany; made New York concerto début (Bernstein conducting) in 1963 and celebrated the 25th anniversary of that début with televised concert, 1988.

Wat Tyler, opera by A. Bush, produced in Leipzig, 1953. Libretto by Nancy Bush (the composer's wife) about the leader of the Peasants' Revolt in England, 1381.

Wayenberg, Daniel [Ernest Joseph Carel] (b. 1929), French-born pianist of Dutch family, resident in France. Also composer of a symphony, concerto for three pianos and orchestra, etc.

Webbe, Samuel (1740–1816), British organist, composer of vocal music from Roman Catholic Masses and motets to glees and catches; father of Samuel Webbe (below).

Webbe, Samuel (c. 1770–1843), pianist, organist, composer of vocal music, etc.; also writer of textbooks. Son of the above.

Webber, Andrew Lloyd and **Julian Lloyd,** ➤Lloyd Webber.

Weber, surname of two unrelated composers (separately below): the surname alone indicates reference to C. M. von Weber.

Weber, Ben [forenames originally William Jennings Bryan] (1916–79), American composer who abandoned medicine for music, largely self-taught; works include a piano concerto, a 'symphony' for baritone and chamber orchestra on poems by Blake, piano solos, ballet *Pool of Darkness*.

Weber, Carl Maria [Friedrich Ernst] **von** (1786–1826), German composer, also conductor and pianist. Exponent of German ➤Romantic opera, particularly in *Der* ➤*Freischütz*, a lasting international success. Other operas include ➤*Abu Hassan,* ➤*Euryanthe* and ➤*Oberon* – the last written in English for England; Weber died in London after superintending the first production. (He had poor health, and was financially driven to over-work.) Also wrote incidental music to plays, including ➤*Preciosa* and ➤*Turandot*; two piano concertos and *Konzertstück* for piano and orchestra; two concertos and a concertino for clarinet; a bassoon concerto; ➤*Aufforderung zum Tanz* ('Invitation to the Dance') and other piano solos; church music, songs, etc. Also writer on music; wrote an unfinished novel *A Composer's Life*, criticism, poems.

Webern, Anton von (1883–1945), Austrian composer, pupil of Schoenberg, whose ➤twelve-note technique he adapted with a special concern for the relationship between a particular tone-quality and a particular note. His works, mainly vocal or in the nature of chamber music, are few (but have been highly influential since 1950) and tend to extreme brevity: no. 4 of his *Five Pieces for Orchestra* (1913), scored for nine instruments including mandolin, takes six and one-third bars and lasts 19 seconds. Other works include a symphony; Variations for orchestra; cantatas; five works for string quartet; songs on texts by Stefan George and others. He was accidentally shot dead in the Allied occupation of Austria.

Wechseldominante, ➤dominant.

Weckerlin, Jean-Baptiste Théodore (1821–1910), French composer of operas, chamber music, etc., and editor of much old French music.

We Come to the River, opera by Henze, produced in London, 1976; libretto by Edward Bond, castigating war and social injustice.

Wedding, The (Rus., *Svadebka*), ballet with music by Stravinsky (for chorus, four pianos and percussion) produced in Paris, 1923 – hence the French title sometimes used, *Les Noces.*

Wedding Day at Troldhaugen, piano piece by Grieg, 1897, later orchestrated, Troldhaugen being the name of the composer's own house near Bergen, Norway.

'Wedge' Fugue, nickname given to the longer of Bach's two Organ Fugues in E minor, composed between 1727 and 1736; the opening subject proceeds in gradually widening intervals.

Weelkes, Thomas (*c.* 1575–1623), English composer of many strongly individual madrigals – including 'As Vesta was from Latmos hill descending' in *The* ➤*Triumphs of Oriana*; also of ➤balletts and other secular vocal music, and of church music. Wrote also pieces for viols, some of the ➤*In nomine* type. Friend of Morley, in whose memory he wrote a three-part song; also organist of Winchester Cathedral.

Weidinger, Anton (1767–1852), Austrian trumpeter; he played the newly evolved keyed trumpet, and for him and his instrument Haydn wrote his Trumpet Concerto (Hob. VIIe: 1), 1796.

Weigl, Joseph (1766–1846), Austrian composer of operas (chiefly comic) in German and Italian; also of church music, etc. Worked in Vienna as conductor of court opera, later as vice-director of royal chapel. Godson of Haydn.

Weigl, Karl (1881–1949), Austrian-born, American-naturalized composer of six symphonies, eight string quartets (no. 2 has a viola d'amore), etc. Also teacher and (1904–6) assistant coach at the Vienna Court Opera under Mahler.

Weihe des Hauses, Die (Ger., 'The Consecration of the House'), title of a German play to which Beethoven wrote an overture and incidental music, 1822. The play, by C. Meisl, was adapted from an earlier play, Kotzebue's *The Ruins of Athens,* to which Beethoven had also written an overture and incidental music.

Weihnachts-Oratorium (Ger.), ➤*Christmas Oratorio.*

Weihnachtssymphonie (Ger., Christmas Symphony), another nickname for Haydn's ➤*Lamentatione* symphony.

Weill, Kurt [Julian] (1900–1950), German-born composer, pupil of Humperdinck and Busoni. Borrowing from some jazz-based idioms, he had early success with *Die* ➤*Dreigroschenoper*), and with ➤*Aufstieg und Fall der Stadt Mahagonny* – both to texts by Brecht with satirical criticism of capitalist society. Penalized by the Nazis as a Jew and a composer of 'decadent' music (➤*entartete Musik*), he settled in USA, 1935 (naturalized 1943). His American works include operas ➤*Street Scene* and *Down in the Valley,* music to various Broadway musical plays including *Lost in the Stars.* Other works include cantata

Lindbergh's Flight (1929), two symphonies.

Weinberger, Jaromir (1896–1967), Czech composer who studied with Reger in Berlin, lived in USA, 1922–6, and settled in USA, 1939. Works include opera ➤*Švanda the Bagpiper*, formerly much performed; also orchestral Variations and Fugue on 'Under the Spreading Chestnut Tree', etc.

Weiner, Leó (1885–1960), Hungarian composer, also noted teacher in Budapest and writer on music. Works include five Divertimentos for orchestra, two violin concertos, works for piano based on Hungarian folk-music.

Weingartner, [Paul] Felix, Count von Münzberg (1863–1942), German conductor (also composer) of unsurpassed reputation (London début 1908), making famous Beethoven recordings in the 1930s.

Weinzweig, John Jacob (b. 1913), Canadian composer, also conductor and teacher. Works include a symphony and *Symphonic Ode* for orchestra; a harp concerto; *Around the stage in 25 minutes during which a variety of instruments are struck* for percussionist.

Weir, Gillian [Constance] (b. 1941), New Zealand organist (also harpsichordist) who trained in London and has been prominent as organ soloist in Britain and elsewhere since 1965; noted interpreter of Messiaen. Created Dame, 1996.

Weir, Judith (b. 1954), British composer. Works include *A Night at the Chinese Opera*, *Blond Eckbert* and *King Harald's Saga*; *Heaven ablaze in his breast* for voices, two pianos and eight dancers; pieces for piano and for organ. CBE, 1995.

Weisgall, Hugo [David] (b. 1912), American composer (born in Czechoslovakia); works include operas *Six Characters in Search of an Author* (after Pirandello), *The Stronger* (after Strindberg) and other operas; also *Proclamations and Prospects* for orchestra, two piano sonatas.

Weiss, Sylvius Leopold (1686–1750), German lutenist and composer for his instrument, working at various courts.

Weissenberg, Alexis (b. 1929), Bulgarian-born pianist who made his début in Israel at 14, then trained at Juilliard School, New York; naturalized French, 1956. Celebrated soloist, e.g. recording with Karajan, Giulini, etc.

Weldon, John (1676–1736), English organist and composer of church and stage music including *The Judgement of Paris*. His music to a Restoration version of Shakespeare's *The Tempest* was formerly attributed to Purcell, his teacher.

Weller, Walter (b. 1939), Austrian conductor, formerly violinist and quartet-leader in Vienna; conducted both concert and opera in Vienna, but his first major post was with the Royal Liverpool Philharmonic Orchestra, 1977–80. Since 1992, conductor of the Royal Scottish National Orchestra.

Wellesz, Egon (1885–1974), Austrian-born composer (pupil of Schoenberg) who settled in England, 1939, as Oxford University lecturer; authority on Byzantine music. Works include *Alkestis* (in German), *Incognita* (in English) and other operas; *The Leaden Echo and the Golden Echo*

(Gerard Manley Hopkins) for soprano and four instruments; Roman Catholic church music; a violin concerto, songs. CBE, 1957.

Wellingtons Sieg, oder Die Schlacht bei Vitoria (Ger., 'Wellington's Victory, or the Battle at Vitoria'), orchestral work by Beethoven, 1813. (He wrote 'Vittoria' by mistake.) Also known as the 'Battle Symphony', it is illustrative of a British and allied victory over Napoleonic forces at Vitoria, Spain, and quotes various national airs.

Wells, H. G. [Herbert George] (1866–1946), British writer. ➤*Half a Sixpence.*

Well-tempered Clavier, The, keyboard work by Bach. ➤*Wohltemperirte Clavier.*

Welser-Möst, Franz [originally Franz Leopold Maria von Bennigsen] (b. 1960), Austrian conductor. After British début with London Philharmonic Orchestra in 1986, became its principal conductor in 1990; under criticism, he left in 1995. Music director of Zurich Opera since 1995.

Welsh National Opera (or **Opera Cenedlaethol Cymru**), British opera company based in Cardiff, achieving full professional status 1970; musical director since 1992 (succeeding Mackerras), Carlo Rizzi.

Wenzinger, August (b. 1905), Swiss cellist, viol-player and conductor; a pioneer in establishing 'authentic' baroque orchestral performances, particularly with the (Swiss) Schola Cantorum Basiliensis, of which he was co-founder in 1933.

Werle, Lars Johan (b. 1926), Swedish composer of operas including The Dream about Thérèse, designed with special instrumentation to be performed 'in the round' (orchestra encircling audience encircling singers) and one on Shakespeare's A Midsummer Night's Dream, also Chants for Dark Hours for mezzo-soprano, flute, guitar and percussion, Pentagram for string quartet.

Werner, Gregor [Joseph] (1693–1766), Austrian composer of 40 Masses, fugues for string quartet, etc.; in service to the Esterházy family, succeeded after his death by Haydn.

Wert, Giaches de [or Jaches de] (1535–96), Flemish composer who went to Italy as a boy chorister and settled there, dying in Mantua. Wrote madrigals, motets, etc., and held court and church musical posts.

Werther, opera by Massenet, produced (in German) in Vienna, 1892; libretto, in French, by É. Blau, P. Milliet and G. Hartmann – after Goethe's The Sorrows of Werther, the hero being driven by sentimental love to suicide.

Wesendonck-Lieder, a set of five songs for female voice by Wagner, published 1862 to poems by his mistress Mathilde Wesendonck (alternatively spelt Wesendonk). The last, Träume ('Dreams'), he also arranged for violin and small orchestra.

Wesker, Arnold (b. 1932), British dramatist. ➤Saxton.

Wesley, Charles (1757–1834), British organist, harpsichordist and composer (concertos, anthems, etc.); a youthful prodigy who did not fulfil his early promise. Pupil of Boyce. Nephew of John Wesley, the founder of Methodism, and brother of Samuel Wesley.

Wesley, Samuel (1766–1837), British organist and composer; despite his family background (see preceding entry) became Roman Catholic, writing Masses, Latin motet *In exitu Israel*, etc. Also composed symphonies, four organ concertos, etc. A head injury in youth caused his later mental instability. Was among the first British enthusiasts for Bach; hence, doubtless, the middle name of his son (below).

Wesley, Samuel Sebastian (1810–76), British composer, illegitimate son of the preceding; also organist, finally at Gloucester Cathedral, attempting a re-invigoration of Anglican cathedral music. Wrote much church music; also choral 'Ode to Labour' and some piano pieces.

West Side Story, musical with text by Arthur Laurents and lyrics by Stephen Sondheim; music by Leonard Bernstein. Produced in New York, 1957. A Romeo and Juliet story in terms of youth gangs in New York.

whip, percussion instrument imitative of the crack of a whip and consisting of two pieces of wood joined in a V-shape: the player snaps the 'arms' loudly together.

whistle (1, verb) to produce a vocal sound through a small aperture in the lips, the pitch being governed by the shaping of the mouth as a resonating chamber. A few professional whistlers have occasionally penetrated to the concert-platform; (2, noun) general name for various wind instruments, usually of primitive construction (and sometimes played with the nose) giving a sound similar to human whistling – such as the ➤tin-whistle.

White, Maude Valérie (1855–1937), British composer, born in France; wrote mainly songs, in French, English and German; also a few piano pieces, etc.

white noise, a hissing, wind-like sound used in electro-acoustic music, the result of all frequencies within the audible ➤spectrum sounding simultaneously at randomly varying amplitudes.

White, Patrick (1912–90), Australian writer. ➤Meale.

White, Robert [or Whyte] (*c*. 1538–74), English composer who died of the plague; wrote church music (chiefly but not entirely to Latin texts), and also music for viols, etc. Married Ellen Tye, probably a daughter of the composer Tye.

White, Willard (b. 1946), Jamaican bass resident in Britain; appeared with New York City Opera from 1974, Welsh National Opera from 1976; roles at Covent Garden have included Klingsor (*Parsifal*) and Porgy (*Porgy and Bess*). CBE, 1995.

White Peacock, The, work for piano by Griffes (1915), later orchestrated; after a poem by 'Fiona Macleod' (William Sharp), and originally forming one of four *Roman Sketches*.

Whithorne (originally Whittern), **Emerson** (1884–1958), American composer – also pianist, pupil of Leschetizky in Vienna; lived for a time in England and China. Works include *New York Days and Nights* and other piano pieces; symphonic poems, chamber music, etc.

Whithorne, Thomas, ➤Whythorne.

Whitlock, Percy [William] (1903–46), British organist, and composer chiefly of organ and church music.

Whitman, Walt (1819–92), American poet. ➤Requiem; ➤*Sea Drift*.

whole-note, the note 𝅝 considered as a time-value. This term is standard North American usage and, as mathematically corresponding to the element of time-signature represented by /1, should clearly be preferred to 'semibreve', still surviving in British use. The corresponding rest is notated 𝄻.

whole-tone, the interval of two semitones, e.g. from C up to the adjacent D – divisible into the two semitones C–C♯ and C♯–D. So *whole-tone scale*, a scale progressing entirely in whole-tones, instead of partly in whole-tones and partly in semitones like the major and minor scales and the old ➤modes. Only two such whole-tone scales are possible – one 'beginning' on C, one on C♯, though in fact each scale can equally well begin on any of its notes, since (owing to the equal intervals) there is no note which presents itself as a point of rest equivalent to a keynote. The scale has been more often used to generate particular chords, melodic figures etc., than complete pieces.

Whyte, Robert, ➤White (R.).

Whythorne, Thomas (1528–96), English composer who travelled in Italy and elsewhere, and wrote music for voices, for viols, etc., including some duos expressly with option for voices or for instruments. His autobiography, written in phonetic script, was rediscovered in 1955.

Widerspänstigen Zähmung, Der (Ger., 'The Taming of the Shrew'), opera by Goetz, produced in Mannheim, 1874; libretto by J. V. Widmann after Shakespeare's play.

Widor, Charles-Marie [-Jean-Albert] (1844–1937), French organist, composer and noted teacher, holder of a church appointment at St Sulpice, Paris, for 64 years. Works include many solos for organ including ten 'symphonies' (source of celebrated ➤Toccata) as well as orchestral symphonies, two piano concertos, operas.

Wiegenlied (Ger.), cradle-song; the one sometimes attributed to Mozart ('Schlafe, mein Prinzchen' – 'Sleep, my little prince') is really by J. Bernhard Flies, an amateur composer born about 1770.

Wiener Blut (Ger., 'Vienna Blood'), operetta compiled from the music of J. Strauss the younger, with the composer's consent, by A. Müller; produced in Vienna, 1899. Libretto by V. Leon and L. Stein. Concerns romantic intrigue in Vienna, 1815, and is named from a Strauss waltz (1871) incorporated in it.

Wiener Sängerknaben, ➤Vienna Boys' Choir.

Wieniawski, Henryk (1835–80), Polish violinist, composer of two concertos (no. 2 is the well-known one) and other music for his instrument. Toured much (in USA with Anton Rubinstein), taught many years at the Brussels Conservatory, and died in Moscow.

Wigglesworth, Mark (b. 1964), British conductor who worked with various British, Continental and North American orchestras, also in opera (music director of Opera Factory, 1991–4), before being appointed conductor of BBC National Orchestra of Wales from 1996.

Wilbye, John (1574–1638), English composer, particularly of madrigals (including 'Flora gave me fairest flowers'). His other works, which are very few, include a little church music (in Latin and English), and some pieces for viols. Contributor to *The* ➤*Triumphs of Oriana*. In service to noble English families.

Wild, Earl (b. 1915), American pianist, celebrated in Liszt and other virtuoso-style music, who made his London début in 1973; performed at President Kennedy's inauguration, 1961.

Wilde, David [Clark] (b. 1935), British pianist who won Liszt-Bartók competition, Budapest, 1961. Concerto soloist with major orchestras, teacher in Hanover; also television presenter, writer and occasional conductor.

Wilde, Oscar (1854–1900), Irish writer. ➤*Salome*; ➤Ibert, ➤Zemlinsky.

Wilder, Thornton (1897–1975), Amercan novelist and dramatist. ➤Reutter.

Wilhelmj, August [Emil Daniel Ferdinand] (1845–1908), German violinist who in 1893 settled in London as teacher, and died there. Wrote cadenzas for celebrated violin concertos, arrangements for violin, etc. – e.g. the so-called *Air on the G String* of Bach (➤air).

Willaert, Adriaan (*c.* 1490–1562), Flemish composer who worked chiefly in Venice as church musician, achieving high influence and dying there. Was one of the first to compose madrigals, to write independent instrumental pieces (of the ➤*ricercar* type) and to employ double choirs antiphonally. Composed Masses, motets, psalm-settings and other works to religious and secular texts.

Willan, Healey (1880–1968), British-born organist and composer who settled in Canada (Toronto University post, 1914). Composed symphony, cantatas, church and organ music, etc.

Willcocks, David [Valentine] (b. 1919), British organist, conductor, and music editor. Music director of the Bach Choir (London) 1960–98; director, Royal College of Music, 1974–85. Knighted, 1977.

Williams, Grace (1906–77), British composer, pupil of Vaughan Williams (no relation) in London and of Wellesz in Vienna. Works include ➤*Penillion* for orchestra, symphonic variations *Owen Glendower* and other works with Welsh associations; also opera *The Parlour*, a trumpet concerto, etc.

Williams, John [Christopher] (b. 1941), Australian guitarist (resident in Britain), for whom works have been written by Takemitsu, Brouwer, Sculthorpe and others; eminent soloist, occasional guitar-duettist with Julian Bream; led his own ensemble embracing jazz and pop as well as classical traditions, 1979–84. OBE, 1980.

Williams, John [Tower] (b. 1932), American conductor and composer; he wrote the music to *Jaws, Close Encounters of the Third Kind* and many other films. Conductor of the Boston Pops Orchestra 1980–95.

Williams, Ralph Vaughan, ➤Vaughan Williams.

Williamson, Malcolm [Benjamin Graham Christopher] (b. 1931), Australian composer resident in Britain since 1953; also organist and pianist. Works include ➤*Our Man in Havana*, *The Violins of St Jacques* and other operas; also three piano concertos, five symphonies, and Roman Catholic church music in popular-song style and recently works recognizing Australian aboriginal culture, including *Requiem for a Tribe Brother* for unaccompanied chorus. Master of the Queen's Music since 1975, he has not substantially associated himself with royal occasions. CBE, 1976.

William Tell, opera by Rossini. ➤*Guillaume Tell*.

Wilson, John (1595–1674), English lutenist, singer, viol-player, and composer of songs (some to words by Shakespeare), catches, psalms, etc. Is thought to be identical with the 'Jack Wilson' who acted in Shakespeare's company in *Much Ado About Nothing*. Later, court musician to Charles I and Charles II.

Wilson, Sandy [forenames originally Alexander Galbraith] (b. 1924), composer of musicals including *The* ➤*Boy Friend*.

Wilson, Thomas [Brendan] (b. 1927), British composer (born in USA of British parents); professor at Glasgow University. Works include four symphonies, concertos for various instruments, opera *The Confessions of a Justified Sinner*.

Wimberger, Gerhard (b. 1923), Austrian composer of *Dame Kobold* (after Calderón) and other operas; *Risonanze* (It., 'resonances') for three orchestral groups; cantatas; etc.

wind band, term used to describe a band of mixed wind instruments (usually with percussion also); ➤military band is, however, the traditional British term (a ➤brass band being of brass alone, not mixed with woodwind). Haydn's so-called *Wind Band Mass* (in B♭, 1802, Hob. XXII: 14; Ger., *Harmoniemesse*), however, got its nickname only because wind instruments are used in it prominently, not exclusively.

Windgassen, Wolfgang (1914–74), German tenor, a leading Wagner singer (Covent Garden, Bayreuth, etc.) of the 1950s and beyond. Was artistic director of Stuttgart Opera, 1972–4.

wind instrument, generic name for musical instruments in which the sound is produced through the vibrations of a column of air which is set in motion by the player's breath – such instruments being commonly divided into ➤woodwind and ➤brass (convenient labels to classify differing types of mechanism, though the implication that all the former are made of wood and the latter of brass is misleading). Instruments in which the effect of the breath is mechanically simulated, e.g. organ and accordion, are not normally understood by the term *wind instruments*, though all may be classified as ➤aerophones.

wind-machine, theatrical 'effects' machine simulating wind (usually by means of the rotation of a fabric-covered barrel) used in a few musical works – e.g. R. Strauss's ➤*Don Quixote*.

Winter Journey, song-cycle by Schubert. ➤*Winterreise*.

Winterreise (Ger., 'Winter Journey'),

song-cycle by Schubert, 1827, on 24 poems by W. Müller about an unrequited love.

'Winter Wind' Study, nickname for Chopin's Study in A minor, op. 25, no. 11, 1834.

wire brush, type of drumstick with a head of several stiff wires, used to give a 'brushing' sound to a side-drum or cymbals – an effect prominent in dance bands of the 1930s, etc.

Wirén, Dag [Ivar] (1905–86), Swedish composer (also critic) who studied in Paris. Works include Serenade (for strings), five symphonies, a violin concerto, piano concerto, cello concerto, stage and film music, five string quartets.

Wise, Michael (c. 1647–87), English singer, organist and composer of anthems, catches, etc.; killed in a street brawl.

Witches' Minuet, ➤Fifths Quartet.

Witt, Jeremias Friedrich (1771–1837), Austrian composer of Masses, orchestral works, etc., including the so-called ➤Jena symphony formerly attributed to Beethoven.

Wittgenstein, Paul (1887–1961), Austrian pianist (naturalized American, 1946) who lost his right arm in World War I and for whom R. Strauss, Ravel, Britten and others wrote piano works for left hand alone (with orchestra). Elder brother of the philosopher Ludwig Wittgenstein.

Wohltemperirte Clavier, Das (Ger., old spelling, 'The Well-tempered Clavier'), title given by Bach to his 24 Preludes and Fugues, 1722, in all the major and minor keys, and commonly extended to a further similar 24

(1744); the title is thus now applied to the two sets together, which are also known as 'The Forty-Eight'. The use of all the major and minor keys demonstrated the facilities offered by the system of 'equal ➤temperament'. The word 'clavier', meaning any keyboard instrument, is correct here – not clavichord, Bach not intending the work exclusively for that instrument.

wolf (1) a jarring sound sometimes occurring through unintentional vibrations on stringed instruments; (2) an out-of-tune effect occurring in certain keys on old organs tuned in 'mean-tone ➤temperament' – not in 'equal temperament' by which all keys are equally 'in tune'.

Wolf, Hugo [Filipp Jakob] (1860–1903), Austrian composer chiefly of songs, usually grouped by their literary sources: ➤Italienisches Liederbuch, ➤Spanisches Liederbuch, ➤Mörike-Lieder (57) and songs to texts by Goethe (51), usually reckoned to constitute a peak within the general German Romantic type of song (a few with orchestral accompaniment as alternative to piano). Other works include opera Der Corregidor and ➤Italienische Serenade. Lived largely in poverty; proved himself unfitted to conducting; was an aggressive music critic (extolling Wagner, decrying Brahms); became insane in 1897 and was confined from 1898 till death.

Wolff, Christian (b. 1934), French-born American composer, naturalized 1946; university teacher of classics and music. Has written music using tapes, music for prepared piano and for non-fixed ensembles ('for one, two or three people' on any instruments), etc., and has evolved his own notation.

Wolf-Ferrari, Ermanno (1876–1948), Italian-born composer, son of a German father and Italian mother; pupil of Rheinberger. Works are principally operas (in Italian, though some were first given in German). They include *I* ➤*quatro rusteghi*, *Il* ➤*segreto di Susanna* and *I* ➤*gioielli della Madonna*. Wrote also chamber music, etc.

Wolkenstein, Oswald von, ➤Oswald von Wolkenstein.

Wolpe, Stefan (1902–72), German-born composer who emigrated to Austria, to Palestine, then (1938) to USA, teaching there. Works include song-settings to Hebrew texts, piano pieces, chamber music, *Solo Piece for Trumpet*, a symphony.

Wolstenholme, William (1865–1931), British organist and composer, blind from birth; composed chiefly for the organ. Also violinist (taught by Elgar) and pianist.

Woman of Arles, The, play by Alphonse Daudet. ➤*Arlésienne*.

Woman's Love and Life, song-cycle by Schumann. ➤*Frauenliebe und -leben*.

Woman without a Shadow, The, opera by R. Strauss. ➤*Frau ohne Schatten*.

WoO, abbr. for German *Werk ohne Opuszahl* (work without opus number), referring particularly to those works by Beethoven to which the composer did not give a number but which were listed in the thematic catalogue by G. Kinsky (1955).

Wood, Charles (1866–1926), Irish organist, composer, professor of music at Cambridge. Composed cantatas, church music, songs, etc.

Wood, Haydn (1882–1959), British composer chiefly famous for 'Roses of Picardy' and similar popular sentimental songs; also wrote a piano concerto, Fantasy Quartet for strings, etc.

Wood, Henry J. [Joseph] (1869–1944), British conductor who in 1895 began a famous series of Promenade Concerts in London ('the Proms') and continued to conduct them until his death. Also arranger: ➤*Fantasia on British Sea Songs*, ➤*Handel in the Strand*, ➤*Toccata and Fugue in D minor*, ➤*Trumpet Voluntary*. Gave more than 700 first (or first British) performances. Knighted, 1911; CH, 1944.

Wood, Hugh [Bradshaw] (b. 1932), British composer, lecturer at Cambridge University. Works include cello concerto, piano concerto, four string quartets. Song-settings of D. H. Lawrence, Ted Hughes, Neruda and others.

Wood, James [Peter] (b. 1953), British percussionist, composer, and conductor, founder (1990) and director of Centre for Microtonal Music; conducted his own *Oreion* at the Proms, 1989; other works include percussion concerto and *Two men meet, each presuming the other to be from a distant planet*, for 24 instrumentalists.

Wood, Thomas (1892–1950), British composer and author. Travelled to Australia and popularized the song 'Waltzing Matilda' outside Australia. Works include cantata *Chanticleer* (after Chaucer; unaccompanied).

wood block (or *Chinese block*), a rectangular block of wood, hollowed out for resonance, and used as a percussion instrument in dance-bands of the 1930s and other entertainment music, also in such works as Walton's *Belshazzar's Feast*.

Woodward, Roger [Robert] (b. 1942), Australian pianist who won the Warsaw International Chopin Competition in 1970. Notable in modern music; works have been written for him by Berio, Boulez, Takemitsu and others. Is also conductor and composer. OBE, 1980.

woodwind, collective name for those types of wind instrument historically and generally made of wood – either blown directly (e.g. flute, recorder), or blown by means of a reed (e.g. clarinet, oboe). The basis is a tube with holes which, closed or opened by the player's fingers directly or by key-mechanism, vary the length of the vibrating air-column and thus vary the pitch of the note emitted. The term is applied also to instruments of this construction but made of metal (e.g. most modern flutes, all saxophones), and so embraces four main 'families' within the symphony orchestra – those represented by ➤flute, ➤oboe, ➤clarinet and ➤bassoon, with their extra high or extra low relations.

Woolrich, John (b. 1954), British composer of *The Barber's Timepiece* and other works for orchestra, viola concerto, *The Death of King Renaud* for string quintet, *Pianobooks I–VI*, *Märchen* (Ger., 'Fairy-Tale') for percussion quartet.

Wordsworth, William (1770–1850), British poet. ➤Bloch (A.).

working-out, synonym for ➤development, e.g. in ➤sonata-form.

World Music, term for an all-embrac-

ing presentation of modern folk and popular music, generally involving performers from Asian and African countries with characteristic instruments, performing in their own languages.

World of the Moon, The, opera by Haydn. ➤*Mondo della luna*.

Wotquenne, Alfred (1867–1939), Belgian musicologist, cataloguer of the works of C. P. E. ➤Bach.

Wozzeck, opera by A. Berg, completed in 1922, produced in Berlin, 1925. Libretto by composer; Wozzeck is a simple, persecuted, feeble-minded private soldier. The play on which the opera is based is by Georg Büchner, 1836; another opera on it, by M. Gurlitt, appeared in 1926.

Wq., abbr. for 'Wotquenne' (in numbering the works of C. P. E. ➤Bach).

Wranitzky, German spelling of Vranický.

Wreckers, The, opera by Ethel Smyth, produced at Leipzig, 1906. Libretto by H. B. Brewster (written originally in French, translated into English, but given in German at the first performance), deals with Cornish community luring boats ashore for gain.

Wührer, Friedrich (1900–1975), Austrian pianist and teacher; first appearance at Salzburg Festival, 1938. His tours in Europe and USA gave prominence to major modern composers including Schoenberg and Webern.

Wunderlich, Fritz (1930–66), German tenor with a distinguished career in concert and opera (Covent Garden from 1965) which was cut short by his early death.

487

Wuorinen, Charles

Wuorinen, Charles (b. 1938), American composer of music for many combinations including *Percussion Symphony* (for 24 percussionists), *Prelude to* ➤*Kullervo* for tuba and orchestra, three string quartets, *Twang* for mezzo-soprano and piano (text by Wallace Stevens); *The Magic Art*, based on music by Purcell, as full evening's work for either full or chamber orchestra.

Wurlitzer, American firm of organ-builders (founded in 1858) which became famous for theatre organs (originally pipe-organs) in the period 1919–39.

Wyner, [originally Weiner] **Yehudi** (b. 1929), Canadian-born American composer of Jewish liturgical music, cello concerto, *On This Most Voluptuous Night* for soprano and seven instruments, etc.; is also pianist, conductor and university teacher.

X

Xenakis, Iannis (b. 1922), Romanian-born composer of Greek parentage; a pioneer in the use of computing in the process of composition, sometimes with a mathematical (➤stochastic) allocation of instrumental notes within a large tapestry of sound. Works include *Eonta* (Gk., 'Beings') for piano and five brass instruments. His *Metastaseis* ('After-standstill') is for 61 individual instrumentalists; used the word *Polytope* ('many-placed') for sound-and-light shows designed for Montreal, Persepolis and elsewhere. Some works, e.g. *Duel* (for two orchestras), have the form of a game with rules (and unpredicted result).

Xerxes, opera by Handel. ➤*Serse*.

xylophone, percussion instrument consisting of tuned wooden bars (hence the name, from Greek for 'wood' and 'sound'), arranged in order as on a piano keyboard and struck with small hard-headed sticks. Compass from middle C upwards for three octaves. Introduced from Eastern Europe; at first with a different (non-piano-like) array of bars – as when first introduced into the concert orchestra in Saint-Saëns's *Danse macabre* (➤*danse*). Thereafter it gained general currency for special effects.

xylorimba, percussion instrument (name joining ➤xylophone and ➤marimba), combining the compass of xylophone and marimba, about five octaves.

Y

Yakobson, Leonid (1904–75), Russian choreographer. ➤*Spartacus*.

Yamash'ta, Stomu (originally Tsutomu Yamashita) (b. 1947), Japanese percussionist (active as soloist in modern music) and composer (*Prisms* for solo percussion, film music, etc.).

Yansons, Arvid (1914–84), Soviet-Latvian conductor, prominently associated with the Hallé Orchestra (Manchester) from 1964. His son, the conductor Mariss ➤Jansons, prefers the original Latvian spelling.

Years of Pilgrimage, four sets of piano pieces by Liszt. ➤*Années de Pèlerinage*.

Yeats, William Butler (1865–1939), Irish poet and dramatist. ➤*Curlew*; ➤Egk.

Yeomen of the Guard, The, or The Merryman and his Maid, operetta by Sullivan, produced in London, 1888. Libretto by W. S. Gilbert, the title referring to the Warders of the Tower of London; set in the 16th century.

Yepes, Narciso (1927–97), Spanish guitarist who has toured internationally since 1948; has also composed film music. Since the mid-1960s, performs on a 16-stringed instrument of his own devising. Dedicatee of works by E. Halffter, Ohana and others.

Yevgeny Onegin, opera by Tchaikovsky, produced in Moscow, 1879. Libretto by composer and K. S. Shilovsky, after Pushkin. The hero lives to regret his blasé rejection of a young woman's love. (The title is often given in English-speaking contexts as *Eugene Onegin*.)

Yevtushenko, Yevgeni (b. 1933), Russian poet. ➤*Babi Yar*.

yodel (Ger., *Jodel*), type of singing for men alternating between natural voice and falsetto, practised particularly in the Swiss and Austrian Alpine region. It is used for simple dance-like tunes.

Yolanta, opera by Tchaikovsky, produced in St Petersburg, 1892. Libretto (after Henrik Hertz) by M. I. Tchaikovsky, the composer's brother: the title-role (in Western form 'Yolande') is that of a blind medieval princess.

Yonge, Nicholas (?–1619), English musician, possibly singer at St Paul's Cathedral, London; published ➤*Musica Transalpina*, introducing the madrigal to England.

Youmans, Vincent (1898–1946), American composer of musicals including ➤*No, No, Nanette* and *Hit the Deck*, 1927. From the former comes the song 'Tea for Two', arranged by Shostakovich as ➤*Tahiti Trot*.

Young, La Monte [Thornton] (b. 1935), American composer who studied with Stockhausen. His works often incorporate non-musical elements – as in *Poem for Chairs* [*Tables, Benches*, etc.] – or may consist of non-musical instructions, e.g. 'Draw a straight line and follow it'; earlier works include a string trio, etc.

Young, William (?–1662), English flautist, violinist and composer who worked abroad and published (at Innsbruck, 1653) the earliest English sonatas for two or more violins with bass viol and continuo – i.e. the type of ➤trio-sonata later used by Purcell. A violinist of the same name active at the court of Charles II, often identified with this William Young, was more probably his son.

Young Lord, The, opera by Henze. ➤*Junge Lord*.

Young Person's Guide to the Orchestra, The, title given to orchestral variations and fugue by Britten (1945) on a theme of Purcell (from the play *Abdelazer*, 1695).

Youth's Magic Horn, The, anthology of German poetry. ➤*Knaben Wunderhorn*.

Yradier, Sebastián (1809–65), Spanish composer of 'La paloma' (Sp., 'The Dove') and other popular songs. The 'habanera' in Bizet's ➤*Carmen* is an adaptation of one of Yradier's songs.

Ysaÿe, Eugène [-Auguste] (1858–1931), Belgian violinist, pupil of Wieniawski and Vieuxtemps; toured much, played many new works (including Franck's Violin Sonata) and led his own celebrated string quartet. Was also conductor (of Cincinnati Symphony Orchestra, 1918–22) and composer of eight concertos and other works for violin and orchestra, six sonatas for unaccompanied violin (highly esteemed by later players), etc.

Yun, Isang (1917–95), Korean-born composer who studied with Blacher in Berlin and settled there; abducted by S. Korean agents, tried in Seoul for sedition and sentenced to life imprisonment, but released after two years; returned to Germany and was naturalized there, 1971. Works include operas *The Dream of Liu-Tung* and *Butterfly Widow*; five symphonies (no. 5 with baritone), three violin concertos, six string quartets; *Images* for flute, oboe, violin and cello.

Z

Z, abbr. for Zimmerman in numbering the works of Henry ➤Purcell.

Zabaleta, Nicanor (1907–93), Spanish harpist who studied in Madrid and Paris and became internationally known; works were specially written for him by Milhaud, Krenek and other composers.

Zachau, Friedrich Wilhelm (1663–1712), German composer, chiefly of church and organ music; teacher of Handel.

Zacher, Gerd (b. 1929), German composer, also organist, giving first performances of works by Kagel, Ligeti, etc. His own works include *The Prayers of Jonah in the Fish's Belly* for soprano and organ, and a *St Luke* ➤*Passion*.

Zadok the Priest, no. 1 of four anthems by Handel for the coronation of George II, 1727; performed at every English coronation since.

Zagrosek, Lothar (b. 1942), Austrian conductor, noted in London and other capitals as a specialist in modern music; music director of Paris Opera 1986–8; of Leipzig City Opera since 1990.

Zakharov, Rostislav (1907–75), Russian choreographer. ➤*Cinderella* (Prokofiev).

Zandonai, Riccardo (1883–1944), Italian composer of operas including *Giulietta e Romeo* (on Shakespeare's *Romeo and Juliet*) and *Francesca da Rimini* (after D'Annunzio's play). Also composed orchestral works, songs, etc.

zapateado (Sp.), vigorous Spanish dance for a single performer, in which the heels tap out rhythmic patterns.

Zappa, Frank [originally Francis Vincent Zappa] (1940–93), American rock songwriter, guitarist and composer, some of whose works have attracted such conductors as Mehta and Boulez, who commissioned *The Perfect Stranger* and gave its first performance (Paris, 1984).

Zar und Zimmermann, oder Die Zwei Peter (Ger., 'Tsar and Carpenter, or The Two Peters'), opera by Lortzing, produced in Leipzig, 1837. Libretto by the composer, after a French play, about Peter the Great when working incognito at a Dutch shipyard.

Zarlino, Gioseffo (1517–90), Italian monk, director of music at St Mark's in Venice, and composer of church music; chiefly famous as theorist, codifying a system of harmony based on major/minor ➤tonality rather than on the older ➤modes.

zarzuela (Sp.), type of traditional Spanish musical stage entertainment, with spoken dialogue, often satirical.

Zauberflöte, Die (Ger., 'The Magic Flute'), opera by Mozart, produced in Vienna, 1791 (K620); libretto by E. Schikaneder, perhaps aided by C. L. Gieseke. The flute secures the passage of the hero through danger to enlightenment; the opera is one of Masonic and humanistic symbolism.

Zelenka, Jan Dismas (1679–1745); Czech composer (also double-bass player) active in Germany; in 1735 became court musical director at Dresden, where he died. Wrote overture *Hypochondria*, 21 Masses, many motets, etc.

Zeller, Carl (1842–98), Austrian composer (and civil servant), whose operettas were successfully produced in Vienna, *Der* ➤*Vogelhändler* lasting longest in popularity.

Zelter, Carl Friedrich (1785–1832), German composer, chiefly of vocal music, including song-settings of Goethe which won Goethe's approval; teacher of Mendelssohn.

Zemlinsky, Alexander von (1872–1942), Austrian composer of operas, including *Eine florentinische Tragödie* ('A Florentine Tragedy'), after Wilde, *Der Zwerg* ('The Dwarf', after Wilde's *The Birthday of the Infanta*), also of two symphonies, etc. Conductor in Vienna and Berlin, mentor (and brother-in-law) of Schoenberg.

Ziehharmonika (Ger.), ➤accordion.

Zigeuner (Ger.), gipsy; so such titles as *Der* ➤*Zigeunerbaron* ('The Gipsy Baron'); *Zigeunerweisen* ('Gipsy Airs'), work for violin and piano (or orchestra) by Sarasate, published in 1878.

Zigeunerbaron, Der (Ger., 'The Gipsy Baron'), operetta by J. Strauss the younger, produced in Vienna, 1885. Libretto by I. Schnitzer. The hero is a young Hungarian landowner regarded by the gipsies as their chief – and eventually made a real baron. The score incidentally quotes the ➤*Rákóczi March*.

Ziloti, Alexander [Ilyich] (1863–1945), Russian pianist and conductor; his piano pupils included his cousin Rakhmaninov. Conducted his own orchestra in St Petersburg, then settled in USA, 1922.

Zimbalist, Efrem [Alexandrovich] (1889–1985), Russian-born American violinist, noted as soloist and as teacher at the Curtis Institute in Philadelphia – he was its director, 1941–68.

Zimerman, Krystian (b. 1956), Polish pianist who won the Warsaw International Chopin Competition, 1975, and later gave the first British performance of Lutosławski's piano concerto, 1989.

Zimmerman, Franklin Bershir (b. 1923), American musicologist, cataloguer of the works of Henry ➤Purcell.

Zimmermann, Bernd [originally Bernhard] **Alois** (1918–70), German composer, pupil of Jarnach, Fortner and Leibowitz; works include two symphonies, a violin concerto, cello concerto; *Requiem for a Young Poet* for speaking and singing choruses, solo singers, jazz group, organ, orchestra and electronics; cantata *Lob der Torheit* ('In Praise of Stupidity', to texts by Goethe); opera *Die* ➤*Soldaten*.

Zimmermann, Tabea (b. 1968), German viola-player, much associated with modern music; gave first performance of Ligeti's viola sonata, 1993; soloist at Salzburg and other festivals, professor in Frankfurt.

Zimmermann, Udo (b. 1945), German composer, administrator since 1990 of Dresden Opera. His works include a concerto for timpani, opera *Die weisse Rose* ('The White Rose', about German conspirators against the Nazis).

Zingarelli, Niccolò Antonio (1752–1837), Italian composer of many operas (including *Giulietta e Romeo*, on Shakespeare's *Romeo and Juliet*), also of church music, etc.: holder of church music posts. Teacher of Bellini.

Zink, the German name for the ➤cornett.

Zipoli, Domenico (1688–1726), Italian composer and Jesuit priest who went as church organist to Argentina, where he died; wrote toccatas and other pieces for harpsichord or organ, also Italian oratorios, etc.

zither, type of flat-backed stringed instrument laid on the knees or table, and plucked; usually, some strings can be 'stopped' (as on a violin), and others are fixed in pitch and used for accompaniment. In its best-known form it is a folk-instrument native to Central Europe; the ➤autoharp is an adaptation.

znamenny chant, English term for Rus. *znammeny raspev* ('chanting by signs'), notation used in 15th–17th centuries for the traditional monophonic chant of the Russian Orthodox church; term also applied to the music itself, not merely its notation.

Zola, Émile (1840–1902), French novelist. ➤Bruneau.

zoppa (It.), a limp; *alla zoppa*, term used of music having a prominent ➤Scots snap or a pronounced regular syncopation.

Zukerman, Pinchas (b. 1948), Israeli violinist who trained in USA, 1962–7; winner of Leventritt Prize (jointly with Kyung-Wha Chung), New York, 1967. Prominent soloist since then, often conducting his own accompaniment in concertos. Is also viola-player and, since 1974, an occasional conductor; was music director of the St Paul (Minnesota) Chamber Orchestra, 1980–86.

Zwilich, Ellen Taaffe (b. 1939), American composer, formerly orchestral violinist. Works include two symphonies (no. 2, Cello Symphony), concerto for (tenor) trombone and another for bass trombone; a 'clarino quartet' for four trumpets, a piano trio.

Zwölf (Ger.), 12; *Zwölftonmusik*, ➤twelve-note music.

READ MORE IN PENGUIN

In every corner of the world, on every subject under the sun, Penguin represents quality and variety – the very best in publishing today.

For complete information about books available from Penguin – including Puffins, Penguin Classics and Arkana – and how to order them, write to us at the appropriate address below. Please note that for copyright reasons the selection of books varies from country to country.

In the United Kingdom: Please write to *Dept. EP, Penguin Books Ltd, Bath Road, Harmondsworth, West Drayton, Middlesex UB7 0DA*

In the United States: Please write to *Consumer Sales, Penguin Putnam Inc., P.O. Box 12289 Dept. B, Newark, New Jersey 07101-5289.* VISA and MasterCard holders call 1-800-788-6262 to order Penguin titles

In Canada: Please write to *Penguin Books Canada Ltd, 10 Alcorn Avenue, Suite 300, Toronto, Ontario M4V 3B2*

In Australia: Please write to *Penguin Books Australia Ltd, P.O. Box 257, Ringwood, Victoria 3134*

In New Zealand: Please write to *Penguin Books (NZ) Ltd, Private Bag 102902, North Shore Mail Centre, Auckland 10*

In India: Please write to *Penguin Books India Pvt Ltd, 11 Community Centre, Panchsheel Park, New Delhi 110017*

In the Netherlands: Please write to *Penguin Books Netherlands bv, Postbus 3507, NL-1001 AH Amsterdam*

In Germany: Please write to *Penguin Books Deutschland GmbH, Metzlerstrasse 26, 60594 Frankfurt am Main*

In Spain: Please write to *Penguin Books S. A., Bravo Murillo 19, 1° B, 28015 Madrid*

In Italy: Please write to *Penguin Italia s.r.l., Via Benedetto Croce 2, 20094 Corsico, Milano*

In France: Please write to *Penguin France, Le Carré Wilson, 62 rue Benjamin Baillaud, 31500 Toulouse*

In Japan: Please write to *Penguin Books Japan Ltd, Kaneko Building, 2-3-25 Koraku, Bunkyo-Ku, Tokyo 112*

In South Africa: Please write to *Penguin Books South Africa (Pty) Ltd, Private Bag X14, Parkview, 2122 Johannesburg*

READ MORE IN PENGUIN

A SELECTION OF MUSICAL HITS

What Jazz is Jonny King

A riveting and enlightening introduction to jazz, from the unique perspective of a professional jazz pianist. 'Exactly what the jazz world needs: a passionate and informative guide to what jazz is all about, written by one of the finest pianists and composers on the scene today' Joshua Redman

X-Ray Ray Davies

'Pop biographies rarely come more enjoyable than this . . . The eye for detail is as precise as in the best of his 1960s music work, and his creativity is sharply evident throughout' *The Times*. '*X-Ray* is that rarest of things: a rock star autobiography that is engaging, entertaining and well written, to boot' *Mail on Sunday*

Dylan: Behind the Shades Clinton Heylin

'The most accurately researched and competently written account of Dylan's life yet' *London Review of Books*. 'Essential reading for anyone who has ever held their flickering cigarette lighter above their head at a Dylan gig' *Daily Mail*

Lady Sings the Blues Billie Holliday with William Duffy

In a memoir that is as poignant, lyrical and dramatic as her legendary performances, Billie Holliday tells her own story, recalling her own dazzling rise to the top, and the darker side of the Holliday legend. 'Skillful, shocking and brutal' *The New York Times*

Bob Marley Cedella Booker with Anthony Winkler

In this intimate portrait, Mother Booker, Bob Marley's mother, tells the full story of her son's life, in a revealing portrait of one of the most loved musical geniuses of the century. 'Poignant and intimate' *Time Out*

READ MORE IN PENGUIN

A SELECTION OF MUSICAL HITS

The Dark Stuff   Nick Kent
Selected Writings on Rock Music 1972–1993

Never afraid to flirt with danger and excess, Nick Kent didn't just know how to write about rock stars . . . he lived in their shadow. From the debauchery of the Rolling Stones on tour, to the violence that surrounded the Sex Pistols, Nick Kent got close to everything that was mad, bad and dangerous to know about rock 'n' roll.

The American Night   Jim Morrison

'A hellfire preacher, part-terrified, part-enraged and mainly fascinated by the drawbacks that being merely human entails . . . refreshing' *Sunday Times*. 'A great American poet' Oliver Stone

Faithfull   Marianne Faithfull with David Dalton

'Marianne Faithfull gives an astonishingly honest and vital description of what it was like to be at the centre of that loony court of the hip, rich, vain and beautiful people of the 1960s . . . her account of sitting with the other disciples at the feet of Bob Dylan at the Savoy Hotel is very funny' *The Times*

Heartache Spoken Here   Stephen Walsh

When his wife took her love to town, Stephen Walsh took himself out on to the lonesome highway, looking for somewhere where people spoke the language of heartache that lives in the great Country songs. 'Country & Western's *Fever Pitch*' *Independent on Sunday*

I, Tina   Tina Turner with Kurt Loder

Ike and Tina Turner were one of the rock sensations of the Sixties. Then Tina made an incredible solo comeback and is now one of the hottest female performers on the pop scene. *I, Tina* tells the astonishing story behind her success. 'A real tearjerker' *Time Out*

READ MORE IN PENGUIN

REFERENCE

The Penguin Dictionary of the Third Reich
James Taylor and Warren Shaw

This dictionary provides a full background to the rise of Nazism and the role of Germany in the Second World War. Among the areas covered are the major figures from Nazi politics, arts and industry, the German Resistance, the politics of race and the Nuremberg trials.

The Penguin Biographical Dictionary of Women

This stimulating, informative and entirely new Penguin dictionary of women from all over the world, through the ages, contains over 1,600 clear and concise biographies on major figures from politicians, saints and scientists to poets, film stars and writers.

Roget's Thesaurus of English Words and Phrases
Edited by Betty Kirkpatrick

This new edition of Roget's classic work, now brought up to date for the nineties, will increase anyone's command of the English language. Fully cross-referenced, it includes synonyms of every kind (formal or colloquial, idiomatic and figurative) for almost 900 headings. It is a must for writers and utterly fascinating for any English speaker.

The Penguin Dictionary of International Relations
Graham Evans and Jeffrey Newnham

International relations have undergone a revolution since the end of the Cold War. This new world disorder is fully reflected in this new Penguin dictionary, which is extensively cross-referenced with a select bibliography to aid further study.

The Penguin Guide to Synonyms and Related Words
S. I. Hayakawa

'More helpful than a thesaurus, more humane than a dictionary, the *Guide to Synonyms and Related Words* maps linguistic boundaries with precision, sensitivity to nuance and, on occasion, dry wit' *The Times Literary Supplement*

READ MORE IN PENGUIN

MUSIC REFERENCE

The Penguin Guide to Compact Discs
Ivan March, Edward Greenfield, Robert Layton

'Within the space of a few years *The Penguin Guide* has become something of an institution, its status earned largely through a cheerful, informative "plain speaking" style, copious entries, and attractive reader-friendly presentation' *CD Review*

The Penguin Encyclopedia of Popular Music Donald Clarke

'There has been a desperate need . . . for a quality reference book on popular music. Covering the huge terrain of "non-classical music this century" . . . this book goes a long way towards satisfying that need . . . the entries are well chosen, considered and informative' *Observer*. 'An indispensable companion' *Q Magazine*

All You Need to Know about the Music Business Donald S. Passman

Recommended by stars and top industry executives alike, *All You Need to Know about the Music Business* is the one essential reference for anyone involved with – or planning to get involved with – the multi-billion dollar music industry.

The Penguin Opera Guide
Edited by Amanda Holden with Nicholas Kenyon and Stephen Walsh

'Remarkably comprehensive . . . The criterion for any guide is whether it can be read not only for reference but for entertainment, and Amanda Holden and her contributors pass this test with first-class honours' *The Times*

The Penguin Guide to Jazz on CD
Richard Cook and Brian Morton

'An incisive account of available recordings, which cuts across the artificial boundaries by which jazz has been divided . . . each page has a revelation; everybody will find their own' *The Times*

READ MORE IN PENGUIN

REFERENCE

The Penguin Dictionary of Troublesome Words Bill Bryson

Why should you avoid discussing the *weather conditions*? Can a married woman be celibate? Why is it eccentric to talk about the aroma of a cowshed? A straightforward guide to the pitfalls and hotly disputed issues in standard written English.

Swearing Geoffrey Hughes

'A deliciously filthy trawl among taboo words across the ages and the globe' Valentine Cunningham, *Observer*, Books of the Year. 'Erudite and entertaining' Penelope Lively, *Daily Telegraph*, Books of the Year.

Medicines: A Guide for Everybody Peter Parish

Now in its seventh edition and completely revised and updated, this bestselling guide is written in ordinary language for the ordinary reader yet will prove indispensable to anyone involved in health care: nurses, pharmacists, opticians, social workers and doctors.

Media Law Geoffrey Robertson QC and Andrew Nichol

Crisp and authoritative surveys explain the up-to-date position on defamation, obscenity, official secrecy, copyright and confidentiality, contempt of court, the protection of privacy and much more.

The Penguin Careers Guide
Anna Alston and Anne Daniel; Consultant Editor: Ruth Miller

As the concept of a 'job for life' wanes, this guide encourages you to think broadly about occupational areas as well as describing day-to-day work and detailing the latest developments and qualifications such as NVQs. Special features include possibilities for working part-time and job-sharing, returning to work after a break and an assessment of the current position of women.

READ MORE IN PENGUIN

DICTIONARIES

Abbreviations
Ancient History
Archaeology
Architecture
Art and Artists
Astronomy
Biographical Dictionary of
  Women
Biology
Botany
Building
Business
Challenging Words
Chemistry
Civil Engineering
Classical Mythology
Computers
Contemporary American History
Curious and Interesting Geometry
Curious and Interesting Numbers
Curious and Interesting Words
Design and Designers
Economics
Eighteenth-Century History
Electronics
English and European History
English Idioms
Foreign Terms and Phrases
French
Geography
Geology
German
Historical Slang
Human Geography
Information Technology

International Finance
International Relations
Literary Terms and Literary
  Theory
Mathematics
Modern History 1789–1945
Modern Quotations
Music
Musical Performers
Nineteenth-Century World
  History
Philosophy
Physical Geography
Physics
Politics
Proverbs
Psychology
Quotations
Quotations from Shakespeare
Religions
Rhyming Dictionary
Russian
Saints
Science
Sociology
Spanish
Surnames
Symbols
Synonyms and Antonyms
Telecommunications
Theatre
The Third Reich
Third World Terms
Troublesome Words
Twentieth-Century History
Twentieth-Century Quotations